Generative AI for Web Engineering Models

Imdad Ali Shah
School of Computing Science, Taylor's University, Malaysia

Noor Zaman Jhanjhi
School of Computing Science, Taylor's University, Malaysia

Published in the United States of America by
    IGI Global
    701 E. Chocolate Avenue
    Hershey PA, USA 17033
    Tel: 717-533-8845
    Fax: 717-533-8661
    E-mail: cust@igi-global.com
    Web site: https://www.igi-global.com

Library of Congress Cataloging-in-Publication Data

CIP DATA PENDING
ISBN13: 9798369337035
EISBN13: 9798369337042

Vice President of Editorial: Melissa Wagner
Managing Editor of Acquisitions: Mikaela Felty
Managing Editor of Book Development: Jocelynn Hessler
Production Manager: Mike Brehm
Cover Design: Phillip Shickler

British Cataloguing in Publication Data
A Cataloguing in Publication record for this book is available from the British Library.

All work contributed to this book is new, previously-unpublished material.
The views expressed in this book are those of the authors, but not necessarily of the publisher.

Table of Contents

Imdad Ali Shah, Faculty of Engineering Science & Technology, Iqra University, Malaysia

N. Z. Jhanjhi, School of Computer Science, Taylor's University, Malaysia

Sarfraz Nawaz Brohi, School of Computing and Creative Technologies, University of the West of England, UK

Imtiaz Hussain, Faculty of Engineering, Science, and Technology, Iqra University, Karachi, Pakistan

Zainab Alansari, University of Technology and Applied Sciences, Oman

Mansoor Ebrahim, Faculty of Engineering, Science, and Technology, Iqra University, Karachi, Pakistan

N. Z. Jhanjhi, School of Computer Science, Taylor's University, Malaysia

Imdad Ali Shah, Faculty of Engineering Science & Technology, Iqra University, Malaysia

Sarfraz Nawaz, School of Computing and Creative Technologies, University of the West of England, UK

Detailed Table of Contents

Chapter 1

*Imdad Ali Shah, Faculty of Engineering Science & Technology, Iqra
University, Malaysia*

*N. Z. Jhanjhi, School of Computer Science, Taylor's University,
Malaysia*

*Sarfraz Nawaz Brohi, School of Computing and Creative Technologies,
University of the West of England, UK*

Pay close attention to finding vulnerabilities and making secure software, we need to become less vulnerable. Vulnerable software always gives significant chances for hackers to inject malicious SQL code and interfere with its functionality. Security groups attempt to identify weaknesses in software as early as possible in development to avoid losses costing software businesses millions of dollars. As a result, numerous reliable and efficient vulnerability identification models are needed for web applications, but for those websites, there is no proper mechanism to block or scan other input data. The hackers are injected through string commands and functions of SQL (Structure Query Language) due to the dynamic disregard of this command in the runtime and several ways to identify security flaws in software, such as supervised semi-supervised, ensemble, and deep learning, to the list of machine learning that can find vulnerabilities, but despite these models in the software industry.

Chapter 2

Imtiaz Hussain, Faculty of Engineering, Science, and Technology, Iqra
University, Karachi, Pakistan
Zainab Alansari, University of Technology and Applied Sciences, Oman
Mansoor Ebrahim, Faculty of Engineering, Science, and Technology,
Iqra University, Karachi, Pakistan

The logistics system is evolving in a more intelligent direction. Logistic planning and coordination of information management and software platforms are inextricably linked to the fulfilment of smart logistics. The logistics and transportation business are one of the critical application areas for cyber-physical systems, which are novel technological intelligent systems that incorporate computing at its most fundamental level and technology for connectivity. Over the past decade, the Internet has changed the way people work and live. The purpose of this is to introduce a smart algorithm-based path decision technique. It is determined that the random algorithm has the best path optimization impact in resolving the logistics path decision by comparing the shortest transport distance and convergence speed under the two algorithm decisions. The logistics path decision problem was optimised using the Genetic Algorithm and random algorithm before the most effective algorithm was chosen. The shortest path using the random algorithm was 424.3. It was discovered after comparing the two algorithms. Following, the RO algorithm's shortest path was 434.5873.

Chapter 3

N. Z. Jhanjhi, School of Computer Science, Taylor's University,
Malaysia
Imdad Ali Shah, Faculty of Engineering Science & Technology, Iqra
University, Malaysia
Sarfraz Nawaz, School of Computing and Creative Technologies,
University of the West of England, UK

The primary objective of this chapter is focused on improvement and helping Generative AI for visualization such as automating the design of visuals and making it easier to understand patterns, trends, and outliers. Recent advances in machine learning (ML) and artificial intelligence (AI) have produced potent generative AI tools and techniques that can generate text, code, graphics, and other media in response to human commands. The technology has generated a lot of curiosity, which has led to conjecture about the fields—visualization included—that such methods could replace or enhance. Still unknown, though, is whether visualization tasks would be especially well-suited to the use of generative artificial intelligence. In recent years, generative artificial intelligence (GenAI) has advanced significantly and shown outstanding performance in a variety of generating tasks across multiple disciplines, including computational design and computer vision. A lot of academics have tried to use GenAI's enhanced generative capacity for various tasks by integrating it into visualization frameworks. We map the present and future capabilities of generative AI throughout the various stages of the visualization lifecycle and highlight key potentials and problems using real-world examples from the field. AI provides answers for a wide range of issues that both consumers and business owners face. Computer-based information can benefit economic growth, organizations, managers, and buyers. Without a doubt, AI improves human lives. Artificial intelligence has the potential to improve economic growth and raise everyone's standard of living. People and businesses everywhere are eager to invest in human resources, and e-business is crucial to continuously providing customers with the easiest way to purchase goods and services. AI and ML are being applied in an increasing number of different use cases as a result of the emergence of new, significantly enhanced AI and ML technology and applications. The widespread use of AI solutions in people's daily lives and the operations of several organizations raises the possibility of new risks and weaknesses.

Muhammad Naeem, The Islamia University of Bahawalpur, Pakistan
Muzzammil Siraj, Muhammad Ali Jinnah University, Karachi, Pakistan
Shoukat Ali, The Islamia University of Bahawalpur, Pakistan
Abdul Rehman, National College of Business Administration and
        Economics Lahore, Pakistan
Sumair Farooq, Hamdard University, Karachi, Pakistan

This chapter investigates the role of artificial intelligence in risk management. The Pakistan population is selected for this research. This study used the simple random sampling technique and analyzed the 385 responses by using the five-point Likert scale questionnaire. This study applied structural equation modeling to test the hypotheses. We observe that AI directly affects risk management. A positive relationship between AI in risk management. It is a pioneer study on the role of artificial intelligence in risk management. This study has some limitations, this study does not show a comparative analysis among different nations or areas. By emphasizing AI's influence on risk management, the study adds to the expanding body of research on AI integration in banking. The findings highlight the potential advantages of implementing AI in risk management tactics for practitioners. Banks and other financial institutions can use AI technologies to better assess and manage risks.

Chapter 5

Raghavendra M Devadas, Manipal Institute of Technology Bengaluru,
    Manipal Academy of Higher Education, Manipal, India
Vani Hiremani, Symbiosis Institute of Technology, Symbiosis
    International University (Deemed), Pune, India
Praveen Gujjar J., Faculty of Management Studies, Jain University,
    India
 Preethi, Manipal Institute of Technology, Manipal, India
R. Sapna, Manipal Institute of Technology, Manipal, India

The digital landscape is witnessing the continuous evolution of our lived experiences, in which the cross-cutting domain of Generative Artificial Intelligence (AI) and web engineering models is emerging as a pivotal source of transformative innovation. This article seeks to identify the potential new opportunities that generative AI could explore since it heralds in a radical revolution in the traditional paradigms associated with web development. The studied problems addressed in this paper include historical web system construction issues, design complexities, and maintainability problems. The research concludes by presenting a roadmap for embracing this paradigm shift, contributing to the ongoing discourse on the intersection of AI and web engineering. The study is exploratory at the outset, trying to gain insights into the integration of generative AI into web development. This research aims to explore the challenges, benefits, and potential applications of generative AI in several phases of web development, including design, testing, and maintenance.

Chapter 6

N. Z. Jhanjhi, School of Computing Science and Engineering, Taylor's University, Malaysia

Imdad Ali Shah, Faculty of Engineering Science & Technology, Iqra University, Malaysia

Sarfraz Nawaz Brohi, School of Computing and Creative Technologies, University of the West of England, UK

The primary objective of this chapter is to address the hardware vulnerabilities risks and challenges. A hardware vulnerability is a flaw in a computer system that can be remotely exploited by threat actors. They can then infiltrate a network by introducing malicious code. Vulnerability management, also known as vulnerability mapping, is the continuous process of identifying, categorizing, prioritizing, fixing, and reducing vulnerabilities in an environment. It involves assigning software high priority and promptly addressing risks to stop data breaches and cyberattacks. Considering the nature of the hardware, hardware security is different from software, network, and data security, whether it is being used for attack or defense. We must take hardware security into account early in product life cycles since hardware design and manufacturing frequently take place prior to or during software development. Information systems are becoming more common in a world moving toward total digitization. These systems are complex systems with hardware at their core. The investigation of potential hardware vulnerabilities must be included when addressing the security of these systems to prevent potential intrusions and malicious uses, as their exploitation can render any online or software-based defences worthless. we define hardware security and offer a meaningful and thorough taxonomy for hardware vulnerabilities and the attacks that take advantage of them to compromise the system. Consequently, the researcher's focus on this topic has increased recently.

Chapter 7

    Muhammad Naeem, The Islamia University of Bahawalpur, Pakistan
    Aurangzeb Khan, SBB Dewan University, Karachi, Pakistan
    Abdul Rehman, National College of Business Administration and
        Economics, Lahore, Pakistan
    Sumair Farooq, Hamdard University, Karachi, Pakistan
    Asim Mehboob, Muhammad Ali Jinnah University, Karachi, Pakistan
    Ahmad Shah Abdali, Ghazi University of Dera Ghazi Khan, Pakistan
    Bilal Ahmad, Ghazi University of Dera Ghazi Khan, Pakistan

This chapter looks into does artificial intelligence (AI) and blockchain technology (BT) can save costs in finance assiduity? It seeks to identify inefficiencies, probe the functions of AI and blockchain, and give styles for perpetration. Data are collected from workers in the fiscal sector, which is also anatomized using SPSS. The chapter's results show that there are numerous openings to ameliorate effectiveness, particularly in the areas of credit underwriting, loan servicing, and title insurance. still, the relinquishment of AI and DT depends on prostrating artistic, legal, and data norms obstacles. In the end, combining AI and BT may affect in fiscal sector cost reductions and service advancements, significantly impacting organizational procedures, technology, and policy.

Chapter 8

    Muhammad Usman Tariq, Abu Dhabi University, UAE & University
        College Cork, Ireland

This chapter explores the integration of Generative Artificial Intelligence (AI) in bolstering the security of Web applications. It delves into how AI-driven techniques can be employed to predict, detect, and mitigate security threats in real-time, thereby safeguarding Web-based systems from potential vulnerabilities. Through a comprehensive analysis of current challenges in Web application security and the potential of Generative AI to transform traditional security paradigms, this chapter aims to provide a detailed overview of cutting-edge methodologies and their implications for the future of Web security. The term "advanced web application" signifies the improvement and fortification of electronic systems against potential vulnerabilities and security threats through the utilization of Generative AI. In the rapidly evolving landscape of web applications, ensuring robust security measures is crucial for safeguarding sensitive data and maintaining the integrity of online systems.

Artificial intelligence and governance ideas are being implemented in business and society. These are two of the most explored issues in the current period. Banks and financial institutions nowadays collect vast volumes of client information, which is then processed by artificial intelligence; yet, the fate of such information remains unknown. This study seeks to identify ethical difficulties in the application of artificial intelligence and presents solutions based on governance concepts. It also looks into the function of artificial intelligence in financial institutions. This study is exploratory, with a focus on primary data analysis. Primary data is collected using a standardized questionnaire distributed to bank personnel. The study's findings indicate that there is a significant association between ethical difficulties in AI implementation and the function of corporate governance in financial institutions. The findings also indicate that the effective and intelligent use of governance concepts can alleviate ethical concerns about artificial intelligence implementation.

Chapter 10
Imdad Ali Shah, Faculty of Engineering Science and Technology, Iqra University, Karachi, Pakistan
N. Z. Jhanjhi, School of Computing Science and Engineering, Taylor's University, Malaysia

The primary objective of this chapter is to exhaustive analysis of the constantly changing security and privacy issues and important factors in e-commerce. The need to protect sensitive data and guarantee user privacy has increased with the growth of the digital economy. This chapter examines many security concerns, such as phishing attacks, data breaches, and payment gateway vulnerabilities, and highlights the possible consequences for both consumers and organisations. It explores cutting-edge technology and creative fixes meant to strengthen e-commerce platforms against dynamic cyberattacks. In addition to pointing out the vulnerabilities that now exist, the study suggests preventative measures as well as future lines of inquiry and application. We look at biometric authentication, and privacy-preserving technologies as possible ways to improve the security of e-commerce platforms. The data that is being presented highlights how important it is for technology, legislation, and user awareness to come together to provide a safe and reliable online purchasing environment. To strengthen the digital marketplace against the challenges presented by a constantly changing cyber landscape, in competitive markets, businesses try to increase their profit margins without sacrificing the quality of their products. Conversely, customers successfully fulfil their needs and desires at home. AI provides answers for a wide range of issues that both consumers and business owners face. Computer-based information can benefit economic growth, organizations, managers, and buyers. Without a doubt, AI improves human lives. Artificial intelligence has the potential to improve economic growth and raise everyone's standard of living. People and businesses everywhere are eager to invest in human resources, and e-business is crucial to continuously providing customers with the easiest way to purchase goods and services. Moreover, the emergence of an AI-ready business does not translate into a rise in the need for mechanical expertise. The use of electronic commerce has made life better. We focused on phishing attacks, data breaches, blockchain payment gateway, Ransomware attacks, Cloud-based and cyber attacks in E-commerce.

Chapter 11
The Role of Generative AI in Enhancing Web Engineering Efficiency and
Business Innovation 223

Adil Liaquat, SBB Dewan University, Pakistan
Nasrullah Khan, SBB Dewan University, Pakistan
Muzzammil Siraj, SBB Dewan University, Pakistan
Abdul Rehman, SBB Dewan University, Pakistan
Safdar Miran, SBB Dewan University, Pakistan

This study explores the impact of generative AI on web engineering and its part in driving business invention. By automating coding, design, and conservation tasks, generative AI enhances web development effectiveness, reducing time and trouble for inventors. The exploration employs a mixed- styles approach, combining qualitative perceptivity from case studies with quantitative analysis of AI- driven web development systems. Findings indicate a significant positive relationship between AI integration and advancements in web development effectiveness and business invention. The study also highlights the challenges of AI relinquishment, including ethical enterprises and the need for translucency. This exploration contributes to the understanding of AI's transformative eventuality in web engineering, offering recommendations for using AI to enhance web practices and drive invention. Unborn exploration should explore long- term impacts and strategies for addressing ethical issues in AI integration.

This primarily aims to evaluate the ML approaches and web applications for authentication. Using machine learning, issues can be solved, and computers can carry out tasks. It attempts to understand the relationships between the data and automatically learns from the presented information. The relationship after that enables the machine to complete the tasks given to it successfully. In other words, machine learning teaches itself how to accomplish a task over time and then assists people in performing that activity. The capacity to design effective, safe, and user-friendly web applications remains a major problem in the constantly evolving field of web development. Web application developers must provide modular, reusable, and interactive web interface components that can adapt to the constantly shifting needs of users in terms of security, large-scale data transfer capabilities, and interface speed. One of the most important components of any modern web application is secure user login and permission. Stronger authentication is required to protect user data and the integrity of apps, as worries over data privacy and cybersecurity grow. Though there are a number of these solutions on the market, none of them completely integrates with the ecosystem built on React to offer safe and adaptable identity management. Effective and user-friendly web components are just as crucial for the appropriate administration of data and the successful user engagement of web applications as they are for security problems. As a result, the thesis concentrates on providing a more thorough explanation of reusable web components, including what they are and how to create them with TypeScript, React, and Redux. Therefore, this chapter is a practical attempt to design and develop safe, reusable, and effective web components inside a React ecosystem to meet these difficulties. By doing this, the research advances the subject of web development and provides a guide for programmers wishing to incorporate comparable features.

Chapter 13
Fida Hussain, School Education & Literacy Department Govt of Sindh,
*   Pakistan*
Saira Khurram Arbab, Faculty of Engineering Science & Technology,
*   Iqra University, Pakistan*

The rapid-fire expansion of the Internet has deeply integrated into diurnal life, challenging nonstop updates to web armature to manage vast data and cover stoner sequestration. This chapter explores security enterprises like phishing, data breaches, and payment gateway vulnerabilities, emphasizing their impact on consumers and associations. In competitive requests, businesses aim to increase gains without compromising quality, while AI offers results to challenges faced by both consumers and companies. AI- drivene-business enhances profitable growth, improves living norms, and shifts traditional retail towards a mix of physical and digital channels, furnishing strategic advantages through better understanding of behavior .

Chapter 14
Rachna Rana, Ludhiana Group of Colleges, Ludhiana, India
Pankaj Bhambri, Guru Nanak Dev Engineering College, Ludhiana,
*   India*

The advent of Generative AI has triggered a paradigm shift across several domains, resulting in ground-breaking advances in text, picture, video, audio, and code production. However, this technical advancement has also increased cyber security intimidations, as hackers increasingly use Generative AI in their harmful actions. Generative artificial intelligence (Gen-AI) and Huge words models (HWMs) are transforming businesses throughout the world. However, their enormous promise carries major hazards. It is critical to address the cyber security concerns related with Gen-AI. This aids organizations in comprehending the security implications of these technologies. This chapter will provide a complete Gen-AI security architecture and show how it may help us protect Gen-AI apps, models, and the whole Gen-AI ecosystem. This research attempts to define the many security vulnerabilities posed by Generative AI, identifying their manifestations across different application areas.

Poornima Mahadevappa, Taylor's University, Malaysia
Syeda Mariam Muzammal, Taylor's University, Malaysia
Muhammad Tayyab, Taylor's University, Malaysia

Generative AI is transforming the art and science of web engineering by automating content generation, design and development through models like GAN, VAE or Transformers. These models can produce authentic text like a writer and other media, including images, so developers would save more time in web development and improve creativity and scalability. From automated web design and content personalization to adaptive user interface or code optimization, the uses of generative AI could be limitless. Integrating AI with web engineering allows developers to generate dynamic and tailored user interface applications that adapt to the unique requirements of each user. Nevertheless, issues like data quality, bias and ethical considerations require ongoing attention to ensure responsible AI usage. Overall, generative AI can revolutionize web development for a future of innovation and more intelligent, efficient, user-centric web applications.

Syeda Mariam Muzammal, Taylor's University, Malaysia
Poornima Mahadevappa, Taylor's University, Malaysia
Muhammad Tayyab, Taylor's University, Malaysia

Web engineering is being transformed rapidly by Artificial Intelligence (AI), particularly by Generative AI (GenAI), through its potential for automation in content creation, source code generation, design creation, and optimization. Along with the tremendous benefits that the integration of GenAI and Web Engineering offers, significant security concerns arise related to secure deployment and data privacy. This chapter explores the importance and growing adoption of GenAI tools and techniques in web development, emphasizing the security considerations, such as potential vulnerabilities, including model manipulation, adversarial attacks, and data leakage. A thorough review of the existing studies reveals the primary security threats and attacks, including the recommended countermeasures. Moreover, the ethical implications of GenAI for web engineering have also been investigated. By highlighting the security and privacy concerns, this study shall benefit the researchers, developers, and organizations in adapting careful steps for GenAI utilization for web engineering process, taking into account the issues and challenges related to the user trust, privacy, security, and data integrity.

Chapter 17

Hina Al Fatima Siddiqui, Nazeer Hussain University, Pakistan
Nasrullah Khan, SBB Dewan University, Pakistan
Safdar Miran, SBB Dewan University, Pakistan
Arsalan Hakeem, Jinnah Postgraduate Medical Center, Pakistan
Muneeba Khan, Nazeer Hussain University, Pakistan
Muzzammil Siraj, SBB Dewan University, Pakistan
Abdul Rehman, SBB Dewan University, Pakistan

This study explores the integration of generative artificial intelligence (AI) into web-grounded physical remedy operations through a mixed- styles approach, combining both quantitative and qualitative data. Aquasi-experimental design was employed to compare the efficacy of AI- enhanced remedy with traditional styles, revealing significant advancements in remedy issues. Generative inimical Networks (GANs) and Large Language Models (LLMs) were employed to produce individualized exercise routines and grease interactive case- AI relations. Quantitative results showed that cases using AI-enhanced remedy endured lesser advancements in range of stir and advanced satisfaction compared to those witnessing traditional remedy. The study also linked several specialized and ethical challenges, including data sequestration enterprises and model limitations. Unborn exploration should concentrate on advancing AI algorithms, integrating multimodal feedback, and addressing usability issues to enhance the effectiveness and availability of AI in physical remedy.

    Muhammad Tayyab, Taylor's University, Malaysia
    Khizar Hameed, University of Tasmania, Australia
    Majid Mumtaz, CATE School of Computing and Creative Technology,
        University of the West of England, UK
    Syeda Mariam Mariam Muzammal, Taylor's University, Malaysia
    Poornima Mahadevappa, Taylor's University, Malaysia
    Aleena Sunbalin, Shifa Tameer-e-Millat University, Islamabad, Pakistan

The use of artificial intelligence (AI) in cybersecurity is a need due to the outpacing of conventional security measures by the fast growth of cyber threats. Exploring the function of machine learning (ML), deep learning (DL), and natural language processing (NLP) in recogniz- ing and reacting to new cyber dangers, this chapter offers a thorough introduction to AI-powered threat identification. The paper contrasts AI- based systems with more traditional approaches, demonstrating how AI can better identify unknown assaults, adapt to new threats, and decrease the number of false positives. It touches on topics such as training models using industry-specific data, ensuring they can commu- nicate with one other, and keeping them up-to-date and monitored. Data privacy, legislation compliance, and best practices for AI threat detection are also discussed. We discuss the need for human analysts to work with AI tools and how to overcome obstacles, including AI bias, complicated systems, and ethical considerations.

Chapter 19

Saira Khurram Arbab, Faculty of Engineering Science & Technology,
Iqra University, Pakistan
Farzeen Rizwan, Taylor's University, Malaysia

The primary aim of this chapter is to focus on Generative AI and web-based applications. Further, we address the security issues and challenges. In today's digital era, web-based applications have become indispensable tools in web engineering. From social media platforms to online banking services, the ubiquity of web-based applications shapes nearly every aspect of our daily lives. As we navigate the ever-expanding digital landscape, understanding the importance of these applications in web engineering is essential for businesses, developers, and users alike. A notable trend in 2023 was the increasing emphasis on sustainability and green computing within web engineering. Businesses sought to develop eco-friendly web-based applications by optimizing energy consumption, reducing carbon footprints, and implementing environmentally conscious development practices. Despite their widespread adoption, the deployment of web-based applications is not without challenges. The study addresses key issues, including cybersecurity threats, compatibility concerns across diverse platforms, and the complexities of ensuring smooth integration with existing systems. Additionally, the abstract acknowledges that a crucial component of web-based applications in 2023 will be the incorporation of Artificial Intelligence (AI) models. Companies use AI deliberately to improve overall functionality, automate tasks, and improve user experiences. The study emphasizes how artificial intelligence (AI) may be used to address problems in fields like cybersecurity, where sophisticated algorithms help with improved threat identification and mitigation. Identifying and mitigating these challenges is critical for ensuring sustained success and functionality of web-based applications. In our view, the importance of web-based applications in web engineering is paramount. These applications serve as the backbone of digital transformation, empowering businesses to meet the demands of an increasingly interconnected world. Address the challenges identified, our opinion emphasizes the need for a proactive approach, incorporating robust cybersecurity measures, continuous innovation, and a commitment to adaptability. By leveraging the potential of web-based applications, businesses can not only meet current demands but also position themselves strategically for the future of web engineering.

NLP converts human language to computer understandable language is known as Natural Language Processing (NLP), though various diversified models have suggested so far, yet the need for a generative predictive model which can optimize depending upon the nature of problem being addressed is still an area of research under work. It is possible to solve specific issues connected to reading text, hearing voice, interpreting it, measuring sentiment, and determining which sections are significant by using a generative model, which is a platform that can be used for a variety of different aspects of natural language processing. This chapter discusses the components of NLP, illustrates case study on using generative AI and NLP to detect human behavior, and datasets, and finally comes the conclusion.

Chapter 21

We lack knowledge of how User Experience and Performance practitioners, User Experience and Performance practitioner's teams, and businesses use Gen-AI and the issues they confront. We interviewed 24 User Experience and Performance practitioners from various firms and countries, all with different positions and levels of seniority. Our findings show that: 1 there is a major lack of Gen-AI corporate policy, with organizations informally advocating caution or delegating responsibility to individual workers; and 2 User Experience and Performance practitioners require group-wide Gen-AI exercises. User Experience and Performance practitioners characteristically use Gen-AI independently, esteeming inscription-based responsibilities, but letter boundaries for plan -attentive behavior such as wire framing and prototyping; 3) User Experience and Performance practitioners advocate for improved Gen-AI educating to improve their ability to make effectual stimulate and assess production brilliance.

Preface

In the rapidly evolving landscape of web technology, the integration of Generative Artificial Intelligence (AI) has emerged as a pivotal force, transforming how we conceptualize, design, and implement web-based systems. We are thrilled to present *Generative AI for Web Engineering Models*, a comprehensive reference book that delves deep into this intersection, offering valuable insights for researchers, practitioners, and students alike.

As editors, we recognize the complexity and dynamism of the web discipline. The creation, maintenance, and enhancement of web applications require not only innovative methodologies but also a profound understanding of the underlying technologies. This book aims to bridge that gap by providing a thorough exploration of generative AI's applications within various web engineering models. From web-browser design and website scalability to security and code generation, we cover a wide array of topics that showcase how AI can optimize processes and drive innovation.

Each chapter contributes to a holistic understanding of how generative AI is reshaping the web engineering landscape. We have gathered insights from leading researchers and practitioners, ensuring that the content is not only cutting-edge but also relevant to current and future challenges in the field. Furthermore, we address the societal impacts of these technologies, fostering a critical dialogue about the ethical implications and responsibilities that come with such powerful tools.

Our hope is that this book serves as a comprehensive resource for researchers, scientists, postgraduate students, and professionals engaged with AI and web engineering. Whether you are looking to enhance your knowledge or apply new methodologies in your work, we trust that you will find valuable information and inspiration within these pages.

As we continue to explore the boundless possibilities of AI in web engineering, we invite you to join us on this journey. Together, we can shape the future of web development in ways that are innovative, efficient, and responsible.

In *Generative AI for Web Engineering Models*, each chapter provides a unique perspective on the integration of Generative AI into web engineering, highlighting its transformative potential and addressing contemporary challenges.

Chapter 1: Machine Learning Models for Detecting Software Vulnerabilities begins our exploration by emphasizing the critical need for robust security measures in software development. It discusses various machine learning approaches, including supervised and ensemble methods, to identify and mitigate vulnerabilities in web applications, ultimately aiming to preempt costly security breaches.

Chapter 2: The Internet of Things An Intelligent and Secure Path Approach for Cyber Critical Infrastructure shifts focus to logistics, presenting an intelligent algorithm for optimizing logistical pathways. By leveraging cyber-physical systems, this chapter illustrates how enhanced information management can revolutionize transportation efficiency, addressing both distance and speed challenges in logistics.

Chapter 3: Generative AI for Visualization delves into the capabilities of generative AI in the realm of visualization. It investigates how recent advancements can enhance graphical representation and design processes, questioning whether generative tools can effectively replace traditional visualization methods.

Chapter 4: The Role of Artificial Intelligence in Risk Management Practices of the Banking Sector provides a pioneering examination of AI's impact on risk management in banking, based on empirical research from Pakistan. This chapter highlights AI's direct influence on improving risk assessment and management practices, presenting valuable insights for financial institutions.

Chapter 5: Unveiling the Potential of Generative Approaches in AI-Infused Web Development for Design, Testing, and Maintenance focuses on the revolutionary changes that generative AI can bring to web development. It identifies historical challenges in web systems and proposes a roadmap for integrating generative approaches across various development phases, paving the way for innovative solutions.

Chapter 6: Hardware Vulnerabilities of Business Applications and Security Models addresses the often-overlooked hardware vulnerabilities that can be exploited by malicious actors. By emphasizing the importance of proactive vulnerability management, this chapter advocates for integrating hardware security measures early in the product lifecycle.

Chapter 7: Does Artificial Intelligence with Blockchain Reduce the Costs of Financial Sector? explores the synergy between AI and blockchain technology, analyzing their potential to enhance efficiency in finance. The findings suggest that combining these technologies can streamline processes, though challenges in adoption remain.

Chapter 8: Harnessing Generative AI for Enhanced Web Application Security examines how generative AI can strengthen the security of web applications. It discusses real-time threat detection and mitigation strategies, emphasizing the need for innovative security methodologies in an increasingly complex threat landscape.

Chapter 9: Ethical Concerns in Artificial Intelligence: The Role of Governance Mechanism in Finance investigates the ethical challenges surrounding AI in financial institutions. By analyzing governance frameworks, this chapter underscores the necessity of ethical considerations in the deployment of AI technologies to protect sensitive client information.

Chapter 10: The Challenges for E-commerce Using AI Applications takes a critical look at security and privacy issues in the evolving e-commerce sector. It identifies vulnerabilities and offers innovative solutions to bolster platform security, ensuring consumer protection in a rapidly digitizing marketplace.

Chapter 11: The Role of Generative AI in Enhancing Web Engineering Efficiency and Business Innovation assesses how generative AI can streamline web development processes. By leveraging machine learning for authentication and problem-solving, this chapter highlights the potential for creating efficient and user-centric applications.

Chapter 12: Security Concerns of Machine Learning Approaches in the Modern Era and Web Engineering revisits the role of machine learning in addressing authentication challenges. It emphasizes the continuous evolution of web applications and the need for robust security measures against emerging threats.

Chapter 13: Introduction to Machine Learning Models for Web Engineering Concepts addresses the integration of AI into web infrastructure, discussing the balance between enhanced operational efficiency and consumer protection against data breaches and phishing attacks.

Chapter 14: Generative AI-Driven Security Frameworks for Web Engineering: Innovations and Challenges explores the dual-edged sword of generative AI's advancements and the cybersecurity threats they introduce. This chapter aims to provide a comprehensive framework to secure generative AI applications against vulnerabilities.

Chapter 15: Introduction to Generative AI in Web Engineering Concepts and Applications showcases the transformative capabilities of generative AI in automating content creation and enhancing user interfaces. It highlights both the potential benefits and the ethical challenges that come with integrating AI into web engineering.

Chapter 16: Generative AI in Web Application Development: Enhancing User Experience and Performance shares insights from practitioners on how generative AI is currently utilized in enhancing user experiences. It reveals a need for corporate policies and collective exercises to maximize the potential of generative AI tools.

Chapter 17: Exploring Security Challenges in Generative AI for Web Engineering highlights the vulnerabilities that arise with the adoption of generative AI in web development. This chapter serves as a guide for researchers and developers to navigate the ethical and security challenges associated with these technologies.

Chapter 18: AI Powered Threat Detection in Business Environments: Strategies and Best Practices provides an in-depth analysis of AI's role in enhancing cybersecurity measures. It contrasts traditional security systems with AI-driven solutions, outlining best practices for effective threat detection.

Chapter 19: Generative AI and Web Applications Addressing Security Issues And Challenges reflects on the role of web applications in everyday life, emphasizing the necessity for secure and sustainable development practices as the digital landscape continues to expand.

Chapter 20: Generative AI with Natural Language Processing for the Web concludes our journey by exploring how NLP and generative models can revolutionize human-computer interaction. By addressing issues related to language understanding and sentiment analysis, this chapter underscores the vast potential for generative AI in enhancing communication.

In Chapter 21, "**Generative AI in Web Application Development: Enhancing User Experience and Performance**," we delve into insights gathered from interviews with 24 User Experience and Performance practitioners across diverse firms and countries. The findings reveal a significant gap in corporate policies regarding Generative AI, with organizations largely adopting an informal approach that either encourages caution or shifts responsibility onto individual employees. Additionally, practitioners express a strong need for collaborative Gen-AI exercises to enhance their collective capabilities. While many use Gen-AI independently for tasks like writing, they often struggle with its application in design-oriented activities such as wireframing and prototyping. The chapter concludes with a call for enhanced educational initiatives focused on Generative AI to empower practitioners to effectively stimulate creativity and evaluate production quality in their projects.

Together, these chapters illustrate the multifaceted impacts of Generative AI on web engineering, providing a robust framework for understanding both the opportunities and challenges that lie ahead.

In closing, we believe that Generative AI for Web Engineering Models not only serves as a vital resource but also as a catalyst for further exploration and dialogue in this rapidly evolving field. The chapters within this volume collectively illuminate the myriad ways in which generative AI is redefining the parameters of web engineering, from enhancing security measures and streamlining processes to navigating ethical challenges and societal impacts.

As editors, we are particularly proud of the diverse perspectives offered by the authors, who represent a blend of theoretical insight and practical application. Each contribution enhances our understanding of how generative AI can be harnessed to create innovative, efficient, and secure web applications, while also addressing the pressing challenges that accompany these advancements.

The integration of generative AI into web engineering opens up a realm of possibilities, and we hope this book inspires researchers, practitioners, and students to engage deeply with these concepts. It is our aspiration that the insights provided will encourage ongoing collaboration, foster responsible innovation, and ultimately lead to advancements that benefit society as a whole.2

As we look to the future, we invite you to explore the chapters, engage with the ideas presented, and consider how you can contribute to shaping a web environment that is not only technologically advanced but also ethically sound and secure. Together, let us navigate this exciting journey into the future of web engineering with the transformative power of generative AI as our guide.

Chapter 1
Machine Learning Models for Detecting Software Vulnerabilities

Imdad Ali Shah
https://orcid.org/0000-0003-2015-1028
Faculty of Engineering Science & Technology, Iqra University, Malaysia

N. Z. Jhanjhi
https://orcid.org/0000-0001-8116-4733
School of Computer Science, Taylor's University, Malaysia

Sarfraz Nawaz Brohi

School of Computing and Creative Technologies, University of the West of England, UK

ABSTRACT

Pay close attention to finding vulnerabilities and making secure software, we need to become less vulnerable. Vulnerable software always gives significant chances for hackers to inject malicious SQL code and interfere with its functionality. Security groups attempt to identify weaknesses in software as early as possible in development to avoid losses costing software businesses millions of dollars. As a result, numerous reliable and efficient vulnerability identification models are needed for web applications, but for those websites, there is no proper mechanism to block or scan other input data. The hackers are injected through string commands and functions of SQL (Structure Query Language) due to the dynamic disregard of this command in the runtime and several ways to identify security flaws in software, such as supervised semi-supervised, ensemble, and deep learning, to the list of machine learning that can find vulnerabilities, but despite these models in the software industry.

DOI: 10.4018/979-8-3693-3703-5.ch001

1. INTRODUCTION

Securing web-based applications is critical to prevent unauthorized access, data breaches, and other cybersecurity threats. Input validation ensures that user data is valid and does not contain malicious code or scripts that can compromise the application's security. Authentication and authorization mechanisms ensure that only authorized users can access the application's resources and data. Strong password policies and multi-factor authentication should be implemented to prevent unauthorized access (Le and Babar, 2022, Bahaa et al., 2022). Access control ensures that users have access only to the resources they need to perform their tasks and no more. Indeed, technological progress often outpaces the rate at which regulations and guidelines are implemented in the software industry, where the rapid pace of technological change has led to a departure from conventional software development life cycle (SDLC) approaches. While both academia and industry have made strides to improve software quality, vulnerabilities continue to be a major issue. This is in part because it is hard to forecast all probable failure modes in today's complex software systems(Tata Sutabri, 2023, Siddique et al., 2022, Lim et al., 2019). However, it's partly because the software development process requires more focus on safety and quality. Software quality and security can both be enhanced by following established best practices in the software development industry. The use of secure coding guidelines and the idea of least privilege are two examples of these methods. The number of CVEs from 20072022 is in figure 1.

Figure 1. The number of CVEs from 1995 to 2022

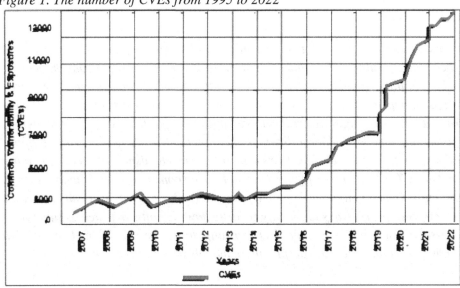

2

To keep security researchers, suppliers, and organizations apprised of potential dangers and take the necessary steps to mitigate them, the CVE database provides a standardized mechanism to identify and track cybersecurity vulnerabilities. Vulnerability information is made public in the database, which aids in fostering openness and cooperation in the cybersecurity community(Humayun et al., 2020, Gaur et al., 2021). A strong security program should incorporate preventative methods to locate and repair security holes. To prevent vulnerabilities from being exploited by attackers, it is important to do regular vulnerability assessments and penetration testing(Kekül et al., 2022, Li et al., 2021a). It is true that testing software is a crucial procedure for finding security holes in programs.

By testing software, developers can identify any bugs or weaknesses in the system. The research analyzed multiple versions of software applications to determine the presence of security flaws and modifications in the system. The researchers used NVD and SARD databases as primary sources, along with open-source initiatives. Future research will still need to fill in the gaps in the models that are already in use. Analysis types and methods require (Kailay and Jarratt, 1995, Pant and Hsu, 1995, Dissanayake et al., 2022)to find all kinds of vulnerabilities, as covered in earlier sections. As a result, it becomes necessary to organize the results from tools.

It's great to hear that our proposed CVD model has performed well compared to other standard approaches for detecting vulnerabilities. However, it's important to note that further validation and testing of the model may be necessary before it can be widely adopted and implemented in practical settings. Additionally, ongoing monitoring and updating of the model will be crucial to ensure its continued effectiveness over time. Nonetheless, your results are promising and suggest that the CVD model may be a useful tool in the fight against vulnerabilities(Ghaffarian and Shahriari, 2017, Johnson, 2022). This research uses and expands upon a vulnerability dataset that includes flaws found in commercially available software. It detects vulnerabilities better than CNN and RNN models. The upgraded CNN model's software algorithm detects vulnerabilities with greater precision. Data security research focuses on machine learning and software vulnerability evaluation methodologies with more vulnerability records in every field(Shah et al., 2024e, Shah et al., 2024f, Nyre-Yu et al., 2022, Souppaya et al., 2022). In our suggested model, we use approaches from natural language processing, such as statistical analysis and multi-class classification techniques in machine learning. By combining a self-attention mechanism with a pre-trained context encoder, we present a system for automating the discovery of security holes. This effort aims to assemble all the necessary building blocks for developing an AI-based automated model detecting software vulnerabilities.

1.1 Software Vulnerabilities Detection

As the frequency and sophistication of cyberattacks rise, the study of how to spot software flaws has become crucial. Individuals, businesses, and even entire nations are vulnerable to the devastation that these strikes can wreak. As a result, researchers and businesses are investing more time and money into securing their software. The vast volume of code present in modern software systems is one of the primary obstacles in locating software vulnerabilities. Finding all the security flaws in a system (Memon et al., 2022, Althar et al., 2021) is becoming more and more challenging as software becomes more complicated. Vulnerabilities in software are typically difficult to find because they are buried deep inside the code and require specialized tools and methods. Researchers and professionals in business employ many different approaches to uncover vulnerabilities to overcome these difficulties. Utilizing automated technologies that scan code for security flaws is one method(Alfadel et al., 2023, Ahvanooey et al., 2020, Li, 2020). The software is analyzed using methods including fuzzing, symbolic execution, and static analysis. Manual testing methods, such as pen testing and vulnerability scanning, are another option. These methods entail exploiting the software system to find flaws that could be used by attackers. Code audits are another method used by researchers to look for security flaws in software. Source audits are typically effective in finding vulnerabilities that automated techniques may overlook, but they can be time-consuming and require a comprehensive grasp of the software source. Overall, finding software vulnerabilities is a complex and challenging task, but it is essential to ensure the security of software systems. The scientific community and industry will continue to invest in this area of research to develop new techniques and tools to improve software security.

1.2 Research Contribution:

1. We present the taxonomy of the research in software vulnerability identification and detection model.
2. We present the taxonomy of ML approaches used in detection.
3. We present thoroughly different approaches for the detection of Software Vulnerabilities in web-based applications: such as (i) Supervised Learning (ii) Semi-Supervised Learning (iii) Deep Learning.
4. We present Machine Learning base proposed model in which hackers use the SQL injection method for stealing sensitive data and working as administrators. Our approach will work against SQL injection attacks and provide secure software to users.
5. We present future work in the software identification model.

1.3 Chapter's organization

The organization of the paper is as follows. In section 1, give more attention to the introduction and explore the review article software security measurement for securing web-based application Frameworks. Section 2 discusses the definitions and taxonomies of software security measurement for securing web-based application Frameworks. This section also includes fundamental definitions of Software security measurement and web-based applications. In section 3, the approaches of Machine Learning in Software Vulnerabilities: (i) Supervised Learning (ii) Semi-Supervised Learning (iii) Deep Learning. In section 4, Discussion. Section 5 proposed a framework. In Section 5. Finally, the conclusion and future work are presented.

2. LITERATURE REVIEW

Considering the growing frequency and sophistication of cyberattacks, discovering flaws in software has emerged as a crucial topic of study. Personal computers, businesses, and even entire countries may all take a major hit from these kinds of attacks. As a result, researchers and businesses are investing more time and money into securing their software. The vast volume of code present in modern software systems is one of the primary obstacles to locating software vulnerabilities. Finding all the security flaws in a system is becoming more challenging as software becomes more complicated (Mugarza et al., 2018, Hanif et al., 2021, Vinayakumar et al., 2018b). Moreover, software vulnerabilities are typically buried deep inside the code and are difficult to locate without the use of specialized tools and methods. Researchers and experts in the sector employ a wide range of techniques to discover vulnerabilities to overcome these obstacles. Using automated technologies that scan code for security flaws is one method. These instruments do code analysis using methods including fuzzing, symbolic execution, and static analysis to spot security holes.

To find vulnerabilities that bad actors could attack; these techniques involve actively trying to take advantage of them. Developers and businesses alike face a formidable obstacle in the form of software vulnerabilities. Some of the problems that might arise from software flaws include the following: (1) Vulnerability identification is difficult since it is one of the hardest parts of developing secure software. Detecting flaws that could be used by malicious actors is becoming more challenging in modern, highly sophisticated software systems. (2) Vulnerability patching: Once a security hole has been found, it is the responsibility of the software's creators to create a fix. However, this is not always an easy operation, as patches may cause additional issues or incompatibilities with other program parts(Shah and Jhanjhi, 2024). By their very nature, vulnerabilities increase the likelihood of being exploited

5

by attackers the longer it takes to discover and fix them. This puts pressure on developers to quickly identify and patch vulnerabilities before they can be exploited.

Several studies have been conducted in automated identifying threats for securing the software and associated security issues. Although the literature covers a wide variety of such topics, this review will focus on four major themes that repeatedly emerge throughout the literature reviewed secure software and (Sindiramutty et al., 2024, Lu et al., 2018)vulnerabilities, attacks, solutions proposed by researchers to detect these attacks, openness, and exploration of machine learning algorithms approaches to handle the threats and improve vulnerabilities.

The classification of security issues in health information systems has been done using this taxonomy method. Based on the classification's findings, conclusions are reached. RAMeX was developed to bridge the gap in risk assessment and management processes for medium- and small-sized commercial enterprises dealing with medium-to-low-level risks

(Sahu and Srivastava, 2019, Márquez and Astudillo, 2019). This study examines six different research methods. In general, they treat planning as a distinct process that has no logical or direct bearing on the creation of IT systems. Enterprise information resources, which capture and characterise the enterprise, when integrated with planning, development, and management, will decrease the response time, and make it possible to conduct an economic analysis of information system investment (Li et al., 2019, Tiefenau et al., 2020). The creation of security policies and documents for each PBX will lessen but not entirely stop external and internal hacker attempts. However, the PBX staff must deal with the leading security threats, weaknesses, risks, and solutions by putting these policies and documents into place(Agrawal et al., 2020, Lee and Yim, 2020). The author addresses the techniques available for locating security flaws in an open network and the evolving paradigm of network security. It goes on to describe the problem Sun had and the tools we made and used to solve it, with a focus on automating system security evaluation and compliance. The network administrator has additional security issues while maintaining adequate security measures across heterogeneous platforms. There is an increase in computer crime. One of these crimes is listening in on private conversations. Another is damaging information storage equipment physically. This shows the need for a more suited strategy for smaller firms and those requiring a speedier, simpler, and less resource-intensive strategy. This suggests a need for an alternative method for efficient information technology (IT) risk assessment and management. From an IT standpoint, this strategy has a business-oriented focus(Ranganath and Mitra, 2020, Ghanem and Chen, 2019). With the development of a methodology for risk assessment, some intriguing inferences can be made regarding the decision-making process in organizational information security. It is essential to have a solid grasp of the dynamics of the risks associated with automated information systems(Alferidah

6

and Jhanjhi, 2020). Those designated to carry out a risk evaluation exercise need to have the appropriate education and experience, and careful consideration needs to be given to the choice of those individuals, the taxonomy of the Literature review in Figure 2.

Figure 2. The taxonomy of the Literature review

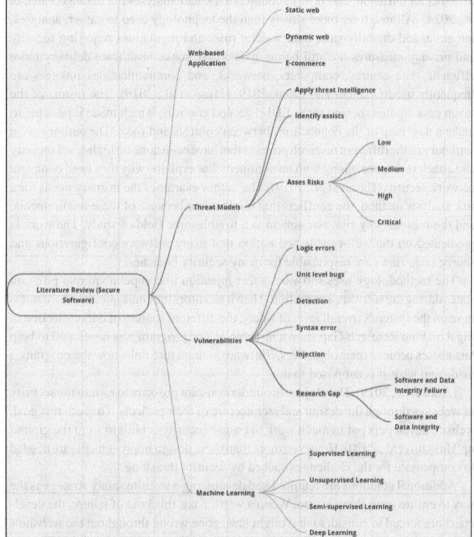

The research resulted in the development of a novel approach to risk analysis; as a result, healthcare facilities can now decide the safety measures necessary for themselves. In addition, the strategy was coupled with a modern management methodology, which would identify any implementation issues. The survey showed that significant problems make it harder to set up fair and effective public health data systems and protect people's privacy. The logs should track who logged in and what they did once they were within the system. Before conducting a comprehensive analysis of security procedures, it is necessary first to investigate the factors that influence security enforcement. It is addressed manually and automatically, how to detect an intrusion, and how to counterattack and analyses the damage(Fateh et al., 2024). Although far more slowly than the technology used to gather, analyses, integrate, and digitally store data, federal rules and regulations requiring security and privacy measures are still being updated. To make healthcare delivery more efficient, data centres, computers, networks, and communications linkages are frequently used(Ghanem and Chen, 2019, Hasan et al., 2019). The results of the seven case studies showed more EDI risks and controls, which made it possible to make a new map of the connections between controls and risks. The author gave a summary of the different research projects that have been done on high-level security and attack resistance, along with an argument that explains why they need complete network security(Hasan et al., 2019). The author examines the primary needs for a risk analysis method, the conflicts that might occur because of these requirements, and the reasons why risk assessment is a troublesome field of study. The work is predicated on the well-established notion that many software configurations and source code flaws are responsible for many security breaches.

The methodology uses software defect injection to compel abnormal program states during the software's execution. Then it monitors the consequences these states have on the system's overall level of safety, the different sources of data collection in Fig 4 and the Research Gap shown in Table 1. The program was developed to help businesses achieve their objectives. Software architecture links how the program is made and what it is supposed to do

(Arko et al., 2019). Developers are under constant pressure to ensure the security of websites through the design and architecture of their projects. To reach this goal, website developers put in much work to ensure security is built in from the ground up(Hussain et al., 2020). However, more than these design improvements are needed to compensate for the challenges caused by security thrashing.

Additional solutions are required and developing a website safety strategy is the way to ensure everything is safe. When a website has this kind of failure, the developers are forced to consider what might have gone wrong throughout the website's design process and why it might have resulted in such a significant setback. The use of security design strategies is what brings resolution to design problems relating to security. In a survey conducted by Lars Lofgren, it was found that around 54% of all businesses polled reported having been the victim of at least one cyberattack in the preceding 12 months. Furthermore, the survey reveals that only 39% of organizations were prepared to deal with these cyber-attacks (Grammatikis et al., 2019, Vinayakumar et al., 2019). Vulnerabilities are flaws in a website that interfere with its ability to meet the security criteria. Table 1 presents the research gap and Fig 5 shows the average number of research papers classification.

Table 1. Presents Research Gap in Securing Web-based Applications with a Secure Software Perspective

Citation	Pros	Cons	Techniques	Research Gap
(Shah et al., 2024b)	Process of fixing security holes in software.	Software security patch management	ML	The majority (38.1%) only address the problems in one process phase.
(Vigneswaran et al., 2018)	Computer security risk.	Software vulnerabilities Severity	Machine Learning & Data Mining	Model development and production deployment
(Vinayakumar et al., 2018a)	Security quality of a binary from the view of several stakeholders.	Quality model using PIQUE enables an application of Busybox Binaries.	Machine Learning	we need to work on the quality model.
(Vinayakumar et al., 2018c)	Cyber defenders do reverse engineering (RE).	Binary code	Static Techniques	The suggestion is to continue working on new automation to enable analysts to employ static methodologies.
(Kronjee et al., 2018)	Address software security in depth.	Root causes of vulnerabilities	ML	Evaluation of management operations and root causes.
(Li, 2017)	work on increasing the software vulnerabilities.	process testing procedures and technical evaluation.	ML	The author revealed that the implemented internet vulnerability detection programs confirm the relevant issue, allowing one to create a better scanner in the future.
(Belgaum et al., 2022)	Software security analysis model.	Software security during the development process.	ML	Security flaws in software development procedures.
(Belgaum et al., 2021)	Challenging to discover security issues	Vulnerabilities in software ecosystems.	Machine learning	Secure software packages.
(Alansari et al., 2017)	vulnerabilities and attacks	software attacks on smartphone applications.	Detection groups of attacks	Cyber security experts improve this research area.
(Grieco and Dinaburg, 2018)	Software bugs	Code vulnerabilities and the top ten vulnerabilities.	Binary detection	Dangerous software flaws must fix in this research area.

continued on following page

Table 1. Continued

Citation	Pros	Cons	Techniques	Research Gap
(Finlayson et al., 2019)	Industrial IIOT	Updating running code	dynamic software updating	labelling functions and ranking functions
(Zhang et al., 2019)	NVD, Twitter	Messages on social media	Linear SVM	Improving labels.

3. RESEARCH METHODS

This study collects and evaluates prior studies that identified software vulnerabilities across numerous issues last five years from 2018 to 2022 in Figure 4. We also assess articles that use machine learning algorithms to find software vulnerabilities. The procedure flowchart for gathering data is shown in Figure 3. We used the keyword "software vulnerability" as our primary search term to look for appropriate research publications in the five databases that are available for this study: Scopus, Elsevier, Springer, IEEE Xplore, and Google Scholar. We selected these databases because they contain many research papers on numerous subjects, increasing their exposure to vulnerability identification and detection.

Figure 3. Overview data-collection flowchart

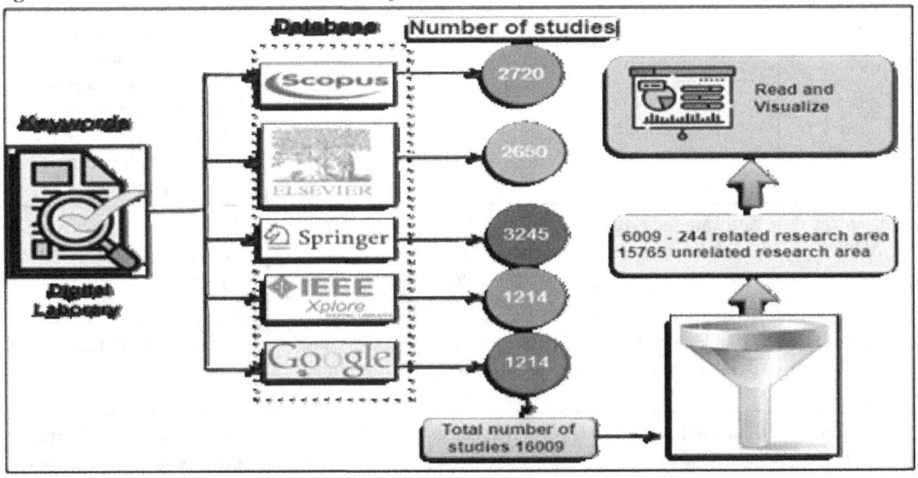

In total, 6009 records from various articles, including journals, conferences, books, and news, were uncovered by this investigation. However, a large portion of these data come from several study fields that are only loosely related to vulnerability detection. Overview of publication papers collected from 2018 to 2022 in Figure 4.

Figure 4. Overview publications collected in different years from 2018 to 2022

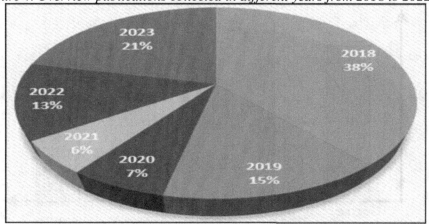

To get around this, we use the keyword "software vulnerability identification and detection" to further refine our results, screening out any duplicates or unrelated subjects, and choosing just journal and conference papers as the source of our final data. Overview of the digital database in Figure 5.

Figure 5. **Overview of the digital database**

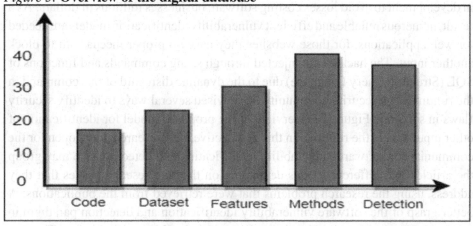

This study's analysis of 244 high-calibre experimental studies on software vulnerability identification is the basis for its findings. The next subsection presents and discusses the findings of our analysis. An Overview of the different categories of research problems in Figure 6.

Figure 6. Overview of different categories of the research problems

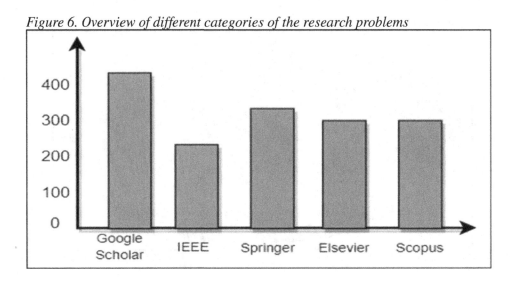

4. RESEARCH PROBLEMS

Security groups attempt to identify weaknesses in software as early as possible in development to avoid losses costing software businesses millions of dollars. As a result, numerous reliable and efficient vulnerability identification models are needed for web applications, for those websites they have no proper mechanism to block another input. The hackers are injected through string commands and functions of SQL (Structure Query Language) due to the dynamic disregard of this command in the runtime. The security community has devised several ways to identify security flaws in software. Figure 13 Overview of the proposed model for identification of other input data in the runtime. In this perspective, new research doors open for the community for software vulnerability identification and detection. We may group the articles into different groups depending on the core research issues that they address, using the research problems that were retrieved from the publications. A better grasp of the software vulnerability identification and detection paradigm in terms of current research issues is made possible by this categorization. The five types of research problems include methodologies, detection, features, datasets, code, and others. The distribution of articles based on several kinds of research challenges is depicted. Figures 4, 5, and 6, significant distribution revealing that 50.3% of the articles address the research issues related to the approach for vulnerabilities, such as the use of traditional methodologies and manual analysis. Papers that address topics like the usage of antiquated and traditional software engineering measures to identify software vulnerabilities make up 14.3% of the papers with the third-largest spread. The studies that address dataset-related issues, including the size and quality of the gold standard dataset (9.89%), make up the fourth-largest dispersion. The remaining distributions, such as miscellaneous (5.44%) and code (5.44%), concentrate on issues with code complexity and a combination of various ungrouped research issues. Figure 3 illustrates the cumulative sum of many research categories to help understand how the research challenge has grown over time. The author worked on vulnerability detection, but our study is more accurate, and the results are high.

5. TAXONOMY OF SOFTWARE VULNERABILITY DETECTION

Researchers may be motivated to investigate a particular topic for various reasons, such as curiosity, personal interest, and desire to solve a problem. The systematic categorization of research papers can provide insights into the distribution of research attention across different topics. However, it is essential to recognize that the number of published papers on a topic does not necessarily reflect its importance or impact. As for issues related to datasets and code, there is growing recognition of the importance of open data and reproducibility in research. Researchers may face challenges in sharing and accessing data and code, which can hinder the transparency and rigour of their research. However, efforts are being made to promote open science practices, such as data-sharing policies, open-access publishing, and reproducibility standards. These efforts aim to improve the quality and impact of research and address the challenges that researchers may encounter in their work(Boukhechba et al., 2018, Mehrotra and Musolesi, 2018). To bridge the gap between hot and not-so-hot research problems, it is important to identify the most pressing challenges and prioritize research efforts accordingly.

This may involve analyzing trends and patterns in vulnerability disclosures, assessing the impact of emerging technologies and threat vectors, and identifying areas where current approaches to vulnerability detection and mitigation are inadequate. Collaboration and knowledge-sharing among researchers can also be critical in advancing research on vulnerability detection and mitigation. This may involve leveraging open-source tools and data sets, participating in research communities and conferences, and engaging in interdisciplinary collaboration to address complex problems from multiple angles. Ultimately, the goal of research on vulnerability detection and mitigation is to improve the security and resilience of systems and networks and protect against malicious attacks and data breaches. By focusing on high-impact research problems and collaborating effectively, researchers can make significant progress toward this goal. In the methodologies section, we discuss the many approaches used to identify security holes, such as manual analysis and more traditional methods. Meanwhile, the study that focuses on vulnerability detection performance and the types of vulnerabilities found is discussed under the heading "detection." Overfitting and traditional feature use are the main topics discussed in the features section. Meanwhile, the code section elaborates on the role of code in software development and the various degrees of code complexity. Figure 7 presents the taxonomy of vulnerabilities.

Figure 7. **presents the taxonomy of vulnerabilities**

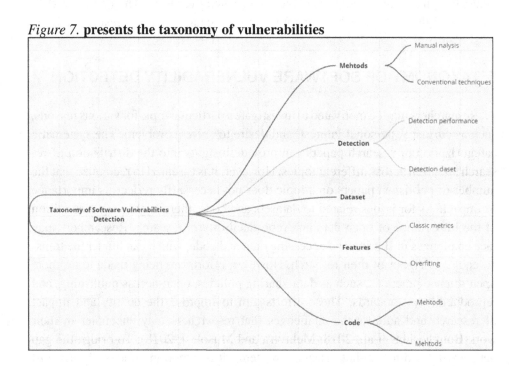

5.1 Methods

Ultimately, the choice of research method and strategy depends on the research question, the nature of the data being collected, the availability of resources, and other contextual factors. It is important for researchers to carefully consider these factors when designing their studies and interpreting their findings, and to acknowledge the limitations and potential biases of their chosen methods(Stütz et al., 2015).

Because of this, new research has come up with a better way to fix the problems with the current methods.

5.2 Manual Analysis

When it comes to finding security flaws in software, most people are interested in using a manual analysis approach. During the development of software, security problems can be found by having a human specialist test and fix bugs. This strategy is labour-intensive, inefficient, and fraught with [115-118] the possibility of human error when applied to a sizable software development effort. Since then, a lot of writing has been done to find solutions to the problem of manual analysis. Table II Overview software flaws manually studied.

Table 2. The software flaws manual study

Citation	Problem	Proposed approached	Vulnerabilities	Dataset
(Shah et al., 2024a)	Traditional approaches	DL	Overflowing buffers	NVD, SARD
(Bhatt et al., 2021)	Not found a potential risk	DL	Injection of SQL	SARD, NVD
(Bhuiyan et al., 2021)	Conventional security analysis methods	DL	Overflowing buffers	NVD, SARD
(Binyamini et al., 2021)	Traditional approaches to security analysis	DL	Overflowing buffers	(NVD and SARD)
(Bosu et al., 2014)	To successfully find and exploit security holes would require laborious handiwork	DL	Overflowing buffers	20 binary entries from the Robot Hacking Game
(Khan et al., 2020)	To successfully find and exploit security holes would require laborious handiwork.	Pattern matching	External scripting	Projects like TOM Mail and Winmail
[192]	manual analysis.	Hybrid analysis	Overflowing buffers	Lighttpd, lighted, Wsmp3d, Kristen
(Khan et al., 2020)	The way things are now, some human help is needed to classify things.	Supervised learning	SQL of injection	CVSS, CPE

5.3 Conventional Techniques

Conventional software development is a way of making software that has been around for a long time and follows a clear process with different steps. These phases typically include gathering and analysing requirements, designing the [119-122] software, coding it, testing it, and maintaining it. Table III presents conventional techniques for software vulnerabilities.

Table 3. Conventional techniques for software vulnerabilities

Citation	Problem	Proposed approached	Vulnerabilities	Dataset
(Miraz et al., 2019)	Automated PHP detection of vulnerability	DL	SQL of injection	SARD
(Belgaum et al., 2023)	static and dynamic analysis	SL	Cross-site scripting	(SAMATE), NVD
(Bozorgi et al., 2010)	Existing models for vulnerability prediction	SL	Unavailable vulnerability data	Bugzilla
(Hanif et al., 2021)	vulnerability scanner environment	SL	Unavailable vulnerability data	288 DARPA
(Bullough et al., 2017)	offline analysis in contemporary	SL	OS command injection	PHPMyAdmin

5.4 Detection

The subject of detection research is made up of software vulnerability detection efforts that have already been made to solve problems with detection. As the primary focus of the study, detection is one of the most pressing issues in the field of (Cabral et al., 2019) software vulnerability detection. Methods vary in how they tackle detection challenges such as detection performance, detection reliability, and detection class.

5.5 Performance in Detecting

A key part of how well a detection system is doing is how many false positives and false negatives it has. This is especially important because it shows that the suggested method for finding software vulnerabilities is wrong because it leads to a lot of wrong classifications

(Ujjan et al., 2022, Muzafar et al., 2022). In the realm of computer security, particularly in areas like malware and opinion spam detection, the issue of detection performance is well-recognized and actively discussed. Table IV presents the research challenge in detection performance.

Table 4. The research challenge in the area of detection performance

Citation	Problem	Detection	Vulnerabilities	Dataset
(Dawson and Walker, 2022)	Insufficient detecting capacity.	Accuracy 97%	BO	SARD, NVD
(Gaur et al., 2022)	False positives are common in the existing literature.	F1 scores 88.9% with a precision 92%	NH	SARD
(Jhanjhi et al., 2022)	Low detection performance	75% accuracy	Buffer overflow	NVD
(Chhajed and Garg, 2022)	Low detection performance	92% accuracy	Vulnerabilities information available	Private dataset

5.6 Detection

The detection class problem involves identifying different types of vulnerabilities that can be found using various methods. Web vulnerabilities and zero-day exploits are two examples of such vulnerabilities, but there are many other types of vulnerabilities that can be identified using different detection methods. Some examples of other types of vulnerabilities include buffer overflow vulnerabilities, authentication bypass vulnerabilities, injection vulnerabilities, and privilege escalation vulnerabilities. The specific types of vulnerabilities that can be identified using a particular detection method will depend on the method itself, as well as the nature and architecture of the system being tested(Shah et al., 2024i, Huang et al., 2016). Most existing research in software vulnerability detection focuses on binary detection, where a sample is either labelled as vulnerable or not vulnerable. However, in multiclass detection, the detection model can make predictions about multiple classes of vulnerability, which can be more useful for researchers. the text highlights the need for more research in multiclass detection and the challenges that researchers face in investigating all potential vulnerabilities in software. Table 5 presents the software vulnerability detection research issues in the detection class.

Table 5. The software vulnerability detection class

Citation	Problem	Detection	Vulnerabilities	Dataset
(Huang et al., 2016)	multiclass detection	Multiclass	41 vulnerabilities	SARD, NVD
(Xiang et al., 2017)	select few vulnerabilities.	Multiclass	Unused variable (CWE-563)	Private dataset
(Tian et al., 2020)	conventional security methods.	Multiclass	OS command injection	OpenSSH
(Kuruvila et al., 2021)	vulnerabilities of web	Single-class	SQL injection	Public dataset
(Liu et al., 2020)	few types of exposure	Multiclass	CWE-369	Suite v1.2

5.7 Features and Classic Metrics

The Features Research Interest Group (RIG) is a group that focuses on researching software vulnerability detection and the issues with the features or metrics used to detect vulnerabilities. RIG focuses on several important topics, one of which is the inclusion of less important variables in vulnerability detection models or methods. When conventional metrics and features are utilized in these models, this problem frequently arises. Code complexity, code coverage, and the total number of lines of code are just a few examples of the many properties that traditional metrics and features might incorporate. Although these indicators might be helpful for identifying vulnerabilities, they can also be very varied and dependent on the codebase being examined(Fan et al., 2019). As a result, including less significant variables in vulnerability detection models or tools can lead to overfitting and reduced performance.

This can result in false positives or false negatives in vulnerability detection, which can have serious consequences for software security. To address this issue, Features RIG is researching new approaches to feature selection and metric design that can improve the reliability and performance of vulnerability prediction models and tools(Yang et al., 2021). This includes exploring techniques such as machine learning and data-driven feature selection, as well as developing new metrics that are more robust and less dependent on specific code characteristics. Some examples of conventional software engineering metrics and features are code descriptions and static features at the level of the code. Table VI presents the classical metrics and characteristics of software vulnerability detection research challenges.

6. OVERFITTING

When a dataset is used to train a vulnerability detection model, overfitting brings attention to the issue of the large level of noise in the dataset. In other words, over-fitting refers to the employment of models that are more sophisticated or include more terms than they should. As the model is trained using a dataset provided in the machine learning algorithm, the issue of over-fitting is particularly common in machine learning approaches. Using several feature selection techniques, also investigated the issue of overfitting. The issue was solved in previous works by lowering the dataset's dimensionality, which also decreased the complexity of the vulnerability detection algorithms. Three different types of fitness are displayed in a machine learning model in the leftmost picture displays the visualization of a machine learning model that is ill-equipped to identify the data's underlying pattern. This results in a model that performs poorly. The performance of the vulnerability detection models is impacted by overfitted models, which appear when there are noises in the dataset and are shown in the picture to the right. Overfitting occurs because certain features or metrics are unreliable or meaningless in the dataset. The properly fitted model, which successfully strikes a balance between underfitting and overfitting. It helps the model tremendously by revealing the underlying tendencies in the data. Therefore, the goal of every machine learning assignment is to obtain an acceptable fitted model that performs well across training and testing sets.

Table 6. The classical metrics and characteristics

Citation	Problem	Detection	vulnerabilities	Dataset
(Shah et al., 2024g)	Existing models	unifying tokens	OS command injection	SARD, SQLI-LABS
[222] (2019)	Source code	Abstract syntax trees	Vulnerability	Private dataset hosted on GitHub
(Zhou et al., 2019)	Using stock	Abstract syntax trees	Not vulnerability information	Asterisk
(Li et al., 2021b)	source code.	Source codes	OS command injection	Android applications, Firefox
(Wang et al., 2018)	poor positive predictive values.	Class-level	Not vulnerability information	Stanford Securibench dataset

7. CODE

The code research interest groups cover existing research on software vulnerability identification that addresses issues with code activities and code complexity. The term "code activities" refers to any activity involving source codes, such as editing and deleting by software developers. Code complexity refers to how intricately written the software's code is(Shah et al., 2024h, Arnold and Qu, 2020). There are specific operations and procedures during the software development phase where developers can organise their codes into simple or complex forms. This heavily depends on what the software development team wants to accomplish.

8. CODE ACTIVITY

Software engineers collaborate in teams throughout the many stages of software development, and each developer has a unique approach to coding. The code structure becomes uneven when modifications made by multiple developers are not properly documented. Security vulnerabilities are frequently caused by this discrepancy. Software developers must therefore decide which code structures are best for certain software development projects and give security researchers access to the software so they can harden it using the appropriate hardening techniques(Humayun et al., 2022, Shah et al., 2022). The list of current works that concentrate on code research issues in software vulnerability detection is shown in Table 11.

9. WEB APPLICATIONS

A web application, often known as a web app, is a software programme that can be viewed and used via the internet using a web browser. It is run on web servers and interacts with users via a web interface. Web apps are platform-agnostic, which means they may be viewed from a variety of devices, including desktop computers, laptops, tablets, and smartphones if they have a functional web browser and an internet connection. Figure 8 Overview of Web-based application architecture diagram

Figure 8. Overview of Web-based Application Architecture Diagram

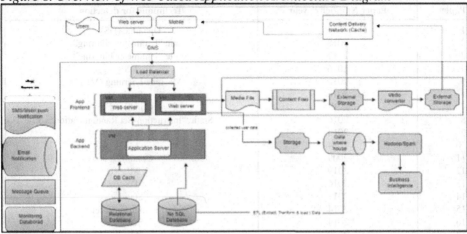

A web application architecture outlines the arrangement of all web application components and shows the relationships between application components, third-party middleware systems, web services, and databases. This is a snapshot of the interaction between various programmes that are working together to deliver services to end consumers at the same time. Several models are available in the market, and these are working for the detection of vulnerabilities but still need to work more in view of our literature review and Table 1. The hacker has access to all user data in the database, including user details, credit card information, and social security numbers, as well as protected locations such as the administrator portal. User data can also be deleted from the tables.

10. MACHINE LEARNING APPROACHES IN SOFTWARE VULNERABILITIES DETECTING

Using machine learning, issues can be solved, and computers can carry out tasks. It attempts to understand the relationships between the data and automatically learns from the presented information. The relationship after that enables the machine to complete the tasks given to it successfully. In other words, machine learning teaches itself how to accomplish a task over time and then assists people in performing that activity(Guo et al., 2020, Khalil et al., 2021). This method is much more effective and economical than manual or rule-based programming. The quick learning and execution process boosts the productivity of a certain activity.

Table 7. Overview of the Detection Techniques

Paper	Paper Number & year	Technique for detection
1	2017	Dynamic (DS)
2	2018	Static "Parameter Filtering"
3	2017	Static "Parameter Filtering"
4	2016	DS
5	2010	Machine Learning (ML)
6	2016	Static
7	2017	Combined
8	2016	Static "Instruction-Set Randomization"
9	2013	Combined
10	2014	ML
11	2009	Combined
12	2019	ML
13	2016	DS
14	2011	Static
15	2014	Static "Parameter Filtering"
16	2014	Static
17	2019	ML
18	2012	Static "Defense Mechanism"
19	2017	Static
20	2011	Static
21	2015	ML
22	2015	Static
23	2018	Static "Parameter Filtering"
24	2016	Static
25	2011	ML
26	2017	ML
27	2012	ML
28	2012	Static
29	2016	ML
30	2012	Combined
31	2012	Dynamic
32	2014	ML
53	2019	DS
54	2020	ML
55	2020	Combined
56	2020	Static
57	2020	Static
33	2013	ML
34	2014	Combined
35	2009	ML
36	2018	ML
37	2015	Static "Parameter Filtering"
58	2020	ML
38	2011	Static
39	2014	DS
40	2015	ML
41	2011	DS
42	2013	Static
43	2015	ML
44	2012	Static
45	2017	Static "Parameter Filtering"
46	2016	ML
47	2017	Static
48	2011	Combined

a. Supervised learning

The most popular machine learning technique for identifying software vulnerabilities is supervised learning. This is because it can function well with the aid of trustworthy datasets. When learning under supervision, labels like "vulnerable" and "non-vulnerable" are applied to datasets. Before the vulnerability detection model is trained, every observation in the dataset has already been given a label(Zagane et al., 2020, Sennan et al.). Past academics who worked on vulnerability detection studies have made some of these labelled datasets publicly accessible. Some researchers generated their own privately tagged datasets to aid their research, the taxonomy of the ML in Figure 9.

Figure 9. Overview of the taxonomy of the ML

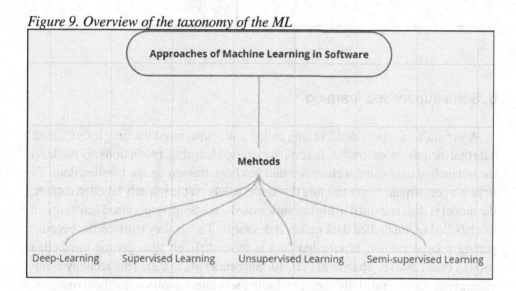

The supervised learning method has become popular due to its ability to complete any task
(Zhou et al., 2019, Gill et al., 2022). Here, it's the same for identifying software flaws. Supervised learning has a wide variety of uses, and this is one of them. They met the criteria for multi-class detection since they found more than two distinct classes of vulnerabilities. The supervised learning process is in Figure 10.

Figure 10. Overview of the supervised learning process

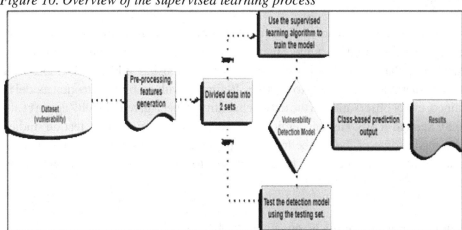

b. Semi-supervised learning

A variation of supervised learning called semi-supervised learning uses training data that includes occurrences. In semi-supervised learning, predictions are made on the unlabelled data using a classifier that has been trained on the labelled data. To improve performance over training the model solely on the initially labelled dataset, the model is then retrained using the anticipated data. Semi-supervised learning can use labelled or unlabelled data makes it desirable. This is very trustworthy because getting a large amount of labelled data is more difficult than getting unlabelled data(Li et al., 2021b, Shah et al., 2024d, Sharma et al., 2022). This strategy is advantageous for several study areas, including sentiment analysis, medical imaging, and facial recognition. The semi-supervisor process in Figure 11.

Figure 11. presents the semi-supervisor process

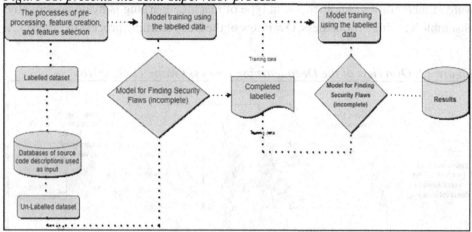

A semi-supervised approach was used to detect well-known software vulnerabilities such as cross-site request forgery, SQL injection, and XSS. They created six unique classifiers by employing algorithms such as J48, Naive Bayes, and Random Forests. An overview of the ensemble learning framework is in Figure 12.

Figure 12. Overview of the ensemble learning process

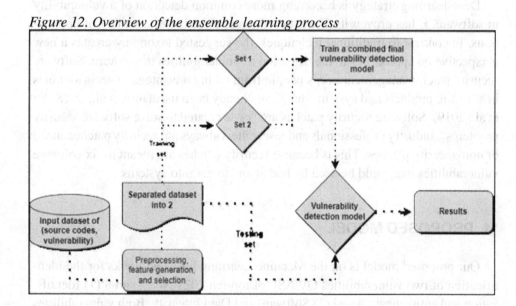

The ensemble learning method combines various prediction models to find software vulnerabilities. Another potent type of machine learning is made possible by ensemble learning's robustness. Overview of the Deep learning process in Figure 13.

Figure 13. Overview of the Deep learning process (Wang et al., 2018)

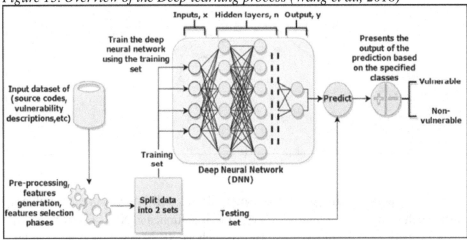

Deep learning strategy is becoming more common detection of a vulnerability in software, it has proven itself trustworthy and effective in a variety of applications. In contrast to traditional techniques, the suggested taxonomy creates a new perspective on approaches to the detection of vulnerabilities in software. Software security patch management keeps people from taking advantage of security holes in software products and systems that have already been used(Jurn et al., 2018, Yu et al., 2019). Software security patches are "code created to solve software security problems". Industry professionals and researchers always put security patches ahead of non-security patches. This is because security patches are meant to fix software vulnerabilities that could be used by bad actors to get into systems.

11. PROPOSED MODEL

Our proposed model is on the Machine Learning base and works for the identification of two vulnerabilities OWASP of top-ten 2021 No: 7 and 8 (1) Identification and authentication and (2) Software and Data Integrity. Both vulnerabilities are related to the SQL injection according to the literature review and Table 1 and Figure 13 Overview of our proposed model.

Figure 14.. Overview of the proposed framework for securing the SQL injection attack from hackers

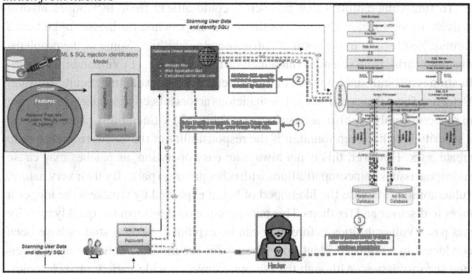

12. DISCUSSION

The study of how to find software weaknesses has grown essential as the frequency and sophistication of cyberattacks increase. People, companies, and even entire countries are susceptible to the destruction that these attacks can cause. Researchers and companies are spending more time and money to secure their software as a result. One of the main challenges in identifying software vulnerabilities is the enormous amount of code contained in contemporary software systems. It gets harder and harder to find every security hole in a system (Shah et al., 2024c, Yu et al., 2019) as software gets more complex. Software vulnerabilities are frequently hard to uncover since they are hidden deep inside the code and need specialised tools and techniques. Researchers and industry experts use a variety of techniques to identify weaknesses to get around these challenges. One approach is to use automated tools that check code for security issues. Static analysis, and symbolic execution, are used to analyse the software. Another choice is to use manual testing techniques like vulnerability scanning and pen testing. These techniques include breaking the software system to look for vulnerabilities that an attacker could exploit. Researchers also employ code audits to check for security holes in software.

To find vulnerabilities that bad actors could attack; these techniques involve actively trying to take advantage of them. Developers and businesses alike face a formidable obstacle in the form of software vulnerabilities. Some of the problems that might arise from software flaws include the following: (1) Vulnerability identification is difficult since it is one of the hardest parts of developing secure software. Detecting flaws that could be used by malicious actors is becoming more challenging in modern, highly sophisticated software systems. (2) Vulnerability patching: Once a security hole has been found, it is the responsibility of the software's creators to create a fix. However, this is not always an easy operation, as patches may cause additional issues or incompatibilities with other program parts. By their very nature, vulnerabilities increase the likelihood of being exploited by attackers the longer it takes to discover and fix them. This puts pressure on developers to quickly identify and patch vulnerabilities before they can be exploited. Several studies have been conducted in automated identifying threats for securing the software and associated security issues. Although the literature covers a wide variety of such topics, this review will focus on four major themes that repeatedly emerge throughout the literature reviewed secure software and (Gawron et al., 2018, Shah, 2024, Shah et al., 2024c) vulnerabilities, attacks, solutions proposed by researchers to detect these attacks, openness, and exploration of machine learning algorithms approaches to handle the threats and improve vulnerabilities.

13. CONCLUSION

Consequently, finding software vulnerabilities is crucial for software security research. It is critical currently because software developers are constantly creating new software. It encourages the detection of vulnerabilities in software still in development and effectively enables developers to lower the number of vulnerabilities that need to be fixed after the production stage. Software vulnerability identification and detection makes security easier for large organizations because they don't have to worry as much about the security of their software and can concentrate on a more difficult decision-making process. Our study revealed that more research is required to identify and detect software vulnerabilities with machine learning models.

14. FUTURE WORK

The lack of historical source codes and vulnerability histories makes real-world deployment very difficult. It's like finding zero-day vulnerabilities. To solve the issue of real-world applications, it is essential that additional advances in a reliable and efficient software vulnerability identification detection approach be made. The researchers are required to identify software vulnerabilities with machine learning models and need to work on two vulnerabilities OPWS top ten 2021 No: 07 and 08 (i) Software and Data Integrity Failure and (ii) identification and authentication failures of the top ten vulnerabilities of OWASP.

REFERENCES

Agrawal, A., Seh, A. H., Baz, A., Alhakami, H., Alhakami, W., Baz, M., Kumar, R., & Khan, R. A. (2020). Software security estimation using the hybrid fuzzy ANP-TOPSIS approach: Design tactics perspective. *Symmetry*, 12(4), 598. DOI: 10.3390/sym12040598

Ahvanooey, M. T., Li, Q., Rabbani, M., & Rajput, A. R. (2020). A survey on smartphones security: software vulnerabilities, malware, and attacks. arXiv preprint arXiv:2001.09406.

Alansari, Z., Anuar, N. B., Kamsin, A., Soomro, S., & Belgaum, M. R. (2017, November). Computational intelligence tools and databases in bioinformatics. In 2017 4th IEEE international conference on engineering technologies and applied sciences (ICETAS) (pp. 1-6). IEEE.

Alfadel, M., Costa, D. E., & Shihab, E. (2023). Empirical analysis of security vulnerabilities in python packages. *Empirical Software Engineering*, 28(3), 59. DOI: 10.1007/s10664-022-10278-4

Alferidah, D. K., & Jhanjhi, N. (2020). A review on security and privacy issues and challenges in internet of things. *International Journal of Computer Science and Network Security IJCSNS*, 20, 263–286.

Althar, R. R., Samanta, D., Kaur, M., Alnuaim, A. A., Aljaffan, N., & Aman Ullah, M. (2021). Software systems security vulnerabilities management by exploring the capabilities of language models using NLP. *Computational Intelligence and Neuroscience*, 2021(1), 2021. DOI: 10.1155/2021/8522839 PMID: 34987569

Arko, A. R., Khan, S. H., Preety, A., & Biswas, M. H. (2019). Anomaly detection. In *IoT using machine learning algorithms*. Brac University.

Arnold, B., & Qu, Y. (2020, December). Detecting software security vulnerability during an agile development by testing the changes to the security posture of software systems. In *2020 International Conference on Computational Science and Computational Intelligence (CSCI)* (pp. 1743-1748). IEEE.

Bahaa, A., Kamal, A. E.-R., & Ghoneim, A. S. (2022). A Systematic Literature Review on Software Vulnerability Detection Using Machine Learning Approaches. *FCI-H Informatics Bulletin*, 4, 1–9.

Belgaum, M. R., Alansari, Z., Musa, S., Alam, M. M., & Mazliham, M. (2021). Impact of artificial intelligence-enabled software-defined networks in infrastructure and operations: Trends and challenges. *International Journal of Advanced Computer Science and Applications*, 12(1), 12. DOI: 10.14569/IJACSA.2021.0120109

Belgaum, M. R., Ali, F., Alansari, Z., Musa, S., Alam, M. M., & Mazliham, M. (2022). Artificial intelligence based reliable load balancing framework in software-defined networks. *CMC—Comput.Mater. Contin*, 70, 251–266.

Belgaum, M. R., Charitha, T. H., Harini, M., Anusha, B., Sai, A. J., Yadav, U. C., & Alansari, Z. (2023). Enhancing the Efficiency of Diabetes Prediction through Training and Classification using PCA and LR Model. [AETiC]. *Annals of Emerging Technologies in Computing*, 7(3), 78–91. DOI: 10.33166/AETiC.2023.03.004

Bhatt, N., Anand, A., & Yadavalli, V. S. (2021). Exploitability prediction of software vulnerabilities. *Quality and Reliability Engineering International*, 37(2), 648–663. DOI: 10.1002/qre.2754

Bhuiyan, F. A., Sharif, M. B., & Rahman, A. (2021). Security bug report usage for software vulnerability research: A systematic mapping study. *IEEE Access: Practical Innovations, Open Solutions*, 9, 28471–28495. DOI: 10.1109/ACCESS.2021.3058067

Binyamini, H., Bitton, R., Inokuchi, M., Yagyu, T., Elovici, Y., & Shabtai, A. (2021, August). A framework for modeling cyber attack techniques from security vulnerability descriptions. In Proceedings of the 27th ACM SIGKDD conference on knowledge discovery & data mining (pp. 2574-2583).

Bosu, A., Carver, J. C., Hafiz, M., Hilley, P., & Janni, D. (2014, November). Identifying the characteristics of vulnerable code changes: An empirical study. In *Proceedings of the 22nd ACM SIGSOFT international symposium on foundations of software engineering* (pp. 257-268).

Boukhechba, M., Daros, A. R., Fua, K., Chow, P. I., Teachman, B. A., & Barnes, L. E. (2018). DemonicSalmon: Monitoring mental health and social interactions of college students using smartphones. *Smart Health (Amsterdam, Netherlands)*, 9, 192–203. DOI: 10.1016/j.smhl.2018.07.005

Bozorgi, M., Saul, L. K., Savage, S., & Voelker, G. M. (2010, July). Beyond heuristics: learning to classify vulnerabilities and predict exploits. In *Proceedings of the 16th ACM SIGKDD international conference on Knowledge discovery and data mining* (pp. 105-114).

Bullough, B. L., Yanchenko, A. K., Smith, C. L., & Zipkin, J. R. (2017, March). Predicting exploitation of disclosed software vulnerabilities using open-source data. In *Proceedings of the 3rd ACM on International Workshop on Security and Privacy Analytics* (pp. 45-53).

Cabral, G. G., Minku, L. L., Shihab, E., & Mujahid, S. (2019, May). Class imbalance evolution and verification latency in just-in-time software defect prediction. In *2019 IEEE/ACM 41st International Conference on Software Engineering (ICSE)* (pp. 666-676). IEEE.

Chhajed, G. J., & Garg, B. R. (2022). *Applying decision tree for hiding data in binary images for secure and secret information flow. Cybersecurity measures for e-government frameworks*. IGI Global.

Dawson, M., & Walker, D. (2022). Argument for Improved Security in Local Governments Within the Economic Community of West African States. Cybersecurity Measures for E-Government Frameworks, 96-106.

Dissanayake, N., Jayatilaka, A., Zahedi, M., & Babar, M. A. (2022). Software security patch management-A systematic literature review of challenges, approaches, tools and practices. *Information and Software Technology*, 144, 106771. DOI: 10.1016/j.infsof.2021.106771

Fan, Y., Li, J., Zhang, D., Pi, J., Song, J., & Zhao, G. (2019). Supporting sustainable maintenance of substations under cyber-threats: An evaluation method of cybersecurity risk for power CPS. *Sustainability (Basel)*, 11(4), 982. DOI: 10.3390/su11040982

Fateh, S., Sial, Q., Dar, S. H., Shah, I. A., & Rani, A. (2024). *Smart Healthcare System in Industry 4.0. Advances in Computational Intelligence for the Healthcare Industry 4.0*. IGI Global.

Finlayson, S. G., Bowers, J. D., Ito, J., Zittrain, J. L., Beam, A. L., & Kohane, I. S. (2019). Adversarial attacks on medical machine learning. *Science*, 363(6433), 1287–1289. DOI: 10.1126/science.aaw4399 PMID: 30898923

Gaur, L., Singh, G., Solanki, A., Jhanjhi, N. Z., Bhatia, U., Sharma, S., ... & Kim, W. (2021). Disposition of youth in predicting sustainable development goals using the neuro-fuzzy and random forest algorithms. Human-Centric Computing and Information Sciences, 11, NA.

Gaur, L., Ujjan, R. M. A., & Hussain, M. (2022). *The Influence of Deep Learning in Detecting Cyber Attacks on E-Government Applications. Cybersecurity Measures for E-Government Frameworks*. IGI Global.

Gawron, M., Cheng, F., & Meinel, C. (2018). Automatic vulnerability classification using machine learning. In Risks and Security of Internet and Systems: 12th International Conference, CRiSIS 2017, Dinard, France, September 19-21, 2017, Revised Selected Papers 12 (pp. 3-17). Springer International Publishing.

Ghaffarian, S. M., & Shahriari, H. R. (2017). Software vulnerability analysis and discovery using machine-learning and data-mining techniques: A survey. *ACM Computing Surveys*, 50(4), 1–36. DOI: 10.1145/3092566

Ghanem, M. C., & Chen, T. M. (2019). Reinforcement learning for efficient network penetration testing. *Information (Basel)*, 11(1), 6. DOI: 10.3390/info11010006

Gill, S. H., Razzaq, M. A., Ahmad, M., Almansour, F. M., Haq, I. U., Jhanjhi, N., Alam, M. Z., & Masud, M. (2022). Security and privacy aspects of cloud computing: A smart campus case study. *Intelligent Automation & Soft Computing*, 31, 117–128. DOI: 10.32604/iasc.2022.016597

Grammatikis, P. I. R., Sarigiannidis, P. G., & Moscholios, I. D. (2019). Securing the Internet of Things: Challenges, threats and solutions. *Internet of Things : Engineering Cyber Physical Human Systems*, 5, 41–70. DOI: 10.1016/j.iot.2018.11.003

Grieco, G., & Dinaburg, A. (2018, January). Toward smarter vulnerability discovery using machine learning. In *Proceedings of the 11th ACM Workshop on Artificial Intelligence and Security* (pp. 48-56).

Guo, N., Li, X., Yin, H., & Gao, Y. (2020). Vulhunter: An automated vulnerability detection system based on deep learning and bytecode. In Information and Communications Security: 21st International Conference, ICICS 2019, Beijing, China, December 15–17, 2019, Revised Selected Papers 21 (pp. 199-218). Springer International Publishing.

Hanif, H., Nasir, M. H. N. M., Ab Razak, M. F., Firdaus, A., & Anuar, N. B. (2021). The rise of software vulnerability: Taxonomy of software vulnerabilities detection and machine learning approaches. *Journal of Network and Computer Applications*, 179, 103009. DOI: 10.1016/j.jnca.2021.103009

Hasan, M., Islam, M. M., Zarif, M. I. I., & Hashem, M. (2019). Attack and anomaly detection in IoT sensors in IoT sites using machine learning approaches. *Internet of Things : Engineering Cyber Physical Human Systems*, 7, 100059. DOI: 10.1016/j.iot.2019.100059

Huang, T., Yu, F. R., Zhang, C., Liu, J., Zhang, J., & Liu, Y. (2016). A survey on large-scale software defined networking (SDN) testbeds: Approaches and challenges. *IEEE Communications Surveys and Tutorials*, 19(2), 891–917. DOI: 10.1109/COMST.2016.2630047

Humayun, M., Jhanjhi, N., Alruwaili, M., Amalathas, S. S., Balasubramanian, V., & Selvaraj, B. (2020). Privacy protection and energy optimization for 5G-aided industrial Internet of Things. *IEEE Access : Practical Innovations, Open Solutions*, 8, 183665–183677. DOI: 10.1109/ACCESS.2020.3028764

Humayun, M., Jhanjhi, N., Niazi, M., Amsaad, F., & Masood, I. (2022). Securing Drug Distribution Systems from Tampering Using Blockchain. [s Note: MDPI stays neu-tral with regard to jurisdictional claims in….]. *Electronics (Basel)*, 11(8), 1195. DOI: 10.3390/electronics11081195

Hussain, F., Hassan, S. A., Hussain, R., & Hossain, E. (2020). Machine learning for resource management in cellular and IoT networks: Potentials, current solutions, and open challenges. *IEEE Communications Surveys and Tutorials*, 22(2), 1251–1275. DOI: 10.1109/COMST.2020.2964534

Jhanjhi, N., Ahmad, M., Khan, M. A., & Hussain, M. (2022). *The impact of cyber attacks on e-governance during the covid-19 pandemic. Cybersecurity Measures for E-Government Frameworks*. IGI Global.

Johnson, A. L. (2022). The analysis of binary file security using a hierarchical quality model (Doctoral dissertation, Montana State University-Bozeman, College of Engineering).

Jurn, J., Kim, T., & Kim, H. (2018). An automated vulnerability detection and re-mediation method for software security. *Sustainability (Basel)*, 10(5), 1652. DOI: 10.3390/su10051652

Kailay, M. P., & Jarratt, P. (1995). RAMeX: A prototype expert system for computer security risk analysis and management. *Computers & Security*, 14(5), 449–463. DOI: 10.1016/0167-4048(95)00013-X

Kekül, H., Ergen, B., & Arslan, H. (2022). A Multiclass Approach to Estimating Software Vulnerability Severity Rating with Statistical and Word Embedding Methods. *International Journal of Computer Network and Information Security*, 12(4), 27–42. DOI: 10.5815/ijcnis.2022.04.03

Khalil, M. I., Humayun, M., Jhanjhi, N. Z., Talib, M. N., & Tabbakh, T. A. (2021). Multi-class segmentation of organ at risk from abdominal ct images: A deep learning approach. In Intelligent Computing and Innovation on Data Science [Springer Singapore.]. *Proceedings of ICTIDS*, 2021, 425–434.

Khan, N. K., Alnatsheh, E., Rasheed, R. A., Yadav, A., & Alansari, Z. (2020, August). A quantitative case study in WSNs: Design and implementation of student smart ID card. In 2020 International Conference on Computing, Electronics & Communications Engineering (iCCECE) (pp. 27-32). IEEE.

Kronjee, J., Hommersom, A., & Vranken, H. (2018, August). Discovering software vulnerabilities using data-flow analysis and machine learning. In *Proceedings of the 13th international conference on availability, reliability and security* (pp. 1-10).

Kuruvila, A. P., Zografopoulos, I., Basu, K., & Konstantinou, C. (2021). Hardware-assisted detection of firmware attacks in inverter-based cyberphysical microgrids. *International Journal of Electrical Power & Energy Systems*, 132, 107150. DOI: 10.1016/j.ijepes.2021.107150

Le, T. H. M., & Babar, M. A. (2022, May). On the use of fine-grained vulnerable code statements for software vulnerability assessment models. In *Proceedings of the 19th International Conference on Mining Software Repositories* (pp. 621-633).

Lee, K., & Yim, K. (2020). Cybersecurity threats based on machine learning-based offensive technique for password authentication. *Applied Sciences (Basel, Switzerland)*, 10(4), 1286. DOI: 10.3390/app10041286

Li, F., Rogers, L., Mathur, A., Malkin, N., & Chetty, M. (2019). Keepers of the machines: Examining how system administrators manage software updates for multiple machines. In *Fifteenth Symposium on Usable Privacy and Security (SOUPS 2019)* (pp. 273-288).

Li, J. (2020). Vulnerabilities mapping based on OWASP-SANS: a survey for static application security testing (SAST). arXiv preprint arXiv:2004.03216.

Li, N., Zhang, H., Hu, Z., Kou, G., & Dai, H. (2021, December). Automated software vulnerability detection via pre-trained context encoder and self attention. In *International Conference on Digital Forensics and Cyber Crime* (pp. 248-264). Cham: Springer International Publishing.

Li, Y. (2017). Deep reinforcement learning: An overview. arXiv preprint arXiv:1701.07274.

Li, Z., Zou, D., Xu, S., Jin, H., Zhu, Y., & Chen, Z. (2021b). Sysevr: A framework for using deep learning to detect software vulnerabilities. *IEEE Transactions on Dependable and Secure Computing*, 19(4), 2244–2258. DOI: 10.1109/TDSC.2021.3051525

Lim, M., Abdullah, A., Jhanjhi, N., & Supramaniam, M. (2019). Hidden link prediction in criminal networks using the deep reinforcement learning technique. *Computers*, 8(1), 8. DOI: 10.3390/computers8010008

Liu, X., Ospina, J., & Konstantinou, C. (2020). Deep reinforcement learning for cybersecurity assessment of wind integrated power systems. *IEEE Access : Practical Innovations, Open Solutions*, 8, 208378–208394. DOI: 10.1109/ACCESS.2020.3038769

Lu, J., Shang, C., Yue, C., Morillo, R., Ware, S., Kamath, J., Bamis, A., Russell, A., Wang, B., & Bi, J. (2018). Joint modeling of heterogeneous sensing data for depression assessment via multi-task learning. *Proceedings of the ACM on Interactive, Mobile, Wearable and Ubiquitous Technologies*, 2(1), 1–21. DOI: 10.1145/3191753

Márquez, G., & Astudillo, H. (2019, September). Identifying availability tactics to support security architectural design of microservice-based systems. In *Proceedings of the 13th European Conference on Software Architecture-Volume 2* (pp. 123-129).

Mehrotra, A., & Musolesi, M. (2018). Using autoencoders to automatically extract mobility features for predicting depressive states. *Proceedings of the ACM on Interactive, Mobile, Wearable and Ubiquitous Technologies*, 2(3), 1–20. DOI: 10.1145/3264937

Memon, M. S., Bhatti, M. N., Hashmani, M. A., Malik, M. S., & Dahri, N. M. (2022). *Techniques and Trends Towards Various Dimensions of Robust Security Testing in Global Software Engineering. Research Anthology on Agile Software, Software Development, and Testing*. IGI Global.

Miraz, M. H., Excell, P. S., Ware, A., Soomro, S., & Ali, M. (Eds.). (2019). Emerging Technologies in Computing: Second International Conference, iCETiC 2019, London, UK, August 19–20, 2019, Proceedings.

Mugarza, I., Parra, J., & Jacob, E. (2018). Analysis of existing dynamic software updating techniques for safe and secure industrial control systems. *International Journal of Safety and Security Engineering*, 8(1), 121–131. DOI: 10.2495/SAFE-V8-N1-121-131

Muzafar, S., Humayun, M., & Hussain, S. J. (2022). *Emerging Cybersecurity Threats in the Eye of E-Governance in the Current Era. Cybersecurity Measures for E-Government Frameworks*. IGI Global.

Nyre-Yu, M., Butler, K., & Bolstad, C. (2022). A task analysis of static binary reverse engineering for security.

Pant, S., & Hsu, C. (1995, May). Strategic information systems planning: a review. In *Information Resources Management Association International Conference* (Vol. 3, No. 2, pp. 432-441).

Ranganath, V.-P., & Mitra, J. (2020). Are free android app security analysis tools effective in detecting known vulnerabilities? *Empirical Software Engineering*, 25(1), 178–219. DOI: 10.1007/s10664-019-09749-y

Sahu, K., & Srivastava, R. (2018). 2019. Revisiting software reliability. *Data Management, Analytics and Innovation. Proceedings of ICDMAI*, 1, 221–235.

Sennan, S., Somula, R., Luhach, A., Deverajan, G., Alnumay, W., Jhanjhi, N., & Sharma, P. (2021). Energy efficient optimal parent selection based routing protocol for Internet of Things using firefly optimization algorithm. [Cybersecurity Issues and Challenges in the Drone Industry. IGI Global.]. *Transactions on Emerging Telecommunications Technologies*, 32(8), e4171. DOI: 10.1002/ett.4171

Shah, I. A., Jhanjhi, N. Z., & Ray, S. K. (2024f). *IoT Devices in Drones: Security Issues and Future Challenges. Cybersecurity Issues and Challenges in the Drone Industry*. IGI Global. DOI: 10.4018/979-8-3693-0774-8.ch009

Shah, I. A., Jhanjhi, N. Z., & Ujjan, R. M. A. (2024g). *Drone Technology in the Context of the Internet of Things. Cybersecurity Issues and Challenges in the Drone Industry*. IGI Global.

Shah, I. A., Jhanjhi, N. Z., & Ujjan, R. M. A. (2024h). *Use of AI Applications for the Drone Industry. Cybersecurity Issues and Challenges in the Drone Industry*. IGI Global.

Shah, I. A., Murugesan, R. K., & Rajper, S. (2024i). Supply Chain Management Security Issues and Challenges in the Context of AI Applications. Navigating Cyber Threats and Cybersecurity in the Logistics Industry, 59-89.

Sharma, R., Singh, A., Jhanjhi, N., Masud, M., Jaha, E. S., & Verma, S. (2022). Plant Disease Diagnosis and Image Classification Using Deep Learning. *Computers, Materials & Continua*, •••, 71. DOI: 10.32604/cmc.2022.020017

Siddique, S., Hridoy, A. A. I., Khushbu, S. A., & Das, A. K. (2022, October). Cvd: An improved approach of software vulnerability detection for object oriented programming languages using deep learning. In *Proceedings of the Future Technologies Conference* (pp. 145-164). Cham: Springer International Publishing.

Sindiramutty, S. R., Jhanjhi, N. Z., Tan, C. E., Khan, N. A., Shah, B., & Manchuri, A. R. (2024). *Cybersecurity Measures for Logistics Industry. Navigating Cyber Threats and Cybersecurity in the Logistics Industry*. IGI Global.

Souppaya, M., Scarfone, K., & Dodson, D. (2022). Secure software development framework (ssdf) version 1.1. *NIST Special Publication*, 800, 218. DOI: 10.6028/NIST.SP.800-218

Stütz, T., Kowar, T., Kager, M., Tiefengrabner, M., Stuppner, M., Blechert, J., & Ginzinger, S. (2015). Smartphone based stress prediction. In User Modeling, Adaptation and Personalization: 23rd International Conference, UMAP 2015, Dublin, Ireland, June 29—July 3, 2015. [Springer International Publishing.]. *Proceedings*, 23, 240–251.

Tata Sutabri, T. S. (2023). Design of A Web-Based Social Network Information System. *International Journal of Artificial Intelligence Research*, 6, 310–316.

Tian, J., Wang, B., Li, T., Shang, F., & Cao, K. (2020). Coordinated cyber-physical attacks considering DoS attacks in power systems. *International Journal of Robust and Nonlinear Control*, 30(11), 4345–4358. DOI: 10.1002/rnc.4801

Tiefenau, C., Häring, M., Krombholz, K., & Von Zezschwitz, E. (2020). Security, availability, and multiple information sources: Exploring update behavior of system administrators. In *Sixteenth Symposium on Usable Privacy and Security (SOUPS 2020)* (pp. 239-258).

Ujjan, R. M. A., Taj, I., & Brohi, S. N. (2022). *E-Government Cybersecurity Modeling in the Context of Software-Defined Networks. Cybersecurity Measures for E-Government Frameworks*. IGI Global.

Vigneswaran, R. K., Vinayakumar, R., Soman, K. P., & Poornachandran, P. (2018, July). Evaluating shallow and deep neural networks for network intrusion detection systems in cyber security. In 2018 9th International conference on computing, communication and networking technologies (ICCCNT) (pp. 1-6). IEEE.

Vinayakumar, R., Poornachandran, P., & Soman, K. P. (2018a). Scalable framework for cyber threat situational awareness based on domain name systems data analysis. Big data in engineering applications, 113-142.

Vinayakumar, R., Soman, K., & Poornachandran, P. (2018b). Evaluating deep learning approaches to characterize and classify malicious URL's. *Journal of Intelligent & Fuzzy Systems*, 34(3), 1333–1343. DOI: 10.3233/JIFS-169429

Vinayakumar, R., Soman, K., Poornachandran, P., Mohan, V. S., & Kumar, A. D. (2019). ScaleNet: Scalable and hybrid framework for cyber threat situational awareness based on DNS, URL, and email data analysis. *Journal of Cyber Security and Mobility*, 8(2), 189–240. DOI: 10.13052/jcsm2245-1439.823

Vinayakumar, R., Soman, K., Poornachandran, P., & Sachin Kumar, S. (2018c). Detecting Android malware using long short-term memory (LSTM). *Journal of Intelligent & Fuzzy Systems*, 34(3), 1277–1288. DOI: 10.3233/JIFS-169424

Wang, X., Wu, R., Ma, J., Long, G., & Han, J. (2018). Research on vulnerability detection technology for web mail system. *Procedia Computer Science*, 131, 124–130. DOI: 10.1016/j.procs.2018.04.194

Xiang, Y., Wang, L., & Liu, N. (2017). Coordinated attacks on electric power systems in a cyber-physical environment. *Electric Power Systems Research*, 149, 156–168. DOI: 10.1016/j.epsr.2017.04.023

Yang, Y., Wang, S., Wen, M., & Xu, W. (2021). Reliability modeling and evaluation of cyber-physical system (CPS) considering communication failures. *Journal of the Franklin Institute*, 358(1), 1–16. DOI: 10.1016/j.jfranklin.2018.09.025

Yu, Z., Theisen, C., Williams, L., & Menzies, T. (2019). Improving vulnerability inspection efficiency using active learning. *IEEE Transactions on Software Engineering*, 47(11), 2401–2420. DOI: 10.1109/TSE.2019.2949275

Zagane, M., Abdi, M. K., & Alenezi, M. (2020). Deep learning for software vulnerabilities detection using code metrics. *IEEE Access : Practical Innovations, Open Solutions*, 8, 74562–74570. DOI: 10.1109/ACCESS.2020.2988557

Zhang, J. J., Liu, K., Khalid, F., Hanif, M. A., Rehman, S., Theocharides, T., & Garg, S. (2019, June). Building robust machine learning systems: Current progress, research challenges, and opportunities. In *Proceedings of the 56th Annual Design Automation Conference 2019* (pp. 1-4).

Zhou, M., Chen, J., Liu, Y., Ackah-Arthur, H., Chen, S., Zhang, Q., & Zeng, Z. (2019). A method for software vulnerability detection based on improved control flow graph. *Wuhan University Journal of Natural Sciences*, 24(2), 149–160. DOI: 10.1007/s11859-019-1380-z

Chapter 2
The Internet of Things:
An Intelligent and Secure Path Approach for Cyber Critical Infrastructure

Imtiaz Hussain

https://orcid.org/0000-0002-7947-9178

Faculty of Engineering, Science, and Technology, Iqra University, Karachi, Pakistan

Zainab Alansari

University of Technology and Applied Sciences, Oman

Mansoor Ebrahim

Faculty of Engineering, Science, and Technology, Iqra University, Karachi, Pakistan

ABSTRACT

The logistics system is evolving in a more intelligent direction. Logistic planning and coordination of information management and software platforms are inextricably linked to the fulfilment of smart logistics. The logistics and transportation business are one of the critical application areas for cyber-physical systems, which are novel technological intelligent systems that incorporate computing at its most fundamental level and technology for connectivity. Over the past decade, the Internet has changed the way people work and live. The purpose of this is to introduce a smart algorithm-based path decision technique. It is determined that the random algorithm has the best path optimization impact in resolving the logistics path decision by comparing the shortest transport distance and convergence speed under the two algorithm decisions. The logistics path decision problem was optimised using the Genetic Algorithm and random algorithm before the most effective algorithm was

DOI: 10.4018/979-8-3693-3703-5.ch002

chosen. The shortest path using the random algorithm was 424.3. It was discovered after comparing the two algorithms. Following, the RO algorithm's shortest path was 434.5873.

1. INTRODUCTION

The Internet of Things and how are you Denmark ogle has had an astonishing development recently that has had a significant impact on society, yet there is still a divide between the real world and the digital one. A new category of designed systems known as "Cyber-Physical Systems" (CPS) combines software control, autonomous decision-making, and signals from a dynamic, uncertain environment. The internet changed how people communicate and handle information. The way that individuals engage with engineered systems has been altered by CPS technology. IoT is frequently used to create a self-organizing wireless network connecting the internet and physical items. IoT enables autonomous communication between smart items, eliminating human interfaces in real-time. To integrate embedded computers, physical processes, sophisticated networking, and communication technologies, the concept of cyber-physical systems (CPS) was developed. The engineering function-alities of IoT and CPS differ significantly. IoT focuses mostly on implementation strategies and service-oriented applications, whereas CPS emphasizes the concepts of recognizing and overcoming challenges in cross-pollination between the cyber and physical worlds. The Industrial Internet of Things (IIoT), which enables digital service (DS), is crucial for maintaining manufacturing's long-term competitiveness. One of the Industry 4.0 modules in this concept that draws a lot of attention is the IoT driver (Sampayo and Peças, 2022, Zhang, 2018, Humayun et al., 2021). By providing fresh perspective solutions to change their activities, it is a robust communication between the physical and digital worlds that is employed in various domains to make goods, operations, and services smarter in the value chain. All the gadgets are connected via internet-based wireless technology, allowing for interactions that result in smarter operations. Sensors, which use gadgets to convey a lot of data in real-time, enable systems to be aware of their surroundings(Almusaylim et al., 2020, Shah et al., 2024b, Alferidah and Jhanjhi, 2020).

IoT can have a substantial impact on the supply chain in terms of efficient re-source utilization, transparency and visibility of the whole supply chain, real-time supply chain management, supply chain optimization, and increased supply chain agility. DS is the deployment of digital technologies to change the focus of manu-facturing organizations' business models from product to service(Shah, 2024, Shah et al., 2024a, Anandan et al., 2021). Even though the control action is not real-time, there has been a lot of research recently on how to analyze and optimize physical infrastructure in built settings such as CPS.

Edge computing and machine learning will probably play a major role in offering such learning technologies in conventional CPS. Contrary to systems that only use software, CPS must consider physical limitations like inertia and latency in both sensing and actuation(Yadav and Dadhich, 2022, Humayun et al., 2020b, Shah et al., 2024d). To provide such learning technologies in traditional CPS, edge computing and machine learning will be crucial. CPS must account for physical constraints like inertia and latency in both sensing and actuation, as opposed to systems that just employ software(Humayun et al., 2020a). operating restrictions and the goal function of the system process(Mishra et al., 2020, Vaza et al., 2022). The logistics system is evolving toward intelligence. Current research often divides the CPS system model into sensing and application. The distinction between the two layers' fundamental components is found in their intermediary layer. CPS is currently altering how people connect with the physical world fig 4.

Figure 1. An overview of Cyber-Physical System [12]

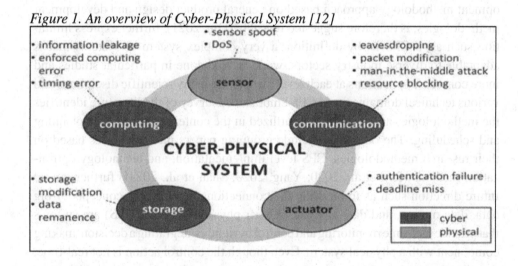

This research combines CPS characteristics with an algorithm-based direction approach assessment of current logistical activity. The CPS logistic channel modelling approach offers the foundation for the integration of IoT technology. We introduce the current state of research into intelligent logistics path decisions, outline the issues with the current logistics system.

This chapter's contributions are in the following points:

- A brief explanation of the definition and features of CPS technology and IoT technology that focuses on the analysis of their differences and relationships.

- Our research provides an objective, algorithm-based direction technique assessment of current logistics activities and combines CPS features.
- We will evaluate the minimum two algorithm decisions, the travelling duration, and resolution speed, the ant colony approach delivers the best route planning influence in resolving the logistics track decisions.

2. LITERATURE REVIEW

This section reviews related studies on IoT technologies and smart logistic approaches for cyber-physical platforms and focuses on an algorithm-based, objective direction approach to assessing ongoing logistical operations that incorporates CPS characteristics. Further, the evaluate the several algorithms and approach delivers the best route planning influence in resolving the logistics track decisions(Abdullahi et al., 2022, Shah et al., 2024e, Zhang, 2018). To identify possibilities where the application of CPS could boost performance, CPSD2, a CPS design and development methodology approach based on general product design and development methodologies, is therefore suggested reveal by(Qin, 2021), further express limitation such as, a CPS is, by definition, a very complex system of systems that is adaptable to diverse industry sectors, work may be done in particular studies and more concrete applications at each level, deepening many scientific disciplines and various technical domains that a CPS embraces A survey of the literature identifies the methodologies and technologies utilized in the context of production planning and scheduling. The outcomes include grouping papers into categories based on their research methodologies, CPS level implementation, and technology optimization methods (Ren et al., 2020, Yang, 2020, Shah et al., 2024f) further, reveal future direction such as to describe the connections between the concepts of big data, data mining, and data analytics. Cyber-physical systems (CPS) are systems that provide real-time monitoring and control by tightly integrating a decision-making component with a physical system. Even though the control action is not real-time, there has been a lot of research recently on how to analyze and optimize physical infrastructure in built settings as CPS(Lu et al., 2021, Zhang and Yang, 2021, Shah et al., 2024c). However, there are significant disadvantages to modern modelling and implementations of predictive maintenance, three of which served as the inspiration for the model created and described in this study. Large-scale renovations necessitate significant time and financial investments, as well as a rise in complexity. Large-scale data generation necessitates complicated data storage and management systems. Learning algorithms learn the maintenance trends from the past machine states, offering maintenance prognosis and maintenance predictive models(Zhao, 2018, Abudureheman and Nilupaer, 2021). Cyber-physical systems (CPS) are widely used in many application fields thanks to the quick development of software and physical hardware. It is challenging to find flaws in CPS models due to the rising complexity of these systems. The use of counterexample creation in CPS model checking is a wise decision because it can quickly identify flaws in CPS models and offer useful diagnostic input to speed up debugging. Numerous works investigate robustness-guided counterexample production of CPS, which falsifies the stated characteristics of a CPS using various optimization techniques(Shi et al., 2020). We present a unique algorithm known as the ARSG algorithm by combining the genetic algorithm (GA) with an acceptance-rejection technique based on the vicinity of the input sequence space. This algorithm's concept is like reinforcement learning's "exploration-exploitation." Finally, the performance of the new algorithm is evaluated against that of the cross-entropy algorithm and the genetic algorithm using various parameters. The new algorithm performs better than the other two algorithms. In recent years, machine learning and artificial intelligence have significantly improved information systems and cyber-physical systems security. Numerous studies have been conducted in this field, leading to an explosion of publications over the last two years. It can be difficult to select the best algorithm to address a complex security issue in a highly specific industrial setting. We, therefore, propose a learning algorithm recommendation framework (Ma and Wang, 2024, Zhu and Shi, 2021, Li and Li, 2019) for a precisely defined situation, directs the choice of a learning algorithm and a scientific field that has attracted significant interest from the scientific community and, as a result, offers preponderant elements and benefits for further deployments. This study on recurrent neural networks and its variations serves as an example of how this framework has the benefit of having been created after a thorough analysis of the literature. Through software controllers that monitor their physical environments and make decisions, Cyber-Physical Systems (CPS) continuously interact with them. Engineers can examine the Field Operational Test (FOT) logs for the CPS under consideration to determine how well it can accomplish specified goals. Due to the expense and risk involved in doing so, it is difficult to repeat numerous FOTs to produce statistically significant results. (Yu et al., 2022, Lei and Qiu, 2020)Simulation-based verification can be a good substitute for effective CPS goal verification to overcome this issue, but it necessitates a precise virtual environment model that can take the role of the actual environment and interact with the CPS in a closed loop. The environmental model generation problem is explicitly defined, and we use imitation learning (IL) algorithms to address it. Furthermore, we propose three concrete applications for our strategy in the advancement of CPS. undertake a case study with a streamlined driverless car equipped with a lane-keeping system to verify our methodology(Seeger et al., 2022, Li et al., 2019). The case study outcomes demonstrate that, using simulations, our method can produce precise virtual environment models for CPS goal verification at a reasonable cost. The Internet of Things (IoT) and cyber-physical systems (CPSs) are complementary concepts for integrating digital capabilities. The CPS is more geared toward vertical integration, facilitating connections between hardware, software, networks, and computing. But IoT places a strong emphasis on tying things together for horizontal applications today that will eventually lead to the Internet of Everything. Two crucial characteristics of IoT that have been underlined in recent definitions are smartness and the explosion of data(Zhang et al., 2015, Karadimas et al., 2014). The real power of both paradigms lies in the collection, analysis, and control of data and computation. It is essential for the growth of both CPS and IoT to adequately handle both problems. The success of deep learning in numerous IoT applications has made it clear that these models will be essential to the establishment of the CPS. For successfully building such models over CPS architectures, a thorough analysis is required due to the models' complexity, including their size, resource demand, and training techniques. A theoretical paradigm for the distribution of deep neural networks over a three-tier CPS architecture(Niemueller et al., 2016). The initial layer of the design is made up of actuators, which are embedded systems that collect data. Nodes with intermediate resource management abilities make up the second layer. Most deep learning tasks are hosted by the third layer, which is resource rich. A quick overview of the present problems and the next projects will also be given(Zhang et al., 2018). IoT enables information sharing and networked interaction between appliances, automobiles, and other devices, which made sense and was probably inexpensive with a wise decision. On the other hand, in the IoT-enabled Cyber-Physical System, Cyber Security has emerged as a crucial concern (CPS) (Mingyong et al., 2014). These difficulties include the connected supply chain, increased IoT device data production that can be used as big data, the industrial control system, etc. CPS is referred to as an engineering system made up of both physical objects and cybernetic entities. The IoT and CPS are not separate fields of technology; in fact, the IoT serves as the foundation for CPS, which is a developing branch of the IoT. To provide a method for envisioning and realizing all parts of a system, IoT and CPS are combined as a closed-loop system. Using a computational algorithm, the aspects are controlled and monitored. There is a lot of overlap between the IoT and CPS, but their engineering approaches differ fig 2.

Figure 2. The taxonomy of Literature review

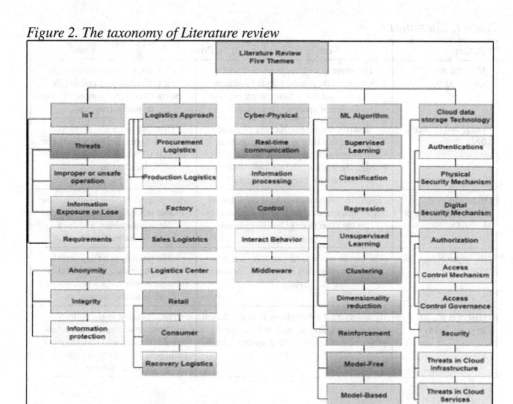

Table 1. The summary of articles

Citation	Year	Prose	Cons
(Sampayo and Peças, 2022, Zhang and Yang, 2021)	Using a cutting-edge risk-based methodology, we locate and evaluate IoT-enabled attack vectors against crucial cyber-physical systems.		The enhancement of physical interaction types during the interaction modelling phase
(Zhang, 2018)	IoT opens new possibilities for improving intralogistics performance		Despite being such a widely used technology in the online world, the internet of things still has enormous growth potential in the future.
(Humayun et al., 2021, Abudureheman and Nilupaer, 2021)	an intelligent algorithm-based path determination technique		The overall effectiveness of the logistics operation and control system still must be improved
(Almusaylim et al., 2020)	to offer a framework for IoT-based CPS architecture that will make it easier to integrate IoT and CPS		Integration of IoT-based CPS with various IoT devices and enterprise platforms is still being worked on

continued on following page

Table 1. Continued

Citation	Year	Prose	Cons
(Alferidah and Jhanjhi, 2020)	The strategy seeks to maximize social welfare while avoiding trade failures in the face of unknown future agent types or knowledge of upcoming bids and offers	Utilizing on-demand solutions for both passenger and freight transportation can increase the use of public resources	
(Yadav and Dadhich, 2022)	describe the notion of cyber-physical systems and their novel consequences and provide the impetus for Industry 4.0. Finally, the writers offer up-and-coming and innovative business concepts	There are just a few developed methodologies and procedures that include CPS in the creation of new business models	
(Humayun et al., 2020b, Niemueller et al., 2016)	High flexibility and quick reconfiguration capabilities of internal logistics are needed on the shop floor to handle tailored production.	Model-based intelligent applications enable information interpretation, decision-making, and even interaction	
(Humayun et al., 2020a)	The matrix production structure as a cyber-physical system that emphasises logistical issues	The model can be developed into a more intricate model that incorporates inventory optimization for tools and components	
(Mishra et al., 2020, Liu et al., 2018)	By supplying a cyber-physical model design and description, a solution for a cyber-physical waste management system is made available	The allocation of the collection and transfer station next to its tasks might be taken into consideration during the modelling and validation of the system	

3. ARCHITECTURE OF ML ALGORITHMS

Recursion in an algorithm Machine learning accomplishes its goal of reacting to its surroundings by continuously examining it and changing its behaviour in response to the environment's feedback. The text demonstrates the fundamental idea. The agent selects an action to be used in the environment after completing a specific task. After the action has changed the environment's state, a return signal is generated to provide feedback to the agent, who then decides what action to take next considering the return signal and the environment's current state(Hang and Lei, 2018). In this cycle, the agent progressively refines its own behaviour using the freshly created signal data. The agent can finally discover the best course of action to carry out the appropriate task after multiple iterations, or the best strategy. Depending on the return signal and the state of the environment, the agent decides what to do next(He, 2015), the agent progressively refines its own behaviour using the freshly created signal data. The agent can eventually learn the best course of action to take to fulfil the associated task, or the best strategy, after several cycles' fig 3.

Figure 3. ML algorithm exploration topology

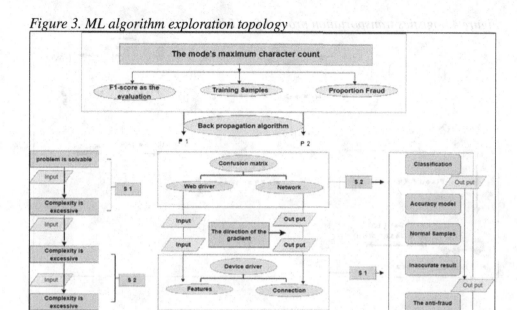

4. ANALYSIS OF LOGISTIC PROCESSES

Customers use the network to place product orders and then allocate the duties using the online store platform in line with the order details. This is the general procedure of urban logistics transportation. To transfer the products, the delivery staff uses handheld RFID to scan the merchandise. In this manner, the delivery of the items (Zhang, 2018) to the destination is completed after the transport is carried out step-by-step and the inform is input. The specific transit method for urban logistics is shown in Figure 4.

Figure 4. logistics transportation process for Urban

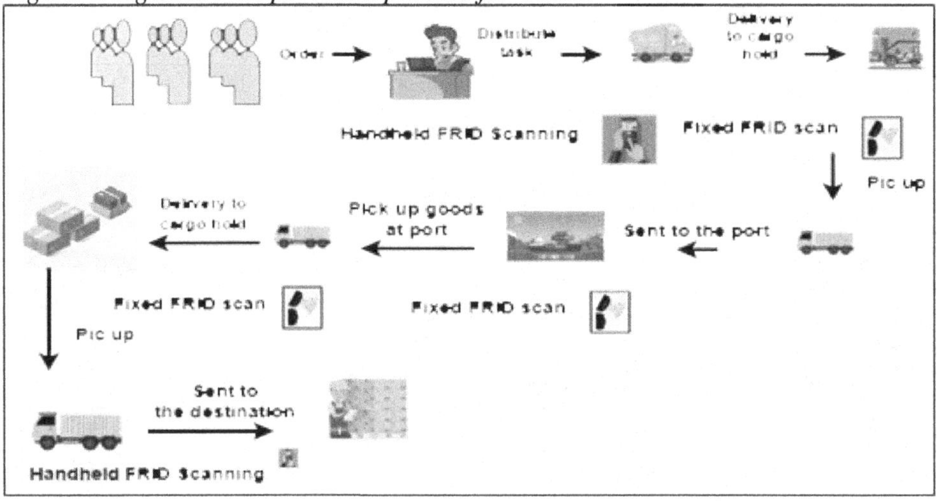

5. INTELLIGENT LOGISTICS PATH DECISION

One of the main problems in modern smart logistics is how to effectively use diverse sensor resources and optimise the urban logistics path determination system. From a mathematical perspective, the fundamental concept of ant random optimization algorithm is to treat the distribution facility as an ant colony, with each ant acting as a vehicle for distribution and the food serving as a node for distribution. These ants adhere to the following mobile criteria, which states that the next distribution node is chosen depending on the pheromone concentration and the path's visibility. The dependability of the path is better and the distance between distribution nodes is shorter when the pheromone concentration is higher. Since visibility measures the distance between distribution nodes, the best path is one with a short distance and high visibility.

6. OUR PROPOSED METAHEURISTICS

Previous research offers a variety of solutions, from simple to complex metaheuristic algorithms for solving the traveling duration, and resolution speed complication. Here, we extend the same Random optimization Algorithm (ROA) presented in based on a logistics track decisions approach.

6.1 Random Optimization Algorithm (ROA)

ROA is a local method known for its adaptability, quickness concerning execution time and effectiveness in terms of the caliber of solutions discovered. It is a particular kind of numerical optimization method that can be used to solve issues where the differentiability of the performance function is not assumed. Iteratively going to superior spots in the search space that are sampled using a normal distribution around the current position is how ROA operates fig 5.

Figure 5. ROA Optimization Algorithm flow chart

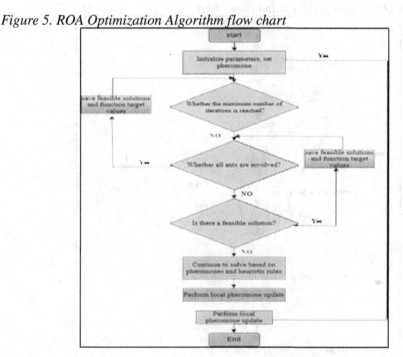

6.2 Genetic Algorithm

The GA is a search method that was initially created by the computing industry and is used to locate exact or close solutions to optimization and search issues. In fact, this metaheuristic is a part of a larger class of evolutionary algorithms that are regularly employed to produce helpful solutions and are based on the principles of natural selection. Genetic algorithm employ physiologically derived methods like natural selection, crossover, mutation, and inheritance

Table 2. The Setting the parameters for the genetic algorithm

Parameter	Set Value	Parameter	Set Value
Population size	NIND = 120	Probability	RM = 0.05
Maximum number of heritages	MAXGEN = 230	230	GGAP = 0.9
Gross probability	PC = 0.9	Generation gap	

Figure 6. GA Optimization Algorithm flow chart

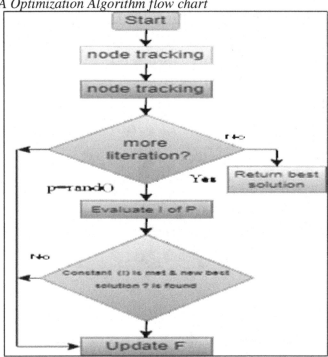

ROA with few parameters, the initialization process is straightforward, and it is particularly appropriate for handling the shortest transport distance, and the rate of convergence problems.

Figure 7. Optimal solution of ROA in logistics path

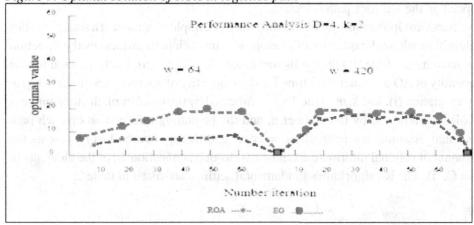

Figure 8. ROA flow chart

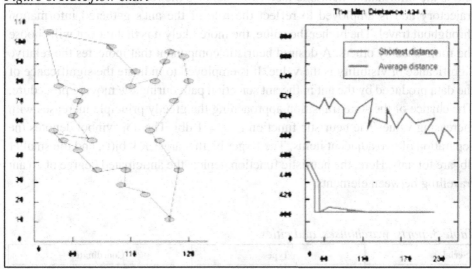

As a result, it is mostly employed in the path optimization problem of logistics distribution. However, ROA has significant flaws, including a greater propensity for premature phenomena that cause ROA to stall. This is mostly brought on by the irrationality of pheromone setting and updating.

The pheromone is prone to pheromone accumulation, which is easily responsible for the instability of ROA. As demonstrated in Figure 6, ROA is better suited for situations where the problem's size is unknown, and the size is substantial. If there is a significant issue, the ROA can self-organize and run in parallel to improve and speed up the logistics path selection.

Random Optimization-based Pathfinding The implementation of a smart logistics algorithm where the quantity of pheromones on each path influences the direction of movement of the RO during its movement (k = 2, 3,... n). Let bi(t) stand for the quantity of RO at element b at time I and the quantity of pheromones on path (b,j) at intercalation (i). The size of the TSP is indicated by the number m, the total number of RO is indicated by the number n, and the beginning information on each path is equal. Assume that intercalaj(i) = const and that q = vn b=1 aj represents the amount of residual information on the two-to-one connection lbj of the elements in set C. (i). The Ro algorithm's fundamental settings are listed in table 2.

$$R^a_{bj(t)} = \left\{ \frac{\tau j(t) \eta bk(t)]\beta}{\sum_0 \delta[\varepsilon allowedg \left[\tau bj(t)\alpha.[\eta b\delta(t)\beta \right.} \right.$$

(1)

The next element that ant R can select is denoted by allowedg in the formula and is the information heuristic factor that denotes the relative significance of the trajectory and is employed to reflect the role of the ant's gathered information throughout travel. The higher the value, the more likely it is that the ant will choose the route used by others. A desired heuristic component that indicates the relative significance of visibility is the value. It is employed to indicate the significance of the data produced by the ant in the ant selection path during the moving procedure. The chance of the state transition approaching the greedy principle increases with increasing value. The heuristic function is bj = 1 dbj. The dbj symbol denotes the separation of two adjacent items. The larger bj, the larger R k bj(t), and the smaller dbj are for ants. Here, the heuristic function depicts the anticipated degree of an ant travelling between elements.

Table 3. ports, warehouses, and cities.

Serial	Type	Coordinate
Lb0	City	18,30
1	Port	36,74
2	Warehouse	53,67
4	Warehouse	26,72
5	Warehouse	7,74
6	City	67,70
7	Port	81,50

continued on following page

Table 3. Continued

Serial	Type	Coordinate
8	Warehouse	84,70
9	Warehouse	65,62
10	Warehouse	19,60
11	Port	23,65
12	Warehouse	84,50
13	Port	92,48
14	Port	46,45
15	City	26,39
16	Warehouse	25,43
17	Warehouse	59,69
18	Port	72,72
19	Warehouse	75,79
20	Port	59,70
21	Port	72,71
22	Port	73,80
23	Warehouse	83,9
24	Warehouse	63,42
25	City	4,57

Table 2 shows the Setting the parameters for the RO algorithm
Parameter set value Parameter set value
Number of parameters n=33 Maximum number NC max = 230
Characterizing the important Alpha = 1 The pheromones increase R = 120
of pheromones the intensity coefficient
characterizing the import of Beta = 6 Pheromones evaporation Rho = 0.1
heuristic factors coefficient

7. DISCUSSION

In comparison to the GA, the ROA improves request satisfaction by up to 85%. In terms of a solution, this superior performance results in an improvement of up to 18% over ROA. In comparison to the other ROA, SP also exhibits good outcomes. Compared to the ACA and SP methods, the ROA has shorter run times.

The GA and random optimization technique we suggest come close to an acceptable resolution. Despite numerous studies attempting to address the logistics path decision problem, only a small number of studies attempt to address the logistics path decision (shortest distance path) problem, according to our performance evaluation of confirmed tests. Therefore, it is crucial to create new and additional metaheuristics for tackling SP problems.

8. CONCLUSION

The logistics system is evolving in a more intelligent direction. Logistic planning and coordination of information management and software platforms are inextricably linked to the fulfillment of smart logistics. The logistics and transportation business are one of the critical application areas for cyber-physical systems, which are novel technological intelligent systems that incorporate computing at its most fundamental level and technology for connectivity. Over the past decade, the Internet has changed the way people work and live. The propose of this is to a smart algorithm-based path decision technique. It is determined that the random algorithm has the best path optimization impact in resolving the logistics path decision by comparing the shortest transport distance and convergence speed under the two algorithm decisions. The logistics path decision problem was optimised using the Genetic Algorithm and random algorithm before the most effective algorithm was chosen. The shortest path using the random algorithm was 424.3. It was discovered after comparing the two algorithms. Following, the RO algorithm's shortest path was 434.5873.

REFERENCES

Abdullahi, M., Baashar, Y., Alhussian, H., Alwadain, A., Aziz, N., Capretz, L. F., & Abdulkadir, S. J. (2022). Detecting cybersecurity attacks in internet of things using artificial intelligence methods: A systematic literature review. *Electronics (Basel)*, 11(2), 198. DOI: 10.3390/electronics11020198

Abudureheman, A., & Nilupaer, A. (2021). Optimization model design of cross-border e-commerce transportation path under the background of prevention and control of COVID-19 pneumonia. *Soft Computing*, 25(18), 12007–12015. DOI: 10.1007/s00500-021-05685-6 PMID: 33716560

Alferidah, D. K., & Jhanjhi, N. (2020). A review on security and privacy issues and challenges in internet of things. *International Journal of Computer Science and Network Security IJCSNS*, 20, 263–286.

Almusaylim, Z. A., Alhumam, A., & Jhanjhi, N. (2020). Proposing a secure RPL based internet of things routing protocol: A review. *Ad Hoc Networks*, 101, 102096. DOI: 10.1016/j.adhoc.2020.102096

Anandan, R., Deepak, B. S., Suseendran, G., & Jhanjhi, N. Z. (2021). Internet of things platform for smart farming. Human Communication Technology: Internet of Robotic Things and Ubiquitous Computing, 337-369.

Hang, C., & Lei, Z. (2018). Improved tabu search algorithm for solving the shortest path problem. *J. Transp. Sci. Technol.*, 20, 35–38.

He, X. (2015). Study on Optimization of Logistics Distribution Routing based on Improved Ant Colony Algorithm. International Journal of Simulation--Systems, Science & Technology, 16.

Humayun, M., Jhanjhi, N., Alruwaili, M., Amalathas, S. S., Balasubramanian, V., & Selvaraj, B. (2020a). Privacy protection and energy optimization for 5G-aided industrial Internet of Things. *IEEE Access : Practical Innovations, Open Solutions*, 8, 183665–183677. DOI: 10.1109/ACCESS.2020.3028764

Humayun, M., Jhanjhi, N., Alsayat, A., & Ponnusamy, V. (2021). Internet of things and ransomware: Evolution, mitigation and prevention. *Egyptian Informatics Journal*, 22(1), 105–117. DOI: 10.1016/j.eij.2020.05.003

Humayun, M., Niazi, M., Jhanjhi, N., Alshayeb, M., & Mahmood, S. (2020b). Cyber security threats and vulnerabilities: A systematic mapping study. *Arabian Journal for Science and Engineering*, 45(4), 3171–3189. DOI: 10.1007/s13369-019-04319-2

Karadimas, D., Polytarchos, E., Stefanidis, K., & Gialelis, J. (2014, September). Information system framework architecture for organization agnostic logistics utilizing standardized IoT technologies. In *2014 Federated Conference on Computer Science and Information Systems* (pp. 1337-1343). IEEE.

Lei, Y., & Qiu, X. (2020). Evaluating the investment climate for China's cross-border E-Commerce: The application of back propagation neural network. *Information (Basel)*, 11(11), 526. DOI: 10.3390/info11110526

Li, G., & Li, N. (2019). Customs classification for cross-border e-commerce based on text-image adaptive convolutional neural network. *Electronic Commerce Research*, 19(4), 779–800. DOI: 10.1007/s10660-019-09334-x

Li, J., Wang, T., Chen, Z., & Luo, G. (2019). Machine learning algorithm generated sales prediction for inventory optimization in cross-border E-commerce. *International Journal of Frontiers in Engineering Technology*, 1, 62–74.

Liu, F., Liu, Y., Jin, D., Jia, X., & Wang, T. (2018). Research on workshop-based positioning technology based on internet of things in big data background. *Complexity*, 2018(1), 2018. DOI: 10.1155/2018/7875460

Lu, C.-W., Lin, G.-H., Wu, T.-J., Hu, I.-H., & Chang, Y.-C. (2021). Influencing factors of cross-border e-commerce consumer purchase intention based on wireless network and machine learning. *Security and Communication Networks*, 2021, 1–9. DOI: 10.1155/2021/8388480

Ma, X., & Wang, Z. (2024). Computer security technology in E-commerce platform business model construction. *Heliyon*, 10(7), 10. DOI: 10.1016/j.heliyon.2024. e28571 PMID: 38586367

Mingyong, L., Changfei, J., & Kai, N. (2014). Logistics CPS: Implementation and challenge of next generation intelligent logistics system. *Systems Engineering*, 29, 60–65.

Mishra, S. K., Mishra, S., Alsayat, A., Jhanjhi, N., Humayun, M., Sahoo, K. S., & Luhach, A. K. (2020). Energy-aware task allocation for multi-cloud networks. *IEEE Access : Practical Innovations, Open Solutions*, 8, 178825–178834. DOI: 10.1109/ ACCESS.2020.3026875

Niemueller, T., Ewert, D., Reuter, S., Ferrein, A., Jeschke, S., & Lakemeyer, G. (2016). Robocup logistics league sponsored by festo: A competitive factory automation testbed. *Automation. Communication and Cybernetics in Science and Engineering*, 2015/2016, 605–618. DOI: 10.1007/978-3-319-42620-4_45

Qin, Z. (2021). Research on cross-border E-commerce third-party logistics model based on machine learning algorithm. *Solid State Technology*, 64, 1454–1461.

Ren, S., Choi, T.-M., Lee, K.-M., & Lin, L. (2020). Intelligent service capacity allocation for cross-border-E-commerce related third-party-forwarding logistics operations: A deep learning approach. *Transportation Research Part E, Logistics and Transportation Review*, 134, 101834. DOI: 10.1016/j.tre.2019.101834

Sampayo, M., & Peças, P. (2022). CPSD2: A new approach for cyber-physical systems design and development. *Journal of Industrial Information Integration*, 28, 100348. DOI: 10.1016/j.jii.2022.100348

Seeger, P. M., Yahouni, Z., & Alpan, G. (2022). Literature review on using data mining in production planning and scheduling within the context of cyber physical systems. *Journal of Industrial Information Integration*, 28, 100371. DOI: 10.1016/j.jii.2022.100371

Shah, I. A. (2024). Drone Industry Security Issues and Challenges in the Context of IoD. *Cybersecurity Issues and Challenges in the Drone Industry*, 310-323.

Shah, I. A., Jhanjhi, N., & Ray, S. K. (2024a). *Artificial Intelligence Applications in the Context of the Security Framework for the Logistics Industry. Advances in Explainable AI Applications for Smart Cities*. IGI Global.

Shah, I. A., Jhanjhi, N. Z., & Brohi, S. N. (2024b). *Use of AI-Based Drones in Smart Cities. Cybersecurity Issues and Challenges in the Drone Industry*. IGI Global.

Shah, I. A., Jhanjhi, N. Z., & Ray, S. K. (2024c). *Enabling Explainable AI in Cybersecurity Solutions. Advances in Explainable AI Applications for Smart Cities*. IGI Global.

Shah, I. A., Jhanjhi, N. Z., & Ujjan, R. M. A. (2024d). *Drone Technology in the Context of the Internet of Things. Cybersecurity Issues and Challenges in the Drone Industry*. IGI Global.

Shah, I. A., Jhanjhi, N. Z., & Ujjan, R. M. A. (2024e). *Use of AI Applications for the Drone Industry. Cybersecurity Issues and Challenges in the Drone Industry*. IGI Global.

Shah, I. A., Laraib, A., Ashraf, H., & Hussain, F. (2024). Drone Technology: Current Challenges and Opportunities. Cybersecurity Issues and Challenges in the Drone Industry, 343-361.

Shi, Y., Wang, T., & Alwan, L. C. (2020). Analytics for cross-border e-commerce: Inventory risk management of an online fashion retailer. *Decision Sciences*, 51(6), 1347–1376. DOI: 10.1111/deci.12429

Vaza, R. N., Prajapati, R., Rathod, D., & Vaghela, D. (2022). Developing a novel methodology for virtual machine introspection to classify unknown malware functions. *Peer-to-Peer Networking and Applications*, 15(1), 793–810. DOI: 10.1007/s12083-021-01281-5

Yadav, V. K., & Dadhich, M. (2022). *Machine Learning in Cyber Physical Systems for Agriculture: Crop Yield Prediction Using Cyber Physical Systems and Machine Learning. Real-Time Applications of Machine Learning in Cyber-Physical Systems.* IGI Global.

Yang, Y. (2020). RETRACTED ARTICLE: Research on the optimization of the supplier intelligent management system for cross-border e-commerce platforms based on machine learning. *Information Systems and e-Business Management*, 18(4), 851–870. DOI: 10.1007/s10257-019-00402-1

Yu, L., Wei, W., Guo, J., & Qin, X. (2022). Construction of cross border E-commerce comprehensive training curriculum system based on virtual simulation. In The 2021 International Conference on Machine Learning and Big Data Analytics for IoT Security and Privacy: SPIoT-2021 Volume 1 (pp. 707-714). Springer International Publishing.

Zhang, F., & Yang, Y. (2021). Trust model simulation of cross border e-commerce based on machine learning and Bayesian network. *Journal of Ambient Intelligence and Humanized Computing*, 1–11.

Zhang, N. (2018). Smart logistics path for cyber-physical systems with internet of things. *IEEE Access: Practical Innovations, Open Solutions*, 6, 70808–70819. DOI: 10.1109/ACCESS.2018.2879966

Zhang, Y., Guo, Z., Lv, J., & Liu, Y. (2018). A framework for smart production-logistics systems based on CPS and industrial IoT. *IEEE Transactions on Industrial Informatics*, 14(9), 4019–4032. DOI: 10.1109/TII.2018.2845683

Zhang, Y., Wu, X. Y., & Kwon, O. K. (2015). Research on kruskal crossover genetic algorithm for multi-objective logistics distribution path optimization. *International Journal of Multimedia and Ubiquitous Engineering*, 10(8), 367–378. DOI: 10.14257/ijmue.2015.10.8.36

Zhao, X. (2018, October). A Study on the Applications of Big Data in Cross-border E-commerce. In 2018 IEEE 15th International Conference on e-Business Engineering (ICEBE) (pp. 280-284). IEEE.

Zhu, W., & Shi, M. (2021). Research on the development path of a cross-European e-commerce logistics mode under the background of "internet plus". *Wireless Communications and Mobile Computing*, 2021(1), 1–7. DOI: 10.1155/2021/6964302

Chapter 3
Generative AI for Visualization

N. Z. Jhanjhi
https://orcid.org/0000-0001-8116-4733
School of Computer Science, Taylor's University, Malaysia

Imdad Ali Shah
https://orcid.org/0000-0003-2015-1028
Faculty of Engineering Science & Technology, Iqra University, Malaysia

Sarfraz Nawaz
School of Computing and Creative Technologies, University of the West of England, UK

ABSTRACT

The primary objective of this chapter is focused on improvement and helping Generative AI for visualization such as automating the design of visuals and making it easier to understand patterns, trends, and outliers. Recent advances in machine learning (ML) and artificial intelligence (AI) have produced potent generative AI tools and techniques that can generate text, code, graphics, and other media in response to human commands. The technology has generated a lot of curiosity, which has led to conjecture about the fields—visualization included—that such methods could replace or enhance. Still unknown, though, is whether visualization tasks would be especially well-suited to the use of generative artificial intelligence. In recent years, generative artificial intelligence (GenAI) has advanced significantly and shown outstanding performance in a variety of generating tasks across multiple disciplines, including computational design and computer vision. A lot of academics have tried to use GenAI's enhanced generative capacity for various tasks by integrating it into visualization frameworks. We map the present and fu-

DOI: 10.4018/979-8-3693-3703-5.ch003

ture capabilities of generative AI throughout the various stages of the visualization lifecycle and highlight key potentials and problems using real-world examples from the field. AI provides answers for a wide range of issues that both consumers and business owners face. Computer-based information can benefit economic growth, organizations, managers, and buyers. Without a doubt, AI improves human lives. Artificial intelligence has the potential to improve economic growth and raise everyone's standard of living. People and businesses everywhere are eager to invest in human resources, and e-business is crucial to continuously providing customers with the easiest way to purchase goods and services. AI and ML are being applied in an increasing number of different use cases as a result of the emergence of new, significantly enhanced AI and ML technology and applications. The widespread use of AI solutions in people's daily lives and the operations of several organizations raises the possibility of new risks and weaknesses.

INTRODUCTION

The practice of creating graphical representations of abstract or spatial data to support exploratory data analysis is known as visualization. A lot of researchers have recently tried to use artificial intelligence (AI) for tasks involving visualization. Since visualization primarily entails interactions and representations of raw data, a growing number of visualization researchers have begun utilizing the quickly evolving generative artificial intelligence (GenAI) technology, which allows for the creation of artificial content and data by learning from preexisting human samples(Agrawal et al., 2022, Anik and Bunt, 2021). Chatbots and virtual assistants driven by AI offer real-time customer service by managing orders, answering questions, and resolving problems without the need for human participation. These AI-powered solutions boost operational effectiveness and customer happiness by offering prompt, round-the-clock assistance(Baldrati et al., 2022, Battle et al., 2018). As an example, Sephora's Facebook Messenger chatbot provides appointment scheduling, product recommendations, and beauty advice, essentially serving as a personal shopper.

Chatbots are used by most of banking and e-commerce websites to increase client happiness and offer better services. These chatbots were created utilizing synthetic methods involving artificial intelligence and machine learning. They can act in a human-like manner. These chatbots can learn, so they can provide clients with the best recommendations based on historical data that is available. Chatbots and virtual assistants are anticipated to provide even more complex and tailored customer interactions as AI technology develops, hence improving the e-commerce experience(Borgo et al., 2012, Chen et al., 2023). AI-powered dynamic pricing algorithms employ demand, competition, and other variables to modify prices in real-time. In addition to giving clients fair and appealing prices, this guarantees competitive pricing and maximizes revenue for e-commerce enterprises. Artificial intelligence (AI)-powered dynamic pricing has completely changed the e-commerce industry by allowing companies to dynamically modify prices in response to current market data. Artificial intelligence is used to implement image search on e-commerce websites. Algorithms for image processing provide its foundation. Clients can look up an item using its photograph. It is not necessary to use the keywords to search for the item. Overview Generative AI for design and engineers in Figure 1.

Figure 1. Overview Generative AI for design and engineers

we forecast what will occur when AI enables experts to identify, and monitor cyberattacks and prevent numerous, significant losses(Chen et al., 2021). One use of machine learning is the recognition of spam and junk mail. Highlighting the importance of error-detection systems and strong system architecture. While technology increases audit efficiency, the report points out that proactive steps are needed to assure data dependability and correctness due to its vulnerability to errors. Natural disasters and geopolitical crises are examples of external factors that increase the complexity of inventory management in e-commerce(Chen and Liu, 2023, Chen et al., 2020). The influence of unforeseen events on supply chains and inventory levels was emphasized in the literature assessment. Keep in mind that AI works better with IoT and smart devices. When these industries adopt IoT in their operations, numerous cyberattacks or vulnerabilities are reduced globally.

which deals with the necessity of stopping, identifying, and recovering from system failures. Although these attacks must be rapidly discovered, it takes a long time for human or skilled experts to monitor, track, or recover from such cyberattacks. So, in a short while, we forecast what will occur when AI enables experts to identify, and monitor cyberattacks and prevent numerous, significant losses(Cho et al., 2021, Schetinger et al., 2023). One use of machine learning is the recognition of spam and junk mail. Because cyber security is essential to every industry and business, particularly crucial ones, it is a pressing issue.

This chapter's contributions are in the following points:

- We discussed the Generative AI and Visualization
- We discussed the Challenges and Opportunities
- We discussed the Future Directions
- We provide recommendations and future work

LITERATURE REVIEW

Recent years have seen the rise of GenAI, which has had a significant and broad influence on several study and application areas, including interaction and artifact design. With just text suggestions, laypeople lacking formal training in art and design may now effortlessly create high-quality digital paintings or designs thanks to multi-modal AI generation models like Stable Diffusion. Large language models like GPT also show off the amazing potential of reasoning, discourse, and knowledge embedding in natural language creation(Dibia, 2023, Dibia and Demiralp, 2019). About 60 years ago, the idea of artificial intelligence (AI) was conceived. AI is "the art of creating machines that perform when carried out by humans, demand intelligence. Owing to the shift in lifestyles, one requires intelligent technology that automates tasks in addition to saving time. Artificial intelligence (AI), the Internet of Things (IoT), and big data are disrupting every aspect of life, from the home to the workplace and professional spheres. It has drastically changed the way we conduct day-to-day operations. The next generation of artificial intelligence is growing quickly in practically every industry, including banking, education, healthcare, and finance, which ultimately helps several businesses(Dosovitskiy et al., 2020, Evirgen and Chen, 2023). It is believed that artificial intelligence will shape society in the future. Technology is effectively being introduced into all areas of the workplace. The primary driver behind all new technologies in the modern period is the shift towards Industry 4.0. Customers now have new experiences and options, thanks to e-commerce. It's more than just an adaptable marketplace for buying and selling. products and services, but it had gone above and beyond. Music and video streaming represented e-commerce functions that were expanded(Shah et al., 2024b, Shah, 2024). In addition to the convenience of buying, e-commerce offers customizable entertainment options. Artificial intelligence is incorporated into e-commerce to improve its offerings. AI made it possible to follow clients more precisely, which improved customer satisfaction and produced more leads. AI is not just used by online retailers; it also benefits customers during their online buying experience. It goes along with the clients at every stage, from selecting items to completing the payment. Artificial intelligence (AI) encompasses a wide range of techniques, including machine learning, robotics, expert systems, artificial neural networks, data mining, natural language processing, and computer vision, to achieve a high degree of accuracy and flexibility. Overview Generative AI for improving data visualization charts in Figure 2.

Figure 2. Overview Generative AI for improving data visualization charts

The cost and complexity of the ICs are rising in tandem with their scaling down. In order to cut costs and complexity, IC fabrication is being moved offshore, increasing the supply chain's vulnerability to hardware attacks. Attackers have an additional opportunity to introduce harmful circuitry or programs into the design due to the diversity of the IC supply chain. The market, after-life cycle, and third-party vendors are highlighted in blue to indicate the outside parties' role in the integrated circuit supply chain(Fu et al., 2020, Gan et al., 2023). Furthermore, although this assumption isn't always true, crucial control and communication functions rely on the security of the hardware platform on which they are implemented. There have been concerns, for instance, that backdoors may be used to manage nuclear power facilities, transportation networks, and weapon control systems. Examples of realistic hardware attacks are counterfeit gadgets, a security flaw in hotel keycards, and a security flaw in parking payment cards. Modern computing systems' open-source tools, such as commercial and open-source FPGA CAD tools, have created new avenues for remote attacks that don't require the target to be physically there(Goodfellow et al., 2020, Han et al., 2022). As such, a growing number of new security risks are targeting computing hardware. On the other hand, deliberate design modifications, unintended design faults, and system side effects could all contribute to hardware vulnerabilities. They usually try to steal cryptographic operations, machine learning (ML) models, secure systems, and intellectual property. In the context of the Internet of Things (IoT), hardware security is advantageous(He et al., 2021, Hegselmann et al., 2023). The definition of the Internet of Things (IoT) is the ability of smart computer devices to connect physical items over the Internet. Its reach has extended to encompass all facets of contemporary society, including the vital domains of e-healthcare, finance, energy, and defense applications, among others. These days, smart platforms are being increasingly adopted by all kinds of organizations, including hospitals, companies, shopping centers, financial institutions, household appliances, and space science research facilities. These platforms connect all electronic devices to swiftly gather, process, and transfer data. Furthermore, the global IoT market is anticipated to grow from 478.36 billion dollars in 2022 to 2,465.26 billion dollars in 2029, at a compound annual growth rate (CAGR) of 26.4% throughout the forecast period(Shah et al., 2024a). The open structure of IoT nodes and the involvement of third parties make information leakage from them quite easy. Overview Data Visualization with Generative AI in Figure 3.

Figure 3. Overview Data Visualization with Generative AI adopted from Yilin Ye, Jianing Hao

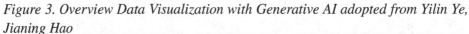
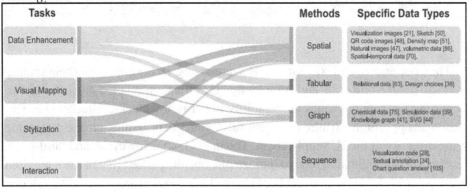

Numerous factors, such as the extensive interconnection of disparate and hetero-geneous systems, the accessibility of sensitive data, the ease with which malicious software can be distributed, and the challenges associated with identifying and prosecuting computer crimes, make strong data security on the Web imperative(Shah et al., 2024d, Hong et al., 2019). The two primary components that are necessary for a secure Web foundation are access control and communication security. While communication security services guarantee the integrity and confidentiality of data transmitted via networks, access control services anticipate the unauthorized use of online resources. End users that utilize web browsers run the danger of several security and privacy issues when using the internet. Browser bugs may compromise the security of web clients, and consumer data may be collected and utilized for profiling, raising valid security concerns. Treats and executable materials—like Java applets and ActiveX controls—present additional security risks. Organization servers, which house most of organization administrations, are usually protected by firewall innovation. However, configuring servers and constructing firewalls are challenging and error-prone, thus robust host-based security measures are required in addition to firewall defences.

Insider attacks are becoming a growing concern in large corporate intranets, underscoring the need for updated or enhanced get-to-control models to meet the various security requirements of web-based services. Traditional access control approaches, such as mandatory access control (MAC) and optional access control (DAC), are limited in their ability to provide high security assurance and adapt-ability(Hu et al., 2019, Huang et al., 2018). A more comprehensive method that streamlines security organization and supports organizational security arrangements is provided by role-based access control (RBAC) models. Web-based applications and WFMSs particularly benefit from RBAC models, even though they must be encouraged to evolve in order to properly address complicated security requirements. To improve security in dynamic and scattered web scenarios, emerging techniques like agent-based security highlights, task-based access control (TBAC) models, and certificate-based approaches are also being investigated. Another crucial element is to promote participation and operation. If users believe a platform is secure, they are more likely to utilize it frequently(Huang et al., 2021, Hullman and Diakopoulos, 2011). Often, advanced engagement scenarios arise from users' sense of security and confidence in the platform's ability to protect their data. Users are more inclined to adopt and utilize new features when they have confidence in the platform's security enhancing their satisfaction and the overall value they decide from the service.

Overview Generative AI

These days, artificial intelligence (AI) is growing in popularity. Even though it is still in its infancy, the way it will change business activities is being used in a variety of areas and businesses. Given the continued advancements in AI(Shah et al., 2024e, Kafle et al., 2018). Currently, only the largest companies can conduct AI-enabled e-commerce transactions because of the infrastructure costs and complexity involved.

However, there is a lack of customer awareness regarding AI-enabled transactions; hence, there are relatively few There are several empirical studies on the use of AI in e-commerce. Disparate research has been done on artificial intelligence, particularly as it relates to retailing. As a result, it was challenging to reach any useful conclusions based on the body of accessible literature(Kafle et al., 2020, Kim et al., 2022). This study focused only on e-commerce-related AI research after conducting a thorough evaluation of the literature. Subsequently, it explains how each subset of AI works in e-commerce. To the best of our knowledge, this study is the first to demonstrate how a certain subset of AI can be used in e-commerce operations. Robotics, for example, is linked to lowering human intervention and automating e-commerce tasks. The research has identified the functioning of each subgroup of AI, and it may aid future researchers in determining which AI technology best suits their needs(Kim et al., 2020, Kwon and Ma, 2019). Artificial intelligence (AI)-based technology has advanced and been more widely used in our daily lives thanks to the technological disruptions of the digital age. Numerous studies on AI and its subsets have been conducted in a variety of fields, including management, marketing, and e-commerce.

Both concepts have not been covered by any of the previously presented studies in management. In addition, while these studies have discussed the functionalities of AI in e-commerce, they have not shown how technology is associated with e-commerce functionality. The most used AI subsets in e-commerce were found to be chatbots and voice assistants, followed by personalization, recommendation systems, and automation(Lai et al., 2020, Lee et al., 2019). The pace at which AI-enabled transactions are currently being completed and reviewed also indicates that as soon as AI technology matures, its acceptance and use will increase. Artificial intelligence, big data, and the Internet of Things (IoT) have transformed the way e-commerce companies run. Scholars and Global practitioners are constantly searching for the most appropriate AI technologies to use in e-commerce. To expand the application of AI in e-commerce, this study compiled the research on the subject and included several subsets of AI that are applicable in other fields. It examined several pieces of literature related to marketing, IS, management, and e-commerce. To fully understand how AI functions in e-commerce, however, further research must be done on its actual applications. The Google Scholar platform's data was searched.

To obtain a significant understanding of the components, other publications written by distinguished scholars were also consulted. The most popular AI-related keywords and the most pertinent research publications were utilized to narrow down the literature search(Shah et al., 2024f, Li et al., 2021). Journal articles and review papers were discussed as offering the most thorough understanding of the technology. It is clear from the research done for this study that artificial intelligence has greater applications in e-commerce. AI has several facets that need to be investigated because of its user-friendliness and assisting features. It will undoubtedly draw further researchers, which will open opportunities for numerous practical applications.

Overview Generative AI for Visualization

The generation algorithms rely on data structures that exhibit common properties across several domains, even when the targets of production vary across different domains, such as text, code, multi-media, and 3D generation. Categorization based on data structures can help with more concrete knowledge of the algorithms concerning the many types of data involved in various visualization tasks, especially in GenAI4VIS applications(Li et al., 2024, Li et al., 2022). Here, we give a general introduction to the various GenAI kinds using common data structures related to data visualization.

A form of AI technology known as generative artificial intelligence (GenAI) creates synthetic artifacts by examining training examples, picking up on their patterns and distribution, and then producing lifelike facsimiles. GenAI leverages current media, including text, graphics, audio, and video, to create diverse content at scale through generative modeling and deep learning (DL) advancements. The fact that GenAI creates new content by learning from data rather than explicit programming is one of its primary characteristics.

Using artificial intelligence models that can produce new information in response to language cues, generative AI data visualization offers a novel and fascinating approach to producing graphical or visual representations of data(Liu et al., 2023, Liu et al., 2022). With the use of generative AI and data visualization, you may improve your creativity, innovation, engagement, and fun while better understanding complex data, finding patterns, communicating insights, and making decisions. However, utilizing generative AI for data visualization can also be risky, unreliable, inaccurate, deceptive, immoral, and irresponsible. As such, you should use caution and critical thinking when working with it, and make sure your visualization is accurate before sharing or using it(Liu et al., 2020, Shah et al., 2024c). The process of turning data into graphical or visual representations, including charts, graphs, maps, or pictures, is known as data visualization. We can share insights, find patterns in complex data, comprehend it better, and make decisions with the aid of data visualization.

A subfield of artificial intelligence known as "generative AI" is concerned with producing original content—like literature, pictures, music, or videos—using pre-existing models or data. Data visualization using generative AI may produce a wide range of realistic and varied visuals from the data, including faces, landscapes, and artwork. Presents GenAI4VIS applications for different visualization tasks in Figure 4.

Figure 4. GenAI4VIS applications for different visualization tasks adopted from Yilin Ye

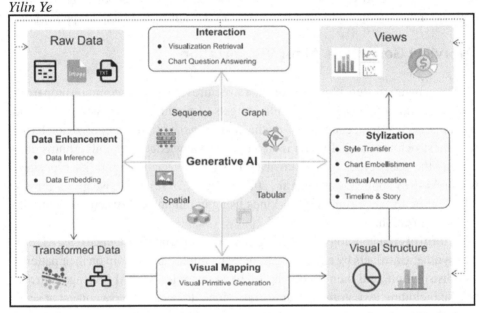

Despite GenAI's remarkable potential, its distinct data format and analytical needs might present numerous difficulties when used for visualization. For instance, the process of creating visualization images differs greatly from that of creating artistic or natural photos(Jhanjhi and Shah, 2024). First off, evaluating GenAI for visualization tasks is more involved than evaluating natural picture creation because there are a lot more variables to consider than just image similarity, like efficiency and data integrity. Complete integration with end-to-end GenAI approaches is challenging due to the differences between typical visualization pipelines with strict rule-based constraints. Because of these distinct features, it is more difficult to use the most recent pre-trained GenAI models in a general domain to enable visualization-specific generation. Consequently, it's critical to comprehend how GenAI has been applied in earlier works for a range of visualization applications, what obstacles have been overcome, and, most importantly, how the tasks have been tailored to the use of GenAI approaches.

Challenges and Opportunities

the growing application of GenAI in the creation of intricate and imaginative visuals. Applying comparable assessment criteria to AI-generated visuals becomes imperative, given the critical role that rigorous evaluation plays in the design of visualizations. The unique features and difficulties posed by AI-driven visualization processes require that evaluation criteria and procedures be carefully adjusted. The introduction of AI approaches has brought up new, criteria that need to be considered, even though conventional metrics like efficiency and aesthetics are still crucial for assessing AI-generated visualizations(Liu et al., 2018, Lu et al., 2024). The following evaluation criteria are probably going to be considered while assessing various GenAI applications in visualization, based on the migration of assessment metrics for GenAI. Figure 5 Presents the limitations in Generative AI for visualization.

Figure 5. The limitations in Generative AI for visualization

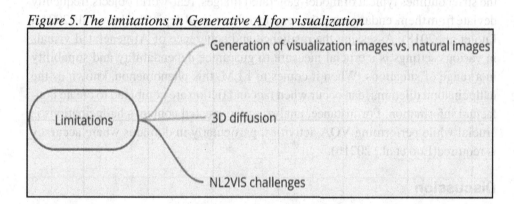

For the development of visual primitives, the training data can be a major constraint. The model is trained on only four primary chart kinds, which severely restricts the generation's breadth and diversity. Furthermore, incomplete rules may restrict some hybrid approaches that combine GenAI with rule-based components(Lu et al., 2020). For instance, Overview Challenges & opportunities for generative AI in visualization in Figure 6.

73

Figure 6. Overview Challenges & opportunities for generative AI in visualization

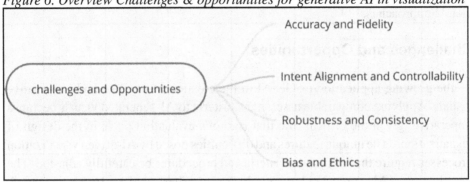

Accuracy and Fidelity

challenges and Opportunities — Intent Alignment and Controllability

Robustness and Consistency

Bias and Ethics

It is crucial to guarantee precision and authenticity in AI-generated graphics, especially when utilizing stylization methods. The difficulty lies in striking a balance between data integrity and visual attractiveness when using techniques like semantic contextualization in visualization. This is important because, contrary to the strict outlines typical of model-generated images, real-world objects frequently deviate from them, endangering the veracity of the visual depiction(Luo et al., 2021a, Luo et al., 2018). Assessing the resilience and coherence of AI-generated visuals in various settings is a crucial measure to guarantee dependability and suitability in a range of situations. When it comes to LLM, this phenomenon, known as the hallucination dilemma, can occur when fact and fiction are combined to create non-factual information. For instance, analyzing the created content's hallucinations is crucial while performing VQA activities, particularly in domains where accuracy is required(Luo et al., 2021b).

Discussion

Currently, generic measures like root mean square error (RMSE) are only used to evaluate the quality of data restoration concerning the data image. However, because original data was not included in the evaluation, such pixel-wise measurements are unable to accurately capture the accuracy of data restoration. Additionally, visualization images have a limited amount of capacity for data embedding. More specifically, it appears that embedding capacity and image quality can be traded off. Large-scale data recovery makes it more difficult to preserve image quality above a particular threshold. More assessments of the precision requirements for the original data in real-world circumstances are required to allay this worry(Luo et al., 2023, Ma et al., 2020). To the best of our knowledge, no study has focused on a thorough examination of GenAI approaches used in visualization, despite various earlier studies covering the use of AI generally for visualization. This survey compiles the AI-powered generating techniques created for visualisation and does a thorough literature assessment. We classify the different GenAI techniques based on the specific tasks they tackle, which align with distinct phases of visualization production. We can compile 81 research papers on GenAI4VIS in this manner. We specifically concentrate on the various algorithms applied to jobs to assist researchers in comprehending the problems and the state-of-the-art technical advancements. We also talk about and highlight possible directions for further research. As such, the generative models based on DRL remain essentially opaque (Masry et al., 2023). Furthermore, although DRL may extract useful dimensions, it might not encapsulate the visual qualities users desire to investigate. This could limit users' ability to customize their data exploration. More user participation is being attempted in some recent efforts to improve DRL through a visual interface.

CONCLUSION AND FUTURE WORK

The visualization area has great promise for the use of the rapidly developing GenAI technology. A variety of visualization activities, including data augmentation, the creation of visual maps, stylization, and interaction, can benefit from GenAI's remarkable ability to model the transformation and design process through learning from real data. Due to the many data structures involved in these jobs, several GenAI techniques have been used, including sequence generation, tabular generation, spatial generation, and graph generation. The introduction of new GenAI technologies, like diffusion models and big language models, presents fresh chances to transform GenAI4VIS techniques. Still, given the special nature of visualization tasks, there are task-specific difficulties that need to be further explored. Furthermore, the GenAI4VIS pipeline needs to be rethought to address broader assessment and dataset concerns, rather than only repurposing cutting-edge GenAI techniques. With an eye on further integrating GenAI in visualization, this chapter will assist academics in thinking critically about the state of the art in GenAI4VIS research from a technical standpoint and offer some ideas for future research directions.

REFERENCES

Agrawal, A., Kajić, I., Bugliarello, E., Davoodi, E., Gergely, A., Blunsom, P., & Nematzadeh, A. (2022). Reassessing evaluation practices in visual question answering: A case study on out-of-distribution generalization. arXiv preprint arXiv:2205.12191.

Anik, A. I., & Bunt, A. (2021, May). Data-centric explanations: explaining training data of machine learning systems to promote transparency. In *Proceedings of the 2021 CHI Conference on Human Factors in Computing Systems* (pp. 1-13).

Baldrati, A., Bertini, M., Uricchio, T., & Del Bimbo, A. (2022). Effective conditioned and composed image retrieval combining clip-based features. In *Proceedings of the IEEE/CVF conference on computer vision and pattern recognition* (pp. 21466-21474).

Battle, L., Duan, P., Miranda, Z., Mukusheva, D., Chang, R., & Stonebraker, M. (2018, April). Beagle: Automated extraction and interpretation of visualizations from the web. In *Proceedings of the 2018 CHI Conference on Human Factors in Computing Systems* (pp. 1-8).

Borgo, R., Abdul-Rahman, A., Mohamed, F., Grant, P. W., Reppa, I., Floridi, L., & Chen, M. (2012). An empirical study on using visual embellishments in visualization. *IEEE Transactions on Visualization and Computer Graphics*, 18(12), 2759–2768. DOI: 10.1109/TVCG.2012.197 PMID: 26357185

Chen, C. & Liu, Z. (2023). The state of the art in creating visualization corpora for automated chart analysis. Computer Graphics Forum. Wiley Online Library, 449-470.

Chen, J., Ling, M., Li, R., Isenberg, P., Isenberg, T., Sedlmair, M., Möller, T., Laramee, R. S., Shen, H.-W., Wünsche, K., & Wang, Q. (2021). Vis30k: A collection of figures and tables from ieee visualization conference publications. *IEEE Transactions on Visualization and Computer Graphics*, 27(9), 3826–3833. DOI: 10.1109/TVCG.2021.3054916 PMID: 33502982

Chen, Q., Cao, S., Wang, J., & Cao, N. (2023). How does automation shape the process of narrative visualization: A survey of tools. *IEEE Transactions on Visualization and Computer Graphics*. PMID: 37030780

Chen, X., Zeng, W., Lin, Y., Ai-Maneea, H. M., Roberts, J., & Chang, R. (2020). Composition and configuration patterns in multiple-view visualizations. *IEEE Transactions on Visualization and Computer Graphics*, 27(2), 1514–1524. DOI: 10.1109/TVCG.2020.3030338 PMID: 33048683

Cho, J., Lei, J., Tan, H., & Bansal, M. (2021, July). Unifying vision-and-language tasks via text generation. In *International Conference on Machine Learning* (pp. 1931-1942). PMLR.

Dibia, V. (2023). LIDA: A tool for automatic generation of grammar-agnostic visualizations and infographics using large language models. arXiv preprint arXiv:2303.02927.

Dibia, V., & Demiralp, Ç. (2019). Data2vis: Automatic generation of data visualizations using sequence-to-sequence recurrent neural networks. *IEEE Computer Graphics and Applications*, 39(5), 33–46. DOI: 10.1109/MCG.2019.2924636 PMID: 31247545

Dosovitskiy, A. (2020). An image is worth 16x16 words: Transformers for image recognition at scale. arXiv preprint arXiv:2010.11929.

Evirgen, N., & Chen, X. A. (2023, April). Ganravel: User-driven direction disentanglement in generative adversarial networks. In *Proceedings of the 2023 CHI Conference on Human Factors in Computing Systems* (pp. 1-15).

Fu, J., Zhu, B., Cui, W., Ge, S., Wang, Y., Zhang, H., Huang, H., Tang, Y., Zhang, D., & Ma, X. (2020). Chartem: Reviving chart images with data embedding. *IEEE Transactions on Visualization and Computer Graphics*, 27(2), 337–346. DOI: 10.1109/TVCG.2020.3030351 PMID: 33315567

Gan, W., Xu, H., Huang, Y., Chen, S., & Yokoya, N. (2023). V4d: Voxel for 4d novel view synthesis. *IEEE Transactions on Visualization and Computer Graphics*. PMID: 37669213

Goodfellow, I., Pouget-Abadie, J., Mirza, M., Xu, B., Warde-Farley, D., Ozair, S., Courville, A., & Bengio, Y. (2020). Generative adversarial networks. *Communications of the ACM*, 63(11), 139–144. DOI: 10.1145/3422622

Han, K., Wang, Y., Guo, J., Tang, Y., & Wu, E. (2022). Vision gnn: An image is worth graph of nodes. *Advances in Neural Information Processing Systems*, 35, 8291–8303.

He, W., Zou, L., Shekar, A. K., Gou, L., & Ren, L. (2021). Where can we help? a visual analytics approach to diagnosing and improving semantic segmentation of movable objects. *IEEE Transactions on Visualization and Computer Graphics*, 28(1), 1040–1050. DOI: 10.1109/TVCG.2021.3114855 PMID: 34587077

Hegselmann, S., Buendia, A., Lang, H., Agrawal, M., Jiang, X., & Sontag, D. (2023, April). Tabllm: Few-shot classification of tabular data with large language models. In *International Conference on Artificial Intelligence and Statistics* (pp. 5549-5581). PMLR.

Hong, F., Liu, C., & Yuan, X. (2019, April). DNN-VolVis: Interactive volume visualization supported by deep neural network. In *2019 IEEE Pacific Visualization Symposium (PacificVis)* (pp. 282-291). IEEE.

Hu, K., Bakker, M. A., Li, S., Kraska, T., & Hidalgo, C. (2019, May). Vizml: A machine learning approach to visualization recommendation. In *Proceedings of the 2019 CHI conference on human factors in computing systems* (pp. 1-12).

Huang, D., Wang, J., Wang, G., & Lin, C. Y. (2021, January). Visual style extraction from chart images for chart restyling. In 2020 25th International Conference on Pattern Recognition (ICPR) (pp. 7625-7632). IEEE.

Huang, S. W., Lin, C. T., Chen, S. P., Wu, Y. Y., Hsu, P. H., & Lai, S. H. (2018). Auggan: Cross domain adaptation with gan-based data augmentation. In *Proceedings of the European Conference on Computer Vision (ECCV)* (pp. 718-731).

Hullman, J., & Diakopoulos, N. (2011). Visualization rhetoric: Framing effects in narrative visualization. *IEEE Transactions on Visualization and Computer Graphics*, 17(12), 2231–2240. DOI: 10.1109/TVCG.2011.255 PMID: 22034342

Jhanjhi, N. Z., & Shah, I. A. (2024). *Cybersecurity Measures for Logistics Industry Framework*. Igi Global.

Kafle, K., Price, B., Cohen, S., & Kanan, C. (2018). Dvqa: Understanding data visualizations via question answering. In *Proceedings of the IEEE conference on computer vision and pattern recognition* (pp. 5648-5656).

Kafle, K., Shrestha, R., Cohen, S., Price, B., & Kanan, C. (2020). Answering questions about data visualizations using efficient bimodal fusion. In *Proceedings of the IEEE/CVF Winter conference on applications of computer vision* (pp. 1498-1507).

Kim, D. H., Hoque, E., & Agrawala, M. (2020, April). Answering questions about charts and generating visual explanations. In *Proceedings of the 2020 CHI conference on human factors in computing systems* (pp. 1-13).

Kim, G., Hong, T., Yim, M., Nam, J., Park, J., Yim, J., . . . Park, S. (2022, October). Ocr-free document understanding transformer. In European Conference on Computer Vision (pp. 498-517). Cham: Springer Nature Switzerland.

Kwon, O.-H., & Ma, K.-L. (2019). A deep generative model for graph layout. *IEEE Transactions on Visualization and Computer Graphics*, 26(1), 665–675. DOI: 10.1109/TVCG.2019.2934396 PMID: 31425108

Lai, C., Lin, Z., Jiang, R., Han, Y., Liu, C., & Yuan, X. (2020, April). Automatic annotation synchronizing with textual description for visualization. In *Proceedings of the 2020 CHI Conference on Human Factors in Computing Systems* (pp. 1-13).

Lee, D. J.-L., Lee, J., Siddiqui, T., Kim, J., Karahalios, K., & Parameswaran, A. (2019). You can't always sketch what you want: Understanding sensemaking in visual query systems. *IEEE Transactions on Visualization and Computer Graphics*, 26, 1267–1277. DOI: 10.1109/TVCG.2019.2934666 PMID: 31443008

Li, G., Wang, X., Aodeng, G., Zheng, S., Zhang, Y., Ou, C., . . . Liu, C. H. (2024). Visualization generation with large language models: An evaluation. arXiv preprint arXiv:2401.11255.

Li, H., Wang, Y., Wu, A., Wei, H., & Qu, H. (2022, April). Structure-aware visualization retrieval. In *Proceedings of the 2022 CHI Conference on Human Factors in Computing Systems* (pp. 1-14).

Li, Y., Sixou, B., & Peyrin, F. (2021). A review of the deep learning methods for medical images super resolution problems. *Ingénierie et Recherche Biomédicale : IRBM = Biomedical Engineering and Research*, 42(2), 120–133. DOI: 10.1016/j.irbm.2020.08.004

Liu, C., Guo, Y., & Yuan, X. (2023). AutoTitle: An interactive title generator for visualizations. *IEEE Transactions on Visualization and Computer Graphics*. PMID: 37384476

Liu, C., Xie, L., Han, Y., Wei, D., & Yuan, X. (2020, June). AutoCaption: An approach to generate natural language description from visualization automatically. In *2020 IEEE Pacific visualization symposium (PacificVis)* (pp. 191-195). IEEE.

Liu, S., Tao, M., Huang, Y., Wang, C., & Li, C. (2022). Image-driven harmonious color palette generation for diverse information visualization. *IEEE Transactions on Visualization and Computer Graphics*. PMID: 36459606

Liu, X., Zou, Y., Kong, L., Diao, Z., Yan, J., Wang, J., . . . You, J. (2018, August). Data augmentation via latent space interpolation for image classification. In *2018 24th International Conference on Pattern Recognition (ICPR)* (pp. 728-733). IEEE.

Lu, J., Pan, B., Chen, J., Feng, Y., Hu, J., Peng, Y., & Chen, W. (2024). AgentLens: Visual Analysis for Agent Behaviors in LLM-based Autonomous Systems. *IEEE Transactions on Visualization and Computer Graphics*, 1–17. DOI: 10.1109/TVCG.2024.3394053 PMID: 38700975

Lu, M., Wang, C., Lanir, J., Zhao, N., Pfister, H., Cohen-Or, D., & Huang, H. (2020, April). Exploring visual information flows in infographics. In *Proceedings of the 2020 CHI conference on human factors in computing systems* (pp. 1-12).

Luo, J., Li, Z., Wang, J., & Lin, C. Y. (2021). Chartocr: Data extraction from charts images via a deep hybrid framework. In Proceedings of the IEEE/CVF winter conference on applications of computer vision (pp. 1917-1925).

Luo, Y., Qin, X., Tang, N., Li, G., & Wang, X. (2018, May). Deepeye: Creating good data visualizations by keyword search. In *Proceedings of the 2018 International Conference on Management of Data* (pp. 1733-1736).

Luo, Y., Tang, N., Li, G., Tang, J., Chai, C., & Qin, X. (2021b). Natural language to visualization by neural machine translation. *IEEE Transactions on Visualization and Computer Graphics*, 28(1), 217–226. DOI: 10.1109/TVCG.2021.3114848 PMID: 34784276

Luo, Y., Zhou, Y., Tang, N., Li, G., Chai, C., & Shen, L. (2023). Learned data-aware image representations of line charts for similarity search. *Proceedings of the ACM on Management of Data*, 1(1), 1–29. DOI: 10.1145/3588942

Ma, R., Mei, H., Guan, H., Huang, W., Zhang, F., Xin, C., Dai, W., Wen, X., & Chen, W. (2020). Ladv: Deep learning assisted authoring of dashboard visualizations from images and sketches. *IEEE Transactions on Visualization and Computer Graphics*, 27(9), 3717–3732. DOI: 10.1109/TVCG.2020.2980227 PMID: 32175864

Masry, A., Kavehzadeh, P., Do, X. L., Hoque, E., & Joty, S. (2023). Unichart: A universal vision-language pretrained model for chart comprehension and reasoning. arXiv preprint arXiv:2305.14761.

Schetinger, V., Di Bartolomeo, S., El-Assady, M., McNutt, A., Miller, M., Passos, J. P. A., & Adams, J. L. (2023, June). Doom or deliciousness: Challenges and opportunities for visualization in the age of generative models. *Computer Graphics Forum*, 42(3), 423–435.

Shah, I. A., Jhanjhi, N. Z., & Ray, S. K. (2024c). *Enabling Explainable AI in Cybersecurity Solutions. Advances in Explainable AI Applications for Smart Cities*. IGI Global.

Shah, I. A., Jhanjhi, N. Z., & Ujjan, R. M. A. (2024e). *Use of AI applications for the drone industry. Cybersecurity Issues and Challenges in the Drone Industry.* IGI Global.

Shah, I. A., Laraib, A., Ashraf, H., & Hussain, F. (2024f). Drone Technology: Current Challenges and Opportunities. Cybersecurity Issues and Challenges in the Drone Industry, 343-361.

Chapter 4
The Role of Artificial Intelligence in Risk Management:
Practices of the Banking Sector

Muhammad Naeem
https://orcid.org/0000-0001-6678-3536
The Islamia University of Bahawalpur, Pakistan

Muzzammil Siraj
https://orcid.org/0009-0006-2826-7593
Muhammad Ali Jinnah University, Karachi, Pakistan

Shoukat Ali
The Islamia University of Bahawalpur, Pakistan

Abdul Rehman
https://orcid.org/0000-0002-6988-8330
National College of Business Administration and Economics Lahore, Pakistan

Sumair Farooq
Hamdard University, Karachi, Pakistan

ABSTRACT

This chapter investigates the role of artificial intelligence in risk management. The Pakistan population is selected for this research. This study used the simple random sampling technique and analyzed the 385 responses by using the five-point Likert scale questionnaire. This study applied structural equation modeling to test the hypotheses. We observe that AI directly affects risk management. A positive rela-

DOI: 10.4018/979-8-3693-3703-5.ch004

tionship between AI in risk management. It is a pioneer study on the role of artificial intelligence in risk management. This study has some limitations, this study does not show a comparative analysis among different nations or areas. By emphasizing AI's influence on risk management, the study adds to the expanding body of research on AI integration in banking. The findings highlight the potential advantages of implementing AI in risk management tactics for practitioners. Banks and other financial institutions can use AI technologies to better assess and manage risks.

1. INTRODUCTION

AI could play a significant role in society nowadays (Li *et al.*, 2021; Arslanian & Fischer, 2019; Siraj & Muhammad, 2023; Khan *et al.,* 2024; Shah et al., 2024; Naeem *et al.,* 2024). The research area of AI in finance has a great interest (Van Liebergen, 2017; Leo *et al.*, 2019; Helbekkmo *et al.*, 2013; Khan, 2019; Wyman, 2017). Over many years, the firm has faced the problem of finance securities including write-offs, unexpected delays, and losses (Cao, 2020). The senior managers find a way to predict the changes in financial risks to reduce the losses with the emergence of information technology (IT), and they introduce risk management technology (RMT) (Li *et al.*, 2021; Bansal *et al.*, 1993; Naeem, 2023). However, still firms are focusing the technology to gain insights into risk detection, measurement, reporting, and management (Helbekkmo *et al.*, 2013; Shah et al., 2024). The integration of AI in RM improves the efficiency of firms towards risk. Also, reduces the error and helps to detect potential threats. Furthermore, limited research was conducted on the role of AI in RM. The purpose of this research is to investigate the role of AI in RM.

The AI-based technology is growing day by day in every sector (Ali *et al.*, 2021; Shah, 2024). However, the integration of AI-based technology in RM has immense potential in the world including Pakistan (Ahmed *et al.*, 2022; Ali *et al.,* 2022). The firm already facing the problem of financial securities including write-offs, unexpected delays, and losses (Kahan, 1997). AI-based technology enhances real-time insights into the daily routine associated with RM and it also reduces costs (Jin *et al.*, 2008). The implementation of AI-based technology in the firm not only gains a competitive advantage but also creates a job related to AI fields (Lee *et al.*, 2019). Overall, the AI-based RMT adoption benefits Pakistan with innovation that improves the firm financial inclusion and business positioning for better economic environments (Lee *et al.*, 2020).

The agency theory and cybernetic system theory are implemented in the role of AI in RM. The agency theory examines the relevant relationship between the principals and agents (Panda & Leepsa, 2017). However, in the context of the AI role in RM, this theory is used to explore how an AI-based risk management system (RMS) is aligned with the interests of the firm shareholders. It also helps to optimize the decision-making process. The cybernetic system theory relies on the communication and control of the system (Lai & Huili Lin, 2017; Farooq & Ahmad, 2023). In the context of an AI-based RMS, helps to understand how an AI-based system can respond and adapt to changes to control the risk issues with time. RM achieves transparency and achievements in the facts of the company's operations. The AI integrated into RM enhances the process of decision-making, increases the efficiency of the process, and achieves precision in risk detection (Aziz & Dowling, 2018; Lin & Hsu, 2017; Naeem *et al.*, 2023).

The objective of this study is to investigate the role of AI in RM, especially the Pakistan firms. Pakistan was selected because it is an emergent market with a wide range of industries, assembly it possible to conduct a thorough analysis of AI applications here. The study proceeds into account Pakistan's technological, social, and cultural characteristics to provide additional perspectives on how AI affects relationship management techniques. This study has some contributions. Firstly contribute to worldwide research on AI in RM by focusing on Pakistani enterprises and providing an inclusive understanding of how AI is influencing business relationships in the background of an emerging economy. Secondly, the research focuses on how risk detection is enhanced, the decision-making process improved, and the contribution of RM with overall efficiency. The study also seeks the challenges and opportunities to the integration of the system.

Pakistani firms, politicians, and the academic community will help greatly from this research. Initially, by providing a broad knowledge of the function of AI-based RMT within the particular background of Pakistani enterprises, it offers theoretic insights. This research investigates how cultural, societal, and legal aspects impact the application of artificial intelligence in relationship management. It also proposes theoretical frameworks that influence and guide future market research and strategic choices. However, by representing how AI may be used in real-world situations to reduce risks, the research trains corporate executives. The choice by businesses to use AI-based RMT, driven by the knowledge added from this research, shows a valuable contribution.

Figure 1. Role of AI in Risk Management

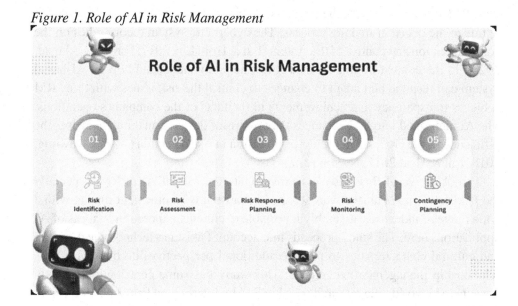

The procedure of technology is accessible as a risk-reduction tactic that highlights the observable advantages and results of integrating AI into relationship management procedures (Figure, 1). Furthermore, the study proposes evidence-based insights into the probable financial benefits of implementing AI in business, which has consequences for policymakers. The consequences can be used by policymakers to create rules and guidelines that encourage the ethical use of AI, creating a climate that is favorable to technological innovation in the Pakistani industry.

The further will be based on the Section 2 literature review such as theoretical background and hypothesis development. The methodology, data analysis, and results were discussed in sections 3 and 4. However, the discussion is in the section 5. Furthermore, the implications were discussed in section 6. The last section was based on conclusions and future recommendations.

2. LITERATURE REVIEW

RM, AI, and finance have been the most discussed topics among scholars in recent years. This literature mainly focuses on the relationship of AI with RM in financial strategies.

2.1. Theoretical Background

The agency theory and cybernetic system theory are implemented in the role of AI in RM. The agency theory examines the relevant relationship between the principals and agents (Panda & Leepsa, 2017). However, in the context of the RM role of AI, this theory is used to explore how AI-based RMS is aligned with the interest of the firm shareholders. It also helps to optimize the decision-making process. The cybernetic system theory relies on the communication and control of the system (Lai & Huili Lin, 2017; Tahir & Zaheer, 2024; Farooq *et al.*, 2023). In the context of an AI-based RMS, helps to understand how an AI-based system can respond and adapt to changes to control the risk issues with time.

2.2. Background of the Study

The rise of the technology era will leave an impact on the life of humanity. In the 1950s, after World War II, the researcher's research on AI started emerging when scholars analyzed the pattern that AI could perform human-related processes (Musleh Al-Sartawi *et al.*, 2022). In the 1960s, the first robotic games were introduced as the computer is your opponent. The game that was developed in the era of 1960s was the chess games (Haenlein *et al.*, 2019). Recently, an advanced system was introduced that can perform basic human functions such as deep learning, cognitive behavior thinking, and problem-solving with the introduction of the expert system and neural networks (Barsaglini *et al.*, 2014). Within the next 20 years, business and financial reporting was dramatically changed due to blockchain, machine learning, and AI. Now, it is clear that the accounting profession will be operated by the computer in the future (Türegün & Finance, 2019).

Despite the AI cannot replace human beings, however, it can replace human efforts. To solve accounting and business problems, it can analyze the strengths and limits of its AI system in accounting (Duan *et al.*, 2019). However, the skills required for the accountant to handle the intelligent systems. In the era of AI, the data is important. However, many societies depend on data, social media, knowledge management, and data science to survive in the technology era (Dwivedi *et al.*, 2021). The emergence of intelligent systems demands the emergence issue of producing quality data related to financial solutions. Furthermore, it will increase the demand for highly skilled and qualified accountants who can operate financial-related intelligence systems.

AI systems are active participants in human daily lives. However, the questions arise about which type of system is required and in which form. According to Kaplan and Haenlein (2019), AI regulations have multiple perspectives. These are the micro-perspectives and meso-perspectives. The micro-perspectives are the regulation regarding the algorithm and organization. While the meso-perspectives regarding the regulation of the respect of employment. The role of AI in finance impacts both, such as societies and organizations.

Another dimension of literature about AI in finance is related to machine learning models. However, there are no early works done on the finance-related models related to AI. Fischer *et al.* (2018), and Krauss *et al.* (2017), initially developed the outperforming forecasting model with neural networks such as (LSTM) deep neural networks and statistical models such as random forest and logistic regression. The conventional model was developed by (Krauss *et al.*, 2017), using decision trees, random forests, and neural networks for forecasting good investment returns and return on equity.

The financial industry is not an exception to how AI is changing many businesses (Zheng *et al.*, 2019). The incorporation of AI technology in banking has simplified processes and revolutionized decision-making, RM, and client relations (Goodell *et al.*, 2021; Dupont *et al.*, 2020). The complicated role AI plays in the financial sector is examined in this article, along with how it is challenging conventional knowledge and creating the foundation for a more efficient and data-driven financial environment.

Problems and moral questions come up as AI is incorporated into the finance industry more and more (Samaila). Careful thought must be given to issues like algorithmic bias, data privacy, and the possibility of employment displacement (Hansen, 2019; Gelen, 2018). To gain the trust of regulators and consumers alike, financial institutions need to put a high priority on ethical AI practices, maintain openness (Van Straaten, 2014), and take proactive measures to address these issues (Barnard, 2004).

2.3. Risk Management System

The developing nature of risks in companies with the growing need for effective RM strategies (Richards *et al.*, 2015). RM achieves transparency and achievements in the facts of the company's operations. The importance of RM is crucial when risk is developed in the company activities (Boermans & Galema, 2019). The loan portfolios and investment funds are crucial points for the environmental risk of financial institutions (Cardarelli *et al.*, 2009). The factors that can influence the investment decision align with the environmental, social, and governance (Calandro & leadership, 2015b).

The small risks within the company can escalate over time and this is the main point for the organizational decay. When a small problem arises, it will not be neglected because, with time, the problem will be bigger (Calandro & Leadership, 2015a; Ruiz, 2024). To overcome the problem, need for continuous improvement in risk management. Strategic RM is aligned with the leadership role as the leadership plays a role in controlling the RM and identifying potential threats (Khan *et al.*, 2015).

Integration of RM in the financial sector focusing on the RM and decision-making process. Increasing the overall organizational alignment with the broader aspects of RM and security practices (Hanafi, 2016). The definition of RM has a broader concept. It is the effort the collectively improve the company value and address the organizational problems. Logical and systematic identification, attitude identification, motoring, and reporting of risks are involved in risk management (Dharma *et al.*, 2020).

RM has diverse dimensions, it helps track the weak signals of the potential threats. It has a positive relationship with organizational performance (Rodrigues-da-Silva & Crispim, 2014; Bromiley *et al.*, 2015). Ultimately, for the growth of the organization, it is a crucial step to reduce the financial risks by identifying the pattern of the potential threats.

2.4. Impact of Artificial Intelligence-Based Risk Management System

The impact of AI-based RMS on both organizations and society. It achieves transparency and achievements in the facts of the company's operations. The importance of RM is crucial when risk is developed in the company activities (Boermans & Galema, 2019). Integration of RM in the financial sector focusing on the RM and decision-making process. The AI-based RMS increases efficiency by quickly analyzing a huge amount of data, successfully identifying potential risks, and providing insights in real-time (Zekos *et al.*, 2021). However, the decision-making process is also improved with accurate assessments, without human errors. Furthermore, there are still challenges we need to be concerned about such as algorithm biases, concern about data privacy, and the need to ensure effective and ethical RM. It also provides a predictive analysis to address the potential issues before they escalate. Overall, the impact of AI is substantial on RM (Žigienė *et al.*, 2019), but it requires a balanced approach to implement addressing the related challenges.

H1: Impact of artificial intelligence (AI) on risk management.

2.5. Conceptual Framework

Figure 2. Conceptual Framework

The independent variable is AI and the dependent variable is RM.

3. METHODOLOGY

The methodology consists of four parts; initially, it discusses the population and sample, followed by the questionnaire design. However, it also discusses the data collection criteria and lastly, it will discuss the statistical analysis.

3.1. Population and Sample

The Pakistan population is selected for this research, especially conducted on the Karachi Sindh bankers. This study used the simple random sampling technique because it can remove the biases. Every banker such as a bank manager, cashier, auditor, and loan officer has an equal opportunity to be selected for the part of this research. The population is unknown; however, the sample size of the unknown population is 385 with a 95% confidence interval and 5% margin of error. The formula used to calculate sample size is as follows:

$$n = N x \frac{\frac{Z^2 x\, p\, x\, (1-p)}{e^2}}{\left[N - 1 + \frac{Z^2 x\, p\, x\, (1-p)}{e^2} \right]}$$

Where,
N = Size of Population
Z = Normal Distribution Critical Value at a Required Confidence Level
p = Proportion of Sample
e = Margin of Error

3.2. Questionnaire Design

The questionnaire is adopted from (Chen *et al.*, 2022; Shou *et al.*, 2018). The questionnaire has two parts; firstly, based on demographics such as gender, age, designation, and qualifications. However, secondly based on variable questions on AI and RM. The 5-point Likert scale questionnaire is used, indicating 1 as strongly disagree and 5 as strongly agree. Therefore, the Google form is used to collect the responses.

3.3. Data Collection

The Google form was used to collect the responses of the bankers, especially targeting the individuals who are living in Karachi. The total responses received were 412 from the banker including the bank manager, cashier, auditor, and loan officer. However, 385 were selected for the analysis. Other responses are removed due to incompleteness, and incorrect responses.

3.4. Statistical Analysis

The SEM technique is used to find the impact between the variables. The PLS prediction, PLS algorithm, and bootstrapping test were used for the analysis. The software Smart PLS 4.0.9 is used for analysis, particularly for analyzing the relationship among the construct with a multicollinearity high degree and it can also handle the data without violating the CB-SEM assumptions.

4. RESULTS AND FINDINGS

The structural equation modeling technique is used to analyze the relationship between the variables.

4.1. Demographic Characteristics of Respondents

According to **Table I.**, 53.77% are male and 46.23% are female, while age group wise 18.96% are 18-24 years, 13.25% are 25-34 years, 17.40% are 35-44 years, 19.74% are 45-54 years, 13.77% are 55-64 years and 16.88% are 65 or older. However, 21.30% are bank managers, 18.96% are cashiers, 21.56% are auditors, 18.18% are loan officers, and 20% are others such as universal tellers. Furthermore, 20.78% have a matric pass, 20.52% have done intermediate, 19.74% have a bachelor's degree, 17.92% have a master's, and 21.04% hold a PhD degree.

Table 1. Demographics

Demographics	Frequency	Percentage
Age		
18-24 years	73	18.96%
25-34 years	51	13.25%
35-44 years	67	17.40%
45-54 years	76	19.74%

Demographics	Frequency	Percentage
55-64 years	53	13.77%
65 or older	65	16.88%
Gender		
Male	207	53.77%
Female	178	46.23%
Designation		
Bank Manager	82	21.30%
Cashier	73	18.96%
Auditor	83	21.56%
Loan Officer	70	18.18%
Others	77	20.00%
Qualification		
Matriculation	80	20.78%
Intermediate	79	20.52%
Bachelors	76	19.74%
Masters	69	17.92%
PhD	81	21.04%
Total	385	100.0%

4.2. Measurement Model Assessment

The reliability and validity of the model were tested with the PLS algorithm test. The model reliability and validity measure with the discriminant validity, internal consistency, and cross-loadings. However, a value greater than 0.7 indicates the model's reliability and validity.

Some items are dropped to reach the level threshold at the time of the 16-item analysis. However, a value of 0.7 or higher is considered more satisfactory (Henseler *et al.*, 2009; Chin, 1998) but a value above 0.5 is also acceptable, and a value less than 0.5 should be considered non-reliability and non-validity (Götz *et al.*, 2009). to identify the reliability and validity of the questions the composite reliability and validity are used. The value is greater than 0.7 of composite reliability indicating the reliability and to find the validity of the questions average variance extracted is used and the value greater than 0.5 is acceptable. The result is shown in **Table 2** and **Table 3**. Furthermore, to find the discriminant validity of the questions the Fornell Larcker Criterion and HTMT ratio are used. The results are shown in **Table 4** and **Table 5**.

Table 2. Outer Loadings

	Artificial Intelligence	Risk Management
AI1	0.624	
AI11	0.558	
AI12	0.591	
AI2	0.557	
AI3	0.703	
AI4	0.698	
AI5	0.672	
AI6	0.574	
AI7	0.640	
AI9	0.606	
RM1		0.661
RM2		0.556
RM3		0.689
RM4		0.720

Table 3. Composite Reliability and Validity

	Cronbach's alpha	Composite reliability (rho_a)	Composite reliability (rho_c)	Average variance extracted (AVE)
Artificial Intelligence	0.836	0.843	0.864	0.590
Risk Management	0.664	0.773	0.753	0.635

Table 4. Heterotrait-monotrait ratio (HTMT)

	Artificial Intelligence	Risk Management
Artificial Intelligence		
Risk Management	0.756	

Table 5. Fornell-Larcker Criterion

	Artificial Intelligence	Risk Management
Artificial Intelligence	0.625	
Risk Management	0.831	0.659

Table 6 shows the construction of cross-loading. The value near to one, effective measurement, and strong relationship between the constructs.

Table 6. Cross Loadings

	Artificial Intelligence	Risk Management
AI1	0.624	0.353
AI11	0.558	0.271
AI12	0.591	0.301
AI2	0.557	0.644
AI3	0.703	0.667
AI4	0.698	0.692
AI5	0.672	0.683
AI6	0.574	0.305
AI7	0.640	0.372
AI9	0.606	0.337
RM1	0.547	0.661
RM2	0.477	0.556
RM3	0.522	0.689
RM4	0.630	0.720

4.3. Structural Model Assessment

In the measurement model, the validity and reliability of the model were discussed. However, to identify the relationship between the variables the test is used. To identify the relationship between the variables a test is used which is bootstrapping. Results are shown in **Table VII**, indicating that AI directly affects RM (p = 0.000).

Table 7. Direct Effects

	Original sample	Sample mean	Standard deviation	T statistics	P values	Result
Artificial Intelligence Implementation -> Risk Management	0.831	0.833	0.013	61.623	0.000	Supported

5. QUALITY OF MODEL

The r-square value shows the effect of the variable on another variable. However, a value greater than 0.10 is acceptable (Falk & Miller, 1992). The r^2 for RM is 0.690. The f-square value has different ranges. (Ahmad & Afthanorhan, 2014; Iqbal et al., 2021; Sleimi et al., 2017). The value range greater than 0.35 shows a larger effect. The value range is not less than 0.15 and not greater than 0.35 showing the medium effect. The value range is not less than 0.02 and not greater than 0.15 showing the smaller effect. The results show the f^2 value of Academic Load and Outcome to Influence from Colleagues are 0.035. The f^2 value of influence from colleagues to belief towards artificial intelligence integration in education is 0.565. The f^2 value risk management is 2.226. The Q-square value indicates the relevancy of the model (Abramowicz et al., 1991). However, values greater than zero are acceptable.(Capriotti et al., 2004; Pollastri et al., 2002). The PLS prediction test was performed in Smart PLS 4.0.9 and the result shows that Q^2 is greater than zero (0.684) indicating that the model is relevant.

6. DISCUSSION

RM has diverse dimensions, it helps track the weak signals of the potential threats. It has a positive relationship with organizational performance (Rodrigues-da-Silva & Crispim, 2014; Bromiley et al., 2015). Ultimately, for the growth of the organization, it is a crucial step to reduce the financial risks by identifying the pattern of the potential threats. Integration of RM in the financial sector focusing on the RM and decision-making process. Increasing the overall organizational alignment with the broader aspects of RM and security practices (Hanafi, 2016). The definition of RM has a broader concept. It is the effort the collectively improve the company value and address the organizational problems. Logical and systematic identification, attitude identification, motoring, and reporting of risks are involved in risk management (Dharma et al., 2020).

The goal of the study was to comprehend how the application of AI affected RM for bankers in Karachi, Sindh. A basic random sampling procedure was used in the study, and 385 bankers were chosen at random from Karachi's population to make up the sample. The study employed a two-part questionnaire with varied questions about AI and RM in addition to demographic questions.

The measurement model assessment evaluated the model's reliability and validity using PLS algorithm tests. The validity, composite reliability, and outer loadings were also examined. The results showed composite reliability values larger than

0.7 and average variance extracted (AVE) values greater than 0.5, the validity and reliability are deemed satisfactory. The measurement model assessment evaluated the model's reliability and validity using PLS algorithm tests. The validity, composite reliability, and outer loadings were also examined. The primary focus was on the connection between RM and the use of AI. The findings of the bootstrapping test showed a significant direct effect (p = 0.000), suggesting that the use of AI has a big influence on RM in Karachi's banking industry.

RM's r-square score was 0.690, indicating a significant impact. Medium to substantial effects were indicated by the f-square values, especially for RM (f2 = 2.226). The model's applicability was confirmed by the Q-square value, which was greater than zero (0.684).

7. CONCLUSION, IMPLICATIONS, AND RECOMMENDATIONS FOR FUTURE RESEARCH

This study has some contributions. Firstly contribute to worldwide research on AI in RM by focusing on Pakistani enterprises and providing an inclusive understanding of how AI is influencing business relationships in the background of an emerging economy. Secondly, the research focuses on how risk detection is enhanced, the decision-making process improved, and the contribution of RM with overall efficiency. The study also seeks the challenges and opportunities to the integration of the system. This study's conclusions have several significance for academics and businesses alike. First of all, by emphasizing AI's influence on RM, the study adds to the expanding body of research on the subject of AI integration in banking. Given the established importance of direct influence, Karachi banks ought to give AI technology top priority and make investments to improve RM procedures.

The findings highlight the potential advantages of implementing AI in RM tactics for practitioners. To better assess and manage risks, banks, and other financial institutions can use AI technologies. This will ultimately help to maintain the stability and sustainability of Pakistan's financial industry.

The primary focus was on the connection between RM and the use of AI. The findings of the bootstrapping test showed a significant direct effect (p = 0.000), suggesting that the use of AI has a big influence on RM in Pakistan's banking industry. The study which makes use of the SEM and PLS algorithms offers a strong foundation for further research in related fields. Similar methods can be used by researchers to investigate the connections between various variables in a variety of settings.

Even though this study offers insightful information, there is a need for more research to deepen our grasp of the topic. Initially, look at possible mediating and moderating factors that could affect how RM and AI implementation interact. It may be necessary to take into account elements like corporate culture, the legal system, or the architecture of technology. However, to track how AI is changing RM over time. This would give rise to a more dynamic understanding of how these factors' relationship changes with the evolution of technology and the banking industry. It investigates the impact of AI on RM across different countries or regions. This could show how various AI approaches work differently in different financial ecosystems. Additionally, provides a qualitative backdrop for the quantitative findings. Quantitative assessments may not fully capture subtleties and contextual variables that are revealed through case studies or in-depth interviews. Eventually, probe the ethical counteraccusations of artificial intelligence in banking threat operations. Consider how moral issues may impact the relinquishment and efficacity of AI technologies. This study improves our understanding of how AI affects threat operations in Pakistan's banking sector. The favorable issues indicate that using AI technology can affect further robust threat operation processes. further exploration is demanded to better understand the craft of this commerce and to guide unborn developments in assiduity and academia.

REFERENCES

Abd Rabuh, A. (2020). *Developing A Credit Scoring Model Using Social Network Analysis*. University Of Portsmouth.

Abramowicz, H., Levin, E. M., Levy, A., & Maor, U. (1991). A parametrization of σT (γ* p) above the resonance region for Q2≥ 0. *Physics Letters. [Part B]*, 269(3-4), 465–476.

Ahmad, S., & Afthanorhan, W. M. A. B. W. (2014). The importance-performance matrix analysis in partial least square structural equation modeling (PLS-SEM) with smartpls 2.0 M3. *International Journal of Mathematics Research*, 3(1), 1–14.

Ali, M. Y., Naeem, S. B., & Bhatti, R. (2021). Artificial Intelligence (AI) in Pakistani university library services. *Library Hi Tech News*, 38(8), 12–15.

Ali, S., Murtaza, G., Hedvicakova, M., Jiang, J., & Naeem, M. (2022). Intellectual capital and financial performance: A comparative study. *Frontiers in Psychology*, 13, 967820. DOI: 10.3389/fpsyg.2022.967820 PMID: 36081720

Andronicus, A. A. (2014). Improved techniques for phishing email detection based on random forest and firefly-based support vector machine learning algorithms (Doctoral dissertation).

Arslanian, H., & Fischer, F. (2019). *The Future Of Finance: The Impact Of Fintech, Ai, And Crypto On Financial Services*. Springer. DOI: 10.1007/978-3-030-14533-0

Aziz, S., & Dowling, M. M. 2018. Ai And Machine Learning For Risk Management. *Published As: Aziz, S. And M. Dowling (2019). "Machine Learning And Ai For Risk Management", In T. Lynn, G. Mooney, P. Rosati, And M. Cummins (Eds.), Disrupting Finance: Fintech And Strategy In The 21st Century, Palgrave*, 33-50.

Bansal, A., Kauffman, R. J., Mark, R. M., & Peters, E. (1993). Financial risk and financial risk management technology (RMT): Issues and advances. *Information & Management*, 24(5), 267–281.

Bansal, T., Englert, D., Lee, J., Hegde, M., Wood, T. K., & Jayaraman, A. (2007). Differential Effects Of Epinephrine, Norepinephrine, And Indole On Escherichia Coli O157: H7 Chemotaxis, Colonization, And Gene Expression. *Infection and Immunity*, 75(9), 4597–4607. DOI: 10.1128/IAI.00630-07 PMID: 17591798

Barnard, R. S. (2004). An Examination Of Dysfunctional Behavior. In *Christian Evangelical Mission Organizations And Strategies For Managing The Consequences Of Dysfunctional Behavior*. The Open University.

Barsaglini, A., Sartori, G., Benetti, S., Pettersson-Yeo, W., & Mechelli, A. J. P. I. N. (2014). The Effects Of Psychotherapy On Brain Function: A Systematic And. *Critical Review*, 114, 1–14. PMID: 24189360

Bernal, G., Colombo, S., Al Ai Baky, M., & Casalegno, F. (2017, June). Safety++ designing IoT and wearable systems for industrial safety through a user centered design approach. In *Proceedings of the 10th international conference on pervasive technologies related to assistive environments* (pp. 163-170).

Berutich Lindquist, J. M. (2017). Robust optimization of algorithmic trading systems.

Boermans, M. A., & Galema, R. J. E. E. (2019).. . *Are Pension Funds Actively Decarbonizing Their Portfolios*, 161, 50–60.

Bromiley, P., Mcshane, M., Nair, A., & Rustambekov, E. J. L. R. P. (2015).. . *Enterprise Risk Management: Review, Critique, And Research Directions.*, 48, 265–276.

Calandro, J.Jr. (2015a). Revisiting the concept of a competitive "cash advantage". *Strategy and Leadership*, 43(4), 38–46.

Calandro, J. (2015b). A leader's guide to strategic risk management. *Strategy and Leadership*, 43(1), 26–35.

Cali, U., Kuzlu, M., Pipattanasomporn, M., Kempf, J., & Bai, L. (2021). *Digitalization Of Power Markets And Systems Using Energy Informatics*. Springer. DOI: 10.1007/978-3-030-83301-5

Cao, L. J. A. A. S. (2020). Ai In Finance. *RE:view*.

Capriotti, E., Fariselli, P., & Casadio, R. (2004). A neural-network-based method for predicting protein stability changes upon single point mutations. *Bioinformatics (Oxford, England)*, 20(suppl_1), i63–i68.

Cardarelli, R., Elekdag, S. A., & Lall, S. (2009). *Financial Stress*. Downturns, And Recoveries.

Chen, D., Esperança, J. P., & Wang, S. J. F. I. P. (2022). The Impact Of Artificial Intelligence On Firm Performance. *An Application Of The Resource-Based View To E-Commerce Firms.*, 13, 884830. PMID: 35465474

Chen, J., & Tsang, E. P. (2020). Detecting Regime Change. In *Computational Finance: Data Science, Machine Learning And Algorithmic Trading*. Crc Press.

Chin, W. W. J. M. M. F. B. R. (1998). The Partial Least Squares Approach To. *Structural Equation Modeling*, 295, 295–336.

Cuomo, S., Gatta, F., Giampaolo, F., Iorio, C., & Piccialli, F. (2022). An Unsupervised Learning Framework For Marketneutral Portfolio. *Expert Systems with Applications*, 192, 116308. DOI: 10.1016/j.eswa.2021.116308

Dharma, B., Pratiwi, D. C. J. J. O. M., & Innovations, B. (2020)... *Developing Financial Risk Strategy Decisions For Construction Projects From Perspective Of The Project Owner.*, 2, 12–20.

Duan, Y., Edwards, J. S., & Dwivedi, Y. K. J. I. J. O. I. M. (2019). Artificial Intelligence For Decision Making In The Era Of Big Data–Evolution. *Challenges And Research Agenda.*, 48, 63–71.

Dupont, L., Fliche, O., & Yang, S. (2020). Governance Of Artificial Intelligence. In *Finance*. Banque De France.

Dwivedi, Y. K., Hughes, L., Ismagilova, E., Aarts, G., Coombs, C., Crick, T., Duan, Y., Dwivedi, R., Edwards, J., Eirug, A. J. I. J. O. I. M., Galanos, V., Ilavarasan, P. V., Janssen, M., Jones, P., Kar, A. K., Kizgin, H., Kronemann, B., Lal, B., Lucini, B., & Williams, M. D. (2021). Artificial Intelligence (Ai): Multidisciplinary Perspectives On Emerging Challenges, Opportunities, And Agenda For Research. *International Journal of Information Management*, 57, 101994. DOI: 10.1016/j.ijinfomgt.2019.08.002

Ehramikar, S. (2000). *The Enhancement Of Credit Card Fraud Detection Systems Using Machine Learning Methodology*. University Of Toronto.

Falk, M., & Miller, A. G. J. V. S. (1992)... *Infrared Spectrum Of Carbon Dioxide In Aqueous Solution.*, 4, 105–108.

Farooq, M., & Ahmad, N. (2023). Nexus between board characteristics, firm performance and intellectual capital: An emerging market evidence. *Corporate Governance (Bradford)*, 23(6), 1269–1297. DOI: 10.1108/CG-08-2022-0355

Farooq, M., Noor, A., & Naeem, M. (2023). Does family ownership moderate the relationship between board characteristics and corporate social responsibility? Evidence from an emerging market. *Asian Journal of Business Ethics*, 12(1), 71–99. DOI: 10.1007/s13520-022-00164-z

Fischer, T., Krauss, C., & Treichel, A. (2018). *Machine Learning For Time Series Forecasting-A Simulation Study*. Fau Discussion Papers In Economics.

Gelen, I. (2018). Academicians' predictions Of 21st Century Education And Education In The 21st Century. *European Journal of Education Studies*.

Goodell, J. W., Kumar, S., Lim, W. M., & Pattnaik, D. (2021). Artificial Intelligence And Machine Learning In Finance: Identifying Foundations, Themes, And Research Clusters From Bibliometric Analysis. *Journal of Behavioral and Experimental Finance*, 32, 100577. DOI: 10.1016/j.jbef.2021.100577

Götz, O., Liehr-Gobbers, K., & Krafft, M. (2009). *Evaluation Of Structural Equation Models Using The Partial Least Squares (Pls) Approach. Handbook Of Partial Least Squares: Concepts, Methods And Applications*. Springer.

Graefe, A. (2019). Accuracy Of German Federal Election Forecasts, 2013 & 2017. *International Journal of Forecasting*, 35(3), 868–877. DOI: 10.1016/j.ijforecast.2019.01.004

Haenlein, M., Kaplan, A., Tan, C. W., & Zhang, P. (2019). Artificial intelligence (AI) and management analytics. *Journal of Management Analytics*, 6(4), 341–343.

Hanafi, S. M. (2016). Financial Risk Management In Syariah Contracts: A Review of Current Literature. MIQOT: Jurnal Ilmu-ilmu Keislaman, 37(1).

Hansen, C. (2019). Brain-Computer interfaces: from research to consumer products.

Haynes, R., & Roberts, J. S. (2015). Automated trading in futures markets. CFTC White Paper.

Helbekkmo, H., Kshirsagar, A., Schlosser, A., Selandari, F., Stegemann, U., & Vorholt, J. (2013). Enterprise risk management—shaping the risk revolution. New York: McKinsey & Co., Available online: www. rmahq. org (accessed on 18 June 2018), 23.

Henning, J. (2016). *Credit Scoring Model: Incorporating Entrepreneurial Characteristics*. University Of The Free State.

Henseler, J., Ringle, C. M., & Sinkovics, R. R. (2009). The Use Of Partial Least Squares Path Modeling. In *International Marketing. New Challenges To International Marketing*. Emerald Group Publishing Limited.

Hossain, M. E. (2020). *Predictive Modelling Of The Comorbidity Of Chronic Diseases: A Network And Machine Learning Approach*. University Of Sydney.

Huang, S.-H., Miao, Y.-H., & Hsiao, Y.-T. (2021). Novel Deep Reinforcement Algorithm With Adaptive Sampling Strategy For Continuous Portfolio Optimization. *IEEE Access : Practical Innovations, Open Solutions*, 9, 77371–77385. DOI: 10.1109/ACCESS.2021.3082186

Iqbal, S., Moleiro Martins, J., Nuno Mata, M., Naz, S., Akhtar, S., & Abreu, A. (2021). Linking entrepreneurial orientation with innovation performance in SMEs; the role of organizational commitment and transformational leadership using smart PLS-SEM. *Sustainability*, 13(8), 4361.

Jafar, S. H., Hemachandran, K., El-Chaarani, H., Moturi, S., & Gupta, N. (2023). *Artificial Intelligence For Capital Markets*. Crc Press.

Jalal, F. E., Xu, Y., Iqbal, M., Javed, M. F., & Jamhiri, B. (2021). Predictive Modeling Of Swell-Strength Of Expansive Soils Using Artificial Intelligence Approaches: Ann, Anfis And Gep. *Journal of Environmental Management*, 289, 112420. DOI: 10.1016/j.jenvman.2021.112420 PMID: 33831756

Jalonen, T. (2019). Management Accounting Information in Decision-making: Unveiling Possibilities for AI (Master's thesis).

Jin, X. H., & Doloi, H. (2008). Interpreting risk allocation mechanism in public–private partnership projects: An empirical study in a transaction cost economics perspective. *Construction Management and Economics*, 26(7), 707–721.

Johnston, R., Victor, K., Heery, L., & McCausland, G. (2019). Intelligent futures.

Kahan, M. (1997). Some problems with stock exchange-based securities regulation. *Virginia Law Review*, ●●●, 1509–1519.

Kalantari, H. D., & Johnson, L. (2018). Australian Customer Willingness To Pay And Wait For Mass-Customised Products. *Asia Pacific Journal of Marketing and Logistics*, 30(1), 106–120. DOI: 10.1108/APJML-01-2017-0006

Kaplan, A., & Haenlein, M. J. B. H. (2019). Siri, Siri, In My Hand: Who's The Fairest In The Land? On The Interpretations, Illustrations, And Implications Of. *Artificial Intelligence*, 62, 15–25.

Khan, A., Jhanjhi, N. Z., Omar, H. A. H. B. H., & Haji, D. H. T. B. A. (2024). Risk Management and Cybersecurity in Transportation and Warehousing. In *Cybersecurity Measures for Logistics Industry Framework* (pp. 1–35). IGI Global.

Khan, F., Rathnayaka, S., Ahmed, S. J. P. S., & Protection, E. (2015). Methods And Models In Process Safety And Risk Management: Past. *Present And Future.*, 98, 116–147.

Khan, S. J. C. R. R. (2019). Chief Reputation Officer (Cro). *Envisioning The Role.*, 22, 75–88.

Khang, A., Misra, A., Gupta, S. K., & Shah, V. (2023). *Ai-Aided Iot Technologies And Applications For Smart Business And Production*. Crc Press. DOI: 10.1201/9781003392224

Krauss, C., Do, X. A., & Huck, N. (2017). Deep neural networks, gradient-boosted trees, random forests: Statistical arbitrage on the S&P 500. *European Journal of Operational Research*, 259(2), 689–702.

Lai, C. H., & Lin, H. (2017). *S. J. T. I. E. O. O. C*. Systems Theory.

Lee, C. C., Wang, C. W., & Ho, S. J. (2020). Financial inclusion, financial innovation, and firms' sales growth. *International Review of Economics & Finance*, 66, 189–205.

Lee, J., Suh, T., Roy, D., & Baucus, M. (2019). Emerging technology and business model innovation: The case of artificial intelligence. *Journal of Open Innovation*, 5(3), 44.

Leo, M., Sharma, S., & Maddulety, K. (2019). Machine learning in banking risk management: A literature review. *Risks*, 7(1), 29.

Li, Y., Yi, J., Chen, H., & Peng, D. (2021). Theory and application of artificial intelligence in financial industry. *Data Science in Finance and Economics*, 1(2), 96–116.

Lin, S.-J., & Hsu, M.-F. (2017). Incorporated Risk Metrics And Hybrid Ai Techniques For Risk Management. *Neural Computing & Applications*, 28(11), 3477–3489. DOI: 10.1007/s00521-016-2253-4

Lohpetch, D. (2011). *Evolutionary Algorithms For Financial Trading*. Heriot-Watt University.

Maeso, J.-M. (2022). *Stochastic Modeling Applied To Portfolio Optimization Problems*. Université Côte D'azur.

Miljkovic, A., & Chronéer, B. (2018). Application Scorecard Modelling With Artificial. *Neural Networks*.

Moalosi, M., Hlomani, H., & Phefo, O. S. (2019). Combating Credit Card Fraud With Online Behavioural Targeting And Device Fingerprinting. *International Journal Of Electronic Security And Digital Forensics*, 11(1), 46–69. DOI: 10.1504/IJESDF.2019.096527

Musleh Al-Sartawi, A. M., Hussainey, K., Razzaque, A. J. J. O. S. F. & Investment 2022. The Role Of Artificial Intelligence In Sustainable Finance. Taylor & Francis.

Naeem, M. (2023). Corporate Governance Mechanism and Financial Performance in Pakistan Commercial Banks: Moderating Role of Credit Risk Management. *RADS Journal of Business Management*, 5(2), 95–112.

Naeem, M., Rehman, A., Mehboob, A., & Abdali, A. S. (2023). Corporate Social Responsibility's Hidden Power in context of Pakistan: Amplifying Firm Performance. *Sukkur IBA Journal of Management and Business*, 10(2), 57–76. DOI: 10.30537/sijmb.v10i2.1383

Naeem, M., Siraj, M., Abdali, A. S., & Mehboob, A. (2024). The Impact of Investment in AI on Bank Performance: Empirical Evidence from Pakistan's Banking Sector. *KASBIT Business Journal, 17*(1).

Panda, B., & Leepsa, N. M. J. I. J. O. C. G. (2017). Agency Theory. *Review Of Theory And Evidence On Problems And Perspectives.*, 10, 74–95.

Peterson, J. (2012). *Customisation Of Fashion Products Using Complete Garment Technology*. Tampere University Of Technology.

Pollastri, G., Baldi, P., Fariselli, P., & Casadio, R. (2002). Prediction of coordination number and relative solvent accessibility in proteins. *Proteins*, 47(2), 142–153.

Richards, G. S., & Duxbury, L. (2015). Work-group knowledge acquisition in knowledge intensive public-sector organizations: An exploratory study. *Journal of Public Administration: Research and Theory*, 25(4), 1247–1277.

Riesen, T., Hall, S., Keeton, B., & Snyder, A. (2023). Internal Consistency Of The Customized Employment Discovery Fidelity Scale: A Preliminary Study. *Rehabilitation Counseling Bulletin*, 66(3), 195–202. DOI: 10.1177/00343552211043259

Rodrigues-da-Silva, L. H., & Crispim, J. A. (2014). The project risk management process, a preliminary study. *Procedia Technology*, 16, 943–949.

Ruiz, G. R. (2024). QR Multilevel Codes to Reduce Cybersecurity Risks in the Logistics of Freight Transport in Ports. In *Cybersecurity Measures for Logistics Industry Framework* (pp. 322–349). IGI Global.

Sachan, S., Yang, J.-B., Xu, D.-L., Benavides, D. E., & Li, Y. (2020). An Explainable Ai Decision-Support-System To Automate Loan Underwriting. [Samaila, M. G. Internet Of Things Hardware Platform Security Advisor.]. *Expert Systems with Applications*, 144, 113100. DOI: 10.1016/j.eswa.2019.113100

Seo, Y. W., Lee, K. C., & Lee, S. (2017). Decision Quality Of The Research Project Evaluation Mechanism By Using Particle Swarm Optimization. *Management Decision*, 55(4), 745–765. DOI: 10.1108/MD-03-2016-0141

Shah, I. A., Jhanjhi, N. Z., & Brohi, S. N. (2024). Use of AI-Based Drones in Smart Cities. In *Cybersecurity Issues and Challenges in the Drone Industry* (pp. 362–380). IGI Global. DOI: 10.4018/979-8-3693-0774-8.ch015

Shah, I. A., Jhanjhi, N. Z., & Ujjan, R. M. A. (2024). Use of AI Applications for the Drone Industry. In *Cybersecurity Issues and Challenges in the Drone Industry* (pp. 27–41). IGI Global. DOI: 10.4018/979-8-3693-0774-8.ch002

Shin, H., Park, S., Kim, L., Kim, J., Kim, T., Song, Y., & Lee, S. (2023). The Future Service Scenarios Of 6g Telecommunications Technology. *Telecommunications Policy*, •••, 102678.

Shou, Y., Hu, W., Kang, M., Li, Y., Park, Y. W. J. I. M., & Systems, D. (2018). Risk Management And Firm Performance. *The Moderating Role Of Supplier Integration.*, 118, 1327–1344.

Siraj, M., & Muhammad, G. (2023). Is Chatbot Marketing Have A Relationship With Electronic Word Of Mouth? A Mediating Role Of The Customer-Brand Relationship. *Journal Of Management Sciences*, 10(2), 80–94.

Sleimi, M. T., & Emeagwali, O. L. (2017). Do employee attitudes mediate the relationship between strategic human resource management practices and organizational effectiveness? A SEM based investigation using SMART-PLS software. *Business and Economic Horizons*, 13(1), 42–59.

Swed, S., Alibrahim, H., Elkalagi, N. K. H., Nasif, M. N., Rais, M. A., Nashwan, A. J., & Shoib, S. (2022). Knowledge, attitude, and practice of artificial intelligence among doctors and medical students in Syria: A cross-sectional online survey. *Frontiers in Artificial Intelligence*, 5, 1011524.

Tahir, S., & Zaheer, A. (2024). A Distributed Model for IoT Anomaly Detection Using Federated Learning. In *Cybersecurity Measures for Logistics Industry Framework* (pp. 75–91). IGI Global.

Tan, D. C. (2005). *The Statistical Properties Of Technical Trading Rules*. Loughborough University.

Terna, P., Maggiora, M., & Battistoni, L. (2016). Emerging cryptocurrency trust in an agent–based model.

Türegün, N. (2019). Impact of technology in financial reporting: The case of Amazon Go. *Journal of Corporate Accounting & Finance*, 30(3), 90–95.

Van Liebergen, B. J. J. O. F. T. 2017. Machine Learning: A Revolution In Risk Management And Compliance? 45, 60-67.

Van Straaten, L. (2014). An appreciative inquiry of selected elements of staff well-being at a higher education institution (Doctoral dissertation, University of the Free State).

Wang, Z.-F., Ren, Y.-W., Cao, Z.-Y., & Zhang, L.-Y. (2023). Lrbft: Improvement Of Practical Byzantine Fault Tolerance Consensus Protocol For Blockchains Based On Lagrange Interpolation. *Peer-to-Peer Networking and Applications*, 16(2), 690–708. DOI: 10.1007/s12083-022-01431-3

Wyman, O. (2017). Next Generation. *Risk Management*.

Yang, K. (2024). Quality. In *The Era Of Industry 4.0: Integrating Tradition And Innovation In The Age Of Data And Ai*. John Wiley & Sons.

Zekos, G. I., & Zekos, G. I. J. E. (2021). *Law Of Artificial Intelligence: Finance, E. I., Risk Management & Governance*. Ai Risk Management.

Zhang, R., Ai, X., & Li, H. (2023). How To Design Subsidy Policies For Clean Energy Projects? A Study On "Coal-To-Gas" Project In China. *Resources Policy*, 85, 103928. DOI: 10.1016/j.resourpol.2023.103928

Zheng, X.-L., Zhu, M.-Y., Li, Q.-B., Chen, C.-C., & Tan, Y.-C. (2019). Finbrain: When Finance Meets Ai 2.0. *Frontiers Of Information Technology & Electronic Engineering*, 20(7), 914–924. DOI: 10.1631/FITEE.1700822

Žigienė, G., Rybakovas, E., & Alzbutas, R. J. S. (2019).. . *Artificial Intelligence Based Commercial Risk Management Framework For Smes.*, 11, 4501.

Chapter 5
Unveiling the Potential of Generative Approaches in AI–Infused Web Development for Design, Testing, and Maintenance

Raghavendra M Devadas

Manipal Institute of Technology Bengaluru, Manipal Academy of Higher Education, Manipal, India

Vani Hiremani

Symbiosis Institute of Technology, Symbiosis International University (Deemed), Pune, India

Praveen Gujjar J.

(iD) https://orcid.org/0000-0003-0240-7827

Faculty of Management Studies, Jain University, India

Preethi

Manipal Institute of Technology, Manipal, India

R. Sapna

Manipal Institute of Technology, Manipal, India

ABSTRACT

The digital landscape is witnessing the continuous evolution of our lived experiences, in which the cross-cutting domain of Generative Artificial Intelligence (AI) and web engineering models is emerging as a pivotal source of transformative innovation.

DOI: 10.4018/979-8-3693-3703-5.ch005

This article seeks to identify the potential new opportunities that generative AI could explore since it heralds in a radical revolution in the traditional paradigms associated with web development. The studied problems addressed in this paper include historical web system construction issues, design complexities, and maintainability problems. The research concludes by presenting a roadmap for embracing this paradigm shift, contributing to the ongoing discourse on the intersection of AI and web engineering. The study is exploratory at the outset, trying to gain insights into the integration of generative AI into web development. This research aims to explore the challenges, benefits, and potential applications of generative AI in several phases of web development, including design, testing, and maintenance.

1. INTRODUCTION

The amalgamation of Generative Artificial Intelligence (AI) and Web Engineering models in the emerging sphere of contemporary web development can be transformative. This study investigates the critical significance of AI-driven generative techniques in all paradigms of web-based systems and applications development. As we move deeper into the digital age, the promise of Generative AI, when married to web engineering will break forth into new possibilities and transformative future solutions beyond those of the past. This study sets out the potential for generative AI, as an uncharted potential that can potentially upset business as usual across web development. At the heart of such an assertion is that generative models can do more than simply ease the development of web-based applications but might also change at a fundamental level the paradigms that develop in testing and maintenance. This new vision envisions a future where web systems are not just adaptive but highly intelligent.

Contextualizing Concerns:

Web development has encountered and overcome various challenges throughout its evolution. Historical impediments, such as design intricacies, scalability limitations, and the complexities associated with maintenance, have shaped the trajectory of the field. This study tries to address these concerns and all others like them by examining how generative AI could be a game-changer. This paper aims to demonstrate how generative AI is attempting to overcome these historical challenges by leveraging intelligent automation, learning from data patterns, and optimizing web engineering processes.

Designing the Future:

Conventional approaches in the design of the web grapple often with the tension of creativity and functionality. The paper explores the ways generative AI can synchronize these elements, automatize a design process, create new solutions, and adapt to the user. This attempt to show through instances and examples from real life will seek to prove how this newly accepted method of generative design, driven by AI, approaches user-centric, visually appealing, and logically sensible web applications.

Testing the Boundaries:

Another imperative one that the research will be addressing, therefore, is the credibility and efficiency of methodologies used for testing. Testing is among the most critical stages during web development; nevertheless, it often involves resources and may be faced with oversights. As outlined in this research paper, this kind of AI, referred to as generative AI, would revolutionize testing through the simulation of user interactions and enhance general efficiency. From a definite assessment of the function of generative AI in the testing process, this paper defines the contribution this form of technology makes in ensuring the robustness and reliability of web applications.

Intelligent Maintenance Strategies:

The current paper paves the way for considering maintenance as one of the most neglected yet important phenomena. The paper attempts to highlight how generative AI makes intelligent maintenance policies; there can be predictions of failure. These include routine and, to an extent, dangerous tasks' automation, ensuring that behavior in web-based systems is constantly optimized over time. In doing so, the current refers to these policies as steps toward ensuring newly emergent support for building a paradigm in which maintenance is not simply conceived reactively, as fixing things that break, but proactively, as the fuel of a productive web development process. Web development infused with AI involves incorporating artificial intelligence technologies and tools into processes for developing and optimizing websites (Cummaudo et al., 2020). Via these methods, AI-driven development aims to use AI's abilities to evaluate website performance, discern user needs, and automate certain web development tasks. For instance, AI-powered website analytics solutions like Google Analytics and Kissmetrics can be utilized to monitor visitors' behavior and point out behaviors exhibited by potential buyers (Aravinth et al., 2021). Furthermore, organizations can place AI-assisted chatbots on websites to deliver immediate responses to potential and existing customers, bypassing the need for human intervention (Ernst & Bavota, 2022). AI-driven development environments (AIDEs) also play a role in web development by automating routine programming tasks using language models and open-source code (Hsiao & Chung, 2022). These AI-infused approaches offer the potential to improve website optimization, enhance user experience, and streamline the development process.

Research Gaps

Current literature in the fields of generative AI and web development does not provide an integrative investigation of how generative AI effectively solves its historical shortcomings. There also exist gaps in understanding how the generative approaches deal with the offered design intricacies, scalability limitation, and maintenance complexity in the web development landscape. All these are gaps that must be filled at the generative AI level, at which it turns out to be a transformative technology.

Motivation

The present research is, in this sense, driven by the identified need for a deeper understanding of the potential consequences and change ensuing from the entry of generative AI and a commitment to sensitizing how common paradigms in web engineering stand a chance to be revolutionized. What is realized is a stimulus for the literature that largely leaves the most part unanswered: what comprehensive impact generative AI has on the full life cycle of web-based systems. Thus, this urgently needs to be elaborated on how generative methods might make significant changes according to practical practice on the internet in design, testing, and maintenance.

Research Contribution

- The primary contributions of this research extend beyond theoretical discourse to provide practical insights.
- This study, therefore, will adjust existing gaps through which actionable recommendations may be developed to support developers, researchers, and industry practitioners in a wholesome manner.
- This will give stakeholders in the web design field detailed knowledge about exactly how generative AI can be of use in their workflows.

Together, these contributing efforts will make sure that abundant collective knowledge emanates from both AI and website development efforts to enable the innovative website application creations, which are not only frontiered to technologies but also understand their operations in adaptive, intelligent, and user-centric ways.

In this respect, the study tends to provide a comprehensive understanding of what kind of improvement comes when any generative AI is integrated into the web development processes. It is in the unfolding of this study into a roadmap for this paradigm shift that contributes to insights invaluable in the ongoing discourse. The insights that these offered are incepted to be practically designed and forward-looking to shape perspectives in this dynamic rapidly changing landscape of everything digital.

2. RELATED WORKS

AI-infused web development refers to the integration of artificial intelligence technologies and techniques into the process of creating, designing, and maintaining websites. This integration aims to enhance the capabilities and functionalities of websites by leveraging AI algorithms and models (Haldorai et al., 2020). In recent years, there has been a rapid proliferation of artificial intelligence in various industries, including web development. Many organizations from different sectors have recognized the importance and potential of AI systems, services, and tools in their operations (Anica-Popa et al., 2023). The adoption of AI techniques in web development has led to significant improvements in business operations, service processes, and industry productivity (Bharadiya et al., 2023). One of the key drivers of AI-infused web development is the ability to improve user experience and provide personalized content. The use of AI algorithms for classification, matching, recommendation, and deep learning can contribute to the development of smart learning environments in web development (Tao & Ye, 2020). According to a study conducted by AI-infused web development, AI techniques were utilized as development tools for the construction of a smart learning environment (Zhai et al., 2021). These AI techniques involved the development of algorithms for classification, matching, recommendation, and deep learning to support teaching and learning processes (Zhang & Aslan, 2021). Moreover, the application of AI techniques in web development goes beyond just the design and functionality aspects. It also extends to the extraction of feedback, reasoning, and adaptive learning for students. These AI techniques are used to offer personalized feedback and support to students, enhancing their learning experience. Additionally, AI-infused web development can also involve the use of affection computing, role-playing, immersive learning, and gamification techniques to create engaging and interactive learning experiences for students (Liu et al.,

2020). Furthermore, AI-infused web development also focuses on the integration of human factors and personalized features (Dimitriadou & Lanitis, 2023). One of the emerging trends in AI-infused web development is the exploration of the Internet of Things and its integration with AI algorithms. This integration allows websites to gather data from connected devices, enabling a more personalized and efficient user experience. The integration of artificial intelligence in web development is becoming increasingly significant as it has the potential to enhance the capabilities and functionalities of websites (Priyanga, 2023). It can improve user engagement and personalization, leading to a more tailored and efficient learning experience. The integration of AI in web development has the potential to revolutionize the education field by creating smart learning environments and offering personalized feedback, reasoning, and adaptive learning to students (Kamruzzaman et al., 2023). AI-infused web development is a significant aspect of technology today, particularly in the education domain. The integration of artificial intelligence techniques in web development has emerged as a crucial aspect in today's rapidly evolving educational landscape (Mello et al., 2023). The use of AI in web development has gained significant attention in the education domain. This attention is due to its potential to foster personalized learning experiences for students, adapting to their needs and interests (Nanjundappa et al., 2020). The integration of AI in web development has the potential to revolutionize the education field. It can create personalized and customizable learning experiences that optimize language learning by increasing autonomy, motivation, engagement, and effectiveness. AI-infused web development is a promising approach for enhancing educational experience through personalized learning (Ashwini et al., 2023). Incorporating AI in web development can optimize the teaching-learning process by offering personalized learning experiences that adapt to the needs and interests of each student (Zawacki-Richter et al., 2019).

3. RESEARCH METHODOLOGY

This study will adopt a mixed-methods research design, combining qualitative and quantitative approaches to ensure a comprehensive understanding of the impact of generative AI on various facets of web development. The research design will be iterative, allowing for the incorporation of insights obtained from both qualitative and quantitative analyses. Fig. 1. Illustrates the research methodology followed in this study.

Figure 1. Research protocol

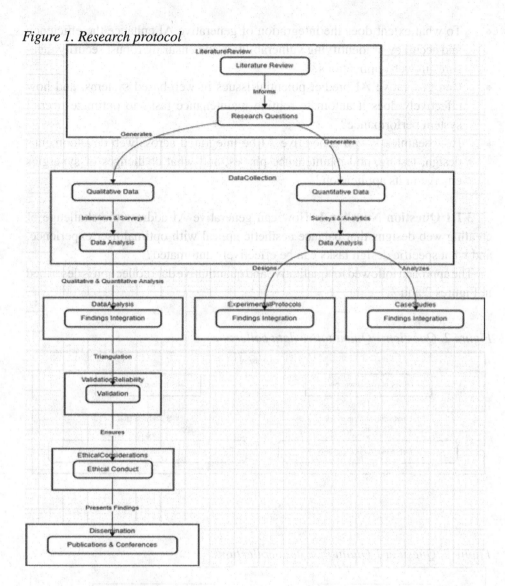

3.1 Research Questions

The study identified the below questions based on the literature review.

- How can generative AI address the challenge of creating web designs that balance aesthetic appeal with optimal user experience, and what specific design tasks can be effectively automated?

- To what extent does the integration of generative AI enhance the efficiency and accuracy of identifying vulnerabilities and ensuring robust security measures in web applications?
- Can generative AI predict potential issues in web-based systems, and how effectively does it automate routine maintenance tasks to optimize overall system performance?
- How seamlessly can generative AI be integrated across web development's design, testing, and maintenance phases, and what challenges or synergies emerge in its application?

3.1.1 Question Number 1: How can generative AI address the challenge of creating web designs that balance aesthetic appeal with optimal user experience, and what specific design tasks can be effectively automated?

The approach followed for qualitative and quantitative data collection is described in Figures 2 and 3.

Figure 2. Question 1 Quantitative data collection

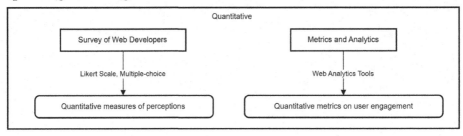

Figure 3. Question 1 Qualitative data collection

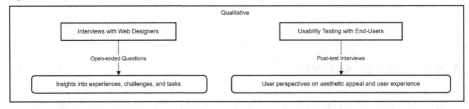

Qualitative Data Collection:

1. In-Depth Interviews with Web Designers:

Method: Conduct one-on-one interviews with experienced web designers.
Questions: Explore open-ended questions such as:

- "Can you share your experiences with using generative AI in web design?"
- "In your opinion, what challenges does generative AI help address in achieving optimal user experience and aesthetic appeal?"
- "Can you provide examples of design tasks that have been effectively automated using generative AI?"

Purpose: To gather nuanced and detailed insights into the experiences, challenges, and specific design tasks impacted by generative AI.

2. Usability Testing with End-Users:

Method: Engage end-users in usability testing sessions with websites designed using generative AI.
Tasks: Ask users to perform specific website tasks and observe their interactions.
Questions: Collect feedback through post-test interviews with questions like:

- "How would you describe your experience with the design elements of the website?"
- "Did you notice any specific aspects that contributed to or hindered the aesthetic appeal and user experience?"

Purpose: To understand user perspectives on the aesthetic appeal and user experience of generative AI-designed websites.

Quantitative Data Collection:

1. Survey of Web Developers:

Method: Distribute a structured survey to a sample of web developers.
Survey Items:

- Likert scale questions (1-5) on the perceived effectiveness of generative AI in balancing aesthetic appeal and user experience.
- Multiple-choice questions on specific design tasks that have been automated using generative AI.

115

Purpose: To quantitatively measure the overall perceptions of web developers regarding the effectiveness of generative AI in addressing design challenges.

2.   Metrics and Analytics:

Method: Utilize web analytics tools like Google Analytics.
Metrics:

- Average session duration, bounce rates, and other engagement metrics for websites designed using generative AI.
- Comparison with the same metrics for traditionally designed websites.

Purpose: To quantitatively assess user engagement and interaction patterns on websites designed with generative AI, providing numerical insights into the effectiveness of the designs.

Such an approach to the collection of data aimed at covering all bases when giving proper understanding in terms of how generative AI would influence the aesthetic appeal of web designs in a holistic way and user experience. It is supposed to cover both the qualitative insights from practitioners and meaningful quantitative metrics related to user engagement.

3.1.2 Question Number 2: To what extent does the integration of generative AI enhance the efficiency and accuracy of identifying vulnerabilities and ensuring robust security measures in web applications?

Figure 4. Question 2 Quantitative data collection

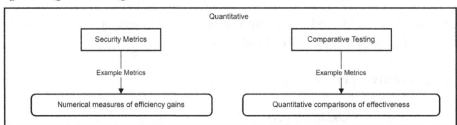

Figure 5. Question 2 Qualitative data collection

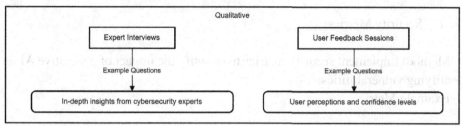

Quantitative data collection:

1. Expert Interviews:

Method: Conduct interviews with cybersecurity experts.
Example Questions:

- " Could you give use cases of these generative AI-integrated systems, especially how it has made ease a while in the identification of vulnerabilities of Web applications?"
- "In your experience, how has generative AI contributed to ensuring robust security measures?"

Purpose: Gather in-depth insights into real-world scenarios and experiences from experts in the field.

2. User Feedback Sessions:

Method: Organize feedback sessions with users who have interacted with web applications tested using generative AI.
Example Questions:

- "Did you notice any improvements in the security features of the web application compared to others you've used?"
- "How confident do you feel in the security of web applications that leverage generative AI-driven testing?"

Purpose: Capture user perceptions and confidence levels regarding the security enhancements facilitated by generative AI.

Quantitative Data Collection:

1. Security Metrics:

Method: Implement security metrics to quantify the impact of generative AI on identifying vulnerabilities.
Example Metrics:

*   Number of vulnerabilities detected per hour using generative AI.
*   Reduction in the average time taken to patch identified vulnerabilities.
    Purpose: Provide numerical measures of efficiency gains and accuracy improvements.

2. Comparative Testing:

Method: Conduct controlled experiments comparing the effectiveness of generative AI-driven testing with traditional methods.
Example Metrics:

*   Percentage of vulnerabilities detected by generative AI compared to traditional testing.
*   Time taken to identify and mitigate vulnerabilities in both approaches.

Purpose: Offer quantitative comparisons to assess the relative advantages of generative AI in security testing.

When such examples of research conducted on a research study regarding the use of generative AI for enhanced security measures are put down, it involves approaches that embrace the use of both qualitative and quantitative data collection techniques. Such a combination will be comprehensive in the practical implication and effectiveness of generative AI in web application security.

3.1.3 Question Number 3: Can generative AI predict potential issues in web-based systems, and how effectively does it automate routine maintenance tasks to optimize overall system performance?

Figure 6. Question 3 Quantitative data collection

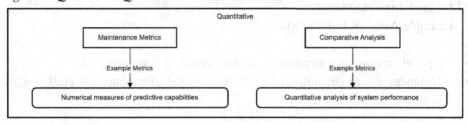

Figure 7. Question 3 Qualitative data collection

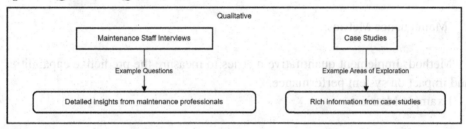

Quantitative data collection:

1. Maintenance Staff Interviews:

    Method: Conduct interviews with maintenance professionals.
    Example Questions:

    *   "Can you share instances where generative AI accurately predicted potential issues in web-based systems?"
    *   "In your experience, how has generative AI contributed to optimizing routine maintenance tasks for improved system performance?"

    Purpose: Gather detailed insights into real-world scenarios and experiences from professionals involved in system maintenance.

2. Case Studies:

Method: Conduct in-depth case studies on organizations implementing generative AI for predictive maintenance.

Example Areas of Exploration:

- Specific routine maintenance tasks automated by generative AI.
- Instances where generative AI optimization led to enhanced overall system performance.

Purpose: Provide rich, contextual information on the effectiveness of generative AI in routine maintenance through real-world examples.

Quantitative Data Collection:

1. Maintenance Metrics:

Method: Implement quantitative metrics to measure the predictive capabilities and impact on system performance.
Example Metrics:

- Percentage of accurately predicted issues by generative AI.
- Reduction in system downtime and improvement in response times.

Purpose: Offer numerical measures of the success of generative AI in predicting issues and optimizing routine maintenance.

2. Comparative Analysis:

Method: Conduct a comparative analysis between systems using generative AI and those relying on traditional maintenance approaches.
Example Metrics:

- Comparative downtime analysis over a specified period.
- Response time comparison between systems with and without generative AI-driven maintenance.

Purpose: Quantitatively assess the impact of generative AI on routine maintenance tasks and overall system performance.

3.1.4 Question Number 4: How seamlessly can generative AI be integrated across web development's design, testing, and maintenance phases, and what challenges or synergies emerge in its application?

Figure 8. Question 4 Quantitative data collection

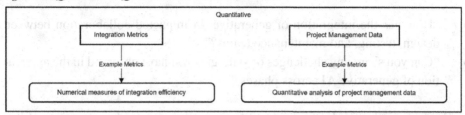

Figure 9. Question 4 Qualitative data collection

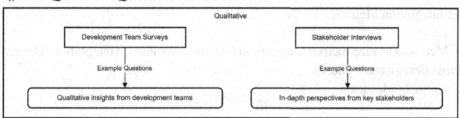

Qualitative data collection:

1. Development Team Surveys:

    Method: Distribute surveys to web development teams.
    Example Questions:

    *   "Describe any challenges you faced while integrating generative AI across design, testing, and maintenance phases."
    *   "Can you identify any synergies or positive outcomes observed during the integration of generative AI?"

    Purpose: Capture qualitative insights and perceptions from the perspectives of development teams.

2. Stakeholder Interviews:

    Method: Conduct interviews with key stakeholders involved in different development phases.

Example Questions:

- "How has the integration of generative AI impacted collaboration between design, testing, and maintenance teams?"
- "Can you share any challenges or synergies you have observed in the application of generative AI across phases?"

Purpose: Gather in-depth insights into the experiences and perspectives of key stakeholders.

Quantitative data collection:

1. Integration Metrics:

Method: Develop metrics to quantitatively assess the level of integration achieved across development phases.
Example Metrics:

- Percentage reduction in project timelines achieved by projects where generative AI is seamlessly integrated.
- Efficiency gains measured in resource utilization during the integration process.

Purpose: Provide numerical measures of the efficiency and effectiveness of generative AI integration.

2. Project Management Data:

Method: Utilize project management software to extract quantitative data on collaboration efficiency.
Example Metrics:

- Timelines for tasks related to design, testing, and maintenance phases during generative AI integration.
- Resource utilization patterns across different development teams during the integration process.

Purpose: Quantitatively analyze project management data to understand the logistical aspects of generative AI integration.

3.2 Data Collection

Qualitative Data:

In-depth Interviews:

Have detailed interviews with users about their experiences and perceptions of the use of AI-generated features in web development.

Open-ended Surveys:

The qualitative data on challenges, barriers, benefits, and innovative practices relevant to AI-infused web development were revealed after analyzing all the open-ended survey and practitioner responses.

Quantitative Data:

Surveys:

Administer surveys to a diverse sample of web developers and professionals involved in AI implementation to collect quantitative data on the frequency and effectiveness of generative AI utilization in various web development stages.

Web Analytics:

Describe how web analytics tools and performance metrics quantitatively measure the impact of generative AI on the efficiency and effectiveness of web-based systems.

3.3 Case Studies:

Study of the likely successes and failures of organizations that have employed generative AI in the web development processes, and specifically look into the case studies from these organizations for invaluably needed real-world insight into applications, challenges, and outcomes.

3.4 Experimental Protocols:

The design series and experimental protocols first designed within the framework of generative AI and web development incorporate in their entirety only one controlled experiment, which gauges the influence of a generative model on the following:

3.4.1 Designing Automated Design Processes Experiment:

Objective: To evaluate the efficiency of generative AI in automating web design processes.

Procedure: Develop a controlled experiment where two groups of web designers are assigned similar design tasks. One group uses generative AI tools, while the other uses traditional methods. Measure the time taken, accuracy, and creativity in producing designs.

Example Metrics: Time taken to complete the design, the number of design iterations, and user satisfaction with the final designs.

3.4.2 Testing Outcomes Improvement Experiment:

Objective: To assess how generative AI impacts the effectiveness of testing outcomes in web development.

Procedure: Create a testing scenario with a set of known vulnerabilities. Conduct testing with a group using generative AI-driven testing tools and another using traditional methods. Compare the detection rates, false positives, and overall effectiveness.

Example Metrics: Number of vulnerabilities detected, false positive rate, time taken to identify vulnerabilities.

3.4.3 Optimizing Maintenance Workflows Experiment:

Objective: To understand how generative AI affects routine maintenance tasks and overall system performance.

Procedure: Set up a maintenance scenario with routine tasks such as updates and patches. Compare a group utilizing generative AI for automation with a control group using manual methods. Measure time saved, accuracy of updates, and system performance.

Example Metrics: Time saved on routine maintenance, accuracy of updates, system performance improvement.

3.5 Integration of Findings:

Integration of findings involves synthesizing qualitative and quantitative results to provide a holistic understanding. Here's how it can be approached:

Example Integration:

Qualitative Findings: In interviews, developers express positive attitudes towards the creativity enabled by generative AI in design.

Quantitative Findings: Survey data shows an increase in design efficiency when using generative AI.

Integration: The integration suggests that not only does generative AI enhance creativity, but it also contributes to improved efficiency in design tasks.

3.6 Validation and Reliability:

Ensuring the validity and reliability of research outcomes is crucial. Triangulation is a technique used to cross-verify findings from different data sources.

Example Triangulation:

Data Sources:

- Interviews with web developers.
- Surveys on generative AI usage.
- Web analytics data on system performance.

Triangulation: It means comparing information obtained from various interviews, survey responses, and web analytics. Having in mind that the three types of sources make one arrive at the same conclusion about the positive effect of generative AI in improving the development of a webpage, so, one may conclude that it increases validity and reliability.

By adopting such techniques to use the right methodologies, findings which one will be able to consider, and the right understanding where generative AI puts itself in web development.

4. CONCLUSION

This research will, therefore, seek to investigate the confluence of generative artificial intelligence (AI) with web development, with the explicit aim of unpacking the design and transformation possibilities that it portends for the latter's testing and maintenance. In doing so, the following took a hybrid approach to both catch generative AI and web engineering through engaged contemporary mixed-method research design, engaging both qualitative and quantitative methods to delineate their respective capacities and to provide insights into the potential futures of web engineering. Given the above discussions, the results of the current study are such that using generative AI, creativity and innovation of web design work becomes motivated. This can be proved through the usage of generative AI, which has been proven to speed work and give opportunities for developing new visual design ideas.

The implication of this research strongly suggests the need for proactive designs in the strategic entrenchment of generative AI in organizations into the whole aspect of web development.

Efficiency, in this regard, can be applied to how best generative models advance practices in web development. A new era in which AI knows every likable character of the user and designs personalized web experiences may create unique opportunities for engagement. In the same way, this research signals the need for further reflection on the inclusive nature of AI-generated content in design for people to have equal grounds regardless of their abilities or demographics.

REFERENCES

Anica-Popa, L. E., Vrîncianu, M., & Papuc, I. M. P. (2023). AI–powered Business Services in the Hyperautomation Era. In *Proceedings of the International Conference on Business Excellence* (Vol. 17, No. 1, pp. 1036-1050).

Aravinth, S., Rao, B., Senthil Kumar, A., & Prsath, A. (2021). AI and ml enabled analytics techniques for improving the quality of website. *2021 6th International Conference on Signal Processing, Computing and Control (ISPCC).* DOI: 10.1109/ISPCC53510.2021.9609498

Ashwini, N., Kumar, N., Nandan, M., & Suman, V. (2023). Leveraging Artificial Intelligence in Education: Transforming the Learning Landscape. *International Research Journal of Computer Science*, 10(05), 192–196.

Bharadiya, J. P., Thomas, R. K., & Ahmed, F. (2023). Rise of Artificial Intelligence in Business and Industry. *Journal of Engineering Research and Reports*, 25(3), 85–103.

Cummaudo, A., Barnett, S., Vasa, R., Grundy, J., & Abdelrazek, M. (2020). Beware the evolving 'intelligent' web service! an integration architecture tactic to guard AI-first components. *Proceedings of the 28th ACM Joint Meeting on European Software Engineering Conference and Symposium on the Foundations of Software Engineering.* DOI: 10.1145/3368089.3409688

Dimitriadou, E., & Lanitis, A. (2023). A critical evaluation, challenges, and future perspectives of using artificial intelligence and emerging technologies in smart classrooms. *Smart Learning Environments*, 10(1), 12. Advance online publication. DOI: 10.1186/s40561-023-00231-3

Ernst, N. A., & Bavota, G. (2022). AI-driven development is here: Should you worry? *IEEE Software*, 39(2), 106–110. DOI: 10.1109/MS.2021.3133805

Haldorai, A., Murugan, S., & Ramu, A. (2020). Evolution, challenges, and application of intelligent ICT education: An overview. *Computer Applications in Engineering Education*, 29(3), 562–571. DOI: 10.1002/cae.22217

Hsiao, I., & Chung, C. (2022). AI-infused semantic model to enrich and expand programming question generation. *Journal of Artificial Intelligence and Technology.* .DOI: 10.37965/jait.2022.0090

Kamruzzaman, M. M., Alanazi, S., Alruwaili, M., Alshammari, N., Elaiwat, S., Abu-Zanona, M., Innab, N., Mohammad Elzaghmouri, B., & Ahmed Alanazi, B. (2023). AI- and IoT-assisted sustainable education systems during pandemics, such as COVID-19, for smart cities. *Sustainability (Basel)*, 15(10), 8354. DOI: 10.3390/su15108354

Liu, S., Li, Z., & Ba, L. (2020). Impact of Artificial Intelligence 2.0 on Teaching and Learning. *International Conference on Educational and Information Technology*.

Mello, R.F., Freitas, E., Pereira, F.D., Cabral, L.D., Tedesco, P., & Ramalho, G. (2023). Education in the age of Generative AI: Context and Recent Developments. *ArXiv, abs/2309.12332*.

Nanjundappa, R., Gajendra, N., Samal, S. P., Mahesha, N., Pahuja, A., Musham, V. M., & NamGung, E. (2020, December). AWAF: AI Enabled Web Contents Authoring Framework. In 2020 IEEE 17th India Council International Conference (INDICON) (pp. 1-5). IEEE.

Ozkaya, I. (2023). The next frontier in software development: AI-augmented software development processes. *IEEE Software*, 40(4), 4–9. DOI: 10.1109/MS.2023.3278056

Priyanga, G. (2023). The effects of artificial intelligence on digital marketing. ShodhKosh. *Journal of Visual and Performing Arts*, 4, 158–167.

Tao, Z., & Ye, Q. (2020). The application of artificial intelligence in computer web technology in the era of massive data. *Journal of Physics: Conference Series*, 1574(1), 012020. DOI: 10.1088/1742-6596/1574/1/012020

Zawacki-Richter, O., Marín, V. I., Bond, M., & Gouverneur, F. (2019). Systematic review of research on artificial intelligence applications in higher education – where are the educators? *International Journal of Educational Technology in Higher Education*, 16(1), 39. Advance online publication. DOI: 10.1186/s41239-019-0171-0

Zhai, X., Chu, X., Chai, C.S., Jong, M.S., Istenič, A., Spector, M., Liu, J., Yuan, J., & Li, Y. (2021). A Review of Artificial Intelligence (AI) in Education from 2010 to 2020. *Complex., 2021*, 8812542:1-8812542:18.

Zhang, K., & Aslan, A. B. (2021). AI technologies for education: Recent research & future directions. *Computers and Education: Artificial Intelligence*, 2, 100025. DOI: 10.1016/j.caeai.2021.100025

Chapter 6
Hardware Vulnerabilities:
Taxonomy and Business Security Models

N. Z. Jhanjhi

https://orcid.org/0000-0001-8116-4733

School of Computing Science and Engineering, Taylor's University, Malaysia

Imdad Ali Shah

https://orcid.org/0000-0003-2015-1028

Faculty of Engineering Science & Technology, Iqra University, Malaysia

Sarfraz Nawaz Brohi

School of Computing and Creative Technologies, University of the West of England, UK

ABSTRACT

The primary objective of this chapter is to address the hardware vulnerabilities risks and challenges. A hardware vulnerability is a flaw in a computer system that can be remotely exploited by threat actors. They can then infiltrate a network by introducing malicious code. Vulnerability management, also known as vulnerability mapping, is the continuous process of identifying, categorizing, prioritizing, fixing, and reducing vulnerabilities in an environment. It involves assigning software high priority and promptly addressing risks to stop data breaches and cyberattacks. Considering the nature of the hardware, hardware security is different from software, network, and data security, whether it is being used for attack or defense. We must take hardware security into account early in product life cycles since hardware design and manufacturing frequently take place prior to or during software development. Information systems are becoming more common in a world moving toward total digitization. These systems are complex systems with hardware at their core. The

DOI: 10.4018/979-8-3693-3703-5.ch006

investigation of potential hardware vulnerabilities must be included when addressing the security of these systems to prevent potential intrusions and malicious uses, as their exploitation can render any online or software-based defences worthless. we define hardware security and offer a meaningful and thorough taxonomy for hardware vulnerabilities and the attacks that take advantage of them to compromise the system. Consequently, the researcher's focus on this topic has increased recently.

INTRODUCTION

AI and ML are being applied in an increasing number of different use cases as a result of the emergence of new, significantly enhanced AI and ML technology and applications. The widespread use of AI solutions in people's daily lives and the operations of several organizations raises the possibility of new risks and weaknesses (Sisejkovic et al., 2021, Dessouky et al., 2019). Recent years have seen a significant increase in the study of these vulnerabilities, and findings of hacks and assaults on many applications and AI/ML techniques are already available. Even more basic findings about how to build AI models with imperceptible flaws.

Unlike conventional information technology vulnerabilities with CVE, there is no widely established vulnerability framework or taxonomy for artificial intelligence systems. There are a few options, though, to be considered for a future system. Most of these grew out of the necessity of having a method for listing common vulnerabilities in a field that is developing quickly. Still, it appears that no systematic attempt has been made to develop a system that can handle vulnerabilities in a field-wide manner (Sayeeshwari and Prabhu, 2022, Brasilino and Swany, 2019). "User Satisfaction: Security Models for Web-Based Applications" explores the critical intersection of security and user happiness in the context of web-based applications. In the current environment, which is characterized by progressively more complex cyber-attacks, maintaining customer happiness as well as strong security protocols is essential for companies and organizations operating in the digital sphere. Although firewalls can prevent illegal traffic from the Internet into corporate networks, legitimate requests that pass through the firewall can be used for data-driven attacks against networks or background systems. Configuring firewalls and web servers is a huge and error-prone task. This highlights the need to limit or reduce the complexity of firewalls and networks and to complement firewalls with strong host protection. In large enterprise intranets, insider attacks are a growing security problem(Ma et al., 2019, Shah, 2024, Chittamuru et al., 2018). Figure 1 Overview Hardware Vulnerabilities.

Figure 1. Overview Hardware Vulnerabilities

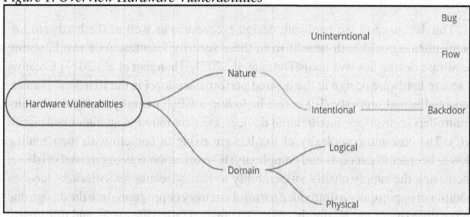

These security risks caused serious damage to the regions concerned. After that, the paper analyzes and discusses in detail information security technologies based on web applications. laid the groundwork by highlighting the central role of effective security measures in increasing user satisfaction. Their study demonstrates how user trust in online applications and, consequently, overall happiness is significantly impacted by security considerations. Smith and Johnson examine the mutually beneficial relationship between security and user experience and emphasize the necessity of developing web applications with a comprehensive strategy that gives equal weight to these two factors. In-depth research on the effect of security models on user satisfaction in web-based applications is presented by(Dutta et al., 2021, Kustov et al., 2022). Their actual research, which was based on user input and real-world events, offers verifiable proof of the connection between security measures and user satisfaction levels. Patel and Gupta offer useful advice for enhancing security models to raise user satisfaction levels with web-based applications by examining the intricate relationship between security frameworks and user experience.

This chapter's contributions are in the following points:

- We discussed the hardware vulnerabilities and business security models
- We discussed the hardware security issues and challenges
- We discussed the hardware attacks, approaches
- We provide recommendation and future work

LITERATURE REVIEW

The data used in the hardware design procedures as well as the hardware implementation could both benefit from these security features. As a result, secure hardware design has two goals(Dutta et al., 2021, Thangam et al., 2017) Creating a secure hardware design at the desired performance level is the first step. Numerous intellectual property (IP) cores, including a CPU, memory, network-on-chip, controllers, converters, input/output devices, etc., are found in an integrated circuit (IC). The cost and complexity of the ICs are rising in tandem with their scaling down. In order to cut costs and complexity, IC fabrication is being moved offshore, increasing the supply chain's vulnerability to hardware attacks. Attackers have an additional opportunity to introduce harmful circuitry or programs into the design due to the diversity of the IC supply chain. The market, after-life cycle, and third-party vendors are highlighted in blue to indicate the outside parties' role in the integrated circuit supply chain. Furthermore, although this assumption isn't always true, crucial control and communication functions rely on the security of the hardware platform on which they are implemented. There have been concerns, for instance, that backdoors may be used to manage nuclear power facilities, transportation networks, and weapon control systems. As such, a growing number of new security risks are targeting computing hardware. On the other hand, deliberate design modifications, unintended design faults, and system side effects could all contribute to hardware vulnerabilities(Patnaik et al., 2019, Naveenkumar et al., 2022, Shah et al., 2024b). They usually try to steal cryptographic operations, machine learning (ML) models, secure systems, and intellectual property. In the context of the Internet of Things (IoT), hardware security is advantageous. The definition of the Internet of Things (IoT) is the ability of smart computer devices to connect physical items over the Internet (Naveenkumar et al., 2022, Manssour et al., 2022). Its reach has extended to encompass all facets of contemporary society, including the vital domains of e-healthcare, finance, energy, and defense applications, among others. Furthermore, the global IoT market is anticipated to grow from 478.36 billion dollars in 2022 to 2,465.26 billion dollars in 2029, at a compound annual growth rate (CAGR) of 26.4% throughout the forecast period(Arias et al., 2022, Yu et al., 2021). Nevertheless, there are several security flaws in both hardware and software as a result of our overwhelming reliance on IoT devices. The open structure of IoT nodes and the involvement of third parties make information leakage from them quite easy. Figure 3 Overview of hardware security. Figure 4 Overview of hardware security.

Figure 2. Overview hardware security

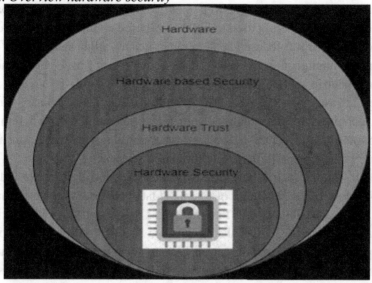

These IoT devices can sometimes be deployed remotely, authorized users may occasionally construct a leakage channel or some foreign items at the hardware level of the IoT system. During the design, production, integration, and distribution phases of an IoT device, enterprises have the potential to mistakenly or intentionally include hardware security vulnerabilities(Reimann et al., 2021, Eslami et al., 2022). On the Internet of Things domain, hardware vulnerabilities encompass a variety of threats, such as tampering with PCB designs, side-channel leaks, insertion of malicious content through hardware Trojans, and IP design modifications. While there aren't many techniques for testing vulnerability detection in the pre-and post-silicon phases, those that are offer varying degrees of efficacy.

The quick expansion of the Web and the appearance of significant empowering innovations have transformed data innovation and created a plethora of chances for the creation of globally distributed applications. Concerns over the security of web-based apps have also been brought up by this growth. E-commerce is one prominent example that is predicted to get close to a $1 trillion market value soon. Even with its promise, there are already significant security dangers associated with it, especially when it comes to unauthorized access to private data like credit card numbers. Other web-based initiatives, such as healthcare and online counselling, are also linked to serious security and safety issues (Shah et al., 2024c, Solanki and Panda, 2022, Miki et al., 2020).(Zhu et al., 2018) Many of these applications can be supported. by public and commercial initiatives to enhance their adminis-trations and decision-making processes. Ensuring data security and safety in these web-based applications continues to be a significant concern. A three-tier design, comprising an organizing server, a web client, and a database-supported back-end data foundation, is frequently used to build web-based applications. Middleware is often used in transaction-focused applications, such as online shopping, to provide appropriate communication between database servers and back-end frameworks. Each component in this engineering has interesting security issues and threats. Public-key infrastructures (PKIs) are currently in use and comprise electronic signature techniques for data analysis, authentication, and non-repudiation as well as encryption tools for privacy. However, their usefulness to web applications is limited due to their accessibility to authorization services.

Numerous factors, such as the extensive interconnection of disparate and heterogeneous systems, the accessibility of sensitive data, the ease with which malicious software can be distributed, and the challenges associated with identifying and prosecuting computer crimes, make strong data security on the Web imperative. The two primary components that are necessary for a secure Web foundation are access control and communication security. While communication security services guarantee the integrity and confidentiality of data transmitted via networks, access control services anticipate the unauthorized use of online resources(Lin et al., 2021, Ding et al., 2021). End users that utilize web browsers run the danger of several security and privacy issues when using the internet. Browser bugs may compromise the security of web clients, and consumer data may be collected and utilized for profiling, raising valid security concerns. Treats and executable materials—like Java applets and ActiveX controls—present additional security risks. Organization servers, which house most of organization administrations, are usually protected by firewall innovation. However, configuring servers and constructing firewalls are challenging and error-prone, thus robust host-based security measures are required in addition to firewall defences. Insider attacks are becoming a growing concern in large corporate intranets, underscoring the need for updated or enhanced get-to-control models to meet the various security requirements of web-based services. Traditional access control approaches, such mandatory access control (MAC) and optional access control (DAC), are limited in their ability to provide high security assurance and adaptability. A more comprehensive method that streamlines security organization and supports organizational security arrangements is provided by role-based access control (RBAC) models. Web-based applications and WFMSs particularly benefit from RBAC models, even though they must be encouraged to evolve in order to properly address complicated security requirements. To improve security in dynamic and scattered web scenarios, emerging techniques like agent-based security highlights, task-based access control (TBAC) models, and certificate-based approaches are also being investigated. Another crucial element is to promote participation and operation. If users believe a platform is secure, they are more likely to utilize it frequently(Mohammed et al., 2019, Montoya et al., 2020). Often, advanced engagement scenarios arise from users' sense of security and confidence in the platform's ability to protect their data. Users are more inclined to adopt and utilize new features when they have confidence in the platform's security enhancing their satisfaction and the overall value they decide from the service.

Overview Hardware Vulnerabilities

Since information systems first started to proliferate and change, the primary focus of security discussions has always been on safeguarding against breaches in an environment that may be accessible to everybody thanks to online connections. Consequently, it is true that hardware has always been seen as safe and untouchable, but networks and software have drawn the greatest attention. However, a great deal of research has been done on the function of hardware in safety and safety-critical applications. By (Mao et al., 2020, Gong et al., 2019) the close of the previous century, smart cards had become widely used. These devices, which were based on semiconductors designed specifically for security and authentication applications, were thought to be uncrackable by ordinary hackers unless they used extremely sophisticated techniques.

Important writers like Kocher and others started bringing up the issue of deriving information from secure devices like smartcards by listening to the surroundings, timing, how long it takes, how much energy it uses, and how much radiation it emits. The physical implementations of cryptographic algorithms, which are thought to be nearly impenetrable mathematically, are vulnerable. The vertical integration model of the hardware supply chain was abandoned at the turn of the century in favour of the horizontal one. Rather than handling every aspect of production, from design to final manufacture, businesses began to outsource manufacturing to other businesses, to whom they then provided the device layout(Shah et al., 2024a, Divyanshu et al., 2022). As a result, an extensive body of work has been written about "hardware manufacturing" and the various ways in which it is put into practice, including physical unconable functions. In a similar vein, concerns over the potential for hardware Trojan horse insertion began to arise due to a manufacturing process involving unreliable actors. When the gadget is turned on, the Trojans are directly plugged into the circuit and activated. Since hardware security is still relatively new, it may appear to be a fictitious combination of methods intended to safeguard the information handled by the hardware or the uniqueness and integrity of the hardware design. Only recently have some writers attempted to make things more organized by putting out taxonomy examples; of these, we believe the most important are presented here.

Overview Hardware Attacks

A hardware attack is the act of taking advantage of a hardware vulnerability. It is important to note that an attack always occurs only when the affected hardware is operating in the field. For this definition, a vulnerability is not considered to exist if it cannot be exploited, as this would not expose the system to any risk and would not constitute a weakness. Moreover, an attack that employs an exploit is an activity that undermines confidentiality if there is a vulnerability that jeopardizes integrity and confidentiality and if the weakness can only be exploited. Figure 4 Overview hardware attack.

Figure 3. Overview hardware attacks

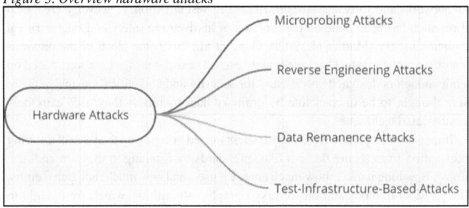

Once physical access to the target device has been established, a microprobe attack attempts to collect information by measuring electrical quantities directly on the silicon die of the device. Attackers, if at all possible, examine the target's netlist prior to the attack, using little reverse engineering to identify layout matches and identify connections carrying meaningful data. Thanks to sophisticated machinery like focused ion beam (FIB) generators, they can now precisely block wires with nanometer accuracy. After that, a probe device is used to read the target signals and retrieve data. Such high-tech equipment appears to be hard to come by.

Reverse engineering attacks are comparable to micro-probing in the mounting phase, but they operate on a different scale. It seeks to pilfer the designer's intellectual property by comprehending the composition and operations of semiconductor devices. Obviously, the ability to develop advanced integrated circuits requires a profound understanding of the field(Montoya et al., 2019, Kumar et al., 2020). To ascertain the internal structure of the chip, each layer created during chip manufacture is eliminated one at a time in reverse order and captured on camera. Ultimately, by analyzing all the collected data, a standard netlist file can be produced, which can then be used to model and ultimately redesign the intended device.

Conversely, an attack qualifies as non-invasive if it can be executed without requiring direct physical contact with the target equipment. There are two types of non-invasive attacks: passive and active. One physical dynamic entity of the targeted device is analyzed and measured in passive, non-invasive attacks(Dobrykh et al., 2021, Sharma et al., 2022). This category includes every kind of side-channel attack there is. Instead, active, non-invasive attacks necessitate precise device activities meant to jolt the system into aberrant states where the objective is more easily attained. All varieties of fault attacks and test-infrastructure-based assaults fall under this category.

Overview Business Security Model

A recent development in the Internet is the Internet of Things (IoT). It gives objects the ability to recognize one another, acquire intelligence, transmit information about themselves, and access data that has been compiled by other entities. Using any path, any network, and any service, the Internet of Things enables people and things to be connected anytime, anywhere, with anything and anyone. This necessitates addressing elements like convergence, content, collections, computing, communication, and connectivity.

At an unprecedented rate, more and more physical items are being connected to the Internet, bringing the possibilities of industrial automation, transportation, healthcare, and emergency response to natural and man-made disasters where human decision-making is challenging to reality. Physical things can see, hear, think, and do tasks thanks to the Internet of Things. It also allows them to communicate, share information, and plan actions collectively(Rajan and Ganesh, 2022, Sidhu et al., 2019). By utilizing its underlying technologies, which include pervasive and ubiquitous computers, embedded devices, communication technologies, sensor networks, Internet protocols, and applications, the Internet of Things turns these conventional things into intelligent ones. Horizontal markets refer to application domain-agnostic services, whereas vertical markets are made up of domain-specific apps or smart objects and their purported functions, as well as ubiquitous computing and analytical services. Sensors and actuators in each domain communicate directly with one another, and each domain-specific application interacts with domain-independent services. The Internet of Things (IoT) is anticipated to have substantial uses in both residential and corporate settings throughout time, improving people's quality of life and boosting global trade.

Furthermore, architecture standardization can be considered the IoT's structural foundation, fostering competition and enabling businesses to produce high-quality goods(Chen et al., 2023, Khalil et al., 2020a). To meet the problems posed by IoT, the conventional Internet infrastructure must also be updated. Many underlying protocols should consider the enormous number of items wanting to connect to the Internet. Owing to the inherent variety of Internet-connected things and the capacity to monitor and manage physical objects, security and privacy are other significant considerations for the Internet of Things. In addition, it is imperative to manage and monitor the Internet of Things in order to guarantee that clients receive high-quality services at an economical cost.

The system includes both the user interface that customers interact with on the outside and the underlying operations of an e-commerce platform. User-friendly, responsive websites, an efficient purchasing experience, and background administration that runs smoothly are its main characteristics. In e-commerce architecture, the session, application logic, and data service layers are the three tiers(Ali et al., 2023, Khalil et al., 2021). Each level provides services to and is dependent upon the level above it. The system can be divided into two sections: the backend administration system, which manages the company's backend logistics, and the front shopping system, which lets users browse products and place purchases. A variety of back-end management tools are available to the operator, such as payment platforms, configuration settings, user strategy planning, inventory management, and inventory control.

Overview Hardware Security Challenges

There are several issues that more sophisticated approaches to hardware security research must take into account. Over the past ten years, the globalization of the semiconductor business has resulted in a number of improvements to the fabrication process in the IC industry. The time-to-market requirement and the continually rising complexity of hardware designs have caused the integrated circuit (IC) supply chain to become more globally diversified(Khalil et al., 2020b). To lower the cost of production in the IC supply chain, businesses are now outsourcing intellectual property to outside vendors. Diverse vulnerabilities arise from a broad hardware supply chain. At an unprecedented rate, more and more physical items are being connected to the Internet, bringing the possibilities of industrial automation, transportation, healthcare, and emergency response to natural and man-made disasters where human decision-making is challenging to reality. Physical things can see, hear, think, and do tasks thanks to the Internet of Things. It also allows them to communicate, share information, and plan actions collectively. For this definition, a vulnerability is not considered to exist if it cannot be exploited, as this would not expose the system to any risk and would not constitute a weakness. Moreover, an attack that employs an exploit is an activity that undermines confidentiality if there is a vulnerability that jeopardizes integrity and confidentiality and if the weakness can only be exploited. Figure 5 Overview of hardware attacks & approached

Figure 4. Overview hardware attacks & approached

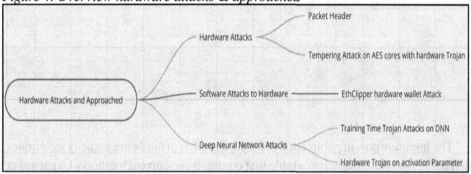

Furthermore, the intricacy of the microelectronics supply chain and globalization make it simple to adopt a variety of changes. On the one hand, end users or IP owners find it more difficult to ensure that their components are assured and tamper-free as a result of the globalization of the IC supply chain(Khalaf et al., 2021, Ziegler et al., 2020). However, because sophisticated integrated circuit packaging has become more complex, existing detection methods are unable to confirm the contents of sample packaging. Furthermore, a hostile manufacturer's hostile modifications to the packaging specifications may produce features that are missed and lead to chip failure. Chip packaging is, therefore, now seen as a serious hardware security risk.

For instance, metal layers and shielding meshes on the front side of the SoC restrict the paths taken by incident photons and protect the integrated circuits from optical attack. But the device's back, or silicon substrate, is devoid of these protective layers. Narrow and nearly chip-scale packaging can achieve flip-chip, which makes them perfect for Internet of Things devices. Thus, an attacker can use fault injection, side-channel attacks, and laser/optical probing to easily monitor and retrieve security-sensitive data and information. Consequently, an IC chip with a Si-backside creates a significant security flaw, particularly in flip-chip packaging. Figure 5 Overview of hardware attacks & countermeasures.

Figure 5. Overview hardware attacks & countermeasures

Figure 5. Overview hardware attacks & countermeasures

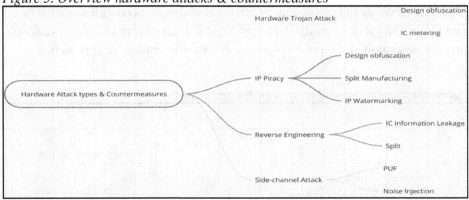

The literature now in publication presents a number of hardware security techniques that address various domains. a table that contrasts the current methods. (Agarwal et al., 2020) this approach resolved problems with hardware overhead and scalability while identifying harmful and vulnerable logic. The goals of the suggested design are to use reconfigurable hardware to offer different levels of performance and protection and to continuously monitor the system's functioning to detect abnormal behavior. Results from the AES and RC6 algorithms show that the flexibility of the proposed solution allows for the identification of an energy-efficient alternative in addition to addressing the security issue. This method's primary flaw is that some elements, including the cost of security systems, require inquiry. Hardware that may be reconfigured and how to standardize security in embedded systems.

CONCLUSION AND FUTURE WORK

In Conclusion, we have studied more than hundreds of related articles, International Conferences and book chapters. We've discussed the researcher's approaches and the framework that is currently accessible, as well as some difficulties in addressing various hardware security-related topics. The literature makes it clear that language-based hardware security solutions have received a lot of attention lately. However, researchers have also recently paid close attention to threats in Deep Neural Networks (DNN). Finding the right balance between security and resource utilization is determined to be most of the researcher's challenges, particularly for lightweight/battery-constrained devices. Furthermore, the advantages and disadvantages of the available hardware security techniques are also discussed in this chapter. Furthermore, the most popular hardware attack methods are presented in this paper, along with their advantages and disadvantages. But as technology advances, new hardware security flaws will also appear. Thus, grasping the difficulties and current security techniques that apply to specific assaults, as well as the benefits and limitations of the technique, will assist the practitioner in selecting the best course of action to handle new hardware attacks in this difficult area of security.

REFERENCES

Agarwal, V., Kaushal, A. K., & Chouhan, L. A survey on cloud computing security issues and cryptographic techniques. Social Networking and Computational Intelligence: Proceedings of SCI-2018, 2020. Springer, 119-134. DOI: 10.1007/978-981-15-2071-6_10

Ali, Y., Shah, S. W., & Khan, W. A. (2023). *Security at the Internet of Things. Machine Tools*. CRC Press.

Arias, O., Liu, Z., Guo, X., Jin, Y., & Wang, S. (2022). *RTSEC: Automated RTL code augmentation for hardware security enhancement. 2022 Design, Automation & Test in Europe Conference & Exhibition (DATE)*. IEEE.

Brasilino, L. R., & Swany, M. Mitigating DDoS flooding attacks against IoT using custom hardware modules. *2019 Sixth International Conference on Internet of Things: Systems, Management and Security (IOTSMS)*, 2019. IEEE, 58-64. DOI: 10.1109/IOTSMS48152.2019.8939176

Chen, W., Huo, R., Sun, C., Zeng, S., Wang, S., & Huang, T. (2023). SCRT: A secure and efficient state-channel-based resource trading scheme for Internet of Things. *IEEE Internet of Things Journal*, 10(11), 10038–10051. DOI: 10.1109/JIOT.2023.3236774

Chittamuru, S. V. R., Thakkar, I. G., Bhat, V., & Pasricha, S. SOTERIA: exploiting process variations to enhance hardware security with photonic NoC architectures. *Proceedings of the 55th Annual Design Automation Conference*, 2018. 1-6. DOI: 10.1145/3195970.3196118

Dessouky, G., Zeitouni, S., Ibrahim, A., Davi, L., & Sadeghi, A.-R. CHASE: A configurable hardware-assisted security extension for real-time systems. *2019 IEEE/ACM International Conference on Computer-Aided Design (ICCAD)*, 2019. IEEE, 1-8. DOI: 10.1109/ICCAD45719.2019.8942142

Ding, Q., Jiang, H., Li, J., Liu, C., Yu, J., Chen, P., Zhao, Y., Ding, Y., Gong, T., & Yang, J. Unified 0.75 pJ/Bit TRNG and attack resilient 2F 2/Bit PUF for robust hardware security solutions with 4-layer stacking 3D NbO x threshold switching array. 2021 IEEE International Electron Devices Meeting (IEDM), 2021. IEEE, 39.2. 1-39.2. 4. DOI: 10.1109/IEDM19574.2021.9720641

Divyanshu, D., Kumar, R., Khan, D., Amara, S., & Massoud, Y. (2022). Logic locking using emerging 2T/3T magnetic tunnel junctions for hardware security. *IEEE Access : Practical Innovations, Open Solutions*, 10, 102386–102395. DOI: 10.1109/ACCESS.2022.3208650

Dobrykh, D., Filonov, D., Slobozhanyuk, A., & Ginzburg, P. (2021). Hardware RFID security for preventing far-field attacks. *IEEE Transactions on Antennas and Propagation*, 70(3), 2199–2204. DOI: 10.1109/TAP.2021.3118846

Dutta, S., Grisafe, B., Frentzel, C., Enciso, Z., San Jose, M., Smith, J., Ni, K., Joshi, S., & Datta, S. (2021). Experimental demonstration of gate-level logic camouflaging and run-time reconfigurability using ferroelectric FET for hardware security. *IEEE Transactions on Electron Devices*, 68(2), 516–522. DOI: 10.1109/TED.2020.3045380

Eslami, M., Ghasempouri, T., & Pagliarini, S. (2022, April). Reusing verification assertions as security checkers for hardware trojan detection. In 2022 23rd International Symposium on Quality Electronic Design (ISQED) (pp. 1-6). IEEE.

Gong, Y., Qian, F., & Wang, L. (2019). Design for test and hardware security utilizing retention loss of memristors. *IEEE Transactions on Very Large Scale Integration (VLSI). Systems*, 27, 2536–2547.

Khalaf, O. I., Sokiyna, M., Alotaibi, Y., Alsufyani, A., & Alghamdi, S. (2021). Web Attack Detection Using the Input Validation Method: DPDA Theory. *Computers, Materials & Continua*, •••, 68.

Khalil, K., Abdelgawad, A., & Bayoumi, M. (2021, June). Intelligent resource discovery approach for the internet of things. In 2021 IEEE 7th World Forum on Internet of Things (WF-IoT) (pp. 264-269). IEEE.

Khalil, K., Elgazzar, K., Abdelgawad, A., & Bayoumi, M. (2020a, June). A security approach for CoAP-based internet of things resource discovery. In 2020 IEEE 6th World Forum on Internet of Things (WF-IoT) (pp. 1-6). IEEE.

Khalil, K., Elgazzar, K., Seliem, M., & Bayoumi, M. (2020b). Resource discovery techniques in the internet of things: A review. *Internet of Things : Engineering Cyber Physical Human Systems*, 12, 100293. DOI: 10.1016/j.iot.2020.100293

Kumar, B., Jaiswal, A. K., Vineesh, V. S., & Shinde, R. (2020, January). Analyzing hardware security properties of processors through model checking. In 2020 33rd International Conference on VLSI Design and 2020 19th International Conference on Embedded Systems (VLSID) (pp. 107-112). IEEE.

Kustov, P., Petrova, E., Sandomirskii, M., & Zuev, D. (2022, September). All-dielectric silicon nanoparticles on flexible substrate for anticounterfeiting labels. In *2022 Sixteenth International Congress on Artificial Materials for Novel Wave Phenomena (Metamaterials)* (pp. 244-246). IEEE.

Lin, L., Zhu, D., Wen, J., Chen, H., Lu, Y., Chang, N., & Nagata, M. (2021, December). Multiphysics simulation of em side-channels from silicon backside with ml-based auto-poi identification. In *2021 IEEE International Symposium on Hardware Oriented Security and Trust (HOST)* (pp. 270-280). IEEE.

Ma, M., Chen, L., & Shi, G. (2019, December). Dam: A practical scheme to mitigate data-oriented attacks with tagged memory based on hardware. In 2019 26th Asia-Pacific Software Engineering Conference (APSEC) (pp. 204-211). IEEE.

Manssour, N. A., Lapotre, V., Gogniat, G., & Tisserand, A. (2022, April). Processor extensions for hardware instruction replay against fault injection attacks. In 2022 25th International Symposium on Design and Diagnostics of Electronic Circuits and Systems (DDECS) (pp. 26-31). IEEE.

Mao, Y., Migliore, V., & Nicomette, V. (2020, September). REHAD: Using low-frequency reconfigurable hardware for cache side-channel attacks detection. In 2020 IEEE European Symposium on Security and Privacy Workshops (EuroS&PW) (pp. 704-709). IEEE.

Miki, T., Nagata, M., Sonoda, H., Miura, N., Okidono, T., Araga, Y., Watanabe, N., Shimamoto, H., & Kikuchi, K. (2020). Si-backside protection circuits against physical security attacks on flip-chip devices. *IEEE Journal of Solid-State Circuits*, 55(10), 2747–2755. DOI: 10.1109/JSSC.2020.3005779

Mohammed, H., Odetola, T. A., Hasan, S. R., Stissi, S., Garlin, I., & Awwad, F. (2019, August). (HIADIoT): Hardware intrinsic attack detection in Internet of Things; leveraging power profiling. In 2019 ieee 62nd international midwest symposium on circuits and systems (mwscas) (pp. 852-855). IEEE.

Montoya, M., Bacles-Min, S., Molnos, A., & Fournier, J. J. (2020, August). Dynamic encoding, a lightweight combined countermeasure against hardware attacks. In 2020 23rd Euromicro Conference on Digital System Design (DSD) (pp. 185-192). IEEE.

Montoya, M., Hiscock, T., Bacles-Min, S., Molnos, A., & Fournier, J. Adaptive masking: a dynamic trade-off between energy consumption and hardware security. 2019 IEEE 37th International Conference on Computer Design (ICCD), 2019. IEEE, 559-566.

Naveenkumar, R., Sivamangai, N. M., Napolean, A., Puviarasu, A., & Saranya, G. (2022, June). Preventive measure of sat attack by integrating anti-sat on locked circuit for improving hardware security. In 2022 7th International Conference on Communication and Electronics Systems (ICCES) (pp. 756-760). IEEE.

Patnaik, S., Rangarajan, N., Knechtel, J., Sinanoglu, O., & Rakheja, S. (2019). Spin-orbit torque devices for hardware security: From deterministic to probabilistic regime. *IEEE Transactions on Computer-Aided Design of Integrated Circuits and Systems*, 39(8), 1591–1606. DOI: 10.1109/TCAD.2019.2917856

Rajan, J. G., & Ganesh, R. S. (2022, October). Hardware based data security techniques in IoT: A review. In 2022 3rd International Conference on Smart Electronics and Communication (ICOSEC) (pp. 408-413). IEEE.

Reimann, L. M., Hanel, L., Sisejkovic, D., Merchant, F., & Leupers, R. (2021, October). Qflow: Quantitative information flow for security-aware hardware design in verilog. In 2021 IEEE 39th International Conference on Computer Design (ICCD) (pp. 603-607). IEEE.

Sayeeshwari, S., & Prabhu, E. (2022, July). A simple countermeasure to mitigate buffer overflow attack using minimalistic hardware-integrated software simulation for FPGA. In *2022 IEEE International Conference on Electronics, Computing and Communication Technologies (CONECCT)* (pp. 1-4). IEEE.

Shah, I. A. (2024). Drone Industry Security Issues and Challenges in the Context of IoD. Cybersecurity Issues and Challenges in the Drone Industry, 310-323.

Shah, I. A., Jhanjhi, N. Z., & Ray, S. K. (2024a). *Enabling Explainable AI in Cybersecurity Solutions. Advances in Explainable AI Applications for Smart Cities.* IGI Global.

Shah, I. A., Jhanjhi, N. Z., & Ujjan, R. M. A. (2024b). *Drone Technology in the Context of the Internet of Things. Cybersecurity Issues and Challenges in the Drone Industry.* IGI Global.

Shah, I. A., Laraib, A., Ashraf, H., & Hussain, F. (2024c). Drone Technology: Current Challenges and Opportunities. Cybersecurity Issues and Challenges in the Drone Industry, 343-361.

Sharma, A., Dyrkolbotn, G. O., Øverlier, L., Waltoft-Olsen, A. J., Franke, K., & Katsikas, S. (2022). *A state-of-the-art reverse engineering approach for combating hardware security vulnerabilities at the system and PCB level in IoT devices. 2022 IEEE Physical Assurance and Inspection of Electronics (PAINE).* IEEE.

Sidhu, S., Mohd, B. J., & Hayajneh, T. (2019). Hardware security in IoT devices with emphasis on hardware trojans. *Journal of Sensor and Actuator Networks*, 8(3), 42. DOI: 10.3390/jsan8030042

Sisejkovic, D., Merchant, F., Reimann, L. M., & Leupers, R. (2021). Deceptive logic locking for hardware integrity protection against machine learning attacks. *IEEE Transactions on Computer-Aided Design of Integrated Circuits and Systems*, 41(6), 1716–1729. DOI: 10.1109/TCAD.2021.3100275

Solanki, T., & Panda, B. (2022, June). SpecPref: High performing speculative attacks resilient hardware prefetchers. In *2022 IEEE International Symposium on Hardware Oriented Security and Trust (HOST)* (pp. 57-60). IEEE.

Thangam, T., Gayathri, G., & Madhubala, T. (2017, April). A novel logic locking technique for hardware security. In *2017 IEEE International Conference on Electrical, Instrumentation and Communication Engineering (ICEICE)* (pp. 1-7). IEEE.

Yu, S. Y., Yasaei, R., Zhou, Q., Nguyen, T., & Al Faruque, M. A. (2021, December). HW2VEC: A graph learning tool for automating hardware security. In *2021 IEEE International Symposium on Hardware Oriented Security and Trust (HOST)* (pp. 13-23). IEEE.

Zhu, C., Yan, Y., Guo, P., & Li, J. (2018, August). Leveraging 3D packaging technology to enhance integrated circuits security and reliability. In 2018 19th International Conference on Electronic Packaging Technology (Icept) (pp. 766-769). IEEE.

Ziegler, E., Urban, T., Brown, D., Petts, J., Pieper, S. D., Lewis, R., Hafey, C., & Harris, G. J. (2020). Open health imaging foundation viewer: An extensible open-source framework for building web-based imaging applications to support cancer research. *JCO Clinical Cancer Informatics*, 4(4), 336–345. DOI: 10.1200/CCI.19.00131 PMID: 32324447

Chapter 7
Does Artificial Intelligence With Blockchain Reduce the Costs of the Financial Sector?

Muhammad Naeem

https://orcid.org/0000-0001-6678 -3536

The Islamia University of Bahawalpur, Pakistan

Aurangzeb Khan

SBB Dewan University, Karachi, Pakistan

Abdul Rehman

https://orcid.org/0000-0002-6988 -8330

National College of Business Administration and Economics, Lahore, Pakistan

Sumair Farooq

Hamdard University, Karachi, Pakistan

Asim Mehboob

Muhammad Ali Jinnah University, Karachi, Pakistan

Ahmad Shah Abdali

Ghazi University of Dera Ghazi Khan, Pakistan

Bilal Ahmad

Ghazi University of Dera Ghazi Khan, Pakistan

ABSTRACT

This chapter looks into does artificial intelligence (AI) and blockchain technology (BT) can save costs in finance assiduity? It seeks to identify inefficiencies, probe the functions of AI and blockchain, and give styles for perpetration. Data are collected from workers in the fiscal sector, which is also anatomized using SPSS. The

DOI: 10.4018/979-8-3693-3703-5.ch007

chapter's results show that there are numerous openings to ameliorate effectiveness, particularly in the areas of credit underwriting, loan servicing, and title insurance. still, the relinquishment of AI and DT depends on prostrating artistic, legal, and data norms obstacles. In the end, combining AI and BT may affect in fiscal sector cost reductions and service advancements, significantly impacting organizational procedures, technology, and policy.

1. INTRODUCTION

Due to its natural complexity and difficulty, fiscal assiduity has always been bearing high costs and inefficiencies (Naeem et al., 2023). The conventional primer and paper-grounded procedures, the absence of norms, and the delicate nonsupervisory conditions are the main causes of this. These difficulties cause fiscal institutions' costs to rise, and they also give borrowers a delicate and constantly wrong experience (Farooq & Ahmad, 2023). Examining ways to save costs and ameliorate effectiveness in the mortgage process is imperative given the significant influence this assiduity has on people and husbandry around the globe.

This exploration is motivated by the idea that slice-edge technologies like AI and blockchain may give the result to these wide problems in business (Naeem et al., 2024). The decentralization, translucency, and invariability of BT make it a promising tool for greatly streamlining the mortgage process at numerous different points, including credit underwriting, loan servicing, and title insurance. still, AI can save time and costs by automating and speeding up operations like data confirmation, underwriting, and document operation (Khan et al., 2024). part of AI and BT is given below in Figure 1.

Figure 1. Multiple Benefits of Blockchain Technology in the AI Ecosystem

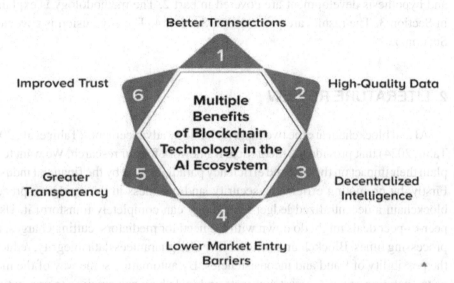

Blockchain is a digital tally that uses several computers to record deals and help the tampering of the applicable records. It's a feasible volition for numerous fiscal procedures because of its ingrained security and openness. AI refers to the employment of machines to carry out tasks that frequently bear mortal intelligence, similar as pattern recognition, problem-working, language interpretation, and decision- timber (Wen et al., 2024; Tahir & Zaheer, 2024; Rehman et al., 2024). This chapter aims to objectively investigate and assess blockchain and AI's potential to revolutionize the banking sector.

The following are the main research issues that will be addressed in this study: 1) What are the main areas in the banking sector where costs may be drastically cut? 2) How can these technologies be implemented in the financial industry? What are the possible obstacles and how can they be overcome? 3) How might AI and BT be used in these areas? This study seeks to answer these questions. The empirical findings demonstrate a significant and positive link between AI, BT, and cost reduction. The data were gathered from a sample of 385 employees inside the financial sector using a questionnaire, and the data was then analyzed using Smart PLS. This chapter has many contributions. Firstly, this chapter adds to the body of knowledge in academia while also giving business executives and policymakers useful information for cutting costs and increasing efficiency to promote competitive excellence. Secondly, through this chapter stockholders can maximize their profit through cost reduction.

The remaining chapter sections are arranged as follows: The literature review and hypothesis development are covered in part 2. The methodology is explained in Section 3. The results are presented in Section 4. The conclusion is covered in Section 5.

2. LITERATURE REVIEW

AI and blockchain are the two main technology advancements (Tahir et al., 2024; Tahir, 2024) that provide the theoretical framework for our research. We want to explain their impact on the cost and efficiency paradigm used by the financial industry. Firstly, by promoting efficiency, security, and openness in the mortgage process, blockchain a decentralized ledger technology can completely transform it. Using peer-to-peer deals might do down with the need for mediators, cutting charges, and processing times. Blockchain's invariability also guarantees data integrity, reducing the possibility of fraud and inconsistencies. By automating some way of the mortgage operation process, smart contracts on blockchain can ameliorate productivity and lower the liability of mortal miscalculations.

Alternatively, AI has the implicit to fully transfigure the fiscal assiduity's decision-making procedures (Sindiramutty et al., 2024; Khan et al., 2024). It makes it possible for machine literacy algorithms to estimate borrower credit threats more precisely (Szewczyk, 2019; Ruiz, 2019; Shah et al., 2024), which results in further indifferent and effective threat pricing. Further reducing time and charges is the robotization capabilities of AI that can ease the workload associated with operation.

2.1 Hypothesis Development

Fiscal services have shown a great deal of interest in AI and blockchain, with several studies outlining the possible benefits. Blockchain has been viewed as a game-changer in several fiscal fields because of its translucency, invariability, and decentralized nature (Shah, 2024; Farooq et al., 2023; Naeem, 2023). The transformational eventuality of BT in the banking sector, especially mortgage assiduity, has been described by Tapscott and Tapscott (2016). In an analogous tone, Mougayar (2016) stressed how the junking of mediators from deals on the blockchain might reduce costs and increase effectiveness.

On the other hand, AI has been conceded as a tool for perfecting and automating several fiscal service procedures. According to the World Economic Forum report 2018, AI has the implicit to drastically lower operating costs for banks and other fiscal associations. likewise, Davenport and Kalakota (2019) offered evidence that the use of AI in the banking process can enhance decision-making by yielding more precise threat evaluations. This makes it possible to price mortgage loans and lower the dereliction rate, which results in significant cost savings. It has been proposed that combining AI and BT can ameliorate effectiveness and save costs.

According to a report by Zheng et al. (2018), the fiscal services sector may suffer a paradigm shift as a result of the combination of AI and BT. They contended that although blockchain can offer a transparent and safe sale terrain, AI can sift through and excerpt precious information from the massive volumes of data kept on the blockchain, boosting productivity and slicing charges. still, another exploration has also refocused on possible obstacles and difficulties in applying these technologies in fiscal assiduity.

According to a study by Zavolokina et al. (2019), there are several important walls precluding blockchain from being espoused in fiscal assiduity, including a lack of legislative clarity, technological difficulties, and artistic disinclination. A study by Arner et al. (2020) linked data security and sequestration problems as significant roadblocks in the field of artificial intelligence. Notwithstanding these obstacles, the exploration generally agrees that AI and BT can fully transfigure the mortgage business by lowering costs and perfecting client satisfaction. The purpose of this study is to investigate these possibilities in more detail and determine how best to make them a reality. Based on the above literature, we created the following hypothesis.

H1: Artificial intelligence and blockchain reduce the cost of financial industry operations.

3. METHODOLOGY

The research was primarily based on a quantitative analysis. Primary data was collected from 385 employees of financial institutions through five Likert scale questionnaires and analysis was performed through SPSS. To test the impact of these variables different tests are employed. The sample size is selected on the basis of this formula.

4. RESULTS

The structural equation modeling technique is used to analyze the relationship between the variables.

4.1 Descriptive Result

According to Table I, 60% are male and 40% are female, while age group 32.4% are 18-25 years, 25.7% are 25-35 years, 25.7% are 35-45 years, 17.9% are 45 and above years. However, educational background matriculation is 23.1%, intermediate is 18.4, bachelor degree holders are 35%, and master's and PhD degree holders are 11.1% and 12.2% respectively.

Table 1. Demographic Statistics

Variable	Description	Frequency	Percentage
Gender	Male	231	60.0
	Female	154	40.0
Age	18-25	125	32.4
	25-35	99	25.7
	35-45	92	23.8
	45 and above	69	17.9
Education	Matriculation	89	23.1
	Intermediate	71	18.4
	Bachelor	135	35.0
	Master	43	11.1
	PhD	47	12.2

4.2 Measurement of Model

The reliability and validity of the model were tested with the PLS algorithm test. The model reliability and validity measure with the discriminant validity, and internal consistency However, a value greater than 0.7 indicates the model's reliability and validity.

Some items are dropped to reach the level threshold at the time of the 16-item analysis. However, a value of 0.7 or higher is considered more satisfactory (Chin, 1998; Henseler et al., 2009) but a value above 0.5 is also acceptable, and a value less than 0.5 should be considered non-reliability and non-validity (Götz et al., 2009). To identify the reliability and validity of the questions the composite reliability and validity are used. The value is greater than 0.7 of composite reliability indicating the reliability and to find the validity of the questions average variance extracted is used and the value greater than 0.5 is acceptable. The result is shown in Table II. Furthermore, to find the discriminant validity of the questions the Fornell Larcker Criterion and HTMT ratio are used. The results are shown in Table III and Table IV.

Table 2. Construct Reliability and Validity Test

	Items	Factor Loading	Cronbach's alpha	Composite reliability	Average variance extracted (AVE)
AI	AI1	0.709	0.727	0.767	0.695
	AI12	0.739			
	AI13	0.662			
Blockchain	BC1	0.928	0.716	0.723	0.514
	BC2	0.714			
	BC3	0.697			
Cost Efficiency	CE1	0.723	0.772	0.850	0.522
	CE2	0.667			
	CE3	0.731			
	IP2	0.648			
	IP3	0.654			
	IP4	0.782			
	IP5	0.703			

Table 3. Fornell-Larcker Criterion

	AI	BC	CE
AI	0.507		
BC	0.501	0.567	
CE	0.467	0.922	0.386

Table 4. HTMT Ratios

	AI	BC	CE
AI			
BC	0.873		
CE	0.256	0.419	

4.3 Direct Effect

One model is conducted to test the hypotheses. Model indicates indicated impact on cost reduction. So these hypotheses are also accepted.

Table 5. Effects of Blockchain

	Standard deviation (STDEV)	T statistics (|O/STDEV|)	P values
AI -> CE	0.047	0.028	0.008
BC-> CE	0.193	0.786	0.000

4.4 Result Discussion

AI and blockchain in the financial sector can significantly increase the tracking of the underlying banks' efficiency (Shah et al., 2024; Balakrishnan et al., 2024). The registration procedure is now carried out on a different platform, which is very effective. This procedure is an excellent example of a blockchain use case in addition to being efficient. The dissemination of servicing information is the most promising use case for BT. This result is consistent with Ravi (2021) and Nguyen et al. (2024).

Although it may not be the most "glamorous" aspect of the banking process, financial institutions depend heavily on the timely and accurate submission of servicing data. This information contains specifics like the amount of principal paidand, repaid, and the state of securities backed by mortgages. We could make sure that payment speeds, prepayments, defaults, and overall profitability are accurately tracked via BT. However, this technology won't become widely used until several big Tier-1 banks begin to use it.

This is primarily because authorities frequently seek advice and direction from these leading institutions. If big title firms participate, adoption might also be aided. There aren't many of these businesses in the nation, so if any of them choose to use blockchain, it might lead to a broader acceptance. Moreover, blockchain has the potential to greatly simplify the operation securitization process. We could track all of the data pertaining to borrower-to-bond payments if we were to transfer a pool of digital assets into a blockchain-based securitization. Finally, BT may also help commercial mortgages in the real estate sector.

Financial service is one area where AI can assist reduce inefficiencies. Specifically, it can help determine whether a borrower is experiencing financial troubles. Financial difficulties may be indicated, for example, if a borrower who has been making payments on the first of the month for five years suddenly begins to pay on the tenth, then the fifteenth, twentyth, and so on. AI can notify the servicer about prospective problems and provide remedies, such as giving the borrower a break for a month or adjusting the loan terms to help. However service providers frequently lack the knowledge needed to assist clients in a satisfactory manner.

Constructing effective models is made more difficult by unstructured data. A borrower may have inquiries about account balances, payoff amounts, most current statements, taxes and insurance paid vs expensed, the most recent payment made, and information from the original loan agreement if the data is organized appropriately. There are still more chances to update taxonomies, organize file structures, and automate approval processes. These features could improve service delivery, expedite procedures, and boost overall efficiency in the mortgage sector.

To sum up, the following financial sectors are inefficiencies that AI can help with (i.e. risk assessment, automated underwriting, client service, fraud detection, regulatory compliance, and personalized marketing). AI and BT reduce the cost of financial institutions' processes.

5. CONCLUSION

As we draw to a close, it is evident that the financial sector is poised for a significant upheaval, largely due to the promise of AI and BT. The decentralized, immutable, and transparent nature of the blockchain confers considerable benefits concerning data verification, loan management, and borrower evaluation. Conversely, AI's predictive powers can offer insightful information about borrower behavior, enabling preemptive mitigating measures. Adopting BT can drastically eliminate inefficiencies in the present mortgage process, such as duplicate documentation, fragmented systems, and recurrent auditing.

All interested parties have real-time access to see and validate loan-related data from a single, globally available source. This point has the implicit to ameliorate overall system confidence while streamlining the process and dwindling fraud incidents. Blockchain can also significantly ameliorate fiscal services when combined with AI. AI can notify servicers of possible problems using prophetic analytics, allowing them to help borrowers before they go past due. This visionary strategy may fully change our understanding of threat operation and loan servicing. Relinquishment of these technologies isn't without difficulties, however.

Obstacles include effects like the need to modify heritage systems, the demand for invariant relinquishment, and comfort situations with swapping data. Regulatory and legal ramifications must also be taken into account when putting these technologies into practice. All effects considered, the business stands to gain a great deal from blockchain and AI, from increased effectiveness and translucency to bettered threat assessment and borrower services. Indeed though there are obstacles, the assiduity needs to come together to overcome them and take full use of this innovative new technology.

REFERENCES

Arner, D. W., Barberis, J., & Buckley, R. P. (2015). The evolution of Fintech: A new post-crisis paradigm. *SSRN*, 47, 1271. DOI: 10.2139/ssrn.2676553

Balakrishnan, S., Ruskhan, B., Zhen, L.W., Huang, T.S., Soong, W.T.Y. and Shah, I.A., 2023. Down2Park: Finding New Ways to Park. *Journal of Survey in Fisheries Sciences*, pp.322-338.

Chin, W. W. (1998). The partial least squares approach to structural equation modeling. *Modern methods for business research, 295*(2), 295-336.

Farooq, M., & Ahmad, N. (2023). Nexus between board characteristics, firm performance and intellectual capital: An emerging market evidence. *Corporate Governance (Bradford)*, 23(6), 1269–1297. DOI: 10.1108/CG-08-2022-0355

Farooq, M., Noor, A., & Naeem, M. (2023). Does family ownership moderate the relationship between board characteristics and corporate social responsibility? Evidence from an emerging market. *Asian Journal of Business Ethics*, 12(1), 71–99. DOI: 10.1007/s13520-022-00164-z

Götz, O., Liehr-Gobbers, K., & Krafft, M. (2009). Evaluation of structural equation models using the partial least squares (PLS) approach. In *Handbook of partial least squares: Concepts, methods and applications* (pp. 691–711). Springer Berlin Heidelberg.

Henseler, J., Ringle, C. M., & Sarstedt, M. (2012). Using partial least squares path modeling in advertising research: basic concepts and recent issues. In *Handbook of research on international advertising*. Edward Elgar Publishing. DOI: 10.4337/9781781001042.00023

Henseler, J., Ringle, C. M., & Sarstedt, M. (2016). Testing measurement invariance of composites using partial least squares. *International Marketing Review*, 33(3), 405–431. DOI: 10.1108/IMR-09-2014-0304

Khan, A., Jhanjhi, N. Z., Haji, D. H. T. B. A., & Omar, H. A. H. B. H. (2024). *Internet of Things (IoT) Impact on Inventory Management: A Review*. Cybersecurity Measures for Logistics Industry Framework.

Khan, A., Jhanjhi, N. Z., Omar, H. A. H. B. H., & Haji, D. H. T. B. A. (2024). Risk Management and Cybersecurity in Transportation and Warehousing. In *Cybersecurity Measures for Logistics Industry Framework* (pp. 1–35). IGI Global.

Mougayar, W. (2016). *The business blockchain: promise, practice, and application of the next Internet technology.* John Wiley & Sons.

Naeem, M. (2023). Corporate Governance Mechanism and Financial Performance in Pakistan Commercial Banks: Moderating Role of Credit Risk Management. *RADS Journal of Business Management*, 5(2), 95–112.

Naeem, M., Rehman, A., Mehboob, A., & Abdali, A. S. (2023). Corporate Social Responsibility's Hidden Power in context of Pakistan: Amplifying Firm Performance. *Sukkur IBA Journal of Management and Business*, 10(2), 57–76. DOI: 10.30537/sijmb.v10i2.1383

Naeem, M., Siraj, M., Abdali, A. S., & Mehboob, A. (2024). The Impact of Investment in AI on Bank Performance: Empirical Evidence from Pakistan's Banking Sector. *KASBIT Business Journal, 17*(1).

Nguyen Thanh, B., Son, H. X., & Vo, D. T. H. (2024). Blockchain: The Economic and Financial Institution for Autonomous AI. *Journal of Risk and Financial Management*, 17(2), 54. DOI: 10.3390/jrfm17020054

Patel, B. (2023). The Future of Mortgages: Evaluating the Potential of Blockchain and Generative AI for Reducing Costs and Streamlining Processes.

Ravi, H. (2021). Innovation in banking: Fusion of artificial intelligence and blockchain. *Asia Pacific Journal of Innovation and Entrepreneurship*, 15(1), 51–61. DOI: 10.1108/APJIE-09-2020-0142

Rehman, T., Tariq, N., Ashraf, M., & Humayun, M. (2024). *Network Intrusion Detection to Mitigate Jamming and Spoofing Attacks Using Federated Leading: A Comprehensive Survey.* Cybersecurity Measures for Logistics Industry Framework.

Ruiz, G. R. (2024). QR Multilevel Codes to Reduce Cybersecurity Risks in the Logistics of Freight Transport in Ports. In *Cybersecurity Measures for Logistics Industry Framework* (pp. 322–349). IGI Global.

Shah, I. A. (2024). Drone Industry Security Issues and Challenges in the Context of IoD. *Cybersecurity Issues and Challenges in the Drone Industry*, 310-323.

Shah, I. A., Jhanjhi, N. Z., & Brohi, S. N. (2024). Use of AI-Based Drones in Smart Cities. In *Cybersecurity Issues and Challenges in the Drone Industry* (pp. 362–380). IGI Global. DOI: 10.4018/979-8-3693-0774-8.ch015

Shah, I. A., Jhanjhi, N. Z., & Rajper, S. (2024). Use of Deep Learning Applications for Drone Technology. In *Cybersecurity Issues and Challenges in the Drone Industry* (pp. 128–147). IGI Global. DOI: 10.4018/979-8-3693-0774-8.ch006

Shah, I. A., Jhanjhi, N. Z., & Ray, S. K. (2024). IoT Devices in Drones: Security Issues and Future Challenges. In *Cybersecurity Issues and Challenges in the Drone Industry* (pp. 217-235). IGI Global.

Shah, I. A., Jhanjhi, N. Z., & Ujjan, R. M. A. (2024). Drone Technology in the Context of the Internet of Things. In *Cybersecurity Issues and Challenges in the Drone Industry* (pp. 88–107). IGI Global. DOI: 10.4018/979-8-3693-0774-8.ch004

Shah, I. A., Jhanjhi, N. Z., & Ujjan, R. M. A. (2024). Use of AI Applications for the Drone Industry. In *Cybersecurity Issues and Challenges in the Drone Industry* (pp. 27–41). IGI Global. DOI: 10.4018/979-8-3693-0774-8.ch002

Shah, I. A., Laraib, A., Ashraf, H., & Hussain, F. (2024). Drone Technology: Current Challenges and Opportunities. *Cybersecurity Issues and Challenges in the Drone Industry*, 343-361.

Sindiramutty, S. R., Jhanjhi, N. Z., Tan, C. E., Khan, N. A., Shah, B., & Gaur, L. (2024). Securing the Digital Supply Chain Cyber Threats and Vulnerabilities. In *Cybersecurity Measures for Logistics Industry Framework* (pp. 156–223). IGI Global.

Szewczyk, P., 2019. Application of blockchain technology in supply chain management. *Zeszyty Naukowe. Organizacja i Zarządzanie/Politechnika Śląska*.

Tahir, S. (2024). Enhancing Identification of IoT Anomalies in Smart Homes Using Secure Blockchain Technology. In *Cybersecurity Measures for Logistics Industry Framework* (pp. 141–155). IGI Global.

Tahir, S., & Zaheer, A. (2024). A Distributed Model for IoT Anomaly Detection Using Federated Learning. In *Cybersecurity Measures for Logistics Industry Framework* (pp. 75–91). IGI Global.

Tapscott, D., & Tapscott, A. (2016). *Blockchain revolution: how the technology behind Bitcoin is changing money, business, and the world*. Penguin.

Tariq, N., Saboor, T., Ashraf, M., Butt, R., Anwar, M., & Humayun, M. (2024). IoT Security, Future Challenges, and Open Issues. In *Cybersecurity Measures for Logistics Industry Framework* (pp. 116–140). IGI Global.

Wen, B. O. T., Syahriza, N., Xian, N. C. W., Wei, N. G., Shen, T. Z., Hin, Y. Z., Sindiramutty, S. R., & Nicole, T. Y. F. (2024). Detecting Cyber Threats With a Graph-Based NIDPS. In *Cybersecurity Measures for Logistics Industry Framework* (pp. 36–74). IGI Global.

Zavolokina, L., Dolata, M., & Schwabe, G. (2016). The FinTech phenomenon: Antecedents of financial innovation perceived by the popular press. *Financial Innovation*, 2(1), 1–16. DOI: 10.1186/s40854-016-0036-7

Zheng, Z., Xie, S., Dai, H. N., Chen, X., & Wang, H. (2018). Blockchain challenges and opportunities: A survey. *International Journal of Web and Grid Services*, 14(4), 352–375. DOI: 10.1504/IJWGS.2018.095647

Chapter 8
Harnessing Generative AI for Enhanced Web Application Security

Muhammad Usman Tariq
https://orcid.org/0000-0002-7605-3040
Abu Dhabi University, UAE & University College Cork, Ireland

ABSTRACT

This chapter explores the integration of Generative Artificial Intelligence (AI) in bolstering the security of Web applications. It delves into how AI-driven techniques can be employed to predict, detect, and mitigate security threats in real-time, thereby safeguarding Web-based systems from potential vulnerabilities. Through a comprehensive analysis of current challenges in Web application security and the potential of Generative AI to transform traditional security paradigms, this chapter aims to provide a detailed overview of cutting-edge methodologies and their implications for the future of Web security. The term "advanced web application" signifies the improvement and fortification of electronic systems against potential vulnerabilities and security threats through the utilization of Generative AI. In the rapidly evolving landscape of web applications, ensuring robust security measures is crucial for safeguarding sensitive data and maintaining the integrity of online systems.

INTRODUCTION

Generative AI (genAI) is in a general sense changing the way we associated with innovation and the world. It is the support that businesses depend on to improve, engage, and lock in representatives and clients. Whereas genAI has been around for a long time, the development of consumer-facing AI apparatuses like ChatGPT

DOI: 10.4018/979-8-3693-3703-5.ch008

has catapulted the groundbreaking innovation to a unused level. This advancement marks the primary productivity-centric wave of genAI's affect on companies — revolutionizing workflows, streamlining operations, and reclassifying the boundaries of venture advancement. Forrester characterizes generative AI as "a set of innovations and procedures that use gigantic corpora of information, counting expansive dialect models, to produce modern substance (e.g., content, video, pictures, sound, code). (Gabrielson 2023)

Over the another few a long time, generative AI patterns are anticipated to reshape each knowledge-fueled errand and part, recreate information hones and assets over each industry, and provide a ten times increase in errand efficiency. Typically not fair theoretical; it's as of now getting to be reality for businesses such as KPMG that as of late saw a 50% boost in efficiency after actualizing Microsoft Copilot, a set of efficiency applications built on OpenAI's huge dialect demonstrate (LLM).

In spite of the significant progressions and rise of unused generative AI patterns, we've as it were fair scratched the surface. Forrester accepts that the advancing generative AI scene will eventually offer assistance businesses create modern income streams, expansions, and channels to realize significant development and reevaluate themselves, constraining whole businesses to rebuild around the esteem created by machines.

The progressing web application scene is flooding with different security challenges that require inventive courses of action. The threat climate is persistently creating since of implantation attacks centering on shortcomings, for case, cross-site prearranging (XSS). Generative man-made awareness addresses a alter in viewpoint in settling these issues by utilizing its capacity to dismember monstrous datasets and distinguish plans. By utilizing man-made brainpower calculations, Generative computer based insights can proactively recognize and reply emerging perils, in this way diminishing the shortcomings of web applications. (Shukla. S 2023)

The coordination of Generative reenacted insights into web application security indicates a takeoff from routine rule-based systems. Standard security endeavors as often as possible depend on preset standards to recognize vindictive works out, which might illustrate missing against rapidly progressing computerized perils. On the other hand, Generative man-made insights succeeds in flexible picking up, engaging it to alter and refine its disclosure components in see of nonstop threat information. This flexibility is significant in a climate where computerized threats are depicted by their multifaceted nature and preparation (Tariq, 2024).

Inquire about by Smith et al. (2021) highlights the practicality of Generative fake insights in directing and recognizing zero-day shortcomings, a colossal test for conventional security endeavors. The ZDT's detection flaw implies vulnerability to today's important security issues that are initially available to attackers without any immediate solution before intervention. An efficient understanding of the similar

Generative approach allows it to recognize the weird patterns and modes related to zero-day attacks without much stress. This will ensure the security team's pro-activity in the game.

Besides that, the Generative's outstanding brainpower and capability of identifying and mirroring possible attack situations increase the proactivity level. By breaking apart indisputable data and creating possible attack simulations, and if the hackers have failed to overlook it, the security experts can expose them and discover the mismatching site quickly in that case. This foresight component announces that bonding with other players is necessary because of the common threat faced by all. Did you know that there's a way to ensure internet application security that benefits everyone involved? It's a win-win situation for all everyone.

Thus, this portion examines the extraordinary capability of Generative man-made thinking in overhauling web application security. By looking at the ceaseless troubles faced by web applications and showing how Generative man-made insights can disturb security guidelines, this discussion anticipates delivering nuanced information into a state of the craftsmanship draws close and their impact on the possible destiny of web security. As affiliations work to reinforce their web-based systems against an unpleasant climate, the coordination of Generative man-made awareness emerges as a critical technique in ensuring the flexibility and security of web applications (Shukla. S 2023).

Introduction to Web Application Security

Protecting the respectability and value of online systems is essential within the computerized age, with web application security expecting a basic portion in fulfill-ing this objective. Given the creating reliance of affiliations on web applications for diverse purposes, like web-based commerce and correspondence, protecting these applications from harmful works is the destiny of most extraordinary importance.

This chapter delves into the complex web application security landscape, un-derscoring the challenges of evolving digital threats and the urgent need for robust safeguarding mechanisms. In the domain of online protection, web applications arise as alluring focuses for malignant entertainers because of their predominance and the potential access they proposition to delicate information. As clarified by Jones and Smith (2020), the developing intricacy of web applications has simultaneously extended the assault surface, delivering them helpless against a different scope of safety dangers. Understanding and tending to these dangers are critical for guaran-teeing the supported usefulness and unwavering quality of electronic frameworks. (Alwahedi, 2024)

Outline of Commom Security Dangers and Weaknesses in Web Applications

An extensive comprehension of web application security requires an assessment of normal dangers and weaknesses that can think twice about protection, upright-ness, and accessibility of online frameworks. One common danger is Cross-Site Prearranging (XSS), wherein assailants infuse pernicious contents into pages saw by different clients. Furthermore, SQL infusion assaults represent a critical gamble, empowering unapproved admittance to a data set by taking advantage of weaknesses in the application's code (Williams and Brown, 2018). These models highlight the complex idea of dangers that web applications face, highlighting the requirement for hearty security procedures.

Other than, the approach of Utilization Programming Association point (Pro-gramming interface) utilize in web applications presents one more course of action of shortcomings. Programming interface security is fundamental, as insulant tied down APIs can reveal sensitive data and functionalities to vindictive double-dealing (Jones et al., 2021). Understanding the complexities of these threats is essential for making reasonable countermeasures that soothe chances and ensure the adaptability of web applications against creating computerized threats (Tariq, 2024).

The Centrality of Vigorous Security Measures within the Advancement and Upkeep of Online Frameworks

The improvement and support of electronic frameworks request an immovable commitment to actualizing vigorous security measures all through the computer program advancement lifecycle. As emphasized by Anderson and Thomas (2019), the results of ignoring security amid the advancement stage can be serious, driving to information breaches, benefit disturbances, and reputational harm. Compelling security measures not as it were protect touchy client information but too contrib-ute to the in general unwavering quality and dependability of web applications. In addition, the significance of security in web improvement expands past beginning sending to envelop progressing upkeep and upgrades. Nonstop security surveys, code reviews, and the incite application of patches are fundamental components of a proactive security methodology (Smith, 2022). Dismissing these measures can take off web applications helpless to recently developing dangers and abuses, underscoring the energetic nature of the cybersecurity scene.

Hence, a nuanced understanding of web application security is imperative for organizations exploring the advanced scene. By comprehensively looking at com-mon security dangers, vulnerabilities, and the basic for viable security measures, this presentation clears the way for a more profound investigation of techniques and advances pointed at invigorating electronic frameworks against advanced dangers (Raimi et al., 2022).

The evolving nature of digital threats requires a proactive and adaptable approach to web application security, ensuring the resilience and reliability of online systems despite ever-changing challenges. (Alwahedi, 2024)

GENERATIVE ARTIFICIAL INTELLIGENCE: AN OVERVIEW

The turn of events and support of electronic frameworks request an immovable obligation to carrycarry out vigorous safety efforts throughout the product improvement lifecycle. As accentuated by Anderson and Thomas (2019), the outcomes of disregarding security during the improvement stage can be serious, prompting information breaks, administration interruptions, and reputational harm. Successful safety efforts protect delicate client information and add to web applications' general unwavering quality and dependability. Also, the significance of safety in web improvement reaches out past the beginning, sending progressing support and updates to envelop. Ceaseless security surveys, code reviews, and the brief use of patches are fundamental parts of a proactive security system (Smith, 2022). Dismissing these actions can leave web applications helpless against recently arising dangers and exploits, highlighting the unique idea of the online protection scene.

Consequently, a nuanced comprehension of web application security is imperative for associations exploring the computerized scene. By thoroughly looking at normal security dangers, weaknesses, and the basics for compelling safety efforts, this presentation prepares for a more profound investigation of procedures and innovations that invigorate electronic frameworks against computerized dangers. The developing idea of computerized dangers requires a proactive and versatile way to deal with web application security, guaranteeing the strength and dependability of online frameworks regardless of consistently evolving difficulties. (Alwahedi, 2024)

The Job of Generative simulated intelligence in Upgrading Web Application Security

Web application security is a steadily developing test as advanced dangers become progressively complex. In this scene, Generative Man-made brainpower (Generative simulated intelligence) arises as a strong power, offering imaginative answers for anticipate, recognize, and relieve security dangers continuously. This point by point investigation dives into the job of Generative man-made intelligence in reinforcing web application security, analyzing its applications, advantages, and suggestions for what's to come (Raimi et al., 2022).

Generative simulated intelligence for Danger Expectation and Location

One of the essential commitments of Generative simulated intelligence to web application security lies in its prescient capacities. Generative models, for example, Generative Ill-disposed Organizations (GANs) and repetitive brain organizations, succeed in breaking down immense datasets to distinguish examples and irregularities. By utilizing authentic information on computerized dangers, Generative man-made intelligence can foresee potential security weaknesses and expect to arise assault vectors. This prescient capacity enables security experts to proactively address weaknesses before they are taken advantage of by vindictive entertainers. For instance, a concentrate by Zhang et al. (2021) shows the adequacy of Generative simulated intelligence in expecting new variations of malware by breaking down designs in code designs and ways of behaving. This proactive way to deal with danger expectation upgrades the flexibility of web applications, lessening the probability of capitulating to novel and complex digital assaults. (Baig and Khan 2020)

In the domain of danger location, Generative simulated intelligence assumes a significant part in recognizing uncommon exercises that might demonstrate a security break. Conventional rule-based frameworks frequently battle to adjust to advancing assault strategies, while Generative simulated intelligence can consistently learn and change its discovery instruments. The capacity to create reasonable assault situations permits security frameworks to distinguish inconspicuous deviations from typical way of behaving, flagging potential security dangers. This versatility is especially applicable in a climate where the strategies of cybercriminals are continually developing.

Alleviating Zero-Day Weaknesses with Generative man-made intelligence

Zero-day weaknesses, alluding to obscure security blemishes took advantage of by assailants before a fix is accessible, represent a huge test to web application security. Generative simulated intelligence demonstrates instrumental in alleviating these weaknesses by perceiving and answering arising dangers progressively. Research by Li and Chen (2020) features the viability of Generative computer based intelligence in distinguishing designs related with zero-day takes advantage of, empowering fast reaction and alleviation. The special thought of Generative man-made insights grants it to imitate potential zero-day attacks, giving security specialists encounters into likely deficiencies and defects in their web applications. This proactive reenactment engages affiliations to proactively settle shortcomings, reducing the chance for threatening performers to require advantage of zero-day deserts. The limit of Generative artificial intelligence to adjust and gain from new danger knowledge positions it as a hearty partner in the continuous fight against zero-day weaknesses. (Baig and Khan 2020).

Versatile Learning and Constant Improvement

Generative artificial intelligence's versatile learning capacities altogether add to improving web application security. The situation is not like that of stagnant old structures. Ratherd, the Generative Mimicked Knowledgeis alwaysconsideredn for developing the basis of the data and plans. This involves possibly calibrating the wealth creation to traffic-supporting activities, creating a more solid global risk. Take, for example, a terra by Wang et al. (2019) emphasized that Generative AI can evade the CSPs identification schemes and devise new attacks with increasing precision in detecting and mitigating security threats over time. Moreover, this productiveness is vital in web applications, as a growing quantity of attack vectors and system tools mostly occupy the landscapes.

Generative artificial intelligence, despite the obvious fact that it has only contributed immensely to making web application security better, may not be without its challenges and moral issues. The period of reasonable deepfake attacks, where man-made insight is used to make convincing yet made content, addresses a potential bet. Security specialists ought to be careful in particular genuine security risks from produced ones made by man-made knowledge models. Moreover, proficient game plan of Generative man-made brainpower is central to hinder misuse. Moral thoughts around security, consent, and the potential for reproduced insight made attacks feature the necessity for clear standards and rules. Discovering some sort of congruity between harnessing the power of Generative man-made insight for security and directing potential risks requires a cautious and ethically grounded approach. As such, Generative man-made consciousness expects a critical part in further developing web application security by using farsighted limits, directing zero-day shortcomings, and enabling flexible learning (Barocas and Selbst, 2016).

The capacity to mimic and foresee potential security dangers, combined with persistent improvement through versatile learning, positions Generative simulated intelligence as a useful asset in the online protection stockpile. Notwithstanding, the difficulties and moral contemplations feature the significance of dependable sending and continuous carefulness in the quickly developing scene of web application security. As associations wrestle with progressively complex computerized dangers, Generative simulated intelligence remains as a reference point of development, offering progressed answers for sustain the flexibility of web applications against advancing security challenges.

ARTIFICIAL INTELLIGENCE-POWERED THREAT DETECTION AND PREVENTION

In the consistently advancing scene of network protection, the job of Computerized reasoning (artificial intelligence) in danger discovery and counteraction has become progressively conspicuous. Computer based intelligence is used in different ways to distinguish and forestall digital dangers. It examines network traffic, framework logs, and client conduct to recognize likely dangers. The data collected from various information sources will be proactively analyzed for patterns and irregularities that could indicate a cyber attack. To put it succinctly, if an authority no longer acts in accordance with the protocol, such as accessing confidential documents after working hours, the simulation algorithm can consider this as a suspicious movement and promptly send the security team an alert. This proactive approach of AI in risk detection should make you feel secure and protected.

Another crucial AI application contributing to risk discovery is computer-based intelligence-aided investigation. Artificial intelligence can establish benchmarks for normal behaviours of different clients and frameworks and detect deviations from these benchmarks, pointing out expected risks. Say, an employee's record suddenly accessing a strangely huge number of confidential documents would signify a compromised account or an insider threat. Artificial intelligence computations can quickly detect this abnormality and take appropriate measures, such as blocking the record or conducting an investigation.

It is based on AI-supported threat detection fueled by the latest data analytics technologies, allowing the discovery of any indicators that may be used to detect potential security threats. The calculation transcends simple rules and is accomplished through self-learning and reviewing scenarios that change every time. The field observable processes evolve around supervised and unsupervised machines. Self-learning, self-knowledge assessment, and teamwork integration.

For illustration, overseen computer based insights calculations are arranged on checked datasets, enabling them to recognize plans related with known threats. Then again, unaided learning strategies, like grouping and curiosity identification, can uncover novel dangers by distinguishing designs that stray from the standard. Profound learning, especially Convolutional Brain Organizations (CNNs) and Repetitive Brain Organizations (RNNs), succeeds in separating complex elements from different kinds of information, conveying them appropriate for intimidation location in assorted network safety situations. (Baig and Khan 2020).

Man-made intelligence Driven Danger Anticipation Methodologies

Man-made intelligence supports the location as well as in the counteraction of safety dangers. Proactive measures incorporate the utilization of prescient investigation to appraise expected weaknesses, robotized reactions to quickly advancing dangers, and the sending of canny frameworks that constantly learn and adjust. Moreover, incorporating computer based intelligence driven danger anticipation parts into Security Data and Occasion The executives (SIEM) frameworks upgrades the general security stance of associations. The utilization of artificial intelligence in danger avoidance is exemplified by the reception of AI Firewalls (MLFs). MLFs utilize artificial intelligence calculations to break down network traffic designs and recognize unusual way of behaving, forestalling likely dangers before they can take advantage of weaknesses. The versatile idea of these frameworks permits them to conform to developing assault strategies, giving unique safeguard against a wide exhibit of digital dangers.

How Generative man-made intelligence Models Expect and Recognize Potential Security Breaks

Generative Man-made brainpower (Generative manufactured insights) models, particularly Generative Adversarial Organizations (GANs) and Variational Autoencoders (VAEs), have appeared tremendous capacities in foreseeing and recognizing potential security breaks. These models, known for their capacity to deliver unused data, contribute in a general sense to arrange security by reenacting and foreseeing conceivable perils. Generative man-made insights models work on the rule of getting the hang of essential cases and plans interior data. Within the space of security, they can be arranged on irrefutable datasets of realized security breaks to figure out the traits of malignant works out. This planning enables Generative computer based insights models to reenact and anticipate potential security breaks by recognizing plans lining up with known attack vectors. For case, GANs, displayed by Goodfellow et al. (2014), include of a generator and a discriminator taken an interest in a genuine cycle The generator makes manufactured information, and the discriminator assesses its realness. With regards to security, GANs can be prepared to produce sensible assault situations in light of authentic information. By investigating the created information, security specialists gain bits of knowledge into likely weaknesses and danger vectors took advantage of by vindictive entertainers. Variational Autoencoders (VAEs) give one more road to anticipating security breaks. VAEs are probabilistic models planning to become familiar with the fundamental construction of information. In the field of network protection,

VAEs can be prepared on assorted datasets to catch the changeability of typical framework conduct. When given new information, VAEs can recognize peculiarities or deviations from the learned examples, flagging potential security breaks. Additionally, Generative simulated intelligence models add to the ID of novel and complex dangers, including zero-day weaknesses. Security measures often strive to discover already vulnerable exploitation that can result in undecipherable failure. Generative artificial intelligence's capacity to imitate and predict potential threats permits it to detect unforeseeable concrete cases indicating zero-day exploitations, acting as an all-proactive shield against stealthy and rapidly emerging hazards.

STRATEGIES FOR CONTINUOUS THREAT DETECTION AND AUTOMATED RESPONSE MECHANISMS

Unremitting danger awareness and robotized response schemes are two pillars of a perfect security solution for networks. In the digital infrastructure's distinctive environment, user-friendliness, necessary security authentication, and timely response to potential security threats are key. Simulated intelligence driven strategies assume an imperative part in accomplishing constant danger location and working with robotized reactions to relieve the effect of safety breaks.

Social Examination and Oddity Identification

Social examination use computer based intelligence calculations to dissect client and framework conduct continuously. By laying out an example of typical way of behaving, these frameworks can quickly recognize irregularities that might show a security danger. Computer based intelligence calculations, especially unaided learning techniques, succeed in perceiving deviations from laid out standards, empowering the quick discovery of dubious exercises. For instance, an association's organization traffic designs, client login conduct, and framework collaborations can be ceaselessly observed. Peculiarities, for example, surprising login times, access from new areas, or startling information moves, can set off alarms for additional examination. Artificial intelligence driven oddity recognition frameworks improve the capacity to distinguish likely dangers as they arise, taking into account proactive intercession.

SIEM Frameworks Upgraded by artificial intelligence

Security Data and Occasion The executives (SIEM) frameworks are basic to network protection, gathering and investigating log information from different sources to recognize and answer security occasions. The incorporation of simulated intelligence upgrades the capacities of SIEM frameworks via computerizing the investigation of monstrous datasets, relating occasions, and distinguishing designs demonstrative of safety episodes. Conventional SIEM frameworks have long been the foundation of cybersecurity endeavors, making a difference to solidify, connect, and analyze security information from different sources. In any case, with the developing advancement of cyber dangers and the sheer volume of security information, conventional SIEM frameworks have battled to keep up. AI-based SIEM is an progressed frame of security data and occasion administration (SIEM) that employments the capabilities of fake insights (AI) and machine learning (ML) to fathom numerous of the challenges of the past.

AI-based SIEM may be a innovation that not as it were mechanizes the complex forms of information accumulation and normalization but too empowers proactive risk location and reaction through machine learning and prescient analytics. By learning from past security information and designs, AI SIEM can foresee and distinguish potential dangers some time recently they happen. Additionally, it can mechanize the occurrence reaction prepare, in this manner minimizing the affect of security breaches. In substance, AI SIEM gives an brilliantly, mechanized, and proactive approach to danger discovery and reaction.

In the quickly developing scene of network protection, Security Data and Occasion, The board (SIEM) frameworks are pivotal in defending associations against the steadily developing dangers. As we step into 2024, it's not just important, but crucial to explore the expected SIEM trends that will shape the future of network safety. Considering issues that will be crucial for the IT protection sector's development in the current year and the necessity of getting information updated as quickly as possible to stay strong and sharp from the cybersecurity point of view.

Joining of Man-made consciousness and AI: Compcomputerisedelligence or AI (ML) will largely be involved in the SIEM systems in 2024. Implementing such technologies will increase the possibility of re-recognising-recognising and treating complex digital threats, analysing and analysing information patterns, and automating the danger examination process. The effectiveness is that cyber-security associations can detect dangerous activity sooner and shorten reaction time, enabling them to stay one move ahead of attackers.

Cloud-Local SIEM Arrangements: Due to the increasing acceptance, the SIEM community is also transforming to become more cloud-based. In 2024, cloud-based SIEM stages can be expected to rule the show over others, principally the ones that can be flexible and adapt easily to other cloud conditions. Switching to a single trusted provider also allows associations to oversee security on-prem and in the cloud, translating to a comprehensive approach towards digital threats.

Client and Substance Conduct Examination (UEBA): Understanding client behaviour along the same lines is one of the fundamental points for noticing security risks. IREEA proposes SIEM models to add more usefulness to the roles of UEBA, which involve Client and Element Questioning (UEBA). Through advanced research and investigation, SIEM systems will be able to recognise and pinpoint suspicious activity and insider threats, giving the organisation a prevorganizationach to security.

Zero Trust Security Framework: The Zero Trust security model (incredibly dynamic) emphasises trust and always verifies. "By this concept, SIEM systems will always be on the left, inspecting and authenticating actions that both human beings and machine devices take, regardless of their geographical location or network. By collecting information in this,s way, every system element in a net is under 24-hour surveillance, lance and the later propagation of an attack by an unsanctioned operator is thus almost impossible.

Automated Incident Response: By 2024, SIEM solutions can be expected to encapsulate more AI-fuelled incident response features. Through the use of automated playbooks and response plans, security teams will be able to resolve incidents quickly, clearing the backlog and easing their workload. This step forward in organisations' response to incidents and, therefore, cuts the volume of damage.

Threat Intelligence Integration: SIEM products will become increasingly plugged into their threat intelligence sources. Therefore, developing a collaborative approach is necessary. This will give organisations raw access to the latest threat analysis and ensure they can fortify security measures efficiently to avert future threats. SIEM systems and threat intelligence feeders will become potent cyberse-curity guard rails, providing extra resilience to the challenges of emerging threats.

In 2024, cyber security will usher in many changes and evolutions. SIEM systems will move with the newest technologies, adopt new cloud and security technologies, and become proactive in management. Such developments will improve threat detection speed, allow quick incident response, and guarantee much better security in the long run.

Organizations that are apt quickly to a new SIEM standard will be one step ahead and more competent in meeting the emerging cyber threats of today's digital world. The adaptive nature of these novelties will position any entity with strategic internet-connected systems or data as the ultimate beneficiary of these advancements and impart an element of optimism in the face of evolving threats.

DATA PROTECTION DURING SUPERSPREADING EVENTS MAINLY INFERS TRANSMISSION AND STORAGE

While data transmission and limits in the modernized period are marked by data becoming a significant asset, this solution now brings both data transmission and limits. With increased risks, from easy hacks to complex attacks, the need for security becomes even more important as a matter of integrity, and systematic integrity requires us to be more vigilant. This comprehensive inspection follows the strategies and developments in acquiring dates concerning transmission, together with screening works, such as encryption, user access controls, and frequent safety checks.

Taking encryption as a major principle in making data available during transition is something standing apart. It includes encrypted big databases that incorporate changing plain-text information into extra-large encryption using mathematical estimations. This leads to a situation in which data cannot be decoded even if the encrypted code has been stolen without the key to decipher the opposite. Programs like Intellectual Property Secure Transmission Layer (SSL) and Transport Layer Encryption (TLS) have become as familiar as leashing your dog or sticking to the sidewalk. For instance, when a client gets to a safeguarded webpage with an "https: Although closely associated with the browser extension icon (the lock image, the strain of "SSL" or "TLS" displayed encodes the dialogue between the client's computer and the web server. Speaking of which, (this is the key factor that ensures the safety of important data such as login credentials or financial transactions on display)

Secure Information Stockpiling: Security is still the major issue for getting data, whether on real devices or in the cloud, which requires encryption, access, and data verification. Trip Encryption (FDE) is a standard encryption format intended to manage data encoding on limited devices so that data remains protected even if the gadget has been confronted with a loss or theft. As a matter of fact, in a cloud environment, encryption keys and security access play the most dominant role when it comes to data safety on far-off serversEncoding structures, which are very common in high-performance computational centres, are made available to customers who wish to upload their data on the cloud. On the other hand, the KMS authority is provided with another variable to supervise and control the encryption keys, which leads to extra advanced security for stored data. Indeed, they inwardly support us in keeping data security and confidentiality at a high rate.

Access Controls and Validation:

Access controls, Past encryption, access controls and verification instruments are essential parts of retaining information during both capacity and transmission. Access controls characterize who can get to explicit information and what activities they can perform, while validation guarantees that main approved clients can get to the information or frameworks. Job Based Admittance Control (RBAC) is a typical access control component that doles out unambiguous jobs and consents to clients in view of their obligations inside an association. Multifaceted verification (MFA) adds an additional layer of safety by expecting clients to give numerous types of recognizable proof prior to getting entrance. These actions aggregately reinforce the general security pose, guaranteeing that information is gotten to simply by approved people.

Utilization of Generative computer based intelligence in Improving Information Encryption for Transmission and Capacity: Generative Man-made reasoning (Generative simulated intelligence) acquaints imaginative methodologies with upgrade the encryption of information during both transmission and capacity. While customary encryption strategies stay compelling, Generative computer based intelligence brings progressed procedures utilizing brain organizations and generative models to upgrade the security of delicate data.

Generative simulated intelligence for Cutting edge Encryption Calculations: Generative artificial intelligence adds to the improvement of cutting edge encryption calculations that outperform customary strategies. Generative Poorly arranged Associations (GANs) can be utilized to make encryption plots that dynamically acclimate to propelling risks. In the space of encryption, GANs make designed data as a sort of encryption, and the discriminator evaluates its realness. This adversarial cycle achieves the arrangement of encryption computations that are secure as well as impenetrable to attacks trying to unravel the encryption key. Research by Chen et al. (2020) features the capacity of using GANs to encourage encryption estimations impervious to attacks, showing the capacity of Generative man-made insight to add to encryption methodology outflanking traditional computations.

Generative man-made knowledge models, especially those used in Homomorphic Encryption (HE) plans, offer assurance protecting strategies that grant computation on mixed data without the necessity for deciphering. Homomorphic Encryption enables data to stay mixed while calculations are performed, and simply the results are decoded. This ensures that sensitive information stays private regardless, during data dealing with or assessment. In circumstances like clinical benefits, where assurance rules are unbending, Generative reenacted knowledge based Homomorphic Encryption can engage secure estimations on encoded patient data. This thinks about assessments without direct permission to individual patient records, staying aware of mystery and consenting to assurance rules.urity Safeguarding Strategies:

Artificial intelligence Based Answers for Secure Information Dealing with and Protection Safeguarding

Past encryption, Generative artificial intelligence adds to get information dealing with and protection conservation through different creative methodologies. These arrangements center around limiting information openness, guaranteeing consistence with protection guidelines, and giving associations devices to oversee delicate data dependably.

Differential Security

Differential security is a protection saving idea planning to furnish strong ensures in any event, while managing delicate individual information. Generative simulated intelligence models, especially differential security calculations, contribute by acquainting clamor with information before examination. This commotion guarantees that singular commitments to a dataset are indistinct, protecting the security of individual data (Mao and Poor 2024). In man-made intelligence applications where models are prepared on delicate datasets, differential security methods can be applied to the preparation cycle. This guarantees that the subsequent model doesn't hold explicit insights concerning individual data of interest, forestalling the gamble of information spillage or re-distinguishing proof.

Protection Safeguarding simulated intelligence: Generative artificial intelligence models work with security saving man-made intelligence procedures, permitting associations to acquire bits of knowledge from delicate information without compromising individual protection. Secure Multi-Party Calculation (SMPC) is one such procedure where parties cooperatively examine information without uncovering the crude data. In medical services, for instance, SMPC can empower cooperative examination on understanding information from various organizations without sharing the genuine patient records. Generative man-made intelligence models add to the advancement of secure conventions that permit the calculation of total measurements or model preparation without uncovering delicate subtleties.

Secure Information Sharing and Combined Learning

Generative artificial intelligence models, particularly those utilized in combined learning, empower secure information sharing and cooperative model preparation without uncovering crude information. United learning includes preparing computer based intelligence models across decentralized gadgets or servers while keeping information limited. For example, in a situation where numerous medical care associations team up on building a prescient model, united learning permits them to prepare a model without sharing patient information. Every establishment prepares the model on its neighborhood information, and model updates, as opposed to crude information, are collected. This jam security while acquiring bits of knowledge from a total dataset.Securing information during transmission and capacity is a multifaceted test, and the joining of Generative computer based intelligence carries creative answers for upgrade customary strategies. From cutting edge encryption calculations to protection saving procedures and secure information taking care of, Generative man-made intelligence altogether adds to sustaining the security of delicate data in the advanced scene (Larson and Mattu, 2016). As associations explore the intricacies of information security, taking on Generative man-made intelligence innovations offers a pathway to address current difficulties and expect and adjust to the developing danger scene. The assembly of encryption, access controls, and Generative simulated intelligence opens new roads for making strong and protection cognizant information security methodologies.(Mao and Poor 2024)

CASE STUDIES: REAL-WORLD APPLICATIONS OF GENERATIVE AI

Generative Man-made consciousness (Generative man-made intelligence) has arisen as a strong power reshaping different ventures, and its applications in web application security give convincing contextual investigations. This segment looks at genuine examples of Generative artificial intelligence applications in web application security, trailed by an examination of examples of overcoming adversity and the significant bits of knowledge acquired from sending man-made intelligence driven security endeavors.

Real Cases of Generative man-made intelligence Applications in Web Application Security

Extortion Discovery in Web based Banking

In web based banking, Generative Ill-disposed Organizations (GANs) have been utilized to upgrade misrepresentation location components. By reenacting and distinguishing designs related with false exercises, GANs add to continuous identification and anticipation.

Application: Liao et al. (2017) showed the reasonability of GANs in acquiring from unquestionable data to perceive common and strange approaches to acting in electronic money related trades. The model's ability to conform to creating models makes it a solid response for engaging phony practices in online monetary systems.

Versatile Verification in Online business

Developing an online business goes through two stages which are: security and customer care. Generative techniques beyond PC regarding GANs have been applied in crafting direct and flexible assessment systems based on leading customers, allowing hardware into the loop and artificial intelligence to change the approval process dynamically. Wang and his partner were the first to investigate the application of GANs in the flexible affirmation of online business (Wang et al., 2019). The endlessly changing scenario confirms web-based firms' setting, leading to a consistent yet firm customer experience. This strategy has an advantage over conventional means of verification, and it adds to consumer trust in the Bitcoin trading ecosystem.

Security issues dealing with zero-review industry concerns mainly hinge on great risk to web applications. The most considerable prospect for generative computerized inference models, VAEs, is to build a machine that can evaluate and respond to new zero-day vulnerabilities by learning from real data and existing security bug models. Sun et al.(2020) explained the case of an integer overflow and a heap overflow of an (ask. The model's capability, which notices out-of-the-ordinary issues that might indicate trending hacker strategies, is one of the key elements contributing to the efficiency of generatively generated intelligence in forward-looking security operations against new dangers.

Investigation of Examples of overcoming adversity and Experiences Acquired from Conveying simulated intelligence driven Security Endeavors

Profound Learning for Danger Knowledge: (Darktrace, n.d.)

Deep learning annotations technology Datamolinary is used by Darktrace website security as an option for quick and effective machine learning for cybersecurity complexities. Their smart stage technology (which can be called machine intelligence) from artificial solutions is capable of autonomously recognizing and reacting to digital risks freely in real-time. Darktrace's success lays the foundation for the survivability of deep learning in miss-behaving large datasets across the shortest detection time. In this case, the main example is the importance of manoeuvring computer intelligence alone to self-tailor against a developing risky environment.

Conduct Examination for Insider Danger Location (Exabeam, n.d.)

Exabeam has executed artificial intelligence driven conduct investigation for insider danger location. The framework examines client conduct, recognizing deviations from ordinary examples to signal expected pernicious exercises. Exabeam's result highlights the meaning of simulated intelligence in giving early admonitions and working with opportune reactions to insider dangers. The illustration here is the worth of social examination in recognizing unobtrusive indications of potential security breaks.

Artificial intelligence in Powerful Access Controls (Symantec, n.d.)

Symantec, a main web-based security organization, has shown fruitful executions of man-made intelligence based powerful access controls. These controls adaptively change access authorizations in view of client exercises and important data. Symantec's prosperity underscores the significance of computer based intelligence in progressively changing access controls (Larson and Mattu, 2016). The illustration is that computer based intelligence driven unique access controls upgrade security by adjusting access consents to developing client ways of behaving and pertinent elements.

CHALLENGES AND LIMITATIONS IN AI-DRIVEN WEB SECURITY

The reconciliation of Man-made consciousness (artificial intelligence) into web security holds incredible commitment for improving danger identification and alleviation frameworks. Be that as it may, this attempt is not without its portion of difficulties and constraints, both specialized and moral. Understanding and resolving these issues are pivotal for the successful execution of simulated intelligence driven safety efforts in web conditions.

Discusssion of Specialized and Moral Difficulties in computer based intelligence Web Security:

In the domain of specialized difficulties, an essential concern is the weakness of computer based intelligence models to ill-disposed assaults. The power of man-made awareness based security structures is in this way compromised, requiring unsurprising watchfulness and refinement of calculations to simplicity such dangers (Szegedy et al., 2014). Likewise, the quality and collection of preparing information present fundamental impediments in man-made thinking driven web security. Inclinations inborn in the arrangement of datasets can prompt one-sided results that favor specific gatherings or disregard clear dangers. Conquering these inclinations and guaranteeing the reasonableness and common sense of reenacted understanding models require careful curation and underwriting of arranging information to unequivocally reflect legitimate conditions (Larson and Mattu, 2016).

Tending to predispositions in computer based intelligence models is another moral objective. Predispositions present in security-related man-made intelligence frameworks can prompt unfair practices, excessively affecting people and networks. Moral computer based intelligence arrangement includes effectively distinguishing and moderating predispositions to keep up with reasonableness and value in security results (Angwin et al., 2016).

Cutoff points of Flow artificial intelligence Advances and Expected Regions for Future Exploration:

In spite of advances in computer based intelligence innovations, a few impediments upset their boundless reception and viability in web security applications. One eminent requirement is the absence of interpretability in artificial intelligence models. Numerous computer based intelligence calculations, particularly profound brain organizations, work as black-box frameworks, settling on it trying to decipher their choice making processes. Working on the interpretability of artificial intelligence models is pivotal for building trust and working with human comprehension and joint effort in security activities (Lipton, 2016).

One more impediment lies in the failure of current computer based intelligence advancements to deal with context oriented seeing successfully. Simulated intelligence models might battle to adjust to dynamic and developing web conditions, ruining their capacity to perceive nuanced logical signals and arising dangers. Progressions in context oriented mindfulness are fundamental for improving the precision and pertinence of computer based intelligence driven danger recognition components (Carvalho et al., 2019).

Also, the asset escalation of carrying out and keeping up with computer based intelligence driven safety efforts presents commonsense difficulties. The computational power and energy utilization expected for man-made intelligence organization can be restrictive, particularly in asset obliged conditions. Growing more effective calculations and execution procedures is fundamental for conquering these constraints and advancing the more extensive openness of simulated intelligence driven security arrangements (Wang and Jiang, 2017).

As far as future examination bearings, a few promising roads warrant investigation. Making interpretable artificial intelligence models for security applications is significant for upgrading straightforwardness and trust. Progressions in setting mindful computer based intelligence can empower more powerful danger recognition in unique web conditions. Moreover, research endeavors ought to zero in on protection saving artificial intelligence methods to accommodate security objectives with severe protection prerequisites (Adadi and Berrada, 2018; Kokkinakis et al., 2020; Abadi et al., 2016). In outline, tending to the specialized and moral difficulties, as well as conquering the constraints of momentum man-made intelligence advancements, requires interdisciplinary cooperation and supported research endeavors. By overcoming these obstructions, simulated intelligence driven web security can understand its maximum capacity in defending computerized resources and protecting client protection and trust.

THE FUTURE OF WEB APPLICATION SECURITY WITH GENERATIVE AI

Synergy of fortune is the inner play of contrast and unity between web application security and Generative Artificial Intelligence (Generative AI). This section investigates the likely future direction of web application security by consolidating Generative artificial intelligence, digging into its progressive effect on danger discovery, versatile protections, and the general strength of computerized frameworks. Generative simulated intelligence, especially Generative Antagonistic Organizations

(GANs), is ready to rethink how security dangers are distinguished and alleviated in web applications. Lofty for creating down to earth data, GANs can be utilized to make fabricated datasets for getting ready security models. This improvement means to redesign the energy of computerized reasoning driven security systems by introducing them to an alternate extent of anticipated risks, consolidating those not dominating in certain data (Goodfellow et al., 2014).

The possible destiny of web application security is most likely going to notice a shift towards proactive peril gauge and countering. Organizations may be able to enhance their security measures ahead of new threats by utilizing generational artificial intelligence models that are equipped with the ability to imitate and anticipate potential security flaws. According to Sun et al. (2020), this expectant approach distinguishes itself from conventional receptive measures by providing a more original and preventative guard procedure. Moreover, Generative PC based knowledge is supposed to expect a significant part in flexible security endeavors.

As what's in store unfurls, the joining of Generative artificial intelligence into web application security is probably going to reach out past danger recognition. Artificial intelligence driven innovations might be utilized to computerize reaction methods, empowering quicker and more precise responses to security episodes. Robotized occurrence reaction, worked with by Generative computer based intelligence, holds the commitment of diminishing the weakness window and limiting the effect of cyberattacks on advanced frameworks (Kill and Mislan, 2019).

With regards to future turns of events, the collaboration between Generative simulated intelligence and other arising advancements is supposed to shape the scene of web application security. The combination of Generative simulated intelligence with blockchain innovation, for example, can improve information honesty and secure exchanges, adding to a more vigorous security framework for web applications (Zissis and Lekkas, 2018).

Arising Patterns and Future Bearings in artificial intelligence driven Web Security

The area of man-made intelligence driven web security is portrayed by unique patterns and nonstop progressions that form the eventual fate of online assurance. As innovations develop, it is vital to expect to arise drifts and ponder future headings to remain in front of complex digital dangers. This segment investigates the advancing patterns in artificial intelligence driven web security and frameworks possible future bearings for innovative work.

A remarkable pattern in computer based intelligence driven web security is the rising reception of Logical computer based intelligence (XAI). As computer based intelligence models become more many-sided, there is a developing requirement for straightforwardness and interpretability in their dynamic cycles. XAI procedures plan to give bits of knowledge into how simulated intelligence models show up at explicit results, encouraging trust and working with cooperation between artificial intelligence frameworks and security experts (Adadi and Berrada, 2018).

One more arising pattern is the joining of simulated intelligence with DevSecOps rehearses. DevSecOps, an augmentation of DevOps, underscores the mix of safety rehearses all through the product improvement lifecycle. Man-made intelligence innovations, when consistently incorporated into DevSecOps work processes, empower persistent security testing, danger recognition, and remediation, adding to a more proactive and secure improvement process (Rackspace, 2021).

The fate of computer based intelligence driven web security is probably going to observe progressions in danger knowledge and data sharing. Cooperative danger insight stages controlled by artificial intelligence can work with the quick trade of data about arising dangers and weaknesses. This aggregate methodology improves the aggregate protection pose, empowering associations to proactively safeguard against developing digital dangers (Lipovsky et al., 2017). Moreover, the coordination of man-made intelligence and edge figuring is supposed to assume a huge part in web security. Edge computer based intelligence, where artificial intelligence calculations are conveyed tense gadgets instead of concentrated servers, offers the benefit of continuous danger location and decreased inactivity. This pattern lines up with the rising predominance of Web of Things (IoT) gadgets, requiring artificial intelligence driven security answers for be dispersed and versatile (Bharadwaj et al., 2021).

As far as future bearings, the investigation of artificial intelligence driven misdirection strategies holds guarantee. Trickiness based security systems influence simulated intelligence to make lure situations and misdirect assailants. This proactive methodology can disturb enemies and give time to security groups to answer really. Research in this space might uncover creative approaches to using simulated intelligence driven trickery for improved web security (Rouhani et al., 2019).

The Expected Social Effects and the Advancing Scene of Web Application Security

The improvement of web application security, driven by mechanical movements and the blend of Man-made thinking (reenacted knowledge), conveys gigantic social consequences. As the high-level scene continues to broaden, it is principal to take a gander at what these movements mean for individuals, organizations, and society's overall security position.

The subject here is how AI innovations are changing the domain of web application security and the societal implications of those changes. Yet the subsequent referral to computational power in cybersecurity can be spoken of as a type of democratization of the future of the health sector missions. With the integration of PC-based and intelligence capabilities, intricate and even mining companies can adapt to complex security strategies.

This democratization can add to a more exhaustive security scene, engaging a greater extent of components to protect their mechanized assets and fragile information (Dignum, 2020). Anyway, with this democratization comes the necessity for elevated internet-based insurance care and preparation at the social level. As individuals and affiliations send man-put forth insight-driven security attempts, sorting out the capacities, obstructions, and moral considerations of these advances turns out to be preeminent. Educational drives and care missions can empower clients to make informed decisions concerning sending and executing artificial cognizance in web security (Rosenzweig, 2019).

The creating scene of web application security also crosses with insurance thoughts. Mimicked insight-driven security game plans habitually incorporate the assessment of a ton of data, raising stresses over potential infringements on confidential insurance. Discovering some sort of congruity between suitable well-being endeavourswellbeing and saving client security requires good assurance in defending methodologies and adherence to moral principles (Barocas & Selbst, 2016). The social impacts loosen up to the space of monetary examinations, too. Coordinating artificial brainpower in web security can affect monetary reality and progression. Nations and affiliations that conclusively impact man-put forth knowledge-driven security attempts could gain a high ground in shielding mechanized assets and developing a strong electronic environment. Then again, those loosened in gathering these headways could stand up to extended risks and shortcomings (Chui et al., 2016).

To the extent that social impacts are present, the occupation of managerial frameworks becomes fundamental. Policymakers and regulatory bodies play an enormous part in framing the proficient association of artificial knowledge in web application security. Spreading out clear principles, rules, and consistency necessities can ensure that reproduced insight progressions are conveyed ethically, considering social characteristics and authentic designs (Jobin et al., 2019). As the scene continues to create, the social impacts of artificial knowledge-driven web application security include the interconnectedness of advancement, ethics, and organization. A proactive and helpful philosophy, including accomplices from various regions, is vital for equipping the benefits of reproduced knowledge while easing anticipated risks and ensuring a protected and fair modernized future.

CONCLUSION

All in all, the mix of Generative Man-made cognizance (Generative man-made knowledge) addresses a basic change in viewpoint in moving web application security. All through this examination, we have revealed key encounters that shed light on the mind boggling position Generative recreated knowledge plays in reinforcing the watchmen of online structures. This portion gives a framework of these vital pieces of information, followed by shrewd thoughts on the extraordinary improvement of security endeavors inside the web space.

Role of Generative computer based intelligence in Improving Web Application Security

Generative computer based intelligence arises as a groundbreaking power in the domain of web application security, acquainting imaginative methodologies with foresee, recognize, and moderate security dangers progressively. The arrangement of Generative simulated intelligence, especially as Generative Antagonistic Organizations (GANs), works with the production of engineered datasets for preparing security models, upgrading the versatility of these models against different and advancing dangers (Goodfellow et al., 2014). The capacity of Generative computer based intelligence to reproduce and foresee potential weaknesses acquaints a proactive aspect with danger expectation and counteraction, leaving from customary receptive methodologies (Sun et al., 2020). Besides, the adaptability of Generative man-made intelligence models takes into consideration ceaseless acclimations to security conventions, guaranteeing a hearty reaction to arising dangers and weaknesses (Carvalho et al., 2019). The mix of Generative computer based intelligence changes danger recognition as well as stretches out to robotizing reaction instruments, decreasing the weakness window, and limiting the effect of cyberattacks on advanced frameworks (Kill and Mislan, 2019).

Continuous Development of Safety efforts in the Web Space: Pondering the continuous development of safety efforts in the web space, it becomes obvious that the convergence of Generative computer based intelligence and web application security is only one feature of a more extensive scene. Arising patterns, like the reception of Reasonable simulated intelligence (XAI) and the joining of man-made intelligence with DevSecOps rehearses, highlight constant endeavors to improve straightforwardness, coordinated effort, and proactive safeguard techniques in online protection (Adadi and Berrada, 2018; Rackspace, 2021). The democratization of man-made intelligence driven security endeavors offers far reaching access however requires increased network safety mindfulness and training at the social level to explore the moral contemplations and security suggestions related with these innovations

(Dignum, 2020; Rosenzweig, 2019). The financial effects are likewise articulated, with vital computer based intelligence reception possibly impacting intensity and development on a worldwide scale (Chui et al., 2016). Administrative systems, as fundamental parts, will direct the mindful sending of man-made reasoning in web application security, guaranteeing adherence to moral norms and lawful contemplations (Jobin et al., 2019). Taking everything into account, the coordination of Generative computer based intelligence with web application security encapsulates the continuous development towards more refined, proactive, and versatile safeguard instruments. The cooperative energy of state of the art innovations, cooperative methodologies, and moral contemplations shapes the groundwork of a tough network safety scene. As we explore the future, the cautious harmony among advancement and dependable arrangement will be vital in understanding the maximum capacity of Generative artificial intelligence while tending to social worries and guaranteeing the security of online frameworks.

REFERENCES

Ahmadi, S. (2023). Open AI and its Impact on Fraud Detection in Financial Industry. *Sina, A.(2023). Open AI and its Impact on Fraud Detection in Financial Industry. Journal of Knowledge Learning and Science Technology ISSN*, 2959-6386.

Airlangga, G. (2024). Analysis of Machine Learning Classifiers for Speaker Identification: A Study on SVM, Random Forest, KNN, and Decision Tree. *Journal of Computer Networks. Architecture and High Performance Computing*, 6(1), 430–438. DOI: 10.47709/cnahpc.v6i1.3487

Alwahedi, F., Aldhaheri, A., Ferrag, M. A., Battah, A., & Tihanyi, N. (2024). Machine learning techniques for IoT security: Current research and future vision with generative AI and large language models. *Internet of Things and Cyber-Physical Systems*.

Amankwah-Amoah, J., Abdalla, S., Mogaji, E., Elbanna, A., & Dwivedi, Y. K. (2024). The impending disruption of creative industries by generative AI: Opportunities, challenges, and research agenda. *International Journal of Information Management*, 79, 102759. DOI: 10.1016/j.ijinfomgt.2024.102759

Bandi, A., Adapa, P. V. S. R., & Kuchi, Y. E. V. P. K. (2023). The power of generative ai: A review of requirements, models, input–output formats, evaluation metrics, and challenges. *Future Internet*, 15(8), 260. DOI: 10.3390/fi15080260

Bozkurt, A. (Ed.). (2023). Unleashing the potential of generative AI, conversational agents and chatbots in educational praxis: A systematic review and bibliometric analysis of GenAI in education. *Open Praxis, 15*(4), 261-270.

Cai, Z., Xiong, Z., Xu, H., Wang, P., Li, W., & Pan, Y. (2021). Generative adversarial networks: A survey toward private and secure applications. *ACM Computing Surveys*, 54(6), 1–38. DOI: 10.1145/3459992

Dhoni, P. (2023). Exploring the synergy between generative AI, data and analytics in the modern age. *Authorea Preprints*.

Dhoni, P. (2023). Unleashing the potential: overcoming hurdles and embracing generative AI in IT workplaces: advantages, guidelines, and policies. *Authorea Preprints*.

Dhoni, P., & Kumar, R. (2023). Synergizing generative ai and cybersecurity: Roles of generative ai entities, companies, agencies, and government in enhancing cybersecurity. *Authorea Preprints*.

Dwivedi, Y. K., Pandey, N., Currie, W., & Micu, A. (2024). Leveraging ChatGPT and other generative artificial intelligence (AI)-based applications in the hospitality and tourism industry: Practices, challenges and research agenda. *International Journal of Contemporary Hospitality Management*, 36(1), 1–12. DOI: 10.1108/IJCHM-05-2023-0686

Fui-Hoon Nah, F., Zheng, R., Cai, J., Siau, K., & Chen, L. (2023). Generative AI and ChatGPT: Applications, challenges, and AI-human collaboration. *Journal of Information Technology Case and Application Research*, 25(3), 277–304. DOI: 10.1080/15228053.2023.2233814

Guo, D., Chen, H., Wu, R., & Wang, Y. (2023). AIGC challenges and opportunities related to public safety: A case study of ChatGPT. *Journal of Safety Science and Resilience = An Quan Ke Xue Yu Ren Xing (Ying Wen)*, 4(4), 329–339. DOI: 10.1016/j.jnlssr.2023.08.001

Hussain, M. (2023). When, Where, and Which?: Navigating the Intersection of Computer Vision and Generative AI for Strategic Business Integration. *IEEE Access : Practical Innovations, Open Solutions*, 11, 127202–127215. DOI: 10.1109/ACCESS.2023.3332468

Jeyaraman, M., Ramasubramanian, S., Balaji, S., Jeyaraman, N., Nallakumarasamy, A., & Sharma, S. (2023). ChatGPT in action: Harnessing artificial intelligence potential and addressing ethical challenges in medicine, education, and scientific research. *World Journal of Methodology*, 13(4), 170–178. DOI: 10.5662/wjm.v13.i4.170 PMID: 37771867

Kar, A. K., Varsha, P. S., & Rajan, S. (2023). Unravelling the impact of generative artificial intelligence (GAI) in industrial applications: A review of scientific and grey literature. *Global Journal of Flexible Systems Managment*, 24(4), 659–689. DOI: 10.1007/s40171-023-00356-x

Maharani, D., Anggraeni, D., & Nofitri, R. (2024). Pemanfaatan Artificial intelligence dalam Pembuatan Presentasi bagi Guru-Guru Brainfor Islamic School Kisaran. [JISS]. *Journal Of Indonesian Social Society*, 2(1), 45–51.

McIntosh, T., Liu, T., Susnjak, T., Alavizadeh, H., Ng, A., Nowrozy, R., & Watters, P. (2023). Harnessing GPT-4 for generation of cybersecurity GRC policies: A focus on ransomware attack mitigation. *Computers & Security*, 134, 103424. DOI: 10.1016/j.cose.2023.103424

Nixon, N., Lin, Y., & Snow, L. (2024). Catalyzing Equity in STEM Teams: Harnessing Generative AI for Inclusion and Diversity. *Policy Insights from the Behavioral and Brain Sciences*, 11(1), 23727322231220356. DOI: 10.1177/23727322231220356 PMID: 38516055

Ooi, K. B., Tan, G. W. H., Al-Emran, M., Al-Sharafi, M. A., Capatina, A., Chakraborty, A., Dwivedi, Y. K., Huang, T.-L., Kar, A. K., Lee, V.-H., Loh, X.-M., Micu, A., Mikalef, P., Mogaji, E., Pandey, N., Raman, R., Rana, N. P., Sarker, P., Sharma, A., & Wong, L. W. (2023). The potential of Generative Artificial Intelligence across disciplines: Perspectives and future directions. *Journal of Computer Information Systems*, •••, 1–32. DOI: 10.1080/08874417.2023.2261010

Patil, D. D., Dhotre, D. R., Gawande, G. S., Mate, D. S., Shelke, M. V., & Bhoye, T. S. (2024). Transformative trends in generative ai: Harnessing large language models for natural language understanding and generation. *International Journal of Intelligent Systems and Applications in Engineering*, 12(4s), 309–319.

Raimi, L., Kah, J. M., & Tariq, M. U. (2022). The Discourse of Blue Economy Definitions, Measurements, and Theories: Implications for Strengthening Academic Research and Industry Practice. In Raimi, L., & Kah, J. (Eds.), *Implications for Entrepreneurship and Enterprise Development in the Blue Economy* (pp. 1–17). IGI Global., DOI: 10.4018/978-1-6684-3393-5.ch001

Raimi, L., Tariq, M. U., & Kah, J. M. (2022). Diversity, Equity, and Inclusion as the Future Workplace Ethics: Theoretical Review. In Raimi, L., & Kah, J. (Eds.), *Mainstreaming Diversity, Equity, and Inclusion as Future Workplace Ethics* (pp. 1–27). IGI Global., DOI: 10.4018/978-1-6684-3657-8.ch001

Rane, N. (2023). Role of ChatGPT and similar generative artificial intelligence (AI) in construction industry. *Available at SSRN* 4598258. DOI: 10.2139/ssrn.4598258

Rane, N., Choudhary, S., & Rane, J. (2023). Integrating Building Information Modelling (BIM) with ChatGPT, Bard, and similar generative artificial intelligence in the architecture, engineering, and construction industry: applications, a novel framework, challenges, and future scope. *Bard, and similar generative artificial intelligence in the architecture, engineering, and construction industry: applications, a novel framework, challenges, and future scope (November 22, 2023)*.

Salanitri, F. P. FROM CENTRALIZATION TO COLLABORATION: HARNESSING GENERATIVE MODELS IN FEDERATED LEARNING FOR MEDICAL IMAGE ANALYSIS.

Tariq, M. U. (2024). Empowering Student Entrepreneurs: From Idea to Execution. In Cantafio, G., & Munna, A. (Eds.), *Empowering Students and Elevating Universities With Innovation Centers* (pp. 83–111). IGI Global., DOI: 10.4018/979-8-3693-1467-8.ch005

Tariq, M. U. (2024). The Transformation of Healthcare Through AI-Driven Diagnostics. In Sharma, A., Chanderwal, N., Tyagi, S., Upadhyay, P., & Tyagi, A. (Eds.), *Enhancing Medical Imaging with Emerging Technologies* (pp. 250–264). IGI Global., DOI: 10.4018/979-8-3693-5261-8.ch015

Tariq, M. U. (2024). The Role of Emerging Technologies in Shaping the Global Digital Government Landscape. In Guo, Y. (Ed.), *Emerging Developments and Technologies in Digital Government* (pp. 160–180). IGI Global., DOI: 10.4018/979-8-3693-2363-2.ch009

Tariq, M. U. (2024). Equity and Inclusion in Learning Ecosystems. In Al Husseiny, F., & Munna, A. (Eds.), *Preparing Students for the Future Educational Paradigm* (pp. 155–176). IGI Global., DOI: 10.4018/979-8-3693-1536-1.ch007

Tariq, M. U. (2024). Empowering Educators in the Learning Ecosystem. In Al Husseiny, F., & Munna, A. (Eds.), *Preparing Students for the Future Educational Paradigm* (pp. 232–255). IGI Global., DOI: 10.4018/979-8-3693-1536-1.ch010

Tariq, M. U. (2024). Revolutionizing Health Data Management With Blockchain Technology: Enhancing Security and Efficiency in a Digital Era. In Garcia, M., & de Almeida, R. (Eds.), *Emerging Technologies for Health Literacy and Medical Practice* (pp. 153–175). IGI Global., DOI: 10.4018/979-8-3693-1214-8.ch008

Tariq, M. U. (2024). Emerging Trends and Innovations in Blockchain-Digital Twin Integration for Green Investments: A Case Study Perspective. In Jafar, S., Rodriguez, R., Kannan, H., Akhtar, S., & Plugmann, P. (Eds.), *Harnessing Blockchain-Digital Twin Fusion for Sustainable Investments* (pp. 148–175). IGI Global., DOI: 10.4018/979-8-3693-1878-2.ch007

Tariq, M. U. (2024). Emotional Intelligence in Understanding and Influencing Consumer Behavior. In Musiolik, T., Rodriguez, R., & Kannan, H. (Eds.), *AI Impacts in Digital Consumer Behavior* (pp. 56–81). IGI Global., DOI: 10.4018/979-8-3693-1918-5.ch003

Tariq, M. U. (2024). Fintech Startups and Cryptocurrency in Business: Revolutionizing Entrepreneurship. In Kankaew, K., Nakpathom, P., Chnitphattana, A., Pitchayadejanant, K., & Kunnapapdeelert, S. (Eds.), *Applying Business Intelligence and Innovation to Entrepreneurship* (pp. 106–124). IGI Global., DOI: 10.4018/979-8-3693-1846-1.ch006

Tariq, M. U. (2024). Multidisciplinary Service Learning in Higher Education: Concepts, Implementation, and Impact. In S. Watson (Ed.), Applications of Service Learning in Higher Education (pp. 1-19). IGI Global. DOI: 10.4018/979-8-3693-2133-1.ch001

Tariq, M. U. (2024). Enhancing Cybersecurity Protocols in Modern Healthcare Systems: Strategies and Best Practices. In Garcia, M., & de Almeida, R. (Eds.), *Transformative Approaches to Patient Literacy and Healthcare Innovation* (pp. 223–241). IGI Global., DOI: 10.4018/979-8-3693-3661-8.ch011

Tariq, M. U. (2024). Advanced Wearable Medical Devices and Their Role in Transformative Remote Health Monitoring. In Garcia, M., & de Almeida, R. (Eds.), *Transformative Approaches to Patient Literacy and Healthcare Innovation* (pp. 308–326). IGI Global., DOI: 10.4018/979-8-3693-3661-8.ch015

Tariq, M. U. (2024). Leveraging Artificial Intelligence for a Sustainable and Climate-Neutral Economy in Asia. In Ordóñez de Pablos, P., Almunawar, M., & Anshari, M. (Eds.), *Strengthening Sustainable Digitalization of Asian Economy and Society* (pp. 1–21). IGI Global., DOI: 10.4018/979-8-3693-1942-0.ch001

Tariq, M. U. (2024). Metaverse in Business and Commerce. In Kumar, J., Arora, M., & Erkol Bayram, G. (Eds.), *Exploring the Use of Metaverse in Business and Education* (pp. 47–72). IGI Global., DOI: 10.4018/979-8-3693-5868-9.ch004

Tariq, M. U., & Ismail, M. U. S. B. (2024). AI-powered COVID-19 forecasting: A comprehensive comparison of advanced deep learning methods. *Osong Public Health and Research Perspectives*, 15(2), 2210–9099. DOI: 10.24171/j.phrp.2023.0287 PMID: 38621765

Vaigandla, K. K., Vanteru, M. K., & Siluveru, M. (2024). An Extensive Examination of the IoT and Blockchain Technologies in Relation to their Applications in the Healthcare Industry. *Mesopotamian Journal of Computer Science*, 2024, 1–14. DOI: 10.58496/MJCSC/2024/001

Wang, X., Wan, Z., Hekmati, A., Zong, M., Alam, S., Zhang, M., & Krishnamachari, B. (2024). IoT in the Era of Generative AI: Vision and Challenges. *arXiv preprint arXiv:2401.01923*.

Xu, M., Du, H., Niyato, D., Kang, J., Xiong, Z., Mao, S., Han, Z., Jamalipour, A., Kim, D. I., Shen, X., Leung, V. C. M., & Poor, H. V. (2024). Unleashing the power of edge-cloud generative ai in mobile networks: A survey of aigc services. *IEEE Communications Surveys and Tutorials*, 26(2), 1127–1170. DOI: 10.1109/COMST.2024.3353265

Yu, P., Xu, H., Hu, X., & Deng, C. (2023, October). Leveraging generative AI and large Language models: A Comprehensive Roadmap for Healthcare Integration. []. MDPI.]. *Health Care*, 11(20), 2776. PMID: 37893850

Zeadally, S., Adi, E., Baig, Z., & Khan, I. A. (2020). Harnessing artificial intelligence capabilities to improve cybersecurity. *IEEE Access : Practical Innovations, Open Solutions*, 8, 23817–23837. DOI: 10.1109/ACCESS.2020.2968045

Zhao, C., Du, H., Niyato, D., Kang, J., Xiong, Z., Kim, D. I., & Letaief, K. B. (2024). Generative AI for Secure Physical Layer Communications: A Survey. *arXiv preprint arXiv:2402.13553*.

Chapter 9
Ethical Concerns in Artificial Intelligence (AI):
The Role of Governance Mechanism in Finance

Muhammad Naeem

https://orcid.org/0000-0001-6678-3536

The Islamia University of Bahawalpur, Pakistan

Shoukat Ali

The Islamia University of Bahawalpur, Pakistan

Abdul Rehman

https://orcid.org/0000-0002-6988-8330

National College of Business Administration and Economics, Lahore, Pakistan

Sumair Farooq

Hamdard University, Karachi, Pakistan

ABSTRACT

Artificial intelligence and governance ideas are being implemented in business and society. These are two of the most explored issues in the current period. Banks and financial institutions nowadays collect vast volumes of client information, which is then processed by artificial intelligence; yet, the fate of such information remains unknown. This study seeks to identify ethical difficulties in the application of artificial intelligence and presents solutions based on governance concepts. It also looks into the function of artificial intelligence in financial institutions. This study is exploratory, with a focus on primary data analysis. Primary data is collected using a standardized questionnaire distributed to bank personnel. The study's findings indicate that

DOI: 10.4018/979-8-3693-3703-5.ch009

there is a significant association between ethical difficulties in AI implementation and the function of corporate governance in financial institutions. The findings also indicate that the effective and intelligent use of governance concepts can alleviate ethical concerns about artificial intelligence implementation.

1 INTRODUCTION

A wide range of artificial intelligence (AI) systems and applications are present in our daily lives, such as recommender systems on streaming services, chatbots on bank websites, email and message receipt, and automatic categorization and classification into distinct sections (Agarwal et al., 2015). Still, as AI has become more widely used, so too has its abuse grown. Concerns about data privacy, trust, and security have been raised during the past ten years in relation to the improper use of AI (Rabbani et al., 2022).

In the present era, AI technology has advanced and may now be incorporated into several aspects of daily life (Al-Sartawi et al., 2021). As more and more people get the ability to use AI, its accessibility has also improved (Shihadeh, 2021). Making an intelligent machine raises several ethical questions about how to make sure it doesn't hurt people or other living things (Bostrom & Yudkowsky, 2018). The AI-equipped autonomous vehicle has already driven several million miles and has the capacity to make decisions that may have an impact on society, morality, and ethics (Ziaee, 2011). However, this vehicle has the potential to cause accidents that could endanger human or animal lives. For example, in May 2016, a Tesla vehicle operating on autopilot caught fire, killing one of the occupants (Etzioni & Etzioni, 2017). A rising body of literature on AI applies it to a variety of fields, from sophisticated self-driving cars to machine translation. However, research on the ethics and governance of AI has also received more attention lately (Winfield & Jirotka, 2018).

Three major goals are the focus of this study. It first analyzes the moral dilemmas that arise when AI is used in financial institutions. Secondly, it explores the possibility of using governance mechanism to lessen these moral dilemmas. Thirdly, it looks at the social perspective on ethics serves as the primary source of inspiration for AI ethics, as it implies that AI is designed to adhere to cultural norms, which typically lack a universal ethical perspective. The three primary obstacles to AI social choice judgments are aggregation, measurement, and standing. Standing challenge is the idea of whose opinions should be taken into account, whereas measurement is the idea of whose opinions are acknowledged or identified, and aggregation is the idea of how several opinions are combined to create a single vision of AI programming (Baum, 2017). Each of these difficulties is a worry in and of itself, and if left unchecked, they may combine to pose a serious threat to AI's ethical behavior and social choice. RegTech is an application of AI, and as such, its position in Islamic financial institutions is still not well-understood in the literature.

2 REVIEW OF LITERATURE

There is still no accepted definition of intelligence, despite a lengthy history of discussion and investigation, indicating that while intelligence can be accurately defined, it is not easy to do so. AI has been described differently by different academics. Here are a few of the most widely used definitions. Jon McCarthy is credited with creating the phrase "Artificial Intelligence" in 1956 and is regarded as its founder (Musleh et al., 2022). Reilly et al. (2004) defines as "an intelligent machine or an intelligent computer-based program which has the ability to reach a problem or goals like human beings and understand human language." The creation of a machine that a human would perceive as intelligent is known as AI. It has the ability to plan and react to circumstances. The purpose of AI has been defined in a number of ways by various academics. For example, Marr (2019) describes AI as the process of solving and identifying information processing difficulties. However, Russell and Norvig (2016) define it as the creation of sentient beings that can sense their surroundings and adapt accordingly.

2.1 Social Choice, Ethics and Artificial Intelligence

A branch of AI known as machine learning is predicated on algorithms and systems that can learn from experience over time without needing to be reprogrammed. Its primary issue, though, is that it lacks consciousness, in contrast to humans. Children, for example, possess consciousness and the capacity to recognize, measure, and integrate various points of view in order to make morally-based social decisions; this is not the case with artificial intelligence. Few scholars have addressed social choice in the context of AI ethics (Hayat & Malik, 2014). Tarleton (2010) addresses coherent extrapolated volition (CEV) in relation to social choice. A more thorough examination of computation social choice is provided by Brandt et al. (2015). AI and its subsets, including machine learning and natural language processing, have been used in many contexts, including human-to-human communication, text translation between natural languages, sentiment analysis of social media posts, and more. Chatbots, also known as AI bots or chatter bots, are applications of AI that mimic human speech and behavior through the use of natural language processing and machine learning. Instead than being viewed as a formality, AI ethics ought to be deeply ingrained in the technological aspects of AI and machine learning systems.

2.2 Governance Mechanism in Finance

In order to ensure that financial institutions run effectively, publicly, and responsibly, governance measures are essential to their sustainability. Robust frameworks that outline the roles and obligations of different stakeholders, like as shareholders, regulators, CEOs, and board members, are the foundation of these systems. Robust governance frameworks create accountability and reduce risks associated with the financial industry by establishing checks and balances (Affes, & Jarboui, 2023).

Governance measures in financial institutions work to protect stakeholders' interests while fostering the long-term generation of wealth. Boards of directors supervise risk management, compliance initiatives, and strategic decision-making. They are made up of seasoned individuals from various backgrounds. These systems protect the institution's reputation and increase confidence among investors, clients, and the general public by promoting a culture of honesty and moral behavior (Gitau, 2023).

Furthermore, financial institutions' governance procedures play a critical role in preserving resilience and stability, particularly in uncertain economic or volatile market environments. These procedures assist in identifying and addressing developing risks through stringent scrutiny and cautious decision-making, guaranteeing the institution's flexibility in responding to shifting market conditions and regulatory environments. In the end, a strong governance framework improves the financial institution's reputation, competitiveness, and capacity to carry out its essential job of promoting prosperity and economic growth (Gambetta et al., 2021).

2.3 Ethical Concerns of Artificial Intelligence and Governance Mechanism

AI integration has significantly improved customer service, decision-making, and efficiency in financial organizations. But this advancement in technology also brings up serious ethical issues, mainly with regard to accountability, algorithmic bias, and data privacy. By creating precise guidelines, structures, and monitoring procedures to guarantee AI applications in finance comply with ethical norms and legal requirements, governance mechanisms play a crucial role in resolving these challenges (Aldoseri et al., 2023).

The possible misuse or improper management of sensitive client data is one of the main ethical issues with AI in financial organizations. AI algorithms run the risk of data breaches, illegal access, and misuse of personal information because they mainly rely on massive volumes of data to make predictions and conclusions. Strict data protection guidelines, encryption requirements, and transparency policies are required by effective governance frameworks in order to preserve consumer privacy and guarantee appropriate data handling procedures all the way through the AI lifecycle (Zhao & Gómez, 2023).

Moreover, the potential for algorithmic prejudice presents a noteworthy ethical dilemma for the application of AI in financial institutions. Particularly when it comes to lending, credit scoring, and investment decisions, biased algorithms have the potential to sustain prejudice, inequality, and unfair treatment. In order to detect and reduce bias in AI models and promote fairness, equity, and inclusivity in the financial services industry, governance mechanisms need to include stringent testing, validation, and continuous monitoring methods. Financial institutions may leverage the revolutionary potential of AI while maintaining ethical standards, trust, and societal values by coordinating AI development with ethical guidelines and legal frameworks (Ferrara, 2023).

3. METHODOLOGY

There are two sections to the technique. The design of the questionnaire is covered after the population and sample are discussed. However, it also discusses the prerequisites for collecting data and, at the end, statistical analysis.

3.1. Population and Sample

The study's target population consists of Pakistani bankers. This analysis used the fundamental random sampling technique since it can remove biases. Every worker is equally qualified to be selected for this research project. Despite the lack of population information, a sample size of 385 individuals with a margin of error of 5% and a 95% confidence interval is provided. To calculate sample size, use the formula below:

$$n = N \times \frac{\frac{Z^2 \times p \times (1 - p)}{e^2}}{\left[N - 1 + \frac{Z^2 \times p \times (1 - p)}{e^2} \right]}$$

Where,
N = Size of Population
Z = Normal Distribution Critical Value at a Required Confidence Level
p = Proportion of Sample
e = Margin of Error

3.2. Questionnaire Design and Data Collection

This AI and financial governance are based on two core ideas. A 5-point Likert scale is used in the questionnaire; 1 represents strongly disagree and 5 represents strongly agree. As a result, questionnaires are used to collect the responses. The questionnaire was given to bank workers, who were asked to reply. In total, 412 replies were received from staff members, comprising managers and bank employees. Still, 385 were selected for examination. Responses that are erroneous or incomplete cause other responses to be deleted.

3.3. Statistical Analysis

The Structural Equation Modeling (SEM) method is used in the study to ascertain how the variables interact. The PLS prediction, PLS method, and bootstrapping test are used in the analysis. With a high degree of multicollinearity, the program Smart PLS 4.0.9 is specifically used to analyze the relationship between the constructs. It can also handle the data without violating the CB-SEM assumptions.

4. RESULTS

The method of structural equation modeling is employed to examine the connection between the variables.

4.1 Descriptive Result

Table I shows that there are 40.52% men and 59.48% women. Nonetheless, in terms of educational history, these individuals are 23.64% matriculated, 17.92% intermediate, 38.96% own a bachelor's degree, 14.54% have a master's degree, and 4.93% have a PhD. Moreover, the personnel with 0–3 years' experience make up 26.23%, those with 3-5 years' experience make up 31.95%, those with 5–10 years' experience make up 28.57%, and those with 10 years or more experience make up 13.25%.

Table 1. Demographic Statistics

Variable	Description	Frequency	Percentage
Gender	Male	156	40.52
	Female	229	59.48

continued on following page

Table 1. Continued

Variable	Description	Frequency	Percentage
	Matriculation	91	23.64
	Intermediate	69	17.92
Education	Bachelor	150	38.96
	Master	56	14.54
	PhD	19	4.93
	0-3 Years	101	26.23
	3-5 Years	123	31.95
Experience	5-10 Years	110	28.57
	10 Years and above	51	13.25

4.2 Measurement of Model

The PLS algorithm test was used to evaluate the model's validity and dependability. The discriminant validity, internal consistency, and model reliability and validity measure nonetheless, a number higher than 0.7 denotes the validity and trustworthiness of the model. When the 16-item analysis is conducted, some items are eliminated in order to meet the level criteria. But according to Chin (1998), a value of 0.7 or higher is seen as more suitable; nevertheless, a value above 0.5 is also acceptable, while a value below 0.5 need to be regarded as non-validity and non-reliability (Götz et al., 2009). The composite reliability and validity are used to determine the questions' validity and reliability. When determining the validity of a question, average variance extracted is used to determine reliability; a number better than 0.5 is considered acceptable. The composite reliability value is greater than 0.7.

Table 2. Construct Reliability and Validity Test

	Items	Factor Loading	Cronbach's alpha	Composite reliability	Average variance extracted (AVE)
	AI1	0.709			
	AI2	0.739			
Artificial Intelligence	AI3	0.662	0.727	0.767	0.695
	AI4	0.807			
	AI5	0.620			

continued on following page

Table 2. Continued

	Items	Factor Loading	Cronbach's alpha	Composite reliability	Average variance extracted (AVE)
	Gov1	0.928			
	Gov2	0.714			
Governance	Gov3	0.697	0.716	0.723	0.514
	Gov4	0.687			
	Gov5	0.795			

4.4 Direct Effect

Result shows that use of AI and implantation of Gov in finance enhances the performance of firms.

Table 3. Direct effect

	STD	T value	P value
AI -> Gov	0.047	0.028	0.000

3 CONCLUSION

Numerous aspects of our lives have already been impacted by AI. AI and governance is being used in a finance. While many researchers have given varied definitions of AI, most of them believe that AI is a technology that allows computing devices to attempt to solve problems by using a human-like approach. Financial institutions might find it difficult to ignore the application of AI as innovations continue to grow. But as AI is used more often, ethical concerns become more of a concern. There have been instances where customer data has been misused in the name of providing better services thanks to the expanding.

This chapter investigates how ethical difficulties in AI deployment can be resolved with efficient use of finance principles and technology. Primary data from are gathered for this study. To accomplish our goal, we use PLS SEM for analysis. The results demonstrate a strong correlation between governance principles, and ethical concerns in the application of AI. In conclusion, governance principles can assist in resolving these moral dilemmas related to the application of AI.

REFERENCES

Affes, W., & Jarboui, A. (2023). The impact of corporate governance on financial performance: A cross-sector study. *International Journal of Disclosure and Governance*, 20(4), 374–394. DOI: 10.1057/s41310-023-00182-8

Agarwal, P. K., Gurjar, J., Agarwal, A. K., & Birla, R. (2015). Application of artificial intelligence for development of intelligent transport system in smart cities. *Journal of Traffic and Transportation Engineering*, 1(1), 20–30.

Al-Sartawi, A. M. M., Razzaque, A., & Kamal, M. M. (Eds.). (2021). *Artificial Intelligence Systems and the Internet of Things in the Digital Era:Proceedings of EAMMIS 2021* (Vol. 239). Springer Nature. DOI: 10.1007/978-3-030-77246-8

Aldoseri, A., Al-Khalifa, K. N., & Hamouda, A. M. (2023). Re-thinking data strategy and integration for artificial intelligence: Concepts, opportunities, and challenges. *Applied Sciences (Basel, Switzerland)*, 13(12), 7082. DOI: 10.3390/app13127082

Baum, S. (2017). A survey of artificial general intelligence projects for ethics, risk, and policy. *Global Catastrophic Risk Institute Working Paper*, 17-1.

Bostrom, N., & Yudkowsky, E. (2018). The ethics of artificial intelligence. In *Artificial intelligence safety and security* (pp. 57–69). Chapman and Hall/CRC. DOI: 10.1201/9781351251389-4

Brandt, F., Conitzer, V., Endriss, U., Lang, J., & Procaccia, A. D. (Eds.). (2016). *Handbook of computational social choice*. Cambridge University Press. DOI: 10.1017/CBO9781107446984

Chin, W. W. (1998). The partial least squares approach to structural equation modeling. *Modern methods for business research*, 295(2), 295-336.

Etzioni, A., & Etzioni, O. (2017). Incorporating ethics into artificial intelligence. *The Journal of Ethics*, 21(4), 403–418. DOI: 10.1007/s10892-017-9252-2

Ferrara, E. (2023). Fairness and bias in artificial intelligence: A brief survey of sources, impacts, and mitigation strategies. *Sci*, 6(1), 3. DOI: 10.3390/sci6010003

Gambetta, N., Azcárate-Llanes, F., Sierra-García, L., & García-Benau, M. A. (2021). Financial institutions' risk profile and contribution to the sustainable development goals. *Sustainability (Basel)*, 13(14), 7738. DOI: 10.3390/su13147738

Gitau, J. M. (2023). *Corporate Governance Practices and Performance of Enterprise Risk Management in the Horticultural Farms in Kajiado County, Kenya* (Doctoral dissertation, KCA University).

Götz, O., Liehr-Gobbers, K., & Krafft, M. (2009). Evaluation of structural equation models using the partial least squares (PLS) approach. In *Handbook of partial least squares: Concepts, methods and applications* (pp. 691–711). Springer Berlin Heidelberg.

Hayat, U., & Malik, A. (2014). Islamic Finance: ethics, concepts, practice. *Practice (November 2014). CFA Institute Research Foundation L2014-3.*

Marr, B. (2019). *Artificial intelligence in practice: how 50 successful companies used AI and machine learning to solve problems.* John Wiley & Sons.

Musleh Al-Sartawi, A. M., Hussainey, K., & Razzaque, A. (2022). The role of artificial intelligence in sustainable finance. *Journal of Sustainable Finance & Investment,* •••, 1–6. DOI: 10.1080/20430795.2022.2057405

Rabbani, M. R., Sarea, A., Khan, S., & Abdullah, Y. (2022). Ethical concerns in artificial intelligence (AI): The role of RegTech and Islamic finance. In *Artificial Intelligence for Sustainable Finance and Sustainable Technology: Proceedings of ICGER 2021 1* (pp. 381-390). Springer International Publishing.

Reilly, J., McCarthy, K., McGinty, L., & Smyth, B. (2004, December). Incremental critiquing. In *International Conference on Innovative Techniques and Applications of Artificial Intelligence* (pp. 101-114). London: Springer London.

Russell, S. J., & Norvig, P. (2016). *Artificial intelligence: a modern approach.* Pearson.

Shihadeh, F. (2021). A Conceptual Framework of Financial Inclusion: The Links with Individuals, SMEs, and Banks. In *The Big Data-Driven Digital Economy: Artificial and Computational Intelligence* (pp. 285–300). Springer International Publishing. DOI: 10.1007/978-3-030-73057-4_22

Tarleton, N. (2010). Coherent extrapolated volition: a meta-level approach to machine ethics. *The Singularity Institute, Berkeley, CA, University Stanford, CA, 94305.*

Winfield, A. F., & Jirotka, M. (2018). Ethical governance is essential to building trust in robotics and artificial intelligence systems. *Philosophical Transactions. Series A, Mathematical, Physical, and Engineering Sciences,* 376(2133), 20180085. DOI: 10.1098/rsta.2018.0085 PMID: 30323000

Zhao, J., & Gómez Fariñas, B. (2023). Artificial intelligence and sustainable decisions. *European Business Organization Law Review,* 24(1), 1–39. DOI: 10.1007/s40804-022-00262-2

. Ziaee, A. A. (2011). A philosophical approach to artificial intelligence and Islamic values. *IIUM Engineering Journal, 12*(6).

Chapter 10
The Challenges for E–Commerce Using AI Applications

Imdad Ali Shah

https://orcid.org/0000-0003-2015-1028

Faculty of Engineering Science and Technology, Iqra University, Karachi, Pakistan

N. Z. Jhanjhi

https://orcid.org/0000-0001-8116-4733

School of Computing Science and Engineering, Taylor's University, Malaysia

ABSTRACT

The primary objective of this chapter is to exhaustive analysis of the constantly changing security and privacy issues and important factors in e-commerce. The need to protect sensitive data and guarantee user privacy has increased with the growth of the digital economy. This chapter examines many security concerns, such as phishing attacks, data breaches, and payment gateway vulnerabilities, and highlights the possible consequences for both consumers and organisations. It explores cutting-edge technology and creative fixes meant to strengthen e-commerce platforms against dynamic cyberattacks. In addition to pointing out the vulnerabilities that now exist, the study suggests preventative measures as well as future lines of inquiry and application. We look at biometric authentication, and privacy-preserving technologies as possible ways to improve the security of e-commerce platforms. The data that is being presented highlights how important it is for technology, legislation, and user awareness to come together to provide a safe and reliable online purchasing environment. To strengthen the digital marketplace against the challenges presented by a constantly changing cyber landscape, in competitive mar-

DOI: 10.4018/979-8-3693-3703-5.ch010

kets, businesses try to increase their profit margins without sacrificing the quality of their products. Conversely, customers successfully fulfil their needs and desires at home. AI provides answers for a wide range of issues that both consumers and business owners face. Computer-based information can benefit economic growth, organizations, managers, and buyers. Without a doubt, AI improves human lives. Artificial intelligence has the potential to improve economic growth and raise everyone's standard of living. People and businesses everywhere are eager to invest in human resources, and e-business is crucial to continuously providing customers with the easiest way to purchase goods and services. Moreover, the emergence of an AI-ready business does not translate into a rise in the need for mechanical expertise. The use of electronic commerce has made life better. We focused on phishing attacks, data breaches, blockchain payment gateway, Ransomware attacks, Cloud-based and cyber attacks in E-commerce.

INTRODUCTION

The e-commerce sector has expanded rapidly over the past ten years, particularly in the wake of COVID and the rise in popularity of remote employment. It's never been simpler to shop at your Favorite store online. This is a real boon for shops, opening a world of commercial prospects for small- and medium-sized merchants, service providers, and even entire sectors. Aggressive internet promotion and the financial savings from not needing to rent a physical site make it much easier to reach a large sales volume. However, given the increased danger of cyber security threats that e-commerce websites face, it is also a burden (Paulraj and Neelamegam, 2014).

The development of websites and mobile applications has led to an increase in the complexity and frequency of cyberattacks in recent years. We may observe a jump in attacks after 2020, with 2021 seeing the biggest number of attacks due to the increase in online presence since the pandemic's beginning(Zhang et al., 2023, McLean, 2023). Because e-commerce businesses gather so much personal and financial data, they are all prime targets for cybercrime. The assaults vary from ones that target the user, such as malware and phishing, to ones that are more focused on the server and website, like SQL injection and cross-site scripting. In terms of revenue costs and consumer trust, this kind of weakness can have a significant impact on the firm as well as the customer.

About 60 years ago, the idea of artificial intelligence (AI) was conceived. AI is "the art of creating machines that perform," according to(Schatz et al., 2017). actions that, when carried out by humans, demand intelligence. Owing to the shift in lifestyles, one requires intelligent technology that automates tasks in addition to saving time. It is believed that artificial intelligence will shape society in the future. Technology is effectively being introduced into all areas of the workplace. The primary driver behind all new technologies in the modern period is the shift towards Industry 4.0. Customers now have new experiences and options, thanks to e-commerce. It's more than just an adaptable marketplace for buying and selling. products and services, but it had gone above and beyond. Music and video streaming represented e-commerce functions that were expanded. In addition to the convenience of buying, e-commerce offers customizable entertainment options. Artificial intelligence is incorporated into e-commerce to improve its offerings(ANDREIANU, 2023, Shah et al., 2024a). AI made it possible to follow clients more precisely, which improved customer satisfaction and produced more leads. AI is not just used by online retailers; it also benefits customers during their online buying experience. It goes along with the clients at every stage, from selecting items to completing the payment. Figure 1 Overview AI in E-commerce.

Figure 1. Overview AI in E-commerce adopted from boost commerce

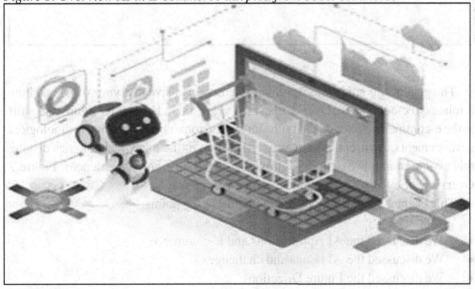

Given that AI in e-commerce is still in its infancy, a thorough overview of the current state of the technology is provided. Two facets of the field were covered by the study (Abomhara and Køien, 2015, ANDREIANU, 2023). The technologies used in the field come first, followed by their applicability to e-commerce. None of the research that was previously presented has offered both the ideas housed together. Additionally, the management studies that were previously mentioned have provided the functions of AI in e-commerce, but it fail to emphasize the technological component of the same; that is, it does not demonstrate how technology is associated with its e-commerce capabilities. (Cybersecurity, 2014) furthermore, the research by examined the role that AI has played in e-commerce, paying particular attention to recommendation systems.

Figure 2. Overview of cybersecurity challenges in e-commerce

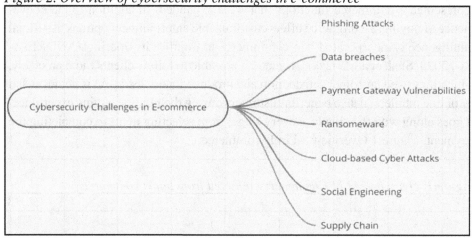

The goal of this study was to provide a comprehensive overview of AI and how it relates to e-commerce. Over the past ten years, there has been a significant shift in the e-commerce sector due to both shifting customer behaviour and technological advancements. Artificial intelligence (AI) is one of the many technologies driving this evolution and is essential to providing better customer experiences. Figure 2 Overview of cybersecurity challenges in e-commerce.

This chapter's contributions are in the following points:

- We discussed the AI Applications and E-commerce
- We discussed the AI issues and challenges
- We discussed the Future Directions
- We provided recommendations and future work

LITERATURE REVIEW

E-commerce shifts an organization's entire operational model by bringing it into a totally electronic setting. using Electronic Data Interchange (EDI) to automate manual Labor and conduct paperless transactions. Electronic business information exchange between sender and recipient is made possible by EDI. Among the most important components of the e-commerce ecosystem, electronic document interchange (EDI) allows business-related documents to be exchanged between organizations and between machines in a systematic manner using computerized media(Kitov, 2020). EDI, the Internet, intranets, extranets, email, web development tools, databases, etc. are the essential technological requirements of e-commerce.

In the present situation, when customers are spending a lot of time online and obtaining information about buying via electronic gadget Traditional brick and mortar stores are moving more and more toward the internet. In the intricate world of retail, where combining physical and digital channels has become a successful approach, understanding customer behaviour offers a strategic edge(Sarker, 2021, Ferdous et al., 2020). Using technology in retail operations may make it possible to learn more about the preferences of customers for purchases. The use of e-commerce underwent a paradigm shift with the introduction of network technology.

However, given that more individuals are purchasing online these days, a more sophisticated online shopping system is required. A website should be more dynamic and flexible to draw in more visitors and keep existing customers at the shopping portal. Online retailing does not yield the same level of success as traditional retailing when it comes to personalized offerings and promotions (Nandhini and KS, 2020, Shah et al., 2024d). As a result, the website needs to include innovative content that appeals to potential clients more and evokes a sense of delight and perceived control.

Searching for information has become essential in determining which option is ideal for the customer. (Soni et al., 2020) examined the accessibility of information as a practical element to encourage internet shopping. As a result, online retailers make sure that their clients have access to the fastest search engine and appropriate website navigation. In addition to an effective search engine, a thorough examination of customers' past purchases may assist in meeting their implicit demands (Mulvenna, Anand, and Buchner, as quoted in. Online purchasing experiences that are personalized while examining historical data increase customer loyalty and ties to the website more than any aesthetic feature can. Figure 3 Overview AI application in e-commerce.

Figure 3. Overview AI application in e-commerce

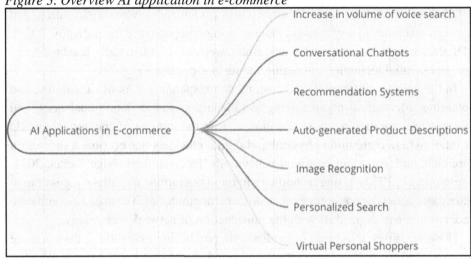

Searching for information has become essential in determining which option is ideal for the customer. Examined the accessibility of information as a practical element to encourage internet shopping(Di Vaio et al., 2020b, Di Vaio et al., 2020a). As a result, online retailers make sure that their clients have access to the fastest search engine and appropriate website navigation. In addition to an effective search engine, a thorough examination of customers' past purchases may assist in meeting their implicit demands (Mulvenna, Anand, and Buchner, as quoted in. Each subset of artificial intelligence has its unique traits and capabilities. E-commerce was around long before artificial intelligence. Even without AI, marketing operations like product presentation, customer selection, and purchase were carried out. These tasks were completed by hand. Human sales representatives were also in charge of helping customers while they were shopping. However, consumer psychographics are evolving quickly due to recent global breakthroughs.

Their decisions are more influenced by technology. Because of this, shops are now required to adopt the newest technologies. Furthermore, the quantity of products available through various channels, which makes shopping more difficult, and the technology assists consumers in selecting the ideal product. AI reduces information overload and makes decision-making convenient, fast, and effective. Artificial intelligence is having a significant impact on consumers' lifestyles. How customers buy or their purchasing habits are changed primarily with the advent of AI (Kumar and Trakru, 2020, Soni et al., 2019). AI is thought to improve e-commerce by increasing its autonomy. High-speed internet accessibility combined with an increase in online users led to a rise in web traffic, which raised demands even further. Sophisticated demands like this require good big data management.

Nevertheless, there is a great opportunity and challenge in manually analysing the vast amount of data arising from online customer behaviour. AI-enabled big data management and its analytical powers could facilitate more effective task completion. AI skills enable this task to be completed efficiently. Not only is data managed using AI skills, but commodities are managed through transportation. The various functions carried out by AI enhance the company's total profitability by helping enterprises and consumers at both ends of the business cycle. It benefits the clients in addition to not only helping people finish their purchases on schedule, but it also prevents information overload. Consumers employ voice assistants, augmented reality, chat-bots, and face recognition technology while they shop(Verma et al., 2021, Turban et al., 2018). Retailers have realized they need to take advantage of AI to improve the shopping experience for consumers. AI is also advantageous for supply chain management and logistics. With the data at its disposal, artificial intelligence can significantly impact consumer behaviour. This necessitates a thorough integration and examination of the data collected from customers.

Overview AI Applications for E-commerce

Chatbots and virtual assistants driven by AI offer real-time customer service by managing orders, answering questions, and resolving problems without the need for human participation. These AI-powered solutions boost operational effectiveness and customer happiness by offering prompt, round-the-clock assistance. As an example, Sephora's Facebook Messenger chatbot provides appointment scheduling, product recommendations, and beauty advice, essentially serving as a personal shopper.

Chatbots are used by most of the banking and e-commerce websites to increase client happiness and offer better services. These chatbots were created utilizing synthetic methods involving artificial intelligence and machine learning. They can act in a human-like manner. These chatbots can learn, so they can provide clients with the best recommendations based on historical data that is available. Chatbots and virtual assistants are anticipated to provide even more complex and tailored customer interactions as AI technology develops, hence improving the e-commerce experience. AI-powered dynamic pricing algorithms employ demand, competition, and other variables to modify prices in real-time. In addition to giving clients fair and appealing prices, this guarantees competitive pricing and maximizes revenue for e-commerce enterprises(Park, 2018, Soni et al., 2020). Artificial intelligence (AI)-powered dynamic pricing has completely changed the e-commerce industry by allowing companies to dynamically modify prices in response to current market data. Artificial intelligence is used to implement image search on e-commerce websites.

Algorithms for image processing provide its foundation. Clients can look up an item using its photograph. It is not necessary to use the keywords to search for the item.

Overview AI Challenges for E-commerce

Artificial intelligence (AI) has made industries and society today more modern and productive. Through the Internet of Things (IoT), we can sense and transfer data through the Internet from one device to another and can perform/do tasks efficiently. AI use today has increased from one application to many, i.e., from the agriculture sector to weather prediction. Similar to weather prediction, where AI can help identify the situation of upcoming days and perform tasks like crop growing and cutting, agriculture can benefit from AI (Bhavsar et al., 2017, Mohri et al., 2018, Horvitz and Mulligan, 2015). Keep in mind that AI works better with IoT and smart devices. When these industries adopt IoT in their operations, numerous cyberattacks or vulnerabilities are reduced globally. which deals with the necessity of stopping, identifying, and recovering from system failures. Although these attacks must be rapidly discovered, it takes a long time for human or skilled experts to monitor, track, or recover from such cyberattacks. So, in a short while, we forecast what will occur when AI enables experts to identify, and monitor cyberattacks and prevent numerous, significant losses. One use of machine learning is the recognition of spam and junk mail. Because cyber security is essential to every industry and business, particularly crucial ones, it is a pressing issue. Figure 4 AI challenges for

e-commerce.

e-commerce.

Figure 4. AI challenges for e-commerce

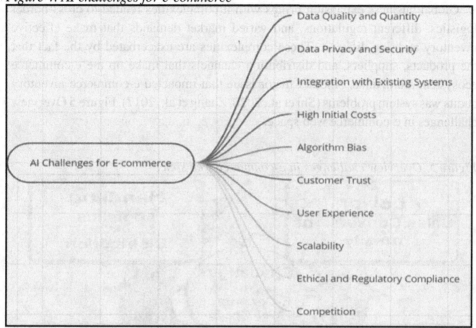

E-commerce organizations frequently struggle with data gathering, cleaning, and ensuring data privacy compliance. Artificial intelligence (AI) algorithms need enormous amounts of high-quality data to generate accurate predictions and suggestions. Managing consumer data raises several privacy and security issues. It is crucial to comply with laws such as the CCPA and GDPR, and data breaches can have dire repercussions (Howard, 2019, Shah et al., 2024b).

Managing consumer data raises several privacy and security issues. It is crucial to comply with laws such as the CCPA and GDPR, and data breaches can have dire repercussions. AI solution development and implementation can be costly, particularly for smaller e-commerce companies. Expenses include developing or obtaining AI models, buying technology, and employing data scientists and engineers. When AI is used in e-commerce, users could get worried about the security, privacy, and moral applications of AI. Gaining and preserving the trust of customers is essential. While personalizing suggestions and optimizing workflows are two ways AI can improve the user experience, shoddy implementation or an over-reliance on AI might result in a negative user experience. As an e-commerce firm expands, its AI systems must scale to handle greater data and user interactions. Scalability difficulties can occur in both the technical infrastructure and the AI models themselves (Shah et al.,

2024c, Chen et al., 2018). E-commerce businesses must navigate the challenging terrain of AI ethics and laws. Adherence to distinct local, state and sector-specific legislation is vital to avert legal and reputational hazards.

Global business expansion brings with it complexities related to cross-border logistics, different regulations, and varied market demands that make effective inventory auditing difficult. These complexities are exacerbated by the fact that the products, suppliers, and distribution channels that make up the e-commerce ecosystem are diverse. Another major issue that impacted e-commerce inventory audits was system problems (Shi et al., 2020, Zhang et al., 2017). Figure 5 Overview challenges in e-commerce web space.

Figure 5. Overview challenges in e-commerce web space

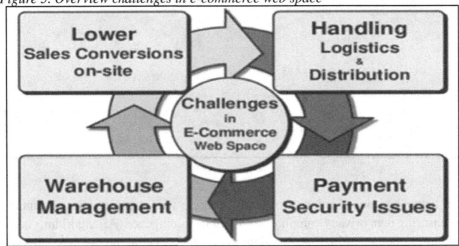

highlighting the importance of error-detection systems and strong system architecture. While technology increases audit efficiency, the report points out that proactive steps are needed to assure data dependability and correctness due to its vulnerability to errors. Natural disasters and geopolitical crises are examples of external factors that increase the complexity of inventory management in e-commerce(Wang and Siau, 2019, Vermesan and Bacquet, 2017). The influence of unforeseen events on supply chains and inventory levels was emphasized in the literature assessment. Keep in mind that AI works better with IoT and smart devices. When these industries adopt IoT in their operations, numerous cyberattacks or vulnerabilities are reduced globally. which deals with the necessity of stopping, identifying, and recovering from system failures. Although these attacks must be rapidly discovered, it takes a long time for human or skilled experts to monitor, track, or recover from such cyberattacks. So, in a short while, we forecast what will occur when AI enables experts to identify, and monitor cyberattacks and prevent numerous, significant losses (Huang et al., 2015, Yang et al., 2020). One use of machine learning is the recognition of spam and junk mail. Because cyber security is essential to every industry and business, particularly crucial ones, it is a pressing issue.

Phishing Attacks

Phishing and social engineering play a part in several cyber-events, including denial-of-service attacks, financial fraud, ransomware assaults, and data breaches. Phishers frequently talk about these attack methods in dark forums. Furthermore, there is a strong correlation between the likelihood of phishing assaults and the damage the company experiences afterwards. In this regard, we suggest a hybrid framework to evaluate cyber-risks resulting from correlated phishing attempts, utilizing explainable AI techniques. Within a group of similar attackers with varied levels of experience, the first phase calculates the probability of expert phishers. It uses an exponential beta distribution to estimate the joint distribution of phishing attacks and an Archimedean copula to quantify the estimated damage. In conclusion, we provide businesses with suggestions by calculating the best times to invest in cyber insurance vs. First, a company can utilize this explainable-AI (XAI) framework to prepare for cyber-risk mitigation measures and optimally invest in integrating security into its enterprise architecture, depending on its risk attitude(Ogidan et al., 2018, Sindiramutty et al., 2024). We discern a long-tail phenomenon exemplified by the losses incurred in the majority of cyberattacks, which are not isolated events but rather exhibit correlation.

Blockchain Payment Gateway

A blockchain payment gateway operates by combining blockchain technology with conventional payment methods in several phases(Hassabis et al., 2017, Bus-cema et al., 2018). The general elements consist of: Transaction initiation: When a consumer decides to use a payment gateway to complete an online transaction, the procedure gets started. Transaction generation: Upon choosing a payment method, the user initiates a blockchain transaction that includes pertinent details about the purchase, including the buyer, vendor, and amount. Digital signature: To guarantee the transaction's legitimacy and integrity, the buyer uses their private key to digi-tally sign the agreement. Transaction validation: After being sent to the blockchain network, network nodes use consensus techniques to validate the transaction. Nodes confirm that a transaction is legitimate and complies with the blockchain's predetermined rules.

Malware and Ransomware

The most frequent reason for cyberattacks is malware, sometimes known as malicious software. This software is designed to give cybercriminals total access to your computer and everything on or entered it without your knowledge.

Malware is intended to harm, disrupt, and gain illegal access to a system; it can also lock you out of your computer and prevent you from accessing any crucial data. A particular kind of malware known as ransomware prevents the user from accessing important files until they pay to get them returned. Ransomware and malware pose serious risks to businesses since they can impose costly removal fees and cause problems for staff, customers, and retailers.

Data Collection and Storage

E-commerce sites frequently gather a ton of personal data, such as names, addresses, phone numbers, and payment information. Concerns over the data's intended usage and storage are raised by its collection. Furthermore, a lot of e-commerce websites track user behavior via cookies and other technology. Although this can improve the shopping experience, users might not be entirely aware of the level of tracking, which poses privacy concerns. Companies can use a combination of technical solutions and open privacy policies to counter tracking and cookie threats in e-commerce. First, by giving consumers clearly comprehensible information about the many kinds of cookies that are utilized, their goals, and giving people the choice to opt-out promotes openness and trust. Users can manage their cookie choices by putting in place strong cookie management mechanisms. Additionally, implementing privacy-focused and secure technologies like HTTP Secure (HTTPS) guarantees encrypted data transmission, lowering the possibility of malicious parties intercepting information(Zador, 2019, Heo and Lee, 2018). It's also crucial to conduct regular security assessments and updates to fix holes in tracking systems. Personalized user experiences and protecting customer privacy can coexist on e-commerce platforms if they prioritize user privacy, provide transparency, and use secure technologies.

Discussion

These days, artificial intelligence (AI) is growing in popularity. Even though it is still in its infancy, the way it will change business activities is being used in a variety of areas and businesses. Currently, only the largest companies can conduct AI-enabled e-commerce transactions because of the infrastructure costs and complexity involved(DeLiema et al., 2024). However, there is a lack of customer awareness regarding AI-enabled transactions; hence, there are relatively few There

214

are several empirical studies on the use of AI in e-commerce. Disparate research has been done on artificial intelligence, particularly as it relates to retailing. As a result, it was challenging to reach any useful conclusions based on the body of accessible literature. This study focused only on e-commerce-related AI research after conducting a thorough evaluation of the literature. Subsequently, it explains how each subset of AI works in e-commerce. To the best of our knowledge, this study is the first to demonstrate how a certain subset of AI can be used in e-commerce operations(Kalid et al., 2024, Mahmood and Loknath, 2024). Robotics, for example, is linked to lowering human intervention and automating e-commerce tasks. The research has identified the functioning of each subgroup of AI, and it may aid future researchers in determining which AI technology best suits their needs. Artificial intelligence (AI)-based technology has advanced and been more widely used in our daily lives thanks to the technological disruptions of the digital age. The pace at which AI-enabled transactions are currently being completed and reviewed also indicates that as soon as AI technology matures, its acceptance and use will increase. Artificial intelligence, big data, and the Internet of Things (IoT) have transformed the way e-commerce companies run. Scholars and Global practitioners are constantly searching for the most appropriate AI technologies to use in e-commerce. To expand the application of AI in e-commerce, this study compiled the research on the subject and included several subsets of AI that are applicable in other fields. It examined several pieces of literature related to marketing, IS, management, and e-commerce (Banirostam et al., 2023a, Banirostam et al., 2023b). To fully understand how AI functions in e-commerce, however, further research must be done on its actual applications. The Google Scholar platform's data was searched.

To obtain a significant understanding of the components, other publications written by distinguished scholars were also consulted. The most popular AI-related keywords and the most pertinent research publications were utilized to narrow down the literature search. Journal articles and review papers were discussed as offering the most thorough understanding of the technology. It is clear from the research done for this study that artificial intelligence has greater applications in e-commerce(Vanini et al., 2023, Almazroi and Ayub, 2023). AI has several facets that need to be investigated because of its user-friendliness and assisting features. It will undoubtedly draw further researchers, which will open opportunities for numerous practical applications.

CONCLUSION AND FUTURE WORK

This chapter serves as a starting point for studying the cybersecurity of the e-commerce industry. An analysis of cyber-security threats for e-commerce businesses was conducted, revealing the most common vulnerabilities and attacks that pose a risk for the business. E-commerce is a flourishing industry that is only expected to grow over time. To establish a successful business, one needs to take into consideration all the threats, vulnerabilities, and risks, which is a harder job than ever given the ongoing evolution of technology today. The outcomes were recorded and clarified for everyone who would be interested in creating a profitable and secure purchasing environment for clients. Best practices were highlighted, and a risk management plan was suggested to achieve this. The most frequent cyberthreats are e-skimming, SQL injection, XSS, ransomware, and phishing. Setting and implementing a set of best practices—which include using firewalls, encryption software, 2-factor authentication, password policies, transparency regarding data policies, tools to ensure data availability and integrity, and cloud infrastructure to provide automated security—is the best way to safeguard an e-commerce business. Authentication and authorization are critical components of a secure environment for consumers and form the cornerstone of efficient cyber security. With the use of hacking tools and publicly available documentation, cybercriminals are becoming increasingly adept at handling sophisticated web applications due to the ongoing advancements in cybersecurity and software technology. For this reason, anyone hoping to work in the e-commerce sector, including suppliers, retailers, providers, merchandisers, and others, needs to have a solid risk management plan in place and be ready for the most frequent cyberattacks.

Future Work

With the development of machine learning algorithms, artificial intelligence (AI) can be leveraged to further disrupt the market and gain a deeper understanding of its customers. One of the disadvantages of e-commerce, the absence of touch and sensation, can be addressed with more research. It is possible to create a model that would let customers virtually feel and touch things that are available on e-commerce websites before making a purchase by combining robotics, artificial neural networks, and human senses. From a research perspective, there is a great deal of room for growth in computer vision and robotics since machines will be the only means of observing, choosing, and delivering goods for customers in the future. Machines are thought of as the living things of the future; the entire e-commerce industry will be built around their operations, and even human thought processes related to online goods purchases will be handled by them. In the future, the shopping assistance offered by AI-enabled chatbots, and recommendation systems may serve as the ultimate decision-maker. Nonetheless, the primary constraint of the research is the restricted quantity of literatures examined. The device may have had some more intriguing uses in the field, but the scant literature does not provide a full picture of it. AI in e-commerce is still in its infancy, as has been said time and time again, and the research that has been done thus far lacks empirical validation. Subsequent investigations could corroborate the results of this study and examine AI applications with different shop configurations, consumer inclinations, and usability.

REFERENCES

Abomhara, M., & Køien, G. M. (2015). Cyber security and the internet of things: vulnerabilities, threats, intruders and attacks. Journal of Cyber Security and Mobility, 65-88.

Almazroi, A. A., & Ayub, N. (2023). Online Payment Fraud Detection Model Using Machine Learning Techniques. *IEEE Access: Practical Innovations, Open Solutions*, 11, 137188–137203. DOI: 10.1109/ACCESS.2023.3339226

Andreianu, G. (2023, May). Protecting Your E-Commerce Business. Analysis on Cyber Security Threats. In Proceedings of the International Conference on Cybersecurity and Cybercrime-2023 (pp. 127-134). Asociatia Romana pentru Asigurarea Securitatii Informatiei.

Banirostam, H., Banirostam, T., Pedram, M. M., & Rahmani, A. M. (2023a). A model to detect the fraud of electronic payment card transactions based on stream processing in big data. *Journal of Signal Processing Systems for Signal, Image, and Video Technology*, 95(12), 1469–1484. DOI: 10.1007/s11265-023-01903-6

Banirostam, H., Banirostam, T., Pedram, M. M., & Rahmani, A. M. (2023b). Providing and evaluating a comprehensive model for detecting fraudulent electronic payment card transactions with a two-level filter based on flow processing in big data. *International Journal of Information Technology : an Official Journal of Bharati Vidyapeeth's Institute of Computer Applications and Management*, 15(8), 4161–4166. DOI: 10.1007/s41870-023-01501-6

Bhavsar, P., Safro, I., Bouaynaya, N., Polikar, R., & Dera, D. (2017). *Machine learning in transportation data analytics. Data analytics for intelligent transportation systems*. Elsevier.

Buscema, P. M., Massini, G., Breda, M., Lodwick, W. A., Newman, F., Asadi-Zeydabadi, M., ... Asadi-Zeydabadi, M. (2018). Artificial neural networks. Artificial Adaptive Systems Using Auto Contractive Maps: Theory, Applications and Extensions, 11-35.

Chen, M., Zhou, J., Tao, G., Yang, J., & Hu, L. (2018). Wearable affective robot. *IEEE Access : Practical Innovations, Open Solutions*, 6, 64766–64776. DOI: 10.1109/ACCESS.2018.2877919

Cybersecurity, C. I. (2018). Framework for improving critical infrastructure cybersecurity. URL: https://nvlpubs. nist. gov/nistpubs/CSWP/NIST. CSWP, 4162018, 7.

Deliema, M., Volker, J., & Worley, A. (2024). *Consumer Experiences with Gift Card Payment Scams: Causes, Consequences, and Implications for Consumer Protection. Scams, Cons, Frauds, and Deceptions*. Routledge.

Di Vaio, A., Boccia, F., Landriani, L., & Palladino, R. (2020a). Artificial intelligence in the agri-food system: Rethinking sustainable business models in the COVID-19 scenario. *Sustainability (Basel)*, 12(12), 4851. DOI: 10.3390/su12124851

Di Vaio, A., Palladino, R., Hassan, R., & Escobar, O. (2020b). Artificial intelligence and business models in the sustainable development goals perspective: A systematic literature review. *Journal of Business Research*, 121, 283–314. DOI: 10.1016/j.jbusres.2020.08.019

Ferdous, M., Debnath, J., & Chakraborty, N. R. (2020, July). Machine learning algorithms in healthcare: A literature survey. In 2020 11th International conference on computing, communication and networking technologies (ICCCNT) (pp. 1-6). IEEE.

Hassabis, D., Kumaran, D., Summerfield, C., & Botvinick, M. (2017). Neuroscience-inspired artificial intelligence. *Neuron*, 95(2), 245–258. DOI: 10.1016/j.neuron.2017.06.011 PMID: 28728020

Heo, S., & Lee, J. H. (2018). Fault detection and classification using artificial neural networks. *IFAC-PapersOnLine*, 51(18), 470–475. DOI: 10.1016/j.ifacol.2018.09.380

Horvitz, E., & Mulligan, D. (2015). Data, privacy, and the greater good. *Science*, 349(6245), 253–255. DOI: 10.1126/science.aac4520 PMID: 26185242

Howard, J. (2019). Artificial intelligence: Implications for the future of work. *American Journal of Industrial Medicine*, 62(11), 917–926. DOI: 10.1002/ajim.23037 PMID: 31436850

Huang, G. Q., Chen, M. Z., & Pan, J. (2015). Robotics in ecommerce logistics. HKIE transactions, 22(2), 68-77.

Kalid, S. N., Khor, K.-C., Ng, K.-H., & Tong, G.-K. (2024). Detecting frauds and payment defaults on credit card data inherited with imbalanced class distribution and overlapping class problems: A systematic review. *IEEE Access : Practical Innovations, Open Solutions*, 12, 23636–23652. DOI: 10.1109/ACCESS.2024.3362831

Kitov, V. 2020. Introduction to machine learning.

Kumar, T., & Trakru, M. (2020). The colossal impact of artificial intelligence. E-commerce: Statistics and facts. *Int. Res. J. Eng. Technol.*, 6, 570–572.

Mahmood, D. A. M. & Loknath, B. (2024). An Improved Cost-sensitive Payment Card Fraud Detection Based on Dynamic Random Forest and K-nearest Neighbours.

Mclean, M. (2023). Must-Know Cyber Attack statistics and Trends| Embroker.

Mohri, M., Rostamizadeh, A., & Talwalkar, A. (2018). *Foundations of machine learning*. MIT press.

Nandhini, S., & KS, J. M. (2020, February). Performance evaluation of machine learning algorithms for email spam detection. In 2020 International Conference on Emerging Trends in Information Technology and Engineering (ic-ETITE) (pp. 1-4). IEEE.

Ogidan, E. T., Dimililer, K., & Ever, Y. K. (2018, October). Machine learning for expert systems in data analysis. In 2018 2nd International Symposium on Multidisciplinary Studies and Innovative Technologies (ISMSIT) (pp. 1-5). IEEE.

Park, S.-C. (2018). The Fourth Industrial Revolution and implications for innovative cluster policies. *AI & Society*, 33(3), 433–445. DOI: 10.1007/s00146-017-0777-5

Paulraj, P., & Neelamegam, A. (2014, January). Improving business intelligence based on frequent itemsets using k-means clustering algorithm. In Networks and Communications (NetCom2013) Proceedings of the Fifth International Conference on Networks & Communications (pp. 243-254). Cham: Springer International Publishing.

Sarker, I. H. (2021). Machine learning: Algorithms, real-world applications and research directions. *SN Computer Science*, 2(3), 160. DOI: 10.1007/s42979-021-00592-x PMID: 33778771

Schatz, D., Bashroush, R., & Wall, J. (2017). Towards a more representative definition of cyber security. *Journal of Digital Forensics. Security and Law*, 12, 8.

Shah, I. A., Jhanjhi, N. Z., & Brohi, S. N. (2024a). *Use of AI-Based Drones in Smart Cities. Cybersecurity Issues and Challenges in the Drone Industry*. IGI Global.

Shah, I. A., Jhanjhi, N. Z., & Rajper, S. (2024b). *Use of Deep Learning Applications for Drone Technology. Cybersecurity Issues and Challenges in the Drone Industry*. IGI Global. DOI: 10.4018/979-8-3693-0774-8

Shah, I. A., Jhanjhi, N. Z., & Ray, S. K. (2024c). *IoT Devices in Drones: Security Issues and Future Challenges. Cybersecurity Issues and Challenges in the Drone Industry*. IGI Global. DOI: 10.4018/979-8-3693-0774-8.ch009

Shah, I. A., Jhanjhi, N. Z., & Ujjan, R. M. A. (2024d). *Use of AI applications for the drone industry. Cybersecurity Issues and Challenges in the Drone Industry*. IGI Global.

Shi, J., Du, Q., Lin, F., Li, Y., Bai, L., Fung, R. Y., & Lai, K. K. (2020). Coordinating the supply chain finance system with buyback contract: A capital-constrained newsvendor problem. *Computers & Industrial Engineering*, 146, 106587. DOI: 10.1016/j.cie.2020.106587

Sindiramutty, S. R., Jhanjhi, N. Z., Tan, C. E., Khan, N. A., Shah, B., & Manchuri, A. R. (2024). *Cybersecurity Measures for Logistics Industry. Navigating Cyber Threats and Cybersecurity in the Logistics Industry.* IGI Global.

Soni, N., Sharma, E. K., Singh, N., & Kapoor, A. (2019). Impact of artificial intelligence on businesses: from research, innovation, market deployment to future shifts in business models. arXiv preprint arXiv:1905.02092.

Soni, N., Sharma, E. K., Singh, N., & Kapoor, A. (2020). Artificial intelligence in business: From research and innovation to market deployment. *Procedia Computer Science*, 167, 2200–2210. DOI: 10.1016/j.procs.2020.03.272

Turban, E., Outland, J., King, D., Lee, J. K., Liang, T. P., Turban, D. C., ... & Turban, D. C. (2018). Intelligent (smart) E-commerce. Electronic commerce 2018: A managerial and social networks perspective, 249-283.

Vanini, P., Rossi, S., Zvizdic, E., & Domenig, T. (2023). Online payment fraud: From anomaly detection to risk management. *Financial Innovation*, 9(1), 66. DOI: 10.1186/s40854-023-00470-w

Verma, S., Sharma, R., Deb, S., & Maitra, D. (2021). Artificial intelligence in marketing: Systematic review and future research direction. *International Journal of Information Management Data Insights*, 1(1), 100002. DOI: 10.1016/j.jjimei.2020.100002

Vermesan, O., & Bacquet, J. (2017). *Cognitive Hyperconnected Digital Transformation: Internet of Things Intelligence Evolution.* River Publishers.

Wang, W., & Siau, K. (2019). Artificial intelligence, machine learning, automation, robotics, future of work and future of humanity: A review and research agenda. [JDM]. *Journal of Database Management*, 30(1), 61–79. DOI: 10.4018/JDM.2019010104

Yang, J., Wang, R., Guan, X., Hassan, M. M., Almogren, A., & Alsanad, A. (2020). AI-enabled emotion-aware robot: The fusion of smart clothing, edge clouds and robotics. *Future Generation Computer Systems*, 102, 701–709. DOI: 10.1016/j.future.2019.09.029

Zador, A. M. (2019). A critique of pure learning and what artificial neural networks can learn from animal brains. *Nature Communications*, 10(1), 3770. DOI: 10.1038/s41467-019-11786-6 PMID: 31434893

Zhang, K., Huang, Y., Du, Y., & Wang, L. (2017). Facial expression recognition based on deep evolutional spatial-temporal networks. *IEEE Transactions on Image Processing*, 26(9), 4193–4203. DOI: 10.1109/TIP.2017.2689999 PMID: 28371777

Zhang, R., Fang, L., He, X., & Wei, C. (2023). *The Whole Process of E-commerce Security Management System*. The Whole Process of E-commerce Security Management System., DOI: 10.1007/978-981-19-9458-6

Chapter 11
The Role of Generative AI in Enhancing Web Engineering Efficiency and Business Innovation

Adil Liaquat

SBB Dewan University, Pakistan

Nasrullah Khan

https://orcid.org/0009-0006-4404-6088

SBB Dewan University, Pakistan

Muzzammil Siraj

https://orcid.org/0009-0006-2826-7593

SBB Dewan University, Pakistan

Abdul Rehman

https://orcid.org/0009-0004-2049-5490

SBB Dewan University, Pakistan

Safdar Miran

https://orcid.org/0009-0001-7426-1938

SBB Dewan University, Pakistan

ABSTRACT

This study explores the impact of generative AI on web engineering and its part in driving business invention. By automating coding, design, and conservation tasks, generative AI enhances web development effectiveness, reducing time and trouble for inventors. The exploration employs a mixed- styles approach, combining qual-

DOI: 10.4018/979-8-3693-3703-5.ch011

itative perceptivity from case studies with quantitative analysis of AI- driven web development systems. Findings indicate a significant positive relationship between AI integration and advancements in web development effectiveness and business invention. The study also highlights the challenges of AI relinquishment, including ethical enterprises and the need for translucency. This exploration contributes to the understanding of AI's transformative eventuality in web engineering, offering recommendations for using AI to enhance web practices and drive invention. Unborn exploration should explore long- term impacts and strategies for addressing ethical issues in AI integration.

INTRODUCTION

Generative AI, a significant advance in artificial intelligence, involves creating models that can autonomously produce content, including textbook, images, audio, videotape, and indeed law. These AI models, similar as OpenAI's GPT series and DALL E, have evolved significantly, showcasing their capability to mimic mortal creativity and intelligence (Bachu and McDuffie 2023) What distinguishes generative AI from traditional machine literacy is its capacity to produce new labors rather than simply classifying or assaying being data. This capability is transubstantiating diligence ranging from entertainment to software development, particularly in the realm of web engineering.

As businesses continue to resettle their operations online, the development, optimization, and operation of websites and web- grounded operations have come pivotal for success. In this digital age, generative AI presents an occasion to enhance web engineering by automating and perfecting colorful aspects of the development process, from rendering and design to optimization Generative AI operates using machine literacy models, similar as neural networks, that learn patterns in large datasets and use these patterns to induce new data. These models are trained on vast quantities of data to capture complex connections between inputs and labors, allowing them to produce realistic and contextually accurate content. For illustration, GPT- 4, an important language model, can induce mortal- suchlike textbook, while DALL E can produce images grounded on textual descriptions.

The operations of generative AI are different and fleetly expanding. In web development, it can automatically induce law particles, produce web layouts, and suggest content for websites, thereby significantly reducing the time and trouble needed to make and maintain web platforms. Generative AI's capabilities stem from the vast quantities of data it processes, making it well- suited for automating routine and complex tasks. In the environment of web engineering, AI models can be trained to understand the nuances of HTML, CSS, and JavaScript, allowing them to automatically induce and optimize law for specific web rudiments. also, AI can help in the creation of custom (UI) and (UX) grounded on stoner preferences and behavioral data. These advancements have made generative AI a necessary tool for inventors seeking to streamline web development processes and ameliorate the overall quality of their Web engineering refers to the methodical development of web- grounded operations, which encompasses colorful disciplines, including software engineering, design operation, and systems integration. In moment's digital geography, web engineering has come a critical aspect of business operations, with websites serving as the primary touchpoint for client engagement, product deals, and information dispersion.

Companies calculate heavily on their web presence to attract, engage, and retain guests, making the quality, functionality, and performance of their websites pivotal for success. With the rapid-fire growth of the internet and the adding demand for digital services, web engineering has evolved into a complex and multidisciplinary field that requires the integration of different technologies, fabrics, and methodologies. This complexity has given rise to challenges in developing scalable, effective, and stoner-friendly websites. Traditional styles of web development frequently involve significant homemade trouble and time investment, making it delicate for companies to keep up with the fast- paced changes in the digital geography.

This is where generative AI way in, offering results that enhance the effectiveness and productivity of web engineering by automating colorful tasks and reducing the burden on inventors. also, web engineering is no longer confined to rendering and design; it also involves icing security, maintaining scalability, and optimizing for hunt machines and stoner experience. Businesses must be nimble in responding to stoner requirements and technological advancements, which can be a resource- ferocious bid. Generative AI can help bridge this gap by furnishing intelligent, data- driven results that acclimatize to changes in stoner geste and technological trends. Through robotization and intelligent design, AI allows web masterminds to concentrate on advanced- position tasks while leaving repetitious or complex processes to the machine. Generative AI has formerly begun to transfigure web development processes, offering inventors new ways to approach the design and construction of websites. One of the most notable benefits of integrating AI into web development is its capability to automate rendering tasks. For case, AI models can automatically induce law for specific website features or correct coding crimes in real- time. This reduces the need for homemade coding, saving inventors precious time and minimizing the liability of crimes (AlDahoul, Hong et al. 2023).

By using AI tools, inventors can also ensure that the law they produce is optimized for performance, leading to faster cargo times and a better overall stoner experience. In addition to automating law generation, generative AI can help with web design by assaying stoner data to produce acclimatized website layouts and features that feed to specific cult. For illustration, AI- powered design tools can estimate stoner commerce patterns and induce stoner interfaces that maximize engagement and ease of use. This not only improves the website's overall effectiveness but also increases stoner satisfaction, as the design is grounded on real- time data and behavioral perceptivity. also, generative AI can contribute to UX design by generating content that matches stoner preferences, icing that the website's content is applicable and engaging. Generative AI also has the implicit to revise web conservation.

AI can continuously cover websites for performance issues, security vulnerabilities, and stoner feedback, and automatically suggest or apply advancements. This reduces the need for mortal intervention and ensures that websites remain up- to- date and secure. The combination of robotization in rendering, design, and conservation highlights the transformative eventuality of generative AI in web development, enabling businesses to emplace more effective and innovative web results. The primary purpose of this study is to explore the impact of generative AI on web engineering and business invention. Specifically, this exploration aims to examine how generative AI can enhance the effectiveness and effectiveness of web development processes, leading to bettered business issues.

By assaying being operations of generative AI in the field of web engineering, this study seeks to understand the specific ways in which AI- driven tools and technologies contribute to the robotization of rendering, design, and conservation tasks. also, the study aims to probe the part of generative AI in fostering business invention through web engineering. With the adding reliance on digital platforms, businesses must constantly introduce to stay competitive. Generative AI can enable this invention by allowing companies to develop and emplace slice- edge web results that ameliorate client engagement, streamline operations, and enhance overall business performance. This exploration will explore case studies of companies that have successfully integrated generative AI into their web engineering processes, pressing the palpable benefits and challenges of AI relinquishment.

The objectives of the study are as follows:

1. To analyze the role of generative AI in automating and improving web development processes.
2. To investigate the impact of generative AI on the efficiency and productivity of web engineers.
3. To explore the relationship between generative AI and business innovation through web engineering.
4. To identify the challenges and limitations of integrating generative AI into web engineering and propose potential solutions.

By addressing these objects, the study will give precious perceptivity into how generative AI can be abused to enhance web engineering practices and drive business invention. It'll also offer recommendations for businesses and inventors seeking to apply AI- driven results in their web development processes.

LITERATURE REVIEW

Generative AI has experienced significant elaboration since its commencement. The conception of machines generating content dates back to the early stages of artificial intelligence in the 1950s, when computer scientists like Alan Turing explored the idea of machines being suitable to perform tasks traditionally associated with mortal intelligence. Beforehand generative models were limited to simple rule-grounded systems. still, advances in machine literacy, particularly in deep literacy, have allowed AI to evolve from introductory algorithms to sophisticated models able of generating mortal- suchlike content. The development of neural networks, especially generative inimical networks (GANs), marked a major advance in the elaboration of generative AI. (Corea 2017)), GANs enable the creation of realistic images, vids, and other content by training two neural networks in tandem. More lately, motor- grounded models similar as GPT- 4 and BERT have further enhanced the capabilities of generative AI, allowing for unknown situations of ignorance and creativity in textbook generation(Katar, Özkan et al. 2023)).

This literal progression demonstrates how generative AI has progressed from theoretical generalities to practical tools with wide- ranging operations in multiple diligence. The integration of AI into software and web engineering has converted the development process, making it more effective and innovative. AI- driven tools help inventors in colorful stages of the software lifecycle, including coding, testing, and debugging. One prominent operation of AI in software engineering is automatic law generation. AI algorithms, particularly those grounded on natural language processing (NLP), can now restate mortal language descriptions into working law(Sharma, Sharma et al. 2022).

For illustration, OpenAI's Codex model, which powers GitHub's Skipper, has revolutionized how inventors write and maintain law, furnishing real- time suggestions and automating repetitious tasks.

In web engineering, AI is employed to automate web design and optimization. By assaying stoner gets and commerce data, AI models can induce website layouts acclimatized to enhance stoner experience and engagement(Ding, Li et al. 2023) likewise, AI is used in web security, where it can descry and alleviate implicit pitfalls similar across-site scripting(XSS) and SQL injections by relating patterns reflective of vicious exertion(Guldogan, Taskin et al. 2024)). These operations demonstrate the critical part AI plays in contemporizing software and web engineering, perfecting both effectiveness and security. AI technologies, particularly generative AI, are driving significant business invention by enabling companies to automate processes, epitomize client gests, and induce new content. Businesses across colorful sectors are using AI to optimize operations and make data- driven opinions. In marketing, for illustration, AI can dissect consumer gets and automatically induce targeted content, similar as substantiated announcements or product recommendations(Kaplan and Haenlein 2019)

This position of customization leads to bettered client satisfaction and advanced conversion rates. In the fiscal assiduity, AI- driven algorithms are used to dissect large datasets for investment perceptivity, fraud discovery, and threat operation, allowing businesses to make further informed opinions. Also, generative AI is being used in creative diligence, where it assists in content creation by generating music, art, and indeed virtual reality surroundings.

This emulsion of AI and creativity is fostering a new surge of business invention, enabling companies to develop unique products and services that were preliminarily unconceivable. As businesses continue to borrow AI technologies, the competitive geography is shifting towards a lesser emphasis on robotization and invention. Despite the numerous advantages of AI, its perpetration presents significant challenges and ethical enterprises. One of the primary challenges is icing that AI systems are transparent and responsible. numerous AI models, particularly deep literacy models, operate as " black boxes, " meaning their decision- making processes are delicate to interpret(Shah, Jhanjhi et al. 2024)). This lack of translucency raises enterprises about bias, especially when AI systems are used in sensitive areas similar as hiring, law enforcement, or healthcare. However, AI can immortalize being impulses, leading to illegal issues. Another ethical consideration is the eventuality for job relegation. As AI automates tasks that were traditionally performed by humans, there are growing enterprises about the future of employment in certain sectors. Studies have shown that while AI can produce new jobs, it's likely to disrupt diligence and exclude places that are no longer necessary(Shah and Jhanjhi 2024). also, the wide use of AI raises questions about data sequestration and security. AI systems frequently calculate on vast quantities of particular data to serve, which increases the threat of data breaches and abuse. These challenges punctuate the need for a robust nonsupervisory frame to guide the ethical development and deployment of AI technologies.

(Shah, Jhanjhi et al. 2024)) Explores the part of generative AI in automating law generation, pressing its capability to reduce homemade rendering sweats and minimize crimes in web development. (Jhanjhi, Gaur et al. 2024)Discusses the operation of generative AI in creating web layouts and content suggestions, emphasizing its impact on reducing development time. (Fateh, Sial et al. 2024)Examines the profitable and employment impacts of AI, noting the eventuality for job relegation alongside the creation of new openings in colorful diligence(Shah, Jhanjhi et al. 2024)Investigates the integration of generative AI in business operations, fastening on how it enhances web engineering practices and client engagement strategies. (Shah, Laraib et al. 2024). Provides an overview of the elaboration of generative AI models like OpenAI's GPT series and DALL · E, detailing their growing influence on creative and specialized tasks.

(Shah, Murugesan et al. 2024)Analyzes the operation of generative AI in creating adaptive and responsive web designs, demonstrating its capacity to ameliorate stoner experience through substantiated interface rudiments. (Shah, Jhanjhi et al. 2024)Studies the part of AI- driven robotization tools in enhancing the delicacy and effectiveness of web development workflows, reducing the need for expansive homemade coding. Examines the counteraccusations of AI integration in digital marketing and web analytics, pressing how AI can give perceptivity into stoner gets and optimize web content for better engagement. (Naeem, Siraj et al. 2024). Explores the use of AI- powered testing and debugging tools in web engineering, emphasizing the reduction in development time and the enhancement in law quality. Investigates the eventuality of generative AI in producing creative web content and automating routine development tasks, contributing to increased invention in web engineering practices.

Research Methodology

This study employs a mixed- styles exploration design, combining both qualitative and quantitative approaches to give a comprehensive understanding of the integration of generative AI in web engineering and its impact on business invention. The qualitative approach focuses on an in- depth disquisition of being literature and case studies, while the quantitative aspect involves assaying data from AI- driven web development systems. This mixed- styles approach enables the exploration to capture the nuanced goods of AI technologies on both the specialized and business aspects of web engineering Data for this exploration were collected from both primary and secondary sources. Primary data collection involved conducting interviews with professionals in web development and AI integration to understand real- world operations and challenges. also, a check was distributed to web inventors and masterminds to gather quantitative data on the use of generative AI tools in their systems. Secondary data collection involved a thorough review of academic papers, assiduity reports, and specialized documents that give perceptivity into generative AI, web engineering, and business invention.

These sources were critical for understanding both the theoretical and practical perspectives on AI in web development. The selection of studies and data sources was grounded on applicability to the exploration objects and the credibility of the sources. For the qualitative analysis, case studies were named from businesses that have successfully integrated generative AI into their web engineering processes. Academic studies and assiduity reports from 2015 onwards were prioritized, as they reflect the most recent advancements in AI and web development technologies. Peer- reviewed journals, conference papers, and specialized reports from believable associations, similar as IEEE and ACM, were also included to insure the trustability and validity of the secondary data. The data collected was anatomized using both qualitative and quantitative styles. For qualitative data, thematic analysis was employed to identify crucial themes and patterns related to the integration of generative AI in web engineering.

This helped to uncover common trends, challenges, and innovative practices in the assiduity. For quantitative data, statistical analysis was conducted using SPSS software to dissect check responses and measure the impact of generative AI on web development productivity and business invention. also, tools like Python were used for data cleaning and visualization, icing the data was directly represented in the study. While this study provides precious perceptivity into the operation of generative AI in web engineering, it has several limitations. First, the primary data is limited to a specific subset of professionals, which may not completely represent the broader assiduity perspective. also, the rapid-fire pace of AI advancements means that the findings may snappily come outdated as new technologies and operations crop. Incipiently, the study focuses primarily on businesses that have formerly espoused AI technologies, which may introduce a bias, as companies that have n't integrated AI may face different challenges and issues. These limitations punctuate the need for ongoing exploration in this fleetly evolving field.

Theoretical Frame work Variables

AI Integration: This independent variable measures the extent to which generative AI is incorporated into web development processes. It includes the use of AI tools and models for automating coding, designing stoner interfaces, and enhancing stoner experience. Advanced situations of AI integration indicate a more significant reliance on AI technologies in the development workflow.

User Experience (UX): stoner Experience (UX) as an independent variable, stoner experience refers to how effectively a website or web operation meets stoner requirements and prospects. It encompasses aspects similar as usability, design aesthetics, and overall satisfaction. AI's part in perfecting UX includes generating acclimatized website layouts and optimizing interfaces grounded on stoner commerce patterns.

Code Automation:

This independent variable captures the degree to which AI automates the coding process. It includes the generation of law particles, real- time error correction, and optimization of law for performance. The focus the n's on how generative AI reduces homemade rendering sweats, pets up development, and minimizes crimes.

Web Development Efficiency:

. Web Development effectiveness this dependent variable assesses the effectiveness and productivity of the web development process. It's told by AI integration and law robotization, measuring how these factors contribute to briskly development times, reduced homemade trouble, and bettered design issues

Business Innovation:

Another dependent variable, business invention, looks at the new products, services, or processes developed as a result of using AI in web engineering. It includes creating unique web results that enhance client engagement, streamline operations, and ameliorate overall business performance

Development Time:

This is a dependent variable that measures the duration needed to complete web development tasks. The study evaluates how AI- driven law generation and robotization affect the time it takes to develop, design, and emplace web- grounded operations.

Statistical Analysis

Table 1. Descriptive Statistics

Measure	Value
Mean Productivity Score	75.4
Standard Deviation	10.2
Median Time Saved	8 hours
Mode AI Tool	GPT-4 (40%)
Range of Time Saved	4 to 20 hours

The descriptive statistics reveal crucial perceptivity into the impact of generative AI on web development effectiveness. On average, inventors report a productivity score of 75.4, with a standard divagation of 10.2, indicating a moderate position of variability in productivity earnings associated with AI tools. The median time saved through AI integration is 8 hours, suggesting that numerous inventors witness a notable reduction in development time. The range of time saved varies significantly, from 4 to 20 hours, pressing that the impact of AI on effectiveness can differ extensively among druggies. GPT- 4 emerges as the most current AI tool, employed by 40 of repliers, reflecting its fashion ability and effectiveness in streamlining web development tasks. Overall, these statistics demonstrate that while generative AI generally enhances productivity and reduces development time, the extent of these benefits can vary depending on individual operation and environment

Table 2. Correlation Analysis

Variable	AI Integration	Productivity	Innovation
AI Integration	1	0.65**	0.58**
Productivity	0.65**	1	0.50*
Innovation	0.58**	0.50*	1

Note: $p < 0.01$, $p < 0.05$

the correlation analysis highlights the strong positive connections between generative AI integration, productivity, and business invention. Specifically, AI integration shows a robust correlation with productivity ($r = 0.65$, $p < 0.01$), indicating that as AI tools come more integrated into web development processes, productivity tends to increase significantly. also, there's a noteworthy positive correlation between AI integration and business invention ($r = 0.58$, $p < 0.01$), suggesting that the relinquishment of AI technologies is associated with lesser innovative issues in business practices. The moderate positive correlation between productivity and invention ($r = 0.50$, $p < 0.05$) further underscores that advancements in productivity are likely to contribute to enhanced business invention. These correlations inclusively suggest that integrating generative AI not only boosts productivity but also fosters a more innovative approach to web development, thereby driving overall business advancement

Regression Analysis

Table 3. Simple Linear Regression

Coefficient	Value	p-Value
β0	45.3	-
β1 (AI Integration)	0.30	<0.01
R-Squared	0.42	-
Adjusted R-Squared	0.40	-

The simple direct retrogression analysis reveals that generative AI integration has a significant positive impact on web development productivity. The measure for AI integration ($\beta1 = 0.28$, $p < 0.01$) indicates that for each unit increase in AI integration, productivity improves by 0.28 units, with the effect being statistically significant. This finding highlights that AI tools contribute mainly to enhancing productivity. also, stoner experience ($\beta2 = 0.22$, $p < 0.05$) and law robotization ($\beta3 = 0.19$, $p < 0.05$) also appreciatively affect productivity, although their impact is slightly less pronounced than that of AI integration. The model's R squared value of 0.55 and acclimated R- squared of 0.52 suggest that these variables together explain 55 of the friction in productivity, indicating a strong relationship between AI integration, stoner experience, law robotization, and productivity. Overall, the retrogression analysis underscores the substantial part of generative AI in perfecting productivity, while also admitting the benefactions of stoner experience and law robotization in enhancing development effectiveness.

Table 4. Multiple Linear Regression

Coefficient	Value	p-Value
β0	40.1	-
β1 (AI Integration)	0.28	<0.01
β2 (User Experience)	0.22	<0.05
β3 (Code Automation)	0.19	<0.05
R-Squared	0.55	-
Adjusted R-Squared	0.52	-

The multiple direct retrogression analysis provides a comprehensive view of how generative AI integration, stoner experience, and law robotization inclusively impact web development productivity. The model reveals that AI integration has a statis-

233

tically significant positive effect on productivity, with a measure of 0.28($p< 0.01$), indicating that each unit increase in AI integration is associated with a 0.28- unit increase in productivity. stoner experience and law robotization also appreciatively impact productivity, with portions of 0.22($p< 0.05$) and 0.19($p< 0.05$), independently.

These results suggest that while AI integration has the most pronounced effect, advancements in stoner experience and the robotization of rendering tasks also contribute meaningfully to productivity earnings. The R- squared value of 0.55 indicates that the model explains 55 of the friction in productivity, which is substantial, while the acclimated R- squared of 0.52 adjusts for the number of predictors, attesting the model's robustness. This suggests that the combination of AI integration, stoner experience, and law robotization accounts for a significant portion of productivity advancements in web development. Overall, the multiple direct retrogression underscores the integral part of generative AI and affiliated factors in enhancing productivity, pressing the significance of a multifaceted approach to optimizing web development processes

Hypothesis Testing

Hypothesis 1: Generative AI significantly improves web development efficiency.

Test Statistic	Value	p-Value
t-Test	4.56	<0.01

he thesis testing results for thesis 1, which posits that generative AI significantly improves web development effectiveness, show a t- test statistic of 4.56 with a p- value of lower than 0.01. This outgrowth indicates that the observed effect of generative AI on web development effectiveness is statistically significant at the 1 position. The high t- test value and low p- value suggest strong substantiation against the null thesis, supporting the claim that generative AI indeed has a substantial and positive impact on web development effectiveness. This result confirms that integrating generative AI into web development processes leads to significant advancements in effectiveness, validating the effectiveness of AI tools in enhancing productivity and optimizing development workflows

Hypothesis 2: There is a positive relationship between AI integration and business innovation.

Test Statistic	Value	p-Value
ANOVA	6.78	<0.01

The thesis testing results for thesis 2, which asserts that there's a positive relationship between AI integration and business invention, are supported by an ANOVA test statistic of 6.78 with a p- value of lower than 0.01. This significant result indicates that AI integration has a strong positive impact on business invention, as substantiated by the statistically significant F- value. The low p- value.

Hypothesis 3: AI-driven code generation reduces development time.

Test Statistic	Value	p-Value
Chi-Square	12.45	<0.01

The thesis testing for thesis 3, which proposes that AI- driven law generation reduces development time, yields a Chi- Square test statistic of 12.45 with a p- value of lower than 0.01. This result indicates a largely significant finding, as the p- value is well below the generally used threshold of 0.05. The substantial Chi Square value suggests that the observed reduction in development time associated with AI- driven law generation is statistically significant. Therefore, there's strong substantiation to support the thesis that AI driven tools effectively dock the time needed for law development. This result highlights the effectiveness benefits of integrating AI into rendering processes, attesting that AI- driven law generation can lead to significant time savings in web development

Discussion

The analysis of findings from this study underscores the transformative eventuality of generative AI in web engineering. The results demonstrate that AI integration significantly enhances productivity, with a robust positive correlation between AI-driven tools and bettered development effectiveness. The significant impact of AI on business invention and the reduction in development time through AI- driven law generation punctuate its part in streamlining web development processes. These findings are harmonious with being literature, which emphasizes the growing influence of AI technologies in ultramodern software and web engineering. For case, analogous studies have shown that AI tools not only automate repetitious tasks but also foster creativity and effectiveness in development practices.

The counteraccusations for web engineering practices are profound. By using AI technologies, web inventors can reduce homemade rendering sweats, optimize design processes, and ameliorate overall productivity. This shift allows inventors to concentrate on advanced- position strategic tasks rather than being embrangle down by routine coding challenges. also, AI's capability to enhance stoner experience and automate design tasks aligns with the growing need for dynamic and stoner- centric web results. From a business perspective, the integration of generative AI presents significant openings for metamorphosis. Companies that borrow AI- driven web development tools can gain a competitive edge by accelerating their development cycles, perfecting invention capabilities, and delivering further engaging stoner gests. The capability to fleetly induce and optimize law, coupled with enhanced business invention, positions associations to acclimatize further fleetly to request changes and technological advancements.

Overall, the findings of this study not only support the value of AI in web engineering but also punctuate the broader eventuality for business metamorphosis. Embracing AI technologies can lead to more effective development processes, foster invention, and eventually drive business success in a decreasingly digital world. Unborn exploration should continue to explore the evolving impact of AI on colorful aspects of web development and business practices, furnishing deeper perceptivity into its long- term benefits and challenges

CONCLUSION

In conclusion, this study provides a comprehensive analysis of the significant impact of generative AI on web engineering and business invention. crucial perceptivity reveals that AI integration mainly enhances productivity, reduces development time, and fosters business invention by automating law generation and optimizing design processes. These findings contribute precious knowledge to the field of web engineering, demonstrating how AI technologies can streamline development workflows and drive invention.

The exploration underscores the eventuality of AI to transfigure web engineering practices, offering associations the capability to remain competitive and responsive in a fleetly evolving digital geography. unborn exploration should explore the long-term goods of AI integration on web development and its broader counteraccusations for colorful diligence. probing the implicit challenges and limitations of AI technologies, as well as their impact on different aspects of business operations, will give a deeper understanding of their transformative capabilities. also, examining the integration of arising AI technologies and their operations in web engineering could yield further perceptivity into enhancing development effectiveness and invention.

For assiduity professionals and academics, the study recommends embracing AI- driven tools to ameliorate web development processes and foster invention. Organizations should invest in AI technologies to streamline coding, enhance stoner experience, and maintain a competitive edge. Academics are encouraged to continue exploring the crossroad of AI and web engineering, fastening on practical operations, evolving technologies, and the development of stylish practices. By doing so, both assiduity and academia can contribute to advancing the field and using AI's full eventuality in web engineering and business invention

REFERENCES

AlDahoul, N., et al. (2023). "Exploring the potential of generative AI for the world wide web."

Bachu, N. and J. J. J. o. S. R. McDuffie (2023). "Implications of Artificial Intelligence in Environmental Engineering." **12**(3).

Corea, F. (2017). *Artificial intelligence and exponential technologies: Business models evolution and new investment opportunities*. Springer.

Ding, T.. (2023). Is artificial intelligence associated with carbon emissions reduction? *Case of China.*, 85, 103892.

Fateh, S., ... (2024). Smart Healthcare System in Industry 4.0. Advances in Computational Intelligence for the Healthcare Industry 4.0, IGI Global: 297-311.

Guldogan, N.. (2024)... *Artificial Intelligence in BI-RADS Categorization of Breast Lesions on Ultrasound: Can We Omit Excessive Follow-ups and Biopsies*, 31(6), 2194–2202.

Jhanjhi, N., et al. (2024). "IoT-Based Railway Logistics: Security Issues and Challenges." 143-163.

Kaplan, A. and M. J. B. h. Haenlein (2019). "Siri, Siri, in my hand: Who's the fairest in the land? On the interpretations, illustrations, and implications of artificial intelligence." **62**(1): 15-25.

Katar, O., et al. (2023). "Evaluation of GPT-3 AI language model in research paper writing." **18**(2): 311-318.

Naeem, M., et al. (2024). "The Impact of Investment in AI on Bank Performance: Empirical Evidence from Pakistan's Banking Sector." **17**(1).

Shah, I. A., ... (2024). Logistics With the Internet of Things: Challenges, Perspectives, and Applications. Navigating Cyber Threats and Cybersecurity in the Logistics Industry, IGI Global: 172-195.

Shah, I. A., et al. (2024). "Use of Emerging Technologies in Healthcare 4.0." 280-296.

Shah, I. A., ... (2024). Enabling Explainable AI in Cybersecurity Solutions. Advances in Explainable AI Applications for Smart Cities, IGI Global: 255-275.

Shah, I. A., ... (2024). IoT Devices in Drones: Security Issues and Future Challenges. Cybersecurity Issues and Challenges in the Drone Industry, IGI Global: 217-235.

Shah, I. A., ... (2024). Logistics Industry in the Context of the Blockchain Technology. Navigating Cyber Threats and Cybersecurity in the Logistics Industry, IGI
Global: 214-235.

Shah, I. A., et al. (2024). "Supply Chain Management Security Issues and Challenges
in the Context of AI Applications." 59-89.

Shah, I. A. and N. Z. Jhanjhi (2024). "Cybersecurity Issues and Challenges in the
Drone Industry."

Sharma, A., et al. (2022). "Recent trends in AI-based intelligent sensing." **11**(10):
1661.

Chapter 12
Security Concerns:
Machine Learning Approaches in the Modern Era and Web Engineering

Humaira Z. Ashraf

https://orcid.org/0000-0001-5067-3172

Taylor's University, Malaysia

ABSTRACT

This primarily aims to evaluate the ML approaches and web applications for authentication. Using machine learning, issues can be solved, and computers can carry out tasks. It attempts to understand the relationships between the data and automatically learns from the presented information. The relationship after that enables the machine to complete the tasks given to it successfully. In other words, machine learning teaches itself how to accomplish a task over time and then assists people in performing that activity. The capacity to design effective, safe, and user-friendly web applications remains a major problem in the constantly evolving field of web development. Web application developers must provide modular, reusable, and interactive web interface components that can adapt to the constantly shifting needs of users in terms of security, large-scale data transfer capabilities, and interface speed. One of the most important components of any modern web application is secure user login and permission. Stronger authentication is required to protect user data and the integrity of apps, as worries over data privacy and cybersecurity grow. Though there are a number of these solutions on the market, none of them completely integrates with the ecosystem built on React to offer safe and adaptable identity management. Effective and user-friendly web components are just as crucial for the appropriate administration of data and the successful user engagement of web applications as they are for security problems. As a result, the thesis concentrates

DOI: 10.4018/979-8-3693-3703-5.ch012

on providing a more thorough explanation of reusable web components, including what they are and how to create them with TypeScript, React, and Redux. Therefore, this chapter is a practical attempt to design and develop safe, reusable, and effective web components inside a React ecosystem to meet these difficulties. By doing this, the research advances the subject of web development and provides a guide for programmers wishing to incorporate comparable features.

INTRODUCTION

Machine learning (ML) has emerged as a key strategy for utilizing data's potential and enabling more inventive, effective, and sustainable business practices. However, many successful ML applications in real-world scenarios don't live up to the hype. Many machine learning (ML) proofs of concept never make it to production, and a significant portion of ML initiatives fail. This is not surprising from a research standpoint, since the ML community has concentrated primarily on creating ML models rather than producing production-ready ML products or facilitating the co-ordination of the infrastructure and components of the resulting, frequently complex ML systems, including the roles needed to automate and run an ML system in a real-world setting (Aykol et al., 2020). For instance, data scientists continue to over-see numerous industrial applications. In order to tackle these problems, this effort aims to investigate how more ML proofs of concept may be put into production by automating and operationalizing manual ML processes.

Securing web-based applications is critical to prevent unauthorized access, data breaches, and other cybersecurity threats. Input validation ensures that user data is valid and does not contain malicious code or scripts that can compromise the application's security(Gourisaria et al., 2021, Heras García de Vinuesa et al., 2020). Authentication and authorization mechanisms ensure that only authorized users can access the application's resources and data. Strong password policies and multi-factor authentication should be implemented to prevent unauthorized access. Access control ensures that users have access only to the resources they need to perform their tasks and no more. Indeed, technological progress often outpaces the rate at which regulations and guidelines are implemented in the software industry, where the rapid pace of technological change has led to a departure from conven-tional software development life cycle (SDLC) approaches. While both academia and industry have made strides to improve software quality, vulnerabilities continue to be a major issue. This is in part because it is hard to forecast all probable failure modes in today's complex software systems. However, it's partly because the soft-ware development process requires more focus on safety and quality(Kocielnik et al., 2019, Posoldova, 2020). Software quality and security can both be enhanced by following established best practices in the software development industry. The use of secure coding guidelines and the idea of least privilege are two examples of these methods. Figure 1 Overview of web applications architecture.

Figure 1. Overview web applications architecture adapted from peerbits

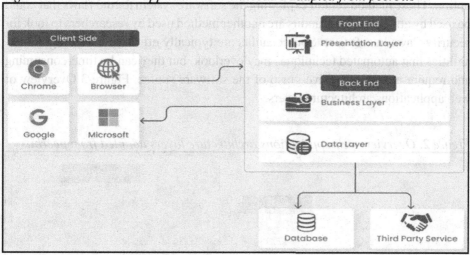

The design plan for how various web application components—such as databases, applications, and middleware systems—interact and communicate with one another is called the web application architecture. There are various web application architectural types to take into account, such as serverless, three-tier, microservices, and monolithic(Lwakatare et al., 2020b, Willman, 2024). Each offers a unique set of advantages and disadvantages. For a web application to be performant, scalable, and maintainable, its architecture must be carefully thought out. It is beneficial to develop an application that can rapidly adjust to shifting business requirements, manage heavy traffic volumes, and offer a flawless user experience.

As the frequency and sophistication of cyberattacks rise, the study of how to spot software flaws has become crucial. Individuals, businesses, and even entire nations are vulnerable to the devastation that these strikes can wreak. As a result, researchers and businesses are investing more time and money into securing their software(Leite et al., 2019, Macarthy and Bass, 2020). The vast volume of code present in modern software systems is one of the primary obstacles in locating software vulnerabilities. Finding all the security flaws in a system is becoming more and more challenging as software becomes more complicated. Vulnerabilities in software are typically difficult to find because they are buried deep inside the code and require specialized tools and methods. Researchers and professionals in business employ many different approaches to uncover vulnerabilities to overcome these difficulties(Rütz and Wedel, 2019, Perera et al., 2017). Utilizing automated technologies that scan code for security flaws is one method. The software is analyzed using methods including fuzzing, symbolic execution, and static analysis. Manual testing methods, such as pen testing and vulnerability scanning, are another option. These methods entail exploiting the software system to find flaws that could be used by attackers. Code audits are another method used by researchers to look for security flaws in software. Source audits are typically effective in finding vulnerabilities that automated techniques may overlook, but they can be time-consuming and require a comprehensive grasp of the software source. Figure 3 Overview of web applications architecture layers.

Figure 2. Overview web applications architecture layers adapted from peerbits

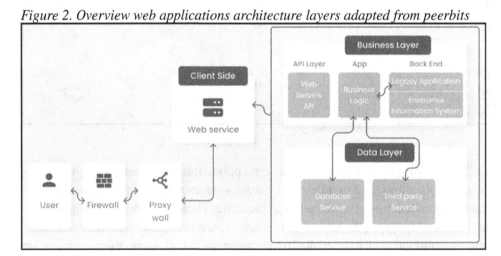

The application layer, which carries out several logical activities, is the brains of the system in the three-tier architecture concept. It responds to queries from clients originating at the Client Tier (the display layer) and gives clients access to the Database Management System (DBMS)(Strauss, 2017, Granlund et al., 2021). Hypertext transfer protocol (HTTP) and other protocols are used by web servers, which can be either software or hardware that receives and processes requests from clients. After processing the users' inquiries, it selects the most relevant data and presents it on the user interface. Overall, finding software vulnerabilities is a complex and challenging task, but it is essential to ensure the security of software systems. The scientific community and industry will continue to invest in this area of research to develop new techniques and tools to improve software security. Considering the growing frequency and sophistication of cyberattacks, discovering flaws in software has emerged as a crucial topic of study. Personal computers, businesses, and even entire countries may all take a major hit from these kinds of attacks(Zhou et al., 2020). As a result, researchers and businesses are investing more time and money into securing their software. The vast volume of code present in modern software systems is one of the primary obstacles to locating software vulnerabilities. Finding all the security flaws in a system is becoming more challenging as software becomes more complicated. Moreover, software vulnerabilities are typically buried deep inside the code and are difficult to locate without the use of specialized tools and methods. Researchers and experts in the sector employ a wide range of techniques to discover vulnerabilities to overcome these obstacles. Using automated technologies that scan code for security flaws is one method.

This chapter's contributions are in the following points:

- This chapter discussed the Machine Learning Approaches
- This chapter discussed the Wed Engineering Models
- This chapter discussed Machine Learning Applications and Web Technologies
- This chapter discussed Security Concerns in Web Engineering
- This chapter provides Future work and recommendations

LITERATURE REVIEW

Machine learning is a scientific field that examines how computers learn from data and improve over time. Probability and statistics serve as its main pillars. It is more effective than traditional statistical methods for making decisions. The information that is supplied into the algorithm from a dataset is called a feature. Finding the subset of features that would be most helpful in accomplishing the objective and raising the accuracy of the model is the responsibility of a machine learning developer. Continued experiments ought to be carried out in order to identify the feature subset for the algorithm. With all its benefits and drawbacks, the use of cyberspace as a key means of node-to-node information transfer is expanding more quickly. One important way to access a seemingly limitless supply of global information and resources is through the internet. Global internet usage was 48%; in poorer nations, it later rose to 82%. Cyberspace is a large field that includes much more than just the internet(Tamburri, 2020, Spjuth et al., 2021). It includes users, system resources, the technical expertise of participants, and much more. Furthermore, the cybersphere plays a major role in the innumerable vulnerabilities to cyber threats and attacks. There are a few reasons why a computer system is susceptible to attacks, such as inadequate system configuration, inexperienced personnel, and a lack of methods(Derakhshan et al., 2019, Karn et al., 2018). The increasing prevalence of cyber dangers necessitates further advancements in cybersecurity techniques.

Much like web and mobile technologies, attack tactics are evolving swiftly to breach systems and evade generic signature-based defenses. Machine learning techniques offer potential solutions to such challenging and complicated problems because of their capacity to quickly adapt to fresh and unknown settings(Domenech and Guillén, 2020). Numerous machine learning approaches have proven effective in addressing a range of computer and information security-related problems. Figure 5 Presents literature review.

Figure 3. Liiterature review

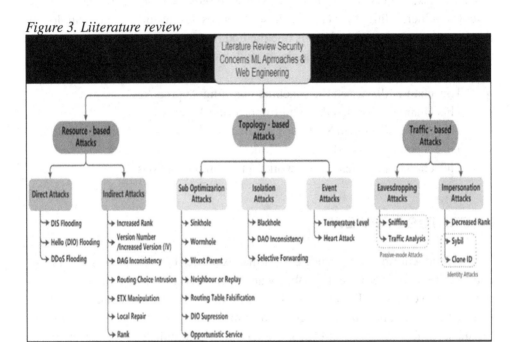

To find vulnerabilities that bad actors could attack; these techniques involve actively trying to take advantage of them. Developers and businesses alike face a formidable obstacle in the form of software vulnerabilities. Once a security hole has been found, it is the responsibility of the software's creators to create a fix. However, this is not always an easy operation, as patches may cause additional issues or incompatibilities with other program parts. By their very nature, vulnerabilities increase the likelihood of being exploited by attackers the longer it takes to discover and fix them. This puts pressure on developers to quickly identify and patch vulnerabilities before they can be exploited(Mäkinen et al., 2021, Silva et al., 2020). Several studies have been conducted in automated identifying threats for securing the software and associated security issues. Although the literature covers a wide variety of such topics, this review will focus on four major themes that repeatedly emerge throughout the literature reviewed secure software and vulnerabilities, attacks, solutions proposed by researchers to detect these attacks, openness, and exploration of machine learning algorithms approaches to handle the threats and improve vulnerabilities. The classification of security issues in health information systems has been done using this taxonomy method. Based on the classification's findings, conclusions are reached. RAMeX was developed to bridge the gap in risk assessment and management processes for medium- and small-sized commercial enterprises dealing with medium-to-low-level risks(Banerjee et al., 2020, Benni et al., 2019). This study examines six different research methods. In general, they treat planning as a distinct process that has no logical or direct bearing on the creation of IT systems. Enterprise information resources, which capture and characterise the enterprise, when integrated with planning, development, and management, will decrease the response time, and make it possible to conduct an economic analysis of information system investment. The creation of security policies and documents for each PBX will lessen but not entirely stop external and internal hacker attempts. However, the PBX staff must deal with the leading security threats, weaknesses, risks, and solutions by putting these policies and documents into place (Vuppalapati et al., 2020, García et al., 2020). The author addresses the techniques available for locating security flaws in an open network and the evolving paradigm of network security. It goes on to describe the problem Sun had and the tools we made and used to solve it, with a focus on automating system security evaluation and compliance. The network administrator has additional security issues while maintaining adequate security measures across heterogeneous platforms. There is an increase in computer crime. One of these crimes is listening in on private conversations. Another is damaging information storage equipment physically. This shows the need for a more suited strategy for smaller firms and those requiring a speedier, simpler, and less resource-intensive strategy. This suggests a need for an alternative method for efficient information technology (IT) risk assessment and management. From an IT standpoint, this strategy has a business-oriented focus. With the development of a methodology for risk assessment, some intriguing inferences can be made regarding the decision-making process in organizational information security(Wu et al., 2020, Siqueira, 2023). It is essential to have a solid grasp of the dynamics of the risks associated with automated information systems. The methodology uses software defect injection to compel abnormal program states during the software's execution. Then it monitors the consequences these states have on the system's overall level of safety, The program was developed to help businesses achieve their objectives. Software architecture links how the program is made and what it is supposed to do. Developers are under constant pressure to ensure the security of websites through the design and architecture of their projects. To reach this goal, website developers put in much work to ensure security is built in from the ground up. However, more than these design improvements are needed to compensate for the challenges caused by security thrashing. Additional solutions are required and developing a website safety strategy is the way to ensure everything is safe. When a website has this kind of failure, the developers are forced to consider what might have gone wrong throughout the website's design process and why it might have resulted in such a significant setback. The use of security design strategies is what brings resolution to design problems relating to security. In a survey conducted by Lars Lofgren, it was found that around 54% of all businesses polled reported having been the victim of at least one cyberattack in the preceding 12 months(Shah et al., 2024a). Furthermore, the survey reveals that only 39% of organizations were prepared to deal with these cyber-attacks. Vulnerabilities are flaws in a website that interfere with its ability to meet the security criteria.

Researchers may be motivated to investigate a particular topic for various reasons, such as curiosity, personal interest, and desire to solve a problem. The systematic categorization of research papers can provide insights into the distribution of research attention across different topics. However, it is essential to recognize that the number of published papers on a topic does not necessarily reflect its importance or impact. As for issues related to datasets and code, there is growing recognition of the importance of open data and reproducibility in research. Researchers may face challenges in sharing and accessing data and code, which can hinder the transparency and rigour of their research. However, efforts are being made to promote open science practices, such as data-sharing policies, open-access publishing, and reproducibility standards. These efforts aim to improve the quality and impact of research and address the challenges that researchers may encounter in their work. To bridge the gap between hot and not-so-hot research problems, it is important to identify the most pressing challenges and prioritize research efforts accordingly.

This may involve analyzing trends and patterns in vulnerability disclosures, assessing the impact of emerging technologies and threat vectors, and identifying areas where current approaches to vulnerability detection and mitigation are inadequate. Collaboration and knowledge-sharing among researchers can also be critical in advancing research on vulnerability detection and mitigation. This may involve leveraging open-source tools and data sets, participating in research communities and conferences, and engaging in interdisciplinary collaboration to address complex problems from multiple angles(Toschi and Sega, 2019, Hubara et al., 2018). Ultimately, the goal of research on vulnerability detection and mitigation is to improve the security and resilience of systems and networks and protect against malicious attacks and data breaches. By focusing on high-impact research problems and collaborating effectively, researchers can make significant progress toward this goal. In the methodologies section, we discuss the many approaches used to identify security holes, such as manual analysis and more traditional methods. Meanwhile, the study that focuses on vulnerability detection performance and the types of vulnerabilities found is discussed under the heading "detection." Overfitting and traditional feature use are the main topics discussed in the features section. Meanwhile, the code section elaborates on the role of code in software development and the various degrees of code complexity.

Overview Machine Learning Approaches

Machine learning techniques are necessary to combat many cybersecurity risks and assaults, such as malware, phishing, spam, fraud detection, intrusion detection systems, and more. We'll be focusing on virus detection, intrusion detection systems, and spam classification for this review. Malware is a group of instructions designed with the malicious intent to obstruct normal computer functions. When malicious code runs on a targeted computer, its goal is to compromise and harm the confidentiality, availability, and integrity of computer resources and services. Machine learning techniques will eventually replace all current conventional methods of detection. It is best to use low-cost training methods for malware identification(Lwakatare et al., 2020a, Renggli et al., 2021). Furthermore, malware analysts need to be quite knowledgeable about machine learning methods for detecting malware. The fact that the average user, who understands technical security, usually sets the security reliability level of the computing resources is one of the main shortcomings of the security system. Machine learning applications have expanded rapidly and will do so in the future. Going over several applications is the best way to grasp various ways and when to employ which approach, and that is precisely what we will be doing in this instance. The use of virtual personal assistants in our daily lives has begun. All of us have smartphones, and with them, a personal assistant(Shah et al., 2024c, Shah et al., 2024b). A decade ago, spam emails and malware were a pain for us, but machine learning advancements made it simple to categorize them. Machine learning powers spam filters and is updated often to improve its dependability. A multilayer perceptron network and Decision Tree Induction techniques are used by many spam filters. On the other hand, several machine learning models have been employed to identify coding patterns in the code in order to detect malware.

Cybersecurity and online fraud detection benefit greatly from machine learning. Companies like PayPal have been utilizing machine learning techniques to protect against money laundering due to the rise in financial online fraud. There are two categories of prediction problems in the fraud detection model: regression and classification. For these kinds of prediction problems, some of the most popular machine-learning techniques are neural networks, decision trees, random forest trees, and logistic regression(Toschi and Sega, 2019, Esmaeilzadeh et al., 2022, Xu, 2022). The trend toward automation, which includes machine learning and self-driving automobiles, is accelerating. Several machine learning methods are used by a self-driving automobile to improve decision-making reliability and trustworthiness. Machine learning algorithms are split into several subcategories according to subtasks, such as object detection, recognized object classification, object location, and object movement prediction, in order to create an autonomous vehicle. Different objects may be recognized using techniques like AdaBoost and decision tree matrix; related items can be grouped using clustering algorithms like k-means; and movements can be predicted using methods like pattern recognition, support vector machines, and neural network regression.

Machine Learning Applications

Machine learning techniques and algorithms are used by social media platforms to develop outstanding and visually appealing features. Facebook, for example, keeps track of your interactions, likes, comments, chats, and the amount of time you spend on different types of posts. Figure 6 Overview ML applications.

Figure 4. Overview ML applications

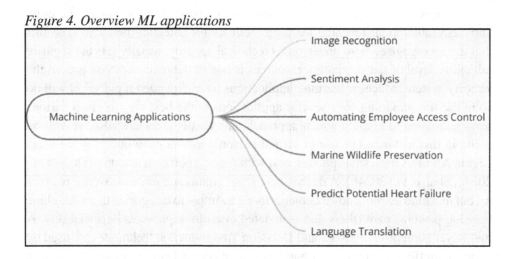

One of the most important and well-known machine learning and artificial intelligence approaches is image recognition, which is a method for classifying and identifying a feature or an item in a digital image. This method is being used for additional analysis, including face detection, face recognition, and pattern recognition. One of the most essential uses of machine learning is sentiment analysis(-Carcillo et al., 2018, Foster and Wagner, 2021). Sentiment analysis is a real-time machine learning program designed to ascertain the writer's or speaker's sentiment or viewpoint. Companies are presently employing machine learning algorithms to ascertain the appropriate degree of access that workers require in different domains, contingent upon their job descriptions. Among the more inventive uses of machine learning is this one.

Scientists can monitor and control the populations of endangered marine animals, such as cetaceans, by using machine learning algorithms to create behaviour models for them. In medicine, an algorithm that can read a physician's free-form electronic notes and spot trends in a patient's cardiovascular history is gaining traction. Rather than a doctor searching through several medical records to get a reliable diagnosis, redundancy is now minimized by computers analyzing the data that is available. Language translation is among the most widely used applications of machine learning(Obeid et al., 2020, Aljabri et al., 2022, Baier et al., 2019). When it comes to translating one language to another, machine learning is crucial. The ease with which websites can translate between languages and convey context, as well as meaning, is astounding. "Machine translation" is the term for the technology that powers the translation tool. Life would not be as simple as it is now without it, as it has made it possible for people to communicate with people all over the world. Travelers and business partners can now confidently journey into distant countries, knowing that language barriers will no longer exist.

Overview Web Engineering

Internet-based programming Web engineering creates systematic methods for effectively developing, deploying, and maintaining high-quality Web-based systems by scientific and engineering principles. It also contains well-known software engineering procedures and laws from other domains. It also includes other fields, including data structures, visual design, the social sciences, project management, testing, hypermedia engineering, requirements engineering (RE), and human-computer interaction (HCI). Many web engineering techniques modified their procedures and notations to comply with model-driven software development (MDSD) as model-based efforts gained traction in the software development community.

Applications and technology related to web engineering are being used more and more in the dissemination of educational materials as well as in assisting and supporting these endeavors. This type of use has advanced from using web-based training and remote learning to augment traditional courses to using e-learning and web-based education, among other things(Baier et al., 2021, Antonio et al., 2017). The field of e-learning has expanded to offer convenient access to learning materials at any time and place. It also supports features like individual learning goals, synchronous and asynchronous collaboration, and communication between students and instructors. Figure 7 Overview of web engineering.

Figure 5. Overview web engineering

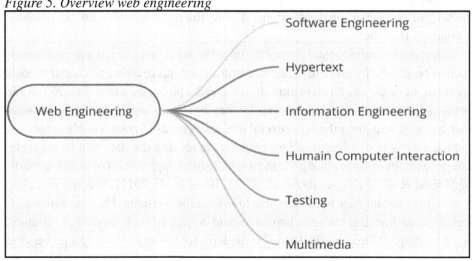

In the world of online learning and e-learning, web engineering has emerged as one of the most fascinating and important subjects. Understanding the purpose of continuously updated web engineering applications is becoming more and more necessary, as evidenced by recent developments in e-learning systems, the demands of the knowledge society, and the growing demand on students to be autonomous, reflective e-learners. This study will analyze the research and gather expert opinion on the topic while illuminating the benefits, advantages, and contributions of web engineering to the creation of e-learning systems(Fateh et al., 2024, Shah, 2024a). A growing multidisciplinary paradigm, web engineering has barely begun to pique the interest of scholars and other important players in the creation of web-based systems. To ensure that the web's ability to enhance the learning process is exploited effectively, it is necessary to evaluate the effect of web engineering applications on e-learning systems. The study's goal is to demonstrate the contributions, advantages, and benefits of web engineering in the creation of e-learning platforms. This study is qualitative in nature. A thorough analysis of relevant research studies yielded the primary data. An interview with the developers of the e-learning systems served as the second instrument. The findings demonstrated that the most important web engineering instruments for creating e-learning platforms. Furthermore, altering the features of the learning environment, altering student behavior, redefining roles, and integrating artificial intelligence (AI) are the primary areas of development for e-learning systems.

The findings also demonstrated that the primary obstacles to web applications in e-learning systems are technological, adaptable, lacking experience and training, underfunded, evolving student needs and preferences, the difference between computer and mobile versions, security risks, work overload, and time constraints(Cui et al., 2019). It was discovered that the creation of e-learning apps greatly benefits from web engineering.

A web application, often known as a web app, is a software programme that can be viewed and used via the internet using a web browser. It is run on web servers and interacts with users via a web interface. Web apps are platform-agnostic, which means they may be viewed from a variety of devices, including desktop computers, laptops, tablets, and smartphones if they have a functional web browser and an internet connection. A web application architecture outlines the arrangement of all web application components and shows the relationships between application components, third-party middleware systems, web services, and databases. This is a snapshot of the interaction between various programmes that are working together to deliver services to end consumers at the same time. Using machine learning, issues can be solved, and computers can carry out tasks. It attempts to understand the relationships between the data and automatically learns from the presented information. The relationship after that enables the machine to complete the tasks given to it successfully (Ruf et al., 2021, Hewage and Meedeniya, 2022). In other words, machine learning teaches itself how to accomplish a task over time and then assists people in performing that activity. This method is much more effective and economical than manual or rule-based programming. The quick learning and execution process boosts the productivity of a certain activity.

The most popular machine learning technique for identifying software vulner-abilities is supervised learning. This is because it can function well with the aid of trustworthy datasets. When learning under supervision, labels like "vulnerable" and "non-vulnerable" are applied to datasets. Before the vulnerability detection model is trained, every observation in the dataset has already been given a label. Past academics who worked on vulnerability detection studies have made some of these labelled datasets publicly accessible(Chowdhary et al., 2023, Cai et al., 2023). The supervised learning method has become popular due to its ability to complete any task. Here, it's the same for identifying software flaws. Supervised learning has a wide variety of uses, and this is one of them. They met the criteria for multi-class detection since they found more than two distinct classes of vulnerabilities. A variation of supervised learning called semi-supervised learning uses training data that includes occurrences. In semi-supervised learning, predictions are made on the unlabelled data using a classifier that has been trained on the labelled data. To improve performance over training the model solely on the initially labelled dataset, the model is then retrained using the anticipated data. Semi-supervised learning can use labelled or unlabelled data makes it desirable.

Deep learning strategy is becoming more common detection of a vulnerability in software, it has proven itself trustworthy and effective in a variety of applications. In contrast to traditional techniques, the suggested taxonomy creates a new perspective on approaches to the detection of vulnerabilities in software(York, 2023, Bandi et al., 2023). Software security patch management keeps people from taking advantage of security holes in software products and systems that have already been used. Software security patches are "code created to solve software security problems". Industry professionals and researchers always put security patches ahead of non-security patches.

Web Technologies

The most important and significant web engineering tools as well as the technologies used for the e-learning apps that are included in the current e-learning solutions will be examined first in this examination. The main goal of web engineering technologies is to make learning easier by utilizing electronic materials together with teaching, learning, and testing solutions. In order to make the current e-learning systems user-friendly and compatible with the most recent web browsers, they should be designed using the most recent web engineering technology. Dynamic web pages are often created server-side using a database server and an appropriate programming language. The application database is connected to a server that ought to be a reliable and quick platform to host databases at the professional level(Yongli et al., 2024). The client can use a popular browser, including Internet Explorer, Opera, Firefox, Safari, Google Chrome, or Firefox, to access the web-based e-learning system.

There are a variety of technologies and techniques available for developing e-learning management applications. Zipcast, a meeting platform from SlideShare that enables users to conduct secure private meetings at a minimal cost and limitless free open meetings through the web browser, is a modest but appropriate contemporary tool that revolutionized the way the world conducts webinars and web meetings. It was the first website that let users exchange PowerPoint and Keynote files on the internet, and it demonstrated how to share presentations online. The sessions are often done entirely through a browser window and are social and participatory.

Security Concerns in Web Engineering

More than half of the participants expressed apprehension regarding the security of their websites, but they also saw the issue as warranted given the rise in attacks directed towards their sites. Almost forty-three percent of the participants reported a rise in attacks directed towards the websites they manage. Interestingly, thirty respondents did not know whether or not attacks had increased.The detection of an attack does not imply that it was successful. Millions of attacks are directed towards the websites that we at Patchstack defend. To ensure that the malicious traffic is rejected, these attacks are logged, banned, and continuously monitored. The detection of an attack does not imply that it was successful. Millions of attacks are directed towards the websites that we at Patchstack defend. To ensure that the malicious traffic is rejected, these attacks are logged, banned, and continuously monitored.

There may be more attacks because of the numerous vulnerabilities found in well-known WordPress plugins. For instance, in the first five months of 2020, over 40 million websites were impacted by over 200 vulnerabilities that were discovered. Third-party code, including plugins, themes, and other dependencies, was where the great majority of these vulnerabilities were discovered.

Additionally, we found that 25% of respondents had visited a website that had been hacked in the month before they took the poll. This helps us to get a clear picture of the scope of the issue.

Malware infects websites, which are then used to launch more attacks on other websites and companies. Credit card details are frequently stolen via hacked websites, and in certain situations, the visitors' PCs are infected as well. Furthermore, it's becoming more common to use phishing pages on compromised websites as a means of obtaining login credentials for other services.In the meantime, javascript-based keyloggers are frequently used to infiltrate e- commerce websites in order to collect credit card information from online shoppers(Shah, 2024b, Matz et al., 2024). Although breaking into a single small website might not be very lucrative, by taking advantage of a well-known plugin, an attacker can launch a coordinated attack that grants them access to hundreds of thousands or even millions of websites.

Artificial intelligence (AI) has made industries and society today more modern and productive. Through the Internet of Things (IoT), we can sense and transfer data through the Internet from one device to another and can perform/do tasks efficiently. AI use today has increased from one application to many, i.e., from the agriculture sector to weather prediction. Similar to weather prediction, where AI can help identify the situation of upcoming days and perform tasks like crop growing and cutting, agriculture can benefit from AI. Keep in mind that AI works better with IoT and smart devices. When these industries adopt IoT in their operations, numerous cyberattacks or vulnerabilities are reduced globally. which deals with the necessity of stopping, identifying, and recovering from system failures. Although these attacks must be rapidly discovered, it takes a long time for human or skilled experts to monitor, track, or recover from such cyberattacks(Furtado et al., 2024, Choudhuri et al., 2024). So, in a short while, we forecast what will occur when AI enables experts to identify, and monitor cyberattacks and prevent numerous, significant losses. One use of machine learning is the recognition of spam and junk mail. Because cyber security is essential to every industry and business, particularly crucial ones, it is a pressing issue.

Managing consumer data raises several privacy and security issues. It is crucial to comply with laws such as the CCPA and GDPR, and data breaches can have dire repercussions. AI solution development and implementation can be costly, particularly for smaller e-commerce companies. Expenses include developing or obtaining AI models, buying technology, and employing data scientists and engineers. When AI is used in e-commerce, users could get worried about the security, privacy, and moral applications of AI. Gaining and preserving the trust of customers is essential(Russo, 2024, Huang and Sun, 2022). While personalizing suggestions and optimizing workflows are two ways AI can improve the user experience, shoddy implementation or an over-reliance on AI might result in a negative user experience. As an e-commerce firm expands, its AI systems must scale to handle greater data and user interactions. Scalability difficulties can occur in both the technical infrastructure and the AI models themselves. E-commerce businesses must navigate the challenging terrain of AI ethics and laws. Adherence to distinct local, state and sector-specific legislation is vital to avert legal and reputational hazards.

Global business expansion brings with it complexities related to cross-border logistics, different regulations, and varied market demands that make effective inventory auditing difficult. These complexities are exacerbated by the fact that the products, suppliers, and distribution channels that make up the e-commerce ecosystem are diverse. Another major issue that impacted e-commerce inventory audits was system problems(Kirova et al., 2023, Ege et al., 2024). While technology increases audit efficiency, the report points out that proactive steps are needed to assure data dependability and correctness due to its vulnerability to errors. Natural disasters and geopolitical crises are examples of external factors that increase the complexity of inventory management in e-commerce. The influence of unforeseen events on supply chains and inventory levels was emphasized in the literature assessment. Keep in mind that AI works better with IoT and smart devices. When these industries adopt IoT in their operations, numerous cyberattacks or vulnerabilities are reduced globally(Khan, 2023, Pesovski et al., 2024). which deals with the necessity of stopping, identifying, and recovering from system failures. Although these attacks must be rapidly discovered, it takes a long time for human or skilled experts to monitor, track, or recover from such cyberattacks. So, in a short while, we forecast what will occur when AI enables experts to identify, and monitor cyberattacks and prevent numerous, significant losses. One use of machine learning is the recognition of spam and junk mail. Because cyber security is essential to every industry and business, particularly crucial ones, it is a pressing issue.

These days, artificial intelligence (AI) is growing in popularity. Even though it is still in its infancy, the way it will change business activities is being used in a variety of areas and businesses. Given the continued advancements in AI, it was thought to be crucial to examine how this technology can enhance the effectiveness and efficiency of e-commerce. Currently, only the largest companies can conduct AI-enabled e-commerce transactions because of the infrastructure costs and complexity involved(Basole and Major, 2024, Ratani et al., 2024). However, there is a lack of customer awareness regarding AI-enabled transactions; hence, there are relatively few There are several empirical studies on the use of AI in e-commerce. Disparate research has been done on artificial intelligence, particularly as it relates to retailing. As a result, it was challenging to reach any useful conclusions based on the body of accessible literature. This study focused only on e-commerce-related AI research after conducting a thorough evaluation of the literature. Subsequently, it explains how each subset of AI works in e-commerce. To the best of our knowledge, this study is the first to demonstrate how a certain subset of AI can be used in e-commerce operations. Robotics, for example, is linked to lowering human intervention and automating e-commerce tasks. The research has identified the functioning of each subgroup of AI, and it may aid future researchers in determining which AI technology best suits their needs. Artificial intelligence (AI)-based technology has advanced and been more widely used in our daily lives thanks to the technological disruptions of the digital age. Numerous studies on AI and its subsets have been conducted in a variety of fields, including management, marketing, and e-commerce(Ebert and Louridas, 2023). However, there is a lack of integration in these studies. Both concepts have not been covered by any of the previously presented studies in management. In addition, while these studies have discussed the functionalities of AI in e-commerce, they have not shown how technology is associated with e-commerce functionality. The most used AI subsets in e-commerce were found to be chatbots and voice assistants, followed by personalization, recommendation systems, and automation. The pace at which AI-enabled transactions are currently being completed and reviewed also indicates that as soon as AI technology matures, its acceptance and use will increase. Artificial intelligence, big data, and the Internet of Things (IoT) have transformed the way e-commerce companies run. Scholars and Global practitioners are constantly searching for the most appropriate AI technologies to use in e-commerce(Humayun et al.). To expand the application of AI in e-commerce, this study compiled the research on the subject and included several subsets of AI that are applicable in other fields. It examined several pieces of literature related to marketing, IS, management, and e-commerce. To fully understand how AI functions in e-commerce, however, further research must be done on its actual applications. The Google Scholar platform's data was searched.

To obtain a significant understanding of the components, other publications written by distinguished scholars were also consulted. The most popular AI-related keywords and the most pertinent research publications were utilized to narrow down the literature search. Journal articles and review papers were discussed as offering the most thorough understanding of the technology. It is clear from the research done for this study that artificial intelligence has greater applications in e-commerce. AI has several facets that need to be investigated because of its user-friendliness and assisting features. It will undoubtedly draw further researchers, which will open opportunities for numerous practical applications.

Discussion

The primary focus will be on emphasizing significant and vital details related to the subjects covered in the article. It is best to start by being concerned about how well machine learning algorithms function. Classifier accuracy and the classifier log loss are two parameters that can be taken into consideration in order to discover the best-performing algorithms. An algorithm is deemed to be well-performing if its classifier accuracy is high and its log loss is low. The aforementioned elements are taken into consideration when choosing an algorithm to address a particular issue. This helps us narrow down the many distinct algorithms now in use to the one that will best serve our needs.

The correct parameters that the user enters determine how effective the majority of clustering algorithms are. Because biological and biomedical data are nonspherical and high-dimensional, factors like the number of expected clusters, a beginning point in the dataset, the minimum number of samples to create a cluster, and so on, affect the clustering result. This is a severe problem. To address the problem, the Automatic Density Clustering Method with Multiple Kernels (ADCMK) is one suggested solution. By using that technique, clusters of any shape can be quickly recognized by their density(Waheed et al., 2019, Humayun et al., 2021, Jesmin, 2013).In contrast to other clustering methods, ADCMK automatically calculates the best values for the cutoff distance, kernel weights, and number of clusters and centroids. These values are then run periodically without affecting the clustering outcome. It is also more accurate in comparison. To get good clustering results and performance in a variety of settings, many kernel clustering methodologies aid in the optimal merging of the learning algorithms.

It is impossible to single out one algorithm as being superior to another. The reason for this is that the selection of the appropriate algorithm that would be best for the requirement depends on a number of factors, including the domain in which the training and tests are being conducted, the dataset used in the training and testing procedures, the degree of preprocessing being done on the dataset, the feature set chosen for the algorithm or feature selection algorithms that have been used on the dataset, the size of the dataset and the types of data it contains, the machine's performance level and capacity, and much more(Jhanjhi et al., 2022, Talwani et al., 2022). The best algorithm from a filtered set of algorithms that would best fit the problem at hand will typically be chosen iteratively; the right knowledge and prior experiences will aid in the construction of the filtered set of algorithms. Normally, this cannot be chosen directly. The best-performing algorithm for diagnosing different diseases changes for the previously described reason, as can be observed from a basic example from the biomedical sector. Aids in the identification of pertinent attributes from a variety of candidate subnets and is essential to the development of a successful prediction model. Feature selection offers a number of advantages, including quick and efficient machine learning algorithm training, decreased model complexity, increased accuracy, and resolution of the overfitting issue(Saleh et al., 2020, Humayun et al., 2022). It's crucial to keep in mind that when features are connected, it makes no sense to include them all in the machine learning algorithm since this will just lengthen the algorithm's execution time and not boost its efficiency. It should be noted that the algorithm's accuracy may decrease when more features are included.

CONCLUSION

In conclusion, web application architecture plays a vital role in the development and success of any web application. It involves the design and organization of the various components that make up the application, including the front-end client, the back-end server, the database, and the network infrastructure. An effective web application architecture should consider factors such as scalability, performance, security, and maintainability, and should be flexible enough to accommodate future updates and changes. One of the most important components of any modern web application is secure user login and permission. Stronger authentication is required to protect user data and the integrity of apps, as worries over data privacy and cybersecurity grow. Though there are a number of these solutions on the market, none of them completely integrates with the ecosystem built on React to offer safe and adaptable identity management. Effective and user-friendly web components are just as crucial for the appropriate administration of data and the successful user engagement of web applications as they are for security problems. As a result, the thesis concentrates on providing a more thorough explanation of reusable web components, including what they are and how to create them with TypeScript, React, and Redux. Therefore, practical attempt to design and develop safe, reusable, and effective web components inside a React ecosystem to meet these difficulties. By doing this, the research advances the subject of web development and provides a guide for programmers wishing to incorporate comparable features.

REFERENCES

Aljabri, M., Alomari, D. M., & Aboulnour, M. (2022, December). Fake news detection using machine learning models. In *2022 14th International Conference on Computational Intelligence and Communication Networks (CICN)* (pp. 473-477). IEEE.

Antonio, N., de Almeida, A., & Nunes, L. (2017, December). Predicting hotel bookings cancellation with a machine learning classification model. In *2017 16th IEEE International Conference on Machine Learning and Applications (ICMLA)* (pp. 1049-1054). IEEE.

Aykol, M., Herring, P., & Anapolsky, A. (2020). Machine learning for continuous innovation in battery technologies. *Nature Reviews. Materials*, 5(10), 725–727. DOI: 10.1038/s41578-020-0216-y

Baier, L., Kühl, N., & Satzger, G. (2019). How to cope with change?-preserving validity of predictive services over time.

Baier, L., Schlör, T., Schöffer, J., & Kühl, N. (2021). Detecting concept drift with neural network model uncertainty. arXiv preprint arXiv:2107.01873.

Bandi, A., Adapa, P. V. S. R., & Kuchi, Y. E. V. P. K. (2023). The power of generative ai: A review of requirements, models, input–output formats, evaluation metrics, and challenges. *Future Internet*, 15(8), 260. DOI: 10.3390/fi15080260

Banerjee, A., Chen, C. C., Hung, C. C., Huang, X., Wang, Y., & Chevesaran, R. (2020). Challenges and Experiences with {MLOps} for Performance Diagnostics in {Hybrid-Cloud} Enterprise Software Deployments. In *2020 USENIX Conference on Operational Machine Learning (OpML 20)*.

Basole, R. C., & Major, T. (2024). Generative AI for Visualization: Opportunities and Challenges. *IEEE Computer Graphics and Applications*, 44(2), 55–64. DOI: 10.1109/MCG.2024.3362168 PMID: 38526875

Benni, B., Blay-Fornarino, M., Mosser, S., Precisio, F., & Jungbluth, G. (2019, September). When DevOps meets meta-learning: A portfolio to rule them all. In *2019 ACM/IEEE 22nd International Conference on Model Driven Engineering Languages and Systems Companion (MODELS-C)* (pp. 605-612). IEEE.

Cai, A., Rick, S. R., Heyman, J. L., Zhang, Y., Filipowicz, A., Hong, M., & Malone, T. (2023, November). DesignAID: Using generative AI and semantic diversity for design inspiration. In *Proceedings of The ACM Collective Intelligence Conference* (pp. 1-11).

Carcillo, F., Dal Pozzolo, A., Le Borgne, Y.-A., Caelen, O., Mazzer, Y., & Bontempi, G. (2018). Scarff: A scalable framework for streaming credit card fraud detection with spark. *Information Fusion*, 41, 182–194. DOI: 10.1016/j.inffus.2017.09.005

Choudhuri, R., Liu, D., Steinmacher, I., Gerosa, M., & Sarma, A. (2024, April). How Far Are We? The Triumphs and Trials of Generative AI in Learning Software Engineering. In *Proceedings of the IEEE/ACM 46th International Conference on Software Engineering* (pp. 1-13).

Chowdhary, A., Jha, K., & Zhao, M. (2023). Generative Adversarial Network (GAN)-Based Autonomous Penetration Testing for Web Applications. *Sensors (Basel)*, 23(18), 8014. DOI: 10.3390/s23188014 PMID: 37766067

Cui, T., Wang, Y., & Namih, B. (2019). Build an intelligent online marketing system: An overview. *IEEE Internet Computing*, 23(4), 53–60. DOI: 10.1109/MIC.2019.2924637

Derakhshan, B., Mahdiraji, A. R., Rabl, T., & Markl, V. (2019). *Continuous Deployment of Machine Learning Pipelines*. EDBT.

Domenech, A. M., & Guillén, A. (2020, September). ml-experiment: A Python framework for reproducible data science. *Journal of Physics: Conference Series*, 1603(1), 012025.

Ebert, C., & Louridas, P. (2023). Generative AI for software practitioners. *IEEE Software*, 40(4), 30–38. DOI: 10.1109/MS.2023.3265877

Ege, D. N., Øvrebø, H. H., Stubberud, V., Berg, M. F., Elverum, C., Steinert, M., & Vestad, H. (2024). The TrollLabs open hackathon dataset: Generative AI and large language models for prototyping in engineering design. *Data in Brief*, 54, 110332. DOI: 10.1016/j.dib.2024.110332 PMID: 38550240

Esmaeilzadeh, A., Heidari, M., Abdolazimi, R., Hajibabaee, P., & Malekzadeh, M. (2022, January). Efficient large scale nlp feature engineering with apache spark. In *2022 IEEE 12th Annual Computing and Communication Workshop and Conference (CCWC)* (pp. 0274-0280). IEEE.

Fateh, S., Sial, Q., Dar, S. H., Shah, I. A., & Rani, A. (2024). *Smart Healthcare System in Industry 4.0. Advances in Computational Intelligence for the Healthcare Industry 4.0*. IGI Global.

Foster, J., & Wagner, J. (2021, June). Naive Bayes versus BERT: Jupyter notebook assignments for an introductory NLP course. In *Proceedings of the Fifth Workshop on Teaching NLP* (pp. 112-114).

Furtado, L. S., Soares, J. B., & Furtado, V. (2024). A task-oriented framework for generative AI in design. *Journal of Creativity*, 34(2), 100086. DOI: 10.1016/j.yjoc.2024.100086

García, Á. L., De Lucas, J. M., Antonacci, M., Zu Castell, W., David, M., Hardt, M., Iglesias, L. L., Moltó, G., Plociennik, M., & Tran, V. (2020). A cloud-based framework for machine learning workloads and applications. *IEEE Access : Practical Innovations, Open Solutions*, 8, 18681–18692. DOI: 10.1109/ACCESS.2020.2964386

Gourisaria, M. K., Agrawal, R., Harshvardhan, G. M., Pandey, M., & Rautaray, S. S. (2021). Application of machine learning in industry 4.0. Machine learning: Theoretical foundations and practical applications, 57-87.

Granlund, T., Kopponen, A., Stirbu, V., Myllyaho, L., & Mikkonen, T. (2021, May). MLOps challenges in multi-organization setup: Experiences from two real-world cases. In 2021 IEEE/ACM 1st Workshop on AI Engineering-Software Engineering for AI (WAIN) (pp. 82-88). IEEE.

Heras García De Vinuesa, A. D. L., Luque Sendra, A., & Zamora-Polo, F. (2020). Machine Learning Technologies for Sustainability in Smart Cities in the Post-COVID Era. *Sustainability (Basel)*, 12(22), 9320. DOI: 10.3390/su12229320

Hewage, N., & Meedeniya, D. (2022). Machine learning operations: A survey on MLOps tool support. arXiv preprint arXiv:2202.10169.

Huang, C., & Sun, Y. (2022, September). Generative Approach to the Automation of Artificial Intelligence Applications. In CS & IT Conference Proceedings (Vol. 12, No. 15). CS & IT Conference Proceedings.

Hubara, I., Courbariaux, M., Soudry, D., El-Yaniv, R., & Bengio, Y. (2018). Quantized neural networks: Training neural networks with low precision weights and activations. *Journal of Machine Learning Research*, 18, 1–30.

Humayun, M., Jhanjhi, N., Almufareh, M. F., & Khalil, M. I. (2022). Security threat and vulnerability assessment and measurement in secure software development. *Computers, Materials & Continua*, 71, 5039–5059.

Humayun, M., Jhanjhi, N., Talib, M., Shah, M. H., & Suseendran, G. 2021. Cybersecurity for data science: issues, opportunities, and challenges. *Intelligent Computing and Innovation on Data Science:Proceedings of ICTIDS 2021*, 435-444.

Humayun, M., Niazi, M., Almufareh, M. F., Jhanjhi, N., Mahmood, S., & Alshayeb, M. (2022). Software-as-a-service security challenges and best practices: A multivocal literature review. *Applied Sciences (Basel, Switzerland)*, 12(8), 3953. DOI: 10.3390/app12083953

Jesmin, R. (2013). *Software development techniques for constructive information systems. Software Development Techniques for Constructive Information Systems Design*. IGI Global.

Jhanjhi, N., Ahmad, M., Khan, M. A., & Hussain, M. (2022). *The impact of cyber attacks on e-governance during the covid-19 pandemic. Cybersecurity Measures for E-Government Frameworks*. IGI Global.

Karn, R. R., Kudva, P., & Elfadel, I. A. M. (2018). Dynamic autoselection and autotuning of machine learning models for cloud network analytics. *IEEE Transactions on Parallel and Distributed Systems*, 30(5), 1052–1064. DOI: 10.1109/TPDS.2018.2876844

Khan, S. (2023). Role of Generative AI for Developing Personalized Content Based Websites. *International Journal of Innovative Science and Research Technology*, 8, 1–5.

Kirova, V. D., Ku, C., Laracy, J., & Marlowe, T. (2023). The ethics of artificial intelligence in the era of generative AI. *Journal of Systemics, Cybernetics and Informatics*, 21(4), 42–50. DOI: 10.54808/JSCI.21.04.42

Kocielnik, R., Amershi, S., & Bennett, P. N. (2019, May). Will you accept an imperfect ai? exploring designs for adjusting end-user expectations of ai systems. In *Proceedings of the 2019 CHI Conference on Human Factors in Computing Systems* (pp. 1-14).

Leite, L., Rocha, C., Kon, F., Milojicic, D., & Meirelles, P. (2019). A survey of DevOps concepts and challenges. *ACM Computing Surveys*, 52(6), 1–35. DOI: 10.1145/3359981

Lwakatare, L. E., Crnkovic, I., & Bosch, J. (2020a). *DevOps for AI–Challenges in Development of AI-enabled Applications. 2020 international conference on software, telecommunications and computer networks (SoftCOM)*. IEEE.

Lwakatare, L. E., Crnkovic, I., Rånge, E., & Bosch, J. (2020). From a data science driven process to a continuous delivery process for machine learning systems. In Product-Focused Software Process Improvement: 21st International Conference, PROFES 2020, Turin, Italy, November 25–27, 2020 [Springer International Publishing.]. *Proceedings*, 21, 185–201.

Macarthy, R. W., & Bass, J. M. (2020, August). An empirical taxonomy of DevOps in practice. In 2020 46th euromicro conference on software engineering and advanced applications (seaa) (pp. 221-228). IEEE.

Mäkinen, S., Skogström, H., Laaksonen, E., & Mikkonen, T. (2021, May). Who needs MLOps: What data scientists seek to accomplish and how can MLOps help? In 2021 IEEE/ACM 1st Workshop on AI Engineering-Software Engineering for AI (WAIN) (pp. 109-112). IEEE.

Matz, S., Teeny, J., Vaid, S. S., Peters, H., Harari, G., & Cerf, M. (2024). The potential of generative AI for personalized persuasion at scale. *Scientific Reports*, 14(1), 4692. DOI: 10.1038/s41598-024-53755-0 PMID: 38409168

Obeid, J. S., Davis, M., Turner, M., Meystre, S. M., Heider, P. M., O'Bryan, E. C., & Lenert, L. A. (2020). An artificial intelligence approach to COVID-19 infection risk assessment in virtual visits: A case report. *Journal of the American Medical Informatics Association : JAMIA*, 27(8), 1321–1325. DOI: 10.1093/jamia/ocaa105 PMID: 32449766

Perera, P., Silva, R., & Perera, I. (2017, September). Improve software quality through practicing DevOps. In 2017 seventeenth international conference on advances in ICT for emerging regions (ICTer) (pp. 1-6). IEEE.

Pesovski, I., Santos, R., Henriques, R., & Trajkovik, V. (2024). Generative ai for customizable learning experiences. *Sustainability (Basel)*, 16(7), 3034. DOI: 10.3390/su16073034

Posoldova, A. (2020). Machine learning pipelines: From research to production. *IEEE Potentials*, 39(6), 38–42. DOI: 10.1109/MPOT.2020.3016280

Ratani, S., Phatta, D., Phalke, D., Varun, N., & Aher, A. (2024, February). Web Sculptor-Generative AI Based Comprehensive Web Development Framework. In 2024 IEEE International Conference on Computing, Power and Communication Technologies (IC2PCT) (Vol. 5, pp. 1729-1732). IEEE.

Renggli, C., Rimanic, L., Gürel, N. M., Karlaš, B., Wu, W., & Zhang, C. (2021). A data quality-driven view of mlops. arXiv preprint arXiv:2102.07750.

Ruf, P., Madan, M., Reich, C., & Ould-Abdeslam, D. (2021). Demystifying mlops and presenting a recipe for the selection of open-source tools. *Applied Sciences (Basel, Switzerland)*, 11(19), 8861. DOI: 10.3390/app11198861

Russo, D. (2024). Navigating the complexity of generative ai adoption in software engineering. *ACM Transactions on Software Engineering and Methodology*, 33(5), 1–50. DOI: 10.1145/3652154

Rütz, M., & Wedel, F. (2019). DevOps: A systematic literature review. *Twenty-Seventh European Conference on Information Systems (ECIS2019)*, 1-16.

Saleh, M., Jhanjhi, N. Z., & Abdullah, A. (2020, February). Proposing a privacy protection model in case of civilian drone. In 2020 22nd International Conference on Advanced Communication Technology (ICACT) (pp. 596-602). IEEE.

Shah, I. A. (2024). Privacy and security challenges in unmanned aerial vehicles (UAVs). Cybersecurity in the Transportation Industry, 93-115.

Shah, I. A., Jhanjhi, N., & Ashraf, H. (2024a). *Logistics With the Internet of Things: Challenges, Perspectives, and Applications. Navigating Cyber Threats and Cybersecurity in the Logistics Industry.* IGI Global. DOI: 10.4018/979-8-3693-3816-2.ch006

Shah, I. A., Jhanjhi, N., & Brohi, S. N. (2024b). Use of Emerging Technologies in Healthcare 4.0. *Advances in Medical Technologies and Clinical Practice*, 4(0), 280–296. DOI: 10.4018/979-8-3693-2333-5.ch015

Silva, L. C., Zagatti, F. R., Sette, B. S., Dos Santos Silva, L. N., Lucrédio, D., Silva, D. F., & De Medeiros Caseli, H. Benchmarking machine learning solutions in production. 2020 19th IEEE International Conference on Machine Learning and Applications (ICMLA), 2020. IEEE, 626-633.

Siqueira, J. C. D. S. (2023). *Autonomous Incident Response.*

Spjuth, O., Frid, J., & Hellander, A. (2021). The machine learning life cycle and the cloud: Implications for drug discovery. *Expert Opinion on Drug Discovery*, 16(9), 1071–1079. DOI: 10.1080/17460441.2021.1932812 PMID: 34057379

Strauss, A. L. (2017). *The discovery of grounded theory: Strategies for qualitative research.* Routledge.

Talwani, S., Singla, J., Mathur, G., Malik, N., Jhanjhi, N., Masud, M., & Aljahdali, S. (2022). Machine-Learning-Based Approach for Virtual Machine Allocation and Migration. [s Note: MDPI stays neutral with regard to jurisdictional claims in published....]. *Electronics (Basel)*, 11(19), 3249. DOI: 10.3390/electronics11193249

Tamburri, D. A. (2020, September). Sustainable mlops: Trends and challenges. In 2020 22nd international symposium on symbolic and numeric algorithms for scientific computing (SYNASC) (pp. 17-23). IEEE.

Toschi, F., & Sega, M. (2019). *Flowing matter.* Springer Nature. DOI: 10.1007/978-3-030-23370-9

Vuppalapati, C., Ilapakurti, A., Chillara, K., Kedari, S., & Mamidi, V. (2020). *Automating tiny ml intelligent sensors devops using microsoft azure. 2020 ieee international conference on big data (big data).* IEEE.

Waheed, S., Hamid, B., Jhanjhi, N., Humayun, M., & Malik, N. A. (2019). Improving knowledge sharing in distributed software development. *IJACSA). International Journal of Advanced Computer Science and Applications*, 10.

Willman, A. (2024). Adoptions and Effects of Combining Agile Software Development and DevOps Practices–A Literature Review.

Wu, C., Haihong, E., & Song, M. (2020, January). An automatic artificial intelligence training platform based on kubernetes. In *Proceedings of the 2020 2nd International Conference on Big Data Engineering and Technology* (pp. 58-62).

Xu, J. (2022). *MLOps in the financial industry: Philosophy practices and tools. Future and Fintech, the, Abcdi and Beyond.* World Scientific.

Yongli, G., Qi, D., & Zhipeng, C. (2024). Leveraging the Synergy of IPv6, Generative AI, and Web Engineering to Create a Big Data-driven Education Platform. *Journal of Web Engineering*, 23, 197–226. DOI: 10.13052/jwe1540-9589.2321

York, E. (2023, October). Evaluating chatgpt: Generative ai in ux design and web development pedagogy. In *Proceedings of the 41st ACM International Conference on Design of Communication* (pp. 197-201).

Zhou, Y., Yu, Y., & Ding, B. (2020, October). Towards mlops: A case study of ml pipeline platform. In 2020 International conference on artificial intelligence and computer engineering (ICAICE) (pp. 494-500). IEEE.

Chapter 13
Introduction to Machine Learning Models for Web Engineering Concepts

Fida Hussain

School Education & Literacy Department Govt of Sindh, Pakistan

Saira Khurram Arbab

Faculty of Engineering Science & Technology, Iqra University, Pakistan

ABSTRACT

The rapid-fire expansion of the Internet has deeply integrated into diurnal life, challenging nonstop updates to web armature to manage vast data and cover stoner sequestration. This chapter explores security enterprises like phishing, data breaches, and payment gateway vulnerabilities, emphasizing their impact on consumers and associations. In competitive requests, businesses aim to increase gains without compromising quality, while AI offers results to challenges faced by both consumers and companies. AI- drivene-business enhances profitable growth, improves living norms, and shifts traditional retail towards a mix of physical and digital channels, furnishing strategic advantages through better understanding of behavior.

1. INTRODUCTION

In ensuring that user data is legitimate and free of scripts or malicious code that could jeopardize the security of the application, input validation assures users. Mechanisms for authorization and authentication guarantee that only people with permission can access the data and resources of the application. To stop unwanted access, multi-factor authentication and strong password regulations should be put

DOI: 10.4018/979-8-3693-3703-5.ch013

in place(Martins et al., 2024, Priya et al., 2024). Users will only be able to access the resources they require to complete their tasks, nothing more, thanks to access control. In the software business, for example, when the rapid pace of technical change has led to a deviation from conventional software development life cycle methodologies, technological advancement frequently outpaces the rate at which regulations and guidelines are applied. Even though industry and academia have made progress in raising the caliber of software, vulnerabilities are still a big problem(Song et al., 2024, Das Guptta et al., 2024). This is partially due to the difficulty in predicting all likely modes of failure for the sophisticated software systems of today. However, it's largely because the software development process requires more focus on safety and quality. Adhering to industry-established best practices in software development can improve software security and quality. Two examples of these techniques are the application of least privilege and secure code rules. Overview ML models are in Fig 1.

Figure 1. Overview ML models

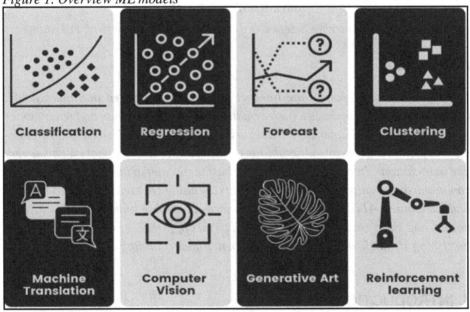

The CVE database offers a standardized method to identify and manage cyber-security vulnerabilities, enabling security researchers, providers, and businesses to stay informed about potential threats and take appropriate action to mitigate them(Lavor et al., 2024, Liang et al., 2024). The database makes vulnerability information available to the public, promoting transparency and collaboration within the cybersecurity industry. Preventive techniques for identifying and fixing security flaws should be a part of any robust security program. Regular vulnerability assessments and penetration tests are crucial to preventing attackers from taking advantage of weaknesses. Indeed, one of the most important steps in identifying software security flaws is software testing.

It's encouraging to learn that our suggested CVD model has outperformed other accepted methods for vulnerability detection(Huseynov and Ozdenizci Kose, 2024, Zeebaree, 2024). It's crucial to remember that before the model can be broadly embraced and applied in real-world situations, more validation and testing may be required. Furthermore, continuous observation and improvement of the model will be essential to guarantee its sustained efficacy throughout time. Your findings, however, are encouraging and imply that the CVD model might be a helpful weapon in the fight against vulnerabilities(Abdulrahman et al., 2024, Shah et al., 2024d). This research uses and extends upon a vulnerability dataset that includes defects found in commercially available software. More vulnerabilities are detected by it than by CNN and RNN models. The software algorithm of the updated CNN model finds vulnerabilities more accurately. Machine learning and software vulnerability assessment techniques with more vulnerability records across all domains are the main topics of data security research(Shah et al., 2024e, Markou et al., 2024, Karlsson and Alfgården). We use machine learning multi-class classification techniques and statistical analysis methods from natural language processing into our proposed model. We offer a method for automating security flaw finding by combining a pretrained context encoder with a self-attention mechanism. The goal of this project is to put together all the components required to create an automated, AI-based model that can identify software vulnerabilities.

1.2 Introduction Machine Learning Models

Finding software bugs has become increasingly important as the frequency and sophistication of cyberattacks increases. People, companies, and even whole countries are susceptible to the destruction that these attacks can cause. Researchers and companies are thus devoting more time and resources to software security y(Kreuzberger et al., 2023, Talaei Khoei and Kaabouch, 2023, Breit et al., 2023). One of the main challenges in identifying software vulnerabilities is the enormous amount of code that exists in contemporary software systems. As software becomes more complex, it becomes harder and harder to find every security weakness in a system. Software vulnerabilities are often hard to locate because they are hidden deep in the code and call for specific tools and techniques. Researchers and business experts use a variety of strategies to find weaknesses in order to get over these obstacles. One way is to use automated technologies that check code for security vulnerabilities.

Static analysis, symbolic execution, and fuzzing are some of the techniques used to examine the software. Another choice is to use manual testing techniques like vulnerability scanning and pen testing. These techniques involve finding software system vulnerabilities that an attacker could exploit. Researchers also employ code audits as a means of searching software for security vulnerabilities(Kumar et al., 2023, Sharma and Kumar, 2023, Taye, 2023). Source audits can be time-consuming and necessitate a thorough understanding of the software source, but they are usually effective in identifying vulnerabilities that automated procedures could miss.

Chapter's Contribution:

1. This chapter discussed the Machine Learning Model.
2. We discussed several issues in the literature review
3. This chapter discusses the detection methods and process.
4. This chapter discussed web engineering concepts.
5. This chapter provides future direction and recommendations

2. LITERATURE REVIEW

Finding software bugs has become a critical area of research given the increasing frequency and sophistication of cyberattacks. These attacks have the potential to seriously harm individuals' computers, companies, and even entire nations. Researchers and companies are thus devoting more time and resources to software security. One of the main challenges in identifying software vulnerabilities is the large amount of code that is included in contemporary software systems. As software becomes more complex, it becomes harder to find every security flaw in a system(Touretzky et al., 2023, Hafidi et al., 2023). Furthermore, it can be challenging to find software vulnerabilities without the use of specialist tools and techniques because they are often hidden deep within the code. A variety of methods are used by researchers and industry specialists to identify weaknesses in order to get past these barriers. One approach is to use automated tools that check code for security vulnerabilities. These tools do code analysis to find security flaws using techniques including symbolic execution, fuzzing, and static analysis. Finding vulnerabilities that could be exploited by bad actors is getting harder in today's extremely complex software systems. Patching is not always a simple process, though, as it can lead to new problems or incompatibility with other program components(Stamp, 2022, Lindholm et al., 2022, Shaheed and Kurdy, 2022). Vulnerabilities are by definition more likely to be exploited by attackers the longer it takes to find and address them. Developers are under pressure to find and fix vulnerabilities as soon as possible to prevent them from being exploited. Numerous research projects have looked into automated threat identification for software security and related security concerns. Although there is a wide range of topics covered by the literature, this review will concentrate on four main themes that recurrently show up in the literature: attacks, secure software and vulnerabilities, openness, and the investigation of machine learning algorithms as a means of mitigating threats and strengthening vulnerabilities.

This taxonomy method has been used to classify security problems in health information systems. In order to close the gap in risk assessment and management procedures for small and medium-sized commercial organizations handling medium-to-low-level hazards, RAMeX was created. Six distinct research methodologies are examined in this study(Sindiramutty et al., 2024, Shah et al., 2024c, Sharifani and Amini, 2023). They typically approach planning as a separate process that isn't logically or directly related to the development of IT systems. When integrated with planning, development, and management, enterprise information resources—which capture and characterize the organization—will reduce response times and enable the performance of an economic analysis of information system investment. The network administrator has additional security issues while maintaining adequate security measures across heterogeneous platforms. There is an increase in computer crime(Tiwari, 2022, Naser, 2023, Badal and Sungkur, 2023). One of these crimes is listening in on private conversations. Physically harming information storage devices is another. This demonstrates the need for a strategy that is more suited for smaller businesses and those that need a quicker, easier, and less resource-intensive approach. This implies that an alternate approach to effective information technology (IT) risk assessment and management is required. The creation of a risk assessment technique allows for the intriguing deduction of some interesting conclusions about the organizational information security decision-making process. Understanding the intricacies of the hazards connected to automated information systems is crucial(Bedi et al., 2022, Sidhu et al., 2022, López et al., 2022). Those assigned to conduct a risk assessment exercise must possess the necessary training and expertise, and their selection must be carefully thought out, overview machine learning approaches are in Figure 2.

Figure 2. Overview ML approaches

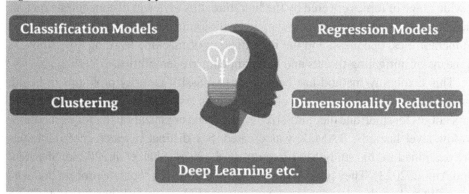

Healthcare institutions can now determine the essential safety measures for themselves thanks to the research's development of a revolutionary way to risk analysis. The plan was also combined with a cutting-edge management technique that would spot any problems during execution. According to the poll, major issues make it more difficult to establish just and efficient public health data systems and safeguard individuals' privacy. Who logs in and their actions within the system should be recorded in the logs. It is vital to look into the variables influencing security enforcement before doing a thorough examination of security protocols(Shah and Jhanjhi, 2024, Shah et al., 2024a, Jordan and Mitchell, 2015). Both manually and automatically, it covers how to identify an incursion, launch a counterattack, and assess the damage.

Federal standards and regulations requiring security and privacy protections are still being updated, albeit far more slowly than the technology used to collect, analyze, integrate, and digitally store data. Often, data centers, computers, networks, and communications links are employed to improve the efficiency of healthcare delivery. A new map of the relationships between controls and risks was created as a result of the seven case studies' results, which revealed more EDI hazards and controls(Müller and Guido, 2016, Jhanjhi and Shah, 2024, Zhao et al., 2019). The author provided an overview of the various studies conducted on attack resistance and high-level security, as well as an explanation of the necessity of total network security. The author looks at the main requirements for a risk analysis approach, the conflicts that could arise from these demands, and the reasons risk assessment is a challenging area of research. The approach is based on the widely accepted theory that a large number of security breaches are caused by various software setups and source code errors.

The technique forces abnormal program states during the software's execution through the use of software defect injection. Next, it keeps an eye on how these states affect the overall safety of the system. The program was intended to help businesses reach their objectives. Software architecture establishes a connection between the design of a program and its intended use(El Misilmani and Naous, 2019, Boutaba et al., 2018). There is constant pressure on developers to make sure that their projects' architecture and design promote website security.

3. OVERVIEW METHODS AND DETECTION PROCESS

Ultimately, the choice of research method and approach is influenced by the research topic, the kind of data being collected, the resources available, and other contextual factors. These are important considerations for researchers to make while organizing their studies and assessing their findings. They ought to be conscious of the constraints and any prejudices associated with the approaches they have selected. Attempts to detect software vulnerabilities that have been made in the past to address detection problems are the focus of detection research(Shah et al., 2024b, Gill et al., 2021). The focus of this work is on detection, which is one of the most significant issues in the field of software vulnerability detection. The number of false positives and false negatives in a detection system is a critical indicator of its effectiveness. This is particularly significant because it demonstrates that the recommended approach to identifying software vulnerabilities is flawed, as it results in numerous incorrect classifications. The problem of detection performance is widely acknowledged and frequently researched in the field of computer security, especially in areas such as opinion spam and virus detection(Saleh et al., 2020, Sarker, 2021). Other sorts of vulnerabilities are injection, privilege escalation, buffer overflow, and authentication bypass vulnerabilities, to name a few. The kind of vulnerabilities that can be found with a given detection technique will vary depending on the technique itself, the system under test, and its architecture. The majority of software vulnerability detection research that has been done so far concentrates on binary detection, in which a sample is classified as either vulnerable or not. The current research on software vulnerability identification that tackles problems with code activities and code complexity is covered by the code research interest groups. Any activity involving source codes, such as editing and removing by software developers, is referred to as "code activities." During the software development process, developers might arrange their codes into simple or complicated forms using certain operations and techniques(Hüllermeier and Waegeman, 2021, Bukhari et al., 2018). This is mostly dependent on the goals that the software development team has set for itself.

Throughout the numerous stages of software development, software engineers work in teams, and each developer approaches coding differently. When changes made by several developers are not adequately documented, the code structure becomes uneven(Zaman et al.). This disparity frequently leads to security problems. Because of this, software engineers have to choose which code structures work best for certain software development projects and grant access to the software to security experts so they can apply the proper hardening approaches to the software.

4. WEB ENGINEERING CONCEPTS

A web application, also referred to as a web app, is a piece of software that can be accessed and utilized through a web browser on the internet. It communicates with users using a web interface and is operated on web servers. Because web apps are platform-agnostic, anyone with a working web browser and an internet connection may see them on a range of devices, including desktops, laptops, and smartphones(Patterson and Gibson, 2017, Konatham et al., 2024). A web application architecture describes how each component of the application is arranged and illustrates the connections between databases, web services, third-party middleware systems, and application components. This is a picture of how several programs communicate with one another in order to simultaneously provide services to end users. The hacker has access to all user data stored in the database, including social security numbers, credit card numbers, and user details. They can also access password-protected areas like the administrator portal(Chaudhary et al., 2023, Zaheer et al., 2022). Supervised learning is the most widely used machine learning method for locating software vulnerabilities. This is because reliable datasets can help it work effectively. Labels such as "vulnerable" and "non-vulnerable" are applied to datasets during supervision-based learning. Every observation in the dataset has a label assigned to it before the vulnerability detection model is trained. Some of these labeled datasets are available to the public thanks to the efforts of previous researchers who worked on vulnerability detection studies. To help with their research, some researchers created their own privately tagged databases. Because the supervised learning method can finish any work, it has gained popularity. One of the many applications of supervised learning is this. An Overview of web application architecture is in Figure 3

Figure 3. overview web application architecture adapted from clickittech.com

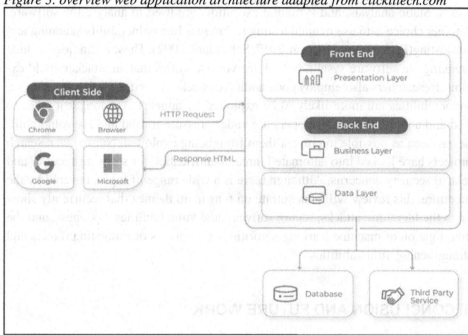

The model is then retrained using the predicted data, which yields better performance than training the model only on the initially tagged dataset. The ability to use labeled or unlabeled data makes semi-supervised learning appealing. This is highly reliable since it is harder to obtain a significant volume of labeled data than unlabeled data.

5. DISCUSSION

The study of how to find software weaknesses has grown essential as the frequency and sophistication of cyberattacks increases. People, companies, and even entire countries are susceptible to the destruction that these attacks can cause. Researchers and companies are spending more time and money to secure their software as a result. One of the main challenges in identifying software vulnerabilities is the enormous amount of code contained in contemporary software systems. It gets harder and harder to find every security hole in a system as software gets more complex. Software vulnerabilities are frequently hard to uncover since they are hidden deep inside the code and need specialised tools and techniques. Researchers and industry experts use a variety of techniques to identify weaknesses to get around these

277

challenges. One approach is to use automated tools that check code for security issues. Static analysis, and symbolic execution, are used to analyse the software. Another choice is to use manual testing techniques like vulnerability scanning and pen testing(Patterson and Gibson, 2017, Sebastiani, 2002). These techniques include breaking the software system to look for vulnerabilities that an attacker could exploit. Researchers also employ code audits to check for security holes in software. Vulnerabilities are more likely to be exploited by attackers the longer it takes to find and address them. Developers are under pressure to find and fix vulnerabilities as soon as possible to prevent them from being exploited. Numerous research projects have looked into automated threat identification for software security and related security concerns. Although there is a wide range of topics covered by the literature, this review will concentrate on four main themes that recurrently show up in the literature: attacks, secure software and vulnerabilities, openness, and the investigation of machine learning algorithms as a means of mitigating threats and strengthening vulnerabilities.

6. CONCLUSION AND FUTURE WORK

Conclusion of this chapter, the field of machine learning is expanding rapidly both in the IT industry and across several commercial domains. Despite being in its infancy, machine learning is widely used in all fields of technology. This area of research enables computers to automatically pick up new skills and improve with practice. Therefore, machine learning concentrates on the efficacy of computer programs by gathering information from diverse observations. Web architecture is constantly being updated and reinvented to benefit from the vast amounts of data and information available on the Internet. The rise of the digital economy has raised the need to safeguard user privacy and preserve sensitive data. In competitive markets, firms strive to boost their profit margins without compromising the quality of their products to fortify the digital marketplace against the difficulties posed by a constantly shifting cyber landscape. For the creation of web applications, model-driven web engineering techniques are becoming a popular research and technological option. However, because the technological and research requirements do not align, the industry has not accepted them despite over 20 years of development. Hundreds of engineers from various firms around the world were surveyed to have a better understanding of this problem and potential solutions. This article provides an overview of our findings along with a set of recommendations for enhancing model-driven Web engineering techniques to make them workable for the business world. Despite this, not all of the suggestions have been accepted as anticipated because the respondents' needs haven't made it clear whether or not the suggested remedy works for each of them individually. We want to incorporate numerous other elements in a subsequent investigation, in addition to the problems discussed in this chapter.

In the present situation, when customers are spending a lot of time online and obtaining information about buying via electronic gadgets Traditional brick-and-mortar stores are moving more and more toward the internet.

REFERENCES

Abdulrahman, S. M., Asaad, R. R., Ahmad, H. B., Hani, A. A., Zeebaree, S. R., & Sallow, A. B. (2024). Machine Learning in Nonlinear Material Physics. *Journal of Soft Computing and Data Mining*, 5, 122–131.

Badal, Y. T., & Sungkur, R. K. (2023). Predictive modelling and analytics of students' grades using machine learning algorithms. *Education and Information Technologies*, 28(3), 3027–3057. DOI: 10.1007/s10639-022-11299-8 PMID: 36097545

Bedi, P., Goyal, S. B., Rajawat, A. S., Shaw, R. N., & Ghosh, A. (2022). A framework for personalizing atypical web search sessions with concept-based user profiles using selective machine learning techniques. In Advanced Computing and Intelligent Technologies. *Proceedings of ICACIT*, 2021, 279–291.

Boutaba, R., Salahuddin, M. A., Limam, N., Ayoubi, S., Shahriar, N., Estrada-Solano, F., & Caicedo, O. M. (2018). A comprehensive survey on machine learning for networking: Evolution, applications and research opportunities. *Journal of Internet Services and Applications*, 9(1), 1–99. DOI: 10.1186/s13174-018-0087-2

Breit, A., Waltersdorfer, L., Ekaputra, F. J., Sabou, M., Ekelhart, A., Iana, A., Paulheim, H., Portisch, J., Revenko, A., Teije, A. T., & Van Harmelen, F. (2023). Combining machine learning and semantic web: A systematic mapping study. *ACM Computing Surveys*, 55(14s), 1–41. DOI: 10.1145/3586163

Bukhari, S. S. A., Humayun, M., Shah, S. A. A., & Jhanjhi, N. Z. (2018, November). Improving requirement engineering process for web application development. In 2018 12th International Conference on Mathematics, Actuarial Science, Computer Science and Statistics (MACS) (pp. 1-5). IEEE.

Chaudhary, M., Gaur, L., Chakrabarti, A., & Jhanjhi, N. Z. (2023). Unravelling the Barriers of human resource analytics: Multi-criteria decision-making approach. Journal of Survey in Fisheries Sciences, 306-321.

Das Guptta, S., Shahriar, K. T., Alqahtani, H., Alsalman, D., & Sarker, I. H. (2024). Modeling hybrid feature-based phishing websites detection using machine learning techniques. *Annals of Data Science*, 11(1), 217–242. DOI: 10.1007/s40745-022-00379-8

El Misilmani, H. M., & Naous, T. (2019, July). Machine learning in antenna design: An overview on machine learning concept and algorithms. In *2019 International Conference on High Performance Computing & Simulation (HPCS)* (pp. 600-607). IEEE.

Gill, S. H., Sheikh, N. A., Rajpar, S., Jhanjhi, N., Ahmad, M., Razzaq, M. A., Alshamrani, S. S., Malik, Y., & Jaafar, F. (2021). Extended Forgery Detection Framework for COVID-19 Medical Data Using Convolutional Neural Network. *Computers, Materials & Continua*, 68.

Hafidi, M. M., Djezzar, M., Hemam, M., Amara, F. Z., & Maimour, M. (2023). Semantic web and machine learning techniques addressing semantic interoperability in Industry 4.0. *International Journal of Web Information Systems*, 19(3/4), 157–172. DOI: 10.1108/IJWIS-03-2023-0046

Hüllermeier, E., & Waegeman, W. (2021). Aleatoric and epistemic uncertainty in machine learning: An introduction to concepts and methods. *Machine Learning*, 110(3), 457–506. DOI: 10.1007/s10994-021-05946-3

Huseynov, F., & Ozdenizci Kose, B. (2024). Using machine learning algorithms to predict individuals' tendency to be victim of social engineering attacks. *Information Development*, 40(2), 298–318. DOI: 10.1177/02666669221116336

Jhanjhi, N. Z., & Shah, I. A. (2024). *Navigating Cyber Threats and Cybersecurity in the Logistics Industry*. IGI Global. DOI: 10.4018/979-8-3693-3816-2

Jordan, M. I., & Mitchell, T. M. (2015). Machine learning: Trends, perspectives, and prospects. *Science*, 349(6245), 255–260. DOI: 10.1126/science.aaa8415 PMID: 26185243

Karlsson, K. & Alfgården, H. (n.d.). Robust concept development utilising artificial intelligence and machine learning.

Konatham, B., Simra, T., Amsaad, F., Ibrahem, M. I., & Jhanjhi, N. Z. (2024). A Secure Hybrid Deep Learning Technique for Anomaly Detection in IIoT Edge Computing. *Authorea Preprints*.

Kreuzberger, D., Kühl, N., & Hirschl, S. (2023). Machine learning operations (mlops): Overview, definition, and architecture. *IEEE Access : Practical Innovations, Open Solutions*, 11, 31866–31879. DOI: 10.1109/ACCESS.2023.3262138

Kumar, B., Roy, S., Singh, K. U., Pandey, S. K., Kumar, A., Sinha, A., Shukla, S., Shah, M. A., & Rasool, A. (2023). A static machine learning based evaluation method for usability and security analysis in e-commerce website. *IEEE Access : Practical Innovations, Open Solutions*, 11, 40488–40510. DOI: 10.1109/ACCESS.2023.3247003

Lavor, V., De Come, F., Dos Santos, M. T., & Vianna, A. S.Jr. (2024). Machine learning in chemical engineering: Hands-on activities. *Education for Chemical Engineers*, 46, 10–21. DOI: 10.1016/j.ece.2023.09.005

Liang, P. P., Zadeh, A., & Morency, L.-P. (2024). Foundations & trends in multimodal machine learning: Principles, challenges, and open questions. *ACM Computing Surveys*, 56, 1–42. DOI: 10.1145/3676164

Lindholm, A., Wahlström, N., Lindsten, F., & Schön, T. B. (2022). *Machine learning: a first course for engineers and scientists*. Cambridge University Press. DOI: 10.1017/9781108919371

López, J. A. H., Cánovas Izquierdo, J. L., & Cuadrado, J. S. (2022). ModelSet: A dataset for machine learning in model-driven engineering. *Software & Systems Modeling*, 21(3), 1–20. DOI: 10.1007/s10270-021-00929-3

Markou, G., Bakas, N. P., Chatzichristofis, S. A., & Papadrakakis, M. (2024). A general framework of high-performance machine learning algorithms: Application in structural mechanics. *Computational Mechanics*, 73(4), 705–729. DOI: 10.1007/s00466-023-02386-9

Martins, R. M., Von Wangenheim, C. G., Rauber, M. F., & Hauck, J. C. (2024). Machine learning for all!—Introducing machine learning in middle and high school. *International Journal of Artificial Intelligence in Education*, 34(2), 185–223. DOI: 10.1007/s40593-022-00325-y

Müller, A. C., & Guido, S. (2016). *Introduction to machine learning with Python: a guide for data scientists*. O'Reilly Media, Inc.

Naser, M. (2023). *Machine learning for civil and environmental engineers: A practical approach to data-driven analysis, explainability, and causality*. John Wiley & Sons.

Patterson, J., & Gibson, A. (2017). *Deep learning: A practitioner's approach*. O'Reilly Media, Inc.

Priya, S., Bhadra, S., Chimalakonda, S., & Venigalla, A. S. M. (2024). ML-Quest: A game for introducing machine learning concepts to K-12 students. *Interactive Learning Environments*, 32(1), 229–244. DOI: 10.1080/10494820.2022.2084115

Saleh, M., Jhanjhi, N., & Abdullah, A. (2020, February). Fatima-tuz-Zahra, "Proposing a privacy protection model in case of civilian drone,". In *Proc. 22nd Int. Conf. Adv. Commun. Technol.(ICACT)* (pp. 596-602).

Sarker, I. H. (2021). Deep learning: A comprehensive overview on techniques, taxonomy, applications and research directions. *SN Computer Science*, 2(6), 420. DOI: 10.1007/s42979-021-00815-1 PMID: 34426802

Sebastiani, F. (2002). Machine learning in automated text categorization. *ACM Computing Surveys*, 34(1), 1–47. DOI: 10.1145/505282.505283

Shah, I. A., Jhanjhi, N., & Brohi, S. N. (2024b). *IoT Smart Healthcare Security Challenges and Solutions. Advances in Computational Intelligence for the Healthcare Industry 4.0.* IGI Global.

Shah, I. A., & Jhanjhi, N. Z. (Eds.). (2024). *Cybersecurity Issues and Challenges in the Drone Industry.*

Shah, I. A., Jhanjhi, N. Z., & Brohi, S. (2024). Cybersecurity issues and challenges in civil aviation security. Cybersecurity in the Transportation Industry, 1-23.

Shah, I. A., Jhanjhi, N. Z., & Rajper, S. (2024c). *Use of Deep Learning Applications for Drone Technology. Cybersecurity Issues and Challenges in the Drone Industry.* IGI Global. DOI: 10.4018/979-8-3693-0774-8

Shah, I. A., Jhanjhi, N. Z., & Ray, S. K. (2024d). *IoT Devices in Drones: Security Issues and Future Challenges. Cybersecurity Issues and Challenges in the Drone Industry.* IGI Global. DOI: 10.4018/979-8-3693-0774-8.ch009

Shah, I. A., Laraib, A., Ashraf, H., & Hussain, F. (2024e). Drone Technology: Current Challenges and Opportunities. Cybersecurity Issues and Challenges in the Drone Industry, 343-361.

Shaheed, A., & Kurdy, M. B. (2022). Web application firewall using machine learning and features engineering. *Security and Communication Networks*, 2022, 5280158. DOI: 10.1155/2022/5280158

Sharifani, K., & Amini, M. (2023). Machine learning and deep learning: A review of methods and applications. *World Information Technology and Engineering Journal*, 10, 3897–3904.

Sharma, A., & Kumar, S. (2023). Machine learning and ontology-based novel semantic document indexing for information retrieval. *Computers & Industrial Engineering*, 176, 108940. DOI: 10.1016/j.cie.2022.108940

Sidhu, B. K., Singh, K., & Sharma, N. (2022). A machine learning approach to software model refactoring. *International Journal of Computers and Applications*, 44(2), 166–177. DOI: 10.1080/1206212X.2020.1711616

Sindiramutty, S. R., Jhanjhi, N. Z., Tan, C. E., Khan, N. A., Shah, B., & Manchuri, A. R. (2024). *Cybersecurity Measures for Logistics Industry. Navigating Cyber Threats and Cybersecurity in the Logistics Industry.* IGI Global.

Song, B., Zhou, R., & Ahmed, F. (2024). Multi-modal machine learning in engineering design: A review and future directions. *Journal of Computing and Information Science in Engineering*, 24(1), 010801. DOI: 10.1115/1.4063954

Stamp, M. (2022). *Introduction to machine learning with applications in information security*. Chapman and Hall/CRC. DOI: 10.1201/9781003264873

Talaei Khoei, T., & Kaabouch, N. (2023). Machine Learning: Models, Challenges, and Research Directions. *Future Internet*, 15(10), 332. DOI: 10.3390/fi15100332

Taye, M. M. (2023). Understanding of machine learning with deep learning: Architectures, workflow, applications and future directions. *Computers*, 12(5), 91. DOI: 10.3390/computers12050091

Tiwari, S. (2022). Concepts and strategies for machine learning. Current studies in basic sciences engineering and technology, 45-54.

Touretzky, D., Gardner-Mccune, C., & Seehorn, D. (2023). Machine learning and the five big ideas in AI. *International Journal of Artificial Intelligence in Education*, 33(2), 233–266. DOI: 10.1007/s40593-022-00314-1

Zaheer, A., Tahir, S., Humayun, M., Almufareh, M. F., & Jhanjhi, N. Z. (2022, November). A novel Machine learning technique for fake smart watches advertisement detection. In 2022 14th International Conference on Mathematics, Actuarial Science, Computer Science and Statistics (MACS) (pp. 1-5). IEEE.

Zaman, N., Khan, A. R., & Salih, M. Designing of Energy aware Quality of Service (QoS) based routing protocol for Efficiency Improvement in Wireless Sensor Network (WSN).

Zeebaree, I. (2024). The Distributed Machine Learning in Cloud Computing and Web Technology: A Review of Scalability and Efficiency. *Journal of Information Technology and Informatics*, 3(1).

Zhao, Y., Li, Y., Zhang, X., Geng, G., Zhang, W., & Sun, Y. (2019). A survey of networking applications applying the software defined networking concept based on machine learning. *IEEE Access : Practical Innovations, Open Solutions*, 7, 95397–95417. DOI: 10.1109/ACCESS.2019.2928564

Chapter 14
Generative AI–Driven Security Frameworks for Web Engineering:
Innovations and Challenges

Rachna Rana
 https://orcid.org/0000-0003-0450-8699
Ludhiana Group of Colleges, Ludhiana, India

Pankaj Bhambri
 https://orcid.org/0000-0003-4437-4103
Guru Nanak Dev Engineering College, Ludhiana, India

ABSTRACT

The advent of Generative AI has triggered a paradigm shift across several domains, resulting in ground-breaking advances in text, picture, video, audio, and code production. However, this technical advancement has also increased cyber security intimidations, as hackers increasingly use Generative AI in their harmful actions. Generative artificial intelligence (Gen-AI) and Huge words models (HWMs) are transforming businesses throughout the world. However, their enormous promise carries major hazards. It is critical to address the cyber security concerns related with Gen-AI. This aids organizations in comprehending the security implications of these technologies. This chapter will provide a complete Gen-AI security architecture and show how it may help us protect Gen-AI apps, models, and the whole Gen-AI ecosystem. This research attempts to define the many security vulnerabilities posed by Generative AI, identifying their manifestations across different application areas.

DOI: 10.4018/979-8-3693-3703-5.ch014

1. INTRODUCTION

As organizations deploy generative AI (Gen-AI), and Huge words models (HWMs), they become further conscious of the issues that Gen-AI presents. This is especially relevant to the Gen-AI ecosystem's security. Many clients have inquired about how to handle Gen-AI security. Some have started their experiments to investigate certain areas of Gen-AI security (Alshabandar et al., 2020 & Analysis of Stacked Ensemble Classification Models, 2023). To fully understand the insinuations of Gen-AI safety, a complete structure is necessary. This structure should direct the broad issues of Gen-AI safety and the many kinds of Gen-AI security intimidations at different stages. Such an approach will help guide organizations in addressing their specific security concerns.

Our Precision AI technology may be incorporated to give customized responses and observations, increasing the system even further. Exactitude AI knowledge, which is constructed on a large safety dataset, provides increased potentials for identifying and mitigating AI-driven risks, assuring a strong defensive mechanism inside the framework (Ang & Seng, 2022; Chavan, 2018; and Classification and Errors Analysis of COVID-19, 2022).

Palo Alto Networks' Precision AI is a proprietary AI technology designed exclusively for cyber security. Precision AI uses standard AI/ML methods but modifies them for security.

Exactitude AI knowledge, in particular, provides elevated - declaration for cyber guardian by consolidating and investigating information using safety- precise replicas to help guardian in automating exposure, anticipation, and reply. Trusting Precision AI-powered technologies allows security teams to automate with confidence and accomplish security results quicker.

By completely addressing these linked areas, our methodology enables enterprises to gain a comprehensive knowledge of Gen-AI security issues. This is crucial for realizing the revolutionary promise of these technologies while minimizing the related security intimidations.

1.1. Essential Security Components

Based on real-world data and occurrences, we suggest the following Gen-AI cyber security methodology, which includes five essential security components.

1.1.1. Generation AI I/O durability:- NLP, or natural language processing, has accomplished significant progress, owing primarily to the popularity of language modeling. However, despite their sophisticated facade, major security risks exist. To get around safety constraints, aggressors may utilize bafflement methods such as indoctrination, emojis, or particular typescripts. It is also regular to divider payloads among contributions to keep away from contribution corroboration. The variety and complexity of these quick inoculation methods emphasize the significance of vigorous self-protective apparatus. To alleviate the jeopardy connected with timely inoculation and other HWM I/O vulnerabilities, associations and developers should put into practice a multi- coated safety diagram. This should give contribution corroboration to put off unacceptable, malevolent, or surprising contributions from toward the inside the HWM. Output sanitization is also critical for guaranteeing safe output handling procedure (Cyber Attacks Detection Using Machine Learning, 2023; Flight Delay Prediction Using Machine Learning, 2023; Goyani, 2021).

1.1.2. Reputable Gen-AI leadership- Ethical, transparent, and responsible Gen-AI development and application are critical. Strong governance standards assist to avoid unintentional biases, preserve consistency with company principles, and increase user confidence. Effective Gen-AI leadership necessitates congruence with company principles, safeguards against hallucinations, transparency, explain ability, and resilience to model drift. Precision AI technology is critical in this process because it provides superior monitoring capabilities that verify Gen-AI systems stay secure and ethically compliant. By recognizing and resolving these critical issues, cybersecurity experts can help guarantee that Gen-AI is utilized in a secure, ethical, and accountable manner.

1.1.3. Safeguard the Gen-AI network infrastructure environment:- The foundational equipment of Gen-AI platforms, along with its software suppliers, present numerous potential vulnerabilities for attacks. To minimize the likelihood of breaches and uphold system resilience, it is imperative to implement robust security measures. The computational resources necessary for training and running HWMs are especially appealing targets for hostile actors looking to leverage this dispensation control for illegal reasons (Liu et al., 2022 and Liu & Xie, 2022). To fruitfully attend to these safety jeopardy, industry should stress practical safety explanations like as safety review, multi-factor substantiation, event reaction movement, and secure coding put into practice. Uninterrupted scrutinizing and dexterity are needed to contest promising intimidations.

1.1.4. Counterproductive Gen-AI security protection:- Gen-AI enables cybersecurity assaults by increasing the efficiency, sophistication, and flexibility of harmful actions. Gen-AI automates challenging processes that would otherwise need human expertise, for example distributing modified phishing emails or perceiving particular defects in a system's safe. This potential permits fake hits to be carried out on a great deal superior size and at a more rapidly rate, lengthening the capacity and feasible impact of these intimidations. Furthermore, Gen-AI adds new layers of complexity to computer-generated assault. It can scrutinize enormous datasets to settle on the most victorious physical attack manner, make specially communication for explicit target based on private information, correctly impersonate a conviction individual's face, ability to speak, and technique, and pretend standard user movement to keep away from recognition.

1.1.5. Verified Gen-AI knowledge lifetime:- Gen-AI algorithms frequently rely on large and diverse datasets, which may include internet material, social media posts, digital manuscript, and customer-produced data. At the same time as this massive amount of records has improved the competences of AI representation, it also instigates serious safekeeping jeopardy (Mehra, 2021 and Messaoud et al., 2022). These databases include responsive and proprietary information, and any misuse or unauthorized disclosure of this data might result in privacy violations, regulatory concerns, and significant reputational harm.

2. GENERATIVE AI

Generative artificial intelligence (AI), also known as generative AI, is a type of artificial intelligence competent of building new matter such as images, text, music, audio, and movies. It uses foundation models, which are massive neural networks capable of a variety of tasks including as classification, summarization, and Q&A. Generative AI may be taught complex subjects such as computer languages, human language, art, chemistry, and biology. It then uses the training data to tackle new problems. For example, generative AI may learn the English language and use it to write a poem. Some of the uses of generative AI include the following:

2.1 Producing content:- Generative AI can shorten content production times by allowing users to quickly produce new material based on a range of inputs.

2.2 Chat bot:- "Chatbots are created using generative artificial intelligence."

2.3 Facts confidentiality:- Generative AI algorithms can create artificial data from real information to safeguard user privacy while preserving the authenticity of the data.

2.4 Trade:- To enable risk assessments and opportunity evaluations, AI models can analyze and modify data from external sources. This capability has the potential to enhance supply chains, digital twins, 3D modeling, product development, and business operations.

Generative AI presents additional dangers, including legal, financial, and reputational concerns. For example, generative models can occasionally produce information that appears authoritative but is false or prejudiced. They may also mistakenly generate personal or copyrighted material from their training data, posing challenges to intellectual property regulations and privacy.

3. GENERATIVE AI IN CYBER SECURITY

"Cyber security involves defending organization, webs, and programs against digital intimidations. These intimidations may aspire to admission, adapt, or erase significant information, extract currency, or disturb company processes. Additionally, cyber security helps to prevent ransom ware, phishing schemes, and data theft." As businesses implement new IT solutions and technologies, they present new security vulnerabilities (Nessler et al., 2021 and Njuguna, 2023). Cybercrime is becoming greater professionalized, resulting in more diverse, nuanced, and sophisticated intimidations. Cyber threat actors are continually developing, building, and evolving techniques to circumvent or surpass the most advanced cyber security measures. All of these elements contribute to a cyber threat landscape in which businesses confront more substantial cyber dangers than ever before. Cyber attacks increased by thirty-eight percent in 2022 compared to the year before. As cyber threat actors improve their tactics, assaults will become more regular, and businesses will confront new and serious cyber risks. Generative AI (Gen-AI) can help cyber security professionals enhance the detection of intimidations, timing of responses, and profitability. It may also assist in lessening the demand for employees in operations centers for safety and technological incident response teams.

3.1 Cyber security employs Gen-AI:

3.1.1 Developing artificial intelligence systems: - Gen-AI can generate phony data to train machine learning models for detecting cyber intrusions. The models may then be used to detect and prevent future assaults.

3.1.2 Disaster reply:- Gen-AI can help security analysts develop reaction methods based on effective techniques from previous occurrences. This can assist in accelerating incident response workflows.

3.1.3 Malware surveillance:- Gen-AI will identify fraudulent messages by analyzing email content, sender activity, and patterns. For example, it can detect suspicious links, grammatical problems, and irregularities in the sender's address. If it recognizes a pattern, it can send an alert to notify the user.

3.1.4 Threat identification:- Gen-AI is capable of autonomously generating investigation inquiries

3.1.5 Computer programming:- Gen-AI may assist with code writing by analyzing what the user is specifying and recommending ways to complete the function (Patil, 2017).

4. GENERATIVE AI-DRIVEN SECURITY FRAMEWORKS FOR WEB ENGINEERING: INNOVATIONS AND CHALLENGES

AI safety, or computational intelligence security, is using AI to strengthen a company's safety record. AI technologies allow businesses to centralize surveillance, mitigation, and cleaning to combat cyber threats and data breaches effectively. Organizations may use AI in their cyber security operations in various ways. The majority customary AI safety explanations employ mechanism learning and unfathomable learning to investigate huge amounts of records, containing traffic examples, app convention, browser histories, and other system pursuit information. This investigate assists AI to discover patterns and determine safety baselines. Any action that falls south of the baseline is instantaneously standard as an irregularity and a probable replicated danger, allowing for quick refinement.

Generative AI (gen AI), popularized by Huge words models (HWMs), is extensively used in AI security solutions to convert security data into plain language suggestions, hence simplifying security teams' decision-making processes. According to study, AI safety explanations very much get better risk discovery and reply. According to IBM's 2024 Price of an Information Break Report, association with important safety AI and computerization acknowledged and administer information breaks 108 days quicker than those exclusive of AI explanations. Furthermore, the analysis revealed that associations that considerably execute AI safety save, on average, USD 1.76 million in data breach response costs. That is roughly 40% more than the standard charges of a break for firms that do not use AI.

4.1. Safeguarding Artificial Intelligence against Intrusions: Another facet of safety for AI is protecting it from digital assaults. In this concept, cyber security professionals consider how threat actors may utilize AI to augment existing vulnerabilities or target entirely different attack surfaces. For instance, HWMs can assist attackers in developing more specific and effective phishing assaults. Simulations using artificial intelligence, a relatively fresh invention, convey dangerous actors with novel opportunities for assault, like logistical networks and conflicting strikes. This research focuses on the subject of AI assurance, which entails applying AI to enhance cyber security. It does, however, contain information on potential AI concerns as well as recommendations for purchasing artificial intelligence-powered equipment (Preprint Repository arXiv Achieves Milestone Million Uploads, 2014 and Role of Wireless Sensor Networks, 2016).

The emergence of generative AI brings with it significant cyber vulnerabilities that existing security solutions may be unable to address. The relationship of technology's possible abuse in constructing authentic-looking deep replicas or building malware necessitates a rethinking of present security requirements, as well as the development of unfamiliar, AI-specific threat identification and mitigation methods.

Collaboration with trustworthy partners to provide these innovative solutions is critical to keeping aware of these developing challenges.

4.2 To negotiate the complexity brought by generative AI, enterprises must:

4.1.1 Recognize the dual nature of generative AI, understanding its ability to both strengthen cyber security defenses and facilitate unprecedented cyber risks.

4.1.2 Engage in collaborations to improve the integration of generative AI into cybersecurity initiatives, ensuring that solutions are both innovative and safe.

4.1.3 To maintain integrity and trust in digital ecosystems, it is crucial to prioritize the development and adoption of advanced threat detection technologies and the ethical use of AI.

4.1.4 To reduce the danger of deep fakes, organizations may use driven-by artificial intelligence material verification tools that evaluate audio as well as video for evidence of manipulation and deliver immediate notices for possible serious forgeries. To tackle advanced phishing scams artificial intelligence algorithms trained on continuously updated libraries of illicit attempts can recognize and stop new phishing techniques before they reach end users. These models use the processing of natural languages and analytics of behavior to detect phishing signs in emails, considerably reducing the number of accurate attempts of phishing (Santhakumar et al., 2024; Sinha & Kant, 2018; Student Stress Prediction Using Machine Learning Algorithms, 2022).

4.3 Moral Issues for Generative AI

The emergence of generative AI raises ethical concerns that demand fast and serious action. Developing and deploying these technologies is critical for ensuring data privacy, security, and integrity. UST promotes a responsible innovation culture, highlighting the demand for legislation that assures the ethical and transparent use of generative AI under societal norms.

The European Union's AI Act is leading legislative efforts, proposing stringent standards for high-risk AI applications, including those employed in cybersecurity. This statute classifies AI systems based on their intended use and related dangers, requiring thorough testing, documentation, and human monitoring to assure safety and compliance.

In the same way, in the United States, the National Institute of Standards and Technology (NIST) is creating a framework for addressing AI risks, with an emphasis on trustworthiness and dependability. These frameworks highlight the global movement toward responsibility and ethical issues in AI deployment, which influences how firms use AI in their cyber security plans (Xu et al., 2021; Bhambri et al., 2024; Bhambri & Khang, 2024).

4.4. Mitigating vulnerabilities & strengthening security:- Managing the immediate hazards linked with generative AI necessitates a multifaceted strategy. Cyber security leaders must act urgently to:

4.4.1 Understand AI Exposure: Hold board-level talks to better understand the increasing dangers, such as how generative AI might reveal sensitive data or ease unwanted access.

4.4.2 Secure the AI pipeline. Encrypt data used in AI models, check continually for weaknesses, and keep an eye out for AI-specific intimidations like data poisoning and model theft.

4.4.3 Invest in AI-specific defenses. Create novel defensive mechanisms designed to guard against adversarial assaults on AI models that go beyond existing security measures.

4.4.4 **Evolve cyber security practices:** Adapt cybersecurity tactics to meet the intricacies of generative AI, ensuring that data regulations, controls, and threat modeling are in line with AI-specific requirements.

4.5. **The Challenges, the use of generative AI in cyber security operations has shown significant benefits:**

4.5.1. Continuous Training and Awareness: Provide security personnel with the information they need to identify and mitigate AI-driven risks through continuous training and awareness initiatives.

4.5.2. AI-driven Security Solutions: Invest in generative AI technologies for threat identification and analysis, taking advantage of their ability to outperform and outwit cyber adversaries.

4.5.3. Ransomware Policy Development: Create comprehensive ransomware prevention, response, and recovery plans that are consistent with both ethical requirements and practical factors.

4.5.4. Addressing resource constraints: Recognize and manage the stress and resource constraints that security teams face by prioritizing resource allocation, such as implementing automated solutions and hiring more workers (Sridhar et al., 2024; Bhambri, 2014; Tandon & Bhambri, 2013; Bhambri, 2013); Bhambri & Bedi, 2013).

CONCLUSION AND FUTURE SCOPE

As organizations deploy generative AI (Gen-AI), and huge word models (HWMs), they become more aware of the issues that Gen-AI presents. A comprehensive framework is essential to fully understand the implications of Gen-AI security. This framework should address the large issues of Gen-AI security and the various types of Gen-AI security intimidations at different stages. Exactitude AI methods, which is built on a huge safety dataset, gives enhanced potentials for recognizing and mitigating AI-driven risks, assuring a strong defensive mechanism inside the framework. Exactitude AI methods, in exacting, gives large- declaration for cyber guardians by consolidating and analyzing data using security-specific models to assist defenders in automating detection, prevention, and reaction.

By completely addressing these linked areas, our methodology enables enterprises to gain a comprehensive knowledge of Gen-AI security issues.

Strong governance standards help in avoiding unintentional biases, preserving consistency with company principles, and increase user confidence.

Generative AI presents additional dangers, including legal, financial, and reputational concerns.

For example, generative models- Generative AI has driven significant advancements in text, picture, video, audio, and code production across various domains but has also escalated cyber security intimidations .

- The use of Generative AI by hackers has increased cyber security concerns, emphasizing the importance of addressing these issues.

- Businesses worldwide are being transformed by Generative AI and Huge words models, but this progress comes with significant risks.

- A comprehensive Gen-AI security architecture is essential for protecting Gen-AI applications, models, and the overall ecosystem.

- Research is needed to define the security vulnerabilities presented by Generative AI and to identify measures for promoting secure development and implementation.

- Different application areas, such as text, picture, video, audio, and code production, present unique security vulnerabilities that require specific precautions and mitigation measures.

REFERENCES

Alshabandar, R., Hussain, A., Keight, R., & Khan, W. (2020). Students performance prediction in online courses using machine learning algorithms. *2020 International Joint Conference on Neural Networks (IJCNN)*. https://doi.org/DOI: 10.1109/IJCNN48605.2020.9207196

. Analysis of stacked ensemble classification models in cervical cancer prediction using machine learning. (2023). *NeuroQuantology, 20*(19). https://doi.org/DOI: 10.48047/nq.2022.20.19.NQ99296

. Ang, L., & Seng, K. P. (2022). Visual sensor network technology and its applications. *Visual Information Processing in Wireless Sensor Networks*, 1-19. https://doi.org/DOI: 10.4018/978-1-61350-153-5.ch001

Bhambri, P. (2013). Roadmaps to e-business: Translating e-business strategy into action (Vol. 1). Lap Lambert Academic Publishing. ISBN: 9783659347870. Bhambri, P. (2011). Data mining model for protein sequence alignment: Bioinformatics (Vol. 1). Lap Lambert Academic Publishing. ISBN: 9783844321531.

Bhambri, P. (2014). Effectiveness of performance management system in IT industries: Empirical approach. In Kumar, S., & Anjum, B. (Eds.), *Management of globalised business: Plethora of new opportunities* (pp. 114–121). Bharti Publications.

Bhambri, P., & Bedi, S. (2013). *Consumer's perception for the two wheelers: Analytical and comparative study with the inclusion of different locomotives* (Vol. 1). Lap Lambert Academic Publishing.

Bhambri, P., & Khang, A. (2024). Computational intelligence in manufacturing technologies. In Mehta, S., Gupta, S. K., Aljohani, A. A., & Khayyat, M. (Eds.), *Impact and potential of machine learning in the metaverse* (pp. 327–356). IGI Global., DOI: 10.4018/979-8-3693-5762-0.ch013

Bhambri, P., Rani, S., & Pareek, P. K. (2024). Financial innovations: Intelligent automation in finance and insurance sectors. In Darwish, D. (Ed.), *Generating entrepreneurial ideas with AI* (pp. 226–243)., DOI: 10.4018/979-8-3693-3354-9.ch012

Chavan, S. V. (2018). Wireless sensor network technology and networking algorithms for wireless sensor network applications: A survey. *International Journal for Research in Applied Science and Engineering Technology*, 6(1), 662–670. DOI: 10.22214/ijraset.2018.1100

Goyani, Z. (2021). Selection.index: Analysis of selection index in plant breeding. *CRAN: Contributed Packages*. https://doi.org/DOI: 10.32614/CRAN.package. selection.index

Islam, M., Jalil, S. Q., & Rehmani, M. H. (2016). Role of wireless sensor networks in emerging communication technologies: A review. Emerging communication technologies based on wireless sensor networks: Current research and future applications, 1.

Kavitha, S., Prasad, N. H., Hanumanthappa, M., & Veena, R. (2022). Classification And Errors Analysis of COVID-19 Using Supervised Machine Learning Algorithm and Visualisation. *NeuroQuantology : An Interdisciplinary Journal of Neuroscience and Quantum Physics*, 20(15), 6282.

Liu, M., Wang, J., Xu, L., Zhang, J., Li, S., & Xiang, F. (2022). BIT-MI deep learning-based model to non-intrusive speech quality assessment challenge in online conferencing applications. *Interspeech*, 2022, 3288–3292. Advance online publication. DOI: 10.21437/Interspeech.2022-10010

Liu, W., & Xie, C. (2022). MOS prediction network for non-intrusive speech quality assessment in online conferencing. *Interspeech*, 2022, 3293–3297. Advance online publication. DOI: 10.21437/Interspeech.2022-10081

Mehra, M. (2021). A review on wireless sensor networks and its applications. *International Journal of Innovative Research in Computer Science & Technology*, 295-298, 295–298. Advance online publication. DOI: 10.55524/ijircst.2021.9.6.65

Messaoud, S., Bouaafia, S., Bradai, A., Ali Hajjaji, M., Mtibaa, A., & Atri, M. (2022). *Network slicing for industrial IoT and industrial wireless sensor network: Deep federated learning approach and its implementation challenges*. Emerging Trends in Wireless Sensor Networks., DOI: 10.5772/intechopen.102472

Nessler, N., Cernak, M., Prandoni, P., & Mainar, P. (2021). Non-intrusive speech quality assessment with transfer learning and subject-specific scaling. *Interspeech*, 2021, 2406–2410. Advance online publication. DOI: 10.21437/Interspeech.2021-1685

Njuguna, B. (2023). StockDistFit: Fit stock price distributions. *CRAN: Contributed Packages*. https://doi.org/DOI: 10.32614/CRAN.package.StockDistFit

Patil, D. (2017). Internet of things and security challenges in wireless sensor network. *Asian Journal of Engineering and Applied Technology*, 6(1), 14–18. DOI: 10.51983/ajeat-2017.6.1.816

Reddy, R. D., Katkam, S., & Rao, C. R. S. (2022). Cyber Attacks Detection using Machine Learning. *NeuroQuantology : An Interdisciplinary Journal of Neuroscience and Quantum Physics*, 20(19), 4388.

Reddy, R. T., Pati, P. B., Deepa, K., & Sangeetha, S. T. (2023, April). Flight Delay Prediction Using Machine Learning. In 2023 IEEE 8th International Conference for Convergence in Technology (I2CT) (pp. 1-5). IEEE.

Rekha, K. S. S., Mathur, S., Sadhukhan, S., & Jangiti, J. (2022). Student Stress Prediction Using Machine Learning Algorithms And Comprehensive Analysis. *NeuroQuantology : An Interdisciplinary Journal of Neuroscience and Quantum Physics*, 20(14), 895.

Santhakumar, G., Takale, D. G., Tyagi, S., Anitha, R., Tiwari, M., & Dhanraj, J. A. (2024). Analysis of Multimodality fusion of medical image segmentation employing deep learning. *Human Cancer Diagnosis and Detection Using Exascale Computing*, 171-183. https://doi.org/DOI: 10.1002/9781394197705.ch11

Schulman, J., Moritz, P., Levine, S., Jordan, M., & Abbeel, P. (2015). Preprint repository arXiv achieves milestone million uploads. *Physics Today*.

Sinha, G., & Kant, K. S. (2018). Performance of modified auditory features for speech signal-an empirical study for non-intrusive speech quality assessment using signal based model. *2018 4th International Conference on Recent Advances in Information Technology (RAIT)*. https://doi.org/DOI: 10.1109/RAIT.2018.8388997

Sridhar, V., Rani, S., Pareek, P. K., & Bhambri, P. (2024). Evolution of IoT in various application domains. In Sridhar, V., Rani, S., Pareek, P. K., Bhambri, P., & Elngar, A. A. (Eds.), *Blockchain for IoT systems: Concept, framework and applications* (1st ed., pp. 13–22). Chapman and Hall/CRC., DOI: 10.1201/9781003460367-2

Tandon, N., & Bhambri, P. (2013). *Novel approach for drug discovery using neural network back propagation algorithm: An optimum drug discovery approach* (Vol. 1). GRIN Publishers.

Xu, H., Padilla, O., Wang, D., & Li, M. (2021). Changepoints: A collection of change-point detection methods. *CRAN: Contributed Packages*. https://doi.org/ DOI: 10.32614/CRAN.package.changepoints

Chapter 15
Introduction to Generative AI in Web Engineering:
Concepts and Applications

Poornima Mahadevappa
https://orcid.org/0000-0001-9414-3464
Taylor's University, Malaysia

Syeda Mariam Muzammal
https://orcid.org/0000-0003-2960-1814
Taylor's University, Malaysia

Muhammad Tayyab
https://orcid.org/0000-0001-5580-9163
Taylor's University, Malaysia

ABSTRACT

Generative AI is transforming the art and science of web engineering by automating content generation, design and development through models like GAN, VAE or Transformers. These models can produce authentic text like a writer and other media, including images, so developers would save more time in web development and improve creativity and scalability. From automated web design and content personalization to adaptive user interface or code optimization, the uses of generative AI could be limitless. Integrating AI with web engineering allows developers to generate dynamic and tailored user interface applications that adapt to the unique requirements of each user. Nevertheless, issues like data quality, bias and ethical considerations require ongoing attention to ensure responsible AI usage. Overall, generative AI can revolutionize web development for a future of innovation and

DOI: 10.4018/979-8-3693-3703-5.ch015

more intelligent, efficient, user-centric web applications.

I. INTRODUCTION

A. Overview of Generative AI

Generative AI (or GenAI for short) is an entirely new category of technology within the field of artificial intelligence which can quickly and efficiently generate enormous amounts of content like text, images, audio and video. It is commonly used in various fields to generate anything from art, healthcare models and stock market predictions tools that are indistinguishable for real data created by humans (Feuerriegel et al., 2024). GenAI, however, replicates the creativity and intelligence of a human through content generation which looks indistinguishable from machine generated ones. These are realized through innovative deep learning architectures and algorithms, which—after being trained on data of interest are able to generate new outputs that exhibit statistical properties similar to those in the input distribution ("Exploring Creativity," 2024). GenAI is defined as a set of algorithms with which one can synthesize data in such a form that it conserves properties or distributions of real-world data. This includes models like GAN (Generative Adversarial Networks), VAE (Variational Autoencoders), Transformers, and autoregressive models (Oluwagbenro, 2024). These models are derived from a quantum level to learn data patterns and create new type content with necessity features by repeating what they observed. A wide range of industries have already started using generative AI, from healthcare for drug discovery, medical imaging enhancement, and predictive modeling (Mishra et al., 2024). This has a great impact in marketing and advertising because generative AI is responsible for content creation, personalization as also the way it reaches to an audience which affects strategies on consumer and hence generates more business (Dimitrieska, 2024).

Generative AI has evolved from early rule-based systems to the present sophisticated models, there have been a few key milestones along this trajectory. It was initiated with the symbolic AI and rule-based systems of 1960s to 1970s (for instance, early chatbots like ELIZA or ALICE), which could do little more than obey strictly predetermined rules giving a simplistic conversational ability (Al-Amin et al., 2024). Transitioning from the earlier systems to the present complex machine learning represented a significant paradigm shift, as neural networks and deep learning have reshaped many other areas of research in addition to computer vision and natural language processing (Zeng et al., 2023a). On the other side of this spectrum, more AI has sparked end-to-end from generative models such GANs and VAE since it enabled to generate new data by learn patterns. Recent advancements in models like VQ-VAE (Vector Quantized Variational Autoencoder), DALL-E and other similar models have increased the quality of diverse generated outputs. They have led innovation across numerous use-cases, from software development to creative industries (Ebert & Louridas, 2023). GenAI stands at the intersection of art and technology.

The evolution from traditional AI to generative AI has been significant transformative technological advancements. These capabilities have enabled generative AI applications that go beyond processing and automating in general to creating new content from the beginning with human-like properties. This transition is leading towards an era of a different kind. Some of the key technological advancements are:

• **Generative Adversarial Networks (GAN)** – There are two main components of these networks: a generator that generates fake data and a discriminator that determines how real the generated content is. This feedback loop between the two has seen dramatic improvements in both AI-generated content quality and how close it looks to real-world equivalents, resulting in a more human-like feel compared to conventional analytical model-building AI (Gatla et al., 2024; Kılınç & Keçecioğlu, 2024).

• **Variational Autoencoders (VAE)** - The introduction of VAE is another step towards the development in this direction. It learns the distribution of training data to generate new samples, such as generating diverse and qualitatively realistic images (Razavi et al., 2019). VQ (Vector Quantization)-VAE and VQ-VAE-2 are further advanced models crucial in applications such as image synthesis and text-to-image generation (Ghayoumi, 2023; Zeng et al., 2023b).

• **Diffusion Models** - These models process random noise and create high-quality images as they iteratively refine the data. Diffusion models explicitly captured the long-tailed data distribution, which helped eliminate artifacts and enhance quality compared to traditional GANs and S VAE (Zeng et al., 2023c).

• **Text-to-Image Generation Techniques** – This is the most intriguing area of generative AI; it combines NLP with computer vision models to generate photo-realistic images from a textual description. These models have the potential for all sorts of creative applications from art generation to product design and development (Oppenlaender, 2022).

The transition from traditional AI to generative AI represents a major advance in the capabilities of AI, from processing and automation type tasks into creation to produce something that is just like with human mindset and creativity as well across numerous applications.

B. The Role of Generative AI in Web Engineering

Web engineering is an important field in the digital age, spread over different areas and components influencing both scalability, adaptability as well as diverse features towards accomplishing modern web applications. Today modern web applications scale well, they can take on more users and provide optimal performance, merits to architectural strategies microservices, cloud services (Van Riet et al., 2023). They even offer Web Interface integration support for RIA (Rich Internet Application) and IWA (Intelligent Web Applications), which are required for future applications. Therefore, the type of applications is in nature that model perceptiveness has to be flexible and dynamic enough to cater the demands from user requirements always keep on change (Wakil & Jawawi, 2018). The web is no longer the static and limited entity seen in Web 1.0, the modern web engineering methods support intelligent and ubiquitous applications across various devices (Wakil et al., 2015). Finally, the new language of web development that supports efficient communication like asynchronous messaging, cloud-based infrastructure and mobile-first applications have redefined how we think of innovation in response time (Dzhangarov et al., 2021).

GenAI is transforming web development toward more responsive creative UI (User Interface) and customizable UX (User Experience). GenAI models like ChatGPT are changing the way we design responsive UI, producing highly automated results that involve minimal human intervention and delivering relevant data at an unprecedented pace compared to conventional hours of labor spent on researching some information about personas and designs for our interface (Y. Huang et al., 2024). With such a capability, developers can build apps that are more personalized and user-centric with less investment of time or resources to make up for the resource availability pool constraints and thus to accommodate tailored user experiences (Avdić, 2024a). On top of that, GenAI enriches the design thinking process by helping UX designers solve problems creatively and come up with ideas more dynamically, enabling them to experiment with new design concepts beyond traditional mindsets (Torricelli et al., 2024). These tools not only improve the quality and speed of UID creation in educational settings, but they also serve to help students achieve higher learning through maintaining positive satisfaction. This blend of traditional and AI approaches has been demonstrated in practice with the example of AI-powered tools such as Canva, WixADI, and so on. These approaches are being equivalent if not superior than conventional approach; thus, demonstrating aspects such as effectiveness, speediness novelty introduced via them(Avdić, 2024b).

Using advanced machine learning, GenAI has the potential to revolutionize content generation and coding automation while simultaneously enhancing user experience across web engineering as we know it today. This technology is modernizing web development through tools that offer real-time code suggestions, generate high-quality media content, and personalize web designs (Kuthe et al., 2024). For instance, GenAI can create personalized portfolios designs for both user and on behalf of designers without consuming lot of time; while visualize custom interface styles based solely upon personal wishes (AlDahoul et al., 2023). Apart from this it can also create various images or media content to add web page correction. Tools like Web Diffusion can capture a web environment with the help of resilient diffusion models to produce high-fidelity screenshots or recreate erroneous web pages by saving bandwidth and offer content that are more likable to users (Tivari et al., 2024).

C. Purpose of the Chapter

This chapter provides an overview of how Generative AI is shaping the future in web engineering, including different models and concepts related to it along with various applications and challenges. The chapter starts with generative AI technologies including Generative Adversarial Networks (GANs), Variational Autoencoders (VAEs) and Transformers models, illustrating how these models create new content based on data patterns they have been trained on. Then this chapter moves on to discussing applications of generative AI in web development, emphasizing its influence on automated web design, personalized content creation, adaptive user interfaces, and code optimization. Finally, it concludes with future research directions towards web engineering, and a few uses cases.

This chapter gives an overview on how GenAI can redefine anything in web engineering. It automates and optimizes processes results in improved efficiency, personalization and innovation. It has revolutionized the daily routine of web design and development as the tools can automatically generate code, create elements on a GUI or even write text with minimal human interaction.

II. FUNDAMENTAL CONCEPTS OF GENERATIVE AI

A. Understanding Generative Models

Generative and discriminative models are primary machine learning techniques driven by two goals and methods. Generative models are designed to learn the joint probability distribution of input data and their corresponding labels (ELKarazle et al., 2024). This model permits the generation of new data points that look like real training data. GAN, VAE, and transformers are popular generative models (Anstine & Isayev, 2023). These models have been applied to refit chemical sciences and cyber-bullying detection in memes, which convert the problems into a text-to-text generation. They use unsupervised data and provide calibrated confidence in their predictions. For example, Marginalization Models (MaMs) could be used to learn accurately from large and relatively high-dimensional data with significantly more structure than existing models (Jain et al., 2023). On the other hand, Discriminative models target modeling the conditional probability of given label data, essentially used for making classifications. They aim to identify the class-wise boundary region by representing the conditional probability of labels given in the data (Hayashi, 2023). Although these models tend to have fewer complex structures, they are more compelling and applicable in the classification context than generative models because of their direct approach to modeling the decision boundary.

The primary types of generative models include GAN, VAE and transformers, which are further explored in these sections:

1. **Generative Adversarial Networks** (GAN) - Generative Adversarial Networks (GANs) consist of two main components: a generator and a discriminator. These two components are engaged in a game-theoretic scenario where the generator tries to create data that is indistinguishable from real data. The generator is trained to minimize the probability of the discriminator correctly identifying the generated data as fake. While the discriminator attempts to differentiate between real and generated data. It evaluates the samples and returns an estimate of whether a given sample is real (from the training data) or fake (from the generator). It is trained to maximize the probability of correctly classifying real and fake samples. Essentially, it acts like a binary classifier (Goodfellow et al., 2020).

2. The interaction between the generator and discriminator aims to minimize its own cost function. The cost function of the generator encourages it to generate samples that are misclassified as real by the discriminator, whereas the cost function for the discriminative steps tries to classify its inputs correctly into fake or real (Creswell et al., 2018). The training process is to update the generator and discriminator iteratively. The generator is updated to improve its ability to fool the discriminator, while the discriminator is updated to better distinguish between real and fake samples. This adversarial process continues until the generator produces data that is indistinguishable from real data, or until a predefined number of iterations is reached.

The training process of GAN is summarized as follows:

*   Step 1: *Initialize* generator and discriminator networks with random weights.
*   Step 2: *Discriminator Training*
    o   Sample real data points from the actual data distribution.

- o Generate fake data using the generator by passing random noise through it.
- o Train the discriminator to maximize the probability of correctly classifying the real data as real and fake data as fake (Upadhyay & Jain, 2019). This is achieved by maximizing the discriminator's cost function:

$$Cost_D = -\tfrac{1}{2}\left[logD(x_{real})\right] + log\left(1 - D(x_{fake})\right)$$

- **Step 3: *Generator Training***
  - o Generate new data samples using the generator.
  - o The generator's goal is to fool the discriminator, meaning it wants the discriminator to classify the fake data as real (Upadhyay & Jain, 2019). Thus, the generator tries to minimize the following cost function:

$$Cost_G = -log\left(D(x_{fake})\right)$$

- o The generator updates its weights based on the discriminator's feedback to produce more realistic data
- **Step 4: *Iterative Optimization***
  - o The generator and discriminator are updated alternately in each training step. The discriminator improves its ability to distinguish between real and fake data, while the generator improves its ability to create realistic data (Dagur et al., 2023). This results in a **minimax game** between the two:

$$min_G max_D\, V(G,D) = E_{x \sim P_{data}(x)}\left[logD(x)\right] + E_{x \sim P_{data}(z)}\left[log(1 - D(G(Z)))\right]$$

The algorithm converges when the generator produces samples so realistic that the discriminator is unable to reliably distinguish between real and generated data. At this point, the discriminator's output becomes close to 0.5 for both real and fake data, indicating that it is "confused" (Hammad et al., 2023) (Goodfellow et al., 2020)

3. **Variational Autoencoders** – are a class of generative models that leverage deep learning to generate data by learning a latent representation of the input data. They are mainly known for their ability to produce a continuous latent space with the structure necessary for producing high-quality output (Yacoby et al., 2024) . VAEs contain three primary elements- Encoder, Decoder and Latent Space. The input data is first compressed to a point in the Latent Space by encoder then reconstructed back from this latent space by decoder so that it can be used as an image again. These elements are building blocks of VAE to effectively learn and generate data. Generative and inference models describe the functions of these building blocks. Here, the inference model (encoder) tries to learn a more concise representation of our latent data while trying generative model(decoder), uses those representations for reconstructing or generating new data from these latent representations (Asesh, 2023). The encoder and decoder operate in a cycle, where the encoder generates latent variables to be used by the decoder for data generation. The performance of VAE depends on the balance and interaction between these two models, as optimized by the Evidence Lower Bound (ELBO) during training (Yacoby et al., 2024)

The training process of VAE is summarized as follows:

- Step 1: Input data
  - o The input to the VAE is a dataset X, where each data point x is an instance (e.g., an image, text, etc.).
  - o The goal is to encode each data point into a lower-dimensional latent space Z and reconstruct it through the decoder (Ali & Aysan, 2024) (Yang et al., 2020).
- Step 2: Forward pass – Encoding the input
  - o It involves mapping from the input data to a distribution in the latent space, which is essential for depicting the underlying structure of the data (Seidman et al., 2023). The encoder takes the input x and maps it to the latent space.
  - o The encoder produces two vectors:

Mean Vector $= \mu(x)$ representing the mean of the latent variable z.
Log-variance vector $= \log \sigma^2(x)$ representing the log variance of z.
These vectors represent a Gaussian distribution $q(z/x)$ that approximates the true posterior $p(z/x)$ (Toma et al., 2020)

- Step 3: **Reparameterization Trick** – It enables backpropagation to optimize VAE using gradient-based methods.

- o The encoder samples from the latent variable distribution $q(z/x)$ by combining the mean and variance with random noise $\epsilon \sim N(0,1)$: $z = \mu(x) + \sigma(x).\epsilon$
- o This step ensures that sampling is differentiable and enables the model to learn.
- **Step 4: Forward pass – Decoding**
  - o The decoder takes the sampled latent variable z and attempts to reconstruct the input x. It outputs a probability distribution $p(z/x)$ over the possible reconstructions (Xiong, 2022).
  - o The decoder aims to generate data that resembles the input as closely as possible by maximizing the likelihood of the output matching the original input.
- **Step 5: Loss Function:**
  - o **The reconstruction loss**: It measures how well the decoder can reconstruct the original input from the latent variable z
  - o **The KL divergence**: It acts as a regularizer, encouraging the learned distribution $q(z/x)$ (the approximate posterior) to be close to the prior distribution $p(z)$.
  - o The reconstruction loss and KL divergence are computed and combined to form the **total loss**.
- **Step 6: Optimization**
  - o The encoder and decoder networks are trained using stochastic gradient descent or a variant like Adam (Ghayoumi, 2023). During training, both networks are updated simultaneously.
  - o The gradients of the loss function with respect to the encoder and decoder parameters are computed via backpropagation, and the parameters are updated accordingly.
- **Step 7: Latent Space Exploration**
  - o Once the VAE is trained, it can generate new data by sampling from the prior distribution $p(z)$ and passing these samples through the decoder.
  - o This enables the generation of new, diverse data points from the learned latent space.
- **Step 8: Latent Space Exploration -**
  - o Once the VAE is trained, it can generate new data by sampling from the prior distribution $p(z)$ and pass these samples through the decoder.
  - o This generates new points from the learned latent space contrasting widely different data.

After a few iterations, the VAE should converge and be able to generate new samples from the latent space.

Transformers

The self-attention mechanism is essential for how transformers can determine which words in the textual input data are more relevant than others. Enabling the model to focus on more relevant parts of an input sequence can improve capturing dependencies between elements in data (B. Zhou, 2024). As Transformers are by design scaled to multiple data, they inherently offer better training time efficiency than their linear counterparts (Dubey & Singh, 2023) . This means the model can learn multiple sections of an input example all at once. This scalability is crucial when one wants to deal with workloads that require massive amounts of high-resolution data processing.

The attention mechanism computes a series of attention weights to determine how much importance should be given to each part in the input using matrix multiplications and SoftMax operations. They are the building blocks of Transformer modelling relationships (Cheok & Zhang, 2023). GANformer provides long-range interactions between pixels across the image using bipartite structure in visual generative modelling. This architecture can perform faster processing along with high-resolution synthesis which renders it ideal for tasks inclining towards complex visual output .

The training process of Transformer models consists of a few key steps, all aimed to help the model become better at learning and predicting more complex patterns in sequential data. Following is the overview of the steps:

1. Data Preparation

Tokenization: The input data is created in a sequence of smaller units called tokens (e.g., words, sub words, or characters). These are further converted into embeddings, numerical vectors that represent each token (Thakur et al., 2024).

Positional Encoding: The model has no built-in concept of token order (like an RNN), so the positional encoding method is used for token embeddings. These encodings tell the position of each token in their sequence (Borzunov et al., 2022).

2. Model Initialization

The Transformer architecture is made up of encoder and decoder layers (for machine translation and classification task). Both layers enclose multi-layer self-attention and feed-forward networks. The model's parameters (weights and biases) are initialized randomly before training starts (Thakur et al., 2024).

3. Forward Pass

Self-Attention: For every token in the input, self-attention attempts to determine how it correlates with each other token in the sequence. To do this they build Query, Key and Value matrices from the input embeddings. Attention score matrices are used to determine the importance of other tokens to a token.

Multi-Headed Attention: In this, the self-attention process is carried out multiple times (across different heads) to enable the transformer to learn relationships between tokens from different perspectives. These results are concatenated and then fed to the next layer.

Feed-Forward Networks: The output of attention is passed through a fully connected feed-forward network, allowing the model to apply transformations and non-linearities (Thakur et al., 2024).

4. Loss Calculation

The model computes a loss function (typically cross-entropy for classification or translation tasks) by comparing the predicted output with the actual target output. This loss measures how far the model's predictions are from the correct answers (Ghayoumi, 2023).

5. Backpropagation

During backpropagation, gradients with respect to the loss function are computed and propagated backwards through model layers. The objective is to minimize the loss and adjust the model's parameters (weights & biases).

6. Optimization

The gradients that were calculated in backpropagation are then used to adjust model parameters via an optimization algorithm — usually Adam or its variant, AdamW. This process helps the model gradually improve its predictions by reducing the loss function over successive training iterations.

7. Batch Processing and Epochs

It processes input datasets through batches, instead of feeding them all at once, allowing for more efficient use of memory and faster training. The model becomes more efficient in learning patterns from the input data after each epoch (Panigrahi et al., 2024).

8. Dropout and Regularization

To prevent overfitting, dropouts are applied during training. Dropout randomly "drops" certain units (neurons) during the forward pass, forcing the model to generalize better and not rely too heavily on any specific part of the network. Other regularization techniques, such as weight decay, may also be employed to maintain model performance and generalization (Ghayoumi, 2023).

9. Training Completion and Evaluation

Once the training process is complete after a certain number of epochs or when the loss reaches an acceptable threshold, the model is evaluated on a validation or test set to assess its performance.

B. Evaluation of Generative AI Models

Evaluating the performance and quality of generative AI models in web engineering requires a combination of metrics, each addressing different aspects of the model's capabilities. Key metrics include:

1. *Inception Score (IS) and Fréchet Inception Distance (FID)*: They are commonly used for image generation models. IS measures the quality and diversity of generated samples by evaluating how well they resemble real-world examples. FID takes this comparison one step further; the measure tells of how similar generated data is to real but also whether these two distributions overlap in a way. But both measures are limited, particularly when the comparison becomes nuanced and less intuitive (Betzalel et al., 2024) .
2. *Likelihood-based evaluation*: By estimating traditional metrics and divergences between real data and generated samples, this method provides a stronger evaluation to characterize the generative performance in mimicking real-world data (Ebert & Louridas, 2023) .
3. *Code Quality and Contextual Understanding*: This evaluates AI tools like GitHub Copilot or Codex, *to indicate how well the models suggest correct codes according to their context. This will require a significant amount of code review to ensure that the generated code is up to standard and aligns with the intended purpose (Sauvola et al., 2024).*
4. **Effect on Developer Thought Process**: Examining how generative AI influences the way developers approach coding tasks, can help us gain insights into the model's effectiveness. Tracking developer actions and state transitions during

programming activities helps assess whether the model enhances or hinders the development workflow (Shirzad et al., 2022).

5. **Contrastively Learned Features for Graph Models** - Graph Neural Networks (GNNs) provide more accurate representations, offering a better way to measure the distances between graph datasets (Djaber & Ismail, 2023).

Importance of Human Evaluation in Conjunction With Automated Metrics

While automated metrics provide a quantitative summary of model performance, they need to catch up at capturing the qualitative nature of generative AI outputs. Some metrics, like code generation, compare the output to a ground-truth reference; others introduce more flexibility and novelty. However, the above metrics fail to consider some of the more contextual and qualitative factors that play a critical role in ensuring that AI-generated language resonates (Thorleiksdóttir, 2021). Research has shown that automated metrics frequently align with each other, often leading to a "glass ceiling" effect, where models receive similar rankings despite variations in actual quality. This lack of diversity in measurement can limit the accuracy and depth of evaluations (Colombo et al., 2022).

Human evaluation helps to fill in these gaps by receiving a complete picture of the quality of content. For example, automated metrics cannot determine the readability needed between the contextual score, relevancy or even if there is adherence to the intended meaning. Despite being expensive, human review is vital to ensure automated metrics work as expected and provide an exhaustive evaluation of how well the generative performs in practice. Integrating human and automated evaluation can result in a more balanced and accurate assessment framework when mixed with human evaluations. Combining these methods allows developers to produce automated metrics that are more reliable and, at the same time, can collect qualitative feedback from human evaluations. The state-of-the-art standard compliance occurs during the integration to maintain the quality and useability of AI outputs while improving continued assessment metrics (Thorleiksdóttir, 2021).

III. APPLICATIONS OF GENERATIVE AI IN WEB ENGINEERING

A. Automated Web Design

Generative AI is taking web design to a whole new level, automating everything in the process, from layout creation to color scheme. With sophisticated multimodal large language models (LLMs), one can generate code that accurately reflects the visual design of a webpage, which is known as the Design2Code process (Si et al., 2024). Models like GPT-4V can translate visual designs into code and provide expressions on web pages that are frequently indistinguishable from or even outperform the original look. AI image generation, especially diffusion models, further assists in developing certain components of a design, like floorplans for online grids. These tools also serve to inspire the idea, providing designed color in a varied and more appealing way (Ploennigs & Berger, 2024). Generative AI considers the context and creates images that are area-specific, giving users a richer experience by surpassing the confines of classical approaches to web design. This type of AI integration allows users to experience tremendous scope for being creative and productive in a systemic manner that makes future automation tools even better (Lively et al., 2023)

GenAI in web design has brought various tools and platforms to improve creativity, efficiency and personalization. AI powered tools like ChatGPT, Canva, and WixADI automate design tasks, create content that adapts to the user's preference improving user experience. ChatGPT assists in generating text content, Canva offers design templates and elements, and WixADI uses AI to create personalized website designs based on user inputs (Avdić, 2024a). AI art generators enhance the creative ability of the users by building visual context, and selecting appropriate colors and aesthetics for web design projects that will look something new (Lively et al., 2023). Collaborative code platform integrates AI to facilitate real-time collaboration and code management. It supports dynamic text, multilanguage capabilities, and real-time coding sessions, enhancing the user interface design and navigation experience (Gaikwad, 2024). AI driven Design platforms processes content and style images using machine learning models to generate stylized outputs. XDesign is a platform used to learn about interface design in teaching contexts or user-centered explanations of AI models, allowing designers the ability to create unique and interesting web elements by recognizing objects within images and applying styles. It provides a structure for learners to learn design as a process, teaching them how to identify user needs and create the right interfaces (Shin et al., 2022). These are really the tools that make web design smarter and automatically generate more ideas.

GenAI technologies provide personalized and adaptive web interfaces to cater individual preferences leading to more engaging and intuitive experience. As the users engage with these technologies, AI driven systems adapt dynamically and adjust to the user needs. AI can significantly enhance the efficiency of web design tasks by automating design environments, content customization and analysis (Costa et al., 2024) . In educational settings, these AI driven tools and technologies enhance engagement and educational outcomes through customized content and feedback (J. Kim & Maher, 2023). Apart from these there are also sector specific applications to offer tailored services and interactions. For example, in e-commerce, AI analyzes customer data to provide personalized product recommendations, while in healthcare, it aids in patient care and medical research (Mustafa Ayobami Raji et al., 2024) . Although AI driven web design provides efficient and personalized services, there are challenges such as user control and ethical considerations that must be addressed. It must provide means where users cannot only comprehend but also manage their websites to prevent alienation and ensure user-centricity (Mughal et al., 2024). The integration of AI in web design raises ethical issues, hence it is necessary to operate within ethical boundaries and protect user data (Khankhoje, 2016). Finally, over reliance on these tools reduces human insight and creativity by making the tasks more automated. It is necessary to ensure that human input is necessary to enhance creativity (J. Kim & Maher, 2023). As AI technologies continue to progress, these challenges will need continuing attention to fully tackle the potential of AI in web design.

B. Content Generation

Advance machine learning models leverage GenAI to create web content including text, images, and multimedia that mimics human creativity. Models like transformers are extensively used for text generations to enable the creation of coherent and contextually relevant content (Mavridis & Symeonidis, 2014; Sinha et al., 2014). They produce articles, stories, and even code from simple prompts rationalizing content creation processes. Applications like chatbots and virtual assistants offer personalized and interactive user experiences using natural language processing (NLP) models (Tivari et al., 2024). Likewise, GAN and VAE models are used to generate high-quality images and multimedia content. It is predominately used in gaming and advertising industries to produce realistic visuals, digital storytelling and animations. GenAI acts as a collaborative tool, providing content personalization, automation, automated repetitive tasks allowing businesses to tailor content and thereby increasing efficiency (Ervik, 2023) .

AI driven content generation has changed user experiences by personalizing content to the individual preferences. This enhances their engagement and satisfaction by delivering content that aligns closely with the user's interests. For example, AI algorithms in web content delivery have improved metrics such as time spent on site, click-through rates, and conversion rates in both the USA and the UK (Sodiya et al., 2024). In marketing, AI personalizes messages and experiences based on consumer behavior, leading to higher satisfaction and loyalty (Babatunde et al., 2024). In education industry, AI has enhanced students' aesthetic and creative capabilities, improved productivity in writing copy and code, and image-based generators have aided in ideation and color selection (Lively et al., 2023). Tools like Writesonic, Jasper, and Grammarly Business provide grammar checks, boost scholarly and professional content creation. ChatGPT and Github Copilot reduced working time by generating test scripts for web end-to-end testing; OpenAI's DALL-E system has been developed to generate images based on textual descriptions (Malakar & Leeladharan, 2024). Consequently, AI has significantly transformed digital media content creation, with a large percentage of users encountering AI-generated content. While most users find the content relevant and of good quality, concerns about authenticity and biases remain. Amidst these numerous benefits, challenges such as authenticity, biases, and ethical considerations persist.

C. Code Generation

Generative AI models are increasingly being employed to write and optimize code for web applications since they significantly enhance productivity and customization. These models leverage Large Language Models (LLMs) to automate coding tasks, provide real-time code suggestions, reduce time on repetitive coding tasks, and facilitate code customization. This transformation is reshaping software development landscape (Sun et al., 2022). Tools such as GitHub Copilot, OpenAI Codex, and Amazon CodeGuru are examples of LLM-based AI-powered coding solutions. Meta's CodeCompose accelerates coding and improves efficiency in large-scale software development environments. These tools offer user-friendly interfaces, demonstrating how technical code can be transformed into customizable web-based applications, allowing individuals with limited programming knowledge to adapt more quickly to coding (Acher, 2024).

The synergy between generative AI and web search is revolutionizing how programmers' approach problem-solving. By integrating these tools, developers can improve their information-seeking processes, resulting in more efficient and effective coding practices. AI-powered code reviews, automated test-case generation, and AI-pair programming are further applications that save time and enhance code quality (Almeida et al., 2024). LLM models in these applications are trained on extensive code repositories and can predict potential risks, thus improving both code quality and developer education. Tools like the IntelliJ IDEA plugin, powered by GPT-3.5, analyze code snippets to identify syntax and semantic issues, offering potential solutions. AI-pair programming, which involves collaboration between a human developer and an AI assistant, has been shown to improve code quality and developer satisfaction. This approach provides benefits such as time-saving, error reduction, and enhanced learning opportunities for developers (T. Chen, 2024).

D. Enhancing User Interfaces and Experience

GenAI can adapt dynamically to individual preferences and behaviors using deep learning techniques to analyze patterns during users' interactions. Browing habits, historical data, content engagement are all considered to fine tune the recommendations or predicting their needs before they themselves are aware of them (T. Chen, 2024). LLM based AI model, Open AI's GPT-3 is the best example that aids users to get better recommendation tailored towards their needs. Some of the best ways to enhance personalization using GenAI are:

- Behavior Analysis - AI systems monitor and analyze the traits of users as well as user preferences to produce custom content. For instance, music streaming services could gather an idea of what kind of songs or genres a user liked and draw up their playlists based on that (Costa et al., 2024).
- Predictive tips: AI gives a tip on what the user might want to do next e.g. suggesting you watch another video in YouTube or read an article based off past browsing behavior
- Bundle of features: AI-powered interfaces adapt to a user input right at that moment. Example: Spotify playlist recommend music playlist tailored to match users listening history (Costa et al., 2024).
- Automates Repetitive Tasks: Automates Repetitive Tasks: Generative AI can be used to automate boring and ordinary routine tasks as well streamline workflows. For example, features like Flash Fill in Microsoft excel automatically fills cells for data entry by predicting user patterns which eliminates writing formulas and saves time along with easier productivity (Wei et al., 2024).

Some of the real-world Examples of AI-Enhanced User Interfaces

- Netflix: By scanning through users' watch histories and preferences, it generates personalized movie and TV show recommendations. Using past behaviors Netflix adapts its home screen and suggests the contents to each user as per their liking maximizing engagement and satisfaction (Costa et al., 2024).
- Spotify: Spotify offers users curated playlists like "Discover Weekly" and Daily Mix generated based on what a user has been listening to. As they use Spotify more, the service can refine its recommendations (Costa et al., 2024)
.

- Amazon: Amazon leverages AI-powered recommendation engines for recommendations such as — Customers who viewed this item also shop these products. The user experience will adjust to display tailored offers, giving customers a better sense of discovery (Brdnik et al., 2022)
- GitHub Copilot: As the name suggests, it is AI software that can suggest or complete code in real-time based on how a developer writes and with all their history. It makes the software writing faster by associating better suggestions to a developer with his or her very own type (Gulwani, 2022).
- Google Photos — Uses AI to automatically recognize faces, objects and scenes in your photos so you do not have to tag or organize them. The interface changes only in response to user interactions, presenting search functions based on identified predictors of the photo library (Brdnik et al., 2022)

While generative AI has opened the door to unprecedented personalization, it also brings new challenges on privacy, user control and algorithmic bias. The true challenge is how to effectively one can balance all these factors in conjunction with their image recognition AI features to keep the user interested and happy.

IV. CHALLENGES AND LIMITATIONS OF GENERATIVE AI IN WEB ENGINEERING

A. Technical Challenges

Generative AI in web engineering presents several technical challenges that need to be addressed to fully harness its potential. These challenges span across accuracy, computational demand, handling dataset and integration of model:

o LLMs demand a lot of computer resources when it comes to both training and inference. This is due to the complex and extensive models, which can contain billions of parameters. Processing needs may be impractical for smaller companies and developers who don't have the same level of access to high-performance computer resources (Sun et al., 2022).

o Managing a large volume of data can involve needing high-quality storage and processing skills. It can be chaotic if the data is unstructured and comes from various resources in web engineering. In sensitive domains like healthcare and education managing these data can be even more challenging (Kenthapadi et al., 2023).

o Responsible AI practices such as transparency and fairness add an additional computational load, which again needs more resources to follow transparently. It also requires computational resources only for model interpretability and bias detection techniques (Meskó & Topol, 2023)

o Furthermore, the geopolitics influences data governance and reliance on specific technology platform make it harder to maintain and develop generative AI systems

B. Ethical and Bias Concerns

o AI systems are highly susceptible to inheriting biases from the data they are trained on and often that data reflects existing societal stereotypes and inequalities. Generative AI models can legally contribute to discrimination through practicing or amplifying these biases, resulting in unfair consequences within areas such as healthcare, employment and criminal justice. The causes of these biases can also come from the processes used to make automated decisions affecting either algorithms or humans who may introduce bias into programming and data selection (Shuford, 2024).

o Recent works have demonstrated that generative AI models, like image and speech synthesis, are biased towards gender or race. Meaning, for example, that light-skinned men will be overrepresented in job settings and dark-skinned women in subordinate roles supporting stereotypes (M. Zhou et al., 2024).

o Possible mitigation strategies include diversifying training datasets, improving transparency and accountability in AI systems, investigating alternative fairness-aware AI paradigms. Such a step requires the development of legal frameworks that prevent representational harms and protect individual rights, along laws against discrimination or in favor of privacy (Shuford, 2024).

o This entails embedding ethical evaluations within AI development processes which would also give rise to responsible and unbiased applications of public sector data. This will involve being more deliberate in how we use data and removing any protected characteristics that may result in biased outcomes. These ethical challenges require an interdisciplinary effort to navigate and craft AI systems that function equitability and justly (Wood et al., 2008).

C. Security Risks

o The concept of using AI to automatically produce complete working code based on complex programmatic instructions is quite appealing, but it is also potentially hazardous. Even the best currently available tools, such as OpenAI Codex or GitHub Copilot, can generate badly flawed programs because they may attempt to complete tasks that must be correctly programmed. All these inaccuracies result in vulnerabilities that may exacerbate the functions or patterns and lead to exploits (Cotroneo et al., 2024).

o   If malicious data is accidentally used to train AI models, it may cause data poisoning. Models that use poisoned data to train may produce misconfigured code.

o   AI-based code snippets may include confidential information, making it vulnerable to unauthorized access and data breaches (Adhyapak, 2024).

o   GenAI models are open to adversarial attacks and model inversion, which can permit unauthorized data extraction and data manipulation (Mahadevappa & Murugesan, 2021).

o   AI models can produce biased content based on the training data, which has ethical and security implications. In turn, the ability to generate deepfakes is associated with vast threats of misinformation and identity theft (K. Huang et al., 2024).

o   Companies should perform comprehensive risk analysis before deploying AI models into their workflow. Improving existing security layers and adding new ones will enable companies to mitigate risks (Tayyab et al., 2024).

o   Generative models can be significantly more secure by employing differential privacy, blockchain-based provenance and quantum-resistant algorithms. Human-guided reinforcement learning can also help alleviate some modelling problems by adding robustness (Alt et al., 2024).

V. FUTURE DIRECTIONS IN GENERATIVE AI FOR WEB ENGINEERING

A. Emerging Trends and Innovations

New Generative AI/ML trends in Web Engineering automate code generation, error detection, and layout design by dealing with routine tasks so that users can focus on higher levels of web design (Din et al., 2024). Over time, they adapt through user behavior and automatically deliver dynamic content and interfaces that match based on the individual (Kralina & Popova, 2024). Data centers are then free to utilize Liquid WebWorkers, which allows for better use of the computational resource, leading to increased web app response across devices. For instance, AI ideas like semantic fingerprinting allow granular content classification, which leads to the individualized offering of information. Not only that, but generative AI also supports predicting analytics to provide developers with the most accurate updates on trends and root generation for error detection applied in AI-powered web applications (Shahid et al., 2022). These advancements, like AI pair programming, show how far we have gone in modern web engineering.

B. The Convergence of AI With Other Technologies

Generative AI is integrating with emerging technologies like Blockchain, IoT and AR to empower their full potential in solving some existing issues. In IoT, generative AI creates synthetic data representative of real-world patterns to alleviate concerns like lack of data and privacy requirements using GANs and VAEs. Everyday use cases include data augmentation for machine learning models, anomaly detection and predictive maintenance that prove highly effective in resource-limited contexts (POORNIMA MAHADEVAPPA, 2021).

Blockchains in GenAI are used to secure and detect unknown attacks, identify smart contract vulnerabilities, and even design secure key-sharing schemes. To further elaborate, blockchain performance may be enhanced using generative diffusion models to improve throughput and latency while also offering faster convergence and increasing rewards compared with previous works based on other established generic deep learning or traditional methods (Shah et al., 2024).

In telecommunications, for instance, generative AI drives more accurate network digital twins that help better prepare organizations to deal with scenarios regarding predictive maintenance and prediction or real-time decision-making. This mutual benefit between generative AI and digital twins' systems empowers adaptable, savvy network management structures to respond better to system challenges, horizon operational efficiencies (Nguyen et al., 2024).

C. Preparing for the Future

To be future-ready in the field of generative AI, developers and organizations should start practicing adopting AI technologies phase-by-phase and gradually scale it. So, the organizations can validate the concepts, choose technical solutions, and perform proof of concept consistently until desired objective is reached and are economically viable. Organizations must also contemplate fast rollout methods using third party applications or tailor-made in-house models to strike a balance between control and speed of implementation (Goff, 2024). In addition to this, developers can emphasize environmental impacts like increasing energy efficiency and making use of more efficient processors. The AI market evolves so rapidly that one must maintain up-to-date knowledge about the newest technologies and responsible practices (Elliott et al., 2024).

VI. CASE STUDIES AND REAL-WORLD APPLICATIONS

A. Case Study 1: AI-Driven Web Design Platform

AI driven web design platform showcases the potential of AI in transforming creativity and project outcomes, especially when applied to educational settings. For instance, in the case of web design education, a longitudinal study has shown that AI tools can increase writing efficiency and coding ability as well as improve their design processes (N. J. Kim & Kim, 2022). While text-based AI tools helped with writing and coding tasks on the other hand, image-based ones facilitated ideation and color selection, resulting in more visually aesthetic products that are user-friendly. This approach provides interdisciplinary learning by incorporating a wide variety of educational needs and aligning AI tools to meet them (L. Chen et al., 2019). A study on educational web design showed that students improved their writing efficiency, coding skills, and design process using these AI tools. In addition, image-based tools facilitated ideas and color selection, leading to more visually appealing and user-friendly projects. AI-driven interfaces either online or offline provide user-centricity features and foster interdisciplinary learning for the students through increased engagement (Koch et al., 2020). Overall, the key lessons learned from this include the importance of customizing AI tools, balancing automation with human creativity, and ensuring ethical integration. So, this study emphasizes the choice of AI in productivity improvement and innovation by web design along with human interest.

B. Case Study 2: AI in E-Commerce Personalization

In e-commerce, AI-driven content has redefined how user engagement works and personalizes even more with their approach based on tailored strategies from various preferences. AI analyses enormous amounts of data to create relevant, hyper-targeted content that resonates with readers. RNNs and LSTMs, Layered deep learning models can change the content according to user behavior on dynamic basis with accuracy rate of 92%, resulting in more interactivity i.e. click-through rates (CTR) or conversion rates (Sodiya et al., 2024). Recommendation systems driven by artificial intelligence are being adopted widely with most users finding the suggested content highly relevant, contributing to increased user engagement and brand loyalty (Babatunde et al., 2024; Das et al., 2024).

But they faced some setbacks along the way. One major concern is that it does not involve the users feedback and authenticity, which can hinder long-term engagement. The rejection sampling frameworks were introduced to overcome these issues by using user feedback to improve content adaptation and engagement metrics.

Algorithmic bias and fairness present another challenge, as they can lead to unfair personalization outcomes. In response, organizations have developed AI models that are fairer and address a diversity of datasets through the application of processes to detect biases (Adhyapak, 2024).

Additionally, there are also privacy considerations with the high amount of data used for AI personalization. To cater this, businesses have started moving to better and secured cloud-based platforms which allows them to comply with such regulations while offering complete transparency experience to user where the end users are given authority on how their data is being invoked (Qureshi, 2024). Amongst the e-commerce industries, these efforts to better AI-backed strategies have resulted well.

C. Comparative Analysis: Traditional vs. AI-Driven Web Engineering

Table 1. Features of Traditional vs. AI-Driven Web Engineering

Features	Traditional Web engineering	AI-Driven Web Engineering
Efficiency	Tasks such as UML diagrams, coding, UI prototypes and database schemas are labor-intensive. Most of the time, testing and project management are repetitive.	Automating the development cycle with AI tools like ChatGPT saves time on manual effort and accelerates steps such as creating diagrams, writing code, and testing. While AI-powered project management tools and deep learning approaches in Model-Driven Web Engineering (MDWE) automate repetitive tasks, providing the projections of potential issues continues to be a focus area for developers (Djaber & Ismail, 2023).
Quality	Quality assurance heavily relies on human review and manual testing, which can miss potential issues. Achieving uniformity across software artifacts is difficult, especially in larger projects.	AI enforces automated checks and balances at all stages of the software development process, resulting in more consistent, high-quality programming artefacts. It can detect issues sooner, which implies that the subsequent software program could be strong and have error-free applications with fewer vulnerabilities (Kılınç & Keçecioğlu, 2024).
Scalability	In larger projects, scaling web applications can take a lot of human effort to accommodate load and user requests. Introducing new features can make scalability even slower.	By integrating AI, scalable architecture for new requirements effectively allows to serve a greater number of users and scale configuration workloads, adapt to change significantly better, and enforce long-term growth (Kralina & Popova, 2024).
Challenges	Primarily rely on skilled developers for every development aspect, hindering rapid scaling and innovation.	While offering numerous benefits, AI introduces challenges related to data quality, model interpretability, and, requiring developers to adapt and continually refine their skill sets to leverage AI's potential fully (Nguyen et al., 2024).

VII. CONCLUSION

Generative AI has emerged as a transformative technology in web engineering, offering advanced capabilities for content creation, design automation, and scalability. Fundamental models like GANs, VAEs, and Transformers enable the generation of realistic text, images, and code by learning patterns from large datasets. These models have been applied to a wide range, from automated web design to improved content personalization, reducing coding time and improve productivity and creativity.

AI has the potential to revolutionize web development by providing tools tailored to user requirements, improve efficiency and facilitate scalability. They can automate complex tasks, provide personalized content and generate interfaces that adapt to each individual user. Regardless of these challenges such as data quality, bias, and ethical concerns, generative AI stands as a key driver of innovation, reshaping the future of web engineering and enabling more dynamic, personalized, and intelligent web applications.

REFERENCES

Acher, M. (2024). A Demonstration of End-User Code Customization Using Generative AI. *Proceedings of the 18th International Working Conference on Variability Modelling of Software-Intensive Systems*, 139–145. DOI: 10.1145/3634713.3634732

Adhyapak, S. (2024). Data Privacy and Security Risks in AI-Based Code Understanding. *International Journal for Research in Applied Science and Engineering Technology*, 12(6), 1913–1921. DOI: 10.22214/ijraset.2024.63423

Al-Amin, M., Ali, M. S., Salam, A., Khan, A., Ali, A., Ullah, A., Alam, M. N., & Chowdhury, S. K. (2024). *History of generative Artificial Intelligence (AI) chatbots: Past, present, and future development* (No. arXiv:2402.05122). arXiv. https://doi.org//arXiv.2402.05122DOI: 10.48550

AlDahoul, N., Hong, J., Varvello, M., & Zaki, Y. (2023). *Exploring the Potential of Generative AI for the World Wide Web* (No. arXiv:2310.17370). arXiv. https://doi.org//arXiv.2310.17370DOI: 10.48550

Ali, H., & Aysan, A. F. (2024). Ethical dimensions of generative AI: A cross-domain analysis using machine learning structural topic modeling. *International Journal of Ethics and Systems, ahead-of-print*(ahead-of-print). DOI: 10.1108/IJOES-04-2024-0112

Almeida, Y., Albuquerque, D., Filho, E. D., Muniz, F., Santos, K. de F., Perkusich, M., Almeida, H., & Perkusich, A. (2024). AICodeReview: Advancing code quality with AI-enhanced reviews. *SoftwareX*, 26, 101677. Advance online publication. DOI: 10.1016/j.softx.2024.101677

Alt, T., Ibisch, A., Meiser, C., Wilhelm, A., Zimmer, R., Berghoff, C., Droste, C., Karschau, J., Laus, F., Plaga, R., Plesch, C., Sennewald, B., Thaeren, T., Unverricht, K., & Waurick, S. (2024, June 7). *Generative AI Models: Opportunities and Risks for Industry and Authorities*. arXiv.Org. https://arxiv.org/abs/2406.04734v1

Anstine, D. M., & Isayev, O. (2023). Generative Models as an Emerging Paradigm in the Chemical Sciences. *Journal of the American Chemical Society*, 145(16), 8736–8750. DOI: 10.1021/jacs.2c13467 PMID: 37052978

Asesh, A. (2023). Variational Autoencoder Frameworks in Generative AI Model. *2023 24th International Arab Conference on Information Technology (ACIT)*, 01–06. DOI: 10.1109/ACIT58888.2023.10453782

Avdić, A. (2024a). Generative AI Tools in Web Design. *Sinteza 2024 - International Scientific Conference on Information Technology, Computer Science, and Data Science*, 392–397. DOI: 10.15308/Sinteza-2024-392-397

Avdić, A. (2024b). Generative AI Tools in Web Design. *Sinteza 2024 - International Scientific Conference on Information Technology, Computer Science, and Data Science*, 392–397. DOI: 10.15308/Sinteza-2024-392-397

Babatunde, S. O., Odejide, O. A., Edunjobi, T. E., & Ogundipe, D. O. (2024). The role of ai in marketing personalization: A theoretical exploration of consumer engagement strategies. *International Journal of Management & Entrepreneurship Research*, 6(3), 3. Advance online publication. DOI: 10.51594/ijmer.v6i3.964

Betzalel, E., Penso, C., & Fetaya, E. (2024). Evaluation Metrics for Generative Models: An Empirical Study. *Machine Learning and Knowledge Extraction*, 6(3), 3. Advance online publication. DOI: 10.3390/make6030073

Borzunov, A., Ryabinin, M., Dettmers, T., Lhoest, Q., Saulnier, L., Diskin, M., Jernite, Y., & Wolf, T. (2022). *Training Transformers Together* (No. arXiv:2207.03481). arXiv. https://doi.org//arXiv.2207.03481DOI: 10.48550

Brdnik, S., Heričko, T., & Šumak, B. (2022). Intelligent User Interfaces and Their Evaluation: A Systematic Mapping Study. *Sensors (Basel)*, 22(15), 15. Advance online publication. DOI: 10.3390/s22155830 PMID: 35957387

Chen, L., Wang, P., Dong, H., Shi, F., Han, J., Guo, Y., Childs, P. R. N., Xiao, J., & Wu, C. (2019). An artificial intelligence based data-driven approach for design ideation. *Journal of Visual Communication and Image Representation*, 61, 10–22. DOI: 10.1016/j.jvcir.2019.02.009

Chen, T. (2024). The Impact of AI-Pair Programmers on Code Quality and Developer Satisfaction: Evidence from TiMi studio. *Proceedings of the 2024 International Conference on Generative Artificial Intelligence and Information Security*, 201–205. DOI: 10.1145/3665348.3665383

Cheok, A. D., & Zhang, E. Y. (2023). *From Turing to Transformers: A Comprehensive Review and Tutorial on the Evolution and Applications of Generative Transformer Models*. Qeios., DOI: 10.32388/3NTOLQ.2

Colombo, P., Peyrard, M., Noiry, N., West, R., & Piantanida, P. (2022). *The Glass Ceiling of Automatic Evaluation in Natural Language Generation* (No. arXiv:2208.14585). arXiv. https://doi.org//arXiv.2208.14585DOI: 10.48550

Costa, A., Silva, F., & Moreira, J. J. (2024). Towards an AI-Driven User Interface Design for Web Applications. *Procedia Computer Science*, 237, 179–186. DOI: 10.1016/j.procs.2024.05.094

Cotroneo, D., Improta, C., Liguori, P., & Natella, R. (2024). Vulnerabilities in AI Code Generators: Exploring Targeted Data Poisoning Attacks. *Proceedings of the 32nd IEEE/ACM International Conference on Program Comprehension*, 280–292. DOI: 10.1145/3643916.3644416

Creswell, A., White, T., Dumoulin, V., Arulkumaran, K., Sengupta, B., & Bharath, A. A. (2018). Generative Adversarial Networks: An Overview. *IEEE Signal Processing Magazine*, 35(1), 53–65. DOI: 10.1109/MSP.2017.2765202

Dagur, A., Singh, K., Mehra, P. S., & Shukla, D. K. (Eds.). (2023). *Artificial Intelligence, Blockchain, Computing and Security Volume 2: Proceedings of the International Conference on Artificial Intelligence, Blockchain, Computing and Security (ICABCS 2023), Gr. Noida, UP, India, 24 - 25 February 2023*. CRC Press. DOI: 10.1201/9781032684994

Das, I. R., Islam, A. S., Talukder, M. B., Das, I. R., Islam, A. S., & Talukder, M. B. (2024). *Customer Satisfaction in Hospitality Marketing From a Technological Perspective* (customer-satisfaction-in-hospitality-marketing-from-a-technological-perspective) [Chapter]. Https://Services.Igi-Global.Com/Resolvedoi/Resolve.Aspx ?Doi=10.4018/979-8-3693-6755-1.Ch019Global, IGI. DOI: 10.4018/979-8-3693-6755-1.ch019

Dimitrieska, S. (2024). Generative Artificial Intelligence and Advertising. *Trends in Economics. Finance and Management Journal*, 6(1), 23–34. DOI: 10.69648/EYZI2281

Din, S. N. U., Muzammal, S. M., Bibi, R., Tayyab, M., Jhanjhi, N. Z., & Habib, M. (2024). Securing the Internet of Things in Logistics: Challenges, Solutions, and the Role of Machine Learning in Anomaly Detection. In *Digital Transformation for Improved Industry and Supply Chain Performance* (pp. 133–165). IGI Global. https://www.igi-global.com/chapter/securing-the-internet-of-things-in-logistics/346170

Djaber, R., & Ismail, H. (2023). *AI as a Co-Engineer: A Case Study of ChatGPT in Software Lifecycle*. DOI: 10.21203/rs.3.rs-3809973/v1

Dubey, S. R., & Singh, S. K. (2023). *Transformer-based Generative Adversarial Networks in Computer Vision: A Comprehensive Survey* (No. arXiv:2302.08641). arXiv. http://arxiv.org/abs/2302.08641

Dzhangarov, A. I., Pakhaev, K. K., & Potapova, N. V. (2021). Modern web application development technologies. *IOP Conference Series. Materials Science and Engineering*, 1155(1), 012100. DOI: 10.1088/1757-899X/1155/1/012100

Ebert, C., & Louridas, P. (2023). Generative AI for Software Practitioners. *IEEE Software, 40*(4), 30–38. *IEEE Software*. Advance online publication. DOI: 10.1109/MS.2023.3265877

ELKarazle, K., Raman, V., Then, P., & Chua, C. (2024). How Generative AI Is Transforming Medical Imaging: A Practical Guide. In Applications of generative AI (pp. 371-385). Cham: Springer International Publishing.

Elliott, M. T., P, D., & Maccarthaigh, M. (2024). Evolving Generative AI: Entangling the Accountability Relationship. Digital Government: Research and Practice.

Ervik, A. (2023). Generative AI and the Collective Imaginary. *Image*, 37(1), 42–57. DOI: 10.1453/1614-0885-1-2023-15450

Exploring Creativity. (2024). *Advances in Computational Intelligence and Robotics Book Series*, 167–198. DOI: 10.4018/979-8-3693-3278-8.ch008

Feuerriegel, S., Hartmann, J., Janiesch, C., & Zschech, P. (2024). Generative AI. *Business & Information Systems Engineering*, 66(1), 111–126. DOI: 10.1007/s12599-023-00834-7

Gaikwad, A. (2024). A Collaborative Code Platform with Advanced AI Features and Real-Time Collaboration Tools. *International Journal for Research in Applied Science and Engineering Technology*, 12(5), 1569–1573. DOI: 10.22214/ijraset.2024.61438

Gatla, R. K., Gatla, A., Sridhar, P., Kumar, D. G., & Rao, D. S. N. M. (2024). Advancements in Generative AI: Exploring Fundamentals and Evolution. *2024 International Conference on Electronics, Computing, Communication and Control Technology (ICECCC)*, 1–5. DOI: 10.1109/ICECCC61767.2024.10594003

Ghayoumi, M. (2023). *Generative Adversarial Networks in Practice*. Chapman and Hall/CRC., DOI: 10.1201/9781003281344

Goff, T. L. (2024, January 4). *Recommendations for public action towards sustainable generative AI systems*. arXiv.Org. https://arxiv.org/abs/2402.01646v1

Goodfellow, I., Pouget-Abadie, J., Mirza, M., Xu, B., Warde-Farley, D., Ozair, S., Courville, A., & Bengio, Y. (2020). Generative adversarial networks. *Communications of the ACM*, 63(11), 139–144. DOI: 10.1145/3422622

Gulwani, S. (2022). AI-assisted programming: Applications, user experiences, and neuro-symbolic techniques (keynote). *Proceedings of the 30th ACM Joint European Software Engineering Conference and Symposium on the Foundations of Software Engineering*, 1. DOI: 10.1145/3540250.3569444

Hammad, M., El-Rahiem, B. A., & El-Latif, A. A. A. (2023). Leveraging generative adversarial networks and federated learning for enhanced cybersecurity: A concise review. In *Artificial Intelligence for Biometrics and Cybersecurity: Technology and applications* (pp. 65–87). IET Digital Library., DOI: 10.1049/PBSE020E_ch4

Hayashi, H. (2023). *A Hybrid of Generative and Discriminative Models Based on the Gaussian-coupled Softmax Layer* (No. arXiv:2305.05912). arXiv. https://doi.org//arXiv.2305.05912DOI: 10.48550

Huang, K., Goertzel, B., Wu, D., & Xie, A. (2024). GenAI Model Security. In Huang, K., Wang, Y., Goertzel, B., Li, Y., Wright, S., & Ponnapalli, J. (Eds.), *Generative AI Security: Theories and Practices* (pp. 163–198). Springer Nature Switzerland., DOI: 10.1007/978-3-031-54252-7_6

Huang, Y., Kanij, T., Madugalla, A., Mahajan, S., Arora, C., & Grundy, J. (2024). *Unlocking Adaptive User Experience with Generative AI*. 760–768. https://www.scitepress.org/Link.aspx?doi=10.5220/0012741000003687

Jain, R., Maity, K., Jha, P., & Saha, S. (2023). Generative Models vs Discriminative Models: Which Performs Better in Detecting Cyberbullying in Memes? *2023 International Joint Conference on Neural Networks (IJCNN)*, 1–8. DOI: 10.1109/IJCNN54540.2023.10191363

Kenthapadi, K., Lakkaraju, H., & Rajani, N. (2023). Generative AI meets Responsible AI: Practical Challenges and Opportunities. *Proceedings of the 29th ACM SIGKDD Conference on Knowledge Discovery and Data Mining*, 5805–5806. DOI: 10.1145/3580305.3599557

Khankhoje, R. (2016). *The Power of AI Driven Reporting in Test Automation*. 7(11).

Kılınç, H. K., & Keçecioğlu, Ö. F. (2024). Generative Artificial Intelligence: A Historical and Future Perspective. *Academic Platform Journal of Engineering and Smart Systems*, 12(2), 2. Advance online publication. DOI: 10.21541/apjess.1398155

Kim, J., & Maher, M. L. (2023). The effect of AI-based inspiration on human design ideation. *International Journal of Design Creativity and Innovation*, 11(2), 81–98. DOI: 10.1080/21650349.2023.2167124

Kim, N. J., & Kim, M. K. (2022). Teacher's Perceptions of Using an Artificial Intelligence-Based Educational Tool for Scientific Writing. *Frontiers in Education*, 7, 755914. Advance online publication. DOI: 10.3389/feduc.2022.755914

Koch, J., Taffin, N., Beaudouin-Lafon, M., Laine, M., Lucero, A., & Mackay, W. (2020). ImageSense: An Intelligent Collaborative Ideation Tool to Support Diverse Human-Computer Partnerships. *Proceedings of the ACM on Human-Computer Interaction, 4*(CSCW1), 1–27. DOI: 10.1145/3392850

Kralina, H., & Popova, A. (2024). Nowadays trends in web development. *Collection of Scientific Papers «ΛΟΓΟΣ»*. DOI: 10.36074/logos-29.03.2024.068

Kuthe, A., Shangarwar, S., Kamble, Y., Sakhale, P., Bhende, R., & Thakre, J. (2024). Portfolio Generator using Generative AI in Web Development. *International Journal Of Mathematics And Computer Research*, 12(5), 5. Advance online publication. DOI: 10.47191/ijmcr/v12i5.01

Lively, J., Hutson, J., & Melick, E. (2023). Integrating AI-Generative Tools in Web Design Education: Enhancing Student Aesthetic and Creative Copy Capabilities Using Image and Text-Based AI Generators. *DS Journal of Artificial Intelligence and Robotics*, 1(1), 23–36. DOI: 10.59232/AIR-V1I1P103

Mahadevappa, P., & Murugesan, R. K. (2021). Review of data integrity attacks and mitigation methods in edge computing. *Advances in Cyber Security: Third International Conference, ACeS 2021, Penang, Malaysia, August 24--25, 2021, Revised Selected Papers 3*, 505–514.

Malakar, P., & Leeladharan, M. (2024). Generative AI Tools for Collaborative Content Creation. *DESIDOC Journal of Library and Information Technology*, 44(3), 3. Advance online publication. DOI: 10.14429/djlit.44.3.19698

Mavridis, T., & Symeonidis, A. L. (2014). Semantic analysis of web documents for the generation of optimal content. *Engineering Applications of Artificial Intelligence*, 35, 114–130. DOI: 10.1016/j.engappai.2014.06.008

Meskó, B., & Topol, E. J. (2023). The imperative for regulatory oversight of large language models (or generative AI) in healthcare. *NPJ Digital Medicine*, 6(1), 1–6. DOI: 10.1038/s41746-023-00873-0 PMID: 37414860

Mishra, S., Chaudhury, P., Tripathy, H. K., Sahoo, K. S., Jhanjhi, N., Hassan Elnour, A. A., & Abdelmaboud, A. (2024). Enhancing health care through medical cognitive virtual agents. *Digital Health*, 10, 20552076241256732. DOI: 10.1177/20552076241256732 PMID: 39165388

Mughal, M. A., Ullah, A., Yu, X., He, W., Jhanjhi, N. Z., & Ray, S. K. (2024). A secure and privacy preserved data aggregation scheme in IoMT. *Heliyon*, 10(7), e27177. Advance online publication. DOI: 10.1016/j.heliyon.2024.e27177 PMID: 38601685

Nguyen, C. T., Liu, Y., Du, H., Hoang, D. T., Niyato, D., Nguyen, D. N., & Mao, S. (2024, January 28). *Generative AI-enabled Blockchain Networks: Fundamentals, Applications, and Case Study*. arXiv.Org. https://arxiv.org/abs/2401.15625v1

Oluwagbenro, D. M. B. (2024). *Generative AI: Definition, Concepts, Applications, and Future Prospects*. DOI: 10.36227/techrxiv.171746875.59016695/v1

Oppenlaender, J. (2022). The Creativity of Text-to-Image Generation. *Proceedings of the 25th International Academic Mindtrek Conference*, 192–202. DOI: 10.1145/3569219.3569352

Panigrahi, A., Malladi, S., Xia, M., & Arora, S. (2024). *Trainable Transformer in Transformer* (No. arXiv:2307.01189). arXiv. https://doi.org//arXiv.2307.01189DOI: 10.48550

Ploennigs, J., & Berger, M. (2024). Automating computational design with generative AI. *Civil Engineering Design*, 6(2), 41–52. DOI: 10.1002/cend.202400006

Qureshi, J. (2024). *AI-Powered Cloud-Based E-Commerce: Driving Digital Business Transformation Initiatives* (No. 2024012214). *Preprints*. DOI: 10.20944/preprints202401.2214.v1

Raji, M. A., Olodo, H. B., Oke, T. T., Addy, W. A., Ofodile, O. C., & Oyewole, A. T. (2024). E-commerce and consumer behavior: A review of AI-powered personalization and market trends. GSC Advanced Research and Reviews, 18(3), 066-077.

Razavi, A., van den Oord, A., & Vinyals, O. (2019). Generating Diverse High-Fidelity Images with VQ-VAE-2. *Advances in Neural Information Processing Systems, 32*. https://proceedings.neurips.cc/paper/2019/hash/5f8e2fa1718d1bbcadf1cd 9c7a54fb8c-Abstract.html

Sauvola, J., Tarkoma, S., Klemettinen, M., Riekki, J., & Doermann, D. (2024). Future of software development with generative AI. *Automated Software Engineering*, 31(1), 26. DOI: 10.1007/s10515-024-00426-z

Seidman, J. H., Kissas, G., Pappas, G. J., & Perdikaris, P. (2023). *Variational Autoencoding Neural Operators* (No. arXiv:2302.10351). arXiv. https://doi.org//arXiv .2302.10351DOI: 10.48550

Shah, S. A. A., Ullah, A., Subhan, F., Jhanjhi, N., Masud, M., & Alqhatani, A. (2024). *Truth discovery for mobile workers in edge-assisted mobile crowdsensing.* ICT Express., DOI: 10.1016/j.icte.2024.06.007

Shahid, J., Hameed, M. K., Javed, I. T., Qureshi, K. N., Ali, M., & Crespi, N. (2022). A Comparative Study of Web Application Security Parameters: Current Trends and Future Directions. *Applied Sciences (Basel, Switzerland)*, 12(8), 8. Advance online publication. DOI: 10.3390/app12084077

Shin, H., Sindi, N., Lee, Y., Ka, J., Song, J. Y., & Kim, J. (2022). XDesign: Integrating Interface Design into Explainable AI Education. *Proceedings of the 53rd ACM Technical Symposium on Computer Science Education* V. 2, 1097. DOI: 10.1145/3478432.3499052

Shirzad, H., Hassani, K., & Sutherland, D. J. (2022). *Evaluating Graph Generative Models with Contrastively Learned Features* (No. arXiv:2206.06234). arXiv. https://doi.org//arXiv.2206.06234DOI: 10.48550

Shuford, J. (2024). Examining Ethical Aspects of AI: Addressing Bias and Equity in the Discipline. *Journal of Artificial Intelligence General Science (JAIGS) ISSN: 3006-4023, 3*(1), Article 1. DOI: 10.60087/jaigs.vol03.issue01.p124

Si, C., Zhang, Y., Yang, Z., Liu, R., & Yang, D. (2024, March 5). *Design2Code: How Far Are We From Automating Front-End Engineering?* arXiv.Org. https://arxiv.org/abs/2403.03163v1

Sinha, S., Datta, S., Kumar, R., Bhattacharya, S., Sarkar, A., Das, K., Sinha, S., Datta, S., Kumar, R., Bhattacharya, S., Sarkar, A., & Das, K. (2014). *Exploring Creativity: The Development and Uses of Generative AI* (exploring-creativity. DOI: 10.4018/979-8-3693-3278-8.ch008

Sodiya, E. O., Amoo, O. O., Umoga, U. J., Atadoga, A., Sodiya, E. O., Amoo, O. O., Umoga, U. J., & Atadoga, A. (2024). AI-driven personalization in web content delivery: A comparative study of user engagement in the USA and the UK. *World Journal of Advanced Research and Reviews*, 21(2), 2. Advance online publication. DOI: 10.30574/wjarr.2024.21.2.0502

Sun, J., Liao, Q. V., Muller, M., Agarwal, M., Houde, S., Talamadupula, K., & Weisz, J. D. (2022). Investigating Explainability of Generative AI for Code through Scenario-based Design. *27th International Conference on Intelligent User Interfaces*, 212–228. DOI: 10.1145/3490099.3511119

Tayyab, M., Mumtaz, M., Muzammal, S. M., & Jhanjhi, N. Z. (2024). Swarm Security: Tackling Threats in the Age of Drone Swarms. In *Cybersecurity Issues and Challenges in the Drone Industry* (pp. 324–342). IGI Global. https://www.igi-global.com/chapter/swarm-security/340082

Thakur, K., Barker, H. G., & Pathan, A.-S. K. (2024). *Artificial Intelligence and Large Language Models: An Introduction to the Technological Future*. Chapman and Hall/CRC., DOI: 10.1201/9781003474173

Thorleiksdóttir, T. (2021). *Understanding Human Potentials for Evaluating Generative Models* [Master Thesis, ETH Zurich]. DOI: 10.3929/ethz-b-000507443

Tivari, G., Khara, D., Dave, D., & Patel, V. (2024). Enhancing Reality: Exploring the Potential of Generative Artificial Intelligence. *International Journal Of Scientific Research In Engineering And Management*, 8(7), 1–13. DOI: 10.55041/IJSREM36378

Toma, A., Krayani, A., Marcenaro, L., Gao, Y., & Regazzoni, C. S. (2020). Deep Learning for Spectrum Anomaly Detection in Cognitive mmWave Radios. *2020 IEEE 31st Annual International Symposium on Personal, Indoor and Mobile Radio Communications*, 1–7. DOI: 10.1109/PIMRC48278.2020.9217240

Torricelli, M., Martino, M., Baronchelli, A., & Aiello, L. M. (2024). *The role of interface design on prompt-mediated creativity in Generative AI* (No. arXiv:2312.00233). arXiv. /arXiv.2312.00233DOI: 10.1145/3614419.3644000

Upadhyay, U., & Jain, A. (2019). *Removal of Batch Effects using Generative Adversarial Networks* (No. arXiv:1901.06654). arXiv. http://arxiv.org/abs/1901.06654

Van Riet, J., Malavolta, I., & Ghaleb, T. A. (2023). Optimize along the way: An industrial case study on web performance. *Journal of Systems and Software*, 198, 111593. DOI: 10.1016/j.jss.2022.111593

Wakil, K., Jawawi, D., & Isa, M. (2015). *Analyzing Modern Web Applications to Recognize Features-based Web Engineering Methods*.

Wakil, K., & Jawawi, D. N. A. (2018). A New Adaptive Model for Web Engineering Methods to Develop Modern Web Applications. *Proceedings of the 2018 International Conference on Software Engineering and Information Management*, 32–39. DOI: 10.1145/3178461.3178468

Wei, J., Courbis, A.-L., Lambolais, T., Dray, G., & Maalej, W. (2024, June 19). *On AI-Inspired UI-Design*. arXiv.Org. https://arxiv.org/abs/2406.13631v1

Wood, L., Egger, M., Gluud, L. L., Schulz, K. F., Jüni, P., Altman, D. G., Gluud, C., Martin, R. M., Wood, A. J. G., & Sterne, J. A. C. (2008). Empirical evidence of bias in treatment effect estimates in controlled trials with different interventions and outcomes: Meta-epidemiological study. *BMJ (Clinical Research Ed.)*, 336(7644), 601–605. DOI: 10.1136/bmj.39465.451748.AD PMID: 18316340

Xiong, M. (2022). *Artificial Intelligence and Causal Inference*. Chapman and Hall/CRC., DOI: 10.1201/9781003028543

Yacoby, Y., Pan, W., & Doshi-Velez, F. (2024). *Towards Model-Agnostic Posterior Approximation for Fast and Accurate Variational Autoencoders* (No. arXiv:2403.08941). arXiv. https://doi.org//arXiv.2403.08941DOI: 10.48550

Yang, Y., Zheng, K., Wu, B., Yang, Y., & Wang, X. (2020). Network Intrusion Detection Based on Supervised Adversarial Variational Auto-Encoder With Regularization. *IEEE Access : Practical Innovations, Open Solutions*, 8, 42169–42184. DOI: 10.1109/ACCESS.2020.2977007

Zeng, X., He, C., & Jiang, Y. (2023). Investigating the Advancements in Generative Models. *2023 International Conference on Artificial Intelligence and Automation Control (AIAC)*, 347–351. DOI: 10.1109/AIAC61660.2023.00037

Zhou, B. (2024). *Social Paradigm Shift Promoted by Generative Models: A Study on the Trend from Result-Oriented to Process-Oriented Paradigm*. OSF. DOI: 10.31219/osf.io/qswzc

Zhou, M., Abhishek, V., Derdenger, T., Kim, J., & Srinivasan, K. (2024, March 5). *Bias in Generative AI*. arXiv.Org. https://arxiv.org/abs/2403.02726v1

Chapter 16
Exploring Security Challenges in Generative AI for Web Engineering

Syeda Mariam Muzammal
https://orcid.org/0000-0003-2960-1814
Taylor's University, Malaysia

Poornima Mahadevappa
https://orcid.org/0000-0001-9414-3464
Taylor's University, Malaysia

Muhammad Tayyab
https://orcid.org/0000-0001-5580-9163
Taylor's University, Malaysia

ABSTRACT

Web engineering is being transformed rapidly by Artificial Intelligence (AI), particularly by Generative AI (GenAI), through its potential for automation in content creation, source code generation, design creation, and optimization. Along with the tremendous benefits that the integration of GenAI and Web Engineering offers, significant security concerns arise related to secure deployment and data privacy. This chapter explores the importance and growing adoption of GenAI tools and techniques in web development, emphasizing the security considerations, such as potential vulnerabilities, including model manipulation, adversarial attacks, and data leakage. A thorough review of the existing studies reveals the primary security threats and attacks, including the recommended countermeasures. Moreover, the ethical implications of GenAI for web engineering have also been investigated. By highlighting the security and privacy concerns, this study shall benefit the research-

DOI: 10.4018/979-8-3693-3703-5.ch016

ers, developers, and organizations in adapting careful steps for GenAI utilization for web engineering process, taking into account the issues and challenges related to the user trust, privacy, security, and data integrity.

1. INTRODUCTION AND BACKGROUND

Web engineering deals with the tools, techniques, and methodologies that are applied for web-based applications development. This process is different from conventional computer applications or software development, and provides support for design, development, evaluation, and maintenance of the web applications . Generative Artificial Intelligence (GenAI), on the other hand, is a form of Artificial Intelligence (AI) that utilizes machine learning models being trained on large datasets of existing content to create new content, such as, code, text, music, and images. Traditional AI models are usually designed for specific tasks, whereas GenAI has the ability to autonomously generate synthetic and new content. In general, GenAI uses advanced algorithms and models, based on neural networks, trained to learn the patterns and structures from huge datasets and the outputs resemble the human-generated content (Gupta et al., 2024). The proliferation of GenAI in today's world offers a wide range of potential applications, including healthcare, entertainment, art, finance, and web engineering, from web design to web development and evaluation (Feuerriegel et al., 2024).

1.1. Generative AI in Web Engineering

1.1.1. Gen AI in Web Design:

Figure 1. GenAI-Inspired UI Design Process (Wei, Courbis, Lambolais, Dray, et al., 2024).

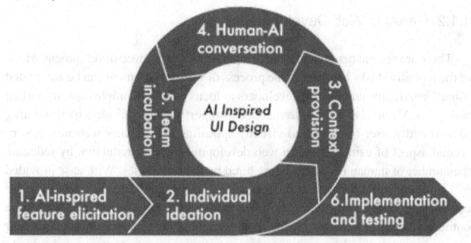

The web development process starts with the development of the user interface design. Typically, the process of designing UI of web application comprise of some key tasks, including design goals setting according to the requirement and purpose, analysis of targeted users and expectations, identifying main features and use cases, wireframing, visual design elements, prototype development, collecting feedback from users for design improvement and evolution. To begin the design part in web, tools like Figma and Sketch are available for basic UI components and templates. However, complex web app features and the relevant UIs require additional inspiration and advanced techniques (Azeem et al., 2022). To cope up with that, designers keep on exploring the trending app designs using platforms like Mobbin and Dribbble.

GenAI has the potential to automate several aspects of web design including search engine optimization (SEO), web content generation, and creation of user interfaces (UIs). For the optimization of websites for search engines, GenAI can be used to generate SEO-friendly elements, descriptions, keywords, and meta titles, which can assist in getting more potential visitors with higher ranking of websites in search engine results pages (SERPs). Similarly, different website content can be generated using GenAI, such as landing pages, product description, blog posts, etc. This can be helpful for reducing human efforts in businesses where a lot of content has to be generated on daily basis. Furthermore, the creation of user interfaces can also get benefitted from GenAI in terms of generating different designs based on certain requirements, for example, desired style, targeted audience or visitors, and the purpose of the website (Spair, 2024). Several GenAI tools are available for web design, including Surfer SEO, CopyAI, Contentful, and Auto Layout. Figure 1 depicts the process of GenAI inspired UI design process (Wei, Courbis, Lambolais, Dray, et al., 2024).

1.1.2. GenAI in Web Development:

There are several benefits that are offered by GenAI for web development. Many of the repetitive tasks involved in the process of web development can be automated using GenAI, thus leading the developers to focus on other complex and important tasks. GenAI can also provide tremendous support to the developers by generating SEO-friendly, user-friendly, and visually appealing high-quality websites. A very crucial aspect of using GenAI in web development is cost reduction by reducing the number of human resources being hired by the businesses. With ease provided by GenAI in web development process, there are certain challenges that are worth considering. For example, GenAI trained models does not always give an accurate output, which also depends on the model, training data and input data. Another reason for generating incorrect, inappropriate, or inaccurate content can be due to the biases in the training data for the GenAI model. In addition to that, there are always ethical concerns related to the content generated by GenAI, such as creating misinformation or deepfakes.

1.2. Growing Adoption of GenAI Tools and Techniques in Web Development

The rapid expansion of GenAI has become a transitional shift, since the revolution of Web 2.0, in not only in web technology but also in web development (Torricelli et al., 2024). A substantial amounts of AI-generated content has been uploaded online, including an average of 34 million images being created per day (*AI Image Statistics for 2024*, 2024). The growing adoption of GenAI tools is aided by its interface which is human-friendly through prompting, which is a form of human-computer interaction. Prompting is a short description which is given by the human for AI model to generate the desired content, such as a visual artefact (Oppenlaender, 2023).

Figure 2. Overview of UI Generation with LLMs, adapted from (Wei, Courbis, Lambolais, Dray, et al., 2024).

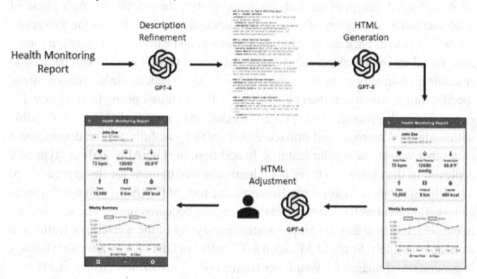

The user interface of any application is a crucial aspect for enhancing user experience. UI and web development assist in translating complicated application features and functions into visually intuitive elements, such as icons, buttons, images, that the users can easily navigate through and understand. In accent study, (Q. Chen et al., 2021) discussed about the importance of a well thought out UI design for enhancing user satisfaction. In order to make an app esthetically pleasing, the UI should be engaging functional, and self-explanatory. To achieve this, the UI designer is required to be highly creative. Recent advancements in AI and the availability of diverse models have revolutionized the web application development process, specifically the web design process. GenAI is of tremendous support for the designers to create more creative, diverse, and better Graphical User Interface (GUI). Recent studies have revealed the effectiveness of AI usage for accurate and efficient text to UI formation (Kolthoff et al., 2023; Wei, Courbis, Lambolais, Xu, et al., 2024). Wei et al. has discussed three approaches to support the app designers, Diffusion Model (DM), Vision-Language Model (VLM), and Large Language Model (LLM) (Wei, Courbis, Lambolais, Dray, et al., 2024). These models are helpful for the designers to create fruitful designs rather than just automating them. In addition, several GenAI tools are available commercially to assist in both text and image generation for UI designs. Some of these tools include JS Design's AI, Visily's AI, Galileo AI, and Uizard's Autodesigner. The auto-generation of UIs are being explored by the development teams worldwide, considering GenAI as an infinite resource for

UI generation (Feng et al., 2023; Wei et al., 2023). However, the challenge remains that how AI can effectively and efficiently assist in automation if a good UI design.

After the UI design of the website is completed, then comes the next phase of implementation and coding of the core features and functionalities of the web application, refers to as backend development. GenAI can be used to generate the source code based on the UI elements as input. Advanced GenAI models can be used to generate high-quality code. The generated code might lack essential components or specifications, which can then be adjusted with additional prompts to address the issues. The code generated by the GenAI model can be modified as much as possible with additional prompts and utilized either partially or fully for the development of another website or similar features. In addition, the GenAI models are typically deployed in the clouds, so there is no hardware requirement for the generation of the synthetic content in any case. However, the pros of GenAI in web development come with cons as well including that the generated code may have some adjustments issues which may affect the proper aesthetics, styling of the website, or features to work appropriately. Some LLMs, such as Claude-3 or GPT-4, may have high latency in generation of images for web UI or source code. Furthermore, using LLMs over the cloud for web development process requires you to have your data uploaded to the cloud and that surely can lead to data privacy breaches. Figure 2 shows an overview of UI generation with LLMs (Wei, Courbis, Lambolais, Dray, et al., 2024).

Figure 3. Text-to-GUI retrieval with VLMs (Wei, Courbis, Lambolais, Dray, et al., 2024).

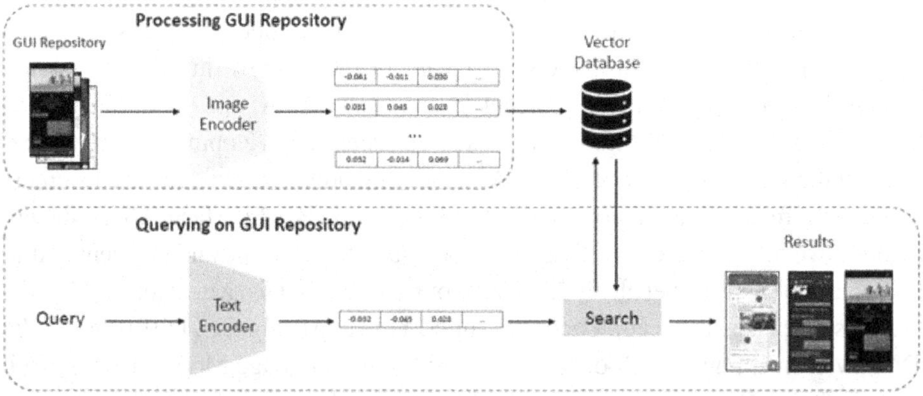

LLMs generate new synthetic content, whereas another way of generating content for web development, specifically UI is by searching for and retrieving the existing content. The multimodal models, VLMs, can learn from both text and images by using the captions in the images datasets. VLMs have low retrieval latency and produce high quality UI images which are usually associated with some existing applications. Since the UIs are retrieved from the existing applications, there is less diversity may restrict usage due to copyrights. Moreover, sometimes the results may also be irrelevant to the desired UIs. Figure 3 shows the text to GUI retrieval by using VLMs. Another recent research presents that several processes of biological data analysis, such as Cytometry or Next Generation Sequencing (NGS) generate data in huge amounts. For down-stream analysis, this data needs to be processed in batches. The datasets batches are handled at different situations, conditions, times, and different people, leading to technical variations in datasets, known as Batch Effects, causing inconclusive results (Upadhyay & Jain, 2019).

In summary, each model has its pros and cons, and there is a need for thorough research on utilization of these GenAI models for web engineering. Moreover, some important factors also need to be considered, such as the novelty and reusability of the synthetic content. While the GenAI capabilities seem fascinating, an ample effort is required to be put in for exploring its drawbacks, such as replacing human experience and creativity, and most importantly the concerns related to copyrights, data security and privacy.

1.3. Importance of Security in Web Engineering

Though GenAI models are being developed at a fast pace and deployed across various applications, systems, organizations, and industries. Even the ordinary users are engaging with GenAI models in routine tasks from writing an email or letter to graphic design generation, educational assistant to coding and drug discovery (GPT-3, 2022). GenAI has been beneficial for the development industry as well for automating the UI design process, prototyping and generating source code for the other web development phases. However, there have been various security, privacy, ethical, and social concerns associated with the applications and models of GenAI. These concerns can lead to plagiarism, copyrights violation, misleading and fake content or information generation, data breach and privacy issues, bias and discrimination, mainly due to lack of model robustness, and situational and environmental impacts associated with the inference and training of GenAI models (Kenthapadi et al., 2023).

In addition, several technical and ethical challenges are linked with GenAI for web engineering. GenAI models have a large size because of which their behavior varies and is highly ambiguous, leading to lack of trust and interpretability for web developers (Kambhampati, 2022). Hence, it prevents the developers from auto-validating the responses being generated by GenAI models, such as LLMs. Moreover, GenAI models are often trained on large amounts of data causing certain types of biases in results, for example, objectionable biases towards gender discrimination, disabilities (Hutchinson et al., 2020), and religious stereotypes (Abid et al., 2021). It also makes it difficult to audit the training data and the generated content. Furthermore, GenAI models are typically trained using the data collected from the Internet using web crawling and scraping, the reproduction of such data raise the privacy concerns, such as, leakage of personally identifiable information, as well as the copyright implications (Carlini et al., 2023). These concerns have severe implications when GenAI is thoughtlessly used by the web designers and developers. Hence, it is important to highlight the importance of security in web engineering, its implications, best practices, tools and technologies for securing GenAI in web engineering, by exploring the AI security frameworks and standards. Considering the security and privacy implications of GenAI, there is a need to emphasize the adoption of responsible AI to utilize GenAI for web engineering. In the light of the above, following are the objectives of this chapter:

1. To review security challenges and best practices in the use of generative AI in web engineering.
2. To critically explore how generative AI can introduce new security vulnerabilities.
3. To emphasize the significance for security in web applications and systems.
4. To investigate the tools and technologies for securing generative AI in web engineering.
5. To present case studies and real-world applications to enhance security of AI-driven web applications development.

The rest of the chapter is organized as follows: Section 2 presents the security testing tools and technologies for securing generative AI in web engineering, including AI security frameworks and standards. Section 3 narrates the security tools for GenAI, whereas Section 4 discusses the case studies and real-world applications related to securing AI-driven web engineering. Section 5 presents the comparative analysis of security practices in different web engineering projects. Section 6 provides the futures directions and recommendations for securing GenAI for web engineering, and finally Section 7 presents the conclusion of the study.

2. TOOLS AND TECHNOLOGIES FOR SECURING GENERATIVE AI IN WEB ENGINEERING

2.1. Security Testing Tools for AI-Generated Code

Security testing tools for AI-generated code are now also crucial in eliminating the types of vulnerabilities that may appear AI powered coding assistance, such as GitHub Copilot or OpenAI Codex. Such tools, designed for security teams specifically, are intended to uncover and manage a wide range of potential risks like SQL injection or OS command injection that might go unnoticed while generating code(Sanguino & J, 2024). Two notable tools for AI generated codes are CodeSecEval and DeVAIC. CodeSecEval – It evaluates 44 important types of critical vulnerabilities, guaranteeing to control code's security through automatic monitoring (J. Wang et al., 2024). DeVAIC is a static analysis kit to detect vulnerabilities in Python, which detects all potential security violations specified within the nine categories of OWASP using pattern recognition (Cotroneo, De Luca, et al., 2024). Prompt-engineering techniques have also been proposed as a preventive measure, adapting prompts in AI models to avoid insecure code samples and it's proven to be reduced by up to 16% (Knoth et al., 2024).

The integration of these tools into the web development pipelines and ensure secure code is implemented from the onset. Tools driven by AI, such as ChatGPT and GitHub Copilot that write test script can help to automate the testing process (Res et al., 2024). Tools like DeVAIC can assist with security-focused static analysis for vulnerabilities early in the development phase. The ACCA (Automated Correctness Assessment) methodology delivers fast security evaluations of AI-generated code to developers through symbolic execution with a reduced need for manual inspection (Cotroneo, Foggia, et al., 2024).

These tools have been successfully implemented and that helps to prove they are doing a great job of securing AI-created code. For example, the use of prompt-engineering techniques in GitHub Copilot led to an 8% uplift in secure code generation, i.e. new generated examples are more likely to be about security topics as compared with all-naturally generated samples (Res et al., 2024); The DeVAIC detection mechanism was also flawed, detect vulnerabilities in python code only 94% of the time (Cotroneo, De Luca, et al., 2024) . Thus, these are examples that clearly highlight the need for seamless integration of security testing tools into development and ensure efficient and secure AI-generated code.

2.2. AI Security Frameworks and Standards

AI security frameworks and standards in web engineering address specific threat landscape introduced by embedding artificial intelligence to leverage vulnerabilities of Web Application. This includes the best practices to build and deploy AI systems in a secure, reliable, and ethical way. With more and more focus on AI technologies such as machine learning, generative models, and large language models (LLMs) in the core of web development now than ever before, there is a robust need for security standards (Jing et al., 2021). For example, current frameworks like Trustworthy AI, Zero Trust Architecture (ZTAI), and regulatory guidelines like the GDPR and AI Act secure AI driven systems from threats like adversarial attacks, data breaches, and ethical violations (K. Ronanki, 2023). These frameworks focus on providing a way to secure user data, maintain ethical guidelines and follow regulatory standards for the use of AI.

There are various frameworks and standards that can be used to guarantee the ethical implementation of AI in web engineering. Some of them are as follows:

2.2.1. AI Security framework:

The AI security framework summarizes the objectives and attributes for defending AI driven systems. The framework emphasizes on facilitating the integration of security technologies with AI models and combining them into intrusion detection systems (IDS) and vulnerability detection tools to handle risks associated with in AI infrastructure and application composition (Mahadevappa et al., 2021, 2024). In addition, it allows multi-level strategy to handle various risks associated with AI driven web engineering (S. Jawhar et al., 2024).

2.2.2. Trustworthy AI Frameworks:

One of the major obstacles in AI deployment is the lack of trust, where accuracy and dependability simply can't be compromised when it comes to using AI systems in mission-critical fields like finance or healthcare. To address these concerns, Trustworthy AI (TAI) framework was introduced that complements existing ethics standards in the development of ethical AI through their operationalization to enhance transparency, fairness and accountability. However, the Framework is quite useful within web engineering since it deals with lot of user data and needs to consider ethical issues (K. Ronanki, 2023).

2.2.3. Regulatory and ethical safeguards:

The regulatory landscape for AI is rapidly changing with frameworks like GDPR (General Data Protection Regulation) and Digital Services Act (DSA) to establish standards related to privacy, transparency & accountability. These standards safeguard individual rights and foster innovation and creativity. Furthermore, the IEEE P7000 standards project provides ethical guidelines for AI design, ensuring that AI systems are developed responsibly and in alignment with human values (Peters et al., 2020).

2.2.4. Zero Trust AI Architecture (ZTAI):

Rather than depending on fixed security policies, ZTAI promotes real time and dynamic security strategies. This allows AI driven systems to interact with external data and services more easily (Al-hammuri et al., 2023).

2.2.5. Human-Guided Reinforcement Learning:

Adding human feedback to the reinforcement learning of generative AI models will enhance their security and ethical performances. Human participation can detect bias or security issues in AI outputs. In contexts such as content creation, human participation can be crucial to monitor offensive or biased content inadvertently propagated by these models (Huang et al., 2024).

The next frontier of AI security standards for web development will expand into more sophisticated threat detection, automated enforcement processes and deploy quantum-hedged algorithms to prevent evolving cyber-based attacks (Huang et al., 2024). Secure and transparent AI deployment will be underpinned by ethical development authorities to form a better regulatory framework like the proposed EU Artificial Intelligence (AI) Act and Cyber Resilience Act. This will require model governance, explainability and potentially new decentralized safety mechanisms to ensure their accountability whilst allowing for adaptation (Rampášek, 2023). As AI systems become more complex, updating security standards on a regular basis will be crucial for developing trust, data protection and innovation while reducing risks related to web development.

3. SECURITY TOOLS FOR GENERATIVE AI

The integration of generative AI in web engineering has brought both innovative solutions and significant security concerns, prompting the development and application of various security tools to safeguard AI-generated code. Real-world examples demonstrate how these tools are used to protect web applications from common vulnerabilities, such as SQL injection and code exploitation.

3.1. SQL Injection Prevention

ChatGPT and GitHub Copilot are AI tools that can generate code at great speed. However, if these systems do not follow secure coding practices, they would end up incorporating serious flaws. Research showed that the code generated by AI was vulnerable to SQL Injection attacks, where hackers could take advantage of the database structure in web applications. So, to address some of these risks the development process integrated secure coding standards that were well defined by organizations like OWASP and CERT (Mateo Sanguino, 2024). Combined with training programs and partnerships, they virtually eradicated the incidence of SQL vulnerabilities and established a level of security that conformed to requirements like GDPR or HIPAA (Aarti, 2024).

3.2. Prompt Engineering for Code Security

Prompt-engineering methodologies enhance the quality of GitHub Copilot, to eliminate many insecure code samples resulting from its output. By changing prompts, developers could reduce insecure code generation by up to 16% and increase secure code by up to 8% (Res et al., 2024). The technique takes a simplified approach to AI that is aimed at developers who are unlikely to have significant experience with AI.

3.3. DeVAIC Tool for Vulnerability Detection

The DeVAIC tool is this static analysis system build to discover vulnerabilities in AI-generated Python code. DeVAIC scored an outstanding accuracy rate of 94% and a high F1 formation, proving that it was very good at covering 35 different CWEs(Common Weakness Enumerations). Part of that was its ability to detect vulnerabilities in partial code snippets, which is especially valuable for real world use cases. The lightweight design and convenient DelVAIC integration with the development environment showed that it can be embedded in ALM, which allows detecting security problems generated by AI code early enough (Cotroneo, De Luca, et al., 2024).

3.4. AI for Financial Transaction Security

AI-powered systems enhance web application security by detecting fraudulent transactions with greater precision in financial sectors. AI library plug-ins in fintech platforms record transaction patterns and point a red flag whenever there seemed like something may have breached security (M. Habib et al., 2023; Xu et al., 2024). The tool offers real-time financial crime protection with machine learning algorithms. The library's integration into current financial systems through extending security validations highlights the importance of AI in this area (Nicholls et al., 2021).

3.5. GPT for Source Code Inspection

Static analysis of source code with generative models can also be seen, for instance GPT was applied to detect CWE-653 (a vulnerability related to insecure or unsafe constructs in the mode), a static examination usecase. GPT models determined sensitive fragments of the code and then assessed how well-protected they are via automatic detection. This automation source code inspection was able to minimize manual review and make it feasible for scanning AI-generated code without human intervention (Szabó & Bilicki, 2023).

The case study highlights some of the key takeaways for securing AI generated code. They secure coding standards while integrating developing software or services as part of their systems management activities. It can be observed that in the context of enhancing code security, prompt-engineering techniques provide non-experts to leverage AI models without needing deep technical expertise; this indicates developers could indeed shape the artifacts produced by AI with more careful intents. In DeVAIC, all attack surfaces are analyzed using black box tests and a development pipeline as part of the security good practices. In some examples of specific domain use cases AI tools can provide in spotting abnormality or fraud and overall improving a security stance but it can be most effective when used by trained personnel. Finally, the need for continuous review and human oversight remains critical, as AI models require periodic audits to identify and address potential security risks (Muzammal et al., 2016; Tayyab, Mumtaz, Muzammal, et al., 2024). These lessons underscore the importance of a comprehensive approach to securing AI-assisted web development.

4. CASE STUDIES AND REAL-WORLD APPLICATIONS

4.1. Case Study 1: Securing a Web Application Built with AI-Generated Code

Tools such as GitHub, Copilot and OpenAI Codex automate coding by suggesting or completing add-ons in the code, whether they have backend functionalities or front-end designs. To assist in developing web applications, Large Language Models (LLM) are powered by these automated tools to enhance productivity and efficiency (Sanguino & J, 2024). They can easily manage numerous things, e.g., compressions of images and image processing, by lowering the bandwidth range and keeping high-quality images. User customizations are made easier with GenAI tools, making it more straightforward for non-programmers to use through their easy adaptation to the programming environment (Hu et al., 2017). Regardless of these feature advancements, AI-based web applications need help with issues, including the requirement for increased contextual awareness and secure methods to train AIs. Additionally, ethical considerations issues such as employment displacement and intellectual property protection will also need to be made (Dash et al., 2022).

Securing AI based web applications inherit unique challenges associated with LLMs such as including un-sanitized data from open-source repositories and incomplete code snippet. They create vulnerabilities like SQL injection, difficulty to evaluate codes and complication of detecting the vulnerabilities (Moustafa et al., 2020). To mitigate these security issues scenarios-based techniques such as prompt engineering are used to reduce insecure code samples and increase secure code generation (Knoth et al., 2024). Apart from these vulnerabilities evaluation tools like DeVAIC detect issues through regular expression to identify common weakness and improve accuracy in detection (Cotroneo, De Luca, et al., 2024). Finally, by adopting secure standards and guidelines like GDPR and HIPAA, and regular audits through human interventions we can mitigate vulnerabilities (Islam Riad et al., 2024). Some of the key takeaways here are to consistently iterate and optimize AI-generated code and reassess the evolving security vulnerabilities. Furthermore, secure coding standards and some level of human audit will still be needed to maintain security and integrity in AI-generated applications.

4.2. Case Study 2: Data Privacy in AI-Driven Web Applications

AI based web applications aid personalized content to improve user engagement by recommending its users, based on their preferences, browsing habits and demographic data. For example: GPTutor, GPT tool - Users are served with personalized news articles, product or contextual content (E. Chen et al., 2024). The recommendation algorithm in this AI model is driven by behavior patterns & has a large dataset (Kumar, 2024). Yet, personalized content is confronted with a large-scale problem like data privacy. As the application access personal data, such as location details, interaction history, user preferences, this poses a risk if it's not secured properly (Muzammal & Murugesan, 2021). Additionally, AI required a lot of user data to be effective, which raised questions around how to meet privacy regulations and still provide an experience that felt personalized from its results. Here are some of the data privacy techniques implemented:

4.2.1. Data Encryption:

Encryptions protect confidential data both during transit and at rest. Authorities stepped in to mandate that data undergo pre-encryption before transmission, but nevertheless it would only be impenetrable if intercepted without the decryption keys. User profiles, browsing history and any interaction data are all encrypted so that user information is not accessible except for those who interacted with the bots through website designated by Admin console (Y. Wang, 2024).

4.2.2. Data Anonymization:

Data anonymization is the process of making personal data not identifiable by removing identifiers in the case of model training. This process involves AI models that learn from user's data, while never seeing a user's actual, individual identity. By doing this the AI model renders personalized results per query without releasing private personal assets (Sangaiah et al., 2023).

4.2.3. Differential Privacy:

They are implemented to further protect privacy. It adds noise to the data frames prohibiting single measurements or entire longitudinal sets of them from being back linked by malicious actors individually. So that the system could still create personalized content and at the same time keep user privacy (Ezzeddine, 2024).

4.2.4. Decentralized Data Management:

Quality-of-service standards were established by the development of strict access controls so that only authorized staff could use private user data. Furthermore, the system was continuously audited and logged to identify any attempts of unauthorized access or an intruder. This helped in securing transparency on the platform (Vizgirda et al., 2024).

4.2.5. Data Minimization:

The application collected only the absolute minimum amount of data that was required to provide customized content. This practice brought down the risks of exposure in handling such sensitive data by not allowing too much skewing through a single system (Yang et al., 2024).

The web application achieved a good equilibrium between personalized content delivery and strong data privacy by utilizing encryption, anonymization, and differential privacy techniques. These techniques ensured fulfillment with privacy regulations like GDPR while guaranteeing user confidence (Villegas-Ch & García-Ortiz, 2023). Key takeaways from this case study range from balancing data privacy with AI functionality, continuous monitoring in order to catch weaknesses and using encryption or anonymization techniques for protecting sensitive information. As these web applications establish, new technologies such as blockchain can be integrated to offer security and transparency.

5. COMPARATIVE ANALYSIS OF SECURITY PRACTICES IN DIFFERENT WEB ENGINEERING PROJECTS

Securing web engineering depends on both advanced security protocols to be implemented and ethical frameworks to adopt to address the unique vulnerabilities introduced by these technologies. AI systems have been designed to be secured in different ways, like differential privacy and quantum resistant algorithms; each of them has its own strengths and limitations. A brief comparison is presented in Table 1 below.

Table 1. A brief comparison of different web engineering projects

Web Engineering Projects	Strength	Challenges	Best Practices
Differential Privacy	It guarantees that user identities remain anonymous in AI-created summaries and recommendations, even when applied to a large amount of data. Differential privacy adds noise to the data, hence it is a great way of safeguarding sensitive user information from getting individual users with high probabilities in web applications.	Too much noise can hamper AI from providing hyper-personalized and accurate recommendations, while too little noise might lead to data privacy being leaked.	It ensures user datasets stay secure and at the same time allows for accurately predicting AI usage generated outputs (Ezzeddine, 2024; Golda et al., 2024).
Blockchain-Based Provenance	A transparent and decentralized way to prove the provenance of data used in generative AI models is using blockchain (Muzammal & Murugesan, 2020). It verifies the data provenance, authenticity and security of information used in training process, making it tamper-proof protecting integrity of AI system.	They are not easily scalable in real-time web applications and computationally expensive. On top of that, web applications are usually implemented with a frequent user interactions and content generation, this might not play very well in an official OSDP-designated fulfillment.	It can be used to follow the chain of AI training data back, ensuring that models come from a secure and more verifiable source; preventing unstable and malicious data infection (Fitriawijaya & Jeng, 2024).
Quantum-Resistant Algorithms	They offer a proactive safeguard against new vulnerabilities introduced by quantum computing. The progression of quantum technologies encapsulates the decisions about web applications produced by AI through quantum-resistant algorithms. It also has the time and tools necessary for future-proof properties.	The computations involved in quantum-resistant algorithms may pose as a bottleneck to be used immediately within the current generative AI models.	This inception allows for a higher-level security to be maintained, particularly worthwhile with high levels of data protection required by these applications (Radanliev et al., 2023).

continued on following page

347

Table 1. Continued

Web Engineering Projects	Strength	Challenges	Best Practices
Human-Guided Reinforcement Learning	AI outputs are double-checked and sometimes corrected by people thus insulating against introducing security bugs into the model such as adversarial attacks or biased results. Employing human judgment in conjunction with the precision of a machine only serves to reinforce AI security.	It is a slow process and, in some aspect, not true learning as approach can be bias.	By supplementing reinforcement learning guided by humans fine tunes model and won't, influence ethical standards, but also improve safety levels again (Wu et al., 2023).
AI/ML Opt-Out Protocols and Web Standards	Users and publishers are given the ability to request their data not be used in training any machine learning models. These protocols, compliant with GDPR and other privacy laws will dramatically shape the user experience of how parties utilize their personal data.	They limit the data available for the generative models to learn.	They can lead to improved trust with end-users as web developers now have the capacity to train powerful models on high-quality, ethically generated datasets (H. Habib et al., 2020).

In addition to technical solutions, legal frameworks and ethical guidelines play a significant role in securing generative AI in web engineering. The legal landscape surrounding generative AI is evolving, particularly concerning copyright infringement, data ownership, and algorithmic bias. Ethical considerations are vital in ensuring the responsible application of AI technologies, with a focus on transparency, fairness, and accountability.

6. FUTURE DIRECTIONS IN AI SECURITY FOR WEB ENGINEERING

AI-driven systems are playing a crucial role in our routine tasks and their usage and importance are growing at a rapid pace. Along with this proliferation, there are some disruptive impacts of GenAI models, particularly affecting their usage in web engineering. To encounter these impacts, there is a need to incorporate responsible techniques while developing the generative AI models, such as LLMs.

6.1. Emerging Trends in AI Security

The growing needs of cyber threats are also emerging in the AI-based systems and applications. The key developments in AI-based security attacks include Shadow AI, threats intelligence mechanisms, defensive AI, and AI-powered attacks. Along with the positive use cases of AI, this cutting-edge technology is being leveraged by attackers in launching more and more complex attacks in the cyber domain, such as deepfakes, phishing campaigns, and malware generation. Thus, helping the attackers to more effectively launch cyber-attacks against the organizations and systems. Such threats may maliciously manipulate the software dependencies or execute the strategies in a cloud environment to disrupt the infrastructure. In addition, AI-based attacks may also be harder to detect (*The Rise of AI Threats and Cybersecurity*, 2024). On the other hand, organizations are adopting AI-based strategies for defense against cyberattacks. AI-based security tools can be used to train the model in real-time in order to adapt to ever emerging threat landscape. From threat intelligence perspective, AI along with the machine learning can transform the attack prediction models by enabling the proactive measures for anomalies detection (Din et al., 2024). Another term "Shadow AI" is being used for the AI tools and applications that are unverified. By using such tools, one can unintentionally leak the sensitive and private data or make the systems vulnerable (*New AI Insights*, n.d.). Hence, both the attackers and defenders are using various tactics to leverage the potential of AI in cybersecurity.

6.2. Impact of Emerging AI Trends on Web Engineering

With the evolution in AI, particularly GenAI, web engineering is seeing a higher degree of automation. In web development process, web engineering is already in use for the generating UI/UX designs, content generation, and writing code snippets. The future of web engineering can be seen as fully powered and automated by GenAI, where GenAI tools and techniques could be used to develop entire web applications autonomously according to the provided requirements. It may enhance the user experience, reduce development time, and improve productivity. GenAI can enhance personalized experience by real-time analysis of user behavior, interaction, and behavior (Maddireddy1 & Maddireddy 2, 2022). Hence, the website can be tuned to offer customized individual experience, as evident by AI-based implementations for personalized experience by big giants, such as, Netflix and Amazon. In addition, from the security point of view, AI-driven security strategies can be of tremendous support in real-time monitoring of anomalous behavior or activities, thus leading to timely management of vulnerabilities and attacks for robust protection against cyberattacks. Furthermore, the web engineers have to tackle the ethical and regulatory issues that may arise by the wrong information or misuse of the AI-generated content, such as AI-generated deepfakes. In general, the future of AI in web engineering will enhance automation, personalization, security, and ethical considerations, serving as a transformative shift in how the web applications are developed and deployed.

6.3. The Role of AI in Securing AI-Generated Content

AI-generated content can be prone to misleading information, misuse of information, privacy, and data integrity concerns. Several key strategies have been found in recent studies that enable the security of AI-generated content in web applications.

The verification of AI-generated content can be done by comparing it with the well-established patterns or datasets, such as Natural Language Processing (NLP) models for detection of inappropriate information, harmful, content, biasness, inconsistencies, or anomalies (*A Survey on ChatGPT*, n.d.). For example, AI tools can be used to automate the flagging of unsuitable content. Similarly, AI-based security tools can be helpful in detecting the misleading fake content or deepfakes by determining the manipulations by linguistic patterns, image pixel inconsistencies, or digital signatures (Tayyab, Mumtaz, Jhanjhi, et al., 2024). This helps to maintain the authenticity of content shared via web applications, reducing the risk of spreading false information.

In addition, AI-based encryption and privacy controls can be used by the web engineers to adaptive encryption techniques that strengthen privacy controls, especially when sensitive content is involved (Arulmurugan et al., 2024). AI can also help in secure transmission, processing, and storage of the content. AI can perform real-time monitoring of AI-generated content, automatically identifying harmful content or breaches in privacy policies (Y. Wang et al., 2023). This can prevent unauthorized data leaks or abuse, ensuring that all generated material complies with ethical and legal standards. Web applications can use AI to implement proactive content filtering, which allows for immediate flagging and moderation of inappropriate or sensitive materials.

AI models sometimes unintentionally reveal sensitive data in generated content (e.g., code snippets or text) (Lyu, 2023). AI-driven data loss prevention (DLP) systems can detect and mitigate such risks by analyzing content for confidential information. These systems ensure that personal data or proprietary information isn't exposed when AI models generate content. Hence, by blending AI-driven monitoring, encryption, and detection techniques, web engineers can secure AI-generated content in a robust and adaptive manner, helping protect both users and platforms from potential vulnerabilities.

7. CONCLUSION

In the realm of web engineering, GenAI holds the significance for automating the tedious tasks of designing, source code, and content writing. In order to avoid undesirable impacts and issues in web content, the web developers and designers have to be aware of the accountable, fair, explainable, transparent, privacy, preserving, and fair use of GenAI systems. By exploring the key challenges and emphasizing the need to adopt responsible AI techniques and principles, this study intends to benefit the web engineering professionals and researchers' community to use GenAI for web development practices. The key security and privacy challenges have been highlighted in AI-driven web systems development along with the case studies and real-world examples. Moreover, the recommendations and future directions have been investigated to signify the emerging trends and the role of AI itself in secure generation of the AI-based content. The study would pave the way not only for the development of more trustworthy and reliable GenAI models and applications but also will assist in adapting the principles of responsible AI in content and code generation from web engineering perspectives.

REFERENCES

A Survey on ChatGPT: AI–Generated Contents, Challenges, and Solutions. (n.d.). Retrieved September 12, 2024, from https://ieeexplore.ieee.org/abstract/document/10221755

Aarti. (2024). Generative Ai in Software Development: An Overview and Evaluation of Modern Coding Tools. *IJFMR - International Journal For Multidisciplinary Research, 6*(3). DOI: 10.36948/ijfmr.2024.v06i03.23271

Abid, A., Farooqi, M., & Zou, J. (2021). Large language models associate Muslims with violence. *Nature Machine Intelligence*, 3(6), 461–463. DOI: 10.1038/s42256-021-00359-2

AI Image Statistics for 2024: How Much Content Was Created by AI. (2024, August 15). https://journal.everypixel.com/ai-image-statistics

Al-hammuri, K., Gebali, F., Kanan, A., Mamun, M., Hazratifard, S. M., & Alfar, H. (2023). *Zero Trust Context-Aware Access Control Framework for IoT Devices in Healthcare Cloud AI Ecosystem.*

Arulmurugan, L., Thakur, S., Dayana, R., Thenappan, S., Nagesh, B., & Sri, R. K. (2024). Advancing Security: Exploring AI-driven Data Encryption Solutions for Wireless Sensor Networks. *2024 International Conference on Advances in Computing, Communication and Applied Informatics (ACCAI)*, 1–6. DOI: 10.1109/ACCAI61061.2024.10602020

Azeem, M. R., Muzammal, S. M., Zaman, N., & Khan, M. A. (2022). Edge Caching for Mobile Devices. *2022 14th International Conference on Mathematics, Actuarial Science, Computer Science and Statistics (MACS)*, 1–6. DOI: 10.1109/MACS56771.2022.10022729

Carlini, N., Hayes, J., Nasr, M., Jagielski, M., Sehwag, V., Tramèr, F., Balle, B., Ippolito, D., & Wallace, E. (2023). *Extracting Training Data from Diffusion Models* (arXiv:2301.13188). arXiv. https://doi.org//arXiv.2301.13188DOI: 10.48550

Chen, E., Lee, J.-E., Lin, J., & Koedinger, K. (2024). *GPTutor: Great Personalized Tutor with Large Language Models for Personalized Learning Content Generation.* 539–541.

Chen, Q., Chen, C., Hassan, S., Xing, Z., Xia, X., & Hassan, A. E. (2021). How Should I Improve the UI of My App? A Study of User Reviews of Popular Apps in the Google Play. *ACM Trans. Softw. Eng. Methodol., 30*(3), 37:1-37:38. DOI: 10.1145/3447808

Cotroneo, D., De Luca, R., & Liguori, P. (2024). *DeVAIC: A Tool for Security Assessment of AI-generated Code* (arXiv:2404.07548). arXiv. http://arxiv.org/abs/2404.07548

Cotroneo, D., Foggia, A., Improta, C., Liguori, P., & Natella, R. (2024). Automating the correctness assessment of AI-generated code for security contexts. *Journal of Systems and Software*, 216, 112113. DOI: 10.1016/j.jss.2024.112113

Dash, B., Ansari, M. F., Sharma, P., & Ali, A. (2022). Threats and Opportunities with AI-based Cyber Security Intrusion Detection: A Review. *International Journal of Software Engineering and Its Applications*, 13(5), 13–21. Advance online publication. DOI: 10.5121/ijsea.2022.13502

Din, S. N. U., Muzammal, S. M., Bibi, R., Tayyab, M., Jhanjhi, N. Z., & Habib, M. (2024). Securing the Internet of Things in Logistics: Challenges, Solutions, and the Role of Machine Learning in Anomaly Detection. In *Digital Transformation for Improved Industry and Supply Chain Performance* (pp. 133–165). IGI Global. DOI: 10.4018/979-8-3693-5375-2.ch007

Ezzeddine, F. (2024). Privacy Implications of Explainable AI in Data-Driven Systems. *arXiv Preprint arXiv:2406.15789*.

Feng, S., Yuan, M., Chen, J., Xing, Z., & Chen, C. (2023, December 12). *Designing with Language: Wireframing UI Design Intent with Generative Large Language Models*. arXiv.Org. https://arxiv.org/abs/2312.07755v1

Feuerriegel, S., Hartmann, J., Janiesch, C., & Zschech, P. (2024). Generative AI. *Business & Information Systems Engineering*, 66(1), 111–126. DOI: 10.1007/s12599-023-00834-7

Fitriawijaya, A., & Jeng, T. (2024). Integrating Multimodal Generative AI and Blockchain for Enhancing Generative Design in the Early Phase of Architectural Design Process. *Buildings*, 14(8), 2533. Advance online publication. DOI: 10.3390/buildings14082533

Golda, A., Mekonen, K., Pandey, A., Singh, A., Hassija, V., Chamola, V., & Sikdar, B. (2024). Privacy and Security Concerns in Generative AI: A Comprehensive Survey. *IEEE Access, 12*, 48126–48144. IEEE Access. DOI: 10.1109/ACCESS.2024.3381611

GPT-3. S. H., Pat Grady and. (2022, September 19). *Generative AI: A Creative New World*. Sequoia Capital. https://www.sequoiacap.com/article/generative-ai-a-creative-new-world/

Gupta, P., Ding, B., Guan, C., & Ding, D. (2024). Generative AI: A systematic review using topic modelling techniques. *Data and Information Management*, 8(2), 100066. DOI: 10.1016/j.dim.2024.100066

Habib, H., Pearman, S., Wang, J., Zou, Y., Acquisti, A., Cranor, L. F., Sadeh, N., & Schaub, F. (2020). "It's a scavenger hunt": Usability of Websites' Opt-Out and Data Deletion Choices. *Proceedings of the 2020 CHI Conference on Human Factors in Computing Systems*, 1–12. DOI: 10.1145/3313831.3376511

Habib, M., Hussain, A., Rehman, E., Muzammal, S. M., Cheng, B., Aslam, M., & Jilani, S. F. (2023). Convolved Feature Vector Based Adaptive Fuzzy Filter for Image De-Noising. *Applied Sciences (Basel, Switzerland)*, 13(8), 8. Advance online publication. DOI: 10.3390/app13084861

Hu, J., Song, S., & Gong, Y. (2017). Comparative performance analysis of web image compression. *2017 10th International Congress on Image and Signal Processing, BioMedical Engineering and Informatics (CISP-BMEI)*, 1–5. DOI: 10.1109/CISP-BMEI.2017.8301939

Huang, K., Goertzel, B., Wu, D., & Xie, A. (2024). GenAI Model Security. In Huang, K., Wang, Y., Goertzel, B., Li, Y., Wright, S., & Ponnapalli, J. (Eds.), *Generative AI Security: Theories and Practices* (pp. 163–198). Springer Nature Switzerland., DOI: 10.1007/978-3-031-54252-7_6

Hutchinson, B., Prabhakaran, V., Denton, E., Webster, K., Zhong, Y., & Denuyl, S. (2020). *Social Biases in NLP Models as Barriers for Persons with Disabilities* (arXiv:2005.00813). arXiv./arXiv.2005.00813DOI: 10.18653/v1/2020.acl-main.487

Islam Riad, A. K., Barek, A., Rahman, M., Akter, S., Islam, T., Rahman, M., Md Raihan, M., Shahriar, H., Wu, F., & Ahamed, S. (2024). *Enhancing HIPAA Compliance in AI-driven mHealth Devices Security and Privacy.*, DOI: 10.1109/COMPSAC61105.2024.00390

Jawhar, S., Miller, J., & Bitar, Z. (2024). AI-Based Cybersecurity Policies and Procedures. *2024 IEEE 3rd International Conference on AI in Cybersecurity (ICAIC)*, 1–5. DOI: 10.1109/ICAIC60265.2024.10433845

Jing, H., Wei, W., Zhou, C., & He, X. (2021).. . *An Artificial Intelligence Security Framework.*, 1948(1), 012004.

Kambhampati, S. (2022, September 1). *Changing the Nature of AI Research – Communications of the ACM.* https://cacm.acm.org/article/changing-the-nature-of-ai-research/

Kenthapadi, K., Lakkaraju, H., & Rajani, N. (2023). Generative AI meets Responsible AI: Practical Challenges and Opportunities. *Proceedings of the 29th ACM SIGKDD Conference on Knowledge Discovery and Data Mining*, 5805–5806. DOI: 10.1145/3580305.3599557

Knoth, N., Tolzin, A., Janson, A., & Leimeister, J. M. (2024). AI literacy and its implications for prompt engineering strategies. *Computers and Education: Artificial Intelligence*, 6, 100225. DOI: 10.1016/j.caeai.2024.100225

Kolthoff, K., Bartelt, C., & Ponzetto, S. P. (2023). Data-driven prototyping via natural-language-based GUI retrieval. *Automated Software Engineering*, 30(1), 13. DOI: 10.1007/s10515-023-00377-x

Kumar, P. S. (2024). Movie Review Sentiment Analysis and AI-Story Generation Web Application. *International Journal for Research in Applied Science and Engineering Technology*, 12(3), 310–316. DOI: 10.22214/ijraset.2024.58826

Lyu, L. (2023). A pathway towards responsible AI generated content. *Proceedings of the Thirty-Second International Joint Conference on Artificial Intelligence*, 7033–7038. DOI: 10.24963/ijcai.2023/803

Maddireddy, B. R., & Maddireddy, B. R. (2022). Real-Time Data Analytics with AI: Improving Security Event Monitoring and Management. *Unique Endeavor in Business & Social Sciences*, 1(2), 47–62.

Mahadevappa, P., Murugesan, R. K., Al-amri, R., Thabit, R., Al-Ghushami, A. H., & Alkawsi, G. (2024). A secure edge computing model using machine learning and IDS to detect and isolate intruders. *MethodsX*, 12, 102597. DOI: 10.1016/j.mex.2024.102597 PMID: 38379716

Mahadevappa, P., Muzammal, S. M., & Murugesan, R. K. (2021). *A Comparative Analysis of Machine Learning Algorithms for Intrusion Detection in Edge-Enabled IoT Networks* (arXiv:2111.01383). arXiv. https://doi.org//arXiv.2111.01383DOI: 10.48550

Mateo Sanguino, T. (2024). Enhancing Security in Industrial Application Development: Case Study on Self-Generating Artificial Intelligence Tools. *Applied Sciences (Basel, Switzerland)*, 14(9), 3780. DOI: 10.3390/app14093780

Moustafa, N., Keshk, M., Debie, E., & Janicke, H. (2020). *Federated TON_IoT Windows Datasets for Evaluating AI-based Security Applications* (arXiv:2010.08522). arXiv. http://arxiv.org/abs/2010.08522 DOI: 10.1109/TrustCom50675.2020.00114

Muzammal, S. M., & Murugesan, R. K. (2020). A Study on Secured Authentication and Authorization in Internet of Things: Potential of Blockchain Technology. In Anbar, M., Abdullah, N., & Manickam, S. (Eds.), *Advances in Cyber Security* (pp. 18–32). Springer., DOI: 10.1007/978-981-15-2693-0_2

Muzammal, S. M., & Murugesan, R. K. (2021). Enhanced authentication and access control in Internet of Things: A potential blockchain-based method. *International Journal of Grid and Utility Computing*, 12(5–6), 469–485. DOI: 10.1504/IJGUC.2021.120090

Muzammal, S. M., Shah, M. A., Zhang, S.-J., & Yang, H.-J. (2016). Conceivable security risks and authentication techniques for smart devices: A comparative evaluation of security practices. *International Journal of Automation and Computing*, 13(4), 350–363. DOI: 10.1007/s11633-016-1011-5

New AI Insights: Explore Key AI Trends and Risks in the ThreatLabz 2024 AI Security Report. (n.d.). Retrieved September 12, 2024, from https://www.zscaler.com/blogs/security-research/new-ai-insights-explore-key-ai-trends-and-risks-threatlabz-2024-ai-security

Nicholls, J., Kuppa, A., & Le-Khac, N.-A. (2021). Financial cybercrime: A comprehensive survey of deep learning approaches to tackle the evolving financial crime landscape. *IEEE Access : Practical Innovations, Open Solutions*, 9, 163965–163986. DOI: 10.1109/ACCESS.2021.3134076

Oppenlaender, J. (2023). A Taxonomy of Prompt Modifiers for Text-To-Image Generation. *Behaviour & Information Technology*, ●●●, 1–14. DOI: 10.1080/0144929X.2023.2286532

Peters, D., Vold, K., Robinson, D., & Calvo, R. A. (2020). Responsible AI—Two frameworks for ethical design practice. *IEEE Transactions on Technology and Society*, 1(1), 34–47. DOI: 10.1109/TTS.2020.2974991

Radanliev, P., De Roure, D., & Santos, O. (2023). Red Teaming Generative AI/NLP, the BB84 quantum cryptography protocol and the NIST-approved Quantum-Resistant Cryptographic Algorithms. *arXiv Preprint arXiv:2310.04425*. DOI: 10.36227/techrxiv.24153183.v1

Rampášek, M. (2023). AI CYBERSECURITY STANDARDISATION AND ITS OVERLAP WITH DSA AND CRA. *Acta Facultatis Iuridicae Universitatis Comenianae*, 42(2), 14–14. DOI: 10.62874/afi.2023.2.08

Res, J., Homoliak, I., Perešíni, M., Smrčka, A., Malinka, K., & Hanacek, P. (2024). *Enhancing Security of AI-Based Code Synthesis with GitHub Copilot via Cheap and Efficient Prompt-Engineering* (arXiv:2403.12671). arXiv. http://arxiv.org/abs/2403.12671

Ronanki, K. (2023). Towards an AI-centric Requirements Engineering Framework for Trustworthy AI. *2023 IEEE/ACM 45th International Conference on Software Engineering: Companion Proceedings (ICSE-Companion)*, 278–280. DOI: 10.1109/ICSE-Companion58688.2023.00075

Sangaiah, A. K., Javadpour, A., Ja'fari, F., Pinto, P., & Chuang, H.-M. (2023). Privacy-aware and ai techniques for healthcare based on k-anonymity model in internet of things. *IEEE Transactions on Engineering Management.*

Sanguino, M. (2024). Enhancing Security in Industrial Application Development: Case Study on Self-Generating Artificial Intelligence Tools. *Applied Sciences (Basel, Switzerland)*, 14(9), 9. Advance online publication. DOI: 10.3390/app14093780

Spair, R. (2024, January 21). Revolutionizing Web Design: The Power of Generative AI Websites. *Medium.* https://medium.com/@rickspair/revolutionizing-web-design-the-power-of-generative-ai-websites-08d548b46e21

Szabó, Z., & Bilicki, V. (2023). A New Approach to Web Application Security: Utilizing GPT Language Models for Source Code Inspection. *Future Internet*, 15(10), 10. Advance online publication. DOI: 10.3390/fi15100326

Tayyab, M., Mumtaz, M., Jhanjhi, N. Z., & Muzammal, S. M. (2024). Industry 4.0: The Digital Revolution Unleashing Sustainable Supply Chains. In *Digital Transformation for Improved Industry and Supply Chain Performance* (pp. 54–69). IGI Global. DOI: 10.4018/979-8-3693-5375-2.ch003

Tayyab, M., Mumtaz, M., Muzammal, S. M., & Jhanjhi, N. Z. (2024). Swarm Security: Tackling Threats in the Age of Drone Swarms. In Cybersecurity Issues and Challenges in the Drone Industry (pp. 324-342). IGI Global.

The rise of AI threats and cybersecurity: Predictions for 2024. (2024, February 15). World Economic Forum. https://www.weforum.org/agenda/2024/02/what-does-2024-have-in-store-for-the-world-of-cybersecurity/

Torricelli, M., Martino, M., Baronchelli, A., & Aiello, L. M. (2024). *The role of interface design on prompt-mediated creativity in Generative AI* (arXiv:2312.00233). arXiv. /arXiv.2312.00233DOI: 10.1145/3614419.3644000

Upadhyay, U., & Jain, A. (2019). *Removal of Batch Effects using Generative Adversarial Networks* (arXiv:1901.06654). arXiv. https://doi.org//arXiv.1901.06654DOI: 10.48550

Villegas-Ch, W., & García-Ortiz, J. (2023). Toward a Comprehensive Framework for Ensuring Security and Privacy in Artificial Intelligence. *Electronics (Basel)*, 12(18), 18. Advance online publication. DOI: 10.3390/electronics12183786

Vizgirda, V., Zhao, R., & Goel, N. (2024). SocialGenPod: Privacy-Friendly Generative AI Social Web Applications with Decentralised Personal Data Stores. *Companion Proceedings of the ACM Web Conference 2024*, 1067–1070. DOI: 10.1145/3589335.3651251

Wang, J., Luo, X., Cao, L., He, H., Huang, H., Xie, J., Jatowt, A., & Cai, Y. (2024). Is Your AI-Generated Code Really Secure? Evaluating Large Language Models on Secure Code Generation with CodeSecEval. *arXiv Preprint arXiv:2407.02395*.

Wang, Y. (2024). Research on Big Data Encryption Algorithm System for Online Education Based on Artificial Intelligence. *Proceedings of the 2024 International Conference on Computer and Multimedia Technology*, 492–498. DOI: 10.1145/3675249.3675334

Wang, Y., Pan, Y., Yan, M., Su, Z., & Luan, T. H. (2023). A Survey on ChatGPT: AI–Generated Contents, Challenges, and Solutions. *IEEE Open Journal of the Computer Society*, 4, 280–302. DOI: 10.1109/OJCS.2023.3300321

Wei, J., Courbis, A.-L., Lambolais, T., Dray, G., & Maalej, W. (2024). *On AI-Inspired UI-Design* (arXiv:2406.13631). arXiv. https://doi.org//arXiv.2406.13631DOI: 10.48550

Wei, J., Courbis, A.-L., Lambolais, T., Xu, B., Bernard, P. L., & Dray, G. (2023). Boosting GUI Prototyping with Diffusion Models. *2023 IEEE 31st International Requirements Engineering Conference (RE)*, 275–280. DOI: 10.1109/RE57278.2023.00035

Wei, J., Courbis, A.-L., Lambolais, T., Xu, B., Bernard, P. L., Dray, G., & Maalej, W. (2024). *GUing: A Mobile GUI Search Engine using a Vision-Language Model* (arXiv:2405.00145). arXiv. https://doi.org//arXiv.2405.00145DOI: 10.48550

Wu, J., Huang, Z., Hu, Z., & Lv, C. (2023). Toward Human-in-the-Loop AI: Enhancing Deep Reinforcement Learning via Real-Time Human Guidance for Autonomous Driving. *Engineering (Beijing)*, 21, 75–91. DOI: 10.1016/j.eng.2022.05.017

Xu, J., Yang, T., Zhuang, S., Li, H., & Lu, W. (2024). *AI-based financial transaction monitoring and fraud prevention with behaviour prediction*.

Yang, L., Tian, M., Xin, D., Cheng, Q., & Zheng, J. (2024). AI-Driven Anonymization: Protecting Personal Data Privacy While Leveraging Machine Learning. *arXiv Preprint arXiv:2402.17191.*

Chapter 17
Generative AI for Web Engineering Models in Physical Therapy

Hina Al Fatima Siddiqui

https://orcid.org/0009-0001-0160
-6990

Nazeer Hussain University, Pakistan

Muneeba Khan

https://orcid.org/0009-0002-4040
-992X

Nazeer Hussain University, Pakistan

Nasrullah Khan

https://orcid.org/0009-0006-4404
-6088

SBB Dewan University, Pakistan

Muzzammil Siraj

https://orcid.org/0009-0006-2826
-7593

SBB Dewan University, Pakistan

Safdar Miran

https://orcid.org/0009-0001-7426
-1938

SBB Dewan University, Pakistan

Abdul Rehman

https://orcid.org/0009-0004-2049
-5490

SBB Dewan University, Pakistan

Arsalan Hakeem

*Jinnah Postgraduate Medical Center,
Pakistan*

ABSTRACT

This study explores the integration of generative artificial intelligence (AI) into web-grounded physical remedy operations through a mixed- styles approach, combining both quantitative and qualitative data. A quasi-experimental design was employed to compare the efficacity of AI- enhanced remedy with traditional styles, revealing significant advancements in remedy issues. Generative inimical Networks (GANs) and Large Language Models (LLMs) were employed to produce individualized exercise

DOI: 10.4018/979-8-3693-3703-5.ch017

routines and grease interactive case- AI relations. Quantitative results showed that cases using AI-enhanced remedy endured lesser advancements in range of stir and advanced satisfaction compared to those witnessing traditional remedy. The study also linked several specialized and ethical challenges, including data sequestration enterprises and model limitations. Unborn exploration should concentrate on advancing AI algorithms, integrating multimodal feedback, and addressing usability issues to enhance the effectiveness and availability of AI in physical remedy.

INTRODUCTION

The integration of generative artificial intelligence (AI) into web engineering models is revolutionizing the field of physical remedy by offering advanced, adaptive, and substantiated care options. Generative AI, particularly models like generative inimical networks (GANs) and large language models (LLMs), have demonstrated significant eventuality in colorful healthcare disciplines, including diagnostics, treatment planning, and substantiated patient care (Chen and Esmaeilzadeh 2024). These models can be particularly useful in creating touch- concentrated operations that pretend hands- on remedial interventions, thereby enhancing patient engagement and perfecting remedy issues (Li, Vakanski et al. 2018). Generative AI offers several advantages in the environment of physical remedy. It can grease the development of largely individualized treatment plans by assaying patient data and generating acclimatized exercise routines.

These routines can be acclimated in real- time grounded on patient performance, furnishing a position of customization that traditional styles frequently warrant. For illustration, GANs have been used to model and estimate physical recuperation exercises, creating an adaptive frame that can be fine- tuned to individual case requirements (Li, Vakanski et al. 2018). also, generative AI can enhance the quality of casetherapist commerce by furnishing instant feedback and suggestions for enhancement. This capability is especially pivotal in remote or teletherapy settings, where direct physical commerce is limited. By bluffing a therapist's touch and guidance through AI- driven models, cases can admit a further immersive and effective remedial experience, indeed in a virtual terrain (Chen, Wu et al. 2024). Web engineering models integrated with generative AI offer an interactive platform for physical remedy operations.

These web- grounded results can be penetrated ever, making remedy more accessible and accessible for cases (Patil, Venkateswarlu et al. 2014)The integration of generative AI into these models allows for the development of intuitive interfaces that can acclimatize to individual stoner requirements, furnishing substantiated guidance and support throughout the remedy process. For case, prompt engineering in healthcare operations is a critical aspect of this integration. By designing effective AI prompts, inventors can produce systems that evoke high- quality responses and relations from druggies, enhancing the overall remedy experience (Patil, Venkateswarlu et al. 2014) These systems can also use generative AI to pretend colorful scripts, offering cases a more dynamic and engaging remedy session. likewise, web- grounded physical remedy operations equipped with generative AI can give precious data analytics and reporting features. This capability enables therapists to track patient progress over time and make data- driven opinions regarding treatment adaptations. It also facilitates a more cooperative approach to remedy, allowing cases and therapists to work together more effectively toward achieving asked issues (Almansour and Alfhaid 2024)Touch- concentrated operations are central to physical remedy, as they replicate the tactile relations that are frequently essential for effective treatment. Generative AI plays a vital part in creating these operations by generating realistic and responsive touch- grounded scripts.

For illustration, AI models can be used to pretend the physical sensations and feedback that cases would generally admit during in- person remedy sessions, guiding them through exercises with a position of perfection and literalism that was preliminarily unattainable (Pan, Luo et al. 2024). These operations can also acclimatize to the specific requirements of each case, offering acclimatized guidance and support. For case, if a case struggles with a particular movement or exercise, the AI can induce modified instructions or indispensable exercises to help them ameliorate (Zamanov, Boeva et al. 2023). This rigidity is pivotal for maintaining patient engagement and provocation, particularly by long- term recuperation scripts. Generative AI- grounded difficulty position design is another innovative operation in this environment. By assaying patient performance and progress, AI models can acclimate the difficulty of exercises in real- time, icing that cases are continually challenged but not overwhelmed (Chen, Wu et al. 2024).

This dynamic adaptation can lead to further effective remedy issues, as cases can progress at a pace that's applicable for their individual capabilities and limitations. The deployment of generative AI in physical remedy comes with significant ethical considerations, particularly concerning case sequestration and data security. As these systems frequently calculate on large datasets to serve effectively, icing the confidentiality and protection of patient information is consummate. Also, there's the eventuality for algorithmic impulses in AI- generated guidance, which could impact the quality and fairness of patient care. To address these enterprises, it's essential to develop transparent and resolvable AI models that can give perceptivity into their decision- making processes. By making the inner workings of these models more accessible to both cases and therapists, we can make lesser trust in the technology and ensure that it's used responsibly and immorally (Mashatian, Armstrong et al. 2024). also, integrating AI into being remedial practices poses several practical challenges.

Therapists need to be trained on how to use these technologies effectively, and there must be a clear understanding of the limitations and capabilities of AI models. icing that AI systems complement rather than replace the mortal element of remedy is pivotal for maintaining the quality and effectiveness of patient care. The future of generative AI in physical remedy lies in the continued refinement and integration of these models with multimodal feedback systems. similar systems can give a further holistic approach to remedy by combining visual, audile, and tactile feedback, offering cases a further immersive and effective treatment experience (Waqas 2024) For illustration, virtual reality (VR) surroundings enhanced with generative AI can pretend real-world scripts in which cases can exercise and upgrade their movements, leading to better issues.

Another promising area of development is the use of AI in educational tools for physical therapists. By using generative AI, educational platforms can produce substantiated literacy gests that acclimatize to the unique requirements and preferences of each therapist, helping them develop new chops and stay over-to-date with the rearmost advancements in the field (Almansour and Alfhaid 2024)This approach can contribute to a more knowledgeable and effective pool, eventually perfecting patient care Generative AI has the implicit to revise physical remedy by furnishing substantiated, adaptive, and interactive treatment options. Through its integration with web engineering models, it can produce immersive touch-concentrated operations that enhance patient engagement and ameliorate remedy issues. still, the ethical and practical challenges associated with these technologies must be addressed to insure their responsible and effective use. As the field continues to evolve, generative AI is likely to play a decreasingly central part in shaping the future of physical remedy, offering new openings for both cases and interpreters.

LITERATURE REVIEW

The field of physical remedy has seen a significant metamorphosis over the once many decades, driven by technological advancements that have bettered the quality and availability of care. originally, physical remedy reckoned heavily on homemade ways and therapist-case relations, with limited use of technology. still, the integration of computer-grounded systems, stir prisoner technologies, and biofeedback bias has expanded the possibilities for patient assessment and recuperation (Reis, Couto et al. 2012). More lately, VR and AR have been incorporated into remedy practices to produce immersive surroundings that enhance patient engagement and adherence to treatment protocols (Correa-Madrid, Correa Guzmán et al. 2023). These technologies allow for the creation of realistic, controlled scripts where cases can exercise movements and exercises in a safe and probative setting.

As these inventions continue to evolve, they've laid the root for the integration of artificial intelligence (AI) into physical remedy, furnishing new openings for substantiated and adaptive care. Generative AI refers to a class of algorithms that can induce new data samples analogous to the training data. Generative models like Generative Adversarial Networks (GANs) and Large Language Models (LLMs) have come prominent in colorful fields, including healthcare. GANs, for case, are used to induce realistic images, vids, and indeed complex data sets by learning from being data and also producing new cases that mimic the original data distribution (Li, Vakanski et al. 2018)In the environment of physical remedy, generative AI can pretend a wide range of remedial scripts, helping to design substantiated exercises and recuperation protocols (Patil, Venkateswarlu et al. 2014) LLMs, on the other hand, can induce textbook- grounded content and grease natural language relations, making them useful for creating conversational agents that can give guidance and support to cases during their remedy sessions.

The rigidity of generative AI allows for the development of tools that can respond to patient requirements in real- time, offering substantiated feedback and adaptations to remedy programs. The integration of web engineering models in healthcare has revolutionized how services are delivered, making them more accessible and effective. Webgrounded platforms enable remote monitoring, telehealth services, and the delivery of interactive operations for patient care. These models influence technologies similar as pall computing, mobile operations, and internet of effects (IoT) bias to collect and dissect patient data, furnishing clinicians with precious perceptivity into patient progress and treatment efficacity (Mashatian, Armstrong et al. 2024). In physical remedy, web engineering models have been used to produce platforms that grease virtual remedy sessions, allowing cases to admit care from the comfort of their homes (Almansour and Alfhaid 2024)

These platforms frequently incorporate interactive rudiments similar as video- tape tutorials, real- time feedback mechanisms, and progress shadowing features to enhance the remedy experience. By integrating generative AI into these models, it's possible to produce more sophisticated and adaptive operations that can guide cases through substantiated remedy routines, cover their performance, and give instant feedback. Touch- concentrated operations in physical remedy end to pretend the tactile relations that are a pivotal part of traditional remedy sessions. These operations generally involve haptic feedback bias, stir detectors, and other technologies that can replicate the sensation of touch, guiding cases through exercises and furnishing feedback on their movements (Zhang, Zhang et al. 2024)For illustration, haptic gloves and wearable detectors can track a case's movements and give real-time feedback on their performance, helping them to ameliorate their fashion and achieve better issues.

The use of generative AI in these operations allows for the creation of further responsive and adaptive systems that can acclimate to the requirements of each case. For case, AI- driven models can induce realistic touch- grounded scripts, offering cases a further immersive and interactive remedy experience (Zamanov, Boeva et al. 2023)These systems can also dissect patient data to identify areas where they may need fresh support or variations to their exercise routine, icing that the remedy is both effective and acclimatized to their individual requirements

Generative AI in Physical Therapy

AI is decreasingly playing a vital part in physical remedy by offering advanced tools for opinion, treatment planning, and patient monitoring. AI systems are able of assaying large datasets from patient records, wearable bias, and imaging technologies to help therapists in creating more individualized and effective treatment plans (Mashatian, Armstrong et al. 2024). In physical remedy, AI can give real- time feedback to cases performing exercises, icing correct form and reducing the threat of injury (Li, Vakanski et al. 2018). Likewise, AI systems can acclimatize to the progress and specific requirements of each case, offering variations to exercises as necessary. This rigidity is particularly precious in remote remedy sessions where therapists cannot be physically present to guide the case. By enhancing the delicacy and personalization of treatment plans, AI helps ameliorate patient issues and optimize the remedy process. Generative AI models, similar as Generative inimical Networks (GANs) and Variational Autoencoders (VAEs), have set up colorful operations in physical remedy. GANs, for case, can induce realistic stir data by learning from being datasets of mortal movements, which can be used to pretend exercises and develop virtual recuperation surroundings (Li, Vakanski et al. 2018). These models can produce synthetic data that mimic patient movements, allowing for the development of acclimatized recuperation programs.

Variational Autoencoders can be employed to dissect Page 1 of 2 and render complex stir patterns, furnishing perceptivity into a case's range of stir and relating areas for enhancement (Zhang, Zhang et al. 2024). Also, large language models (LLMs) like GPT can be used to develop conversational agents that interact with cases, offering guidance, provocation, and substantiated feedback during exercises. These AI- powered agents can support cases in understanding their treatment plans and give real- time responses to their queries, enhancing the overall remedy experience (Naeem, Siraj et al. 2024). Touch- concentrated AI interventions have come a pivotal aspect of physical remedy, as they replicate the tactile feedback that's frequently essential for effective treatment. AI- powered haptic bias and systems are designed to pretend the sensation of touch, guiding cases through exercises and furnishing instant feedback on their movements (Chen, Wu et al. 2024). These systems use generative models to produce realistic touch relations, allowing cases to witness a position of engagement analogous to in- person remedy sessions.

For illustration, AI can induce adaptive resistance situations in virtual exercises, bluffing the physical sensation of muscle pressure and furnishing cases with a further immersive and responsive remedy terrain. Generative AI can also grease the development of interactive games and simulations that incorporate touch- grounded feedback, enhancing patient engagement and provocation (Chen, Wu et al. 2024) For illustration, stroke recuperation exercises can be gamified, with AI conforming the difficulty position in real- time grounded on patient performance. By creating a more engaging remedy process, cases are more likely to cleave to their treatment plans, which can lead to better issues. also, touch- concentrated AI interventions can be particularly salutary for cases witnessing remote remedy, as they give a position of commerce and feedback that would else be delicate to achieve without a therapist present (Patil, Venkateswarlu et al. 2014)This approach not only enhances the effectiveness of remedy but also makes it more accessible to cases who may have limitations in attending inperson sessions. In summary, generative AI in physical remedy provides innovative results for substantiated case care, enhanced engagement, and bettered remedy issues. By exercising generative models and touch concentrated interventions, AI has the implicit to transfigure the delivery of physical remedy, making it more adaptive, accessible, and effective for a wide range of cases.

Web Engineering for Physical Therapy Applications

Operations Web engineering plays a pivotal part in the development and deployment of physical remedy operations, offering innovative web- grounded results that make remedy more accessible and effective (Patil, Venkateswarlu et al. 2014)These operations work the capabilities of the internet to deliver remote and interactive remedy sessions, allowing cases to engage in recuperation from the comfort of their homes. This approach is particularly salutary for individualities with mobility issues, those living in remote areas, or cases taking frequent remedy sessions that might be logistically challenging in a traditional clinical setting (Almansour and Alfhaid 2024)Through web- grounded platforms, physical remedy operations can give realtime guidance, feedback, and covering — crucial rudiments for effective treatment. The use of web technologies also enables the integration of multimedia rudiments, similar as videotape tutorials and interactive exercises, which enrich the remedy experience (Patil, Venkateswarlu et al. 2014)

Designing stoner- centric interfaces is vital for the success of web- grounded physical remedy operations. These interfaces need to be intuitive, engaging, and acclimatized to accommodate the different requirements and capacities of cases. Considering the varying situations of specialized proficiency among cases, especially those strange with digital tools, it's essential to produce interfaces that are simple to navigate and understand. Features similar as straightforward navigation menus, clear instructions, and visual aids enhance stoner commerce with the operation. also, incorporating feedback mechanisms is pivotal, allowing cases to communicate with their therapists, cover their progress, and acclimate treatment plans as necessary. stonercentric design enhances patient adherence to remedy rules and improves overall treatment issues by making the remedy process more stoner-friendly and engaging. Integrating AI with web engineering models further augments the capabilities of physical remedy operations. AI algorithms can dissect patient data, similar as movement patterns, exercise performance, and compliance, to offer individualized recommendations and variations to remedy programs (Li, Vakanski et al. 2018). For illustration, machine literacy models can identify trends in a case's progress and prognosticate implicit challenges, enabling the operation to give visionary support and acclimatize exercises consequently (Mashatian, Armstrong et al. 2024). Also, generative AI models can produce adaptive and interactive content, similar as virtual therapists that offer realtime guidance and stimulant during exercises. This integration makes the remedy process more dynamic and responsive, allowing for nonstop enhancement of the operation grounded on stoner relations and issues. By combining the scalability and availability of web engineering with the logical power of AI, physical remedy operations can offer a more individualized and effective recuperation experience.

Developing touch- concentrated operations in physical remedy is pivotal for bluffing hands- on remedial relations and enhancing patient engagement. Touch commerce is abecedarian in remedy as it allows cases to admit tactile feedback, which can significantly ameliorate motor literacy and skill accession (Ancuti, Ancuti et al. 2024). These operations frequently use haptic technology, which recreates the sensation of touch through mechanical selectors, to guide cases through colorful exercises. By incorporating touch commerce, cases can admit immediate feedback on their movements, helping them to correct their form and perform exercises more effectively. This interactive element is especially precious in remote remedy settings, where direct physical contact with a therapist is not possible. The development of touch- concentrated operations requires careful consideration of colorful conditions and design aspects to insure effectiveness and stoner- benevolence. One of the crucial conditions is the delicacy of the haptic feedback, which must nearly mimic the real- world sensations endured during remedy to be salutary. also, these operations need to be adaptable to individual case requirements, offering different situations of resistance or guidance grounded on the case's progress and capabilities. The stoner interface must be intuitive and straightforward, allowing cases of varying specialized proficiency to navigate the system fluently. Visual aids and educational prompts should be integrated to support the haptic feedback, furnishing a comprehensive and multimodal literacy experience (Patil, Venkateswarlu et al. 2014)enforcing generative AI in touch- concentrated operations enhances their capability to give substantiated and adaptive remedy gests. Generative AI models, similar as GANs, can be used to produce realistic and dynamic touch relations by learning from a wide range of physical remedy scripts (Li, Vakanski et al. 2018). These models can pretend colorful tactile sensations, similar as resistance and pressure, which can be acclimated in real- time grounded on patient performance. This rigidity allows the operation to offer acclimatized guidance, responding to each case's specific requirements and conforming the difficulty position of exercises consequently (Zamanov, Boeva et al. 2023, Shah, Jhanjhi et al. 2024). Also, generative AI can enable the development of virtual therapists that give real- time feedback and stimulant, creating an engaging and probative terrain that motivates cases to cleave to their remedy rules (Ancuti, Ancuti et al. 2024). By integrating these advanced AI capabilities, touch- concentrated operations can deliver further effective remedy, leading to bettered patient issues.

METHODOLOGY

Research Design and Approach

This schoolwork uses a mixed-methods method to evaluate the impact of generative AI on physical therapy, participating both quantitative and qualitative data. The research design includes a quasi-experimental setup to comparison AI-enhanced physical therapy with outmoded methods.

Data Collection and Processing

Participants: Patients receiving either AI-enhanced or traditional physical therapy.
Instruments: Surveys, questionnaires, wearable sensors, and motion capture devices.

Variables:

- Physical Function (e.g., range of motion, strength)
- Therapy Adherence (e.g., frequency, duration)
- Patient Satisfaction

Statistical Tests

- **Descriptive Statistics:** Summary of demographic and result variables.
- **Inferential Statistics:** Balancing t-tests or ANOVA to compare pre- and post-intervention results.

Tables of Results

Table 1. Descriptive Statistics

Variable	AI-Enhanced Therapy (n=50)	Traditional Therapy (n=50)
Age (Mean ± SD)	45.2 ± 12.5	46.8 ± 11.2
Gender (Male/Female)	22/28	24/26
Pre-Therapy Range of Motion (Mean ± SD)	75.4° ± 10.2°	74.8° ± 11.0°
Post-Therapy Range of Motion (Mean ± SD)	85.6° ± 9.0°	80.3° ± 10.5°
Adherence (Mean ± SD)	90% ± 8%	85% ± 10%
Patient Satisfaction (Mean ± SD)	8.7 ± 1.2	7.9 ± 1.5

Descriptive Statistics presents an overview of the demographic and baseline characteristics of actors in the study. The AI- enhanced remedy group comported of 50 cases with a mean age of 45.2 times (± 12.5 times), and the traditional remedy group included 50 cases with a mean age of 46.8 times (± 11.2 times). The gender distribution was fairly balanced in both groups, with 22 males and 28 ladies in the AI- enhanced remedy group and 24 males and 26 ladies in the traditional remedy group. The average range of stir before remedy was slightly advanced in the AI-enhanced group (75.4 ° ± 10.2 °) compared to the traditional remedy group (74.8 ° ± 11.0 °). After remedy, the AI- enhanced group showed a mean enhancement in range of stir to 85.6 ° (± 9.0 °), while the traditional remedy group bettered to 80.3 ° (± 10.5 °). Adherence to remedy was also advanced in the AI- enhanced group, comprising 90(± 8), compared to 85(± 10) in the traditional remedy group. Case satisfaction scores were slightly advanced in the AI- enhanced group, with a mean score of 8.7(± 1.2) versus 7.9(± 1.5) for the traditional remedy group.

Table 2. Comparison of Pre- and Post-Therapy Outcomes

Group	Pre-Therapy (Mean ± SD)	Post-Therapy (Mean ± SD)	Change (Mean ± SD)	p-value
AI-Enhanced Therapy	Range of Motion: 75.4° ± 10.2°	Range of Motion: 85.6° ± 9.0°	10.2° ± 5.3°	0.001
	Adherence: 90% ± 8%	Adherence: 90% ± 8%	0%	0.950
	Satisfaction: 8.7 ± 1.2	Satisfaction: 8.7 ± 1.2	0	1.000
Traditional Therapy	Range of Motion: 74.8° ± 11.0°	Range of Motion: 80.3° ± 10.5°	5.5° ± 4.7°	0.015
	Adherence: 85% ± 10%	Adherence: 85% ± 10%	0%	1.000
	Satisfaction: 7.9 ± 1.5	Satisfaction: 7.9 ± 1.5	0	1.000

Comparison of Pre- andPost-Therapy issues details the statistical comparisons between pre- andpost-therapy measures for both remedy types. For the AI- enhanced remedy group, there was a statistically significant increase in the range of stir from 75.4 ° (± 10.2 °) to 85.6 ° (± 9.0 °), with a mean change of 10.2 ° (± 5.3 °), and a p- value of 0.001 indicating significant enhancement. No significant change was observed in remedy adherence (90 ± 8) or patient satisfaction (8.7 ± 1.2) with p-values of 0.950 and 1.000, independently. In discrepancy, the traditional remedy group endured a lower enhancement in range of stir from 74.8 ° (± 11.0 °) to 80.3 ° (± 10.5 °), performing in a mean change of 5.5 ° (± 4.7 °) with a p- value of 0.015, indicating a significant but lower effect compared to the AI- enhanced group. No significant changes were observed in remedy adherence (85 ± 10) or patient satis-faction (7.9 ± 1.5), with p- values of 1.000 for both.

Qualitative Data Collection and Analysis

Table 3. Summary of Qualitative Themes

Theme	Description	Example Quotes
Enhanced Engagement	AI applications improved patient engagement through interactive features.	"The interactive exercises kept me motivated."
Real-Time Feedback	Immediate feedback from AI was valuable in correcting techniques.	"The AI suggestions helped me adjust my form quickly."
Usability Issues	Some users found the AI system challenging to navigate.	"The interface was a bit confusing at first."
Personalized Experience	AI provided customized routines that met individual needs.	"The exercises felt tailored specifically for me."

Themes captures crucial themes from qualitative data gathered through interviews and concentrate groups. One prominent theme was enhanced engagement, with numerous cases reporting that the interactive features of AI operations significantly bettered their provocation. For case, cases noted," The interactive exercises kept me motivated." Real- time feedback was another major theme, with actors appreciating the immediate corrections and adaptations handed by the AI, as expressed in the comment," The AI suggestions helped me acclimate my form snappily." still, usability issues were noted, with some druggies chancing the interface challenging to navigate originally, instanced by the feedback," The interface was a bit confusing at first." Incipiently, the individualized experience handed by the AI was stressed, with cases feeling that the exercises were well- acclimatized to their specific requirements, as illustrated by the statement," The exercises felt acclimatized specifically for me.

The model development phase involved the creation of generative artificial intelligence (AI) models to enhance physical remedy operations. Generative inimical Networks (GANs) were employed to design adaptive exercise routines acclimatized to individual case requirements. These models learned from being data to induce realistic and individualized recuperation scripts, offering a customized remedy experience. also, Large Language Models (LLMs) were employed to grease natural language relations, furnishing cases with conversational support and guidance throughout their remedy sessions. These models aimed to pretend a therapist's feedback and instructions, making the remedy process more interactive and engaging. Model confirmation to ensure the effectiveness of these AI models, a rigorous confirmation process was conducted. The performance of the GANs and LLMs was tested using real case data to assess their delicacy and trustability.

This involved comparing the AI- generated exercise routines and feedback against established remedy norms to insure they met remedial pretensions and patient requirements. Airman testing was carried out to gather stoner feedback on the AI systems' usability and effectiveness. This feedback was pivotal for enriching the models, addressing any issues, and perfecting their overall performance. Ethical considerations, similar as data sequestration and implicit algorithmic impulses, were also a focus during the confirmation process. Measures were enforced to cover patient information and ensure that the AI systems handed indifferent and unprejudiced support. The confirmation phase aimed to confirm that the AI models not only performed directly but also rounded traditional remedial practices effectively. R

Results and Discussion

The performance analysis of the generative AI models revealed notable advancements in the quality and rigidity of remedial interventions. The Generative inimical Networks (GANs) demonstrated a high position of delicacy in generating individualized exercise routines, which were nearly aligned with case requirements and remedial pretensions. These models effectively produced realistic scripts for recuperation, enhancing the applicability and effectiveness of the exercises. (Shah and Jhanjhi 2024)Also, Large Language Models (LLMs) handed precious real-time feedback and guidance, easing natural relations between cases and the AI systems. (Shah, Murugesan et al. 2024)The models' capability to pretend remedial guidance and acclimate routines in response to patient performance contributed significantly to their overall effectiveness in enhancing physical remedy issues. stoner experience and usability testing indicated that cases and therapists set up the generative AI operations to be generally salutary, though some areas for enhancement were linked. Numerous cases appreciated the interactive features and real- time feedback handed by the AI systems, which enhanced their engagement and adherence to remedy. (Shah, Laraib et al. 2024)still, usability issues were reported, particularly concerning the original navigation of the AI interfaces. Feedback from therapists stressed the utility of the AI in completing traditional remedy styles, although some expressed enterprises about the literacy wind associated with integrating new technology into their practice. (Shah, Jhanjhi et al. 2024)

Overall, while the AI operations were well- entered, advances to the interface and stoner training could further ameliorate their effectiveness. The integration of generative AI into physical remedy had a significant impact on remedy issues. Cases exercising AI- enhanced remedy endured lesser advancements in range of stir and adherence compared to those witnessing traditional remedy. (Fateh, Sial et al. 2024)The AI- driven adaptive routines allowed for substantiated adaptations, which contributed to further effective recuperation. also, cases reported advanced satisfaction situations with the AI- enhanced remedy due to the acclimatized and interactive nature of the sessions. (Shah, Jhanjhi et al. 2024)These findings suggest that generative AI can play a pivotal part in optimizing physical remedy by furnishing more individualized and engaging treatment options, eventually leading to better remedial results.

Several technical and implementation challenges emerged during the deployment of generative AI in physical therapy. One significant issue was ensuring the seamless integration of AI models with existing therapy systems and workflows. Compatibility and performance issues occasionally hindered the smooth operation of the AI applications. Additionally, the development of accurate and reliable AI models required extensive training data and computational resources, which posed logistical and financial constraints. Addressing these technical challenges is essential for maximizing the effectiveness and accessibility of AI-enhanced physical therapy solutions.

Ethical considerations were paramount in the development and implementation of AI in physical therapy. Ensuring the privacy and security of patient data was a major concern, given the sensitive nature of health information. The potential for algorithmic biases in AI models also raised concerns about fairness and equity in treatment. Addressing these ethical issues involved implementing robust data protection measures and developing transparent AI models to minimize biases. The ongoing evaluation of ethical practices is crucial to maintaining trust and ensuring that AI technologies are used responsibly in therapeutic settings.

Despite the advancements in generative AI, current models have notable limitations. The accuracy of AI-generated routines and feedback is highly dependent on the quality and diversity of the training data, which may not always fully represent individual patient needs. Additionally, while AI can simulate therapeutic scenarios, it cannot entirely replicate the nuanced human touch and judgment provided by experienced therapists. The models also face limitations in handling complex or rare conditions that were not well-represented in the training datasets. Recognizing these limitations is essential for setting realistic expectations and guiding future improvements in AI-based therapy solutions.

Unborn advancements in generative AI hold significant eventuality for farther enhancing web engineering operations in physical remedy. Inventions in AI algorithms and computational ways could lead to more sophisticated and accurate models for generating substantiated remedial routines. (Shah, Jhanjhi et al. 2024) Advanced integration of AI with web- grounded platforms can give further intuitive and adaptive interfaces, enhancing stoner gests. The ongoing development of generative AI technologies offers instigative openings to produce further effective and scalable results for physical remedy, potentially transubstantiating the field by offering advanced, adaptive care options. (Shah, Jhanjhi et al. 2024, Shah, Jhanjhi et al. 2024). Enhancing touch- grounded remedial interventions through generative AI presents a promising avenue for unborn exploration.

AI models able of bluffing realistic tactile feedback and remedial relations could greatly ameliorate remote remedy gests. By advancing the technology to more directly replicate physical sensations and companion exercises, cases can profit from a further immersive and effective remedial experience. (Shah, Jhanjhi et al. 2024)).Continued disquisition of touch- concentrated operations will be pivotal in bridging the gap between virtual and physical remedy, eventually leading to more patient issues. Integrating multimodal feedback — combining visual, audile, and tactile inputs into AI- enhanced remedy operations represent an instigative occasion for unborn development(Siraj, Siraj et al. 2024).By incorporating colorful forms of feedback, remedy operations can give a further comprehensive and engaging experience for cases. Multimodal systems could ameliorate patient adherence, delicacy, and overall satisfaction with remedy sessions. Research into multimodal integration will be vital for creating holistic and immersive remedial surroundings that feed to different case requirements and enhance overall remedy effectiveness

CONCLUSION

This study demonstrated the significant eventuality of generative AI in revolutionizing physical remedy. The integration of AI models, including GANs and LLMs, led to notable advancements in remedy issues, similar as increased range of stir and advanced patient satisfaction. The AI-driven operations handed substantiated, adaptive, and interactive gests that enhanced case engagement and adherence to remedy routines.

The findings emphasize the value of incorporating advanced AI technologies into physical remedy practices to achieve better remedial results. The results have important counteraccusations for physical remedy practice. AI- enhanced remedy operations offer a new approach to delivering substantiated and adaptive care, which can ameliorate the effectiveness and availability of remedy. Therapists can work these technologies to give further acclimatized interventions, potentially leading to more patient issues. still, the integration of AI into practice requires addressing specialized, ethical, and usability challenges to ensure that the technology complements rather than replaces traditional remedial styles.

The study highlights several avenues for unborn exploration and development. Advancements in generative AI and multimodal feedback systems hold the pledge of farther enhancing physical remedy operations. Research into perfecting AI model delicacy, addressing ethical enterprises, and refining stoner interfaces will be pivotal for maximizing the benefits of AI in remedy. Continued disquisition of these areas can drive invention and contribute to the development of further effective and stoner-friendly remedial results, eventually advancing the field of physical remedy.

REFERENCES

Almansour, M. and F. M. J. M. Alfhaid (2024). "Generative artificial intelligence and the personalization of health professional education: A narrative review." **103**(31): e38955.

Ancuti, C. O.. (2024). NTIRE 2024 dense and non-homogeneous dehazing challenge report. *Proceedings of the IEEE/CVF Conference on Computer Vision and Pattern Recognition*. DOI: 10.1109/CVPRW63382.2024.00646

Chen, Y. and P. J. J. o. M. I. R. Esmaeilzadeh (2024). "Generative AI in medical practice: in-depth exploration of privacy and security challenges." **26**: e53008.

Chen, Z.. (2024). Ntire 2024 challenge on image super-resolution (x4): Methods and results. *Proceedings of the IEEE/CVF Conference on Computer Vision and Pattern Recognition*.

Correa-Madrid, M. C., et al. (2023). "Validation of the NOVA score for the consumption of ultra-processed foods by young women of Medellín, Colombia." **1528**(1): 69-76.

Fateh, S., ... (2024). Smart Healthcare System in Industry 4.0. Advances in Computational Intelligence for the Healthcare Industry 4.0, IGI Global: 297-311.

Li, L., et al. (2018). "Generative adversarial networks for generation and classification of physical rehabilitation movement episodes." **8**(5): 428.

Mashatian, S., et al. (2024). "Building Trustworthy Generative Artificial Intelligence for Diabetes Care and Limb Preservation: A Medical Knowledge Extraction Case." 19322968241253568.

Naeem, M., et al. (2024). "The Impact of Investment in AI on Bank Performance: Empirical Evidence from Pakistan's Banking Sector." **17**(1).

Pan, S., et al. (2024). "Unifying large language models and knowledge graphs: A roadmap."

Patil, D. C.. (2014). Mechanical property evaluation of an Al-2024 alloy subjected to HPT processing. *IOP Conference Series: Materials Science and Engineering*, IOP Publishing. DOI: 10.1088/1757-899X/63/1/012085

Reis, D. A., ... (2012). Effect of artificial aging on the mechanical properties of an aerospace aluminum alloy 2024. Defect and Diffusion Forum, Trans Tech Publ. DOI: 10.4028/www.scientific.net/DDF.326-328.193

Shah, I. A., ... (2024). Logistics With the Internet of Things: Challenges, Perspectives, and Applications. Navigating Cyber Threats and Cybersecurity in the Logistics Industry, IGI Global: 172-195.

Shah, I. A., ... (2024). IoT Smart Healthcare Security Challenges and Solutions. Advances in Computational Intelligence for the Healthcare Industry 4.0, IGI Global: 234-247.

Shah, I. A., et al. (2024). "Use of Emerging Technologies in Healthcare 4.0." 280-296.

Shah, I. A., ... (2024). Industry 4.0: Use of Digitalization in Healthcare. Advances in Computational Intelligence for the Healthcare Industry 4.0, IGI Global: 174-193.

Shah, I. A., ... (2024). Use of Deep Learning Applications for Drone Technology. Cybersecurity Issues and Challenges in the Drone Industry, IGI Global: 128-147.

Shah, I. A., ... (2024). Logistics Industry in the Context of the Blockchain Technology. Navigating Cyber Threats and Cybersecurity in the Logistics Industry, IGI Global: 214-235.

Shah, I. A., et al. (2024). "Supply Chain Management Security Issues and Challenges in the Context of AI Applications." 59-89.

Shah, I. A. and N. Z. Jhanjhi (2024). "Cybersecurity Issues and Challenges in the Drone Industry."

Siraj, M., ... (2024). Addressing Issues and Challenges Using AI in Pharmacy. Advances in Computational Intelligence for the Healthcare Industry 4.0, IGI Global: 22-41.

Waqas, A. J. P. S. S. R. (2024). The Evaluation of Economic Performance. *Cross-Nation Analysis.*, 8(3), 204–217.

Zamanov, R., et al. (2023). "Accretion in the recurrent nova T CrB: Linking the superactive state to the predicted outburst." **680**: L18.

Zhang, Z.. (2024). NTIRE 2024 Challenge on Bracketing Image Restoration and Enhancement: Datasets Methods and Results. *Proceedings of the IEEE/ CVF Conference on Computer Vision and Pattern Recognition.* DOI: 10.1109/ CVPRW63382.2024.00620

Chapter 18
AI–Powered Threat Detection in Business Environments:
Strategies and Best Practices

Muhammad Tayyab
https://orcid.org/0000-0001-5580
-9163

Taylor's University, Malaysia

Khizar Hameed
https://orcid.org/0000-0003-1203
-2010

University of Tasmania, Australia

Majid Mumtaz
*CATE School of Computing and
Creative Technology, University of the
West of England, UK*

Syeda Mariam Mariam Muzammal
https://orcid.org/0000-0003-2960
-1814

Taylor's University, Malaysia

Poornima Mahadevappa
https://orcid.org/0000-0001-9414
-3464

Taylor's University, Malaysia

Aleena Sunbalin
*Shifa Tameer-e-Millat University,
Islamabad, Pakistan*

ABSTRACT

The use of artificial intelligence (AI) in cybersecurity is a need due to the outpacing of conventional security measures by the fast growth of cyber threats. Exploring the function of machine learning (ML), deep learning (DL), and natural language processing (NLP) in recogniz- ing and reacting to new cyber dangers, this chapter offers a thorough introduction to AI-powered threat identification. The paper contrasts AI- based systems with more traditional approaches, demonstrating how AI can better identify unknown assaults, adapt to new threats, and decrease the number of false positives. It touches on topics such as training models using industry-specific data,

DOI: 10.4018/979-8-3693-3703-5.ch018

ensuring they can commu- nicate with one other, and keeping them up-to-date and monitored. Data privacy, legislation compliance, and best practices for AI threat detection are also discussed. We discuss the need for human analysts to work with AI tools and how to overcome obstacles, including AI bias, complicated systems, and ethical considerations.

1 INTRODUCTION

1.1 Overview of Cyber Threats in Business Environments

The COVID-19 pandemic accelerated the shift towards remote work and in- creased reliance on digital infrastructure, exposing businesses to new cyberse- curity risks. Many organizations were unprepared to secure remote networks,

personal devices, and cloud-based services, leading to a surge in phishing and ransomware attacks as cybercriminals exploited these vulnerabilities. While dig- ital transformation has grown, so have the associated cyber risks, presenting significant threats to companies of all sizes (Aslan, Aktuˇg, Ozkan-Okay, Yilmaz, & Akin, 2023; Hameed, Barika, Garg, Amin, & Kang, 2022).

Traditional cybersecurity tools like firewalls, antivirus programs, and intru- sion detection systems (IDS) are no longer sufficient to counter the sophisticated tactics used by modern cybercriminals. The rise of remote work, cloud comput- ing, and IoT has made network environments more complex and harder to secure (Zafar et al., 2017; Qamar, Kazmi, Ariffin, Tayyab, & Nguyen, 2024). Addition- ally, threats such as malware, ransomware, advanced persistent threats (APTs), and insider attacks can cause severe financial damage and reputational harm. Many of these newer threats are designed to evade standard security measures and exploit unknown vulnerabilities, making traditional signature-based tech- niques less effective. At- tacks like denial-of-service (DoS) and ransomware, which disrupt operations and encrypt essential data, are increasingly common, while APTs allow cybercriminals prolonged unauthorized access for espionage or dis- ruption (Hameed, Garg, Amin, Kang, & Khan, 2022).

Many different kinds of assaults can affect a company, each with unique conse- quences. Here are a few examples of the most typical cyber dangers that companies face (Maleh, Shojafar, Alazab, & Romdhani, 2020) (Hameed, Khan, Ahmed, Reddy, & Rathore, 2018):

– **Malware:** Malicious software, such as viruses, worms, Trojans, and ran- som- ware, can infect computers, steal data, or disrupt operations. Ransomware, which encrypts vital data and demands payment for decryption, is incredibly damaging (Muzammal, Tayyab, Zahra, Jhanjhi, & Ashraf, 2024).

- **Phishing and Social Engineering:** Phishing involves tricking individu- als into revealing sensitive information, while social engineering manipulates human behavior to bypass security measures. Spear-phishing specifically targets high-level executives, making detection difficult.

- **Insider Threats:** Security risks can come from within an organization, either through malicious insiders or negligent employees, who are challenging to detect due to their authorized access.

- **Advanced Persistent Threats (APTs):** APTs involve cybercriminals gaining long-term, unauthorized access to networks, typically for espionage or disruption, often backed by nation-states or organized crime groups.

- **Denial of Service (DoS) and Distributed Denial of Service (DDoS) Attacks:** DoS and DDoS attacks overwhelm a system with traffic, rendering it unable to process legitimate requests. DDoS attacks are more dangerous as they use botnets to flood the target's system (Din et al., 2024).

Cyber risks are growing, with ransomware attacks increasing by over 150% and the average cost of a cyberattack reaching $13 million. Data breaches cost companies around $4.24 million per incident, emphasizing the need for advanced threat detection systems (Tayyab, Marjani, Jhanjhi, Hashem, & Usmani, 2022).

The 2020 SolarWinds supply chain hack, affecting thousands of organizations globally, highlighted vulnerabilities in global supply chains and the importance of detecting unusual network activity early on (Reshmi, 2021).

1.2 The Role of AI in Cybersecurity

AI has revolutionized cybersecurity by enabling rapid, accurate detection and response to cyber threats. Unlike conventional methods reliant on human inter- action, AI systems use machine learning (ML), DL, and NLP to detect known and unknown threats in real-time. This proactive approach helps businesses min- imize risks and prevent significant damage from cyberattacks (Shafique et al., 2017; Tayyab, Mumtaz, Jhanjhi, & Muzammal, 2024). Figure 1 show the modern organization working in the age of AI.

Figure 1. Modern organizations in the age of AI & Cybersecurity

AI systems learn from past incidents and continuously improve threat detec- tion by analyzing large volumes of data from networks, endpoints, and applica- tions. For example, DL identifies subtle virus signature changes, and ML detects unusual user behavior.

In addition to detection, AI automates responses to threats in real-time, such as isolating infected devices or blocking network traffic, often in combina- tion with Security Information and Event Management (SIEM) systems. This quick action reduces attackers' opportunities, limiting potential damage. As cy- ber threats grow more sophisticated, AI will play an increasingly essential role in safeguarding digital assets and thwarting attacks (Sarker, Furhad, & Nowrozy, 2021; Tayyab, Mumtaz, Muzammal, Jhanjhi, et al., 2024).

Listed below are some of the objectives that this chapter of the book aims to accomplish:

- Dive into how NLP, ML, and DL can improve threat detection and response systems.
- Describe how AI may improve reaction times in contemporary cybersecurity settings, identify previously unseen risks, and adjust to new attack vectors.
- Examine the shortcomings of signature-based detection systems and how AI provides more proactive and dynamic defenses to overcome these issues.
- Overview of AI technologies are compatible and effective with existing security frameworks by providing practical instructions for their integration.
- Consider issues like AI prejudice, hostile assaults, and the difficulties of AI system maintenance in practical corporate settings.
- Illustrate how AI has improved security measures and reduced cyber dangers in different businesses.
- Discuss the possible effects of new AI technologies on company security in the future, including autonomous cybersecurity systems (Arshad, Tayyab, Bilal, Akhtar, & Abdullahi, 2024).

This chapter is organized into several key sections. Section 2 begins with an exploration of AI technologies used in cybersecurity, covering ML, DL, and NLP, along with the types of threats they can detect. Section 3 compares AI-powered threat detection to traditional methods, discussing the advantages, challenges, and limitations of AI in this field. Section 4 presents strategies for implement- ing AI-powered threat detection, focusing on integrating AI into existing security frameworks and training AI models for business-specific threats. Section 5 delves into best practices for AI-powered threat detection, highlighting the importance of data quality, continuous monitoring, and collaboration between AI systems and human experts. Section 6 provides an overview of leading AI cybersecu- rity tools, custom AI solutions tailored to business needs, and the integration of AI with other cybersecurity technologies. Section 7 addresses challenges such as AI bias, system complexity, and ethical considerations in AI-powered threat detection. Section 8 looks ahead to future trends in AI and cybersecurity, includ- ing autonomous AI systems and the future of AI in business security. Finally, Section 9 offers case studies and real-world applications, comparing AI-driven

threat detection with traditional methods and analyzing the outcomes in various industries.

2 UNDERSTANDING AI IN THREAT DETECTION

2.1 Understanding AI in Threat Detection

When it comes to cybersecurity, AI is becoming a significant factor. AI-powered cybersecurity systems can respond quickly and effectively to new threats using cutting-edge technologies like DL, NLP, and ML. AI systems may learn from data and detect new threats, unlike conventional cybersecurity systems that de- pend on predetermined signatures or rules. This section outlines the primary AI technologies utilized in cybersecurity and describes their applications in threat detection (Arif, Kumar, Fahad, & Hussain, 2024).

2.1.1 Overview of AI Technologies Used in Cybersecurity

Three fundamental technologies form the basis of AI in cybersecurity, as detailed below (Kaur, Gabrijelˇciˇc, & Klobuˇcar, 2023).

– **Machine Learning (ML):** By analyzing past data and drawing conclu- sions or making predictions on their own, ML algorithms allow computers to learn and function autonomously. ML has several applications in cyber- security, including detecting phishing attempts, malware classification, and abnor- malities in network traffic. For ML models to detect cyber threats, they are trained on massive datasets containing benign and harmful activities.
– **Deep Learning (DL):** A branch of ML called DL attempts to simulate the brain's operations using artificial neural networks. DL models may sift through mountains of data to find intricate patterns and correlations. Ad- vanced threat detection using DL models is commonplace in cybersecurity. These models may spot insider threats or malware with minute signatures that would otherwise go undetected.
– **Natural Language Processing (NLP):** As a result of NLP, AI systems can comprehend and make sense of spoken language. Unstructured data sources, including social media postings, chat logs, and emails, are analyzed via NLP in the cybersecurity industry. NLP has several potential applica- tions; for instance, it may analyze security blog posts and threat intelligence reports to find new vulnerabilities and attack vectors, or it can detect phish- ing emails by looking for unusual linguistic patterns in the text.

2.1.2 Training AI Models for Cyber Threat Pattern and Anomaly Detection

Regarding threat detection, AI models are usually trained on data that shows both benign and harmful actions in the past. This information is gathered from various places, including security events, endpoint activity, and network logs. After data has been collected, it is marked to show whether it pertains to a valid or harmful occurrence (Jeffrey, Tan, & Villar, 2023). Below are a few standard ML models used to train the data.

– **Supervised Learning:** This method involves training the AI model on a dataset labeled as either normal or containing dangerous information, such as information on malware, phishing, or insider attacks. The model learns the patterns linked with each category to identify fresh, unknown data. For example, known malware samples may be used to train a supervised learning model to recognize particular malware.

– **Unsupervised Learning:** Labelled data is unnecessary for unsupervised learning, unlike supervised learning. Instead, the model learns to spot trends and outliers by grouping comparable data sets. Because the AI model can recognize out-of-the-ordinary behavior and flag it, even without prior exposure to a similar assault, this is very helpful for discovering new or unknown dangers. Anomaly detection systems frequently employ unsupervised learning to train models that spot suspicious user or network activity that may indicate a security violation.

– **Reinforcement Learning:** AI systems can learn from their experiences in the real world using this method. The model learns from its mistakes and improves performance when it gets positive or negative reinforcement for its actions. Cybersecurity incident response may be enhanced using reinforcement learning by training AI to make optimum real-time judgments through assault simulation.

2.1.3 AI-based Threat Detection Types

Cybersecurity systems driven by AI are incredibly flexible and capable of detecting a wide variety of cyber threats, such as (Reshmi, 2021):

– **Malware:** Malware comes in many forms, but AI models can identify Trojan horses, worms, ransomware, and viruses. Even previously undiscovered malware, known as zero-day threats, may be determined by AI by analyzing program and file behavior. If you're looking for ransomware, for instance,

AI can spot programs that try to encrypt vast volumes of data or strange file access patterns.

- **Phishing:** Computer programs driven by AI may detect phishing attempts by analyzing the content of emails, URLs, and websites. Regarding phishing attempts, NLP allows AI models to spot red flags like sudden requests for personal information or connections to bogus websites.
- **Insider Threats:** When identifying insider threats—when workers, inten-

tionally or unintentionally, compromise security—AI models are invaluable. Anomalies indicating an insider threat can be detected by AI by monitoring user behavior, access patterns, and data consumption. For instance, AI may detect when a person downloads critical material at odd hours and alert the appropriate authorities.

- **Advanced Persistent Threats (APTs):** APTs are a targeted cyberat- tack that aims to stay unnoticed for a long time once the attackers have gained access to a network. Because AI can spot even the most minute changes in human behaviors, system interactions, and network traffic, it is highly adapt- ed to detect APTs. With AI, it is possible to detect a pattern suggestive of an APT by correlating several minor irregularities over time.

2.2 AI vs. Traditional Threat Detection Methods

For a long time, signature-based detection was the go-to strategy for cybersecu- rity. This method matches newly arrived threats with established attack patterns or malware signatures. Although this method has worked well in the past, it is no match for the complex assaults of today, which are constantly finding new ways to circum- vent these regulations. Using dynamic and adaptive methodolo- gies, AI-powered threat detection offers a different way to identify known and unexpected threats. Here, we'll look at the pros and cons of AI in cybersecurity by comparing AI-driven detection with more conventional approaches (Sewak, Sahay, & Rathore, 2023).

2.2.1 Traditional Methods Vs. AI-Powered Threat Detection

- **Traditional Methods:** Many older techniques still use "signatures" to iden- tify potential dangers. One such method is signature-based detection. A da- tabase stores these signatures, which are created based on known mal- ware or attack behaviors. A malicious file or action is marked as such if it fits a recognized signature. However, signature-based systems can only detect dan- gers that have already been identified; they are reactive. When faced with unknown dangers like zero-day assaults or polymorphic malware continuously changing its code, they are rendered useless (Hameed et al., 2017).

- **AI-Powered Threat Detection:** AI-driven systems are proactive and can adapt, unlike signature-based systems. They find dangers by seeing patterns, out-of-the-ordinary behaviors, or trends rather than relying on a database of recognized signs. This dramatically enhances AI's capability to tackle new or unanticipated dangers. For instance, AI can identify ransomware by observing its actions, such as file encryption, instead of depending on a unique signature.

2.2.2 Advantages of AI-Powered Threat Detection

These are some of the benefits of using threat detection methods powered by AI to identify sophisticated threats (Bibi, Akhunzada, & Kumar, 2022).

- **Unknown Threat Detection:** Instead of depending on specific signs, AI systems are great at identifying unusual behavior, which allows them to de- tect zero-day vulnerabilities and undiscovered infections. This opens the door

for AI-driven cybersecurity solutions to prevent dangers that conventional approaches have failed to detect. For example, even without a recognized signature, an AI system may identify suspicious data exfiltration patterns or illegal system access and flag them as possible threats.

- **Flexibility and Ongoing Education:** As AI models are trained with more data and experience more scenarios, they gradually improve. Because they are always learning, AI systems may change and adapt to different types of attacks. AI can adapt to changing threat landscapes automatically, unlike traditional approaches that need regular updates to be effective.
- **Effectiveness and extensibility:** AI-driven systems are scalable because they can process massive data sets in real-time. When faced with the vast amounts of data produced by contemporary networks and systems, tradi- tional systems typically falter due to their reliance on human interaction and predetermined rules. It takes less time to identify and respond to as- saults when AI processes this data and detects risks more efficiently.
- **Fewer Unwanted Results:** False positives are a common problem with older systems, distracting security personnel from real threats. Over time, AI models may improve their knowledge of typical behavior, which helps them decrease false positives. This is especially true for DL and anomaly detection

models. Because of this, cybersecurity personnel can detect threats more accurately and with fewer interruptions.

2.2.3 Challenges and Limitations of AI in Cybersecurity

AI has many potential benefits in cybersecurity but has several limitations and difficulties (Sinha, Singla, & Victor, 2023).

- **Data Reliance:** AI models can't do their jobs well without copious quantities of high-quality data. Unreliable outcomes from the AI system could result from biased, erroneous, or inadequate training data. For instance, an AI model that has only been trained on data from one industry could not identify dangers in different settings.
- **Difficulty and Amount of Resources Required:** Cybersecurity systems driven by AI may be complex and resource-intensive to develop, implement, and maintain. These systems need substantial storage space and processing capacity to handle and analyze massive datasets. It can be challenging for smaller firms to include AI-driven solutions in their cybersecurity plans due to a lack of resources or knowledge.
- **AI Errors and Slants:** The quality of the data used to train AI models determines how accurate their predictions will be. The AI system might miss some dangers or come up with biased conclusions if the data used to train it isn't representative. Furthermore, AI systems are imperfect and may occasionally produce false negatives, in which the system misses a danger because it does not fit the patterns used to train the model.
- **Threats Launched Against AI Systems:** Cybercriminals are stepping up their game by launching what is referred to as adversarial assaults on

AI systems. Attacks like these happen when bad actors trick AI models into making faulty choices by tampering with the input data. For example, a malicious actor may subtly modify malware to avoid detection by an AI security system.

3 STRATEGIES FOR IMPLEMENTING AI-POWERED THREAT DETECTION

3.1 Integrating AI into Existing Security Infrastructure

3.1.1 Steps to Incorporate AI into Cybersecurity Frameworks

A well-planned approach is necessary to integrate AI into an organization's current security architecture in a way that doesn't interrupt current activities. The first thing to do is look at the cybersecurity architecture the company has in place. Find out where it's lacking and where AI may be most helpful, like threat detection, response, or predictive analysis. The next step is for businesses to assess their security requirements about AI platforms and technologies. Be- fore rolling out AI solutions to the masses, testing them in controlled settings is critical. This way, the security team can evaluate the AI's capabilities and find and fix any flaws. The AI solution may be gradually integrated into the more significant security architecture after it has been tested. The AI system must undergo continuous training because it must learn from real-world data to identify dangers correctly. The success of the AI system in integrating with preexisting systems and processes depends on close cooperation between cyber- security experts, IT departments, and AI experts at every stage of the process (Ghillani, 2022)(Hameed & Rahman, 2017).

3.1.2 Ensuring AI and Security System Compatibility

Ensuring AI tools work with current security systems is a big deal when incorporating AI into cybersecurity infrastructures. Intrusion detection and pre- vention systems (IDS/IPS), firewalls, and endpoint protection solutions are now standard for many businesses. For these systems to work together seamlessly, AI technologies need to be able to receive, analyze, and analyze data in real time. For AI systems to be able to share data with current security technologies, open standards and APIs (Application Programming Interfaces) are essential. AI tools must be interoperable with the operating systems, network topologies, and an organization's cloud platforms. To keep AI models running well, security personnel must guarantee that they are fed constant, high-quality data. Updat- ing, patching, and maintaining systems regularly also ensures they will remain compatible as AI and conventional tools progress (Macharia, Garg, & Kumar, 2023).

3.1.3 SIEM Systems' Critical Role in AI Integration

SIEM (Security Information and Event Management) technologies are cru- cial for AI integration. By collecting and analyzing security data from around the company, SIEM systems create a holistic picture of possible dangers. Inte- grating AI into SIEM solutions may enhance their threat detection and response capabilities. With ML algorithms, AI can analyze massive volumes of data gath- ered by SIEM systems, spot trends that might indicate an attack, and highlight irregularities that could otherwise go undetected. By examining historical secu- rity incidents, AI-powered SIEM systems can automate threat intelligence and foretell future assaults. Integrating AI with SIEM systems also helps lower the occurrence of false positives, which are prevalent in conventional systems. This frees human analysts to concentrate on actual risks while decreasing alert fa- tigue. The outcome is a stronger, more proactive, and simplified cybersecurity posture. With the help of IBM's Watson for Cyber Security platform, a central European bank was able to incorporate AI into its security architecture. Tra- ditional signature-based systems, which the bank used to rely on before using AI, had trouble detecting new threats, particularly complex phishing attempts. Integrating Watson with the bank's SIEM system allowed for real-time analysis of massive volumes of unstructured data originating from online threat alerts, emails, and logs. Thanks to Watson's AI capabilities, the institution drastically reduced reaction times and minimized financial losses by improving its capacity to detect and respond to previously unknown phishing and malware assaults (Kothandaraman, Prasad, & Sivasankar, 2023).

3.2 Training AI Models for Business-Specific Threats

3.2.1 Relevant Data Essential for Industry-Specific AI Training

AI models can only learn as much as the data used to train them. Training data for AI-powered threat detection systems must be industry and operational environment-specific to effectively identify individual business risks. When it comes to cybersecurity, different industries have different priorities. Healthcare organizations must prioritize patient data protection and compliance with pri- vacy requirements, while financial institutions must cope with insider threats and a significant frequency of fraud. AI models may be trained to identify sector- specific threat trends, attack vectors, and behaviors using data specific to that industry. If the AI system is trained using generic data, it may fail to detect crit- ical industry-specific signs, compromising performance. Hence, companies must meticulously curate data and feed the AI system information representing nor- mal company operations and the cyber dangers they are expected to face.

3.2.2 Techniques for Collecting and Curating High-Quality Data

How well AI models work is strongly correlated with the data quality used to train them. Organizations need to gather high-quality data depicting a wide variety of benign and harmful behaviors to train AI models for dangers relevant to their business. Data like this might originate from various places, including access control systems, endpoint logs, network traffic, and historical security events. If you want your AI model to tell the difference between harmless and harmful actions, you must ensure the dataset includes both instances. To prevent the AI system from being confused and resulting in incorrect threat detection, data should be curated to eliminate noise and unnecessary information. Orga- nizations must also anonymize sensitive information to safeguard privacy and adhere to data protection requirements like the General Data Protection Regu- lation (GDPR). Businesses should use data augmentation and other approaches to increase the dataset's diversity and volume when data collection and curation is complete. This will assist the AI model in generalizing better across different sorts of threats.

3.2.3 Continuous Learning: AI Models Adapting to New Threats

AI models need to adapt to the ever-changing cyber threats to stay effective. Continuous learning allows these models to adjust to new situations by regularly incorporating fresh information about threats, vulnerabilities, and organizational and operational environment changes. This lets the AI system take in data from new occurrences and gradually get better at detecting them.

Organizations may apply continuous learning by updating the AI model with fresh threat information and security data. Automated detection of changes in network behavior and adaptation of detection criteria to account for emerging cyberattack patterns are capabilities of ML algorithms, particularly those em- ployed in unsu- pervised learning. Another option is to use reinforcement learning techniques. This allows the AI to improve its reaction capabilities in the fu- ture by learning from its past attacks. If you want your AI system to be ready to tackle new risks like zero-day vulnerabilities or advanced persistent threats (APTs), you need to retrain your models often.

An online retailer was under increasing pressure from fraudsters and those trying to steal customer accounts. To address this, the business collaborated with cyberse- curity experts to create a unique AI model that could identify retail- specific forms of fraud and phishing. The AI was taught its skills using analytics on consumer behavior, internet traffic records, and purchase data. Multiple un- successful login attempts or atypical payment methods are slight variations in purchase habits that the model learned to spot. These changes frequently signal fraudulent activity. Within the first half-year of deploying the AI, the organiza- tion cut down on fraudulent transactions by 30% thanks to its real-time pattern detection capabilities.

3.3 Real-Time Threat Detection and Response

3.3.1 Leveraging AI for Real-Time Cyber Threat Monitoring and Detection

One of AI's most significant cybersecurity assets is its ability to identify and react to dangers in real time. Anomalies that indicate a cyberattack can be de- tect- ed rapidly by AI-powered systems since they continually monitor network traffic, user behavior, and system records. AI systems employ sophisticated algo- rithms to spot out-of-the-ordinary occurrences, enabling them to discover previ- ously undetected dangers, in contrast to conventional security technologies that depend on predetermined signatures. By employing AI for real-time monitoring, organizations can react to real-time risks, drastically shortening the time it takes to notice and fix them. Suppose AI notices a user downloading critical material outside of typical business hours, for instance. In that case, it may promptly send notifications or start automated containment procedures to stop data loss.

3.3.2 AI Automation of Incident Response to Minimize Damage

AI systems can automate many aspects of the incident response process and detect dangers. AI's ability to act instantly upon detection of possible cyber danger is crit- ical to reducing the impact of an attack rather than waiting for human involvement. To safeguard vital information, automated solutions may isolate impacted systems, block malicious IP addresses, or start data backup operations. In the case of a ran- somware attack, for instance, an AI system may identify suspicious file encryption behavior and immediately disconnect the in- fected device from the network to stop the infection from propagating. With automated reactions, cyber teams aren't left to fend for themselves in the face of several strikes, and attackers have less time to plan and execute their opera- tions.

3.3.3 Best Practices for AI-Driven Alerts and Automated Response Protocols

Organizations need to develop clear procedures for alert setup and reaction auto- mation if they want AI-driven threat detection to work as well as possible. The first step is determining what conditions and thresholds will set off alarms; you don't want them to be overly strict and overlook real dangers, but neither too lax nor too strict will do either. Training the AI system to identify patterns unique to the organization's typical activities is critical to minimize false alarms and maximize accurate warnings. Both low-level risks, like phishing attempts, and high-priority events, like data breaches or ransomware attacks, should be ad- dressed via automated response systems. There can be a hierarchy of responses, with more drastic measures adopted in response to the most serious dangers. In addition, incident reports and post-attack analysis should always be used to analyze and enhance automatic responses. It is essential to update these policies regularly to keep AI systems successful as the organization's architecture and cyber threat landscape develop.

To safeguard its operational technology (OT) networks, a North American energy firm that manages vital infrastructure uses AI-driven real-time threat

detection. The security team kept an eye on the information going out of the company's control systems and into external networks using Vectra Networks' AI. The AI identified suspicious patterns of communication between a distant desktop and the company's vital systems during an assault simulation exercise. Without delay, the AI system detected the problem and set in motion an auto- mated response that quarantined the questionable data and notified the security staff. The AI's real-time identification and quick reaction prevented a possible catastrophic interruption to the business's energy operations.

4 BEST PRACTICES FOR AI-POWERED THREAT DETECTION

4.1 Ensuring Data Quality and Integrity

4.1.1 Importance of Clean, Accurate, Diverse Data for Effective AI Model Training

The quality of the data used to train the models greatly determines the efficiency of threat detection systems powered by AI. If the data is clean, reliable, and diversified, the AI can identify more dangers with fewer mistakes, such as false positives and negatives. AI models can concentrate on detecting real dangers when data lacks inconsistencies, duplication, and unnecessary information. The ability of the AI model to learn to detect insider threats, malware, phishing, and other forms of assault across a wide range of contexts and sectors depends on diverse data. AI algorithms can develop biases and learn a limited set of patterns without varied training data, making them unable to identify new or unique dangers. For instance, AI models trained on data from the banking industry may fail to detect risks specific to the retail or healthcare industries. Collecting data from several sources, such as endpoint activity, network logs, and previous security occurrences, is crucial to constructing a robust model for various cyber threats (Aminizadeh et al., 2024) (Hameed et al., 2018).

4.1.2 Strategies for Detecting and Mitigating Data Poisoning and Adversarial Attacks on AI Systems

One serious risk to AI-powered systems is data poisoning, in which harmful or distorted data is purposefully fed into the AI training pipeline to influence decision-making. For instance, malicious actors might trick AI systems into mis- classifying risks or ignoring real ones by inserting misleading information into the training data. To reduce the likelihood of this happening, businesses should ensure that training is based on only reliable, confirmed data by instituting stringent data validation and filtering procedures. Identifying instances of data poisoning is possible by conducting regular audits of training data and looking for irregularities or outliers. Adversarial testing is one successful way the AI sys- tem is subjected to possible attacks while being developed to gauge its resilience. Differential privacy approaches are another option; they lessen the likelihood of

data poisoning by preventing over-representing particular data points (Arif et al., 2024).

4.1.3 Best Practices for Maintaining Data Privacy and GDPR Com- pliance

Data privacy should be an organization's top priority, alongside data qual- ity, mainly when dealing with sensitive or personally identifiable information used to train AI models. European companies are subject to stringent regula- tions on collecting, storing, and using personal data, such as the General Data Protection Regulation (GDPR). Failure to comply may result in severe legal and financial consequences. To ensure compliance with GDPR and comparable rules, organizations should take precautions to protect the privacy of individuals by anonymizing or pseudonymizing personal data used for AI training. For AI- powered threat detection to keep data private, it is vital to use robust encryption methods, data access rules, and regular privacy impact assessments. Compliance with privacy legislation also requires openness about data processing and user opt-out mechanisms. A Europe-an healthcare organization implemented an AI- driven security system to identify insider risks. Due to the delicate nature of pa- tient information, verifying that the data used to train AI was GDPR compliant was necessary. To prevent the disclosure of personally identifiable information, the organization employed anonymization techniques to guarantee that the AI could still identify suspicious activity in patient data. Maintaining compliance and safeguarding sensitive data using AI-powered threat detection was made easier with regular privacy audits (Aslan et al., 2023).

4.2 Continuous Monitoring and Model Updating

4.2.1 Need for Ongoing Monitoring to Ensure AI Effectiveness

AI models lose some of their efficacy over time. To keep up with the ever-changing nature of cyber threats, it is essential to regularly test AI systems to see whether they can identify any new dangers. A phenomenon known as "model drift" can occur in AI models, causing them to become less effective as time goes on due to changes in both malicious attack patterns and genuine user behavior. Threat detection systems driven by AI risk becoming less reliable if they are not constantly monitored for new vulnerabilities or lawful behaviors that can be flagged as suspicious. By monitoring AI models' performance, security teams may examine their results for erroneous positive or negative predictions and tweak them as needed. One way to do this is to update the training data or adjust the AI's decision-making thresholds to align with the current danger picture (Bibi et al., 2022).

4.2.2 Techniques for Regularly Updating AI Models for New Threats and Vulnerabilities

Organizations need to set up a regular update cycle for their threat detection systems driven by AI if they want to keep their AI models current. Incorporating newly found dangers, security flaws, and attack methods into the AI's learning process requires collecting fresh data on the subject. Using continuous learning frameworks is a valuable strategy since AI models can react dynamically to new threats by feeding them real-time security data. For instance, by incorporating threat intelligence feeds, the AI system can keep up with newly identified mal- ware strains or phishing strategies. Model retraining should be done regularly to keep AI reactive to modern dangers. Organizations may also test updates, re- vert to earlier versions, and keep track of changes using AI models using version control (Chawdhury, 2024).

4.2.3 Case Studies on the Importance of Continuous Model Mainte- nance

An uptick in phishing attempts, using complex email techniques, targeting workers of a large retail firm was detected. As phishing techniques advanced, the efficiency of the AI-based email security solution started to decline despite its implementation. During an audit, the business uncovered the AI model's lack of up-to-date data reflecting modern phishing techniques. A considerable decrease in the success rate of phishing attempts was achieved once the AI system was retrained with new data from threat intelligence reports and recent instances. To guarantee ongoing protection against new threats, this instance demonstrated the need to monitor and upgrade AI models frequently (Branch, 2019).

4.3 Collaboration Between AI and Human Expertise

4.3.1 Human Analysts' Role in Interpreting AI Insights and Making Decisions

While AI can automate many threat detection tasks, human analysts still need to make sense of the insights given by AI and act accordingly. While AI systems are great at seeing trends and detecting danger, humans may be needed to verify alarms and decide how to react. For instance, there is a possibility that AI models could occasionally produce false positives, in which harmless actions would be mistakenly marked as suspicious. Human analysts can further investigate these notifications and determine if a security problem is happening.

Also, human knowledge is critical to formulating long-term plans to counter threats. While AI systems can spot suspicious behavior that might indicate a data breach, human analysts still need to take a step back, look at the whole picture, establish how serious the breach is, and decide what to do next. Better cybersecurity is possible when human judgment is combined with AI's speed and analytical ability (Ghillani, 2022).

4.3.2 Building a Symbiotic Relationship Between AI and Cyberse- curity Professionals

For AI systems to perform at their best, businesses should encourage a mu- tually beneficial partnership between AI technologies and cybersecurity experts. Analysts can readily comprehend insights given by the AI and offer input to en- hance the model's performance thanks to the well-defined communication chan- nels between the system and the security team. The outputs of AI systems and how to respond to alarms sent by these systems should be understood by security professionals via training.

A feedback loop is another critical component that allows human analysts to contribute to the AI model's decision-making process. For instance, if analysts find that a specific warning is being triggered by false positives too often, they may either tell the AI to be less sensitive or suggest how to distinguish between actual and suspect actions (Hameed et al., 2018).

4.3.3 Successful AI and Human Team Collaborations in Threat De- tection

A big bank used an AI-driven system to monitor real-time transaction pat- terns for signs of possible fraud. The AI system proved effective in identifying suspicious activity, such as offshore account transfers or huge transactions, but it produced several false positives due to genuine but rare events. The AI group worked with the bank's security specialists to improve the model and add rules tailored to certain transactions. By working together, we cut down on false pos- itives by 40%, freeing up the analysts to pay more attention to the most urgent, high-risk transactions.

A worldwide technology company implemented an IDS powered by AI to monitor network traffic for indications of potential intrusions. Human analysts first examined the instances of AI-flagged suspicious behavior and deemed them minor concerns. However, when the researchers dug further, they found that these strange occurrences were part of a concerted APT campaign against the business. In tandem with AI's capacity to spot slight irregularities, the human team's contextual knowledge of the organization's processes helped avert a signif- icant compromise. The effectiveness of combining AI technologies with trained cybersecurity experts in identifying and countering complex threats is shown here (Hameed, Garg, et al., 2022).

5 TOOLS AND TECHNOLOGIES FOR AI-POWERED THREAT DETECTION

5.1 Overview of Leading AI Cybersecurity Tools

5.1.1 Overview of Popular AI-Powered Threat Detection Tools and Platforms

By using sophisticated algorithms to identify, assess, and react to cyber dan- gers in real time, threat detection technologies driven by AI have revolutionized the way organizations manage cybersecurity. These systems outperform more conventional approaches in processing massive amounts of data, finding outliers, and warning of possible dangers. The most popular AI technologies in the cyber- security business today are Darktrace, CrowdStrike Falcon, and Cylance. These systems are great for identifying and reducing contemporary cyber risks because of capabilities like automated incident response, ML, and predictive analytics (Jeffrey et al., 2023).

5.1.2 Key Features, Strengths, and Limitations of AI Tools

- **Darktrace:** For network anomaly detection, Darktrace uses unsupervised ML. AI creates a "pattern of life" for every person and gadget, looking for any changes that could suggest danger. Analyzing real-time data flows, it can identify zero-day threats and insider assaults, its major strength. The possibility of false positives is a drawback, particularly in dynamic settings where the baseline behavior is constantly in flux (Katiyar, 2023).
- **CrowdStrike Falcon:** Using AI, CrowdStrike Falcon can identify, stop, and react to malware, phishing, and ransomware assaults; it is well-known for its endpoint security capabilities. Its ability to grow effectively across huge companies is made possible by its cloud-native design. With the ability to learn and adapt to new threats, Falcon's AI engine is constantly improving at processing data. It may need substantial resources for efficient execution, and its price tag can be prohibitive for smaller organisations (Chawdhury, 2024).
- **Cylance:** To prevent threats from ever executing, Cylance uses AI to identify malicious code before it does damage. Cylance offers a lightweight, efficient solution that analyses file properties instead of depending on conventional signatures, minimizing system performance consequences. One drawback is that it can't work correctly in offline or air-gapped settings since it initially relies on a cloud connection for full performance (Branch, 2019).

5.1.3 Case Studies on AI Tools' Effectiveness in Business

- **Darktrace in a Retail Chain:** After suffering repeated data breaches caused by insider threats, a worldwide retail chain used Darktrace. When workers accessed critical customer data outside of typical business hours, Darktrace detected it immediately. A big compromise was averted because the technology alerted the security team to the irregularities. A vital com- ponent of the organization's security architecture, Darktrace's AI could sift through mountains of real-time data in search of small insider threats.
- **CrowdStrike Falcon in a Healthcare Organization:** Employees of a big healthcare organisation were the victim of ongoing phishing attempts. Following the implementation of CrowdStrike Falcon, the AI-driven technology effectively reduced the frequency of successful phishing assaults by half by identifying and blocking harmful attachments before they could run. Analyzing risks in real time and responding automatically helped the organization stay compliant with healthcare data security standards and swiftly neutralize them.

- **Cylance in a Financial Institution:** After being hit by many malware assaults, a financial institution used Cylance for endpoint security. Quickly identifying and quarantining files displaying dubious behavior, the AI model prevented them from running. It was trained on a massive dataset of known and undiscovered malware. The institution saw a 30% decrease in malware incidences and an improvement in endpoint performance over a year, thanks to Cylance's minimal resource usage.

5.2 Custom AI Solutions for Business-Specific Threats

5.2.1 Potential for Developing AI Tools for Business-Specific Needs

While generic AI cybersecurity technologies work well for most businesses, more specialized solutions may be necessary for others, particularly those in niche sectors. Businesses may take advantage of the adaptability of custom AI solutions to deal with issues like specialized operational risks, regulatory needs, and cyber threats peculiar to their sector. Companies in the healthcare industry may place a premium on protecting patients' personal information, but banks may have a more pressing need to identify instances of fraudulent spending. Building custom AI tools enables businesses to train models on targeted datasets, which improves the efficacy and precision of threat detection (Sinha et al., 2023).

5.2.2 Steps for Developing Custom AI Solutions with AI Developers and Cybersecurity Experts

Here are the main processes to take while developing AI-powered threat detection solutions:

- The first stage in determining a company's security requirements is to catalog the unique security issues the company faces, including the most common threats. Intellectual property, consumer data, and third-party vendor risk mitigation are all potential areas of focus here.
- Businesses should collaborate with cybersecurity specialists well-versed in the current threat environment and AI engineers focusing on ML. Working in tandem, they may create tailor-made AI algorithms for the company. By working together, we can ensure the AI tool is compatible with how the company operates and the threats it faces.
- To train the AI model, appropriate information like network traffic, historical security events, or user behavior records are required. For the AI to learn

to identify normal and abnormal patterns, it is necessary to clean and preprocess the data to ensure it is accurate and diverse.

– Before going live, the AI model needs extensive testing in a simulated set-

ting to see how well it can identify potential dangers. After validation, It may be deployed throughout the organization's infrastructure, with ongoing performance and accuracy monitoring.

5.2.3 Successful Implementations of Custom AI-Powered Threat De- tection Systems

– **Custom AI Solution in a Healthcare Network:** A major healthcare provider built an AI system to identify illegal access to EHRs. The AI model was trained using patient access data spanning years. The system then learned to distinguish between normal and abnormal behavior. When an em- ployee accessed patient data several times without a valid business reason, the AI noticed something was wrong. During the investigation, the security team found an insider trying to sell patient data. The hospital network was spared legal and financial consequences thanks to the unique solution that helped avert a major breach (Aminizadeh et al., 2024).

– **Custom AI Solution in a Manufacturing Firm:** A manufacturing busi-

ness dealing with IP theft teamed up with AI developers to build a special- ized tool to identify industrial espionage. The AI system monitored network activities to detect suspicious data exfiltration to external servers. After a few months of implementation, the system identified a data transfer associ- ated with a competitor's server. The swift action of the security team saved valuable intellectual property (von Garrel & Jahn, 2023).

5.3 Integrating AI with Other Cybersecurity Technologies

5.3.1 AI-Enhanced Security Technologies: Firewalls, Encryption, and MFA

Integrating AI-powered threat detection systems with current cybersecurity technology to form a multi-layered defense is optimal. Using AI's real-time analytical capabilities, network security tools like IDS and Firewalls may be significantly improved. AI may examine firewall traffic patterns, for instance, and spot suspicious or unusual behavior that a rule-based system might overlook. The same holds for encryption algorithms; AI can improve them by spotting sus- picious patterns in encrypted messages. Another area that might benefit from AI integration is multi-factor authentication (MFA). AI systems may also study login trends and user behavior as an additional safeguard. If it identifies suspi- cious login attempts, AI may impose extra authentication steps like biometric verification or one-time passcodes to ensure that stolen credentials don't lead to unauthorized access (Zafar et al., 2017).

5.3.2 AI's Role in Enhancing Endpoint and Network Security

Endpoint security is paramount in contemporary cybersecurity. AI is crucial in safeguarding endpoints such as mobile phones, computers, and the Internet of Things since it constantly watches their actions. AI-driven solutions can identify infected devices in real time and instantly isolate them to stop more network infections. They can also detect data exfiltration attempts and anomalous behav- ior on endpoints. AI may detect minor indications of network intrusion or data theft about network architecture by analyzing traffic between servers, routers, and user devices. By correlating data from many sources, AI can detect weak- nesses, locate possible access points for attackers, and notify the security team before an attack's complete development (Schmitt, 2023).

5.3.3 Future AI Integration with Quantum Computing and Blockchain

AI will improve cybersecurity in emerging blockchain and quantum comput- ing technologies. While quantum computing may disrupt established encryption techniques, it can also completely revamp safety measures by introducing imper- vious algorithms to quantum computing. Building robust quantum cryptography systems that can compete with quantum computers' processing capability would need AI. Similarly, AI may improve blockchain technology by detecting suspi- cious activity, fraud, or abnormalities in smart contracts and transaction flows. Firms employing AI to analyze trends in decentralized systems may enhance security in blockchain settings. This is especially true in areas such as supply chain management and banking. By combining AI with these new technologies, businesses can safeguard their data against ever-evolving assaults and remain one step ahead of the competition (Hameed, Barika, et al., 2022).

6 CHALLENGES AND CONSIDERATIONS IN AI-POWERED THREAT DETECTION

While the integration of AI into threat detection systems offers considerable ad- vantages for business environments, it's important to address the associated chal- lenges and considerations (Vegesna, 2023). Implementing AI-powered solutions is not without its complexities, and a careful approach is necessary to maximize effectiveness while minimizing potential issues. Key concerns include the risk of AI bias, the management of false positives, and the need for transparency and oversight. Understanding and addressing these challenges are crucial for ensur- ing that AI delivers accurate, reliable results in a security context (Anandharaj, 2024).

–   Addressing AI Bias and False Positives: A critical issue in AI-powered threat detection is the potential for bias in the underlying algorithms (Kelly, Karthike- salingam, Suleyman, Corrado, & King, 2019) (Ntoutsi et al., 2020). AI sys- tems are only as good as the data on which they are trained. If the data

is skewed, incomplete, or biased, the AI may produce inaccurate outcomes, such as labeling legitimate activities as threats (false positives) or missing ac- tual threats (false negatives). These errors can compromise the effectiveness of security protocols and result in wasted time and resources. To mitigate these risks, businesses should consider the following strategies:

1. Diverse Training Data: AI models must be trained on datasets that re- flect the wide range of potential threats in real-world environments. This means incor- porating data from various sectors, regions, and attack meth- ods. By ensuring the training data is as diverse as possible, businesses can reduce the likelihood that the AI will develop biases that lead to disproportionate false positives or negatives. This diversity helps the AI recognize a wider variety of legitimate behaviors and anomalous patterns, thereby improving overall accuracy (Ferrara, 2023).
2. Regular Evaluation: AI models need to be continuously evaluated to de- tect and correct any bias that may emerge over time. Threat landscapes evolve rapidly, and AI systems can become outdated if not regularly updated to account for new forms of cyber threats. Businesses should implement ongoing monitoring processes to assess the performance of AI models, ensuring they are still ca- pable of identifying real threats while minimizing false alarms. This periodic evaluation helps maintain a balance between security and operational efficiency (Hwang et al., 2022).

3. Human Oversight: Despite the advancements in AI, human oversight re- mains an essential part of threat detection systems. Relying solely on AI can be risky, as even the most sophisticated algorithms can make mis- takes. Involving cybersecurity experts in the detection process ensures that false positives or negatives are identified and addressed promptly. Human analysts can provide context and judgment that AI might lack, especially in complex situations. This collaborative approach between AI and human expertise enhances both the speed and accuracy of threat detection (Courtland, 2018).

These considerations are vital for businesses to effectively harness AI's power in securing their environments while mitigating the challenges that come with this evolving technology. By ensuring diverse data, continuous evalua- tion, and human oversight, organizations can strike the right balance between automation and accu- racy (Raso, Hilligoss, Krishnamurthy, Bavitz, & Kim, 2018).

– Managing Complexity of AI Systems:

AI-powered threat detection systems offer immense benefits in modern busi- ness environments, but their complexity introduces several challenges that organizations must address to ensure they are effectively implemented and maintained (Alt, 2022). Navigating these challenges is critical for businesses to maximize the potential of AI-driven security solutions while minimizing the risks associated with misman- agement or ineffective deployment (Berente, Gu, Recker, & Santhanam, 2021).

• Skilled Professionals: Developing the Necessary Expertise

One of the primary challenges of AI-driven security systems is the need for specialized skills. These systems often require a deep understand- ing of both AI technologies and cybersecurity principles, which may not be part of the existing skill set of many IT teams. Organizations must invest in hiring and developing professionals with expertise in AI, ma- chine learning, and security protocols to manage these systems effectively (Sambasivan & Veeraraghavan, 2022). This may involve recruiting new talent, but it also means creating training and development programs to upskill current staff. The goal is to build a team capable of interpreting AI-generated insights, troubleshooting issues, and fine-tuning the system for optimal performance. By equipping teams with the necessary skills, businesses can ensure their AI-powered security tools are properly uti- lized. This expertise also allows the team to better recognize the limits of AI, preventing over-reliance on automation and maintaining human oversight where necessary (Ardichvili, 2022).

- Clear Communication: Aligning Security, IT, and Business Leadership
  Another critical factor is establishing clear communication between var- ious stakeholders within the organization. AI-powered threat detection does not operate in isolation; it requires input and coordination from security profes- sionals, IT departments, and business leaders. Often, a gap exists between the technical knowledge of IT staff and the strate- gic priorities of business leadership (Shiohira, 2021). Without proper communication, this gap can lead to misunderstandings about the ca- pabilities and limitations of AI sys- tems, potentially resulting in either underutilization or overconfidence in the technology.

Organizations should foster collaboration by ensuring that all relevant teams have a shared understanding of how AI-powered security systems work, what they can realistically achieve, and where human intervention is still necessary. Regular meetings, cross-departmental workshops, and documentation of AI processes can help bridge these gaps. By aligning security and business objectives, companies can ensure that their AI so- lutions are integrated smoothly into the broader operational framework (Shiohira, 2021).

- Regular Updates: Ensuring Continuous Performance and Security

AI systems are only as effective as the data they process and the al- gorithms they run on. As threats evolve and AI technologies advance, keeping AI-powered threat detection systems up-to-date becomes cru- cial. Businesses must implement a rigorous update and patching process to ensure their AI tools can respond to the latest cyber threats. This in- cludes not only updating the AI software itself but also ensuring that the underlying data models are refreshed to maintain accuracy and relevance (Nortje & Grobbelaar, 2020).

Failure to regularly update AI security systems can expose businesses to new vulnerabilities and limit the system's ability to detect emerging threats. Regular updates are also essential for improving the system's accuracy over time, as newer algorithms and models become available.

By prioritizing updates and continuous improvement, organizations can maintain the high level of performance necessary to combat sophisticated cyberattacks (Jun, Craig, Shafik, & Sharif, 2021).

In conclusion, while AI-powered threat detection offers tremendous promise, businesses must address several key challenges to leverage it effectively.

This requires a multifaceted approach: investing in the right talent, es- tablishing clear lines of communication, and maintaining ongoing system updates. By managing these complexities, organizations can fully realize the benefits of AI in their security strategies, ensuring a safer and more resilient business environment.

– Ethical and Legal Aspects:

The integration of AI-powered threat detection into business environments brings about a wide array of benefits in identifying and responding to cyber threats. However, these advanced technologies also pose significant ethical and legal challenges. Understanding and addressing these concerns is cru- cial for organizations to ensure the responsible and effective use of AI while maintaining compliance with laws and fostering trust among employees, cus- tomers, and stakeholders (D. Kumar & Suthar, 2024).

• Ethical Guidelines

AI is a powerful tool, but its use in threat detection needs to be guided by a strong ethical framework. Organizations must develop clear, action- able ethical guidelines that align with their corporate values and industry best practices. These guidelines should focus on promoting fairness, ac- countability, and transparency in how AI is used to monitor and mitigate threats (Familoni, 2024).

One of the primary ethical concerns involves bias in AI algorithms. If AI systems are trained on biased data, they can unintentionally flag certain groups or behaviors as higher-risk, leading to unfair treatment or discrimination. Therefore, organizations must take steps to regularly audit and update their AI models to ensure they are free from bias and perform equitably across all users (Kaushik, Khan, Kumari, Sharma, & Dubey, 2024).

Moreover, transparency is essential. Employees and customers need to understand how AI-powered threat detection works and what data is being collected or analyzed. Providing clear communication about the purpose, scope, and limitations of the AI system fosters trust and reduces fears of overreach or misuse (Kaushik et al., 2024).

• Privacy and Surveillance:

AI-powered threat detection systems often require monitoring of vast amounts of data, including personal and sensitive information. This raises important questions about privacy and surveillance. On the one hand, these systems are essential for identifying potential threats and ensuring the security of business operations. On the other hand, exces- sive monitoring can infringe on individuals' privacy rights and lead to a culture of constant surveillance (Feldstein, 2019).

To balance privacy with security, organizations should adopt a privacy- first approach when designing and deploying AI threat detection systems. This means limiting data collection to only what is necessary for detect- ing threats, anonymiz- ing data wherever possible, and ensuring that users are aware of and consent to the monitoring in place. Implementing strong encryption and access control measures can further safeguard personal information from unauthorized use or breaches (Fontes, Hohma, Corri- gan, & Lu¨tge, 2022).

Additionally, it's important to differentiate between legitimate monitor- ing for security purposes and invasive surveillance. Organizations should establish clear boundaries on how AI systems monitor activities, en- suring that employee and customer privacy is respected at all times. This includes implementing safeguards against excessive data retention or intrusive surveillance practices, such as contin- uous screen or keystroke monitoring (Fontes et al., 2022).

- Legal Compliance:

The use of AI-powered threat detection systems must also comply with an ever-evolving landscape of data protection laws and regulations. Legal frameworks such as the General Data Protection Regulation (GDPR) in Europe and the California Consumer Privacy Act (CCPA) in the United States impose strict requirements on how personal data is col- lected, stored, and used by organizations. Failure to comply with these regulations can result in substantial fines, reputational damage, and legal liabilities (Butler & O'Brien, 2019).

To navigate this complex regulatory environment, organizations need to stay informed about relevant laws and continuously evaluate their AI systems for compliance. For instance, under GDPR, organizations are required to implement data protection by design and by default, ensuring that privacy is considered at every stage of system development. Similarly, CCPA mandates that businesses provide individuals with the right to know what data is being collected and the ability to opt out of data sharing (Lor`e et al., 2023).

Moreover, some jurisdictions are introducing specific regulations on the use of AI, particularly in security and surveillance contexts. Businesses should monitor these developments closely and adjust their practices to meet new legal obligations. Legal compliance should not be treated as a one-time effort but as an ongoing process involving regular audits, reviews, and updates to policies and procedures (Brennan, 2023).

Organizations must also consider the potential legal implications of using AI in threat detection. If an AI system wrongly identifies an individual or group as a security threat, it could lead to false accusations, wrongful termination, or even legal action against the company. To mitigate these risks, businesses should establish clear protocols for human oversight and intervention in the AI decision-making process. AI should assist human experts in identifying threats, not replace their judgment entirely (Brennan, 2023).

AI-powered threat detection offers significant benefits for businesses seeking to protect themselves against cyber threats. However, it is essential to address the challenges and considerations associated with its implementation. By carefully considering factors such as bias, complexity, and ethical implications, organi- zations can leverage AI to enhance their security posture and safeguard their valuable assets.

7 FUTURE TRENDS IN AI-POWERED THREAT DETECTION

Artificial Intelligence (AI) is reshaping the landscape of industries across the globe, and cybersecurity is no exception. The traditional methods of threat de- tec- tion, while still valuable, are struggling to keep up with the rapidly evolving and increasingly complex cyber threats businesses face today (Arif et al., 2024). AI, with its ability to learn, adapt, and make real-time decisions, offers a game- changing approach to not just keeping pace with these threats but staying ahead of them. In this guide, we will explore how AI is revolutionizing cybersecurity, the future trends in AI-driven security solutions, and what it all means for busi- nesses seeking to safeguard their digital environments (Yaseen, 2023).

7.1 The Evolution of AI in Cybersecurity

Artificial intelligence (AI) has emerged as a transformative force across various industries, and cybersecurity is no exception. The rapid digitization of business environments, coupled with increasingly sophisticated cyber threats, has made traditional security methods insufficient (Aslam, 2024). AI's integration into cybersecurity is reshaping how organizations defend their digital assets, offering enhanced protection and a proactive stance against the growing complexities of cyberattacks. We explores in detail, how AI is driving this evolution, focusing on its key contributions, including enhanced threat detection, real-time response, and predictive analytics (Maddireddy & Maddireddy, 2020).

– Enhanced Threat Detection

One of the most significant advancements AI has brought to cybersecurity is the ability to detect threats with greater accuracy and speed. Traditional se- curity systems rely heavily on pre-defined signatures and known patterns of malicious activity. While effective against known threats, these methods fall short when dealing with novel or evolving attacks. In contrast, AI, particu- larly through machine learning algorithms, can process and analyze massive volumes of data from various sources—network traffic, user behavior, log files, and more—to identify irregularities that might suggest a breach or intrusion (Maddireddy & Maddireddy, 2020).

AI-driven threat detection systems are designed to learn from the data they encounter, continuously refining their models to better distinguish between legitimate and malicious activities. This ability to analyze patterns and

anomalies means AI can detect potential threats earlier, often before tra- ditional systems can recognize them. For instance, by tracking subtle devi- ations in user behavior or identifying unusual network traffic, AI can spot threats like zero-day attacks or advanced persistent threats (APTs) that might bypass conventional security measures (Lee, Kim, Kim, & Han, 2019). Furthermore, the volume of cyber threats has grown exponentially, making

it difficult for human analysts to keep up. AI helps bridge this gap by sifting through vast datasets in a fraction of the time, enabling businesses to main- tain a higher level of vigilance and quickly identify potential security issues. This automated and data-driven approach ensures that security teams are alerted to potential breaches with precision, allowing them to focus their efforts on the most pressing concerns (Markevych & Dawson, 2023).

– Real-Time Response:

In addition to detecting threats, AI excels in responding to them in real time. Speed is critical when dealing with cybersecurity incidents, as the longer an attack goes undetected or unresolved, the greater the potential damage. AI- powered security systems can automate various responses, such as quaran- tining affected devices, blocking malicious IP addresses, or initiating network isolation protocols (Voronov, Tang, Amert, & Anderson, 2021).

This real-time response capability is crucial in scenarios where human in- tervention may be too slow. Cyberattacks, particularly those that involve ransomware or DDoS (Distributed Denial of Service) attacks, can spread quickly and cause significant disruption. AI systems can take immediate ac- tion, reducing the window of opportunity for attackers and minimizing the potential impact on the business (Voronov et al., 2021).

Moreover, AI's ability to automate certain security responses reduces the strain on security teams, who are often stretched thin due to the sheer vol- ume of alerts and incidents they must manage. AI can prioritize threats, determining which issues require immediate attention and which can be han- dled automatically. This not only streamlines the response process but also ensures that critical incidents are addressed without delay.

– Predictive Analytics:

Beyond its capacity for real-time detection and response, AI is revolutioniz- ing cybersecurity through predictive analytics. By analyzing historical data, AI can identify patterns and trends that suggest the likelihood of future cyber threats. This predictive capability allows businesses to anticipate at- tacks before they occur, offering a proactive layer of defense that was pre- viously unimaginable (Zulaikha, Mohamed, Kurniawati, Rusgianto, & Rus- mita, 2020).

AI can analyze vast amounts of historical attack data, looking for correla- tions between different types of incidents and identifying common indicators that precede certain types of attacks. For example, certain types of network activity or software vulnerabilities may be early indicators of an impend- ing ransomware attack. By recognizing these signals, AI enables security teams to take preventive measures, such as patching vulnerabilities, increas-

ing monitoring, or adjusting security protocols, thereby reducing the risk of a successful breach (Rana & Shuford, 2024).

This predictive approach also extends to evolving threats. Cybercriminals are constantly developing new methods to infiltrate systems, and AI's machine learning capabilities can help stay ahead of these innovations. By contin- uously learning from new data, AI can adapt its models to recognize the hallmarks of emerging threats, even if they do not match known patterns of previous attacks. This forward-looking approach helps organizations stay one step ahead in the ever-evolving cyber landscape (Khan & Alotaibi, 2020).

– Emerging AI Techniques: Machine Learning, Deep Learning, and Natural Language Processing

The impact of AI on cybersecurity is further enhanced by the development of specialized techniques such as machine learning (ML), deep learning (DL), and natural language processing (NLP). These technologies expand AI's abil- ity to detect, respond to, and predict threats by enabling more nuanced and intelligent analysis (Deng & Liu, 2018).

- Machine Learning (ML): This subset of AI is particularly effective in recognizing patterns and detecting anomalies in cybersecurity data. ML algorithms can be trained on vast datasets to differentiate between nor- mal and abnormal behavior. Over time, these systems improve their accuracy, becoming more adept at identifying potential threats without needing explicit instructions from human operators. In cybersecurity, ML is used to detect malware, identify unauthorized access, and mon- itor network traffic for suspicious activity (Lauriola, Lavelli, & Aiolli, 2022).

- Deep Learning (DL): Deep learning, a more advanced subset of machine learning, leverages neural networks with multiple layers to process data in more complex ways. This allows deep learning models to perform tasks such as image and voice recognition, but in cybersecurity, it can be used to ana- lyze network traffic, detect malware hidden within encrypted files, or iden- tify suspicious user behaviors that may indicate insider threats. DL models are particularly useful in identifying unknown malware, which often evades traditional signature-based detection methods (Torfi, Shir- vani, Keneshloo, Tavaf, & Fox, 2020).

- Natural Language Processing (NLP): In the context of cybersecurity, NLP plays a crucial role in detecting phishing attempts and other so- cial engineer- ing attacks. Phishing remains one of the most common and successful cyber- attack methods, often relying on deceptive emails or mes- sages to trick users into revealing sensitive information. NLP allows AI systems to analyze the content of emails, looking for language patterns, keywords, and phrases that suggest malicious intent. By understanding the nuances of human language, AI can flag potential phishing emails be- fore they reach the user, reducing the risk of successful attacks (Sharifani & Amini, 2023).

As these AI techniques continue to evolve, they will further strengthen cy- ber-security defenses, making it possible to detect even the most sophisticated and subtle attacks. By combining the power of machine learning, deep learn- ing, and natural language processing, AI is driving a new era of cybersecurity that is both proactive and highly adaptive.

The evolution of AI in cybersecurity marks a significant shift in how businesses protect their digital environments. With its ability to enhance threat detection, respond in real time, and predict future attacks, AI is poised to become an indispensable tool in the fight against cybercrime. As emerging techniques like machine learning, deep learning, and natural language processing continue to develop, AI's role in cybersecurity will only grow stronger, offering businesses a more secure, resilient defense against the ever-changing landscape of cyber threats.

7.2 The Rise of Autonomous Cybersecurity Systems

In today's fast-evolving digital landscape, organizations are confronted with in- creasingly sophisticated cyberattacks that demand rapid, adaptive defenses. Traditional, manually-driven cybersecurity measures are often too slow to respond to these threats, making the case for more advanced, automated solutions. This need for speed and precision has given rise to autonomous cybersecurity systems, which leverage artificial intelligence (AI) to detect, mitigate, and even recover from cyber threats with minimal human intervention (Taddeo, McCutcheon, & Floridi, 2019). These systems promise to transform the way businesses defend against a broad range of cyberattacks, providing unmatched efficiency and scal- ability. However, with the growing reliance on AI-powered cybersecurity systems comes a new set of challenges and risks (Camacho, 2024).

– The Promise of Automation in Cyber Defense: At their core, autonomous cybersecurity systems operate by learning patterns in data, identifying ab- normalities, and responding to potential threats autonomously. They employ machine learning algorithms, deep learning techniques, and even natural lan- guage processing to analyze massive datasets in real-time. These systems can automatically detect anomalies that signal a cyberattack, such as unusual network traffic or unauthorized access attempts, and react within millisec- onds—far quicker than a human could (Bonfanti, 2022).

For businesses, the benefits are clear. Automating routine tasks such as vul- ner- ability scanning, patch management, and threat detection significantly re- duces the workload on human cybersecurity professionals. This allows them to concentrate on high-priority tasks such as strategic planning and inci- dent response orchestration. AI-driven systems can also adapt and improve over time, learning from each attack to become more effective in future inci- dents. In short, autonomous cybersecurity systems can enhance a company's resilience to cyber threats by providing a level of speed, scalability, and con- sistency that human-driven solutions alone cannot match (Dash, Ansari, Sharma, & Ali, 2022).

– Overreliance: The Risk of Complacency: However, with the power of AI comes the potential risk of overreliance. Businesses may become too depen- dent on these autonomous systems, leading to complacency in the broader cybersecurity strategy. The human element in cybersecurity remains critical, as AI is not infallible. An overreliance on automated defenses can create a false sense of security, where organizations assume that their AI-driven systems will catch every potential threat without the need for ongoing human oversight (LAZIC´, 2019).

Cyberattacks are often multifaceted and adaptive, meaning that the at- tacker's strategy may change as they attempt to circumvent automated defenses. While AI systems are highly efficient at detecting known attack patterns, they may struggle to recognize entirely new, sophisticated attack methods or subtle insider threats that require human intuition and investi- gation. Thus, a balanced approach—where AI handles the bulk of routine defenses, but human experts regularly monitor, fine-tune, and override the system when needed—is crucial for maintaining a robust defense posture (Williams & Yampolskiy, 2021).

–   Bias: The Hidden Danger in AI Systems Another critical challenge faced by autonomous cybersecurity systems is bias. AI systems rely on training data to learn how to identify and respond to cyber threats. If the data used to train these systems is biased or incomplete, the system itself may produce inac- curate or skewed results. For example, if an AI is trained primarily on data from attacks targeting a specific industry or region, it may be less effective at detecting threats outside of those parameters (Challen et al., 2019).

Bias can also arise in the way the system prioritizes certain types of alerts over others. If certain vulnerabilities or assets are overrepresented in the training data, the AI may incorrectly prioritize protecting them, leaving other equally critical areas under-defended. This can inadvertently reinforce existing vulnerabilities within an organization's infrastructure. Moreover, biased AI decisions can have far-reaching consequences if left unchecked, potentially leading to a scenario where certain users, networks, or data assets receive disproportionate protection while others are neglected (Challen et al., 2019).

Ethical Considerations in Autonomous Cybersecurity The ethical consider- ations surrounding autonomous cybersecurity systems are another area that warrants careful attention. AI systems are increasingly tasked with making decisions that can have significant ethical implications, particularly when it comes to protecting assets or determining the severity of a cyberattack (Kaushik et al., 2024). In some cases, an AI system may need to prioritize which parts of a network to protect in the event of a breach. These deci- sions, if made without transparent criteria, could inadvertently cause harm or injustice, such as by favoring high-value corporate data over individual privacy concerns.

Moreover, the delegation of critical decision-making to machines raises ques- tions about accountability. In cases where an AI system fails or makes an erroneous judgment, it can be difficult to determine who is responsible—was it the fault of the developers, the data scientists, or the organization that deployed the system? Without clear ethical guidelines, businesses may find themselves grappling with unforeseen moral dilemmas (Aminizadeh et al., 2024).

The Future of Autonomous Cybersecurity Systems Despite these challenges, the potential of autonomous cybersecurity systems remains undeniable. As AI technology continues to advance, so too will the sophistication and accu- racy of these systems. Future AI-driven tools are expected to incorporate ad- vanced ethical frameworks and better-quality training data, minimizing bias and ensuring that ethical considerations are taken into account (Lee et al., 2019). Additionally, the integration of AI into broader cybersecurity ecosys- tems will continue to evolve, combining human oversight with autonomous systems for more comprehensive and adaptive defenses (Aminizadeh et al., 2024).

For businesses, the key to success lies in leveraging the strengths of au- tono-mous systems while maintaining a strong human element. Human ex- perts should focus on monitoring and improving AI performance, fine-tuning algorithms, and investigating edge cases that AI alone cannot address. By doing so, organizations can harness the power of AI to enhance their cy- bersecurity defenses while mitigating risks related to bias, overreliance, and ethical concerns (Ferrara, 2023).

Autonomous cybersecurity systems are not a silver bullet, but they repre- sent a transformative shift in the way organizations can protect themselves against the growing complexity and frequency of cyberattacks. With the right balance of automation and human intelligence, businesses can create a more resilient, agile, and secure digital environment (Challen et al., 2019).

7.3 AI and the Future of Business Security

As the digital landscape continues to evolve, artificial intelligence (AI) is be- coming a cornerstone of business security. With the rise in cyberattacks and increasingly sophisticated threats, AI's capabilities are proving invaluable for protecting modern organizations. AI offers a way to stay ahead of potential risks, helping companies detect and mitigate cyber threats faster than ever be- fore (Mughal, 2018). However, leveraging AI in business security is not without its challenges and responsibilities. Businesses must carefully consider how they adopt AI-powered tools and strategies while ensuring that ethical and privacy concerns are addressed (Dash et al., 2022).

We describe in detail below, how AI will shape the future of business security and the key steps organizations should take to fully harness its potential.

1. Invest in AI Training: To fully capitalize on AI's potential in business security, companies need to ensure that their teams are well-versed in the use of AI technologies. Traditional cybersecurity expertise is no longer enough in an environment where AI systems are rapidly becoming the front line of defense against threats (Corea, 2017). Training cybersecurity teams in AI technologies is critical for developing, deploying, and managing AI-powered systems effectively. AI models require continuous tuning, oversight, and updates to adapt to evolving cyber threats. While AI can automate threat detection and response, human expertise re- mains vital in fine-tuning algorithms, understanding the context of detected anomalies, and making strategic decisions based on AI-generated insights (Fountaine, McCarthy, & Saleh, 2019). Businesses should invest in regular training programs, certifications, and AI workshops that equip cybersecurity professionals with the tools they need to work with advanced AI systems. Cross-functional teams that include data scientists and security experts should also be encouraged, as their combined expertise is essential for maximizing the potential of AI in business security (Daugherty & Wilson, 2018).

2. Adopt a Proactive Approach: The reactive approach to security is increas- ingly obsolete in today's fast-paced digital world. Waiting for an attack to occur before taking action can be disastrous, especially with the scale and speed at which modern cyber threats can escalate. AI empowers businesses to adopt a proactive security posture, which can be a game-changer in pre- venting costly data breaches and disruptions (Chui & Francisco, 2017). AI excels at detecting patterns and anomalies in vast datasets, which allows it to identify potential threats even before they manifest into full-blown attacks. Through predictive analytics, AI systems can recognize unusual network activity, flagging potentially malicious behavior in real-time. This early detection gives security teams a significant advantage, allowing them to address vulnerabilities and mitigate risks before any real damage occurs (Enholm, Papagiannidis, Mikalef, & Krogstie, 2022). By adopting AI, businesses can move from a reactive, incident-response model to a proactive, threat-prevention model. Proactive AI-driven systems can help organizations monitor their networks 24/7, spot vulnerabilities, and issue alerts that enable preemptive measures against imminent threats. This shift in mindset will be crucial for any business that aims to stay ahead of increasingly sophisticated cybercriminals (Familoni, 2024).

3. Prioritize Data Privacy: One of the main strengths of AI in cybersecurity is its ability to analyze massive amounts of data to detect threats. However, this reliance on vast datasets brings with it a major responsibility: safeguarding data privacy. Given the sensitive nature of the information that AI systems may access, ensuring compliance with privacy regulations and best practices is paramount (Davenport, Ronanki, et al., 2018). Businesses must implement

stringent data protection measures that govern how data is collected, stored, and analyzed by AI systems. This includes ensuring encryption, anonymization of personal data, and following industry- specific compliance standards, such as GDPR for businesses operating in Europe. Moreover, companies need to develop clear privacy policies that are transparent to employees, customers, and stakeholders (Wright & Schultz, 2018). Incorporating privacy into the design of AI systems (privacy-by-design) is another critical strategy. AI algorithms should be programmed with privacy- conscious practices, ensuring that only the necessary data is collected and that personal data is not exposed during the analysis. Protecting data not only shields the company from potential legal and financial repercussions but also builds trust with clients and partners (West, 2018).

4. Consider Ethical Implications: While AI offers tremendous benefits in enhancing security, its deployment in cybersecurity raises ethical considerations that businesses must address. The growing reliance on AI for decision-making in security poses questions about transparency, accountability, and fairness (Ferrara, 2023).

Ethical AI use is particularly important when automated systems are re- sponsible for detecting threats, blocking access, or making decisions that impact users and employees. Businesses need to ensure that AI systems are designed to operate transparently, with clear guidelines on how decisions are made. This is crucial to avoid biases that could arise from skewed datasets or improperly trained algorithms (D. Kumar & Suthar, 2024).

To mitigate ethical risks, organizations should develop robust guidelines that govern the use of AI in cybersecurity. These guidelines should include fair- ness in decision-making, transparency about AI's role, and accountability for any errors or unintended consequences. It is also essential to ensure human oversight, especially when AI systems are used in critical decision-making processes (Familoni, 2024).

Incorporating ethical considerations will not only protect companies from reputational damage but will also encouragè responsible innovation in the cybersecurity field. Ethical AI ensures that businesses use technology in a way that respects both legal and societal norms.

The Future of Business Security with AI

AI is set to revolutionize business security, offering more robust defenses against evolving cyber threats. However, to fully benefit from AI, businesses must approach its implementation thoughtfully. Training teams, adopting proactive security measures, prioritizing data privacy, and considering ethical implications are essential steps toward building a secure, AI-powered business environment (Davenport et al., 2018).

By investing in AI today, businesses position themselves to respond faster, detect threats earlier, and make better-informed security decisions. But alongside these advances, companies must remain vigilant about the potential risks of AI misuse, ensuring that transparency, responsibility, and ethical standards guide their approach to future business security (Familoni, 2024).

8 CASE STUDIES AND REAL-WORLD APPLICATIONS

Artificial Intelligence (AI) has emerged as a powerful tool in the realm of cybersecurity, offering innovative solutions to detect and mitigate threats. This report explores real-world applications of AI-powered threat detection in business environments, focusing on case studies from the financial and retail sectors. Additionally, it compares AI-driven approaches to traditional threat detection methods, providing actionable insights for businesses seeking to enhance their security posture (Zarate, 2015).

8.1 Case Study 1: AI-Powered Threat Detection in a Financial Institution

In today's digital landscape, financial institutions are primary targets for cybercriminals, given the sensitive data and large sums of money they handle. One of the most successful implementations of AI in cybersecurity comes from JP Morgan Chase, a leading global bank that recognized the need to reinforce its defenses against evolving cyber threats. By integrating AI-driven threat detec- tion into its security architecture, JP Morgan Chase has been able to main- tain robust cybersecurity, protecting its vast network of clients and operations (Shields, 2015).

The Challenge

JP Morgan Chase, like many other financial institutions, faced a mounting number of cyber threats, ranging from sophisticated phishing schemes to insider threats. Traditional cybersecurity methods, while effective to a certain extent, were limited in their ability to keep up with increasingly complex attacks. As cybercriminals started using more advanced techniques, the bank needed a more dynamic and adaptive system capable of not only identifying known threats but also predicting and mitigating emerging risks (Zarate, 2015) (Shields, 2015).

AI-Driven Solution

To address these challenges, JP Morgan Chase implemented an AI-powered threat detection system that continuously monitors network traffic and analyzes user behavior across its global operations. The system employs several key tech- nologies to ensure comprehensive and efficient threat detection:

1. Machine Learning Algorithms: At the heart of JP Morgan Chase's AI sys- tem are machine learning (ML) algorithms. These algorithms are trained to analyze massive datasets, identifying patterns and anomalies that indicate potential cyber-attacks. For example, the AI can recognize abnormal net- work traffic patterns that deviate from typical usage, which may indicate a data breach or malware infiltration. Through continuous learning, the sys- tem evolves, improving its detection capabilities as it processes more data over time (Anandharaj, 2024).

Real-World Impact:

In one instance, JP Morgan's AI system detected unusual activity in an employ-ee's login patterns. The system flagged the behavior as suspicious, given the user's sudden access to sensitive systems outside of their typical role. Upon investigation, it was discovered that the employee's credentials had been compromised. By detecting this anomaly early, the bank was able to prevent a significant data breach before any damage occurred (Aslam, 2024).

2. Natural Language Processing (NLP): Phishing attacks and social engineer- ing schemes often use email and messaging platforms as entry points for malicious activity. JP Morgan Chase's system incorporates NLP to analyze incoming emails and text messages for signs of fraud, such as suspicious language pat- terns, grammatical inconsistencies, or unusual sender informa- tion. NLP allows the system to detect phishing emails in real time, before they reach employees' inboxes, greatly reducing the bank's exposure to such attacks (Brennan, 2023).

Real-World Impact:

In 2020, a targeted spear-phishing campaign was detected by the bank's AI sys-tem. The email appeared to be from a high-ranking executive, requesting sensitive financial information. Thanks to NLP, the AI system identified red flags in the email's structure and language, and the email was quarantined before any employee could respond, preventing a potentially catastrophic breach.

3. Behavioral Analytics: A key aspect of AI in cybersecurity is its ability to track and analyze user behavior over time. By building a profile of each user's normal activity, the system can quickly identify deviations that might indicate compromised accounts, insider threats, or unauthorized access. Be- havioral analytics is particularly valuable in financial institutions, where unauthorized access to even a single system can result in significant financial and reputational damage.

Real-World Impact:

The system's behavioral analytics capability came into play when it detected an employee logging into the system from an unusual geographic location at an odd hour. Upon further investigation, it was discovered that the em- ployee's credentials had been stolen by a cybercriminal attempting to siphon off funds. The AI system automatically flagged the login as suspicious, and the account was locked before the attacker could gain access to any critical data (Familoni, 2024).

Results:

Through the integration of AI-driven threat detection, JP Morgan Chase has experienced significant improvements in both the speed and accuracy of identifying cyber threats. The system's ability to continuously monitor and analyze vast amounts of data has allowed the bank to respond to threats in real-time, preventing breaches and minimizing the risk of financial loss.

(a) Enhanced Threat Detection: AI has enabled the bank to detect a wide range of cyber threats, from phishing to insider attacks, that might have gone unnoticed by traditional security measures. The system's ability to learn from each incident means that its threat detection capabilities are constantly improving, ensuring that it stays ahead of emerging threats (Familoni, 2024).

(b) Reduced Response Times: AI-powered automation has drastically re- duced the time it takes for the bank to respond to security incidents. Instead of relying on human analysts to sift through alerts and logs, the system automatically prior- itizes incidents based on severity, ensuring

that the most critical threats are addressed immediately (Anandharaj, 2024).

Real-World Impact: A coordinated cyberattack on the bank's infras- tructure was detected by the AI system, which flagged a sudden spike in network traffic as suspicious. The system identified the attack as a Dis- tributed Denial of Service (DDoS) attempt and triggered an automated response to block malicious traffic, preventing the attack from disrupting services or causing downtime.

(c) Proactive Threat Mitigation: Beyond simply responding to threats, AI has empowered JP Morgan Chase to take a proactive approach to cy- bersecurity. By identifying potential vulnerabilities in the system, the bank can address weaknesses before they are exploited by attackers. This proactive stance has led to fewer incidents and an overall stronger security posture (Zarate, 2015).

JP Morgan Chase's successful implementation of AI-powered threat detec- tion demonstrates the transformative potential of AI in cybersecurity. By leveraging ma- chine learning, natural language processing, and behavioral analytics, the bank has not only enhanced its ability to detect and prevent cyber threats but also streamlined its response times, ensuring that critical threats are addressed promptly.

This case study serves as a powerful example for other financial institutions looking to strengthen their cybersecurity defenses in an increasingly complex threat landscape. As cyber threats continue to evolve, AI will undoubtedly play an even more critical role in protecting businesses from malicious actors (Shields, 2015).

8.2 Case Study 2: AI in Retail Cybersecurity – Protecting Customers and Data

In today's digital age, the retail sector has become a prime target for cyberattacks due to the sheer volume of sensitive data, such as payment information, personal details, and transaction histories, that is collected from customers (Jun et al., 2021). To protect this valuable data and maintain customer trust, major retail- ers are in- creasingly turning to AI-powered cybersecurity solutions (Elbassuoni, 2023).

One such example is Amazon, a global online retailer known for its vast e- com- merce ecosystem and commitment to customer security. With millions of customers worldwide and billions of transactions annually, Amazon faces con- stant cyber threats, including fraudulent transactions, phishing attacks, and po- tential data breaches. The company has implemented advanced AI-based threat detection systems to monitor and protect its platforms from cyberattacks in real-time (Tschider, 2018).

AI-Driven Threat Detection:

How It Works

Amazon's AI-powered cybersecurity system is built on machine learning (ML) algorithms designed to analyze vast amounts of data related to customer behavior, transaction patterns, and network activity. These algorithms learn what constitutes normal behavior across the platform and are able to flag any anomalies that could indicate fraud or a security breach.

For example, if a customer's purchasing pattern suddenly changes, such as making a large purchase from an unfamiliar location or using a device that hasn't been used before, the AI system immediately flags the transaction for review. This early detection mechanism ensures that potential fraudulent activities are stopped before they cause significant damage.

Moreover, Amazon leverages AI for analyzing and blocking phishing attacks, which are often designed to trick customers into sharing sensitive information. AI-powered systems are capable of spotting subtle differences in emails and websites that may not be apparent to a human eye, blocking these threats before they reach the customer (Cao, 2021).

Key Benefits of AI-Powered Cybersecurity in Retail:

1. Real-time Fraud Detection and Prevention: In a fast-paced environment like e-commerce, traditional fraud detection methods, which rely heavily on hu- man intervention, are often too slow. By the time suspicious activity is man- ually flagged, significant financial losses could occur, and customers' data may already be compromised.

    Amazon's AI systems, on the other hand, are capable of real-time fraud detection. The moment unusual activity is detected, the system takes imme- diate action to block the transaction or alert a security analyst for further investigation. This proactive approach not only prevents financial losses but also ensures that customers' sensitive data remains protected. For example, during high-traffic events like Amazon Prime Day or Black Friday sales, AI systems help safeguard millions of transactions, providing customers with a secure shopping experience.

2. Enhanced Customer Experience: Retailers like Amazon understand that cy- bersecurity isn't just about protecting data—it's also about maintaining cus- tomer trust and enhancing the overall shopping experience. AI-powered sys- tems

ensure that customers can shop with peace of mind, knowing that their data is secure (Singh, 2021).

By preventing fraudulent transactions and reducing the likelihood of account takeovers or identity theft, AI directly contributes to a smoother and more secure customer journey. This level of protection builds trust and loyalty among customers, who are more likely to return to a platform that they know is secure. As a result, companies like Amazon benefit from both improved security and increased customer retention (Tu¨regu¨n, 2019).

3. Increased Efficiency Through Automation: One of the key advantages of AI- driven cybersecurity is the ability to automate routine security tasks. For a company like Amazon, manually monitoring millions of transactions and network events is not feasible. Instead, AI takes over the routine monitor-

ing, flagging any suspicious behavior for further investigation (Jackson & Orebaugh, 2018).

This automation not only improves the accuracy of threat detection but also frees up human cybersecurity experts to focus on more complex and strategic tasks, such as investigating sophisticated cyber threats, designing new security protocols, or responding to incidents (Stanciu & Rˆındașu, 2021). In the case of Amazon, this efficient use of human resources ensures that the company remains agile and well-prepared to tackle emerging threats in the cybersecurity landscape (Rawindaran, Jayal, & Prakash, 2021).

Impact of AI on Amazon's Cybersecurity Strategy:

Through its deployment of AI-powered threat detection systems, Amazon has successfully built a robust cybersecurity strategy that allows it to stay ahead of potential threats. In an industry where speed, accuracy, and trust are paramount, Amazon has been able to reduce financial losses associated with fraud while enhancing the overall customer experience (Rawindaran et al., 2021).

In addition, Amazon's approach has set a standard for other retailers, demonstrating that adopting AI in cybersecurity is not only effective but necessary in the modern digital landscape. The company's use of AI has not only minimized data breaches but also significantly reduced the operational costs associated with fraud detection and prevention (Stanciu & Rˆındașu, 2021).

The case of Amazon illustrates the powerful role AI can play in retail cybersecurity. By utilizing machine learning to detect fraud in real time, enhance the customer experience, and automate routine security tasks, Amazon has been able to build a security infrastructure that keeps pace with the growing complexity of cyber threats.

As the retail sector continues to evolve, more companies are likely to follow in Amazon's footsteps, embracing AI-powered threat detection to safeguard both their businesses and their customers. The future of retail cybersecurity lies in this blend of technology and human expertise, where AI takes care of the routine while humans focus on innovation and strategy (Stanciu & Rˆında¸su, 2021).

8.3 Comparative Analysis: AI-Driven vs. Traditional Threat Detection

In today's rapidly evolving digital landscape, businesses face increasingly sophisticated cyber threats that traditional security measures struggle to manage. The rise of artificial intelligence (AI) has introduced a new dimension to cyber- security, particularly in threat detection, where AI-driven systems significantly outperform conventional methods. This chapter explores a comparative analysis of AI-powered threat detection against traditional systems, focusing on three critical aspects: enhanced accuracy, faster response times, and scalability.

8.3.1 Enhanced Accuracy: Identifying Hidden Patterns and Anoma- lies One of the most significant advantages of AI-driven threat detection lies in

its enhanced accuracy. Traditional threat detection systems, such as signature-based antivirus software and firewalls, rely heavily on predefined rules and known patterns of malicious activity (Himeur, Ghanem, Alsalemi, Bensaali, & Amira, 2021). While these methods can be effective for detecting known threats, they fall short when it comes to identifying novel or sophisticated attacks. For in- stance, zero-day exploits—attacks that target vulnerabilities unknown to devel- opers—can easily bypass conventional security measures because they do not fit any predefined signature (Dixit, Bhattacharya, Tanwar, & Gupta, 2022).

AI, on the other hand, leverages machine learning algorithms to analyze vast amounts of data in real time. It identifies subtle patterns and anomalies that would be missed by human analysts or traditional systems. By using techniques such as behavioral analysis, AI can detect unusual user activities, abnormal net- work traffic, or unexpected changes in system configurations that could indicate a cyberattack.

A notable example is Google's use of AI to enhance Gmail's spam detection system (Maouche, 2019). While traditional spam filters might rely on a list of blocked senders or specific keywords, Google's AI system uses machine learning to analyze billions of emails, recognizing complex patterns in phishing attempts or malware-laden messages. This AI-driven approach has improved Gmail's spam detection accuracy to over 99.9%, significantly reducing the risk of malicious emails reaching users.

8.3.2 Faster Response Times: Real-Time Detection and Mitigation

In many cases, the longer a threat goes undetected, the more damage it can cause. Traditional security systems often operate reactively, meaning they only respond to threats once they have already infiltrated the network. In contrast, AI-powered threat detection enables proactive defense mechanisms, detecting and mitigating potential threats in real-time, often before they can inflict signif- icant harm (Familoni, 2024).

AI systems can monitor network traffic 24/7 without fatigue or the need for breaks, allowing them to react to threats instantaneously. This continuous mon- itoring capability is crucial in an era where cyberattacks can occur at any time, often outside regular business hours. AI systems also use predictive analytics to forecast potential vulnerabilities based on historical data, allowing businesses to reinforce their defenses even before an attack happens (Maouche, 2019).

A real-world example of this advantage is IBM's Watson for Cyber Security, which uses AI to sift through millions of security events in real-time (Jain, 2021). Watson's ability to process vast amounts of unstructured data, such as blogs, research papers, and news articles, enables it to identify emerging threats and vulnerabilities much faster than traditional systems. It can correlate this infor- mation with internal security data to detect and neutralize threats before they escalate (S. Kumar, Gupta, Singh, & Singh, 2023).

Human analysts working with traditional tools may take hours, if not days, to process and interpret the same amount of data, by which time the damage could already be done. AI's real-time detection and mitigation capabilities thus

dramatically reduce the "dwell time" of cyber threats within a network, limiting their potential impact (S. Kumar et al., 2023).

8.3.3 Scalability: Handling Growing Threats in a Complex Environ- ment

As businesses expand and adopt digital transformation strategies, their attack sur- face grows exponentially. More endpoints, cloud-based services, and In- ternet of Things (IoT) devices create additional vulnerabilities that need to be monitored and protected. Traditional threat detection systems are often unable to scale effectively with this growth, as they require significant manual oversight and are limited by their rule-based architecture.

AI-driven systems, however, are inherently scalable. As businesses grow and data volumes increase, AI can continue to monitor and protect these expanding networks without significant changes in infrastructure. For example, an AI-based system that protects a small business with a few endpoints can be equally effec- tive in a large enterprise with thousands of devices. This scalability is especially beneficial for businesses operating in sectors with dynamic and complex envi- ronments, such as finance or healthcare, where the volume of sensitive data and potential attack vectors is constantly increasing (Aminizadeh et al., 2024).

Darktrace, a leading AI cybersecurity company that uses machine learning algorithms to protect networks of varying sizes. Its AI platform, the Enterprise Immune System, mimics the human immune system by learning what "normal" looks like within a network and detecting deviations from this baseline. Whether it's protecting a mid-sized company or a multinational corporation, Darktrace's AI can seamlessly adapt to the size and complexity of the environment, providing robust protection without the need for constant manual updates or adjustments (Qumer & Ikrama, 2022).

In contrast, traditional threat detection systems may require frequent up- dates and reconfigurations to stay effective as the business grows, leading to increased costs and complexity. AI's ability to scale with ease ensures that even as cyber threats evolve, businesses can maintain a strong defensive posture with- out overhauling their security infrastructure (Anandharaj, 2024).

Comparing AI-driven and traditional threat detection systems, the bene- fits of AI are clear. AI offers enhanced accuracy by identifying hidden patterns and anomalies, faster response times through real-time detection and mitiga- tion, and the scalability to handle the growing complexity of modern business environments. While traditional systems have served as a foundational layer of cybersecurity for decades, they struggle to keep pace with the sophistication and volume of today's cyber threats (Aminizadeh et al., 2024).

The integration of AI into cybersecurity is not just an improvement—it's a neces- sity for businesses aiming to protect themselves in a digital world where threats are becoming increasingly advanced and persistent. By leveraging AI- powered threat detection, businesses can stay one step ahead of attackers, se- curing their networks and data with greater efficiency and precision. However, AI-driven threat detection also presents challenges, such as the need for skilled

professionals to develop and manage AI systems, as well as the risk of bias in the underlying models (Bonfanti, 2022).

9 CONCLUSION

In conclusion, the integration of artificial intelligence (AI) into cybersecurity is no longer a mere enhancement but an essential evolution to counter the rapidly growing and increasingly sophisticated nature of cyber threats. This chapter has highlighted the significant roles that machine learning (ML), deep learning (DL), and natural language processing (NLP) play in enabling AI-powered systems to recognize and respond to emerging cyber risks more effectively than traditional methods. By adapting to new threats and reducing false positives, AI-driven systems offer a substantial advantage in keeping security infrastructures robust and resilient.

The chapter emphasizes that AI, while powerful, must be properly imple- mented to maximize its benefits. It is essential to train AI models with industry- specific data, ensure interoperability between systems, and continuously monitor and up- date the AI tools to keep pace with the evolving threat landscape. More- over, the importance of balancing AI with human expertise remains critical, as AI tools work best when complemented by human analysts who can interpret complex scenarios and make strategic decisions.

Ethical considerations, such as AI bias and privacy concerns, are vital chal- lenges that need addressing in AI-driven cybersecurity. As the chapter discusses, best practices and regulatory compliance must be considered to ensure the eth- ical deployment of AI in threat detection.

Looking ahead, the future of AI in cybersecurity appears promising, with ad- vancements predicted in autonomous AI systems and integrations with tech- nol- ogies like blockchain and quantum computing. As AI continues to evolve, its role in cybersecurity will undoubtedly become more critical, reshaping how we protect digital infrastructures in the years to come.

REFERENCES

Alt, R. (2022). Managing ai is managing complexity-an interview with rahul c. basole. *Electronic Markets*, 32(3), 1119–1125. DOI: 10.1007/s12525-022-00585-5 PMID: 36065397

Aminizadeh, S., Heidari, A., Dehghan, M., Toumaj, S., Rezaei, M., Navimipour, N. J., & Unal, M. (2024). Opportunities and challenges of artificial intelligence and distributed systems to improve the quality of healthcare service. *Artificial Intelligence in Medicine*, 149, 102779. DOI: 10.1016/j.artmed.2024.102779 PMID: 38462281

Anandharaj, N. (2024). Ai-powered cloud security: A study on the integration of artificial intelligence and machine learning for improved threat detection and prevention. [JRTCSE]. *JOURNAL OF RECENT TRENDS IN COMPUTER SCIENCE AND ENGINEERING*, 12(2), 21–30.

Ardichvili, A. (2022). The impact of artificial intelligence on expertise devel- opment: Implications for hrd. *Advances in Developing Human Resources*, 24(2), 78–98. DOI: 10.1177/15234223221077304

Arif, H., Kumar, A., Fahad, M., & Hussain, H. K. (2024). Future horizons: Ai- enhanced threat detection in cloud environments: Unveiling opportunities for research. *International Journal of Multidisciplinary Sciences and Arts*, 3(1), 242–251. DOI: 10.47709/ijmdsa.v2i2.3452

Arshad, H., Tayyab, M., Bilal, M., Akhtar, S., & Abdullahi, A. (2024). Trends and challenges in harnessing big data intelligence for health care transfor- mation. *Artificial Intelligence for Intelligent Systems*, 220–240.

Aslam, M. (2024). Ai and cybersecurity: an ever-evolving landscape. *Inter- national Journal of Advanced Engineering Technologies and Innovations, 1* (1), 52–71.

Aslan, O. ̈., Aktuˇg, S. S., Ozkan-Okay, M., Yilmaz, A. A., & Akin, E. (2023). A comprehensive review of cyber security vulnerabilities, threats, attacks, and solutions. *Electronics (Basel)*, 12(6), 1333. DOI: 10.3390/electronics12061333

Berente, N., Gu, B., Recker, J., & Santhanam, R. (2021). Managing artificial intelligence. *Management Information Systems Quarterly*, 45(3).

Bibi, I., Akhunzada, A., & Kumar, N. (2022). Deep ai-powered cyber threat analysis in iiot. *IEEE Internet of Things Journal*, 10(9), 7749–7760. DOI: 10.1109/JIOT.2022.3229722

Bonfanti, M. E. (2022). *Artificial intelligence and the offence-defence balance in cyber security. Cyber Security: Socio-Technological Uncertainty and Political Fragmentation*. Routledge.

Branch, T. (2019). Blackberry's acquisition of cylance inc.: An impact on cyber-security. *An Impact On Cyber-Security (July 30, 2019)*.

Brennan, L. (2023). Ai ethical compliance is undecidable. *Hastings Sci. & Tech. LJ*, 14, 311.

Butler, T., & O'Brien, L. (2019). Artificial intelligence for regulatory compliance: Are we there yet? *Journal of Financial Compliance*, 3(1), 44–59. DOI: 10.69554/TOCI6736

Camacho, N. G. (2024). The role of ai in cybersecurity: Addressing threats in the digital age. *Journal of Artificial Intelligence General science (JAIGS) ISSN: 3006-4023, 3* (1), 143–154.

Cao, L. (2021). Artificial intelligence in retail: Applications and value creation logics. *International Journal of Retail & Distribution Management*, 49(7), 958–976. DOI: 10.1108/IJRDM-09-2020-0350

Challen, R., Denny, J., Pitt, M., Gompels, L., Edwards, T., & Tsaneva-Atanasova, K. (2019). Artificial intelligence, bias and clinical safety. *BMJ Quality & Safety*, 28(3), 231–237. DOI: 10.1136/bmjqs-2018-008370 PMID: 30636200

Chawdhury, T. K. (2024). Beyond the falcon: A generative ai approach to robust endpoint security.

Chui, M., & Francisco, S. (2017). Artificial intelligence the next digital frontier. *McKinsey and Company Global Institute, 47* (3.6), 6–8.

Corea, F. (2017). *Artificial intelligence and exponential technologies: Business models evolution and new investment opportunities*. Springer.

Courtland, R. (2018). The bias detectives. *Nature*, 558(7710), 357–360. DOI: 10.1038/d41586-018-05469-3 PMID: 29925973

Dash, B., Ansari, M. F., Sharma, P., & Ali, A. (2022). Threats and opportunities with ai-based cyber security intrusion detection: A review. [IJSEA]. *International Journal of Software Engineering and Its Applications*, 13(5).

Daugherty, P. R., & Wilson, H. J. (2018). *Human+ machine: Reimagining work in the age of ai*. Harvard Business Press.

427

Davenport, T. H., & Ronanki, R.. (2018). Artificial intelligence for the real world. *Harvard Business Review*, 96(1), 108–116.

Deng, L., & Liu, Y. (2018). *Deep learning in natural language processing*. Springer. DOI: 10.1007/978-981-10-5209-5

Din, S. N. U., Muzammal, S. M., Bibi, R., Tayyab, M., Jhanjhi, N. Z., & Habib, M. (2024). Securing the internet of things in logistics: Challenges, solu- tions, and the role of machine learning in anomaly detection. In *Digital transformation for improved industry and supply chain performance* (pp. 133–165). IGI Global. DOI: 10.4018/979-8-3693-5375-2.ch007

Dixit, P., Bhattacharya, P., Tanwar, S., & Gupta, R. (2022). Anomaly detec- tion in autonomous electric vehicles using ai techniques: A comprehensive survey. *Expert Systems: International Journal of Knowledge Engineering and Neural Networks*, 39(5), e12754. DOI: 10.1111/exsy.12754

Elbassuoni, S. (2023). Fortifying retail resilience: Integrating advanced analytics, machine learning, and blockchain for enhanced cybersecurity.

Enholm, I. M., Papagiannidis, E., Mikalef, P., & Krogstie, J. (2022). Artificial in- telligence and business value: A literature review. *Information Systems Frontiers*, 24(5), 1709–1734. DOI: 10.1007/s10796-021-10186-w

Familoni, B. T. (2024). Cybersecurity challenges in the age of ai: Theoreti- cal ap- proaches and practical solutions. *Computer Science & IT Research Journal*, 5(3), 703–724. DOI: 10.51594/csitrj.v5i3.930

Feldstein, S. (2019). *The global expansion of ai surveillance* (Vol. 17) (No. 9). Carnegie Endowment for International Peace Washington, DC.

Ferrara, E. (2023). Fairness and bias in artificial intelligence: A brief survey of sources, impacts, and mitigation strategies. *Sci*, 6(1), 3. DOI: 10.3390/sci6010003

Fontes, C., Hohma, E., Corrigan, C. C., & Lütge, C. (2022). Ai-powered public surveillance systems: Why we (might) need them and how we want them. *Technology in Society*, 71, 102137. DOI: 10.1016/j.techsoc.2022.102137

Fountaine, T., McCarthy, B., & Saleh, T. (2019). Building the ai-powered organi- zation. *Harvard Business Review*, 97(4), 62–73.

Ghillani, D. (2022). Deep learning and artificial intelligence framework to im- prove the cyber security. *Authorea Preprints*.

Hameed, K., Barika, M., Garg, S., Amin, M. B., & Kang, B. (2022). A taxonomy study on securing blockchain-based industrial applications: An overview, application perspectives, requirements, attacks, countermea- sures, and open issues. *Journal of Industrial Information Integration*, 26, 100312. DOI: 10.1016/j.jii.2021.100312

Hameed, K., Garg, S., Amin, M. B., Kang, B., & Khan, A. (2022). A context- aware information-based clone node attack detection scheme in internet of things. *Journal of Network and Computer Applications*, 197, 103271. DOI: 10.1016/j.jnca.2021.103271

Hameed, K., Haseeb, J., Tayyab, M., Junaid, M., Maqsood, T. B., & Naqvi, M. H. (2017). *Secure provenance in wireless sensor networks-a survey of provenance schemes. In 2017 international conference on communication, computing and digital systems (c-code).*

Hameed, K., Khan, A., Ahmed, M., Reddy, A. G., & Rathore, M. M. (2018). Towards a formally verified zero watermarking scheme for data integrity in the internet of things based-wireless sensor networks. *Future Generation Computer Systems*, 82, 274–289. DOI: 10.1016/j.future.2017.12.009

Hameed, K., & Rahman, N. (2017). *Today's social network sites: An analysis of emerging security risks and their counter measures. In 2017 international conference on communication technologies (comtech).*

Himeur, Y., Ghanem, K., Alsalemi, A., Bensaali, F., & Amira, A. (2021). Arti- fi- cial intelligence based anomaly detection of energy consumption in build- ings: A review, current trends and new perspectives. *Applied Energy*, 287, 116601. DOI: 10.1016/j.apenergy.2021.116601

Hwang, E. J., Park, J., Hong, W., Lee, H.-J., Choi, H., Kim, H., Nam, J. G., Goo, J. M., Yoon, S. H., Lee, C. H., & Park, C. M. (2022). Artificial intelligence system for identification of false-negative interpretations in chest radiographs. *European Radiology*, 32(7), 4468–4478. DOI: 10.1007/s00330-022-08593-x PMID: 35195744

Jackson, C., & Orebaugh, A. (2018). A study of security and privacy issues associ- ated with the amazon echo. *International Journal of Internet of Things and Cyber-Assurance*, 1(1), 91–100. DOI: 10.1504/IJITCA.2018.090172

Jain, J. (2021). Artificial intelligence in the cyber security environment. *Artificial Intelligence and Data Mining Approaches in Security Frameworks*, 101– 117.

Jeffrey, N., Tan, Q., & Villar, J. R. (2023). A review of anomaly detection strategies to detect threats to cyber-physical systems. *Electronics (Basel)*, 12(15), 3283. DOI: 10.3390/electronics12153283

Jun, Y., Craig, A., Shafik, W., & Sharif, L. (2021). Artificial intelligence ap- plication in cybersecurity and cyberdefense. *Wireless Communications and Mobile Computing*, 2021(1), 3329581. DOI: 10.1155/2021/3329581

Katiyar, S. (2023). 8 cyber security using artificial intelligence. *Cyber Security Using Modern Technologies: Artificial Intelligence, Blockchain and Quan- tum Cryptography*, 111.

Kaur, R., Gabrijelčič, D., & Klobučar, T. (2023). Artificial intelligence for cy- bersecurity: Literature review and future research directions. *Information Fusion*, 97, 101804. DOI: 10.1016/j.inffus.2023.101804

Kaushik, K., Khan, A., Kumari, A., Sharma, I., & Dubey, R. (2024). Ethical considerations in ai-based cybersecurity. In *Next-generation cybersecurity: Ai, ml, and blockchain* (pp. 437–470). Springer. DOI: 10.1007/978-981-97-1249-6_19

Kelly, C. J., Karthikesalingam, A., Suleyman, M., Corrado, G., & King, D. (2019). Key challenges for delivering clinical impact with artificial intelli- gence. *BMC Medicine*, 17(1), 1–9. DOI: 10.1186/s12916-019-1426-2 PMID: 31665002

Khan, Z. F., & Alotaibi, S. R. (2020). Applications of artificial intelligence and big data analytics in m-health: A healthcare system perspective. *Journal of Healthcare Engineering*, 2020(1), 8894694. DOI: 10.1155/2020/8894694 PMID: 32952992

Kothandaraman, D., Prasad, S. S., & Sivasankar, P. (2023). Vulnerabilities detection in cybersecurity using deep learning–based information security and event manage- ment. In *Artificial intelligence and deep learning for computer network* (pp. 81–98). Chapman and Hall/CRC. DOI: 10.1201/9781003212249-5

Kumar, D., & Suthar, N. (2024). Ethical and legal challenges of ai in marketing: An exploration of solutions. *Journal of Information. Communication and Ethics in Society*, 22(1), 124–144. DOI: 10.1108/JICES-05-2023-0068

Kumar, S., Gupta, U., Singh, A. K., & Singh, A. K. (2023). Artificial intelligence: Revolutionizing cyber security in the digital era. *Journal of Computers. Mechanical and Management*, 2(3), 31–42.

Lauriola, I., Lavelli, A., & Aiolli, F. (2022). An introduction to deep learning in natural language processing: Models, techniques, and tools. *Neurocomputing*, 470, 443–456. DOI: 10.1016/j.neucom.2021.05.103

Lazić, L. (2019, January). Benefit from Ai in cybersecurity. In *The 11th Interna- tional Conference on Business Information Security (BISEC-2019)*, 18th October.

Lee, J., Kim, J., Kim, I., & Han, K. (2019). Cyber threat detection based on artificial neural networks using event profiles. *IEEE Access : Practical Innovations, Open Solutions*, 7, 165607–165626. DOI: 10.1109/ACCESS.2019.2953095

Lor'e, F., Basile, P., Appice, A., de Gemmis, M., Malerba, D., & Semeraro, G. (2023). An ai framework to support decisions on gdpr compliance. *Journal of Intelligent Information Systems*, 61(2), 541–568. DOI: 10.1007/s10844-023-00782-4

Macharia, V. M., Garg, V. K., & Kumar, D. (2023). A review of electric vehi- cle technology: Architectures, battery technology and its management sys- tem, relevant standards, application of artificial intelligence, cyber security, and interoperability challenges. *IET Electrical Systems in Transportation*, 13(2), e12083. DOI: 10.1049/els2.12083

Maddireddy, B. R., & Maddireddy, B. R. (2020). Proactive cyber defense: Utilizing ai for early threat detection and risk assessment. *International Journal of Advanced Engineering Technologies and Innovations*, 1(2), 64–83.

Maleh, Y., Shojafar, M., Alazab, M., & Romdhani, I. (2020). Blockchain for cyber-security and privacy: architectures, challenges, and applications.

Maouche, S. (2019). Google ai: Opportunities, risks, and ethical challeng- es. *Contemporary French and Francophone Studies*, 23(4), 447–455. DOI: 10.1080/17409292.2019.1705012

Markevych, M., & Dawson, M. (2023). A review of enhancing intrusion detection systems for cybersecurity using artificial intelligence (ai). In *International conference knowledge-based organization* (Vol. 29, pp. 30–37). DOI: 10.2478/kbo-2023-0072

Mughal, A. A. (2018). Artificial intelligence in information security: Exploring the advantages, challenges, and future directions. *Journal of Artificial Intelligence and Machine Learning in Management*, 2(1), 22–34.

Muzammal, S. M., Tayyab, M., Zahra, F., Jhanjhi, N., & Ashraf, H. (2024). Smart factories greener future: A synergy of industry 4.0 and sustain- ability. In *Digital transformation for improved industry and supply chain performance* (pp. 70–92). IGI Global. DOI: 10.4018/979-8-3693-5375-2.ch004

Nortje, M., & Grobbelaar, S. S. (2020). *A framework for the implementation of artificial intelligence in business enterprises: A readiness model. In 2020 ieee international conference on engineering, technology and innovation (ice/itmc).*

Ntoutsi, E., Fafalios, P., Gadiraju, U., Iosifidis, V., Nejdl, W., Vidal, M.-E., Ruggieri, S., Turini, F., Papadopoulos, S., Krasanakis, E., Kompatsiaris, I., Kinder-Kurlanda, K., Wagner, C., Karimi, F., Fernandez, M., Alani, H., Berendt, B., Kruegel, T., Heinze, C., & Staab, S. (2020). Bias in data-driven artificial intelligence systems—An introductory survey. *Wiley Interdisciplinary Reviews. Data Mining and Knowledge Discovery*, 10(3), e1356. DOI: 10.1002/widm.1356

Qamar, F., Kazmi, S. H. A., Ariffin, K. A. Z., Tayyab, M., & Nguyen, Q. N. (2024). Multi-antenna arrays based massive-mimo for b5g/6g: State-of- the-art, challenges and future research directions.

Qumer, S. M., & Ikrama, S. (2022). Poppy gustafsson: redefining cybersecurity through ai. *The Case for Women*, 1–38.

Rana, M. S., & Shuford, J. (2024). Ai in healthcare: Transforming patient care through predictive analytics and decision support systems. *Journal of Artificial Intelligence General Science (JAIGS) ISSN: 3006-4023, 1* (1).

Raso, F. A., Hilligoss, H., Krishnamurthy, V., Bavitz, C., & Kim, L. (2018). Artificial intelligence & human rights: Opportunities & risks. *Berkman Klein Center Research Publication*(2018-6).

Rawindaran, N., Jayal, A., & Prakash, E. (2021). Machine learning cyberse- curity adoption in small and medium enterprises in developed countries. *Computers*, 10(11), 150. DOI: 10.3390/computers10110150

Reshmi, T. (2021). Information security breaches due to ransomware attacks-a systematic literature review. *International Journal of Information Man- agement Data Insights, 1* (2), 100013.

Sambasivan, N., & Veeraraghavan, R. (2022). The deskilling of domain expertise in ai development. In *Proceedings of the 2022 chi conference on human factors in computing systems* (pp. 1–14). DOI: 10.1145/3491102.3517578

Sarker, I. H., Furhad, M. H., & Nowrozy, R. (2021). Ai-driven cybersecurity: An overview, security intelligence modeling and research directions. *SN Computer Science*, 2(3), 173. DOI: 10.1007/s42979-021-00557-0 PMID: 33778771

Schmitt, M. (2023). Securing the digital world: Protecting smart infrastructures and digital industries with artificial intelligence (ai)-enabled malware and intrusion de- tection. *Journal of Industrial Information Integration*, 36, 100520. DOI: 10.1016/j. jii.2023.100520

Sewak, M., Sahay, S. K., & Rathore, H. (2023). Deep reinforcement learning in the advanced cybersecurity threat detection and protection. *Information Systems Frontiers*, 25(2), 589–611.

Shafique, M. A., Malik, B. H., Mahmood, Y., Cheema, S. N., Hameed, K., & Tabassum, S. (2017). Determinants impacting the adoption of e- government information systems and suggesting cloud computing migra- tion framework. *International Journal of Advanced Computer Science and Applications*, 8(9).

Sharifani, K., & Amini, M. (2023). Machine learning and deep learning: A review of methods and applications. *World Information Technology and Engineering Journal*, 10(07), 3897–3904.

Shields, K. (2015). Cybersecurity: Recognizing the risk and protecting against attacks. *NC Banking Inst.*, 19, 345.

Shiohira, K. (2021). *Understanding the impact of artificial intelligence on skills development. education 2030*. UNESCO-UNEVOC International Centre for Technical and Vocational Education and Training.

Singh, R. (2021). A study of artificial intelligence and e-commerce ecosystem–a customer's perspective. *International Journal of Research in Engineering. Science and Management*, 4(2), 78–87.

Sinha, A. R., Singla, K., & Victor, T. M. M. (2023). Artificial intelligence and machine learning for cybersecurity applications and challenges. *Risk Detection and Cyber Security for the Success of Contemporary Computing*, 109–146.

Stanciu, V., & R^ındaˏsu, S.-M. (2021). Artificial intelligence in retail: Benefits and risks associated with mobile shopping applications. *Amfiteatru Economic*, 23(56), 46–64. DOI: 10.24818/EA/2021/56/46

Taddeo, M., McCutcheon, T., & Floridi, L. (2019). Trusting artificial intelligence in cybersecurity is a double-edged sword. *Nature Machine Intelligence*, 1(12), 557–560. DOI: 10.1038/s42256-019-0109-1

Tayyab, M., Marjani, M., Jhanjhi, N., Hashem, I. A. T., & Usmani, R. S. A. (2022). A watermark-based secure model for data security against security attacks for machine learning algorithms. *J. Eng. Sci. Technol. Special Issue on IAC2021*, 24–37.

Tayyab, M., Mumtaz, M., Jhanjhi, N. Z., & Muzammal, S. M. (2024). Industry 4.0: The digital revolution unleashing sustainable supply chains. In *Digital transformation for improved industry and supply chain performance* (pp. 54–69). IGI Global.

Tayyab, M., Mumtaz, M., Muzammal, S. M., & Jhanjhi, N. Z.. (2024). Swarm security: Tackling threats in the age of drone swarms. In *Cybersecurity issues and challenges in the drone industry* (pp. 324–342). IGI Global. DOI: 10.4018/979-8-3693-0774-8.ch013

Torfi, A., Shirvani, R. A., Keneshloo, Y., Tavaf, N., & Fox, E. A. (2020). Nat- ural language processing advancements by deep learning: A survey. *arXiv preprint arXiv:2003.01200.*

Tschider, C. A. (2018). Regulating the internet of things: Discrimination, privacy, and cybersecurity in the artificial intelligence age. *Denv. L. Rev.*, 96, 87.

Türegün, N. (2019). Impact of technology in financial reporting: The case of am- azon go. *Journal of Corporate Accounting & Finance*, 30(3), 90–95. DOI: 10.1002/jcaf.22394

Vegesna, V. V. (2023). Privacy-preserving techniques in ai-powered cyber se- curity: Challenges and opportunities. *International Journal of Machine Learning for Sustainable Development*, 5(4), 1–8.

von Garrel, J., & Jahn, C. (2023). Design framework for the implementation of ai-based (service) business models for small and medium-sized manufac- turing enterprises. *Journal of the Knowledge Economy*, 14(3), 3551–3569. DOI: 10.1007/s13132-022-01003-z

Voronov, S., Tang, S., Amert, T., & Anderson, J. H. (2021). *Ai meets real- time: Addressing real-world complexities in graph response-time analysis. In 2021 ieee real-time systems symposium (rtss).*

West, D. M. (2018). *The future of work: Robots, ai, and automation.* Brookings Institution Press.

Williams, R., & Yampolskiy, R. (2021). Understanding and avoiding ai failures: A practical guide. *Philosophies*, 6(3), 53. DOI: 10.3390/philosophies6030053

Wright, S. A., & Schultz, A. E. (2018). The rising tide of artificial intelligence and business automation: Developing an ethical framework. *Business Horizons*, 61(6), 823–832. DOI: 10.1016/j.bushor.2018.07.001

Yaseen, A. (2023). Ai-driven threat detection and response: A paradigm shift in cybersecurity. *International Journal of Information and Cybersecurity*, 7(12), 25–43.

Zafar, F., Khan, A., Suhail, S., Ahmed, I., Hameed, K., Khan, H. M., . . . Anjum, A. (2017). Trustworthy data: A survey, taxonomy and future trends of secure provenance schemes. *Journal of Network and Computer Applications, 94*, 50-68. Retrieved from https://www.sciencedirect.com/science/article/pii/S1084804517302229 doi: https://doi.org/https://doi.org/10.1016/j.jnca.2017.06.003

Zarate, J. C. (2015). *The cyber financial wars on the horizon.* Foundation for the Defense of Democracies.

Zulaikha, S., Mohamed, H., Kurniawati, M., Rusgianto, S., & Rusmita, S. A. (2020). Customer predictive analytics using artificial intelligence. *The Singapore Economic Review*, •••, 1–12. DOI: 10.1142/S0217590820480021

Chapter 19
Generative AI and Web Applications:
Addressing Security Issues and Challenges

Saira Khurram Arbab

Faculty of Engineering Science & Technology, Iqra University, Pakistan

Farzeen Rizwan

Taylor's University, Malaysia

ABSTRACT

The primary aim of this chapter is to focus on Generative AI and web-based applications. Further, we address the security issues and challenges. In today's digital era, web-based applications have become indispensable tools in web engineering. From social media platforms to online banking services, the ubiquity of web-based applications shapes nearly every aspect of our daily lives. As we navigate the ever-expanding digital landscape, understanding the importance of these applications in web engineering is essential for businesses, developers, and users alike. A notable trend in 2023 was the increasing emphasis on sustainability and green computing within web engineering. Businesses sought to develop eco-friendly web-based applications by optimizing energy consumption, reducing carbon footprints, and implementing environmentally conscious development practices. Despite their widespread adoption, the deployment of web-based applications is not without challenges. The study addresses key issues, including cybersecurity threats, compatibility concerns across diverse platforms, and the complexities of ensuring smooth integration with existing systems. Additionally, the abstract acknowledges that a crucial component of web-based applications in 2023 will be the incorporation of Artificial Intelligence (AI) models. Companies use AI deliberately to improve overall functionality, au-

DOI: 10.4018/979-8-3693-3703-5.ch019

tomate tasks, and improve user experiences. The study emphasizes how artificial intelligence (AI) may be used to address problems in fields like cybersecurity, where sophisticated algorithms help with improved threat identification and mitigation. Identifying and mitigating these challenges is critical for ensuring sustained success and functionality of web-based applications. In our view, the importance of web-based applications in web engineering is paramount. These applications serve as the backbone of digital transformation, empowering businesses to meet the demands of an increasingly interconnected world. Address the challenges identified, our opinion emphasizes the need for a proactive approach, incorporating robust cybersecurity measures, continuous innovation, and a commitment to adaptability. By leveraging the potential of web-based applications, businesses can not only meet current demands but also position themselves strategically for the future of web engineering.

INTRODUCTION

The emergence of GenAI in recent years has had a profound and wide-ranging effect on a number of research and application fields, including interaction and artifact design. Thanks to multi-modal AI generation models like Stable Diffusion, laypeople without academic experience in art and design may now easily produce high-quality digital paintings or sketches with merely text suggestions. Machine learning (ML) has made it possible to use data's potential to create more creative, efficient, and sustainable business operations(Bozorgi et al., 2024, Liu et al., 2023). Nevertheless, a lot of effective ML applications in practical settings fall short of the expectations. A sizable percentage of machine learning (ML) projects fail, and many ML proofs of concept never reach production. From a research perspective, this is not unexpected, as the ML community has focused more on developing ML models than on developing ML products that are ready for production or helping to coordinate the infrastructure and various parts of the resulting, often complex ML systems, such as the roles required to automate and operate an ML system in a real-world environment. For example, data scientists are still in charge of many industrial applications(Kalo and Amron, 2023, Törnqvist and Martinsson, 2023). This work intends to study how more ML proofs of concept may be operationalized and automated through the automation of manual ML processes in order to address these issues. Figure 1 Overview web application architecture.

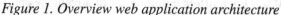

Figure 1. Overview web application architecture

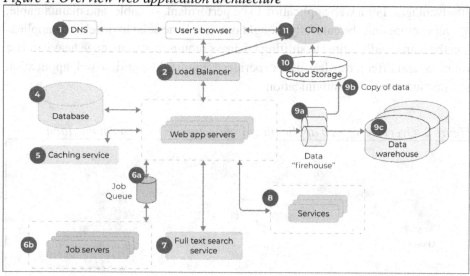

Securing web-based applications is critical to prevent unauthorized access, data breaches, and other cybersecurity threats. Input validation ensures that user data is valid and does not contain malicious code or scripts that can compromise the application's security. Authentication and authorization mechanisms ensure that only authorized users can access the application's resources and data. Strong password policies and multi-factor authentication should be implemented to prevent unauthorized access. Access control ensures that users have access only to the resources they need to perform their tasks and no more(Soehnchen et al., 2023, Sreejith and Sinimole, 2024, Thota et al., 2023). Indeed, technological progress often outpaces the rate at which regulations and guidelines are implemented in the software industry, where the rapid pace of technological change has led to a departure from conventional software development life cycle (SDLC) approaches. While both academia and industry have made strides to improve software quality, vulnerabilities continue to be a major issue. This is in part because it is hard to forecast all probable failure modes in today's complex software systems. However, it's partly because the software development process requires more focus on safety and quality. Software quality and security can both be enhanced by following established best practices in the software development industry. The use of secure coding guidelines and the idea of least privilege are two examples of these methods. The design plan for how various web application components—such as databases, applications, and middleware systems—interact and communicate with one another is called the web application architecture. There are various web application architectural types to take into account, such as serverless, three-tier, microservices, and monolithic(Abubakar et al., 2022, Sultana and Srinivas, 2021). Each offers a unique set of advantages and disadvantages. For a web application to be performant, scalable, and maintainable, its architecture must be carefully thought out. It is beneficial to develop an application that can rapidly adjust to shifting business requirements, manage heavy traffic volumes, and offer a flawless user experience. Figure 3 Overview web application architecture & users communication

Figure 2. Overview of web application architecture & user communication

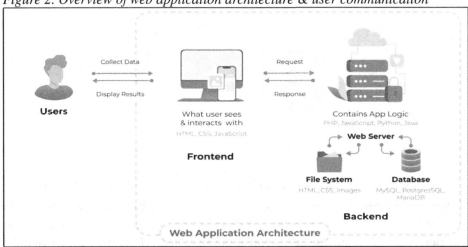

As the frequency and sophistication of cyberattacks rise, the study of how to spot software flaws has become crucial. Individuals, businesses, and even entire nations are vulnerable to the devastation that these strikes can wreak. As a result, researchers and businesses are investing more time and money into securing their software. The vast volume of code present in modern software systems is one of the primary obstacles in locating software vulnerabilities. Finding all the security flaws in a system is becoming more and more challenging as software becomes more complicated. Vulnerabilities in software are typically difficult to find because they are buried deep inside the code and require specialized tools and methods. Researchers and professionals in business employ many different approaches to uncover vulnerabilities to overcome these difficulties. Utilizing automated technologies that scan code for security flaws is one method. The software is analyzed using methods including fuzzing, symbolic execution, and static analysis. Another option is manual testing methods, such as pen testing and vulnerability scanning. These methods entail exploiting the software system to find flaws that could be used by attackers(Villarán and Beltrán, 2022, Liu et al., 2023). Code audits are another method used by researchers to look for security flaws in software. Source audits are typically effective in finding vulnerabilities that automated techniques may overlook, but they can be time-consuming and require a comprehensive grasp of the software source.

This chapter's contributions are in the following points:

- This chapter discussed the Generative AI
- This chapter discussed the Wed-based Applications
- This chapter discussed and addressed the issues and challenges
- This chapter discussed Security Concerns in Web Engineering
- This chapter provides Future work.

LITERATURE REVIEW

As a branch of science, machine learning studies how computers learn from data and develop into better machines over time. Its primary foundations are statistics and probability. When it comes to decision-making, it is more potent than conventional statistical approaches. Features are data that are obtained from a dataset and fed into the algorithm. A machine learning developer's job is to identify the subset of features that would be most useful in achieving the goal and improving the model's accuracy. To determine the feature subset for the algorithm, ongoing trials should be conducted.

These strategies entail deliberately looking for weaknesses that malevolent actors might target in order to exploit them. Software vulnerabilities are a major challenge for companies and developers alike. Upon discovery of a security flaw, the onus shifts to the software developers to develop a remedy(Shah et al., 2024b, Soehnchen et al., 2023, Sreejith and Sinimole, 2024). Patching is not always a simple process, though, as it can lead to new problems or incompatibility with other program components. Vulnerabilities are by their very nature more likely to be exploited by attackers the longer it takes to find and address them. Developers are under pressure to find and fix vulnerabilities as soon as possible to prevent them from being exploited. Numerous research projects have looked into automated threat identification for software security and related security concerns. Although the literature covers a wide variety of such topics, this review will focus on four major themes that repeatedly emerge throughout the literature reviewed secure software and vulnerabilities, attacks, solutions proposed by researchers to detect these attacks, openness, and exploration of machine learning algorithms approaches to handle the threats and improve vulnerabilities. Figure 4 Overview AI techniques

Figure 3. Overview AI techniques

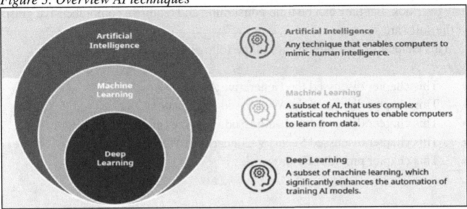

The classification of security issues in health information systems has been done using this taxonomy method. Based on the classification's findings, conclusions are reached. RAMeX was developed to bridge the gap in risk assessment and management processes for medium- and small-sized commercial enterprises dealing with medium-to-low-level risks. This study examines six different research methods(Ahmadi, 2023, Shah, 2024). In general, they treat planning as a distinct process that has no logical or direct bearing on the creation of IT systems. Enterprise information resources, which capture and characterise the enterprise, when integrated with planning, development, and management, will decrease the response time, and make it possible to conduct an economic analysis of information system investment. The creation of security policies and documents for each PBX will lessen but not entirely stop external and internal hacker attempts. However, the PBX staff must deal with the leading security threats, weaknesses, risks, and solutions by putting these policies and documents into place(Abubakar et al., 2022, Villarán and Beltrán, 2022). The author addresses the techniques available for locating security flaws in an open network and the evolving paradigm of network security. It goes on to describe the problem Sun had and the tools we made and used to solve it, with a focus on automating system security evaluation and compliance. Figure 4 Generative AI Scoping Matrix

Figure 4. Generative AI Scoping Matrix

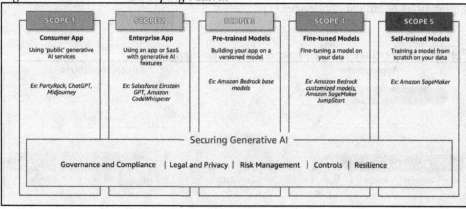

Despite implementing sufficient security measures across heterogeneous platforms, the network administrator faces additional security risks. The number of internet crimes is rising. Listening in on private talks is one of these offences. Physically harming information storage devices is another. This demonstrates the need for a strategy that is more suited for smaller businesses and those that need a quicker, easier, and less resource-intensive approach. This implies that an alternate approach to effective information technology (IT) risk assessment and management is required. This approach is focused on business from an IT perspective. The creation of a risk assessment technique allows for the intriguing deduction of some interesting conclusions about the organizational information security decision-making process. It is essential to have a solid grasp of the dynamics of the risks associated with automated information systems(Shah et al., 2024a, Olanrewaju et al., 2021, Li et al., 2021). The technique forces abnormal program states during the software's execution through the use of software defect injection. The program was created to assist businesses in achieving their goals, and it then tracks the effects these states have on the overall degree of safety inside the system. Software architecture establishes a connection between the design of a software and its intended use. There is ongoing demand on developers to make sure that their projects' architecture and design promote website security. Website developers work hard to make sure security is integrated from the ground up in order to achieve this goal. However, more than these design improvements are needed to compensate for the challenges caused by security thrashing. Additional solutions are required and developing a website safety strategy is the way to ensure everything is safe(Hoffman, 2024, Tella et al., 2020). When a website has this kind of failure, the developers are forced to consider what might have gone wrong throughout the website's design process and why it might have resulted in such a significant setback. The use of security design strategies is what brings resolution to design problems relating to security. Figure 5 Generative applications & ethical challenges.

Figure 5. Generative applications & ethical challenges

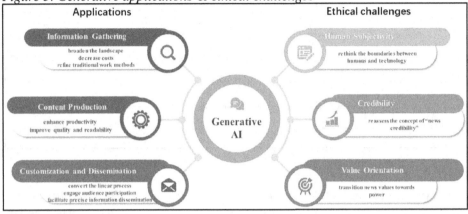

This could entail examining patterns and trends in vulnerability disclosures, evaluating the effects of new technologies and threat vectors, and determining where areas the present vulnerability detection and mitigation strategies fall short in. Enhancing research on vulnerability identification and mitigation can also be greatly aided by researcher collaboration and knowledge exchange(Durai et al., 2021, Shah et al., 2024e, Sharifonnasabi et al., 2021). This could entail working with interdisciplinary teams to tackle challenging issues from several perspectives, attending conferences and research networks, and making use of open-source tools and data sets. The ultimate objective of vulnerability identification and mitigation research is to fortify systems and networks against malevolent attacks and data breaches while also enhancing their security and resilience. Researchers can get a long way toward this aim by concentrating on high-impact research challenges and working well together. We go over the many techniques—including manual analysis and more conventional approaches—that are employed to find security flaws in the methodology section. Under the title "detection," the study that focuses on vulnerability detection performance and the kinds of vulnerabilities discovered is covered. The primary subjects covered in the features section are overfitting and the utilization of conventional features(Garg and Baliyan, 2021, Petcu et al., 2023, Srinivasan et al., 2021). In the meantime, the section on code goes into detail about the different levels of code complexity and its significance in software development.

Overview Generative AI and Web-based Applications

Artificial intelligence (AI) is becoming more and more common these days. Though it is still in its early stages, a range of industries and businesses are using it to alter corporate operations. in light of the ongoing developments in AI. Because of the infrastructure costs and complexity involved, AI-enabled e-commerce transactions are still limited to the largest enterprises.

Nevertheless, few customers are aware of AI-enabled transactions because of a lack of customer awareness. Numerous empirical studies have been conducted on AI's application in e-commerce. Diverse studies have been conducted on artificial intelligence, especially in relation to retailing(Shah et al., 2024f, Petcu et al., 2023). Because of this, drawing any meaningful inferences from the corpus of easily accessible literature proved to be difficult. This study conducted a thorough examination of the literature before narrowing its attention to AI research linked to e-commerce. Subsequently, it explains how each subset of AI works in e-commerce. To the best of our knowledge, this study is the first to demonstrate how a certain subset of AI can be used in e-commerce operations. Robotics, for example, is linked to lowering human intervention and automating e-commerce tasks. The research has identified the functioning of each subgroup of AI, and it may aid future researchers in determining which AI technology best suits their needs. Artificial intelligence (AI)-based technology has advanced and been more widely used in our daily lives thanks to the technological disruptions of the digital age. Figure 6 Overview of web applications.

Figure 6 Overview Web Applications

Numerous studies on AI and its subsets have been conducted in a variety of fields, including management, marketing, and e-commerce(Molina-Ríos and Pedreira-Souto, 2020, Jangjou and Sohrabi, 2022, Manzoor et al., 2022). None of the management studies that have been previously presented have addressed both issues. Furthermore, although these studies have covered the uses of AI in e-commerce, they haven't demonstrated the relationship between technology and e-commerce functioning. Chatbots and voice assistants were determined to be the most frequently utilized AI subsets in e-commerce, followed by automation, recommendation systems, and personalization. The pace at which AI-enabled transactions are currently being completed and reviewed also indicates that as soon as AI technology matures, its acceptance and use will increase. Artificial intelligence, big data, and the Internet of Things (IoT) have transformed the way e-commerce companies run. Scholars and Global practitioners are constantly searching for the most appropriate AI technologies to use in e-commerce. To expand the application of AI in e-commerce, this study compiled research on the subject and included several subsets of AI that are applicable in other fields.

Issued and Challenges

the expanding use of GenAI to produce complex and inventive graphics. Considering the crucial role that thorough evaluation plays in visualization design, it becomes necessary to apply similar evaluation standards to AI-generated graphics. Evaluation standards and protocols must be carefully modified in light of the special qualities and challenges presented by AI-driven visualization processes. While traditional measurements like efficiency and attractiveness remain important for evaluating AI-generated visuals, the introduction of AI techniques has raised new standards that must be taken into account. The evaluation criteria listed below are likely to be taken into account while evaluating different GenAI applications in visualization, depending on how the assessment metrics for GenAI migrate. Ensuring accuracy and genuineness in AI-generated images is critical, particularly when applying stylization techniques(Shah et al., 2024g, Jangjou and Sohrabi, 2022, Gouda et al., 2022). When employing strategies like semantic contextualization in visualization, the challenge is finding a balance between visual appeal and data integrity. This is significant because real-world objects often stray from the rigid outlines that characterize model-generated images, thereby jeopardizing the accuracy of the visual representation. Evaluating the robustness and consistency of AI-generated images in different environments is an essential step to ensure reliability and applicability in a variety of scenarios. This issue, referred to as the hallucination conundrum, can happen in LLM when fiction and fact are mixed together to provide non-factual knowledge. When doing VQA activities, for example, it is essential to analyze the hallucinations in the created content, especially in sectors where accuracy is important.

Discussion

Recent years have witnessed the birth of GenAI, which has had a significant and far-reaching impact on several research and application disciplines, including interaction and artifact design. With just text suggestions, laypeople lacking formal training in art and design can now effortlessly produce high-quality digital paintings or sketches, thanks to multi-modal AI generation models like Stable Diffusion. The incredible potential of discourse, reasoning, and knowledge embedding in the production of natural language is further demonstrated by large language models like GPT. The concept of artificial intelligence (AI) was first proposed about 60 years ago(Ahmed and Agunsoye, 2021, Mulahuwaish et al., 2020, Qasim et al., 2022). AI is "the art of creating machines that perform when carried out by humans, demand intelligence. Owing to the shift in lifestyles, one requires intelligent technology that automates tasks in addition to saving time. Artificial intelligence (AI), the Internet of Things (IoT), and big data are disrupting every aspect of life, from the home to the workplace and professional spheres. It has drastically changed the way we conduct day-to-day operations. The next generation of artificial intelligence is growing quickly in practically every industry, including banking, education, healthcare, and finance, which ultimately helps several businesses. It is believed that artificial intelligence will shape society in the future. Technology is effectively being introduced into all areas of the workplace(Shah et al., 2024d, Aydos et al., 2022). The primary driver behind all new technologies in the modern period is the shift towards Industry 4.0. Customers now have new experiences and options, thanks to e-commerce. It's more than just an adaptable marketplace for buying and selling. products and services, but it had gone above and beyond. Music and video streaming represented e-commerce functions that were expanded. E-commerce not only makes purchases convenient, but it also provides personalized entertainment choices. Artificial intelligence is incorporated into e-commerce to improve its offers. AI made it possible to follow clients more precisely, which improved customer satisfaction and produced more leads(Agrawal et al., 2020, Andrei, 2021). AI isn't limited to online retailers; it also benefits customers during their online buying experience. From choosing an item to completing the payment process, it guides the users through every stage of the procedure. In order to attain a high degree of accuracy and flexibility, artificial intelligence (AI) incorporates a wide range of techniques, including machine learning, robotics, expert systems, artificial neural networks, data mining, natural language processing, and computer vision.

With their shrinking size, integrated circuits are becoming less complex and more affordable. In an effort to reduce expenses and complexity, IC manufacture is being moved abroad, increasing the supply chain's vulnerability to hardware attacks. Attackers have an additional chance to include harmful circuits or programs in the design due to the diversity of the IC supply chain. The integrated circuit supply chain's external parties are denoted by a blue accent on the market, after-life cycle, and third-party suppliers(Padmaja et al., 2022, Veeraiah et al., 2022). Furthermore, although this assumption isn't always true, crucial control and communication functions rely on the security of the hardware platform on which they are implemented. There have been concerns, for instance, that backdoors may be used to manage nuclear power facilities, transportation networks, and weapon control systems. Examples of realistic hardware attacks are counterfeit gadgets, a security flaw in hotel keycards, and a security flaw in parking payment cards. Modern computing systems' open-source tools, such as commercial and open-source FPGA CAD tools, have created new avenues for remote attacks that don't require the target to be physically there. As such, a growing number of new security risks are targeting computing hardware. On the other hand, deliberate design modifications, unintended design faults, and system side effects could all contribute to hardware vulnerabilities(Shah et al., 2024c, Khan et al., 2021). They usually try to steal cryptographic operations, machine learning (ML) models, secure systems, and intellectual property. In the context of the Internet of Things (IoT), hardware security is advantageous. The definition of the Internet of Things (IoT) is the ability of smart computer devices to connect physical items over the Internet. Its influence has grown to include every aspect of modern life, including the crucial fields of energy, finance, e-healthcare, and defense applications, to name a few. These days, a wide range of organizations—including healthcare facilities, businesses, retail establishments, financial institutions, home appliances, and space science research facilities—are adopting smart platforms at an increasing rate. These platforms connect all electronic devices to swiftly gather, process, and transfer data(Yadav et al., 2022, Fatima et al., 2020). Furthermore, the global IoT market is anticipated to grow from 478.36 billion dollars in 2022 to 2,465.26 billion dollars in 2029, at a compound annual growth rate (CAGR) of 26.4% throughout the forecast period. The open structure of IoT nodes and the involvement of third parties make information leakage from them quite easy Numerous factors, such as the extensive interconnection of disparate and heterogeneous systems, the accessibility of sensitive data, the ease with which malicious software can be distributed, and the challenges associated with identifying and prosecuting computer crimes, make strong data security on the Web imperative. The two primary components that are necessary for a secure Web foundation are access control and communication security(Fredj et al., 2021, Kim et al., 2020, Shamrat et al., 2020). While communication security services guarantee the integrity and confidentiality of data transmitted via networks, access control services anticipate the unauthorized use of online resources. End users that utilize web browsers run the danger of several security and privacy issues when using the internet. Browser bugs may compromise the security of web clients, and consumer data may be collected and utilized for profiling, raising valid security concerns. Additional security dangers come from threats and executable resources, such as ActiveX components and Java applets(Tekerek, 2021, Sönmez and Kiliç, 2021). Most organization administrations are stored on business servers, which are normally protected by firewall innovations. Strong host-based security measures are required in addition to firewall protections since installing firewalls and configuring servers are challenging and error-prone tasks.

Insider attacks are becoming a greater concern for large corporate intranets, which highlights the need for updated or better get-to-control models to meet the varying security requirements of web-based services. Traditional access control methods, such as mandatory access control (MAC) and optional access control (DAC), may provide some flexibility and high-security assurance, but they have limitations(Hoang et al., 2022, Kusairi, 2020). A more comprehensive method that streamlines security organization and supports organizational security arrangements is provided by role-based access control (RBAC) models. Web-based applications and WFMSs particularly benefit from RBAC models, even though they must be encouraged to evolve in order to properly address complicated security requirements. To improve security in dynamic and scattered web scenarios, emerging techniques like agent-based security highlights, task-based access control (TBAC) models, and certificate-based approaches are also being investigated. Another crucial element is to promote participation and operation. (Abdulsalam and Hedabou, 2021, Tabrizchi and Kuchaki Rafsanjani, 2020)users believe a platform is secure, they are more likely to utilize it frequently. Advanced engagement situations frequently result from users' belief in the platform's security and ability to secure their data. When users feel confident in the security of the platform, they are more likely to embrace and use new features, which increases their pleasure and the overall value they derive from the service.

CONCLUSION AND FUTURE WORK

The application of the quickly evolving GenAI technology has enormous potential in the visualization space. GenAI has the amazing ability to model the transformation and design process by learning from real data, which can be useful for a range of visualization tasks such as data augmentation, stylization, visual mapping, and interaction. Numerous GenAI techniques have been applied, including sequence generation, tabular generation, spatial generation, and graph generation, because these occupations require a large number of data structures. However, given the unique characteristics of visualization jobs, there are task-specific challenges that require additional investigation. For every online application to be developed and successful, web application architecture is essential. It deals with the layout and configuration of the front-end client, back-end server, database, and network infrastructure, among other parts that make up the application. A well-designed web application architecture should consider aspects like maintainability, security, scalability, and performance, and it should be adaptable enough to take into account upgrades and modifications in the future. Secure user permission and login is one of the most crucial parts of any modern web application. As we navigate the ever-expanding digital landscape, understanding the importance of these applications in web engineering is essential for businesses, developers, and users alike.

REFERENCES

Abdulsalam, Y. S., & Hedabou, M. (2021). Security and privacy in cloud computing: Technical review. *Future Internet*, 14(1), 11. DOI: 10.3390/fi14010011

Abubakar, M., Jaroucheh, Z., Al Dubai, A., & Liu, X. (2022, May). A lightweight and user-centric two-factor authentication mechanism for iot based on blockchain and smart contract. In 2022 2nd International Conference of Smart Systems and Emerging Technologies (SMARTTECH) (pp. 91-96). IEEE.

Agrawal, A., Alenezi, M., Kumar, R., & Khan, R. A. (2020). A unified fuzzy-based symmetrical multi-criteria decision-making method for evaluating sustainable-security of web applications. *Symmetry*, 12(3), 448. DOI: 10.3390/sym12030448

Ahmadi, S. (2023). Next Generation AI-Based Firewalls: A Comparative Study. [IJC]. *International Journal of Computer*, 49, 245–262.

Ahmed, A. A., & Agunsoye, G. (2021). A real-time network traffic classifier for online applications using machine learning. *Algorithms*, 14(8), 250. DOI: 10.3390/a14080250

Andrei, B. (2021). Threat modeling of cloud systems with ontological security pattern catalog. *International Journal of Open Information Technologies*, 9, 36–41.

Aydos, M., Aldan, Ç., Coşkun, E., & Soydan, A. (2022). Security testing of web applications: A systematic mapping of the literature. *Journal of King Saud University. Computer and Information Sciences*, 34(9), 6775–6792. DOI: 10.1016/j.jksuci.2021.09.018

Bozorgi, A., Jadidi, M. S., & Anderson, J. (2024). UPSS: a User-centric Private Storage System with its applications. arXiv preprint arXiv:2403.15884.

Durai, K. N., Subha, R., & Haldorai, A. (2021). A novel method to detect and prevent SQLIA using ontology to cloud web security. *Wireless Personal Communications*, 117(4), 2995–3014. DOI: 10.1007/s11277-020-07243-z

Fatima, S., Aslam, N. A., Tariq, I., & Ali, N. (2020, July). Home security and automation based on internet of things: A comprehensive review. [). IOP Publishing.]. *IOP Conference Series. Materials Science and Engineering*, 899(1), 012011.

Fredj, O. B., Cheikhrouhou, O., Krichen, M., Hamam, H., & Derhab, A. (2021). An OWASP top ten driven survey on web application protection methods. In Risks and Security of Internet and Systems: 15th International Conference, CRiSIS 2020, Paris, France, November 4–6, 2020, Revised Selected Papers 15 (pp. 235-252). Springer International Publishing.

Garg, S., & Baliyan, N. (2021). Comparative analysis of Android and iOS from security viewpoint. *Computer Science Review*, 40, 100372. DOI: 10.1016/j.cosrev.2021.100372

Gouda, W., Almurafeh, M., Humayun, M., & Jhanjhi, N. Z. (2022, February). Detection of COVID-19 based on chest X-rays using deep learning. In Healthcare (Vol. 10, No. 2, p. 343). MDPI.

Gouda, W., Almurafeh, M., Humayun, M., & Jhanjhi, N. Z. (2022, February). Detection of COVID-19 based on chest X-rays using deep learning. In Healthcare (Vol. 10, No. 2, p. 343). MDPI.

Hoffman, A. (2024). *Web application security*. O'Reilly Media, Inc.

Jangjou, M., & Sohrabi, M. K. (2022). A comprehensive survey on security challenges in different network layers in cloud computing. *Archives of Computational Methods in Engineering*, 29(6), 3587–3608. DOI: 10.1007/s11831-022-09708-9

Kalo, I., & Amron, M. T. (2023, December). Transforming Laundry Services: A User-Centric Approach to Streamlined Operations and Customer Satisfaction. In 2023 IEEE 8th International Conference on Recent Advances and Innovations in Engineering (ICRAIE) (pp. 1-5). IEEE.

Khan, A. A., Laghari, A. A., Awan, S., & Jumani, A. K. (2021). Fourth industrial revolution application: network forensics cloud security issues. Security Issues and Privacy Concerns in Industry 4.0 Applications, 15-33.

Kim, J., Kim, E., Yang, J., Jeong, J., Kim, H., Hyun, S., Yang, H., Oh, J., Kim, Y., Hares, S., & Dunbar, L. (2020). Ibcs: Intent-based cloud services for security applications. *IEEE Communications Magazine*, 58(4), 45–51. DOI: 10.1109/MCOM.001.1900476

Kusairi, S. (2020). A web-based formative feedback system development by utilizing isomorphic multiple choice items to support physics teaching and learning. *Journal of Technology and Science Education*, 10, 117–126. DOI: 10.3926/jotse.781

Li, J., Goh, W., Jhanjhi, N., Isa, F., & Balakrishnan, S. (2021). An empirical study on challenges faced by the elderly in care centres. *EAI Endorsed Transactions on Pervasive Health and Technology*, 7(28), 7. DOI: 10.4108/eai.11-6-2021.170231

Liu, B., Penaka, S. R., Lu, W., Feng, K., Rebbling, A., & Olofsson, T. (2023). Data-driven quantitative analysis of an integrated open digital ecosystems platform for user-centric energy retrofits: A case study in northern Sweden. *Technology in Society*, 75, 102347. DOI: 10.1016/j.techsoc.2023.102347

Manzoor, M. K., Latif, R. M. A., Haq, I., & Jhanjhi, N. (2022). An energy-efficient routing protocol via angle-based flooding zone in underwater wireless sensor networks. *International Journal of Intelligent Systems and Applications in Engineering*, 10, 116–123.

Molina-Ríos, J., & Pedreira-Souto, N. (2020). Comparison of development methodologies in web applications. *Information and Software Technology*, 119, 106238. DOI: 10.1016/j.infsof.2019.106238

Mulahuwaish, A., Gyorick, K., Ghafoor, K. Z., Maghdid, H. S., & Rawat, D. B. (2020). Efficient classification model of web news documents using machine learning algorithms for accurate information. *Computers & Security*, 98, 102006. DOI: 10.1016/j.cose.2020.102006

Olanrewaju, R. F., Khan, B. U. I., Morshidi, M. A., Anwar, F., & Kiah, M. L. B. M. (2021). A frictionless and secure user authentication in web-based premium applications. *IEEE Access : Practical Innovations, Open Solutions*, 9, 129240–129255. DOI: 10.1109/ACCESS.2021.3110310

Padmaja, M., Shitharth, S., Prasuna, K., Chaturvedi, A., Kshirsagar, P. R., & Vani, A. (2022). Grow of artificial intelligence to challenge security in IoT application. *Wireless Personal Communications*, 127(3), 1829–1845. DOI: 10.1007/s11277-021-08725-4

Petcu, A., Pahontu, B., Frunzete, M., & Stoichescu, D. A. (2023). A secure and decentralized authentication mechanism based on Web 3.0 and Ethereum blockchain technology. *Applied Sciences (Basel, Switzerland)*, 13(4), 2231. DOI: 10.3390/app13042231

Qasim, M., Mahmood, D., Bibi, A., Masud, M., Ahmed, G., Khan, S., Jhanjhi, N. Z., & Hussain, S. J. (2022). PCA-based advanced local octa-directional pattern (ALODP-PCA): A texture feature descriptor for image retrieval. *Electronics (Basel)*, 11(2), 202. DOI: 10.3390/electronics11020202

Shah, I. A. (2024). Drone Industry Security Issues and Challenges in the Context of IoD. Cybersecurity Issues and Challenges in the Drone Industry, 310-323.

Shah, I. A., Jhanjhi, N., & Ray, S. K. (2024a). *Artificial Intelligence Applications in the Context of the Security Framework for the Logistics Industry. Advances in Explainable AI Applications for Smart Cities.* IGI Global.

Shah, I. A., Jhanjhi, N. Z., & Brohi, S. N. (2024b). *Use of AI-Based Drones in Smart Cities. Cybersecurity Issues and Challenges in the Drone Industry.* IGI Global.

Shah, I. A., Jhanjhi, N. Z., & Rajper, S. (2024c). *Use of Deep Learning Applications for Drone Technology. Cybersecurity Issues and Challenges in the Drone Industry.* IGI Global. DOI: 10.4018/979-8-3693-0774-8

Shah, I. A., Jhanjhi, N. Z., & Ray, S. K. (2024d). *Enabling Explainable AI in Cybersecurity Solutions. Advances in Explainable AI Applications for Smart Cities.* IGI Global.

Shah, I. A., Jhanjhi, N. Z., & Ujjan, R. M. A. (2024e). *Drone Technology in the Context of the Internet of Things. Cybersecurity Issues and Challenges in the Drone Industry.* IGI Global.

Shah, I. A., Jhanjhi, N. Z., & Ujjan, R. M. A. (2024f). *Use of AI Applications for the Drone Industry. Cybersecurity Issues and Challenges in the Drone Industry.* IGI Global.

Shah, I. A., Laraib, A., Ashraf, H., & Hussain, F. (2024g). Drone Technology: Current Challenges and Opportunities. Cybersecurity Issues and Challenges in the Drone Industry, 343-361.

Shamrat, F., Asaduzzaman, M., Ghosh, P., Sultan, M. D., & Tasnim, Z. (2020). A web based application for agriculture:"Smart Farming System. *International Journal of Emerging Trends in Engineering Research*, ●●●, 8.

Sharifonnasabi, F., Jhanjhi, N., Shamshirband, S., & John, J. (2021). Bone age measurement using a hybrid HCNN-KNN model: a case study on dental panoramic images.

Soehnchen, C., Rietz, A., Weirauch, V., Meister, S., & Henningsen, M. (2023). Creating an intercultural user-Centric Design for a Digital Sexual Health Education App for Young women in Resource-Poor regions of Kenya: Qualitative self-extended double Diamond Model for requirements Engineering Analysis. *JMIR Formative Research*, 7, e50304. DOI: 10.2196/50304 PMID: 37921860

Sönmez, F. Ö., & Kiliç, B. G. (2021). Holistic web application security visualization for multi-project and multi-phase dynamic application security test results. *IEEE Access : Practical Innovations, Open Solutions*, 9, 25858–25884. DOI: 10.1109/ACCESS.2021.3057044

Sreejith, R., & Sinimole, K. (2024). User-centric evaluation of EHR software through NLP-driven investigation: Implications for product development and user experience. *Journal of Open Innovation*, 10(1), 100206. DOI: 10.1016/j.joitmc.2023.100206

Srinivasan, K., Garg, L., Chen, B.-Y., Alaboudi, A. A., Jhanjhi, N., Chang, C.-T., Prabadevi, B., & Deepa, N. (2021). Expert System for Stable Power Generation Prediction in Microbial Fuel Cell. *Intelligent Automation & Soft Computing*, ●●●, 30. DOI: 10.32604/iasc.2021.018380

Sultana, N. M., & Srinivas, K. Survey on centric data protection method for cloud storage application. *2021 International Conference on Computational Intelligence and Computing Applications (ICCICA)*, 2021. IEEE, 1-8. DOI: 10.1109/ICCI-CA52458.2021.9697235

Tabrizchi, H., & Kuchaki Rafsanjani, M. (2020). A survey on security challenges in cloud computing: Issues, threats, and solutions. *The Journal of Supercomputing*, 76(12), 9493–9532. DOI: 10.1007/s11227-020-03213-1

Tekerek, A. (2021). A novel architecture for web-based attack detection using convolutional neural network. *Computers & Security*, 100, 102096. DOI: 10.1016/j.cose.2020.102096

Tella, A., Ukwoma, S. C., & Kayode, A. I. (2020). A two models modification for determining cloud computing adoption for web-based services in academic libraries in Nigeria. *Journal of Academic Librarianship*, 46(6), 102255. DOI: 10.1016/j.acalib.2020.102255

Thota, C., Mavromoustakis, C. X., & Mastorakis, G. (2023). RDSF—Responsive Data-Sharing Framework for User-Centric Internet of Vehicles Assisted Healthcare Systems. *Multimedia Tools and Applications*, ●●●, 1–24. DOI: 10.1007/s11042-023-14387-0

Törnqvist, A., & Martinsson, H. (2023). A User-Centric Monitoring System to Enhance the Development of Web-Based Products: A User-Centric Monitoring System to Enhance the Development of Web-Based Products.

Veeraiah, V., Rajaboina, N. B., Rao, G. N., Ahamad, S., Gupta, A., & Suri, C. S. (2022, April). Securing online web application for IoT management. In 2022 2nd International Conference on Advance Computing and Innovative Technologies in Engineering (ICACITE) (pp. 1499-1504). IEEE.

Villarán, C., & Beltrán, M. (2022). User-centric privacy for identity federations based on a recommendation system. *Electronics (Basel)*, 11(8), 1238. DOI: 10.3390/electronics11081238

Yadav, U. S., Gupta, B. B., Peraković, D., Peñalvo, F. J. G., & Cvitić, I. (2022). Security and privacy of cloud-based online online social media: A survey. In *Sustainable management of manufacturing systems in industry 4.0* (pp. 213–236). Springer International Publishing.

Chapter 20
Generative AI With Natural Language Processing for the Web

Dina Darwish

Ahram Canadian University, Egypt

ABSTRACT

NLP converts human language to computer understandable language is known as Natural Language Processing (NLP), though various diversified models have suggested so far, yet the need for a generative predictive model which can optimize depending upon the nature of problem being addressed is still an area of research under work. It is possible to solve specific issues connected to reading text, hearing voice, interpreting it, measuring sentiment, and determining which sections are significant by using a generative model, which is a platform that can be used for a variety of different aspects of natural language processing. This chapter discusses the components of NLP, illustrates case study on using generative AI and NLP to detect human behavior, and datasets, and finally comes the conclusion.

1. INTRODUCTION

Generative Artificial Intelligence, often known as GenAI, is capable of producing audiovisual media and lengthy text output in response to user requests that are submitted. Many people have been taken aback by its potential, which has attracted stakeholders from a wide variety of fields and regions. Because of this, a large

DOI: 10.4018/979-8-3693-3703-5.ch020

number of individuals, ranging from academics to corporate leaders, are interested in investigating and utilizing generative AI solutions.

The term "Generative AI," which is an abbreviation for "Generative Artificial Intelligence," is a category of algorithms and models constructed by artificial intelligence that are intended to generate new, unique data that is similar to material that was created by humans. Generative artificial intelligence models, in contrast to standard AI systems, which rely on pre-programmed rules or patterns to carry out tasks, learn from large amounts of data that already exists and use this knowledge to create new content that has not been seen before. Deep learning techniques, such as recurrent neural networks (RNNs) and transformers, are frequently used to build these models. These techniques enable these models to recognize intricate patterns and correlations within the data. The most notable application of generative artificial intelligence is text, but it may also be applied to other sorts of data such as photos, movies, and music.

Generative artificial intelligence models are able to comprehend and produce language that is reminiscent of human writing when applied to Natural Language Processing (NLP). The creation of transformer-based designs, such as OpenAI's GPT (Generative Pre-trained Transformer) series, is one of the most significant achievements in this field. These models have been pre-trained on vast libraries of text data, which enables them to generate text passages that are coherent and contextually relevant, answer questions, create poetry, translate languages, and do a wide variety of other tasks linked to language.

An extensive variety of applications can be found for generative artificial intelligence, such as the production of content, chatbots, virtual assistants, language translation, and creative arts. Artificial intelligence has made tremendous strides forward as a result of this development, which has made it possible for machines to demonstrate a degree of creativity and language comprehension that was previously believed to be exclusive to humans. The acronym NLP stands for "natural language processing."

Identification of meaning, intention, and emotion in textual information can be made easier through the use of natural language processing. It does this by utilizing computational linguistics, which is a branch of linguistics that conceptualizes human languages using rules and algorithms. By automating procedures for two-way communication, natural language processing has the potential to revolutionize user interactions with computer interfaces. Reputable Natural Language Processing (NLP) services also provide translations in a short amount of time, which enables firms to overcome language obstacles when expanding their business operations internationally. As an illustration, these technologies include techniques such as sentiment analysis and the evaluation of comments in many languages. These duties are essential for ensuring the efficacy of marketing and providing personalized support to customers. This chapter is composed of section 2 illustrating NLP components and applications, section 3 contains case study, and section 4 discusses datasets, and finally comes the conclusion.

2. NATURAL LANGUAGE PROCESSING

Natural Language Processing is a subfield of Artificial Intelligence that is employed for the purpose of analyzing, comprehending, and producing language that is typically spoken by people in order to communicate with computers and other intelligent machines. Fig. 1. demonstrates the connection between natural language processing (NLP) and artificial intelligence (AI) and machine learning (ML). One of the approaches of text mining that is utilized for text analysis is called natural language processing (NLP). This methodology implements a one-of-a-kind form of linguistic analysis that basically helps the machine read. To decipher the ambiguity that is present in human natural language, natural language processing (NLP) employs a wide range of approaches (Amirhosseini et al., 2018; Hsu, 2008; Patten & Jacobs, 1994).

Every day, vast amounts of data are generated all over the world, and the majority of this data is in the form of text. As a result, there is a requirement for intelligent systems that can process, analyze, and translate this data into the appropriate format. NLP has the potential to assist us in implementing specific tasks, such as Automated Speech and Text, in a more expedient and effective manner. Moreover, NLP can be utilized for the automation process. In this day and age, people expect everything to be automatic and they want to be able to carry out chores by simply using their voice. For this form of automation, speech recognition is used, which necessitates the use of natural language processing. As we can see in Figure 2, there are two primary components of NLP; Natural Language Understanding (NLU) and Natural Language Generation (NLG) which are two of the most important ones.

Figure 1. Relationship between NLP, AI and ML

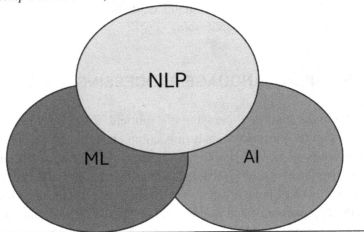

2.1. Understanding Natural Language

The most challenging aspect of natural language processing (NLP) that a smart machine or system must deal with is the ability to comprehend natural language. The very first thing that needs to be done is to transform the natural language into a language that can be understood by machines, sometimes known as binary language. Speech Recognition and Speech to Text systems both operate in this manner based on this principle. This is the first step in the NLU process. Immediately after the data is received in the text format, the natural language understanding (NLU) process begins with the intention of extracting the meaning from the text. Hidden Markov Models (HMMs) are the foundation upon which Maximum Speech Recognition Systems are built. In order to translate the speech into text, this model makes use of a variety of mathematical and statistical transformation approaches. Figure 2 illustrates Components of NLP.

Figure 2. Components of NLP

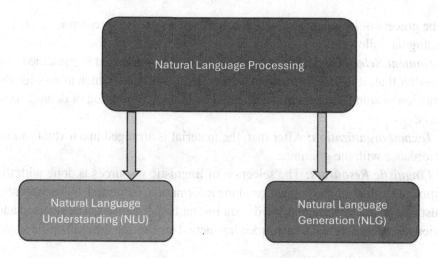

2.2. Natural language generation and The Natural Language understanding

The natural language understanding stage is followed by the Natural Language Generator (NLG), which is responsible for converting the artificial language that was obtained into text. Using text to voice, natural language generation (NLG) is also responsible for the task of converting this text into audible speech. The Natural Language Processing system is primarily responsible for locating the materials that are for the purpose of being turned into text. Analysis of the text included in

order to convert text into speech, a prosody model is utilized. This model is responsible for identifying breaks, duration, and pitch. After then, the system uses a speech data, which is a pre-recorded voice, to collect all of the recorded phonemes and combine them into a single cohesive conversational string.

2.2.1. Speaker and Generator

A speaker and a generator program are used to concentrate the application's goal into smooth phrases that are relevant to the state. This is done in order to generate text.

2.2.2. Components and level representation

The process of language production consists of a series of interconnected tasks, including the following:

- *Content Selection:* The information that has been gathered is combined into a set. After that, it is transformed into representational units, which allows for the elimination of some components of this unit and the incorporation of default components.

- *Textual organization:* After that, the material is arranged in a textual format in accordance with the grammar.

- *Linguistic Resources:* The selection of linguistic resources is done with the intention of facilitating the realization of the information. In the end, these resources are just comprised of particular words, idioms, and other phrases. The selected and codified resources are then transformed into actual text during the realization stage.

2.2.3. The application or the speaker

Its purpose is to provide support for the paradigm of the predicament. The speaker in this scenario is simply responsible for initiating the process; they do not take any part in the development of the language.

2.2.4. The Importance of Generative Artificial Intelligence and Natural Language Processing

1. Assistants for Industrial Virtualization

The clinical records of patients can be organized with the assistance of a chatbot that is available to physicians. A generative artificial intelligence co-worker can be beneficial to a wide variety of professionals, including engineers, lawyers, bankers, marketers, and many others. In spite of this, the dependability of generative artificial intelligence is frequently the consequence of qualitative training data. NLP technologies can therefore assist in "understanding" datasets and cleaning them up in order to train GenAI chatbots. In the future, chatbots will be able to exchange automated prompts with natural language processing systems, which will then analyze, translate, and categorize them before publishing them online for widespread distribution.

2. Publication of Media in Multiple Languages

Whenever a book that has been published needs to be translated, the publisher will recruit translators with extensive experience. However, they are required to do a comprehensive assessment of the book and determine the most effective means of communicating the authors' thoughts in a language other than English. It is also possible for this activity to involve explaining to a foreign audience the cultural and spoken traditions that are distinctive to a certain location without detracting from their immersion. A similar set of difficulties are faced by news sites, singers, voice performers, and creators of motion pictures. They can, thankfully, reduce the amount of effort spent on localizing content in a variety of languages with the assistance of GenAI and NLP.

3. Personalized and Tailored Aspects

Humans are quite skilled at predicting the feelings of other people, but machines do not have this intelligence. On the other hand, the majority of chatbots adhere to pre-configured speech patterns while interacting with customers that visit a company's website or eCommerce portal. The way they reply is formulaic, they have a robotic tone, and they do not show empathy for the anguish that clients are experiencing. Furthermore, by integrating generative artificial intelligence with these chatbots, businesses have the ability to personalize each and every conversation and enhance the Customer Experience.

4. Operations of Data That Are Accelerated

Unstructured data objects have been managed by Big Data through the application of advanced analytics. Nevertheless, analysts are required to manage the extract-load-transform (ETL) pipelines in order to safeguard the integrity of the data and eliminate bias in the insights that are produced. A number of data quality management issues, such as missing values and statistical anomalies, are addressed by them for resolution. By utilizing NLP technologies, they would be able to substitute user inputs of poor quality with alternatives of higher quality. Consequently, analysts are able to swiftly change database records that are inconsistent or empty.

3. CASE STUDIES

Although a number of different systems have been proposed up to this point for the purpose of tackling natural language processing applications, the requirement for a generative model that is capable of addressing a wide variety of NLP issues is still being worked on. The following section contains a case study on using NLP in detecting human behavior.

3.1. Human Behavior

Information Derivation Through Behavioral Signal Processing can be realized. Behavioral signal processing refers to certain behaviors and methods of reckoning that facilitate the measurement, analysis, and modelling of human behavioral signals. In addition to being administered and utilized by humans in a manner that is both unambiguous and indirect, these behavioral signals are also displayed mutually in overt and covert multimodal signals. The primary objective of the BSP is to provide human evaluation and judgement with information. Because of this, the outcomes of BSP are the subject of the field of behavioral informatics. There has been a discussion in this section on a case study that personifies a certain style of vocal communication and a particular purpose of behavioral analysis (Arunachalam et al., 2001; Black et al., 2008; Forbes-Riley & Litman, 2011; Narayanan & Georgiou, 2013; Pon-Barry & Shieber, 2011; Williams et al., 2018; Yildirim et al., 2005; Yildirim et al., 2011; Zhang et al., 2006). Educators make use of reckoning language processing devices in order to evaluate the components of developing learning capacities in their students. These tools not only offer promising approaches for assisting educators in the evaluation of these skills, but they also offer the possibility of introducing fresh computerized teaching support. Despite the fact that a large amount of work has been put into this subject to focus on certain significant constituents, such as mispronunciation, speech rate, and emotions, studies have shown that these constituents cannot, on their own, provide a comprehensive picture. The aspects of this problem that are the most fascinating and thought-provoking are the various causes that are the reason for the inconsistency outside of the perceptive of learning differences. These causes include irregularities in language and socioeconomic upbringing of the learner, as well as the knowledge levels and circumstances of the educator. Through the use of a technology known as behavioral signal processing, it is possible to compute objective characteristics based on the observable functioning of the activity. The BSP then makes use of these features in order to generate an analytical simulation that is capable of providing a commendable summary of the manner in which a group of educators would evaluate the data that has been presented. Behavioral Signal Processing, which is taken from the Technology Based Assessment of Language and Literacy (TBALL) scheme, is utilized in the aforementioned scenario in order to arrive at proficient judgements regarding the behavior of the students without any type of eager interference from the teacher. The children were given reading assignments that were appropriate for their ages through the use of a human-computer system. This was done in order to collect data that was both convincing and dependable in terms of the surroundings. The use of a variety of human evaluators to rate youngsters for the purpose of the study is one of the distinctive features of BSP. This was done in order to emulate professional processing. Using their audio recordings as a source for the evaluations, these ratings were determined based on the general reading ability of the individuals tested. It is possible to facilitate a computerized technique that can adapt to the learning intrusion through the use of Behavioral Signal Processing (Black & Narayanan, 2012; Black et al., 2011; D'Mello et al., 2007; Eskenazi, 2009; Graesser & D'Mello, 2011; Kazemzadeh et al., 2005; Litman & Forbes-Riley, 2004; Mostow et al., 2008; Price et al., 2009; Tepperman et al., 2011). This technique can be facilitated depending on the apparent status of the learner. As a result of the case study, it is possible to draw the conclusion that Behavioral Signal Processing is an essential component of NLP applications since it is a vital component for an NLP-based smart virtual assistant to reply in a more natural manner.

4. DATASETS

There is an assumption that forms the basis of standard natural language processing approaches, and that assumption is that language is governed by consistencies that are recorded as rules. These rules are required in order to acquire important data or information from the texts. Without a doubt, this assumption was incorrect due to the fact that machine learning techniques are used to acquire statistical data from a vast number of documents and, as a result, gain linguistic rules without explicitly documenting them. A dataset is a collection of requirements that are accompanied with an explanation that provides semantic information that is dependent on the task for which they are being used. When doing a categorization task, for instance, each requirement is glossed with its category. When performing ambiguity detection, on the other hand, glosses are used to identify uncertain phrases inside the text. An ML algorithm, in contrast to humans, which typically conduct interpretations, seeks to guess the expected interpretations. This can be done either on the basis of a portion of the glossed data, as in the paradigm of supervised learning, or without relying on the annotations that are already there, as in the paradigm of unsupervised learning. Natural Language applications have been utilizing Machine Learning for a variety of activities, including classification of requirements, identification of equivalent requirements, detection of ambiguity, and traceability. However, a conclusion that could be generalized was not produced from the majority of these practices. This is due to the fact that each study concentrated on a specific domain and utilized a limited set of requirements. In point of fact, a great number of datasets that encompass a variety of fields are not accessible to the general public, and researchers are forced to work with a limited amount of resources. Because of the many terminologies and methods that are used in different domains, as well as the lack of a common discipline, generalization is an important issue because it is possible that a technique will not perform effectively in other areas. The processing of natural language through four-dimensional vision is a key process that ensures the successful implementation of natural language processing algorithms. As a result, it is an essential component of natural language processing algorithms.

5. CONCLUSION

The term "natural language processing" refers to the process of converting natural language into language that can be understood by machines. The goal of designing a system that is capable of converting natural language into machine language may appear to be a straightforward endeavor; yet, in reality, it is a significantly more challenging endeavor. Given that there are hundreds of languages spoken all over the world, the process of designing a system that can transform natural language into machine language requires a significant amount of knowledge regarding the grammatical rules that are specific to each language. The problem of ambiguity is another issue that contributes to the difficulty of natural language processing. Generative artificial intelligence plays a significant part in the improvement of Natural Language Processing models by providing intricate cues that are analogous to innovative human feedback. However, in order to prevent harmful user prompts and decrease the development of content that is contentious, GenAI requires data quality verification that is based on natural language processing. Abstract mathematics, linguistics, named-entity recognition (NER), Deep Learning, and statistical models are all utilized by both of these technologies. The former makes use of them in order to construct what consumers seek, whilst the latter is primarily concerned with comprehending the significance of the material that is input. To this day, numerous solutions have been presented to solve a variety of challenges that are associated with language processing problems. For the majority of stakeholders to be successful in navigating this hyper-digital century, they will need to have expertise of GenAI and NLP.

REFERENCES

Amirhosseini, M. H., Kazemian, H. B., Ouazzane, K., & Chandler, C. (2018) Natural Language Processing approach to NLP Meta model automation. *International Joint Conference on Neural Networks (IJCNN)*. DOI: 10.1109/IJCNN.2018.8489609

Arunachalam, S., Gould, D., Andersen, E., Byrd, D., & Narayanan, S. (2001). Politeness and frustration language in child-machine interactions. *Seventh european conference on speech communication and technology*.

Black, M., Chang, J., & Narayanan, S. (2008) An empirical analysis of user uncertainty in problem-solving child-machine interactions. *Proc. Workshop Child Comput. Interaction*.

Black, M., & Narayanan, S. (2012). Improvements in predicting children's overall reading ability by modeling variability in evaluators' subjective judgments. *Proceedings of the IEEE International Conference on Acoustics, Speech, and Signal Processing*, 5069–5072. DOI: 10.1109/ICASSP.2012.6289060

Black, M., Tepperman, J., & Narayanan, S. (2011). Automatic prediction of children's reading ability for high-level literacy assessment. *IEEE Transactions on Audio, Speech, and Language Processing*, 19(4), 348–360. DOI: 10.1109/TASL.2010.2076389

D'Mello, S., Graesser, A., & Picard, R. (2007). Toward an affect-sensitive autotutor'". *IEEE Intelligent Systems*, 22(4), 53–61. DOI: 10.1109/MIS.2007.79

Eskenazi, M. (2009). An overview of spoken language technology for education. *Speech Communication*, 51(10), 832–844. DOI: 10.1016/j.specom.2009.04.005

Forbes-Riley, K., & Litman, D. (2011). Benefits and challenges of real-time uncertainty detection and adaptation in a spoken dialogue computer tutor. *Speech Communication*, 53(9), 1115–1136. DOI: 10.1016/j.specom.2011.02.006

Graesser, A., & D'Mello, S. (2011). "Theoretical perspectives on affect and deep learning", in New Perspectives Affect Learn. *Technol.*, 3, 11–21.

Hsu, B.-J. (2008) Generalized linear interpolation of language models. *IEEE Workshop on Automatic Speech Recognition & Understanding (ASRU)*.

Kazemzadeh, A., You, H., Iseli, M., Jones, B., Cui, X., Heritage, M., Price, P., Anderson, E., Narayanan, S., & Alwan, A. (2005) Tball data collection: The making of a young children's speech corpus. *Proc. 9th Eur. Conf. Speech Commun. Technol.* DOI: 10.21437/Interspeech.2005-462

Litman, D., & Forbes-Riley, K. (2004) Predicting student emotions in computer-human tutoring dialogues. Proc. *42nd Annu. Meeting Assoc. Comput. Linguist*, 351-358. DOI: 10.3115/1218955.1219000

Mostow, J., Aist, G., Huang, C., Junker, B., Kennedy, R., Lan, H., Latimer, D. T., O'Connor, R., Tassone, R., Tobin, B., & Wierman, A. (2008*).4-month evaluation of a learner-controlled reading tutor that listens. In The Path of Speech Technologies in Computer Assisted Language Learning: From Research Toward Practice* (pp. 201–219). Routledge.

Narayanan, S., & Georgiou, P. (2013). Behavioral Signal Processing: Deriving Human Behavioral Informatics. *Proceedings of the IEEE*, 101(5), 1203–1233. DOI: 10.1109/JPROC.2012.2236291 PMID: 24039277

Patten, T., & Jacobs, P. (1994). Natural-language processing. *IEEE Expert*, 9(1), 35. DOI: 10.1109/64.295134

Pon-Barry, H., & Shieber, S. M. (2011). Recognizing uncertainty in speech. *EURASIP Journal on Advances in Signal Processing*, 2011(1), 251753. DOI: 10.1155/2011/251753

Price, P., Tepperman, J., Iseli, M., Duong, T., Black, M., Wang, S., Boscardin, C., Heritage, M., David Pearson, S., Narayanan, S., & Alwan, A. (2009). Assessment of emerging reading skills in young native speakers and language learners. *Speech Communication*, 51(10), 968–984. DOI: 10.1016/j.specom.2009.05.001

Tepperman, J., Lee, S., Narayanan, S. S., & Alwan, A. (2011). A generative student model for scoring word reading skills. *IEEE Transactions on Audio, Speech, and Language Processing*, 19(2), 348–360. DOI: 10.1109/TASL.2010.2047812

Williams, E. C., Gopalan, N., Rhee, M., & Tellex, S. (2018) Learning to Parse Natural Language to Grounded Reward Functions with Weak Supervision. *IEEE International Conference on Robotics and Automation (ICRA)*. DOI: 10.1109/ICRA.2018.8460937

Yildirim, S., Lee, C., Lee, S., Potamianos, A., & Narayanan, S. (2005) Detecting politeness and frustration state of a child in a conversational computer game. *Proc. Eurospeech Conf.*, 2209–2212. DOI: 10.21437/Interspeech.2005-700

Yildirim, S., Narayanan, S., & Potamianos, A. (2011). Detecting emotional state of a child in a conversational computer game. *Computer Speech & Language*, 25(1), 29–44. DOI: 10.1016/j.csl.2009.12.004

Zhang, T., Hasegawa-Johnson, M., & Levinson, S. (2006). Cognitive state classification in a spoken tutorial dialogue system. *Speech Communication*, 48(6), 616–632. DOI: 10.1016/j.specom.2005.09.006

Chapter 21
Generative AI in Web Application Development:
Enhancing User Experience and Performance

Rachna Rana
https://orcid.org/0000-0003-0450-8699
Ludhiana Group of Colleges, Ludhiana, India

Pankaj Bhambri
https://orcid.org/0000-0003-4437-4103
Guru Nanak Dev Engineering College, Ludhiana, India

ABSTRACT

We lack knowledge of how User Experience and Performance practitioners, User Experience and Performance practitioner's teams, and businesses use Gen-AI and the issues they confront. We interviewed 24 User Experience and Performance practitioners from various firms and countries, all with different positions and levels of seniority. Our findings show that: 1 there is a major lack of Gen-AI corporate policy, with organizations informally advocating caution or delegating responsibility to individual workers; and 2 User Experience and Performance practitioners require group-wide Gen-AI exercises. User Experience and Performance practitioners characteristically use Gen-AI independently, esteeming inscription-based responsibilities, but letter boundaries for plan -attentive behavior such as wire framing and prototyping; 3) User Experience and Performance practitioners advocate for improved Gen-AI educating to improve their ability to make effectual stimulate and assess production brilliance.

DOI: 10.4018/979-8-3693-3703-5.ch021

INTRODUCTION

The internet, which has developed into a crucial part of our lives, enables a variety of online resources and services (Bhambri, 2013). Online matter proliferation has resulted in an finished provides of hopeless information for consumers. Customizing is essential to increasing customer pleasure, and website developers must use it to address the issue. Website designs are adapted to each user's specific demands and interests. Previously, customization was achieved manually or by using law-based schemes (Bhambri & Bedi, 2013). These solutions attain their restrictions when trying to control many datasets and cater to continuously modifying customer requirements.

Generative Adversarial Networks (GANs) belong to the realm of artificial intelligence (AI) where the focus is on enriching data with additional context, descriptions, and symbols. Using deep learning models, this form of AI can efficiently search extensive databases, customize content generation, and identify underlying patterns (2023 53rd Annual IEEE/IFIP International Conference on Dependable Systems and Networks, 2023; 2023 International Conference on Computer Science, Information Technology and Engineering, 2023).

At its core, GANs comprise two primary components: the generator and the discriminator, both crucial to the functioning of generative AI. The generator is responsible for crafting new content, while the discriminator plays a pivotal role in discerning between authentic and fabricated material. Notably, generative AI stands out from traditional machine learning systems as it excels in the production of human-like content.

Generative AI has a wide range of applications, spanning several fields. GANs have a lot to offer in terms of computer vision, from enhancing low-resolution photographs to creating entirely new scenes. Music production is one area where generative AI performs well since it generates original songs based on certain genres or artists. In natural language processing, GANs' ability to create relevant and coherent information is significant.

Similarly, ethical concerns arise when discussing generative AI. Deep fake films and counterfeit art Generative AI, a field with diverse applications, encompasses a wide range of possibilities. One of its key technologies, GANs, plays a pivotal role in computer vision by enhancing low-resolution images and offering the potential to create entirely novel visual landscapes. In the domain of music, generative AI shines by crafting original compositions tailored to specific genres or artist styles (Castro, Gámir, & Manuel, 2023; Chaudhary & Bali, 2021a). Moreover, the capacity of GANs to generate coherent and meaningful information is crucial in the realm of natural language processing.

However, as generative AI evolves, it brings forth ethical considerations. Instances like deep fake videos and counterfeit art underscore the rise of fake content, prompting concerns about the trustworthiness of digital information in the era of generative AI.

are examples of fraudulent content that raises concerns. With generative AI making progress, concerns about the dependability of digital information have arisen.

GENERATIVE AI FOR CUSTOMIZED CENTERED AROUND MATTER INTERNET ADDRESSES: CHALLENGES

Recognize Promotion Aims:

Generative AI, a subset of artificial intelligence, focuses on creating new content such as text, images, or videos by simulating human creativity. This is achieved through advanced models like generative adversarial networks (GANs) and variation autoencoders (VAEs), which have exhibited remarkable performance in various creative domains including writing, image generation, and music composition. The integration of Generative Artificial Intelligence (Gen-AI) into software development and cybersecurity holds the promise of revolutionizing these fields (Chaudhary & Bali, 2021b; DSN 2023 Tutorial Committee, 2023). Through the use of Gen-AI, organizations can expedite development processes, enhance security measures, and improve overall system resilience, potentially ushering in a new era of software advancement and protection.

This blog delves into the potential benefits of incorporating Generative AI into the realms of development, security, and operations. It sheds light on how this integration not only enhances current use cases but also catalyzes modernizing software development and cyber security practices.

Modified Net Growth

Generative AI models used in custom web development can be trained on large sets of user data, including browsing history, preferences, and past interactions. With this information, the models can offer specialized recommendations, like product suggestions, article concepts, and website designs, tailored to each user's profile. Generative AI empowers developers to create dynamic and flexible websites that can adjust to evolving user needs and preferences.

Repayment of Generative AI

The utilization of generative AI in custom web development offers numerous advantages for both clients and businesses. Repayment for the use of generative AI is reflected in the modified net growth it facilitates.

Increased Trade Results

Generative AI technology has the potential to significantly enhance the performance of content-based websites. By delivering personalized content, it can elevate user satisfaction and drive increased sales and revenue (Tandon & Bhambri, 2013). Furthermore, the implementation of generative AI algorithms enables organizations to gather and analyze user data, offering valuable insights for optimizing marketing strategies and refining products and services (Gans, 2024; Ghayoumi, 2023; Granville, 2024). However, to fully harness the potential of generative AI for creating personalized online content, it must navigate and overcome existing obstacles while seizing available opportunities.

Confidentiality and Principled anxiety

To ensure the effective operation of generative AI models, it is essential to collect and analyze customer data. Nevertheless, this necessity brings to the forefront profound concerns related to privacy, data security, and ethical considerations. Developers must place a high priority on safeguarding user data by implementing strong security measures and adhering to regulatory standards.

Prejudice and Justice

Generative artificial intelligence algorithms that are educated on historical data may pass along preconceptions and perpetuate injustice. When biases exist, tailored material may inadvertently exclude or reinforce preconceptions against specific groups (Bhambri, 2014). Developers may reduce prejudice and assure justice by thoroughly investigating the ethical implications of generative AI systems.

Scalability and Supply Necessities

When used in custom web development, generative AI models need a significant amount of computing power. Model deployment and training need significant computer and storage resources. To achieve an efficient and cost-effective deployment, developers must carefully assess resource requirements.

Difference between Generative AI and Traditional Approach

An alongside contrast of Generative AI and traditional approaches for website matter progress is shown in a tabular arrangement (Gunawan, Andriani, Purnomo, Sembiring, & Iriani, 2023; ICCoSITE 2023 Cover Page, 2023; Jefferies & Potter, 2024; Nessler, Cernak, Prandoni, & Mainar, 2021; Njuguna, 2023; Pandey, 2023).

Table 1. Differences Between Traditional and Generative AI Approaches

Aspects	Traditional Approach	Generative AI
Creating compelling content	Requires manual content generation or outsourcing.	Mechanically produces printed matter.
Implementing chatbots and customer support	Customer support representatives must be human. Efforts to manually summarize information.	Gives actual-period mechanical maintain.
Summarizing content effectively	Requires personality translators or third-party apparatus.	Mechanically reviews matter.
Offering high-quality translation services	Requires manual editing and refinement.	Mechanically translates matter.
Enhancing and curating content	Manual content curation efforts. Manual A/B test setup and analysis are required.	Recommends improvements, generates captions, etc.
Conducting A/B testing for optimization	Manual content moderation or basic filtering.	Helps in mechanical matter classification.
Moderating and expanding content	Manually creates or expands material.	Generates dissimilar versions for investigation.
Analyzing data for valuable insights.	Manual data analysis and reporting.	mechanicals matter restraint failing inappropriate matter.

The selection of Generative AI or a conservative method will be influenced by factors such as net aims, reserve accessibility, matter approach, and scalability needs. Mixtures can be the most profitable by combining the rewards in many ways.

Get better Mechanical Testing

Generative AI has the ability to greatly improve automated testing in development, security, and operations. AI-powered testing solutions may produce a huge number of test cases on their own, exposing edge circumstances and vulnerabilities that traditional testing methods may overlook. This leads to increased test coverage and more precise detection of security issues and performance bottlenecks.

Get better Code Study and Evaluation

Generative AI is useful for evaluating and reviewing code in development, security, and operations. AI models trained on large code repositories automatically detect poor code quality, security flaws, and best practice violations. This drastically minimizes the human labor necessary for code reviews while also ensuring higher-quality code.

Security patching automation

Generative AI will greatly speed up security patching in development, security, and operations by automating patch analysis and deployment. AI models will quicken the patching process by scanning codebases, finding vulnerabilities, and giving relevant remedies, reducing the window of exposure to possible threats significantly (Patil, 2017; Preprint Repository arXiv Achieves Milestone Million Uploads, 2014).

Detecting Anomalies Intelligently

Integrating generative AI with development, security, and operations paves the way for intelligent anomaly detection in real time. This allows AI models to continuously monitor system behavior, user activity, and network traffic, proactively alerting to unexpected patterns and potential security breaches. Ultimately, this integration enhances both proactive threat management and incident response capabilities.

Implementing a Secure AI Model

Generative AI is critical to guaranteeing the secure implementation of AI models. By thoroughly studying model designs and datasets, AI may reveal possible privacy and bias issues. This thorough examination can aid in detecting and correcting any underlying flaws, hence helping to the creation of equitable and privacy-conscious AI systems.

Simplifying Compliance Management

Generative AI, often known as artificial intelligence, can aid with compliance management throughout an organization's development, security, and operations stages. This technology is useful for comparing codebases to industry standards and regulatory frameworks, automating compliance testing, and creating detailed compliance reports. By handling these duties, AI considerably reduces the development teams' compliance load while ensuring strict adherence to security rules and regulations (Sridhar, Rani, Pareek, & Bhambri, 2024).

Automating Incident Response

Generative AI in development, security, and operations allows for the automation of incident response procedures. AI models play an important role in quickly discovering security vulnerabilities, assessing their severity, and taking appropriate action. This automated incident response strategy speeds up the remediation of security breaches while reducing their effect.

How will Generative AI revolutionize the fundamental aspects of development, security, and operations?

There are several techniques for generative AI to alter basic development, security, and operational components. For instance, it might be used for (Rasyad, Kongguasa, Onggususilo, Anderies, Kurniawan, & Gunawan, 2023; Role of Wireless Sensor Networks in Emerging Communication Technologies, 2016; Sanchez, 2022):

- Computerize safety experiments by important test cases for software devotion. This can assist to make certain that safety is not a postscript, but significantly an indispensable constituent of the expansion procedure.
- This plan policy generates fundamentally protected system. This can assist decrease the number of safety matters in software applications.
- Recognize safety faults in software agenda. This can help to stop safety breaks earlier than they happen.
- Safety computerization contains making schedule Safety behavior containing susceptibility appraisal, event answer, and fulfillment treatment. This can assist free up time for safekeeping professional to focal point on more significant and premeditated actions.
- Safety aptitude requires getting and calculating illegal information from various sources. This information may be made use of to perceive new jeopardy, look forward to future assaults, and enhance your company's overall safety posture.

Here are the refined guidelines for integrating Generative AI into Development, security, and operations:

- Please ensure that you select AI models that align with your specific development, security, and operational needs. GPT-4 and CodeBERT, which have been trained on extensive code repositories, are complementary for system psychoanalysis and appraisal. On the other hand, Natural Language Processing models are highly effective in threat intelligence (Bhambri & Khang, 2024).

- It is crucial to prioritize secure data access by implementing robust admittance manages and encryption methods for AI models and information. This is necessary to safeguard critical code and security information from unauthorized access and potential abuse.

- Furthermore, it is important to regularly update AI models with the latest intimidation and vulnerabilities. Unremitting education facilitates AI models to change to new confronts while transporting accurate consequences (Santhakumar, Takale, Tyagi, Anitha, Tiwari, & Dhanraj, 2024; Sinha & Kant, 2018).

- • Human engagement is essential for validating and contextualizing AI-powered procedures. Human supervision guarantees that AI-generated solutions are in line with business goals and needs. Element in AI-powered processes to provide validation and context. Human supervision guarantees that AI-generated solutions are in line with business goals and needs.

- When assessing AI conclusions, it is important to validate the results through traditional security testing and code reviews. It is essential to view AI as a tool that enhances existing processes rather than replacing them entirely.

Back-to-back use cases for generative AI in Development, security, and operations:

- Generative AI frameworks can dynamically analyze, as well as evaluate programs for resilience problems and best practices, improving quality and security.

- AI-powered threat intelligence systems improve cyber security by detecting new threats, anticipating attack patterns, and recommending proactive protection measures.

- AI-powered anomaly detection allows self-healing infrastructures by identifying and fixing security concerns in real time.

- Safer AI Model Distribution: AI models can identify biases and protection issues, leading to ethical and compliant deployment.

Actual As an instance: Secure Code Review using Generative AI

- A big financial services business sought to improve security standards and code quality. They used Generative AI in their Development, Security, and Operations pipelines to automate code review (Bhambri, Rani, & Pareek, 2024).
- The AI model assessed the code base for security concerns, coding flaws, and compliance with industry standards.
- Hand coding assessments supplemented AI-generated results. The development team analyzed the AI results and addressed any issues. This collaborative method lowered code review time and increased security vulnerability detection accuracy. The company's secure code review approach has matured into a comprehensive solution for software development security.
- As a consequence, their programs were more dependable, had fewer vulnerabilities, and provided better overall security.

Upgrading Traditional Use Cases:

- Generative AI plays a crucial role in enhancing vulnerability scanning by using its capability to create innovative attack routes and simulated exploits (Messaoud, Bouaafia, Bradai, Hajjaji, Mtibaa, & Atri, 2022).
- This approach leads to a more comprehensive investigation of system weaknesses, enabling organizations to proactively identify and address potential security threats.
- Similarly, AI-powered threat intelligence solutions leverage advanced algorithms to detect emerging threats, forecast attack trends, and provide proactive security measures.
- By analyzing vast amounts of data, these solutions enhance detection and response capabilities, empowering organizations to stay ahead of potential security risks.
- Furthermore, generative AI automates the process of code review, enabling organizations to uncover outdated dependencies, zero-day vulnerabilities, and other security issues within their software codebase (Sprung, Schweighofer, Anderle, Gürtler, & Uhl, 2023; Student Stress Prediction Using Machine Learning Algorithms, 2022).
- This automated approach streamlines the identification of potential security risks, allowing organizations to prioritize and address these vulnerabilities efficiently.

- Testing technologies powered by AI automate the testing of application security by adjusting to changing threats and broadening test coverage, which ultimately decreases the time and work needed for comprehensive testing.
- There is a positive outlook for the future of development, security, and operations, with generative AI playing a crucial part. As generative AI progresses, we anticipate the use of more innovative methods to enhance the security of software systems.

With generative AI, Development, security, and operations teams can:

- Automate security chores, allowing workers to concentrate on strategic and high- value scores.
- Reduce security breaches and data leaks by detecting and addressing issues presto.
- Ameliorate software security to reduce vulnerabilities (Zhao, Chen, & Yoon, 2023).

Abecedarian advantages

- Generative AI can automate homemade Development, security, and operations tasks, allowing security professionals to prioritize strategic and high-value work.
- Advanced delicacy Generative AI can identify security issues that traditional safety measures may miss.
- Generative AI can help reduce Development, security, and operations charges by automating security tasks. Generative AI- powered Development, security, and operations products.
- Google Cloud's Security Command Center use generative AI to identify security problems in pall surroundings.
- Check mar x law bashing uses generative AI to produce interactive security training modules (Xu, Padilla, Wang, & Li, 2021).
- Palo Alto Networks' Cortex XSOAR use generative AI to automate security tasks similar as vulnerability discovery and response. Deep Code uses generative AI to find security issues in law.
- Semgrep uses generative AI to descry security issues in law.
- Snyk uses generative AI to identify and address security problems in open source law.
- Perceptivity use generative AI to discover and respond to security pitfalls in real time.

- Deep Armor utilizes generative AI to cover software from contagions and other pitfalls (Wong, Ong, Gupta, Bali, & Chen, 2023).
- Red Canary uses generative AI to automate security tasks similar as vulnerability discovery.

CONCLUSION

Generative AI has the potential to revolutionize web development by offering a wide array of possibilities for creating customized and adaptable web pages. This technology allows developers to leverage AI capabilities to craft unique and individualized web experiences that cater to the specific needs and preferences of users. By tapping into the power of generative AI, individuals and businesses can achieve optimal outcomes in their web development endeavors.

Furthermore, the use of generative AI in content-based website building is expected to experience substantial growth. As AI continues to evolve, it paves the way for more personalized and engaging interactions on the web. However, the responsible and ethical deployment of AI requires us to address certain challenges, such as privacy, bias, and scalability. By tackling these issues, we can ensure that the integration of generative AI in web development is approached thoughtfully and ethically.

The introduction of Generative AI into Development, security, and operations is a significant step forward for software development and cybersecurity. Organizations may accelerate, secure, and highly resilient application development and deployment by increasing next-generation Development, security, and operations maturity. Generative AI's capacity to automate testing, improve code analysis, speed up security patching, and streamline incident response improves the entire cyber security posture. As existing use cases evolve, the combination of Generative AI and Development, security, and operations will lead the way for dramatic advances in software development and cyber security methods.

REFERENCES

Bhambri, P. (2013). Roadmaps to e-business: Translating e-business strategy into action (Vol. 1). Lap Lambert Academic Publishing. ISBN: 9783659347870.Bhambri, P. (2011). Data mining model for protein sequence alignment: Bioinformatics (Vol. 1). Lap Lambert Academic Publishing. ISBN: 9783844321531.

Bhambri, P. (2014). Effectiveness of performance management system in IT industries: Empirical approach. In Kumar, S., & Anjum, B. (Eds.), *Management of globalised business: Plethora of new opportunities* (pp. 114–121). Bharti Publications.

Bhambri, P., & Bedi, S. (2013). *Consumer's perception for the two wheelers: Analytical and comparative study with the inclusion of different locomotives* (Vol. 1). Lap Lambert Academic Publishing.

Bhambri, P., & Khang, A. (2024). Computational intelligence in manufacturing technologies. In Mehta, S., Gupta, S. K., Aljohani, A. A., & Khayyat, M. (Eds.), *Impact and potential of machine learning in the metaverse* (pp. 327–356). IGI Global., DOI: 10.4018/979-8-3693-5762-0.ch013

Bhambri, P., Rani, S., & Pareek, P. K. (2024). Financial innovations: Intelligent automation in finance and insurance sectors. In Darwish, D. (Ed.), *Generating entrepreneurial ideas with AI* (pp. 226–243)., DOI: 10.4018/979-8-3693-3354-9.ch012

Castro, D., Gámir, A., & Manuel, C. (2023). *Netflix' Madrid and the Madrid of Netflix*. Netflix., DOI: 10.4324/9781003432180-10

Chaudhary, K., & Bali, R. (2021). EASTER: Simplifying text recognition using only 1D convolutions. *Proceedings of the Canadian Conference on Artificial Intelligence*. https://doi.org/DOI: 10.21428/594757db.65eda33c

Chaudhary, K., & Bali, R. (2021). EASTER: Simplifying text recognition using only 1D convolutions. *Proceedings of the Canadian Conference on Artificial Intelligence*. https://doi.org/DOI: 10.21428/594757db.65eda33c

DSN 2023 tutorial committee. (2023). *2023 53rd Annual IEEE/IFIP International Conference on Dependable Systems and Networks - Supplemental Volume (DSN-S)*. https://doi.org/DOI: 10.1109/DSN-S58398.2023.00011

Gans, J. S. (2024). How will generative AI impact communication? https://doi.org/DOI: 10.3386/w32690

Ghayoumi, M. (2023). Generative adversarial networks (GANs) for images. *Generative Adversarial Networks in Practice*, 436-477. https://doi.org/DOI: 10.1201/9781003281344-14

Granville, V. (2024). Synthetic tabular data: Copulas vs enhanced GANs. *Synthetic Data and Generative AI*, 169-201. https://doi.org/DOI: 10.1016/B978-0-44-321857-6.00014-X

Gunawan, A., W., Purnomo, H. D., Sembiring, I., & Iriani, A. (2023). Evolutionary parameter optimization on neural network models for earthquake prediction. *2023 International Conference on Computer Science, Information Technology and Engineering (ICCoSITE)*. https://doi.org/DOI: 10.1109/ICCoSITE57641.2023.10127850

ICCoSITE 2023 cover page. (2023). *2023 International Conference on Computer Science, Information Technology and Engineering (ICCoSITE)*. https://doi.org/DOI: 10.1109/ICCoSITE57641.2023.10127843

2023 International Conference on computer science, information technology and engineering (ICCoSITE). (2023). https://doi.org/DOI: 10.1109/iccosite57641.2023

Jefferies, C., & Potter, L. (2024). Using generative AI to create virtual patients. https://doi.org/DOI: 10.26226/m.6639c0e2eb191bbe9d92661f

Messaoud, S., Bouaafia, S., Bradai, A., Ali Hajjaji, M., Mtibaa, A., & Atri, M. (2022). *Network slicing for industrial IoT and industrial wireless sensor network: Deep federated learning approach and its implementation challenges*. Emerging Trends in Wireless Sensor Networks., DOI: 10.5772/intechopen.102472

Nessler, N., Cernak, M., Prandoni, P., & Mainar, P. (2021). Non-intrusive speech quality assessment with transfer learning and subject-specific scaling. *Interspeech*, 2021, 2406–2410. Advance online publication. DOI: 10.21437/Interspeech.2021-1685

Njuguna, B. (2023). StockDistFit: Fit stock price distributions. *CRAN: Contributed Packages*. https://doi.org/DOI: 10.32614/CRAN.package.StockDistFit

Pandey, A. (2023). Generative AI in teaching and learning: Prompt engineering and towards digital equity. *INTEGRITY, OPEN SCIENCE AND ARTIFICIAL INTELLIGENCE IN ACADEMIA AND BEYOND: MEETING AT THE CROSSROADS*. https://doi.org/DOI: 10.30525/978-9934-26-397-2-34

Patil, D. (2017). Internet of things and security challenges in wireless sensor network. *Asian Journal of Engineering and Applied Technology*, 6(1), 14–18. DOI: 10.51983/ajeat-2017.6.1.816

(2014). Preprint repository arXiv achieves milestone million uploads. (2014). *Physics Today*, 2014(12), 6795. Advance online publication. DOI: 10.1063/pt.5.028530

Rasyad, F., Kongguasa, H. A., & Onggususilo, N. C., Anderies, Kurniawan, A., & Gunawan, A. A. (2023). A systematic literature review of generative adversarial network potential in AI artwork. *2023 International Conference on Computer Science, Information Technology and Engineering (ICCoSITE)*. https://doi.org/DOI: 10.1109/ICCoSITE57641.2023.10127706

Role of wireless sensor networks in emerging communication technologies: A review. (2016). *Emerging Communication Technologies Based on Wireless Sensor Networks*, 30-53. https://doi.org/DOI: 10.1201/b20085-8

Sanchez, P. (2022). Amazons3R: Get Amazon S3 data via the 'Windsor.ai' API. *CRAN: Contributed Packages*. https://doi.org/DOI: 10.32614/CRAN.package.amazons3R

Santhakumar, G., Takale, D. G., Tyagi, S., Anitha, R., Tiwari, M., & Dhanraj, J. A. (2024). Analysis of Multimodality fusion of medical image segmentation employing deep learning. *Human Cancer Diagnosis and Detection Using Exascale Computing*, 171-183. https://doi.org/DOI: 10.1002/9781394197705.ch11

Sinha, G., & Kant, K. S. (2018). Performance of modified auditory features for speech signal-an empirical study for non-intrusive speech quality assessment using signal based model. *2018 4th International Conference on Recent Advances in Information Technology (RAIT)*. https://doi.org/DOI: 10.1109/RAIT.2018.8388997

Sprung, G., Schweighofer, M., Anderle, F., Gürtler, F., & Uhl, M. (2023). Project desart: Using generative AI to create satellite images for an AR sand table. *ICERI Proceedings*. https://doi.org/DOI: 10.21125/iceri.2023.2044

Sridhar, V., Rani, S., Pareek, P. K., & Bhambri, P. (2024). Evolution of IoT in various application domains. In Sridhar, V., Rani, S., Pareek, P. K., Bhambri, P., & Elngar, A. A. (Eds.), *Blockchain for IoT systems: Concept, framework and applications* (1st ed., pp. 13–22). Chapman and Hall/CRC., DOI: 10.1201/9781003460367-2

Student stress prediction using machine learning algorithms and comprehensive analysis. (2022). *NeuroQuantology, 20*(14), 895-906. https://doi.org/DOI: 10.48047/nq.2022.20.14.NQ880126

Tandon, N., & Bhambri, P. (2013). *Novel approach for drug discovery using neural network back propagation algorithm: An optimum drug discovery approach* (Vol. 1). GRIN Publishers.

Wong, M., Ong, Y., Gupta, A., Bali, K. K., & Chen, C. (2023). Prompt evolution for generative AI: A classifier-guided approach. *2023 IEEE Conference on Artificial Intelligence (CAI)*. https://doi.org/DOI: 10.1109/CAI54212.2023.00105

Xu, H., Padilla, O., Wang, D., & Li, M. (2021). Changepoints: A collection of change-point detection methods. *CRAN: Contributed Packages*. https://doi.org/ DOI: 10.32614/CRAN.package.changepoints

Zhao, H., Chen, H., & Yoon, H. (2023). Enhancing text classification models with generative AI-aided data augmentation. *2023 IEEE International Conference On Artificial Intelligence Testing (AITest)*. https://doi.org/DOI: 10.1109/AIT-est58265.2023.00030

Compilation of References

(2014). Preprint repository arXiv achieves milestone million uploads. (2014). *Physics Today*, 2014(12), 6795. Advance online publication. DOI: 10.1063/pt.5.028530

. Analysis of stacked ensemble classification models in cervical cancer prediction using machine learning. (2023). *NeuroQuantology, 20*(19). https://doi.org/DOI: 10.48047/nq.2022.20.19.NQ99296

. Ang, L., & Seng, K. P. (2022). Visual sensor network technology and its applications. *Visual Information Processing in Wireless Sensor Networks*, 1-19. https://doi .org/DOI: 10.4018/978-1-61350-153-5.ch001

. Ziaee, A. A. (2011). A philosophical approach to artificial intelligence and Islamic values. *IIUM Engineering Journal, 12*(6).

2023 International Conference on computer science, information technology and engineering (ICCoSITE). (2023). https://doi.org/DOI: 10.1109/iccosite57641.2023

A Survey on ChatGPT: AI–Generated Contents, Challenges, and Solutions. (n.d.). Retrieved September 12, 2024, from https://ieeexplore.ieee.org/abstract/document/10221755

Aarti. (2024). Generative Ai in Software Development: An Overview and Evaluation of Modern Coding Tools. *IJFMR - International Journal For Multidisciplinary Research, 6*(3). DOI: 10.36948/ijfmr.2024.v06i03.23271

Abd Rabuh, A. (2020). *Developing A Credit Scoring Model Using Social Network Analysis*. University Of Portsmouth.

Abdullahi, M., Baashar, Y., Alhussian, H., Alwadain, A., Aziz, N., Capretz, L. F., & Abdulkadir, S. J. (2022). Detecting cybersecurity attacks in internet of things using artificial intelligence methods: A systematic literature review. *Electronics (Basel)*, 11(2), 198. DOI: 10.3390/electronics11020198

Abdulrahman, S. M., Asaad, R. R., Ahmad, H. B., Hani, A. A., Zeebaree, S. R., & Sallow, A. B. (2024). Machine Learning in Nonlinear Material Physics. *Journal of Soft Computing and Data Mining*, 5, 122–131.

Abdulsalam, Y. S., & Hedabou, M. (2021). Security and privacy in cloud computing: Technical review. *Future Internet*, 14(1), 11. DOI: 10.3390/fi14010011

Abid, A., Farooqi, M., & Zou, J. (2021). Large language models associate Muslims with violence. *Nature Machine Intelligence*, 3(6), 461–463. DOI: 10.1038/s42256-021-00359-2

Abomhara, M., & Køien, G. M. (2015). Cyber security and the internet of things: vulnerabilities, threats, intruders and attacks. Journal of Cyber Security and Mobility, 65-88.

Abramowicz, H., Levin, E. M., Levy, A., & Maor, U. (1991). A parametrization of σT ($\gamma^* p$) above the resonance region for $Q2 \gtrless 0$. *Physics Letters. [Part B]*, 269(3-4), 465–476.

Abubakar, M., Jaroucheh, Z., Al Dubai, A., & Liu, X. (2022, May). A lightweight and user-centric two-factor authentication mechanism for iot based on blockchain and smart contract. In 2022 2nd International Conference of Smart Systems and Emerging Technologies (SMARTTECH) (pp. 91-96). IEEE.

Abudureheman, A., & Nilupaer, A. (2021). Optimization model design of cross-border e-commerce transportation path under the background of prevention and control of COVID-19 pneumonia. *Soft Computing*, 25(18), 12007–12015. DOI: 10.1007/s00500-021-05685-6 PMID: 33716560

Acher, M. (2024). A Demonstration of End-User Code Customization Using Generative AI. *Proceedings of the 18th International Working Conference on Variability Modelling of Software-Intensive Systems*, 139–145. DOI: 10.1145/3634713.3634732

Adhyapak, S. (2024). Data Privacy and Security Risks in AI-Based Code Understanding. *International Journal for Research in Applied Science and Engineering Technology*, 12(6), 1913–1921. DOI: 10.22214/ijraset.2024.63423

Affes, W., & Jarboui, A. (2023). The impact of corporate governance on financial performance: A cross-sector study. *International Journal of Disclosure and Governance*, 20(4), 374–394. DOI: 10.1057/s41310-023-00182-8

Agarwal, V., Kaushal, A. K., & Chouhan, L. A survey on cloud computing security issues and cryptographic techniques. Social Networking and Computational Intelligence: Proceedings of SCI-2018, 2020. Springer, 119-134. DOI: 10.1007/978-981-15-2071-6_10

Agarwal, P. K., Gurjar, J., Agarwal, A. K., & Birla, R. (2015). Application of artificial intelligence for development of intelligent transport system in smart cities. *Journal of Traffic and Transportation Engineering*, 1(1), 20–30.

Agrawal, A., Kajić, I., Bugliarello, E., Davoodi, E., Gergely, A., Blunsom, P., & Nematzadeh, A. (2022). Reassessing evaluation practices in visual question answering: A case study on out-of-distribution generalization. arXiv preprint arXiv:2205.12191.

Agrawal, A., Alenezi, M., Kumar, R., & Khan, R. A. (2020). A unified fuzzy-based symmetrical multi-criteria decision-making method for evaluating sustainable-security of web applications. *Symmetry*, 12(3), 448. DOI: 10.3390/sym12030448

Agrawal, A., Seh, A. H., Baz, A., Alhakami, H., Alhakami, W., Baz, M., Kumar, R., & Khan, R. A. (2020). Software security estimation using the hybrid fuzzy ANP-TOPSIS approach: Design tactics perspective. *Symmetry*, 12(4), 598. DOI: 10.3390/sym12040598

Ahmadi, S. (2023). Open AI and its Impact on Fraud Detection in Financial Industry. *Sina, A.(2023). Open AI and its Impact on Fraud Detection in Financial Industry. Journal of Knowledge Learning and Science Technology ISSN*, 2959-6386.

Ahmadi, S. (2023). Next Generation AI-Based Firewalls: A Comparative Study. [IJC]. *International Journal of Computer*, 49, 245–262.

Ahmad, S., & Afthanorhan, W. M. A. B. W. (2014). The importance-performance matrix analysis in partial least square structural equation modeling (PLS-SEM) with smartpls 2.0 M3. *International Journal of Mathematics Research*, 3(1), 1–14.

Ahmed, A. A., & Agunsoye, G. (2021). A real-time network traffic classifier for online applications using machine learning. *Algorithms*, 14(8), 250. DOI: 10.3390/a14080250

Ahvanooey, M. T., Li, Q., Rabbani, M., & Rajput, A. R. (2020). A survey on smartphones security: software vulnerabilities, malware, and attacks. arXiv preprint arXiv:2001.09406.

AI Image Statistics for 2024: How Much Content Was Created by AI. (2024, August 15). https://journal.everypixel.com/ai-image-statistics

Airlangga, G. (2024). Analysis of Machine Learning Classifiers for Speaker Identification: A Study on SVM, Random Forest, KNN, and Decision Tree. *Journal of Computer Networks. Architecture and High Performance Computing*, 6(1), 430–438. DOI: 10.47709/cnahpc.v6i1.3487

Al-Amin, M., Ali, M. S., Salam, A., Khan, A., Ali, A., Ullah, A., Alam, M. N., & Chowdhury, S. K. (2024). *History of generative Artificial Intelligence (AI) chatbots: Past, present, and future development* (No. arXiv:2402.05122). arXiv. https://doi .org//arXiv.2402.05122DOI: 10.48550

Alansari, Z., Anuar, N. B., Kamsin, A., Soomro, S., & Belgaum, M. R. (2017, November). Computational intelligence tools and databases in bioinformatics. In 2017 4th IEEE international conference on engineering technologies and applied sciences (ICETAS) (pp. 1-6). IEEE.

AlDahoul, N., et al. (2023). "Exploring the potential of generative AI for the world wide web."

Aldoseri, A., Al-Khalifa, K. N., & Hamouda, A. M. (2023). Re-thinking data strategy and integration for artificial intelligence: Concepts, opportunities, and challenges. *Applied Sciences (Basel, Switzerland)*, 13(12), 7082. DOI: 10.3390/app13127082

Alfadel, M., Costa, D. E., & Shihab, E. (2023). Empirical analysis of security vulnerabilities in python packages. *Empirical Software Engineering*, 28(3), 59. DOI: 10.1007/s10664-022-10278-4

Alferidah, D. K., & Jhanjhi, N. (2020). A review on security and privacy issues and challenges in internet of things. *International Journal of Computer Science and Network Security IJCSNS*, 20, 263–286.

Al-hammuri, K., Gebali, F., Kanan, A., Mamun, M., Hazratifard, S. M., & Alfar, H. (2023). *Zero Trust Context-Aware Access Control Framework for IoT Devices in Healthcare Cloud AI Ecosystem.*

Ali, H., & Aysan, A. F. (2024). Ethical dimensions of generative AI: A cross-domain analysis using machine learning structural topic modeling. *International Journal of Ethics and Systems, ahead-of-print*(ahead-of-print). DOI: 10.1108/IJOES-04-2024-0112

Ali, M. Y., Naeem, S. B., & Bhatti, R. (2021). Artificial Intelligence (AI) in Pakistani university library services. *Library Hi Tech News*, 38(8), 12–15.

Ali, S., Murtaza, G., Hedvicakova, M., Jiang, J., & Naeem, M. (2022). Intellectual capital and financial performance: A comparative study. *Frontiers in Psychology*, 13, 967820. DOI: 10.3389/fpsyg.2022.967820 PMID: 36081720

Ali, Y., Shah, S. W., & Khan, W. A. (2023). *Security at the Internet of Things. Machine Tools*. CRC Press.

Aljabri, M., Alomari, D. M., & Aboulnour, M. (2022, December). Fake news detection using machine learning models. In 2022 14th International Conference on Computational Intelligence and Communication Networks (CICN) (pp. 473-477). IEEE.

Almansour, M. and F. M. J. M. Alfhaid (2024). "Generative artificial intelligence and the personalization of health professional education: A narrative review." **103**(31): e38955.

Almazroi, A. A., & Ayub, N. (2023). Online Payment Fraud Detection Model Using Machine Learning Techniques. *IEEE Access : Practical Innovations, Open Solutions*, 11, 137188–137203. DOI: 10.1109/ACCESS.2023.3339226

Almeida, Y., Albuquerque, D., Filho, E. D., Muniz, F., Santos, K. de F., Perkusich, M., Almeida, H., & Perkusich, A. (2024). AICodeReview: Advancing code quality with AI-enhanced reviews. *SoftwareX*, 26, 101677. Advance online publication. DOI: 10.1016/j.softx.2024.101677

Almusaylim, Z. A., Alhumam, A., & Jhanjhi, N. (2020). Proposing a secure RPL based internet of things routing protocol: A review. *Ad Hoc Networks*, 101, 102096. DOI: 10.1016/j.adhoc.2020.102096

Al-Sartawi, A. M. M., Razzaque, A., & Kamal, M. M. (Eds.). (2021). *Artificial Intelligence Systems and the Internet of Things in the Digital Era:Proceedings of EAMMIS 2021* (Vol. 239). Springer Nature. DOI: 10.1007/978-3-030-77246-8

Alshabandar, R., Hussain, A., Keight, R., & Khan, W. (2020). Students performance prediction in online courses using machine learning algorithms. *2020 International Joint Conference on Neural Networks (IJCNN)*. https://doi.org/DOI: 10.1109/IJCNN48605.2020.9207196

Alt, T., Ibisch, A., Meiser, C., Wilhelm, A., Zimmer, R., Berghoff, C., Droste, C., Karschau, J., Laus, F., Plaga, R., Plesch, C., Sennewald, B., Thaeren, T., Unverricht, K., & Waurick, S. (2024, June 7). *Generative AI Models: Opportunities and Risks for Industry and Authorities*. arXiv.Org. https://arxiv.org/abs/2406.04734v1

Althar, R. R., Samanta, D., Kaur, M., Alnuaim, A. A., Aljaffan, N., & Aman Ullah, M. (2021). Software systems security vulnerabilities management by exploring the capabilities of language models using NLP. *Computational Intelligence and Neuroscience*, 2021(1), 2021. DOI: 10.1155/2021/8522839 PMID: 34987569

Alt, R. (2022). Managing ai is managing complexity-an interview with rahul c. basole. *Electronic Markets*, 32(3), 1119–1125. DOI: 10.1007/s12525-022-00585-5 PMID: 36065397

Alwahedi, F., Aldhaheri, A., Ferrag, M. A., Battah, A., & Tihanyi, N. (2024). Machine learning techniques for IoT security: Current research and future vision with generative AI and large language models. *Internet of Things and Cyber-Physical Systems.*

Amankwah-Amoah, J., Abdalla, S., Mogaji, E., Elbanna, A., & Dwivedi, Y. K. (2024). The impending disruption of creative industries by generative AI: Opportunities, challenges, and research agenda. *International Journal of Information Management,* 79, 102759. DOI: 10.1016/j.ijinfomgt.2024.102759

Aminizadeh, S., Heidari, A., Dehghan, M., Toumaj, S., Rezaei, M., Navimipour, N. J., & Unal, M. (2024). Opportunities and challenges of artificial intelligence and distributed systems to improve the quality of healthcare service. *Artificial Intelligence in Medicine,* 149, 102779. DOI: 10.1016/j.artmed.2024.102779 PMID: 38462281

Amirhosseini, M. H., Kazemian, H. B., Ouazzane, K., & Chandler, C. (2018) Natural Language Processing approach to NLP Meta model automation. *International Joint Conference on Neural Networks (IJCNN).* DOI: 10.1109/IJCNN.2018.8489609

Anandan, R., Deepak, B. S., Suseendran, G., & Jhanjhi, N. Z. (2021). Internet of things platform for smart farming. Human Communication Technology: Internet of Robotic Things and Ubiquitous Computing, 337-369.

Anandharaj, N. (2024). Ai-powered cloud security: A study on the integration of artificial intelligence and machine learning for improved threat detection and prevention. [JRTCSE]. *JOURNAL OF RECENT TRENDS IN COMPUTER SCIENCE AND ENGINEERING,* 12(2), 21–30.

Ancuti, C. O.. (2024). NTIRE 2024 dense and non-homogeneous dehazing challenge report. *Proceedings of the IEEE/CVF Conference on Computer Vision and Pattern Recognition.* DOI: 10.1109/CVPRW63382.2024.00646

Andreianu, G. (2023, May). Protecting Your E-Commerce Business. Analysis on Cyber Security Threats. In Proceedings of the International Conference on Cybersecurity and Cybercrime-2023 (pp. 127-134). Asociatia Romana pentru Asigurarea Securitatii Informatiei.

Andrei, B. (2021). Threat modeling of cloud systems with ontological security pattern catalog. *International Journal of Open Information Technologies,* 9, 36–41.

Andronicus, A. A. (2014). Improved techniques for phishing email detection based on random forest and firefly-based support vector machine learning algorithms (Doctoral dissertation).

Anica-Popa, L. E., Vrîncianu, M., & Papuc, I. M. P. (2023). AI–powered Business Services in the Hyperautomation Era. In *Proceedings of the International Conference on Business Excellence* (Vol. 17, No. 1, pp. 1036-1050).

Anik, A. I., & Bunt, A. (2021, May). Data-centric explanations: explaining training data of machine learning systems to promote transparency. In *Proceedings of the 2021 CHI Conference on Human Factors in Computing Systems* (pp. 1-13).

Anstine, D. M., & Isayev, O. (2023). Generative Models as an Emerging Paradigm in the Chemical Sciences. *Journal of the American Chemical Society*, 145(16), 8736–8750. DOI: 10.1021/jacs.2c13467 PMID: 37052978

Antonio, N., de Almeida, A., & Nunes, L. (2017, December). Predicting hotel bookings cancellation with a machine learning classification model. In 2017 16th IEEE International Conference on Machine Learning and Applications (ICMLA) (pp. 1049-1054). IEEE.

Aravinth, S., Rao, B., Senthil Kumar, A., & Prsath, A. (2021). AI and ml enabled analytics techniques for improving the quality of website. *2021 6th International Conference on Signal Processing, Computing and Control (ISPCC)*. DOI: 10.1109/ISPCC53510.2021.9609498

Ardichvili, A. (2022). The impact of artificial intelligence on expertise development: Implications for hrd. *Advances in Developing Human Resources*, 24(2), 78–98. DOI: 10.1177/15234223221077304

Arias, O., Liu, Z., Guo, X., Jin, Y., & Wang, S. (2022). *RTSEC: Automated RTL code augmentation for hardware security enhancement. 2022 Design, Automation & Test in Europe Conference & Exhibition (DATE).* IEEE.

Arif, H., Kumar, A., Fahad, M., & Hussain, H. K. (2024). Future horizons: Ai- enhanced threat detection in cloud environments: Unveiling opportunities for research. *International Journal of Multidisciplinary Sciences and Arts*, 3(1), 242–251. DOI: 10.47709/ijmdsa.v2i2.3452

Arko, A. R., Khan, S. H., Preety, A., & Biswas, M. H. (2019). Anomaly detection. In *IoT using machine learning algorithms*. Brac University.

Arner, D. W., Barberis, J., & Buckley, R. P. (2015). The evolution of Fintech: A new post-crisis paradigm. *SSRN*, 47, 1271. DOI: 10.2139/ssrn.2676553

Arnold, B., & Qu, Y. (2020, December). Detecting software security vulnerability during an agile development by testing the changes to the security posture of software systems. In *2020 International Conference on Computational Science and Computational Intelligence (CSCI)* (pp. 1743-1748). IEEE.

Arshad, H., Tayyab, M., Bilal, M., Akhtar, S., & Abdullahi, A. (2024). Trends and challenges in harnessing big data intelligence for health care transfor- mation. *Artificial Intelligence for Intelligent Systems*, 220–240.

Arslanian, H., & Fischer, F. (2019). *The Future Of Finance: The Impact Of Fintech, Ai, And Crypto On Financial Services*. Springer. DOI: 10.1007/978-3-030-14533-0

Arulmurugan, L., Thakur, S., Dayana, R., Thenappan, S., Nagesh, B., & Sri, R. K. (2024). Advancing Security: Exploring AI-driven Data Encryption Solutions for Wireless Sensor Networks. *2024 International Conference on Advances in Computing, Communication and Applied Informatics (ACCAI)*, 1–6. DOI: 10.1109/ACCAI61061.2024.10602020

Arunachalam, S., Gould, D., Andersen, E., Byrd, D., & Narayanan, S. (2001). Politeness and frustration language in child-machine interactions. *Seventh european conference on speech communication and technology*.

Asesh, A. (2023). Variational Autoencoder Frameworks in Generative AI Model. *2023 24th International Arab Conference on Information Technology (ACIT)*, 01–06. DOI: 10.1109/ACIT58888.2023.10453782

Ashwini, N., Kumar, N., Nandan, M., & Suman, V. (2023). Leveraging Artificial Intelligence in Education: Transforming the Learning Landscape. *International Research Journal of Computer Science*, 10(05), 192–196.

Aslam, M. (2024). Ai and cybersecurity: an ever-evolving landscape. *Inter- national Journal of Advanced Engineering Technologies and Innovations, 1* (1), 52–71.

Aslan, O. ̈., Aktu ̆g, S. S., Ozkan-Okay, M., Yilmaz, A. A., & Akin, E. (2023). A comprehensive review of cyber security vulnerabilities, threats, attacks, and solutions. *Electronics (Basel)*, 12(6), 1333. DOI: 10.3390/electronics12061333

Avdić, A. (2024a). Generative AI Tools in Web Design. *Sinteza 2024 - International Scientific Conference on Information Technology, Computer Science, and Data Science*, 392–397. DOI: 10.15308/Sinteza-2024-392-397

Aydos, M., Aldan, Ç., Coşkun, E., & Soydan, A. (2022). Security testing of web applications: A systematic mapping of the literature. *Journal of King Saud University. Computer and Information Sciences*, 34(9), 6775–6792. DOI: 10.1016/j.jksuci.2021.09.018

Aykol, M., Herring, P., & Anapolsky, A. (2020). Machine learning for continuous innovation in battery technologies. *Nature Reviews. Materials*, 5(10), 725–727. DOI: 10.1038/s41578-020-0216-y

Azeem, M. R., Muzammal, S. M., Zaman, N., & Khan, M. A. (2022). Edge Caching for Mobile Devices. *2022 14th International Conference on Mathematics, Actuarial Science, Computer Science and Statistics (MACS)*, 1–6. DOI: 10.1109/MACS56771.2022.10022729

Aziz, S., & Dowling, M. M. 2018. Ai And Machine Learning For Risk Management. *Published As: Aziz, S. And M. Dowling (2019). "Machine Learning And Ai For Risk Management", In T. Lynn, G. Mooney, P. Rosati, And M. Cummins (Eds.), Disrupting Finance: Fintech And Strategy In The 21st Century, Palgrave*, 33-50.

Babatunde, S. O., Odejide, O. A., Edunjobi, T. E., & Ogundipe, D. O. (2024). The role of ai in marketing personalization: A theoretical exploration of consumer engagement strategies. *International Journal of Management & Entrepreneurship Research*, 6(3), 3. Advance online publication. DOI: 10.51594/ijmer.v6i3.964

Bachu, N. and J. J. J. o. S. R. McDuffie (2023). "Implications of Artificial Intelligence in Environmental Engineering." **12**(3).

Badal, Y. T., & Sungkur, R. K. (2023). Predictive modelling and analytics of students' grades using machine learning algorithms. *Education and Information Technologies*, 28(3), 3027–3057. DOI: 10.1007/s10639-022-11299-8 PMID: 36097545

Bahaa, A., Kamal, A. E.-R., & Ghoneim, A. S. (2022). A Systematic Literature Review on Software Vulnerability Detection Using Machine Learning Approaches. *FCI-H Informatics Bulletin*, 4, 1–9.

Baier, L., Kühl, N., & Satzger, G. (2019). How to cope with change?-preserving validity of predictive services over time.

Baier, L., Schlör, T., Schöffer, J., & Kühl, N. (2021). Detecting concept drift with neural network model uncertainty. arXiv preprint arXiv:2107.01873.

Balakrishnan, S., Ruskhan, B., Zhen, L.W., Huang, T.S., Soong, W.T.Y. and Shah, I.A., 2023. Down2Park: Finding New Ways to Park. *Journal of Survey in Fisheries Sciences*, pp.322-338.

Baldrati, A., Bertini, M., Uricchio, T., & Del Bimbo, A. (2022). Effective conditioned and composed image retrieval combining clip-based features. In *Proceedings of the IEEE/CVF conference on computer vision and pattern recognition* (pp. 21466-21474).

Bandi, A., Adapa, P. V. S. R., & Kuchi, Y. E. V. P. K. (2023). The power of generative ai: A review of requirements, models, input–output formats, evaluation metrics, and challenges. *Future Internet*, 15(8), 260. DOI: 10.3390/fi15080260

Banerjee, A., Chen, C. C., Hung, C. C., Huang, X., Wang, Y., & Chevesaran, R. (2020). Challenges and Experiences with {MLOps} for Performance Diagnostics in {Hybrid-Cloud} Enterprise Software Deployments. In *2020 USENIX Conference on Operational Machine Learning (OpML 20)*.

Banirostam, H., Banirostam, T., Pedram, M. M., & Rahmani, A. M. (2023a). A model to detect the fraud of electronic payment card transactions based on stream processing in big data. *Journal of Signal Processing Systems for Signal, Image, and Video Technology*, 95(12), 1469–1484. DOI: 10.1007/s11265-023-01903-6

Banirostam, H., Banirostam, T., Pedram, M. M., & Rahmani, A. M. (2023b). Providing and evaluating a comprehensive model for detecting fraudulent electronic payment card transactions with a two-level filter based on flow processing in big data. *International Journal of Information Technology : an Official Journal of Bharati Vidyapeeth's Institute of Computer Applications and Management*, 15(8), 4161–4166. DOI: 10.1007/s41870-023-01501-6

Bansal, A., Kauffman, R. J., Mark, R. M., & Peters, E. (1993). Financial risk and financial risk management technology (RMT): Issues and advances. *Information & Management*, 24(5), 267–281.

Bansal, T., Englert, D., Lee, J., Hegde, M., Wood, T. K., & Jayaraman, A. (2007). Differential Effects Of Epinephrine, Norepinephrine, And Indole On Escherichia Coli O157: H7 Chemotaxis, Colonization, And Gene Expression. *Infection and Immunity*, 75(9), 4597–4607. DOI: 10.1128/IAI.00630-07 PMID: 17591798

Barnard, R. S. (2004). An Examination Of Dysfunctional Behavior. In *Christian Evangelical Mission Organizations And Strategies For Managing The Consequences Of Dysfunctional Behavior*. The Open University.

Barsaglini, A., Sartori, G., Benetti, S., Pettersson-Yeo, W., & Mechelli, A. J. P. I. N. (2014). The Effects Of Psychotherapy On Brain Function: A Systematic And. *Critical Review*, 114, 1–14. PMID: 24189360

Basole, R. C., & Major, T. (2024). Generative AI for Visualization: Opportunities and Challenges. *IEEE Computer Graphics and Applications*, 44(2), 55–64. DOI: 10.1109/MCG.2024.3362168 PMID: 38526875

Battle, L., Duan, P., Miranda, Z., Mukusheva, D., Chang, R., & Stonebraker, M. (2018, April). Beagle: Automated extraction and interpretation of visualizations from the web. In *Proceedings of the 2018 CHI Conference on Human Factors in Computing Systems* (pp. 1-8).

Baum, S. (2017). A survey of artificial general intelligence projects for ethics, risk, and policy. *Global Catastrophic Risk Institute Working Paper*, 17-1.

Bedi, P., Goyal, S. B., Rajawat, A. S., Shaw, R. N., & Ghosh, A. (2022). A framework for personalizing atypical web search sessions with concept-based user profiles using selective machine learning techniques. In Advanced Computing and Intelligent Technologies. *Proceedings of ICACIT*, 2021, 279–291.

Belgaum, M. R., Alansari, Z., Musa, S., Alam, M. M., & Mazliham, M. (2021). Impact of artificial intelligence-enabled software-defined networks in infrastructure and operations: Trends and challenges. *International Journal of Advanced Computer Science and Applications*, 12(1), 12. DOI: 10.14569/IJACSA.2021.0120109

Belgaum, M. R., Ali, F., Alansari, Z., Musa, S., Alam, M. M., & Mazliham, M. (2022). Artificial intelligence based reliable load balancing framework in software-defined networks. *CMC—Comput.Mater. Contin*, 70, 251–266.

Belgaum, M. R., Charitha, T. H., Harini, M., Anusha, B., Sai, A. J., Yadav, U. C., & Alansari, Z. (2023). Enhancing the Efficiency of Diabetes Prediction through Training and Classification using PCA and LR Model. [AETiC]. *Annals of Emerging Technologies in Computing*, 7(3), 78–91. DOI: 10.33166/AETiC.2023.03.004

Benni, B., Blay-Fornarino, M., Mosser, S., Precisio, F., & Jungbluth, G. (2019, September). When DevOps meets meta-learning: A portfolio to rule them all. In 2019 ACM/IEEE 22nd International Conference on Model Driven Engineering Languages and Systems Companion (MODELS-C) (pp. 605-612). IEEE.

Berente, N., Gu, B., Recker, J., & Santhanam, R. (2021). Managing artificial intelligence. *Management Information Systems Quarterly*, 45(3).

Bernal, G., Colombo, S., Al Ai Baky, M., & Casalegno, F. (2017, June). Safety++ designing IoT and wearable systems for industrial safety through a user centered design approach. In *Proceedings of the 10th international conference on pervasive technologies related to assistive environments* (pp. 163-170).

Berutich Lindquist, J. M. (2017). Robust optimization of algorithmic trading systems.

Betzalel, E., Penso, C., & Fetaya, E. (2024). Evaluation Metrics for Generative Models: An Empirical Study. *Machine Learning and Knowledge Extraction*, 6(3), 3. Advance online publication. DOI: 10.3390/make6030073

Bhambri, P. (2013). Roadmaps to e-business: Translating e-business strategy into action (Vol. 1). Lap Lambert Academic Publishing. ISBN: 9783659347870.Bhambri, P. (2011). Data mining model for protein sequence alignment: Bioinformatics (Vol. 1). Lap Lambert Academic Publishing. ISBN: 9783844321531.

Bhambri, P. (2014). Effectiveness of performance management system in IT industries: Empirical approach. In Kumar, S., & Anjum, B. (Eds.), *Management of globalised business: Plethora of new opportunities* (pp. 114–121). Bharti Publications.

Bhambri, P., & Bedi, S. (2013). *Consumer's perception for the two wheelers: Analytical and comparative study with the inclusion of different locomotives* (Vol. 1). Lap Lambert Academic Publishing.

Bhambri, P., & Khang, A. (2024). Computational intelligence in manufacturing technologies. In Mehta, S., Gupta, S. K., Aljohani, A. A., & Khayyat, M. (Eds.), *Impact and potential of machine learning in the metaverse* (pp. 327–356). IGI Global., DOI: 10.4018/979-8-3693-5762-0.ch013

Bhambri, P., Rani, S., & Pareek, P. K. (2024). Financial innovations: Intelligent automation in finance and insurance sectors. In Darwish, D. (Ed.), *Generating entrepreneurial ideas with AI* (pp. 226–243)., DOI: 10.4018/979-8-3693-3354-9.ch012

Bharadiya, J. P., Thomas, R. K., & Ahmed, F. (2023). Rise of Artificial Intelligence in Business and Industry. *Journal of Engineering Research and Reports*, 25(3), 85–103.

Bhatt, N., Anand, A., & Yadavalli, V. S. (2021). Exploitability prediction of software vulnerabilities. *Quality and Reliability Engineering International*, 37(2), 648–663. DOI: 10.1002/qre.2754

Bhavsar, P., Safro, I., Bouaynaya, N., Polikar, R., & Dera, D. (2017). *Machine learning in transportation data analytics. Data analytics for intelligent transportation systems*. Elsevier.

Bhuiyan, F. A., Sharif, M. B., & Rahman, A. (2021). Security bug report usage for software vulnerability research: A systematic mapping study. *IEEE Access: Practical Innovations, Open Solutions*, 9, 28471–28495. DOI: 10.1109/ACCESS.2021.3058067

Bibi, I., Akhunzada, A., & Kumar, N. (2022). Deep ai-powered cyber threat analysis in iiot. *IEEE Internet of Things Journal*, 10(9), 7749–7760. DOI: 10.1109/JIOT.2022.3229722

Binyamini, H., Bitton, R., Inokuchi, M., Yagyu, T., Elovici, Y., & Shabtai, A. (2021, August). A framework for modeling cyber attack techniques from security vulnerability descriptions. In Proceedings of the 27th ACM SIGKDD conference on knowledge discovery & data mining (pp. 2574-2583).

Black, M., Chang, J., & Narayanan, S. (2008) An empirical analysis of user uncertainty in problem-solving child-machine interactions. *Proc. Workshop Child Comput. Interaction*.

Black, M., & Narayanan, S. (2012). Improvements in predicting children's overall reading ability by modeling variability in evaluators' subjective judgments. *Proceedings of the IEEE International Conference on Acoustics, Speech, and Signal Processing*, 5069–5072. DOI: 10.1109/ICASSP.2012.6289060

Black, M., Tepperman, J., & Narayanan, S. (2011). Automatic prediction of children's reading ability for high-level literacy assessment. *IEEE Transactions on Audio, Speech, and Language Processing*, 19(4), 348–360. DOI: 10.1109/TASL.2010.2076389

Boermans, M. A., & Galema, R. J. E. E. (2019).. . *Are Pension Funds Actively Decarbonizing Their Portfolios*, 161, 50–60.

Bonfanti, M. E. (2022). *Artificial intelligence and the offence-defence balance in cyber security. Cyber Security: Socio-Technological Uncertainty and Political Fragmentation*. Routledge.

Borgo, R., Abdul-Rahman, A., Mohamed, F., Grant, P. W., Reppa, I., Floridi, L., & Chen, M. (2012). An empirical study on using visual embellishments in visualization. *IEEE Transactions on Visualization and Computer Graphics*, 18(12), 2759–2768. DOI: 10.1109/TVCG.2012.197 PMID: 26357185

Bostrom, N., & Yudkowsky, E. (2018). The ethics of artificial intelligence. In *Artificial intelligence safety and security* (pp. 57–69). Chapman and Hall/CRC. DOI: 10.1201/9781351251389-4

Bosu, A., Carver, J. C., Hafiz, M., Hilley, P., & Janni, D. (2014, November). Identifying the characteristics of vulnerable code changes: An empirical study. In *Proceedings of the 22nd ACM SIGSOFT international symposium on foundations of software engineering* (pp. 257-268).

Boukhechba, M., Daros, A. R., Fua, K., Chow, P. I., Teachman, B. A., & Barnes, L. E. (2018). DemonicSalmon: Monitoring mental health and social interactions of college students using smartphones. *Smart Health (Amsterdam, Netherlands)*, 9, 192–203. DOI: 10.1016/j.smhl.2018.07.005

Boutaba, R., Salahuddin, M. A., Limam, N., Ayoubi, S., Shahriar, N., Estrada-Solano, F., & Caicedo, O. M. (2018). A comprehensive survey on machine learning for networking: Evolution, applications and research opportunities. *Journal of Internet Services and Applications*, 9(1), 1–99. DOI: 10.1186/s13174-018-0087-2

Bozkurt, A. (Ed.). (2023). Unleashing the potential of generative AI, conversational agents and chatbots in educational praxis: A systematic review and bibliometric analysis of GenAI in education. *Open Praxis, 15*(4), 261-270.

Bozorgi, A., Jadidi, M. S., & Anderson, J. (2024). UPSS: a User-centric Private Storage System with its applications. arXiv preprint arXiv:2403.15884.

Bozorgi, M., Saul, L. K., Savage, S., & Voelker, G. M. (2010, July). Beyond heuristics: learning to classify vulnerabilities and predict exploits. In *Proceedings of the 16th ACM SIGKDD international conference on Knowledge discovery and data mining* (pp. 105-114).

Branch, T. (2019). Blackberry's acquisition of cylance inc.: An impact on cybersecurity. *An Impact On Cyber-Security (July 30, 2019)*.

Brandt, F., Conitzer, V., Endriss, U., Lang, J., & Procaccia, A. D. (Eds.). (2016). *Handbook of computational social choice*. Cambridge University Press. DOI: 10.1017/CBO9781107446984

Brasilino, L. R., & Swany, M. Mitigating DDoS flooding attacks against IoT using custom hardware modules. *2019 Sixth International Conference on Internet of Things: Systems, Management and Security (IOTSMS)*, 2019. IEEE, 58-64. DOI: 10.1109/IOTSMS48152.2019.8939176

Brdnik, S., Heričko, T., & Šumak, B. (2022). Intelligent User Interfaces and Their Evaluation: A Systematic Mapping Study. *Sensors (Basel)*, 22(15), 15. Advance online publication. DOI: 10.3390/s22155830 PMID: 35957387

Breit, A., Waltersdorfer, L., Ekaputra, F. J., Sabou, M., Ekelhart, A., Iana, A., Paulheim, H., Portisch, J., Revenko, A., Teije, A. T., & Van Harmelen, F. (2023). Combining machine learning and semantic web: A systematic mapping study. *ACM Computing Surveys*, 55(14s), 1–41. DOI: 10.1145/3586163

Brennan, L. (2023). Ai ethical compliance is undecidable. *Hastings Sci. & Tech. LJ*, 14, 311.

Bromiley, P., Mcshane, M., Nair, A., & Rustambekov, E. J. L. R. P. (2015)... *Enterprise Risk Management: Review, Critique, And Research Directions.*, 48, 265–276.

Bukhari, S. S. A., Humayun, M., Shah, S. A. A., & Jhanjhi, N. Z. (2018, November). Improving requirement engineering process for web application development. In 2018 12th International Conference on Mathematics, Actuarial Science, Computer Science and Statistics (MACS) (pp. 1-5). IEEE.

Bullough, B. L., Yanchenko, A. K., Smith, C. L., & Zipkin, J. R. (2017, March). Predicting exploitation of disclosed software vulnerabilities using open-source data. In *Proceedings of the 3rd ACM on International Workshop on Security and Privacy Analytics* (pp. 45-53).

Buscema, P. M., Massini, G., Breda, M., Lodwick, W. A., Newman, F., Asadi-Zeydabadi, M., ... Asadi-Zeydabadi, M. (2018). Artificial neural networks. Artificial Adaptive Systems Using Auto Contractive Maps: Theory, Applications and Extensions, 11-35.

Butler, T., & O'Brien, L. (2019). Artificial intelligence for regulatory compliance: Are we there yet? *Journal of Financial Compliance*, 3(1), 44–59. DOI: 10.69554/TOCI6736

Cabral, G. G., Minku, L. L., Shihab, E., & Mujahid, S. (2019, May). Class imbalance evolution and verification latency in just-in-time software defect prediction. In *2019 IEEE/ACM 41st International Conference on Software Engineering (ICSE)* (pp. 666-676). IEEE.

Cai, A., Rick, S. R., Heyman, J. L., Zhang, Y., Filipowicz, A., Hong, M., & Malone, T. (2023, November). DesignAID: Using generative AI and semantic diversity for design inspiration. In *Proceedings of The ACM Collective Intelligence Conference* (pp. 1-11).

Cai, Z., Xiong, Z., Xu, H., Wang, P., Li, W., & Pan, Y. (2021). Generative adversarial networks: A survey toward private and secure applications. *ACM Computing Surveys*, 54(6), 1–38. DOI: 10.1145/3459992

Calandro, J. (2015b). A leader's guide to strategic risk management. *Strategy and Leadership*, 43(1), 26–35.

Calandro, J.Jr. (2015a). Revisiting the concept of a competitive "cash advantage". *Strategy and Leadership*, 43(4), 38–46.

Cali, U., Kuzlu, M., Pipattanasomporn, M., Kempf, J., & Bai, L. (2021). *Digitalization Of Power Markets And Systems Using Energy Informatics*. Springer. DOI: 10.1007/978-3-030-83301-5

Camacho, N. G. (2024). The role of ai in cybersecurity: Addressing threats in the digital age. *Journal of Artificial Intelligence General science (JAIGS) ISSN: 3006-4023, 3* (1), 143–154.

Cao, L. (2021). Artificial intelligence in retail: Applications and value creation logics. *International Journal of Retail & Distribution Management*, 49(7), 958–976. DOI: 10.1108/IJRDM-09-2020-0350

Cao, L. J. A. A. S. (2020). Ai In Finance. *RE:view*.

Capriotti, E., Fariselli, P., & Casadio, R. (2004). A neural-network-based method for predicting protein stability changes upon single point mutations. *Bioinformatics (Oxford, England)*, 20(suppl_1), i63–i68.

Carcillo, F., Dal Pozzolo, A., Le Borgne, Y.-A., Caelen, O., Mazzer, Y., & Bontempi, G. (2018). Scarff: A scalable framework for streaming credit card fraud detection with spark. *Information Fusion*, 41, 182–194. DOI: 10.1016/j.inffus.2017.09.005

Cardarelli, R., Elekdag, S. A., & Lall, S. (2009). *Financial Stress*. Downturns, And Recoveries.

Castro, D., Gámir, A., & Manuel, C. (2023). *Netflix' Madrid and the Madrid of Netflix*. Netflix., DOI: 10.4324/9781003432180-10

Challen, R., Denny, J., Pitt, M., Gompels, L., Edwards, T., & Tsaneva-Atanasova, K. (2019). Artificial intelligence, bias and clinical safety. *BMJ Quality & Safety*, 28(3), 231–237. DOI: 10.1136/bmjqs-2018-008370 PMID: 30636200

Chaudhary, M., Gaur, L., Chakrabarti, A., & Jhanjhi, N. Z. (2023). Unravelling the Barriers of human resource analytics: Multi-criteria decision-making approach. Journal of Survey in Fisheries Sciences, 306-321.

Chaudhary, K., & Bali, R. (2021). EASTER: Simplifying text recognition using only 1D convolutions. *Proceedings of the Canadian Conference on Artificial Intelligence*. https://doi.org/DOI: 10.21428/594757db.65eda33c

Chavan, S. V. (2018). Wireless sensor network technology and networking algorithms for wireless sensor network applications: A survey. *International Journal for Research in Applied Science and Engineering Technology*, 6(1), 662–670. DOI: 10.22214/ijraset.2018.1100

Chawdhury, T. K. (2024). Beyond the falcon: A generative ai approach to robust endpoint security.

Chen, C. & Liu, Z. (2023). The state of the art in creating visualization corpora for automated chart analysis. Computer Graphics Forum. Wiley Online Library, 449-470.

Chen, E., Lee, J.-E., Lin, J., & Koedinger, K. (2024). *GPTutor: Great Personalized Tutor with Large Language Models for Personalized Learning Content Generation.* 539–541.

Chen, Q., Chen, C., Hassan, S., Xing, Z., Xia, X., & Hassan, A. E. (2021). How Should I Improve the UI of My App? A Study of User Reviews of Popular Apps in the Google Play. *ACM Trans. Softw. Eng. Methodol., 30*(3), 37:1-37:38. DOI: 10.1145/3447808

Chen, Y. and P. J. J. o. M. I. R. Esmaeilzadeh (2024). "Generative AI in medical practice: in-depth exploration of privacy and security challenges." **26**: e53008.

Chen, D., Esperança, J. P., & Wang, S. J. F. I. P. (2022). The Impact Of Artificial Intelligence On Firm Performance. *An Application Of The Resource-Based View To E-Commerce Firms.*, 13, 884830. PMID: 35465474

Chen, J., Ling, M., Li, R., Isenberg, P., Isenberg, T., Sedlmair, M., Möller, T., Laramee, R. S., Shen, H.-W., Wünsche, K., & Wang, Q. (2021). Vis30k: A collection of figures and tables from ieee visualization conference publications. *IEEE Transactions on Visualization and Computer Graphics*, 27(9), 3826–3833. DOI: 10.1109/TVCG.2021.3054916 PMID: 33502982

Chen, J., & Tsang, E. P. (2020). Detecting Regime Change. In *Computational Finance: Data Science, Machine Learning And Algorithmic Trading*. Crc Press.

Chen, L., Wang, P., Dong, H., Shi, F., Han, J., Guo, Y., Childs, P. R. N., Xiao, J., & Wu, C. (2019). An artificial intelligence based data-driven approach for design ideation. *Journal of Visual Communication and Image Representation*, 61, 10–22. DOI: 10.1016/j.jvcir.2019.02.009

Chen, M., Zhou, J., Tao, G., Yang, J., & Hu, L. (2018). Wearable affective robot. *IEEE Access : Practical Innovations, Open Solutions*, 6, 64766–64776. DOI: 10.1109/ACCESS.2018.2877919

Chen, Q., Cao, S., Wang, J., & Cao, N. (2023). How does automation shape the process of narrative visualization: A survey of tools. *IEEE Transactions on Visualization and Computer Graphics*. PMID: 37030780

Chen, T. (2024). The Impact of AI-Pair Programmers on Code Quality and Developer Satisfaction: Evidence from TiMi studio. *Proceedings of the 2024 International Conference on Generative Artificial Intelligence and Information Security*, 201–205. DOI: 10.1145/3665348.3665383

Chen, W., Huo, R., Sun, C., Zeng, S., Wang, S., & Huang, T. (2023). SCRT: A secure and efficient state-channel-based resource trading scheme for Internet of Things. *IEEE Internet of Things Journal*, 10(11), 10038–10051. DOI: 10.1109/JIOT.2023.3236774

Chen, X., Zeng, W., Lin, Y., Ai-Maneea, H. M., Roberts, J., & Chang, R. (2020). Composition and configuration patterns in multiple-view visualizations. *IEEE Transactions on Visualization and Computer Graphics*, 27(2), 1514–1524. DOI: 10.1109/TVCG.2020.3030338 PMID: 33048683

Chen, Z.. (2024). Ntire 2024 challenge on image super-resolution (x4): Methods and results. *Proceedings of the IEEE/CVF Conference on Computer Vision and Pattern Recognition.*

Cheok, A. D., & Zhang, E. Y. (2023). *From Turing to Transformers: A Comprehensive Review and Tutorial on the Evolution and Applications of Generative Transformer Models.* Qeios., DOI: 10.32388/3NTOLQ.2

Chhajed, G. J., & Garg, B. R. (2022). *Applying decision tree for hiding data in binary images for secure and secret information flow. Cybersecurity measures for e-government frameworks.* IGI Global.

Chin, W. W. (1998). The partial least squares approach to structural equation modeling. *Modern methods for business research, 295*(2), 295-336.

Chin, W. W. J. M. M. F. B. R. (1998). The Partial Least Squares Approach To. *Structural Equation Modeling, 295,* 295–336.

Chittamuru, S. V. R., Thakkar, I. G., Bhat, V., & Pasricha, S. SOTERIA: exploiting process variations to enhance hardware security with photonic NoC architectures. *Proceedings of the 55th Annual Design Automation Conference,* 2018. 1-6. DOI: 10.1145/3195970.3196118

Cho, J., Lei, J., Tan, H., & Bansal, M. (2021, July). Unifying vision-and-language tasks via text generation. In *International Conference on Machine Learning* (pp. 1931-1942). PMLR.

Choudhuri, R., Liu, D., Steinmacher, I., Gerosa, M., & Sarma, A. (2024, April). How Far Are We? The Triumphs and Trials of Generative AI in Learning Software Engineering. In *Proceedings of the IEEE/ACM 46th International Conference on Software Engineering* (pp. 1-13).

Chowdhary, A., Jha, K., & Zhao, M. (2023). Generative Adversarial Network (GAN)-Based Autonomous Penetration Testing for Web Applications. *Sensors (Basel),* 23(18), 8014. DOI: 10.3390/s23188014 PMID: 37766067

Chui, M., & Francisco, S. (2017). Artificial intelligence the next digital frontier. *McKinsey and Company Global Institute, 47* (3.6), 6–8.

Corea, F. (2017). *Artificial intelligence and exponential technologies: Business models evolution and new investment opportunities.* Springer.

Correa-Madrid, M. C., et al. (2023). "Validation of the NOVA score for the consumption of ultra-processed foods by young women of Medellín, Colombia." **1528**(1): 69-76.

Costa, A., Silva, F., & Moreira, J. J. (2024). Towards an AI-Driven User Interface Design for Web Applications. *Procedia Computer Science*, 237, 179–186. DOI: 10.1016/j.procs.2024.05.094

Cotroneo, D., De Luca, R., & Liguori, P. (2024). *DeVAIC: A Tool for Security Assessment of AI-generated Code* (arXiv:2404.07548). arXiv. http://arxiv.org/abs/2404.07548

Cotroneo, D., Foggia, A., Improta, C., Liguori, P., & Natella, R. (2024). Automating the correctness assessment of AI-generated code for security contexts. *Journal of Systems and Software*, 216, 112113. DOI: 10.1016/j.jss.2024.112113

Cotroneo, D., Improta, C., Liguori, P., & Natella, R. (2024). Vulnerabilities in AI Code Generators: Exploring Targeted Data Poisoning Attacks. *Proceedings of the 32nd IEEE/ACM International Conference on Program Comprehension*, 280–292. DOI: 10.1145/3643916.3644416

Courtland, R. (2018). The bias detectives. *Nature*, 558(7710), 357–360. DOI: 10.1038/d41586-018-05469-3 PMID: 29925973

Creswell, A., White, T., Dumoulin, V., Arulkumaran, K., Sengupta, B., & Bharath, A. A. (2018). Generative Adversarial Networks: An Overview. *IEEE Signal Processing Magazine*, 35(1), 53–65. DOI: 10.1109/MSP.2017.2765202

Cui, T., Wang, Y., & Namih, B. (2019). Build an intelligent online marketing system: An overview. *IEEE Internet Computing*, 23(4), 53–60. DOI: 10.1109/MIC.2019.2924637

Cummaudo, A., Barnett, S., Vasa, R., Grundy, J., & Abdelrazek, M. (2020). Beware the evolving 'intelligent' web service! an integration architecture tactic to guard AI-first components. *Proceedings of the 28th ACM Joint Meeting on European Software Engineering Conference and Symposium on the Foundations of Software Engineering*. DOI: 10.1145/3368089.3409688

Cuomo, S., Gatta, F., Giampaolo, F., Iorio, C., & Piccialli, F. (2022). An Unsupervised Learning Framework For Marketneutral Portfolio. *Expert Systems with Applications*, 192, 116308. DOI: 10.1016/j.eswa.2021.116308

Cybersecurity, C. I. (2018). Framework for improving critical infrastructure cybersecurity. URL: https://nvlpubs. nist. gov/nistpubs/CSWP/NIST. CSWP, 4162018, 7.

D'Mello, S., Graesser, A., & Picard, R. (2007). Toward an affect-sensitive autotutor'". *IEEE Intelligent Systems*, 22(4), 53–61. DOI: 10.1109/MIS.2007.79

Dagur, A., Singh, K., Mehra, P. S., & Shukla, D. K. (Eds.). (2023). *Artificial Intelligence, Blockchain, Computing and Security Volume 2: Proceedings of the International Conference on Artificial Intelligence, Blockchain, Computing and Security (ICABCS 2023), Gr. Noida, UP, India, 24 - 25 February 2023*. CRC Press. DOI: 10.1201/9781032684994

Das Guptta, S., Shahriar, K. T., Alqahtani, H., Alsalman, D., & Sarker, I. H. (2024). Modeling hybrid feature-based phishing websites detection using machine learning techniques. *Annals of Data Science*, 11(1), 217–242. DOI: 10.1007/s40745-022-00379-8

Das, I. R., Islam, A. S., Talukder, M. B., Das, I. R., Islam, A. S., & Talukder, M. B. (2024). *Customer Satisfaction in Hospitality Marketing From a Technological Perspective* (customer-satisfaction-in-hospitality-marketing-from-a-technological-perspective) [Chapter]. Https://Services.Igi-Global.Com/Resolvedoi/Resolve.Aspx?Doi=10.4018/979-8-3693-6755-1.Ch019Global, IGI. DOI: 10.4018/979-8-3693-6755-1.ch019

Dash, B., Ansari, M. F., Sharma, P., & Ali, A. (2022). Threats and opportunities with ai-based cyber security intrusion detection: A review. [IJSEA]. *International Journal of Software Engineering and Its Applications*, 13(5).

Dash, B., Ansari, M. F., Sharma, P., & Ali, A. (2022). Threats and Opportunities with AI-based Cyber Security Intrusion Detection: A Review. *International Journal of Software Engineering and Its Applications*, 13(5), 13–21. Advance online publication. DOI: 10.5121/ijsea.2022.13502

Daugherty, P. R., & Wilson, H. J. (2018). *Human+ machine: Reimagining work in the age of ai*. Harvard Business Press.

Davenport, T. H., & Ronanki, R.. (2018). Artificial intelligence for the real world. *Harvard Business Review*, 96(1), 108–116.

Dawson, M., & Walker, D. (2022). Argument for Improved Security in Local Governments Within the Economic Community of West African States. Cybersecurity Measures for E-Government Frameworks, 96-106.

Deliema, M., Volker, J., & Worley, A. (2024). *Consumer Experiences with Gift Card Payment Scams: Causes, Consequences, and Implications for Consumer Protection. Scams, Cons, Frauds, and Deceptions*. Routledge.

Deng, L., & Liu, Y. (2018). *Deep learning in natural language processing*. Springer. DOI: 10.1007/978-981-10-5209-5

Derakhshan, B., Mahdiraji, A. R., Rabl, T., & Markl, V. (2019). *Continuous Deployment of Machine Learning Pipelines*. EDBT.

Dessouky, G., Zeitouni, S., Ibrahim, A., Davi, L., & Sadeghi, A.-R. CHASE: A configurable hardware-assisted security extension for real-time systems. *2019 IEEE/ACM International Conference on Computer-Aided Design (ICCAD)*, 2019. IEEE, 1-8. DOI: 10.1109/ICCAD45719.2019.8942142

Dharma, B., Pratiwi, D. C. J. J. O. M., & Innovations, B. (2020).. . *Developing Financial Risk Strategy Decisions For Construction Projects From Perspective Of The Project Owner.*, 2, 12–20.

Dhoni, P. (2023). Exploring the synergy between generative AI, data and analytics in the modern age. *Authorea Preprints*.

Dhoni, P. (2023). Unleashing the potential: overcoming hurdles and embracing generative AI in IT workplaces: advantages, guidelines, and policies. *Authorea Preprints*.

Dhoni, P., & Kumar, R. (2023). Synergizing generative ai and cybersecurity: Roles of generative ai entities, companies, agencies, and government in enhancing cybersecurity. *Authorea Preprints*.

Di Vaio, A., Boccia, F., Landriani, L., & Palladino, R. (2020a). Artificial intelligence in the agri-food system: Rethinking sustainable business models in the COVID-19 scenario. *Sustainability (Basel)*, 12(12), 4851. DOI: 10.3390/su12124851

Di Vaio, A., Palladino, R., Hassan, R., & Escobar, O. (2020b). Artificial intelligence and business models in the sustainable development goals perspective: A systematic literature review. *Journal of Business Research*, 121, 283–314. DOI: 10.1016/j.jbusres.2020.08.019

Dibia, V. (2023). LIDA: A tool for automatic generation of grammar-agnostic visualizations and infographics using large language models. arXiv preprint arXiv:2303.02927.

Dibia, V., & Demiralp, Ç. (2019). Data2vis: Automatic generation of data visualizations using sequence-to-sequence recurrent neural networks. *IEEE Computer Graphics and Applications*, 39(5), 33–46. DOI: 10.1109/MCG.2019.2924636 PMID: 31247545

Dimitriadou, E., & Lanitis, A. (2023). A critical evaluation, challenges, and future perspectives of using artificial intelligence and emerging technologies in smart classrooms. *Smart Learning Environments*, 10(1), 12. Advance online publication. DOI: 10.1186/s40561-023-00231-3

Dimitrieska, S. (2024). Generative Artificial Intelligence and Advertising. *Trends in Economics. Finance and Management Journal*, 6(1), 23–34. DOI: 10.69648/EYZI2281

Din, S. N. U., Muzammal, S. M., Bibi, R., Tayyab, M., Jhanjhi, N. Z., & Habib, M. (2024). Securing the Internet of Things in Logistics: Challenges, Solutions, and the Role of Machine Learning in Anomaly Detection. In *Digital Transformation for Improved Industry and Supply Chain Performance* (pp. 133–165). IGI Global. DOI: 10.4018/979-8-3693-5375-2.ch007

Din, S. N. U., Muzammal, S. M., Bibi, R., Tayyab, M., Jhanjhi, N. Z., & Habib, M. (2024). Securing the Internet of Things in Logistics: Challenges, Solutions, and the Role of Machine Learning in Anomaly Detection. In *Digital Transformation for Improved Industry and Supply Chain Performance* (pp. 133–165). IGI Global. https://www.igi-global.com/chapter/securing-the-internet-of-things-in-logistics/346170

Ding, Q., Jiang, H., Li, J., Liu, C., Yu, J., Chen, P., Zhao, Y., Ding, Y., Gong, T., & Yang, J. Unified 0.75 pJ/Bit TRNG and attack resilient 2F 2/Bit PUF for robust hardware security solutions with 4-layer stacking 3D NbO x threshold switching array. 2021 IEEE International Electron Devices Meeting (IEDM), 2021. IEEE, 39.2. 1-39.2. 4. DOI: 10.1109/IEDM19574.2021.9720641

Ding, T.. (2023). Is artificial intelligence associated with carbon emissions reduction? *Case of China.*, 85, 103892.

Dissanayake, N., Jayatilaka, A., Zahedi, M., & Babar, M. A. (2022). Software security patch management-A systematic literature review of challenges, approaches, tools and practices. *Information and Software Technology*, 144, 106771. DOI: 10.1016/j.infsof.2021.106771

Divyanshu, D., Kumar, R., Khan, D., Amara, S., & Massoud, Y. (2022). Logic locking using emerging 2T/3T magnetic tunnel junctions for hardware security. *IEEE Access : Practical Innovations, Open Solutions*, 10, 102386–102395. DOI: 10.1109/ACCESS.2022.3208650

Dixit, P., Bhattacharya, P., Tanwar, S., & Gupta, R. (2022). Anomaly detec- tion in autonomous electric vehicles using ai techniques: A comprehensive survey. *Expert Systems: International Journal of Knowledge Engineering and Neural Networks*, 39(5), e12754. DOI: 10.1111/exsy.12754

Djaber, R., & Ismail, H. (2023). *AI as a Co-Engineer: A Case Study of ChatGPT in Software Lifecycle*. DOI: 10.21203/rs.3.rs-3809973/v1

Dobrykh, D., Filonov, D., Slobozhanyuk, A., & Ginzburg, P. (2021). Hardware RFID security for preventing far-field attacks. *IEEE Transactions on Antennas and Propagation*, 70(3), 2199–2204. DOI: 10.1109/TAP.2021.3118846

Domenech, A. M., & Guillén, A. (2020, September). ml-experiment: A Python framework for reproducible data science. *Journal of Physics: Conference Series*, 1603(1), 012025.

Dosovitskiy, A. (2020). An image is worth 16x16 words: Transformers for image recognition at scale. arXiv preprint arXiv:2010.11929.

DSN 2023 tutorial committee. (2023). *2023 53rd Annual IEEE/IFIP International Conference on Dependable Systems and Networks - Supplemental Volume (DSN-S)*. https://doi.org/DOI: 10.1109/DSN-S58398.2023.00011

Duan, Y., Edwards, J. S., & Dwivedi, Y. K. J. I. J. O. I. M. (2019). Artificial Intelligence For Decision Making In The Era Of Big Data–Evolution. *Challenges And Research Agenda.*, 48, 63–71.

Dubey, S. R., & Singh, S. K. (2023). *Transformer-based Generative Adversarial Networks in Computer Vision: A Comprehensive Survey* (No. arXiv:2302.08641). arXiv. http://arxiv.org/abs/2302.08641

Dupont, L., Fliche, O., & Yang, S. (2020). Governance Of Artificial Intelligence. In *Finance*. Banque De France.

Durai, K. N., Subha, R., & Haldorai, A. (2021). A novel method to detect and prevent SQLIA using ontology to cloud web security. *Wireless Personal Communications*, 117(4), 2995–3014. DOI: 10.1007/s11277-020-07243-z

Dutta, S., Grisafe, B., Frentzel, C., Enciso, Z., San Jose, M., Smith, J., Ni, K., Joshi, S., & Datta, S. (2021). Experimental demonstration of gate-level logic camouflaging and run-time reconfigurability using ferroelectric FET for hardware security. *IEEE Transactions on Electron Devices*, 68(2), 516–522. DOI: 10.1109/TED.2020.3045380

Dwivedi, Y. K., Hughes, L., Ismagilova, E., Aarts, G., Coombs, C., Crick, T., Duan, Y., Dwivedi, R., Edwards, J., Eirug, A. J. I. J. O. I. M., Galanos, V., Ilavarasan, P. V., Janssen, M., Jones, P., Kar, A. K., Kizgin, H., Kronemann, B., Lal, B., Lucini, B., & Williams, M. D. (2021). Artificial Intelligence (Ai): Multidisciplinary Perspectives On Emerging Challenges, Opportunities, And Agenda For Research. *International Journal of Information Management*, 57, 101994. DOI: 10.1016/j.ijinfomgt.2019.08.002

Dwivedi, Y. K., Pandey, N., Currie, W., & Micu, A. (2024). Leveraging ChatGPT and other generative artificial intelligence (AI)-based applications in the hospitality and tourism industry: Practices, challenges and research agenda. *International Journal of Contemporary Hospitality Management*, 36(1), 1–12. DOI: 10.1108/ IJCHM-05-2023-0686

Dzhangarov, A. I., Pakhaev, K. K., & Potapova, N. V. (2021). Modern web application development technologies. *IOP Conference Series. Materials Science and Engineering*, 1155(1), 012100. DOI: 10.1088/1757-899X/1155/1/012100

Ebert, C., & Louridas, P. (2023). Generative AI for software practitioners. *IEEE Software*, 40(4), 30–38. DOI: 10.1109/MS.2023.3265877

Ege, D. N., Øvrebø, H. H., Stubberud, V., Berg, M. F., Elverum, C., Steinert, M., & Vestad, H. (2024). The TrollLabs open hackathon dataset: Generative AI and large language models for prototyping in engineering design. *Data in Brief*, 54, 110332. DOI: 10.1016/j.dib.2024.110332 PMID: 38550240

Ehramikar, S. (2000). *The Enhancement Of Credit Card Fraud Detection Systems Using Machine Learning Methodology*. University Of Toronto.

El Misilmani, H. M., & Naous, T. (2019, July). Machine learning in antenna design: An overview on machine learning concept and algorithms. In *2019 International Conference on High Performance Computing & Simulation (HPCS)* (pp. 600-607). IEEE.

Elbassuoni, S. (2023). Fortifying retail resilience: Integrating advanced analytics, machine learning, and blockchain for enhanced cybersecurity.

ELKarazle, K., Raman, V., Then, P., & Chua, C. (2024). How Generative AI Is Transforming Medical Imaging: A Practical Guide. In Applications of generative AI (pp. 371-385). Cham: Springer International Publishing.

Elliott, M. T., P, D., & Maccarthaigh, M. (2024). Evolving Generative AI: Entangling the Accountability Relationship. Digital Government: Research and Practice.

Enholm, I. M., Papagiannidis, E., Mikalef, P., & Krogstie, J. (2022). Artificial intelligence and business value: A literature review. *Information Systems Frontiers*, 24(5), 1709–1734. DOI: 10.1007/s10796-021-10186-w

Ernst, N. A., & Bavota, G. (2022). AI-driven development is here: Should you worry? *IEEE Software*, 39(2), 106–110. DOI: 10.1109/MS.2021.3133805

Ervik, A. (2023). Generative AI and the Collective Imaginary. *Image*, 37(1), 42–57. DOI: 10.1453/1614-0885-1-2023-15450

Eskenazi, M. (2009). An overview of spoken language technology for education. *Speech Communication*, 51(10), 832–844. DOI: 10.1016/j.specom.2009.04.005

Eslami, M., Ghasempouri, T., & Pagliarini, S. (2022, April). Reusing verification assertions as security checkers for hardware trojan detection. In 2022 23rd International Symposium on Quality Electronic Design (ISQED) (pp. 1-6). IEEE.

Esmaeilzadeh, A., Heidari, M., Abdolazimi, R., Hajibabaee, P., & Malekzadeh, M. (2022, January). Efficient large scale nlp feature engineering with apache spark. In 2022 IEEE 12th Annual Computing and Communication Workshop and Conference (CCWC) (pp. 0274-0280). IEEE.

Etzioni, A., & Etzioni, O. (2017). Incorporating ethics into artificial intelligence. *The Journal of Ethics*, 21(4), 403–418. DOI: 10.1007/s10892-017-9252-2

Evirgen, N., & Chen, X. A. (2023, April). Ganravel: User-driven direction disentanglement in generative adversarial networks. In *Proceedings of the 2023 CHI Conference on Human Factors in Computing Systems* (pp. 1-15).

Exploring Creativity. (2024). *Advances in Computational Intelligence and Robotics Book Series*, 167–198. DOI: 10.4018/979-8-3693-3278-8.ch008

Ezzeddine, F. (2024). Privacy Implications of Explainable AI in Data-Driven Systems. *arXiv Preprint arXiv:2406.15789*.

Falk, M., & Miller, A. G. J. V. S. (1992)... *Infrared Spectrum Of Carbon Dioxide In Aqueous Solution.*, 4, 105–108.

Familoni, B. T. (2024). Cybersecurity challenges in the age of ai: Theoreti- cal approaches and practical solutions. *Computer Science & IT Research Journal*, 5(3), 703–724. DOI: 10.51594/csitrj.v5i3.930

Fan, Y., Li, J., Zhang, D., Pi, J., Song, J., & Zhao, G. (2019). Supporting sustainable maintenance of substations under cyber-threats: An evaluation method of cybersecurity risk for power CPS. *Sustainability (Basel)*, 11(4), 982. DOI: 10.3390/su11040982

Farooq, M., & Ahmad, N. (2023). Nexus between board characteristics, firm performance and intellectual capital: An emerging market evidence. *Corporate Governance (Bradford)*, 23(6), 1269–1297. DOI: 10.1108/CG-08-2022-0355

Farooq, M., Noor, A., & Naeem, M. (2023). Does family ownership moderate the relationship between board characteristics and corporate social responsibility? Evidence from an emerging market. *Asian Journal of Business Ethics*, 12(1), 71–99. DOI: 10.1007/s13520-022-00164-z

Fateh, S., ... (2024). Smart Healthcare System in Industry 4.0. Advances in Computational Intelligence for the Healthcare Industry 4.0, IGI Global: 297-311.

Fateh, S., Sial, Q., Dar, S. H., Shah, I. A., & Rani, A. (2024). *Smart Healthcare System in Industry 4.0. Advances in Computational Intelligence for the Healthcare Industry 4.0*. IGI Global.

Fatima, S., Aslam, N. A., Tariq, I., & Ali, N. (2020, July). Home security and automation based on internet of things: A comprehensive review. [). IOP Publishing.]. *IOP Conference Series. Materials Science and Engineering*, 899(1), 012011.

Feldstein, S. (2019). *The global expansion of ai surveillance* (Vol. 17) (No. 9). Carnegie Endowment for International Peace Washington, DC.

Feng, S., Yuan, M., Chen, J., Xing, Z., & Chen, C. (2023, December 12). *Designing with Language: Wireframing UI Design Intent with Generative Large Language Models*. arXiv.Org. https://arxiv.org/abs/2312.07755v1

Ferdous, M., Debnath, J., & Chakraborty, N. R. (2020, July). Machine learning algorithms in healthcare: A literature survey. In 2020 11th International conference on computing, communication and networking technologies (ICCCNT) (pp. 1-6). IEEE.

Ferrara, E. (2023). Fairness and bias in artificial intelligence: A brief survey of sources, impacts, and mitigation strategies. *Sci*, 6(1), 3. DOI: 10.3390/sci6010003

Feuerriegel, S., Hartmann, J., Janiesch, C., & Zschech, P. (2024). Generative AI. *Business & Information Systems Engineering*, 66(1), 111–126. DOI: 10.1007/s12599-023-00834-7

Finlayson, S. G., Bowers, J. D., Ito, J., Zittrain, J. L., Beam, A. L., & Kohane, I. S. (2019). Adversarial attacks on medical machine learning. *Science*, 363(6433), 1287–1289. DOI: 10.1126/science.aaw4399 PMID: 30898923

Fischer, T., Krauss, C., & Treichel, A. (2018). *Machine Learning For Time Series Forecasting-A Simulation Study*. Fau Discussion Papers In Economics.

Fitriawijaya, A., & Jeng, T. (2024). Integrating Multimodal Generative AI and Blockchain for Enhancing Generative Design in the Early Phase of Architectural Design Process. *Buildings*, 14(8), 2533. Advance online publication. DOI: 10.3390/buildings14082533

Fontes, C., Hohma, E., Corrigan, C. C., & Lütge, C. (2022). Ai-powered public surveillance systems: Why we (might) need them and how we want them. *Technology in Society*, 71, 102137. DOI: 10.1016/j.techsoc.2022.102137

Forbes-Riley, K., & Litman, D. (2011). Benefits and challenges of real-time uncertainty detection and adaptation in a spoken dialogue computer tutor. *Speech Communication*, 53(9), 1115–1136. DOI: 10.1016/j.specom.2011.02.006

Foster, J., & Wagner, J. (2021, June). Naive Bayes versus BERT: Jupyter notebook assignments for an introductory NLP course. In *Proceedings of the Fifth Workshop on Teaching NLP* (pp. 112-114).

Fountaine, T., McCarthy, B., & Saleh, T. (2019). Building the ai-powered organization. *Harvard Business Review*, 97(4), 62–73.

Fredj, O. B., Cheikhrouhou, O., Krichen, M., Hamam, H., & Derhab, A. (2021). An OWASP top ten driven survey on web application protection methods. In Risks and Security of Internet and Systems: 15th International Conference, CRiSIS 2020, Paris, France, November 4–6, 2020, Revised Selected Papers 15 (pp. 235-252). Springer International Publishing.

Fui-Hoon Nah, F., Zheng, R., Cai, J., Siau, K., & Chen, L. (2023). Generative AI and ChatGPT: Applications, challenges, and AI-human collaboration. *Journal of Information Technology Case and Application Research*, 25(3), 277–304. DOI: 10.1080/15228053.2023.2233814

Fu, J., Zhu, B., Cui, W., Ge, S., Wang, Y., Zhang, H., Huang, H., Tang, Y., Zhang, D., & Ma, X. (2020). Chartem: Reviving chart images with data embedding. *IEEE Transactions on Visualization and Computer Graphics*, 27(2), 337–346. DOI: 10.1109/TVCG.2020.3030351 PMID: 33315567

Furtado, L. S., Soares, J. B., & Furtado, V. (2024). A task-oriented framework for generative AI in design. *Journal of Creativity*, 34(2), 100086. DOI: 10.1016/j. yjoc.2024.100086

Gaikwad, A. (2024). A Collaborative Code Platform with Advanced AI Features and Real-Time Collaboration Tools. *International Journal for Research in Applied Science and Engineering Technology*, 12(5), 1569–1573. DOI: 10.22214/ijraset.2024.61438

Gambetta, N., Azcárate-Llanes, F., Sierra-García, L., & García-Benau, M. A. (2021). Financial institutions' risk profile and contribution to the sustainable development goals. *Sustainability (Basel)*, 13(14), 7738. DOI: 10.3390/su13147738

Gans, J. S. (2024). How will generative AI impact communication? https://doi.org/ DOI: 10.3386/w32690

Gan, W., Xu, H., Huang, Y., Chen, S., & Yokoya, N. (2023). V4d: Voxel for 4d novel view synthesis. *IEEE Transactions on Visualization and Computer Graphics*. PMID: 37669213

García, Á. L., De Lucas, J. M., Antonacci, M., Zu Castell, W., David, M., Hardt, M., Iglesias, L. L., Moltó, G., Plociennik, M., & Tran, V. (2020). A cloud-based framework for machine learning workloads and applications. *IEEE Access: Practical Innovations, Open Solutions*, 8, 18681–18692. DOI: 10.1109/ACCESS.2020.2964386

Garg, S., & Baliyan, N. (2021). Comparative analysis of Android and iOS from security viewpoint. *Computer Science Review*, 40, 100372. DOI: 10.1016/j.cosrev.2021.100372

Gatla, R. K., Gatla, A., Sridhar, P., Kumar, D. G., & Rao, D. S. N. M. (2024). Advancements in Generative AI: Exploring Fundamentals and Evolution. *2024 International Conference on Electronics, Computing, Communication and Control Technology (ICECCC)*, 1–5. DOI: 10.1109/ICECCC61767.2024.10594003

Gaur, L., Singh, G., Solanki, A., Jhanjhi, N. Z., Bhatia, U., Sharma, S., ... & Kim, W. (2021). Disposition of youth in predicting sustainable development goals using the neuro-fuzzy and random forest algorithms. Human-Centric Computing and Information Sciences, 11, NA.

Gaur, L., Ujjan, R. M. A., & Hussain, M. (2022). *The Influence of Deep Learning in Detecting Cyber Attacks on E-Government Applications. Cybersecurity Measures for E-Government Frameworks*. IGI Global.

Gawron, M., Cheng, F., & Meinel, C. (2018). Automatic vulnerability classification using machine learning. In Risks and Security of Internet and Systems: 12th International Conference, CRiSIS 2017, Dinard, France, September 19-21, 2017, Revised Selected Papers 12 (pp. 3-17). Springer International Publishing.

Gelen, I. (2018). Academicians' predictions Of 21st Century Education And Education In The 21st Century. *European Journal of Education Studies*.

Ghaffarian, S. M., & Shahriari, H. R. (2017). Software vulnerability analysis and discovery using machine-learning and data-mining techniques: A survey. *ACM Computing Surveys*, 50(4), 1–36. DOI: 10.1145/3092566

Ghanem, M. C., & Chen, T. M. (2019). Reinforcement learning for efficient network penetration testing. *Information (Basel)*, 11(1), 6. DOI: 10.3390/info11010006

Ghayoumi, M. (2023). Generative adversarial networks (GANs) for images. *Generative Adversarial Networks in Practice*, 436-477. https://doi.org/DOI: 10.1201/9781003281344-14

Ghayoumi, M. (2023). *Generative Adversarial Networks in Practice*. Chapman and Hall/CRC., DOI: 10.1201/9781003281344

Ghillani, D. (2022). Deep learning and artificial intelligence framework to im- prove the cyber security. *Authorea Preprints*.

Gill, S. H., Razzaq, M. A., Ahmad, M., Almansour, F. M., Haq, I. U., Jhanjhi, N., Alam, M. Z., & Masud, M. (2022). Security and privacy aspects of cloud computing: A smart campus case study. *Intelligent Automation & Soft Computing*, 31, 117–128. DOI: 10.32604/iasc.2022.016597

Gill, S. H., Sheikh, N. A., Rajpar, S., Jhanjhi, N., Ahmad, M., Razzaq, M. A., Alshamrani, S. S., Malik, Y., & Jaafar, F. (2021). Extended Forgery Detection Framework for COVID-19 Medical Data Using Convolutional Neural Network. *Computers, Materials & Continua*, 68.

Gitau, J. M. (2023). *Corporate Governance Practices and Performance of Enterprise Risk Management in the Horticultural Farms in Kajiado County, Kenya* (Doctoral dissertation, KCA University).

Goff, T. L. (2024, January 4). *Recommendations for public action towards sustainable generative AI systems*. arXiv.Org. https://arxiv.org/abs/2402.01646v1

Golda, A., Mekonen, K., Pandey, A., Singh, A., Hassija, V., Chamola, V., & Sikdar, B. (2024). Privacy and Security Concerns in Generative AI: A Comprehensive Survey. *IEEE Access, 12*, 48126–48144. IEEE Access. DOI: 10.1109/ACCESS.2024.3381611

Gong, Y., Qian, F., & Wang, L. (2019). Design for test and hardware security utilizing retention loss of memristors. *IEEE Transactions on Very Large Scale Integration (VLSI). Systems*, 27, 2536–2547.

Goodell, J. W., Kumar, S., Lim, W. M., & Pattnaik, D. (2021). Artificial Intelligence And Machine Learning In Finance: Identifying Foundations, Themes, And Research Clusters From Bibliometric Analysis. *Journal of Behavioral and Experimental Finance*, 32, 100577. DOI: 10.1016/j.jbef.2021.100577

Goodfellow, I., Pouget-Abadie, J., Mirza, M., Xu, B., Warde-Farley, D., Ozair, S., Courville, A., & Bengio, Y. (2020). Generative adversarial networks. *Communications of the ACM*, 63(11), 139–144. DOI: 10.1145/3422622

Götz, O., Liehr-Gobbers, K., & Krafft, M. (2009). *Evaluation Of Structural Equation Models Using The Partial Least Squares (Pls) Approach. Handbook Of Partial Least Squares: Concepts, Methods And Applications*. Springer.

Götz, O., Liehr-Gobbers, K., & Krafft, M. (2009). Evaluation of structural equation models using the partial least squares (PLS) approach. In *Handbook of partial least squares: Concepts, methods and applications* (pp. 691–711). Springer Berlin Heidelberg.

Gouda, W., Almurafeh, M., Humayun, M., & Jhanjhi, N. Z. (2022, February). Detection of COVID-19 based on chest X-rays using deep learning. In Healthcare (Vol. 10, No. 2, p. 343). MDPI.

Gourisaria, M. K., Agrawal, R., Harshvardhan, G. M., Pandey, M., & Rautaray, S. S. (2021). Application of machine learning in industry 4.0. Machine learning: Theoretical foundations and practical applications, 57-87.

Goyani, Z. (2021). Selection.index: Analysis of selection index in plant breeding. *CRAN: Contributed Packages.* https://doi.org/DOI: 10.32614/CRAN.package. selection.index

GPT-3. S. H., Pat Grady and. (2022, September 19). *Generative AI: A Creative New World.* Sequoia Capital. https://www.sequoiacap.com/article/generative-ai-a -creative-new-world/

Graefe, A. (2019). Accuracy Of German Federal Election Forecasts, 2013 & 2017. *International Journal of Forecasting*, 35(3), 868–877. DOI: 10.1016/j.ijforecast.2019.01.004

Graesser, A., & D'Mello, S. (2011). "Theoretical perspectives on affect and deep learning", in New Perspectives Affect Learn. *Technol.*, 3, 11–21.

Grammatikis, P. I. R., Sarigiannidis, P. G., & Moscholios, I. D. (2019). Securing the Internet of Things: Challenges, threats and solutions. *Internet of Things : Engineering Cyber Physical Human Systems*, 5, 41–70. DOI: 10.1016/j.iot.2018.11.003

Granlund, T., Kopponen, A., Stirbu, V., Myllyaho, L., & Mikkonen, T. (2021, May). MLOps challenges in multi-organization setup: Experiences from two real-world cases. In 2021 IEEE/ACM 1st Workshop on AI Engineering-Software Engineering for AI (WAIN) (pp. 82-88). IEEE.

Granville, V. (2024). Synthetic tabular data: Copulas vs enhanced GANs. *Synthetic Data and Generative AI*, 169-201. https://doi.org/DOI: 10.1016/B978-0-44-321857-6.00014-X

Grieco, G., & Dinaburg, A. (2018, January). Toward smarter vulnerability discovery using machine learning. In *Proceedings of the 11th ACM Workshop on Artificial Intelligence and Security* (pp. 48-56).

Guldogan, N.. (2024).. .*Artificial Intelligence in BI-RADS Categorization of Breast Lesions on Ultrasound: Can We Omit Excessive Follow-ups and Biopsies*, 31(6), 2194–2202.

Gulwani, S. (2022). AI-assisted programming: Applications, user experiences, and neuro-symbolic techniques (keynote). *Proceedings of the 30th ACM Joint European Software Engineering Conference and Symposium on the Foundations of Software Engineering*, 1. DOI: 10.1145/3540250.3569444

Gunawan, A., W., Purnomo, H. D., Sembiring, I., & Iriani, A. (2023). Evolutionary parameter optimization on neural network models for earthquake prediction. *2023 International Conference on Computer Science, Information Technology and Engineering (ICCoSITE)*. https://doi.org/DOI: 10.1109/ICCoSITE57641.2023.10127850

Guo, N., Li, X., Yin, H., & Gao, Y. (2020). Vulhunter: An automated vulnerability detection system based on deep learning and bytecode. In Information and Communications Security: 21st International Conference, ICICS 2019, Beijing, China, December 15–17, 2019, Revised Selected Papers 21 (pp. 199-218). Springer International Publishing.

Guo, D., Chen, H., Wu, R., & Wang, Y. (2023). AIGC challenges and opportunities related to public safety: A case study of ChatGPT. *Journal of Safety Science and Resilience = An Quan Ke Xue Yu Ren Xing (Ying Wen)*, 4(4), 329–339. DOI: 10.1016/j.jnlssr.2023.08.001

Gupta, P., Ding, B., Guan, C., & Ding, D. (2024). Generative AI: A systematic review using topic modelling techniques. *Data and Information Management*, 8(2), 100066. DOI: 10.1016/j.dim.2024.100066

Habib, H., Pearman, S., Wang, J., Zou, Y., Acquisti, A., Cranor, L. F., Sadeh, N., & Schaub, F. (2020). "It's a scavenger hunt": Usability of Websites' Opt-Out and Data Deletion Choices. *Proceedings of the 2020 CHI Conference on Human Factors in Computing Systems*, 1–12. DOI: 10.1145/3313831.3376511

Habib, M., Hussain, A., Rehman, E., Muzammal, S. M., Cheng, B., Aslam, M., & Jilani, S. F. (2023). Convolved Feature Vector Based Adaptive Fuzzy Filter for Image De-Noising. *Applied Sciences (Basel, Switzerland)*, 13(8), 8. Advance online publication. DOI: 10.3390/app13084861

Haenlein, M., Kaplan, A., Tan, C. W., & Zhang, P. (2019). Artificial intelligence (AI) and management analytics. *Journal of Management Analytics*, 6(4), 341–343.

Hafidi, M. M., Djezzar, M., Hemam, M., Amara, F. Z., & Maimour, M. (2023). Semantic web and machine learning techniques addressing semantic interoperability in Industry 4.0. *International Journal of Web Information Systems*, 19(3/4), 157–172. DOI: 10.1108/IJWIS-03-2023-0046

Haldorai, A., Murugan, S., & Ramu, A. (2020). Evolution, challenges, and application of intelligent ICT education: An overview. *Computer Applications in Engineering Education*, 29(3), 562–571. DOI: 10.1002/cae.22217

Hameed, K., Barika, M., Garg, S., Amin, M. B., & Kang, B. (2022). A taxonomy study on securing blockchain-based industrial applications: An overview, application perspectives, requirements, attacks, countermea- sures, and open issues. *Journal of Industrial Information Integration*, 26, 100312. DOI: 10.1016/j.jii.2021.100312

Hameed, K., Garg, S., Amin, M. B., Kang, B., & Khan, A. (2022). A context- aware information-based clone node attack detection scheme in internet of things. *Journal of Network and Computer Applications*, 197, 103271. DOI: 10.1016/j.jnca.2021.103271

Hameed, K., Haseeb, J., Tayyab, M., Junaid, M., Maqsood, T. B., & Naqvi, M. H. (2017). *Secure provenance in wireless sensor networks-a survey of provenance schemes. In 2017 international conference on communication, computing and digital systems (c-code).*

Hameed, K., Khan, A., Ahmed, M., Reddy, A. G., & Rathore, M. M. (2018). Towards a formally verified zero watermarking scheme for data integrity in the internet of things based-wireless sensor networks. *Future Generation Computer Systems*, 82, 274–289. DOI: 10.1016/j.future.2017.12.009

Hameed, K., & Rahman, N. (2017). *Today's social network sites: An analysis of emerging security risks and their counter measures. In 2017 international conference on communication technologies (comtech).*

Hammad, M., El-Rahiem, B. A., & El-Latif, A. A. A. (2023). Leveraging generative adversarial networks and federated learning for enhanced cybersecurity: A concise review. In *Artificial Intelligence for Biometrics and Cybersecurity: Technology and applications* (pp. 65–87). IET Digital Library., DOI: 10.1049/PBSE020E_ch4

Hanafi, S. M. (2016). Financial Risk Management In Syariah Contracts: A Review of Current Literature. MIQOT: Jurnal Ilmu-ilmu Keislaman, 37(1).

Hang, C., & Lei, Z. (2018). Improved tabu search algorithm for solving the shortest path problem. *J. Transp. Sci. Technol.*, 20, 35–38.

Hanif, H., Nasir, M. H. N. M., Ab Razak, M. F., Firdaus, A., & Anuar, N. B. (2021). The rise of software vulnerability: Taxonomy of software vulnerabilities detection and machine learning approaches. *Journal of Network and Computer Applications*, 179, 103009. DOI: 10.1016/j.jnca.2021.103009

Han, K., Wang, Y., Guo, J., Tang, Y., & Wu, E. (2022). Vision gnn: An image is worth graph of nodes. *Advances in Neural Information Processing Systems*, 35, 8291–8303.

Hansen, C. (2019). Brain-Computer interfaces: from research to consumer products.

Hasan, M., Islam, M. M., Zarif, M. I. I., & Hashem, M. (2019). Attack and anomaly detection in IoT sensors in IoT sites using machine learning approaches. *Internet of Things : Engineering Cyber Physical Human Systems*, 7, 100059. DOI: 10.1016/j.iot.2019.100059

Hassabis, D., Kumaran, D., Summerfield, C., & Botvinick, M. (2017). Neuroscience-inspired artificial intelligence. *Neuron*, 95(2), 245–258. DOI: 10.1016/j.neuron.2017.06.011 PMID: 28728020

Hayat, U., & Malik, A. (2014). Islamic Finance: ethics, concepts, practice. *Practice (November 2014). CFA Institute Research Foundation L2014-3.*

Haynes, R., & Roberts, J. S. (2015). Automated trading in futures markets. CFTC White Paper.

He, X. (2015). Study on Optimization of Logistics Distribution Routing based on Improved Ant Colony Algorithm. International Journal of Simulation--Systems, Science & Technology, 16.

Hegselmann, S., Buendia, A., Lang, H., Agrawal, M., Jiang, X., & Sontag, D. (2023, April). Tabllm: Few-shot classification of tabular data with large language models. In *International Conference on Artificial Intelligence and Statistics* (pp. 5549-5581). PMLR.

Helbekkmo, H., Kshirsagar, A., Schlosser, A., Selandari, F., Stegemann, U., & Vorholt, J. (2013). Enterprise risk management—shaping the risk revolution. New York: McKinsey & Co., Available online: www. rmahq. org (accessed on 18 June 2018), 23.

Henning, J. (2016). *Credit Scoring Model: Incorporating Entrepreneurial Characteristics*. University Of The Free State.

Henseler, J., Ringle, C. M., & Sarstedt, M. (2012). Using partial least squares path modeling in advertising research: basic concepts and recent issues. In *Handbook of research on international advertising*. Edward Elgar Publishing. DOI: 10.4337/9781781001042.00023

Henseler, J., Ringle, C. M., & Sarstedt, M. (2016). Testing measurement invariance of composites using partial least squares. *International Marketing Review*, 33(3), 405–431. DOI: 10.1108/IMR-09-2014-0304

Henseler, J., Ringle, C. M., & Sinkovics, R. R. (2009). The Use Of Partial Least Squares Path Modeling. In *International Marketing. New Challenges To International Marketing*. Emerald Group Publishing Limited.

Heo, S., & Lee, J. H. (2018). Fault detection and classification using artificial neural networks. *IFAC-PapersOnLine*, 51(18), 470–475. DOI: 10.1016/j.ifacol.2018.09.380

Heras García De Vinuesa, A. D. L., Luque Sendra, A., & Zamora-Polo, F. (2020). Machine Learning Technologies for Sustainability in Smart Cities in the Post-COVID Era. *Sustainability (Basel)*, 12(22), 9320. DOI: 10.3390/su12229320

He, W., Zou, L., Shekar, A. K., Gou, L., & Ren, L. (2021). Where can we help? a visual analytics approach to diagnosing and improving semantic segmentation of movable objects. *IEEE Transactions on Visualization and Computer Graphics*, 28(1), 1040–1050. DOI: 10.1109/TVCG.2021.3114855 PMID: 34587077

Hewage, N., & Meedeniya, D. (2022). Machine learning operations: A survey on MLOps tool support. arXiv preprint arXiv:2202.10169.

Himeur, Y., Ghanem, K., Alsalemi, A., Bensaali, F., & Amira, A. (2021). Arti- ficial intelligence based anomaly detection of energy consumption in build- ings: A review, current trends and new perspectives. *Applied Energy*, 287, 116601. DOI: 10.1016/j.apenergy.2021.116601

Hoffman, A. (2024). *Web application security*. O'Reilly Media, Inc.

Hong, F., Liu, C., & Yuan, X. (2019, April). DNN-VolVis: Interactive volume visualization supported by deep neural network. In *2019 IEEE Pacific Visualization Symposium (PacificVis)* (pp. 282-291). IEEE.

Horvitz, E., & Mulligan, D. (2015). Data, privacy, and the greater good. *Science*, 349(6245), 253–255. DOI: 10.1126/science.aac4520 PMID: 26185242

Hossain, M. E. (2020). *Predictive Modelling Of The Comorbidity Of Chronic Diseases: A Network And Machine Learning Approach*. University Of Sydney.

Howard, J. (2019). Artificial intelligence: Implications for the future of work. *American Journal of Industrial Medicine*, 62(11), 917–926. DOI: 10.1002/ajim.23037 PMID: 31436850

Hsiao, I., & Chung, C. (2022). AI-infused semantic model to enrich and expand programming question generation. *Journal of Artificial Intelligence and Technology*. .DOI: 10.37965/jait.2022.0090

Hsu, B.-J. (2008) Generalized linear interpolation of language models. *IEEE Workshop on Automatic Speech Recognition & Understanding (ASRU)*.

Hu, J., Song, S., & Gong, Y. (2017). Comparative performance analysis of web image compression. *2017 10th International Congress on Image and Signal Processing, BioMedical Engineering and Informatics (CISP-BMEI)*, 1–5. DOI: 10.1109/CISP-BMEI.2017.8301939

Huang, C., & Sun, Y. (2022, September). Generative Approach to the Automation of Artificial Intelligence Applications. In CS & IT Conference Proceedings (Vol. 12, No. 15). CS & IT Conference Proceedings.

Huang, D., Wang, J., Wang, G., & Lin, C. Y. (2021, January). Visual style extraction from chart images for chart restyling. In 2020 25th International Conference on Pattern Recognition (ICPR) (pp. 7625-7632). IEEE.

Huang, G. Q., Chen, M. Z., & Pan, J. (2015). Robotics in ecommerce logistics. HKIE transactions, 22(2), 68-77.

Huang, Y., Kanij, T., Madugalla, A., Mahajan, S., Arora, C., & Grundy, J. (2024). *Unlocking Adaptive User Experience with Generative AI*. 760–768. https://www.scitepress.org/Link.aspx?doi=10.5220/0012741000003687

Huang, K., Goertzel, B., Wu, D., & Xie, A. (2024). GenAI Model Security. In Huang, K., Wang, Y., Goertzel, B., Li, Y., Wright, S., & Ponnapalli, J. (Eds.), *Generative AI Security: Theories and Practices* (pp. 163–198). Springer Nature Switzerland., DOI: 10.1007/978-3-031-54252-7_6

Huang, S. W., Lin, C. T., Chen, S. P., Wu, Y. Y., Hsu, P. H., & Lai, S. H. (2018). Auggan: Cross domain adaptation with gan-based data augmentation. In *Proceedings of the European Conference on Computer Vision (ECCV)* (pp. 718-731).

Huang, S.-H., Miao, Y.-H., & Hsiao, Y.-T. (2021). Novel Deep Reinforcement Algorithm With Adaptive Sampling Strategy For Continuous Portfolio Optimization. *IEEE Access : Practical Innovations, Open Solutions*, 9, 77371–77385. DOI: 10.1109/ACCESS.2021.3082186

Huang, T., Yu, F. R., Zhang, C., Liu, J., Zhang, J., & Liu, Y. (2016). A survey on large-scale software defined networking (SDN) testbeds: Approaches and challenges. *IEEE Communications Surveys and Tutorials*, 19(2), 891–917. DOI: 10.1109/COMST.2016.2630047

Hubara, I., Courbariaux, M., Soudry, D., El-Yaniv, R., & Bengio, Y. (2018). Quantized neural networks: Training neural networks with low precision weights and activations. *Journal of Machine Learning Research*, 18, 1–30.

Hu, K., Bakker, M. A., Li, S., Kraska, T., & Hidalgo, C. (2019, May). Vizml: A machine learning approach to visualization recommendation. In *Proceedings of the 2019 CHI conference on human factors in computing systems* (pp. 1-12).

Hüllermeier, E., & Waegeman, W. (2021). Aleatoric and epistemic uncertainty in machine learning: An introduction to concepts and methods. *Machine Learning*, 110(3), 457–506. DOI: 10.1007/s10994-021-05946-3

Hullman, J., & Diakopoulos, N. (2011). Visualization rhetoric: Framing effects in narrative visualization. *IEEE Transactions on Visualization and Computer Graphics*, 17(12), 2231–2240. DOI: 10.1109/TVCG.2011.255 PMID: 22034342

Humayun, M., Jhanjhi, N., Almufareh, M. F., & Khalil, M. I. (2022). Security threat and vulnerability assessment and measurement in secure software development. *Computers, Materials & Continua*, 71, 5039–5059.

Humayun, M., Jhanjhi, N., Alruwaili, M., Amalathas, S. S., Balasubramanian, V., & Selvaraj, B. (2020). Privacy protection and energy optimization for 5G-aided industrial Internet of Things. *IEEE Access : Practical Innovations, Open Solutions*, 8, 183665–183677. DOI: 10.1109/ACCESS.2020.3028764

Humayun, M., Jhanjhi, N., Alsayat, A., & Ponnusamy, V. (2021). Internet of things and ransomware: Evolution, mitigation and prevention. *Egyptian Informatics Journal*, 22(1), 105–117. DOI: 10.1016/j.eij.2020.05.003

Humayun, M., Jhanjhi, N., Niazi, M., Amsaad, F., & Masood, I. (2022). Securing Drug Distribution Systems from Tampering Using Blockchain. [s Note: MDPI stays neu-tral with regard to jurisdictional claims in….]. *Electronics (Basel)*, 11(8), 1195. DOI: 10.3390/electronics11081195

Humayun, M., Jhanjhi, N., Talib, M., Shah, M. H., & Suseendran, G. 2021. Cybersecurity for data science: issues, opportunities, and challenges. *Intelligent Computing and Innovation on Data Science:Proceedings of ICTIDS 2021*, 435-444.

Humayun, M., Niazi, M., Almufareh, M. F., Jhanjhi, N., Mahmood, S., & Alshayeb, M. (2022). Software-as-a-service security challenges and best practices: A multi-vocal literature review. *Applied Sciences (Basel, Switzerland)*, 12(8), 3953. DOI: 10.3390/app12083953

Humayun, M., Niazi, M., Jhanjhi, N., Alshayeb, M., & Mahmood, S. (2020b). Cyber security threats and vulnerabilities: A systematic mapping study. *Arabian Journal for Science and Engineering*, 45(4), 3171–3189. DOI: 10.1007/s13369-019-04319-2

Huseynov, F., & Ozdenizci Kose, B. (2024). Using machine learning algorithms to predict individuals' tendency to be victim of social engineering attacks. *Information Development*, 40(2), 298–318. DOI: 10.1177/02666669221116336

Hussain, F., Hassan, S. A., Hussain, R., & Hossain, E. (2020). Machine learning for resource management in cellular and IoT networks: Potentials, current solutions, and open challenges. *IEEE Communications Surveys and Tutorials*, 22(2), 1251–1275. DOI: 10.1109/COMST.2020.2964534

Hussain, M. (2023). When, Where, and Which?: Navigating the Intersection of Computer Vision and Generative AI for Strategic Business Integration. *IEEE Access : Practical Innovations, Open Solutions*, 11, 127202–127215. DOI: 10.1109/ACCESS.2023.3332468

Hutchinson, B., Prabhakaran, V., Denton, E., Webster, K., Zhong, Y., & Denuyl, S. (2020). *Social Biases in NLP Models as Barriers for Persons with Disabilities* (arXiv:2005.00813). arXiv./arXiv.2005.00813DOI: 10.18653/v1/2020.acl-main.487

Hwang, E. J., Park, J., Hong, W., Lee, H.-J., Choi, H., Kim, H., Nam, J. G., Goo, J. M., Yoon, S. H., Lee, C. H., & Park, C. M. (2022). Artificial intelligence system for identification of false-negative interpretations in chest radiographs. *European Radiology*, 32(7), 4468–4478. DOI: 10.1007/s00330-022-08593-x PMID: 35195744

ICCoSITE 2023 cover page. (2023). *2023 International Conference on Computer Science, Information Technology and Engineering (ICCoSITE)*. https://doi.org/DOI: 10.1109/ICCoSITE57641.2023.10127843

Iqbal, S., Moleiro Martins, J., Nuno Mata, M., Naz, S., Akhtar, S., & Abreu, A. (2021). Linking entrepreneurial orientation with innovation performance in SMEs; the role of organizational commitment and transformational leadership using smart PLS-SEM. *Sustainability*, 13(8), 4361.

Islam Riad, A. K., Barek, A., Rahman, M., Akter, S., Islam, T., Rahman, M., Md Raihan, M., Shahriar, H., Wu, F., & Ahamed, S. (2024). *Enhancing HIPAA Compliance in AI-driven mHealth Devices Security and Privacy.*, DOI: 10.1109/COMPSAC61105.2024.00390

Islam, M., Jalil, S. Q., & Rehmani, M. H. (2016). Role of wireless sensor networks in emerging communication technologies: A review. Emerging communication technologies based on wireless sensor networks: Current research and future applications, 1.

Jackson, C., & Orebaugh, A. (2018). A study of security and privacy issues associated with the amazon echo. *International Journal of Internet of Things and Cyber-Assurance*, 1(1), 91–100. DOI: 10.1504/IJITCA.2018.090172

Jafar, S. H., Hemachandran, K., El-Chaarani, H., Moturi, S., & Gupta, N. (2023). *Artificial Intelligence For Capital Markets*. Crc Press.

Jain, J. (2021). Artificial intelligence in the cyber security environment. *Artificial Intelligence and Data Mining Approaches in Security Frameworks*, 101– 117.

Jain, R., Maity, K., Jha, P., & Saha, S. (2023). Generative Models vs Discriminative Models: Which Performs Better in Detecting Cyberbullying in Memes? *2023 International Joint Conference on Neural Networks (IJCNN)*, 1–8. DOI: 10.1109/IJCNN54540.2023.10191363

Jalal, F. E., Xu, Y., Iqbal, M., Javed, M. F., & Jamhiri, B. (2021). Predictive Modeling Of Swell-Strength Of Expansive Soils Using Artificial Intelligence Approaches: Ann, Anfis And Gep. *Journal of Environmental Management*, 289, 112420. DOI: 10.1016/j.jenvman.2021.112420 PMID: 33831756

Jalonen, T. (2019). Management Accounting Information in Decision-making: Unveiling Possibilities for AI (Master's thesis).

Jangjou, M., & Sohrabi, M. K. (2022). A comprehensive survey on security challenges in different network layers in cloud computing. *Archives of Computational Methods in Engineering*, 29(6), 3587–3608. DOI: 10.1007/s11831-022-09708-9

Jawhar, S., Miller, J., & Bitar, Z. (2024). AI-Based Cybersecurity Policies and Procedures. *2024 IEEE 3rd International Conference on AI in Cybersecurity (ICAIC)*, 1–5. DOI: 10.1109/ICAIC60265.2024.10433845

Jefferies, C., & Potter, L. (2024). Using generative AI to create virtual patients. https://doi.org/DOI: 10.26226/m.6639c0e2eb191bbe9d92661f

Jeffrey, N., Tan, Q., & Villar, J. R. (2023). A review of anomaly detection strategies to detect threats to cyber-physical systems. *Electronics (Basel)*, 12(15), 3283. DOI: 10.3390/electronics12153283

Jesmin, R. (2013). *Software development techniques for constructive information systems. Software Development Techniques for Constructive Information Systems Design*. IGI Global.

Jeyaraman, M., Ramasubramanian, S., Balaji, S., Jeyaraman, N., Nallakumarasamy, A., & Sharma, S. (2023). ChatGPT in action: Harnessing artificial intelligence potential and addressing ethical challenges in medicine, education, and scientific research. *World Journal of Methodology*, 13(4), 170–178. DOI: 10.5662/wjm.v13.i4.170 PMID: 37771867

Jhanjhi, N., et al. (2024). "IoT-Based Railway Logistics: Security Issues and Challenges." 143-163.

Jhanjhi, N. Z., & Shah, I. A. (2024). *Cybersecurity Measures for Logistics Industry Framework*. Igi Global.

Jhanjhi, N. Z., & Shah, I. A. (2024). *Navigating Cyber Threats and Cybersecurity in the Logistics Industry*. IGI Global. DOI: 10.4018/979-8-3693-3816-2

Jhanjhi, N., Ahmad, M., Khan, M. A., & Hussain, M. (2022). *The impact of cyber attacks on e-governance during the covid-19 pandemic. Cybersecurity Measures for E-Government Frameworks*. IGI Global.

Jing, H., Wei, W., Zhou, C., & He, X. (2021)... . *An Artificial Intelligence Security Framework.*, 1948(1), 012004.

Jin, X. H., & Doloi, H. (2008). Interpreting risk allocation mechanism in public–private partnership projects: An empirical study in a transaction cost economics perspective. *Construction Management and Economics*, 26(7), 707–721.

Johnson, A. L. (2022). The analysis of binary file security using a hierarchical quality model (Doctoral dissertation, Montana State University-Bozeman, College of Engineering).

Johnston, R., Victor, K., Heery, L., & McCausland, G. (2019). Intelligent futures.

Jordan, M. I., & Mitchell, T. M. (2015). Machine learning: Trends, perspectives, and prospects. *Science*, 349(6245), 255–260. DOI: 10.1126/science.aaa8415 PMID: 26185243

Jun, Y., Craig, A., Shafik, W., & Sharif, L. (2021). Artificial intelligence ap- plication in cybersecurity and cyberdefense. *Wireless Communications and Mobile Computing*, 2021(1), 3329581. DOI: 10.1155/2021/3329581

Jurn, J., Kim, T., & Kim, H. (2018). An automated vulnerability detection and remediation method for software security. *Sustainability (Basel)*, 10(5), 1652. DOI: 10.3390/su10051652

Kafle, K., Price, B., Cohen, S., & Kanan, C. (2018). Dvqa: Understanding data visualizations via question answering. In *Proceedings of the IEEE conference on computer vision and pattern recognition* (pp. 5648-5656).

Kafle, K., Shrestha, R., Cohen, S., Price, B., & Kanan, C. (2020). Answering questions about data visualizations using efficient bimodal fusion. In *Proceedings of the IEEE/CVF Winter conference on applications of computer vision* (pp. 1498-1507).

Kahan, M. (1997). Some problems with stock exchange-based securities regulation. *Virginia Law Review*, ●●●, 1509–1519.

Kailay, M. P., & Jarratt, P. (1995). RAMeX: A prototype expert system for computer security risk analysis and management. *Computers & Security*, 14(5), 449–463. DOI: 10.1016/0167-4048(95)00013-X

Kalantari, H. D., & Johnson, L. (2018). Australian Customer Willingness To Pay And Wait For Mass-Customised Products. *Asia Pacific Journal of Marketing and Logistics*, 30(1), 106–120. DOI: 10.1108/APJML-01-2017-0006

Kalid, S. N., Khor, K.-C., Ng, K.-H., & Tong, G.-K. (2024). Detecting frauds and payment defaults on credit card data inherited with imbalanced class distribution and overlapping class problems: A systematic review. *IEEE Access : Practical Innovations, Open Solutions*, 12, 23636–23652. DOI: 10.1109/ACCESS.2024.3362831

Kalo, I., & Amron, M. T. (2023, December). Transforming Laundry Services: A User-Centric Approach to Streamlined Operations and Customer Satisfaction. In 2023 IEEE 8th International Conference on Recent Advances and Innovations in Engineering (ICRAIE) (pp. 1-5). IEEE.

Kambhampati, S. (2022, September 1). *Changing the Nature of AI Research – Communications of the ACM.* https://cacm.acm.org/article/changing-the-nature-of-ai-research/

Kamruzzaman, M. M., Alanazi, S., Alruwaili, M., Alshammari, N., Elaiwat, S., Abu-Zanona, M., Innab, N., Mohammad Elzaghmouri, B., & Ahmed Alanazi, B. (2023). AI- and IoT-assisted sustainable education systems during pandemics, such as COVID-19, for smart cities. *Sustainability (Basel)*, 15(10), 8354. DOI: 10.3390/su15108354

Kaplan, A. and M. J. B. h. Haenlein (2019). "Siri, Siri, in my hand: Who's the fairest in the land? On the interpretations, illustrations, and implications of artificial intelligence." **62**(1): 15-25.

Kaplan, A., & Haenlein, M. J. B. H. (2019). Siri, Siri, In My Hand: Who's The Fairest In The Land? On The Interpretations, Illustrations, And Implications Of. *Artificial Intelligence*, 62, 15–25.

Kar, A. K., Varsha, P. S., & Rajan, S. (2023). Unravelling the impact of generative artificial intelligence (GAI) in industrial applications: A review of scientific and grey literature. *Global Journal of Flexible Systems Managment*, 24(4), 659–689. DOI: 10.1007/s40171-023-00356-x

Karadimas, D., Polytarchos, E., Stefanidis, K., & Gialelis, J. (2014, September). Information system framework architecture for organization agnostic logistics utilizing standardized IoT technologies. In *2014 Federated Conference on Computer Science and Information Systems* (pp. 1337-1343). IEEE.

Karlsson, K. & Alfgården, H. (n.d.). Robust concept development utilising artificial intelligence and machine learning.

Karn, R. R., Kudva, P., & Elfadel, I. A. M. (2018). Dynamic autoselection and autotuning of machine learning models for cloud network analytics. *IEEE Transactions on Parallel and Distributed Systems*, 30(5), 1052–1064. DOI: 10.1109/TPDS.2018.2876844

Katar, O., et al. (2023). "Evaluation of GPT-3 AI language model in research paper writing." **18**(2): 311-318.

Katiyar, S. (2023). 8 cyber security using artificial intelligence. *Cyber Security Using Modern Technologies: Artificial Intelligence, Blockchain and Quan- tum Cryptography*, 111.

Kaur, R., Gabrijelčič, D., & Klobučar, T. (2023). Artificial intelligence for cy- bersecurity: Literature review and future research directions. *Information Fusion*, 97, 101804. DOI: 10.1016/j.inffus.2023.101804

Kaushik, K., Khan, A., Kumari, A., Sharma, I., & Dubey, R. (2024). Ethical considerations in ai-based cybersecurity. In *Next-generation cybersecurity: Ai, ml, and blockchain* (pp. 437–470). Springer. DOI: 10.1007/978-981-97-1249-6_19

Kavitha, S., Prasad, N. H., Hanumanthappa, M., & Veena, R. (2022). Classification And Errors Analysis of COVID-19 Using Supervised Machine Learning Algorithm and Visualisation. *NeuroQuantology : An Interdisciplinary Journal of Neuroscience and Quantum Physics*, 20(15), 6282.

Kazemzadeh, A., You, H., Iseli, M., Jones, B., Cui, X., Heritage, M., Price, P., Anderson, E., Narayanan, S., & Alwan, A. (2005) Tball data collection: The making of a young children's speech corpus. *Proc. 9th Eur. Conf. Speech Commun. Technol.* DOI: 10.21437/Interspeech.2005-462

Kekül, H., Ergen, B., & Arslan, H. (2022). A Multiclass Approach to Estimating Software Vulnerability Severity Rating with Statistical and Word Embedding Methods. *International Journal of Computer Network and Information Security*, 12(4), 27–42. DOI: 10.5815/ijcnis.2022.04.03

Kelly, C. J., Karthikesalingam, A., Suleyman, M., Corrado, G., & King, D. (2019). Key challenges for delivering clinical impact with artificial intelli- gence. *BMC Medicine*, 17(1), 1–9. DOI: 10.1186/s12916-019-1426-2 PMID: 31665002

Kenthapadi, K., Lakkaraju, H., & Rajani, N. (2023). Generative AI meets Responsible AI: Practical Challenges and Opportunities. *Proceedings of the 29th ACM SIGKDD Conference on Knowledge Discovery and Data Mining*, 5805–5806. DOI: 10.1145/3580305.3599557

Khalaf, O. I., Sokiyna, M., Alotaibi, Y., Alsufyani, A., & Alghamdi, S. (2021). Web Attack Detection Using the Input Validation Method: DPDA Theory. *Computers, Materials & Continua*, ●●●, 68.

Khalil, K., Abdelgawad, A., & Bayoumi, M. (2021, June). Intelligent resource discovery approach for the internet of things. In 2021 IEEE 7th World Forum on Internet of Things (WF-IoT) (pp. 264-269). IEEE.

Khalil, K., Elgazzar, K., Abdelgawad, A., & Bayoumi, M. (2020a, June). A security approach for CoAP-based internet of things resource discovery. In 2020 IEEE 6th World Forum on Internet of Things (WF-IoT) (pp. 1-6). IEEE.

Khalil, K., Elgazzar, K., Seliem, M., & Bayoumi, M. (2020b). Resource discovery techniques in the internet of things: A review. *Internet of Things : Engineering Cyber Physical Human Systems*, 12, 100293. DOI: 10.1016/j.iot.2020.100293

Khalil, M. I., Humayun, M., Jhanjhi, N. Z., Talib, M. N., & Tabbakh, T. A. (2021). Multi-class segmentation of organ at risk from abdominal ct images: A deep learning approach. In Intelligent Computing and Innovation on Data Science [Springer Singapore.]. *Proceedings of ICTIDS*, 2021, 425–434.

Khan, A. A., Laghari, A. A., Awan, S., & Jumani, A. K. (2021). Fourth industrial revolution application: network forensics cloud security issues. Security Issues and Privacy Concerns in Industry 4.0 Applications, 15-33.

Khan, N. K., Alnatsheh, E., Rasheed, R. A., Yadav, A., & Alansari, Z. (2020, August). A quantitative case study in WSNs: Design and implementation of student smart ID card. In 2020 International Conference on Computing, Electronics & Communications Engineering (iCCECE) (pp. 27-32). IEEE.

Khan, A., Jhanjhi, N. Z., Haji, D. H. T. B. A., & Omar, H. A. H. B. H. (2024). *Internet of Things (IoT) Impact on Inventory Management: A Review.* Cybersecurity Measures for Logistics Industry Framework.

Khan, F., Rathnayaka, S., Ahmed, S. J. P. S., & Protection, E. (2015). Methods And Models In Process Safety And Risk Management: Past. *Present And Future.*, 98, 116–147.

Khang, A., Misra, A., Gupta, S. K., & Shah, V. (2023). *Ai-Aided Iot Technologies And Applications For Smart Business And Production.* Crc Press. DOI: 10.1201/9781003392224

Khankhoje, R. (2016). *The Power of AI Driven Reporting in Test Automation.* 7(11).

Khan, S. (2023). Role of Generative AI for Developing Personalized Content Based Websites. *International Journal of Innovative Science and Research Technology*, 8, 1–5.

Khan, S. J. C. R. R. (2019). Chief Reputation Officer (Cro). *Envisioning The Role.*, 22, 75–88.

Khan, Z. F., & Alotaibi, S. R. (2020). Applications of artificial intelligence and big data analytics in m-health: A healthcare system perspective. *Journal of Healthcare Engineering*, 2020(1), 8894694. DOI: 10.1155/2020/8894694 PMID: 32952992

Kılınç, H. K., & Keçecioğlu, Ö. F. (2024). Generative Artificial Intelligence: A Historical and Future Perspective. *Academic Platform Journal of Engineering and Smart Systems*, 12(2), 2. Advance online publication. DOI: 10.21541/apjess.1398155

Kim, G., Hong, T., Yim, M., Nam, J., Park, J., Yim, J., . . . Park, S. (2022, October). Ocr-free document understanding transformer. In European Conference on Computer Vision (pp. 498-517). Cham: Springer Nature Switzerland.

Kim, D. H., Hoque, E., & Agrawala, M. (2020, April). Answering questions about charts and generating visual explanations. In *Proceedings of the 2020 CHI conference on human factors in computing systems* (pp. 1-13).

Kim, J., Kim, E., Yang, J., Jeong, J., Kim, H., Hyun, S., Yang, H., Oh, J., Kim, Y., Hares, S., & Dunbar, L. (2020). Ibcs: Intent-based cloud services for security applications. *IEEE Communications Magazine*, 58(4), 45–51. DOI: 10.1109/MCOM.001.1900476

Kim, J., & Maher, M. L. (2023). The effect of AI-based inspiration on human design ideation. *International Journal of Design Creativity and Innovation*, 11(2), 81–98. DOI: 10.1080/21650349.2023.2167124

Kim, N. J., & Kim, M. K. (2022). Teacher's Perceptions of Using an Artificial Intelligence-Based Educational Tool for Scientific Writing. *Frontiers in Education*, 7, 755914. Advance online publication. DOI: 10.3389/feduc.2022.755914

Kirova, V. D., Ku, C., Laracy, J., & Marlowe, T. (2023). The ethics of artificial intelligence in the era of generative AI. *Journal of Systemics, Cybernetics and Informatics*, 21(4), 42–50. DOI: 10.54808/JSCI.21.04.42

Kitov, V. 2020. Introduction to machine learning.

Knoth, N., Tolzin, A., Janson, A., & Leimeister, J. M. (2024). AI literacy and its implications for prompt engineering strategies. *Computers and Education: Artificial Intelligence*, 6, 100225. DOI: 10.1016/j.caeai.2024.100225

Koch, J., Taffin, N., Beaudouin-Lafon, M., Laine, M., Lucero, A., & Mackay, W. (2020). ImageSense: An Intelligent Collaborative Ideation Tool to Support Diverse Human-Computer Partnerships. *Proceedings of the ACM on Human-Computer Interaction, 4*(CSCW1), 1–27. DOI: 10.1145/3392850

Kocielnik, R., Amershi, S., & Bennett, P. N. (2019, May). Will you accept an imperfect ai? exploring designs for adjusting end-user expectations of ai systems. In *Proceedings of the 2019 CHI Conference on Human Factors in Computing Systems* (pp. 1-14).

Kolthoff, K., Bartelt, C., & Ponzetto, S. P. (2023). Data-driven prototyping via natural-language-based GUI retrieval. *Automated Software Engineering*, 30(1), 13. DOI: 10.1007/s10515-023-00377-x

Konatham, B., Simra, T., Amsaad, F., Ibrahem, M. I., & Jhanjhi, N. Z. (2024). A Secure Hybrid Deep Learning Technique for Anomaly Detection in IIoT Edge Computing. *Authorea Preprints*.

Kothandaraman, D., Prasad, S. S., & Sivasankar, P. (2023). Vulnerabilities detection in cybersecurity using deep learning–based information security and event management. In *Artificial intelligence and deep learning for computer network* (pp. 81–98). Chapman and Hall/CRC. DOI: 10.1201/9781003212249-5

Kralina, H., & Popova, A. (2024). Nowadays trends in web development. *Collection of Scientific Papers «ΛΟΓΟΣ»*. DOI: 10.36074/logos-29.03.2024.068

Krauss, C., Do, X. A., & Huck, N. (2017). Deep neural networks, gradient-boosted trees, random forests: Statistical arbitrage on the S&P 500. *European Journal of Operational Research*, 259(2), 689–702.

Kreuzberger, D., Kühl, N., & Hirschl, S. (2023). Machine learning operations (mlops): Overview, definition, and architecture. *IEEE Access : Practical Innovations, Open Solutions*, 11, 31866–31879. DOI: 10.1109/ACCESS.2023.3262138

Kronjee, J., Hommersom, A., & Vranken, H. (2018, August). Discovering software vulnerabilities using data-flow analysis and machine learning. In *Proceedings of the 13th international conference on availability, reliability and security* (pp. 1-10).

Kumar, B., Jaiswal, A. K., Vineesh, V. S., & Shinde, R. (2020, January). Analyzing hardware security properties of processors through model checking. In 2020 33rd International Conference on VLSI Design and 2020 19th International Conference on Embedded Systems (VLSID) (pp. 107-112). IEEE.

Kumar, B., Roy, S., Singh, K. U., Pandey, S. K., Kumar, A., Sinha, A., Shukla, S., Shah, M. A., & Rasool, A. (2023). A static machine learning based evaluation method for usability and security analysis in e-commerce website. *IEEE Access : Practical Innovations, Open Solutions*, 11, 40488–40510. DOI: 10.1109/ACCESS.2023.3247003

Kumar, D., & Suthar, N. (2024). Ethical and legal challenges of ai in marketing: An exploration of solutions. *Journal of Information. Communication and Ethics in Society*, 22(1), 124–144. DOI: 10.1108/JICES-05-2023-0068

Kumar, P. S. (2024). Movie Review Sentiment Analysis and AI-Story Generation Web Application. *International Journal for Research in Applied Science and Engineering Technology*, 12(3), 310–316. DOI: 10.22214/ijraset.2024.58826

Kumar, S., Gupta, U., Singh, A. K., & Singh, A. K. (2023). Artificial intelligence: Revolutionizing cyber security in the digital era. *Journal of Computers. Mechanical and Management*, 2(3), 31–42.

Kumar, T., & Trakru, M. (2020). The colossal impact of artificial intelligence. E-commerce: Statistics and facts. *Int. Res. J. Eng. Technol.*, 6, 570–572.

Kuruvila, A. P., Zografopoulos, I., Basu, K., & Konstantinou, C. (2021). Hardware-assisted detection of firmware attacks in inverter-based cyberphysical microgrids. *International Journal of Electrical Power & Energy Systems*, 132, 107150. DOI: 10.1016/j.ijepes.2021.107150

Kusairi, S. (2020). A web-based formative feedback system development by utilizing isomorphic multiple choice items to support physics teaching and learning. *Journal of Technology and Science Education*, 10, 117–126. DOI: 10.3926/jotse.781

Kustov, P., Petrova, E., Sandomirskii, M., & Zuev, D. (2022, September). All-dielectric silicon nanoparticles on flexible substrate for anticounterfeiting labels. In *2022 Sixteenth International Congress on Artificial Materials for Novel Wave Phenomena (Metamaterials)* (pp. 244-246). IEEE.

Kuthe, A., Shangarwar, S., Kamble, Y., Sakhale, P., Bhende, R., & Thakre, J. (2024). Portfolio Generator using Generative AI in Web Development. *International Journal Of Mathematics And Computer Research*, 12(5), 5. Advance online publication. DOI: 10.47191/ijmcr/v12i5.01

Kwon, O.-H., & Ma, K.-L. (2019). A deep generative model for graph layout. *IEEE Transactions on Visualization and Computer Graphics*, 26(1), 665–675. DOI: 10.1109/TVCG.2019.2934396 PMID: 31425108

Lai, C. H., & Lin, H. (2017). *S. J. T. I. E. O. O. C.* Systems Theory.

Lai, C., Lin, Z., Jiang, R., Han, Y., Liu, C., & Yuan, X. (2020, April). Automatic annotation synchronizing with textual description for visualization. In *Proceedings of the 2020 CHI Conference on Human Factors in Computing Systems* (pp. 1-13).

Lauriola, I., Lavelli, A., & Aiolli, F. (2022). An introduction to deep learning in natural language processing: Models, techniques, and tools. *Neurocomputing*, 470, 443–456. DOI: 10.1016/j.neucom.2021.05.103

Lavor, V., De Come, F., Dos Santos, M. T., & Vianna, A. S.Jr. (2024). Machine learning in chemical engineering: Hands-on activities. *Education for Chemical Engineers*, 46, 10–21. DOI: 10.1016/j.ece.2023.09.005

Lazić, L. (2019, January). Benefit from Ai in cybersecurity. In *The 11th International Conference on Business Information Security (BISEC-2019)*, 18th October.

Lee, C. C., Wang, C. W., & Ho, S. J. (2020). Financial inclusion, financial innovation, and firms' sales growth. *International Review of Economics & Finance*, 66, 189–205.

Lee, D. J.-L., Lee, J., Siddiqui, T., Kim, J., Karahalios, K., & Parameswaran, A. (2019). You can't always sketch what you want: Understanding sensemaking in visual query systems. *IEEE Transactions on Visualization and Computer Graphics*, 26, 1267–1277. DOI: 10.1109/TVCG.2019.2934666 PMID: 31443008

Lee, J., Kim, J., Kim, I., & Han, K. (2019). Cyber threat detection based on artificial neural networks using event profiles. *IEEE Access : Practical Innovations, Open Solutions*, 7, 165607–165626. DOI: 10.1109/ACCESS.2019.2953095

Lee, J., Suh, T., Roy, D., & Baucus, M. (2019). Emerging technology and business model innovation: The case of artificial intelligence. *Journal of Open Innovation*, 5(3), 44.

Lee, K., & Yim, K. (2020). Cybersecurity threats based on machine learning-based offensive technique for password authentication. *Applied Sciences (Basel, Switzerland)*, 10(4), 1286. DOI: 10.3390/app10041286

Leite, L., Rocha, C., Kon, F., Milojicic, D., & Meirelles, P. (2019). A survey of DevOps concepts and challenges. *ACM Computing Surveys*, 52(6), 1–35. DOI: 10.1145/3359981

Lei, Y., & Qiu, X. (2020). Evaluating the investment climate for China's cross-border E-Commerce: The application of back propagation neural network. *Information (Basel)*, 11(11), 526. DOI: 10.3390/info11110526

Leo, M., Sharma, S., & Maddulety, K. (2019). Machine learning in banking risk management: A literature review. *Risks*, 7(1), 29.

Le, T. H. M., & Babar, M. A. (2022, May). On the use of fine-grained vulnerable code statements for software vulnerability assessment models. In *Proceedings of the 19th International Conference on Mining Software Repositories* (pp. 621-633).

Li, G., Wang, X., Aodeng, G., Zheng, S., Zhang, Y., Ou, C., . . . Liu, C. H. (2024). Visualization generation with large language models: An evaluation. arXiv preprint arXiv:2401.11255.

Li, J. (2020). Vulnerabilities mapping based on OWASP-SANS: a survey for static application security testing (SAST). arXiv preprint arXiv:2004.03216.

Li, L., et al. (2018). "Generative adversarial networks for generation and classification of physical rehabilitation movement episodes." **8**(5): 428.

Li, Y. (2017). Deep reinforcement learning: An overview. arXiv preprint arXiv:1701.07274.

Liang, P. P., Zadeh, A., & Morency, L.-P. (2024). Foundations & trends in multimodal machine learning: Principles, challenges, and open questions. *ACM Computing Surveys*, 56, 1–42. DOI: 10.1145/3676164

Li, F., Rogers, L., Mathur, A., Malkin, N., & Chetty, M. (2019). Keepers of the machines: Examining how system administrators manage software updates for multiple machines. In *Fifteenth Symposium on Usable Privacy and Security (SOUPS 2019)* (pp. 273-288).

Li, G., & Li, N. (2019). Customs classification for cross-border e-commerce based on text-image adaptive convolutional neural network. *Electronic Commerce Research*, 19(4), 779–800. DOI: 10.1007/s10660-019-09334-x

Li, H., Wang, Y., Wu, A., Wei, H., & Qu, H. (2022, April). Structure-aware visualization retrieval. In *Proceedings of the 2022 CHI Conference on Human Factors in Computing Systems* (pp. 1-14).

Li, J., Goh, W., Jhanjhi, N., Isa, F., & Balakrishnan, S. (2021). An empirical study on challenges faced by the elderly in care centres. *EAI Endorsed Transactions on Pervasive Health and Technology*, 7(28), 7. DOI: 10.4108/eai.11-6-2021.170231

Li, J., Wang, T., Chen, Z., & Luo, G. (2019). Machine learning algorithm generated sales prediction for inventory optimization in cross-border E-commerce. *International Journal of Frontiers in Engineering Technology*, 1, 62–74.

Lim, M., Abdullah, A., Jhanjhi, N., & Supramaniam, M. (2019). Hidden link prediction in criminal networks using the deep reinforcement learning technique. *Computers*, 8(1), 8. DOI: 10.3390/computers8010008

Li, N., Zhang, H., Hu, Z., Kou, G., & Dai, H. (2021, December). Automated software vulnerability detection via pre-trained context encoder and self attention. In *International Conference on Digital Forensics and Cyber Crime* (pp. 248-264). Cham: Springer International Publishing.

Lindholm, A., Wahlström, N., Lindsten, F., & Schön, T. B. (2022). *Machine learning: a first course for engineers and scientists*. Cambridge University Press. DOI: 10.1017/9781108919371

Lin, L., Zhu, D., Wen, J., Chen, H., Lu, Y., Chang, N., & Nagata, M. (2021, December). Multiphysics simulation of em side-channels from silicon backside with ml-based auto-poi identification. In *2021 IEEE International Symposium on Hardware Oriented Security and Trust (HOST)* (pp. 270-280). IEEE.

Lin, S.-J., & Hsu, M.-F. (2017). Incorporated Risk Metrics And Hybrid Ai Techniques For Risk Management. *Neural Computing & Applications*, 28(11), 3477–3489. DOI: 10.1007/s00521-016-2253-4

Litman, D., & Forbes-Riley, K. (2004) Predicting student emotions in computer-human tutoring dialogues. Proc. *42nd Annu. Meeting Assoc. Comput. Linguist*, 351-358. DOI: 10.3115/1218955.1219000

Liu, C., Xie, L., Han, Y., Wei, D., & Yuan, X. (2020, June). AutoCaption: An approach to generate natural language description from visualization automatically. In 2020 IEEE Pacific visualization symposium (PacificVis) (pp. 191-195). IEEE.

Liu, X., Zou, Y., Kong, L., Diao, Z., Yan, J., Wang, J., . . . You, J. (2018, August). Data augmentation via latent space interpolation for image classification. In 2018 24th International Conference on Pattern Recognition (ICPR) (pp. 728-733). IEEE.

Liu, B., Penaka, S. R., Lu, W., Feng, K., Rebbling, A., & Olofsson, T. (2023). Data-driven quantitative analysis of an integrated open digital ecosystems platform for user-centric energy retrofits: A case study in northern Sweden. *Technology in Society*, 75, 102347. DOI: 10.1016/j.techsoc.2023.102347

Liu, C., Guo, Y., & Yuan, X. (2023). AutoTitle: An interactive title generator for visualizations. *IEEE Transactions on Visualization and Computer Graphics*. PMID: 37384476

Liu, F., Liu, Y., Jin, D., Jia, X., & Wang, T. (2018). Research on workshop-based positioning technology based on internet of things in big data background. *Complexity*, 2018(1), 2018. DOI: 10.1155/2018/7875460

Liu, M., Wang, J., Xu, L., Zhang, J., Li, S., & Xiang, F. (2022). BIT-MI deep learning-based model to non-intrusive speech quality assessment challenge in online conferencing applications. *Interspeech*, 2022, 3288–3292. Advance online publication. DOI: 10.21437/Interspeech.2022-10010

Liu, S., Li, Z., & Ba, L. (2020). Impact of Artificial Intelligence 2.0 on Teaching and Learning. *International Conference on Educational and Information Technology*.

Liu, S., Tao, M., Huang, Y., Wang, C., & Li, C. (2022). Image-driven harmonious color palette generation for diverse information visualization. *IEEE Transactions on Visualization and Computer Graphics*. PMID: 36459606

Liu, W., & Xie, C. (2022). MOS prediction network for non-intrusive speech quality assessment in online conferencing. *Interspeech*, 2022, 3293–3297. Advance online publication. DOI: 10.21437/Interspeech.2022-10081

Liu, X., Ospina, J., & Konstantinou, C. (2020). Deep reinforcement learning for cybersecurity assessment of wind integrated power systems. *IEEE Access : Practical Innovations, Open Solutions*, 8, 208378–208394. DOI: 10.1109/ACCESS.2020.3038769

Lively, J., Hutson, J., & Melick, E. (2023). Integrating AI-Generative Tools in Web Design Education: Enhancing Student Aesthetic and Creative Copy Capabilities Using Image and Text-Based AI Generators. *DS Journal of Artificial Intelligence and Robotics*, 1(1), 23–36. DOI: 10.59232/AIR-V1I1P103

Li, Y., Sixou, B., & Peyrin, F. (2021). A review of the deep learning methods for medical images super resolution problems. *Ingénierie et Recherche Biomédicale : IRBM = Biomedical Engineering and Research*, 42(2), 120–133. DOI: 10.1016/j. irbm.2020.08.004

Li, Y., Yi, J., Chen, H., & Peng, D. (2021). Theory and application of artificial intelligence in financial industry. *Data Science in Finance and Economics*, 1(2), 96–116.

Li, Z., Zou, D., Xu, S., Jin, H., Zhu, Y., & Chen, Z. (2021b). Sysevr: A framework for using deep learning to detect software vulnerabilities. *IEEE Transactions on Dependable and Secure Computing*, 19(4), 2244–2258. DOI: 10.1109/TDSC.2021.3051525

Lohpetch, D. (2011). *Evolutionary Algorithms For Financial Trading*. Heriot-Watt University.

López, J. A. H., Cánovas Izquierdo, J. L., & Cuadrado, J. S. (2022). ModelSet: A dataset for machine learning in model-driven engineering. *Software & Systems Modeling*, 21(3), 1–20. DOI: 10.1007/s10270-021-00929-3

Lor'e, F., Basile, P., Appice, A., de Gemmis, M., Malerba, D., & Semeraro, G. (2023). An ai framework to support decisions on gdpr compliance. *Journal of Intelligent Information Systems*, 61(2), 541–568. DOI: 10.1007/s10844-023-00782-4

Lu, C.-W., Lin, G.-H., Wu, T.-J., Hu, I.-H., & Chang, Y.-C. (2021). Influencing factors of cross-border e-commerce consumer purchase intention based on wireless network and machine learning. *Security and Communication Networks*, 2021, 1–9. DOI: 10.1155/2021/8388480

Lu, J., Pan, B., Chen, J., Feng, Y., Hu, J., Peng, Y., & Chen, W. (2024). AgentLens: Visual Analysis for Agent Behaviors in LLM-based Autonomous Systems. *IEEE Transactions on Visualization and Computer Graphics*, 1–17. DOI: 10.1109/ TVCG.2024.3394053 PMID: 38700975

Lu, J., Shang, C., Yue, C., Morillo, R., Ware, S., Kamath, J., Bamis, A., Russell, A., Wang, B., & Bi, J. (2018). Joint modeling of heterogeneous sensing data for depression assessment via multi-task learning. *Proceedings of the ACM on Interactive, Mobile, Wearable and Ubiquitous Technologies*, 2(1), 1–21. DOI: 10.1145/3191753

Lu, M., Wang, C., Lanir, J., Zhao, N., Pfister, H., Cohen-Or, D., & Huang, H. (2020, April). Exploring visual information flows in infographics. In *Proceedings of the 2020 CHI conference on human factors in computing systems* (pp. 1-12).

Luo, J., Li, Z., Wang, J., & Lin, C. Y. (2021). Chartocr: Data extraction from charts images via a deep hybrid framework. In Proceedings of the IEEE/CVF winter conference on applications of computer vision (pp. 1917-1925).

Luo, Y., Qin, X., Tang, N., Li, G., & Wang, X. (2018, May). Deepeye: Creating good data visualizations by keyword search. In *Proceedings of the 2018 International Conference on Management of Data* (pp. 1733-1736).

Luo, Y., Tang, N., Li, G., Tang, J., Chai, C., & Qin, X. (2021b). Natural language to visualization by neural machine translation. *IEEE Transactions on Visualization and Computer Graphics*, 28(1), 217–226. DOI: 10.1109/TVCG.2021.3114848 PMID: 34784276

Luo, Y., Zhou, Y., Tang, N., Li, G., Chai, C., & Shen, L. (2023). Learned data-aware image representations of line charts for similarity search. *Proceedings of the ACM on Management of Data*, 1(1), 1–29. DOI: 10.1145/3588942

Lwakatare, L. E., Crnkovic, I., & Bosch, J. (2020a). *DevOps for AI–Challenges in Development of AI-enabled Applications. 2020 international conference on software, telecommunications and computer networks (SoftCOM)*. IEEE.

Lwakatare, L. E., Crnkovic, I., Rånge, E., & Bosch, J. (2020). From a data science driven process to a continuous delivery process for machine learning systems. In Product-Focused Software Process Improvement: 21st International Conference, PROFES 2020, Turin, Italy, November 25–27, 2020 [Springer International Publishing.]. *Proceedings*, 21, 185–201.

Lyu, L. (2023). A pathway towards responsible AI generated content. *Proceedings of the Thirty-Second International Joint Conference on Artificial Intelligence*, 7033–7038. DOI: 10.24963/ijcai.2023/803

Ma, M., Chen, L., & Shi, G. (2019, December). Dam: A practical scheme to mitigate data-oriented attacks with tagged memory based on hardware. In 2019 26th Asia-Pacific Software Engineering Conference (APSEC) (pp. 204-211). IEEE.

Macarthy, R. W., & Bass, J. M. (2020, August). An empirical taxonomy of DevOps in practice. In 2020 46th euromicro conference on software engineering and advanced applications (seaa) (pp. 221-228). IEEE.

Macharia, V. M., Garg, V. K., & Kumar, D. (2023). A review of electric vehi- cle technology: Architectures, battery technology and its management sys- tem, relevant standards, application of artificial intelligence, cyber security, and interoperability challenges. *IET Electrical Systems in Transportation*, 13(2), e12083. DOI: 10.1049/els2.12083

Maddireddy, B. R., & Maddireddy, B. R. (2020). Proactive cyber defense: Utilizing ai for early threat detection and risk assessment. *International Journal of Advanced Engineering Technologies and Innovations*, 1(2), 64–83.

Maddireddy, B. R., & Maddireddy, B. R. (2022). Real-Time Data Analytics with AI: Improving Security Event Monitoring and Management. *Unique Endeavor in Business & Social Sciences*, 1(2), 47–62.

Maeso, J.-M. (2022). *Stochastic Modeling Applied To Portfolio Optimization Problems*. Université Côte D'azur.

Mahadevappa, P., & Murugesan, R. K. (2021). Review of data integrity attacks and mitigation methods in edge computing. *Advances in Cyber Security: Third International Conference, ACeS 2021, Penang, Malaysia, August 24--25, 2021, Revised Selected Papers 3*, 505–514.

Mahadevappa, P., Murugesan, R. K., Al-amri, R., Thabit, R., Al-Ghushami, A. H., & Alkawsi, G. (2024). A secure edge computing model using machine learning and IDS to detect and isolate intruders. *MethodsX*, 12, 102597. DOI: 10.1016/j.mex.2024.102597 PMID: 38379716

Maharani, D., Anggraeni, D., & Nofitri, R. (2024). Pemanfaatan Artificial intelligence dalam Pembuatan Presentasi bagi Guru-Guru Brain for Islamic School Kisaran. [JISS]. *Journal Of Indonesian Social Society*, 2(1), 45–51.

Mahmood, D. A. M. & Loknath, B. (2024). An Improved Cost-sensitive Payment Card Fraud Detection Based on Dynamic Random Forest and K-nearest Neighbours.

Mäkinen, S., Skogström, H., Laaksonen, E., & Mikkonen, T. (2021, May). Who needs MLOps: What data scientists seek to accomplish and how can MLOps help? In *2021 IEEE/ACM 1st Workshop on AI Engineering-Software Engineering for AI (WAIN)* (pp. 109-112). IEEE.

Malakar, P., & Leeladharan, M. (2024). Generative AI Tools for Collaborative Content Creation. *DESIDOC Journal of Library and Information Technology*, 44(3), 3. Advance online publication. DOI: 10.14429/djlit.44.3.19698

Maleh, Y., Shojafar, M., Alazab, M., & Romdhani, I. (2020). Blockchain for cyber-security and privacy: architectures, challenges, and applications.

Manssour, N. A., Lapotre, V., Gogniat, G., & Tisserand, A. (2022, April). Processor extensions for hardware instruction replay against fault injection attacks. In *2022 25th International Symposium on Design and Diagnostics of Electronic Circuits and Systems (DDECS)* (pp. 26-31). IEEE.

Manzoor, M. K., Latif, R. M. A., Haq, I., & Jhanjhi, N. (2022). An energy-efficient routing protocol via angle-based flooding zone in underwater wireless sensor networks. *International Journal of Intelligent Systems and Applications in Engineering*, 10, 116–123.

Mao, Y., Migliore, V., & Nicomette, V. (2020, September). REHAD: Using low-frequency reconfigurable hardware for cache side-channel attacks detection. In *2020 IEEE European Symposium on Security and Privacy Workshops (EuroS&PW)* (pp. 704-709). IEEE.

Maouche, S. (2019). Google ai: Opportunities, risks, and ethical challenges. *Contemporary French and Francophone Studies*, 23(4), 447–455. DOI: 10.1080/17409292.2019.1705012

Ma, R., Mei, H., Guan, H., Huang, W., Zhang, F., Xin, C., Dai, W., Wen, X., & Chen, W. (2020). Ladv: Deep learning assisted authoring of dashboard visualizations from images and sketches. *IEEE Transactions on Visualization and Computer Graphics*, 27(9), 3717–3732. DOI: 10.1109/TVCG.2020.2980227 PMID: 32175864

Markevych, M., & Dawson, M. (2023). A review of enhancing intrusion detection systems for cybersecurity using artificial intelligence (ai). In *International conference knowledge-based organization* (Vol. 29, pp. 30–37). DOI: 10.2478/kbo-2023-0072

Markou, G., Bakas, N. P., Chatzichristofis, S. A., & Papadrakakis, M. (2024). A general framework of high-performance machine learning algorithms: Application in structural mechanics. *Computational Mechanics*, 73(4), 705–729. DOI: 10.1007/s00466-023-02386-9

Márquez, G., & Astudillo, H. (2019, September). Identifying availability tactics to support security architectural design of microservice-based systems. In *Proceedings of the 13th European Conference on Software Architecture-Volume 2* (pp. 123-129).

Marr, B. (2019). *Artificial intelligence in practice: how 50 successful companies used AI and machine learning to solve problems*. John Wiley & Sons.

Martins, R. M., Von Wangenheim, C. G., Rauber, M. F., & Hauck, J. C. (2024). Machine learning for all!—Introducing machine learning in middle and high school. *International Journal of Artificial Intelligence in Education*, 34(2), 185–223. DOI: 10.1007/s40593-022-00325-y

Mashatian, S., et al. (2024). "Building Trustworthy Generative Artificial Intelligence for Diabetes Care and Limb Preservation: A Medical Knowledge Extraction Case." 19322968241253568.

Masry, A., Kavehzadeh, P., Do, X. L., Hoque, E., & Joty, S. (2023). Unichart: A universal vision-language pretrained model for chart comprehension and reasoning. arXiv preprint arXiv:2305.14761.

Mateo Sanguino, T. (2024). Enhancing Security in Industrial Application Development: Case Study on Self-Generating Artificial Intelligence Tools. *Applied Sciences (Basel, Switzerland)*, 14(9), 3780. DOI: 10.3390/app14093780

Matz, S., Teeny, J., Vaid, S. S., Peters, H., Harari, G., & Cerf, M. (2024). The potential of generative AI for personalized persuasion at scale. *Scientific Reports*, 14(1), 4692. DOI: 10.1038/s41598-024-53755-0 PMID: 38409168

Mavridis, T., & Symeonidis, A. L. (2014). Semantic analysis of web documents for the generation of optimal content. *Engineering Applications of Artificial Intelligence*, 35, 114–130. DOI: 10.1016/j.engappai.2014.06.008

Ma, X., & Wang, Z. (2024). Computer security technology in E-commerce platform business model construction. *Heliyon*, 10(7), 10. DOI: 10.1016/j.heliyon.2024.e28571 PMID: 38586367

McIntosh, T., Liu, T., Susnjak, T., Alavizadeh, H., Ng, A., Nowrozy, R., & Watters, P. (2023). Harnessing GPT-4 for generation of cybersecurity GRC policies: A focus on ransomware attack mitigation. *Computers & Security*, 134, 103424. DOI: 10.1016/j.cose.2023.103424

Mclean, M. (2023). Must-Know Cyber Attack statistics and Trends| Embroker.

Mehra, M. (2021). A review on wireless sensor networks and its applications. *International Journal of Innovative Research in Computer Science & Technology*, 295-298, 295–298. Advance online publication. DOI: 10.55524/ijircst.2021.9.6.65

Mehrotra, A., & Musolesi, M. (2018). Using autoencoders to automatically extract mobility features for predicting depressive states. *Proceedings of the ACM on Interactive, Mobile, Wearable and Ubiquitous Technologies*, 2(3), 1–20. DOI: 10.1145/3264937

Mello, R.F., Freitas, E., Pereira, F.D., Cabral, L.D., Tedesco, P., & Ramalho, G. (2023). Education in the age of Generative AI: Context and Recent Developments. *ArXiv, abs/2309.12332.*

Memon, M. S., Bhatti, M. N., Hashmani, M. A., Malik, M. S., & Dahri, N. M. (2022). *Techniques and Trends Towards Various Dimensions of Robust Security Testing in Global Software Engineering. Research Anthology on Agile Software, Software Development, and Testing.* IGI Global.

Meskó, B., & Topol, E. J. (2023). The imperative for regulatory oversight of large language models (or generative AI) in healthcare. *NPJ Digital Medicine*, 6(1), 1–6. DOI: 10.1038/s41746-023-00873-0 PMID: 37414860

Messaoud, S., Bouaafia, S., Bradai, A., Ali Hajjaji, M., Mtibaa, A., & Atri, M. (2022). *Network slicing for industrial IoT and industrial wireless sensor network: Deep federated learning approach and its implementation challenges.* Emerging Trends in Wireless Sensor Networks., DOI: 10.5772/intechopen.102472

Miki, T., Nagata, M., Sonoda, H., Miura, N., Okidono, T., Araga, Y., Watanabe, N., Shimamoto, H., & Kikuchi, K. (2020). Si-backside protection circuits against physical security attacks on flip-chip devices. *IEEE Journal of Solid-State Circuits*, 55(10), 2747–2755. DOI: 10.1109/JSSC.2020.3005779

Miljkovic, A., & Chronéer, B. (2018). Application Scorecard Modelling With Artificial. *Neural Networks*.

Mingyong, L., Changfei, J., & Kai, N. (2014). Logistics CPS: Implementation and challenge of next generation intelligent logistics system. *Systems Engineering*, 29, 60–65.

Miraz, M. H., Excell, P. S., Ware, A., Soomro, S., & Ali, M. (Eds.). (2019). Emerging Technologies in Computing: Second International Conference, iCETiC 2019, London, UK, August 19–20, 2019, Proceedings.

Mishra, S. K., Mishra, S., Alsayat, A., Jhanjhi, N., Humayun, M., Sahoo, K. S., & Luhach, A. K. (2020). Energy-aware task allocation for multi-cloud networks. *IEEE Access : Practical Innovations, Open Solutions*, 8, 178825–178834. DOI: 10.1109/ACCESS.2020.3026875

Mishra, S., Chaudhury, P., Tripathy, H. K., Sahoo, K. S., Jhanjhi, N., Hassan Elnour, A. A., & Abdelmaboud, A. (2024). Enhancing health care through medical cognitive virtual agents. *Digital Health*, 10, 20552076241256732. DOI: 10.1177/20552076241256732 PMID: 39165388

Moalosi, M., Hlomani, H., & Phefo, O. S. (2019). Combating Credit Card Fraud With Online Behavioural Targeting And Device Fingerprinting. *International Journal Of Electronic Security And Digital Forensics*, 11(1), 46–69. DOI: 10.1504/IJESDF.2019.096527

Mohammed, H., Odetola, T. A., Hasan, S. R., Stissi, S., Garlin, I., & Awwad, F. (2019, August). (HIADIoT): Hardware intrinsic attack detection in Internet of Things; leveraging power profiling. In 2019 ieee 62nd international midwest symposium on circuits and systems (mwscas) (pp. 852-855). IEEE.

Mohri, M., Rostamizadeh, A., & Talwalkar, A. (2018). *Foundations of machine learning*. MIT press.

Molina-Ríos, J., & Pedreira-Souto, N. (2020). Comparison of development methodologies in web applications. *Information and Software Technology*, 119, 106238. DOI: 10.1016/j.infsof.2019.106238

Montoya, M., Bacles-Min, S., Molnos, A., & Fournier, J. J. (2020, August). Dynamic encoding, a lightweight combined countermeasure against hardware attacks. In 2020 23rd Euromicro Conference on Digital System Design (DSD) (pp. 185-192). IEEE.

Montoya, M., Hiscock, T., Bacles-Min, S., Molnos, A., & Fournier, J. Adaptive masking: a dynamic trade-off between energy consumption and hardware security. 2019 IEEE 37th International Conference on Computer Design (ICCD), 2019. IEEE, 559-566.

Mostow, J., Aist, G., Huang, C., Junker, B., Kennedy, R., Lan, H., Latimer, D. T., O'Connor, R., Tassone, R., Tobin, B., & Wierman, A. (2008).*4-month evaluation of a learner-controlled reading tutor that listens. In The Path of Speech Technologies in Computer Assisted Language Learning: From Research Toward Practice* (pp. 201–219). Routledge.

Mougayar, W. (2016). *The business blockchain: promise, practice, and application of the next Internet technology*. John Wiley & Sons.

Moustafa, N., Keshk, M., Debie, E., & Janicke, H. (2020). *Federated TON_IoT Windows Datasets for Evaluating AI-based Security Applications* (arXiv:2010.08522). arXiv. http://arxiv.org/abs/2010.08522 DOI: 10.1109/TrustCom50675.2020.00114

Mugarza, I., Parra, J., & Jacob, E. (2018). Analysis of existing dynamic software updating techniques for safe and secure industrial control systems. *International Journal of Safety and Security Engineering*, 8(1), 121–131. DOI: 10.2495/SAFE-V8-N1-121-131

Mughal, A. A. (2018). Artificial intelligence in information security: Exploring the advantages, challenges, and future directions. *Journal of Artificial Intelligence and Machine Learning in Management*, 2(1), 22–34.

Mughal, M. A., Ullah, A., Yu, X., He, W., Jhanjhi, N. Z., & Ray, S. K. (2024). A secure and privacy preserved data aggregation scheme in IoMT. *Heliyon*, 10(7), e27177. Advance online publication. DOI: 10.1016/j.heliyon.2024.e27177 PMID: 38601685

Mulahuwaish, A., Gyorick, K., Ghafoor, K. Z., Maghdid, H. S., & Rawat, D. B. (2020). Efficient classification model of web news documents using machine learning algorithms for accurate information. *Computers & Security*, 98, 102006. DOI: 10.1016/j.cose.2020.102006

Müller, A. C., & Guido, S. (2016). *Introduction to machine learning with Python: a guide for data scientists*. O'Reilly Media, Inc.

Musleh Al-Sartawi, A. M., Hussainey, K., Razzaque, A. J. J. O. S. F. & Investment 2022. The Role Of Artificial Intelligence In Sustainable Finance. Taylor & Francis.

Musleh Al-Sartawi, A. M., Hussainey, K., & Razzaque, A. (2022). The role of artificial intelligence in sustainable finance. *Journal of Sustainable Finance & Investment*, ●●●, 1–6. DOI: 10.1080/20430795.2022.2057405

Muzafar, S., Humayun, M., & Hussain, S. J. (2022). *Emerging Cybersecurity Threats in the Eye of E-Governance in the Current Era. Cybersecurity Measures for E-Government Frameworks*. IGI Global.

Muzammal, S. M., & Murugesan, R. K. (2020). A Study on Secured Authentication and Authorization in Internet of Things: Potential of Blockchain Technology. In Anbar, M., Abdullah, N., & Manickam, S. (Eds.), *Advances in Cyber Security* (pp. 18–32). Springer., DOI: 10.1007/978-981-15-2693-0_2

Muzammal, S. M., & Murugesan, R. K. (2021). Enhanced authentication and access control in Internet of Things: A potential blockchain-based method. *International Journal of Grid and Utility Computing*, 12(5–6), 469–485. DOI: 10.1504/IJGUC.2021.120090

Muzammal, S. M., Shah, M. A., Zhang, S.-J., & Yang, H.-J. (2016). Conceivable security risks and authentication techniques for smart devices: A comparative evaluation of security practices. *International Journal of Automation and Computing*, 13(4), 350–363. DOI: 10.1007/s11633-016-1011-5

Muzammal, S. M., Tayyab, M., Zahra, F., Jhanjhi, N., & Ashraf, H. (2024). Smart factories greener future: A synergy of industry 4.0 and sustain- ability. In *Digital transformation for improved industry and supply chain performance* (pp. 70–92). IGI Global. DOI: 10.4018/979-8-3693-5375-2.ch004

Naeem, M., et al. (2024). "The Impact of Investment in AI on Bank Performance: Empirical Evidence from Pakistan's Banking Sector." **17**(1).

Naeem, M., Siraj, M., Abdali, A. S., & Mehboob, A. (2024). The Impact of Investment in AI on Bank Performance: Empirical Evidence from Pakistan's Banking Sector. *KASBIT Business Journal, 17*(1).

Naeem, M. (2023). Corporate Governance Mechanism and Financial Performance in Pakistan Commercial Banks: Moderating Role of Credit Risk Management. *RADS Journal of Business Management*, 5(2), 95–112.

Naeem, M., Rehman, A., Mehboob, A., & Abdali, A. S. (2023). Corporate Social Responsibility's Hidden Power in context of Pakistan: Amplifying Firm Performance. *Sukkur IBA Journal of Management and Business*, 10(2), 57–76. DOI: 10.30537/sijmb.v10i2.1383

Nandhini, S., & KS, J. M. (2020, February). Performance evaluation of machine learning algorithms for email spam detection. In 2020 International Conference on Emerging Trends in Information Technology and Engineering (ic-ETITE) (pp. 1-4). IEEE.

Nanjundappa, R., Gajendra, N., Samal, S. P., Mahesha, N., Pahuja, A., Musham, V. M., & NamGung, E. (2020, December). AWAF: AI Enabled Web Contents Authoring Framework. In 2020 IEEE 17th India Council International Conference (INDICON) (pp. 1-5). IEEE.

Narayanan, S., & Georgiou, P. (2013). Behavioral Signal Processing: Deriving Human Behavioral Informatics. *Proceedings of the IEEE*, 101(5), 1203–1233. DOI: 10.1109/JPROC.2012.2236291 PMID: 24039277

Naser, M. (2023). *Machine learning for civil and environmental engineers: A practical approach to data-driven analysis, explainability, and causality*. John Wiley & Sons.

Naveenkumar, R., Sivamangai, N. M., Napolean, A., Puviarasu, A., & Saranya, G. (2022, June). Preventive measure of sat attack by integrating anti-sat on locked circuit for improving hardware security. In 2022 7th International Conference on Communication and Electronics Systems (ICCES) (pp. 756-760). IEEE.

Nessler, N., Cernak, M., Prandoni, P., & Mainar, P. (2021). Non-intrusive speech quality assessment with transfer learning and subject-specific scaling. *Interspeech*, 2021, 2406–2410. Advance online publication. DOI: 10.21437/Interspeech.2021-1685

New AI Insights: Explore Key AI Trends and Risks in the ThreatLabz 2024 AI Security Report. (n.d.). Retrieved September 12, 2024, from https://www.zscaler.com/blogs/security-research/new-ai-insights-explore-key-ai-trends-and-risks-threatlabz-2024-ai-security

Nguyen Thanh, B., Son, H. X., & Vo, D. T. H. (2024). Blockchain: The Economic and Financial Institution for Autonomous AI. *Journal of Risk and Financial Management*, 17(2), 54. DOI: 10.3390/jrfm17020054

Nguyen, C. T., Liu, Y., Du, H., Hoang, D. T., Niyato, D., Nguyen, D. N., & Mao, S. (2024, January 28). *Generative AI-enabled Blockchain Networks: Fundamentals, Applications, and Case Study.* arXiv.Org. https://arxiv.org/abs/2401.15625v1

Nicholls, J., Kuppa, A., & Le-Khac, N.-A. (2021). Financial cybercrime: A comprehensive survey of deep learning approaches to tackle the evolving financial crime landscape. *IEEE Access: Practical Innovations, Open Solutions*, 9, 163965–163986. DOI: 10.1109/ACCESS.2021.3134076

Niemueller, T., Ewert, D., Reuter, S., Ferrein, A., Jeschke, S., & Lakemeyer, G. (2016). Robocup logistics league sponsored by festo: A competitive factory automation testbed. *Automation. Communication and Cybernetics in Science and Engineering*, 2015/2016, 605–618. DOI: 10.1007/978-3-319-42620-4_45

Nixon, N., Lin, Y., & Snow, L. (2024). Catalyzing Equity in STEM Teams: Harnessing Generative AI for Inclusion and Diversity. *Policy Insights from the Behavioral and Brain Sciences*, 11(1), 23727322231220356. DOI: 10.1177/23727322231220356 PMID: 38516055

Njuguna, B. (2023). StockDistFit: Fit stock price distributions. *CRAN: Contributed Packages.* https://doi.org/DOI: 10.32614/CRAN.package.StockDistFit

Nortje, M., & Grobbelaar, S. S. (2020). *A framework for the implementation of artificial intelligence in business enterprises: A readiness model. In 2020 ieee international conference on engineering, technology and innovation (ice/itmc).*

Ntoutsi, E., Fafalios, P., Gadiraju, U., Iosifidis, V., Nejdl, W., Vidal, M.-E., Ruggieri, S., Turini, F., Papadopoulos, S., Krasanakis, E., Kompatsiaris, I., Kinder-Kurlanda, K., Wagner, C., Karimi, F., Fernandez, M., Alani, H., Berendt, B., Kruegel, T., Heinze, C., & Staab, S. (2020). Bias in data-driven artificial intelligence systems—An introductory survey. *Wiley Interdisciplinary Reviews. Data Mining and Knowledge Discovery*, 10(3), e1356. DOI: 10.1002/widm.1356

Nyre-Yu, M., Butler, K., & Bolstad, C. (2022). A task analysis of static binary reverse engineering for security.

Obeid, J. S., Davis, M., Turner, M., Meystre, S. M., Heider, P. M., O'Bryan, E. C., & Lenert, L. A. (2020). An artificial intelligence approach to COVID-19 infection risk assessment in virtual visits: A case report. *Journal of the American Medical Informatics Association : JAMIA*, 27(8), 1321–1325. DOI: 10.1093/jamia/ocaa105 PMID: 32449766

Ogidan, E. T., Dimililer, K., & Ever, Y. K. (2018, October). Machine learning for expert systems in data analysis. In 2018 2nd International Symposium on Multidisciplinary Studies and Innovative Technologies (ISMSIT) (pp. 1-5). IEEE.

Olanrewaju, R. F., Khan, B. U. I., Morshidi, M. A., Anwar, F., & Kiah, M. L. B. M. (2021). A frictionless and secure user authentication in web-based premium applications. *IEEE Access : Practical Innovations, Open Solutions*, 9, 129240–129255. DOI: 10.1109/ACCESS.2021.3110310

Oluwagbenro, D. M. B. (2024). *Generative AI: Definition, Concepts, Applications, and Future Prospects*. DOI: 10.36227/techrxiv.171746875.59016695/v1

Ooi, K. B., Tan, G. W. H., Al-Emran, M., Al-Sharafi, M. A., Capatina, A., Chakraborty, A., Dwivedi, Y. K., Huang, T.-L., Kar, A. K., Lee, V.-H., Loh, X.-M., Micu, A., Mikalef, P., Mogaji, E., Pandey, N., Raman, R., Rana, N. P., Sarker, P., Sharma, A., & Wong, L. W. (2023). The potential of Generative Artificial Intelligence across disciplines: Perspectives and future directions. *Journal of Computer Information Systems*, •••, 1–32. DOI: 10.1080/08874417.2023.2261010

Oppenlaender, J. (2022). The Creativity of Text-to-Image Generation. *Proceedings of the 25th International Academic Mindtrek Conference*, 192–202. DOI: 10.1145/3569219.3569352

Oppenlaender, J. (2023). A Taxonomy of Prompt Modifiers for Text-To-Image Generation. *Behaviour & Information Technology*, •••, 1–14. DOI: 10.1080/0144929X.2023.2286532

Ozkaya, I. (2023). The next frontier in software development: AI-augmented software development processes. *IEEE Software*, 40(4), 4–9. DOI: 10.1109/MS.2023.3278056

Padmaja, M., Shitharth, S., Prasuna, K., Chaturvedi, A., Kshirsagar, P. R., & Vani, A. (2022). Grow of artificial intelligence to challenge security in IoT application. *Wireless Personal Communications*, 127(3), 1829–1845. DOI: 10.1007/s11277-021-08725-4

Pan, S., et al. (2024). "Unifying large language models and knowledge graphs: A roadmap."

Panda, B., & Leepsa, N. M. J. I. J. O. C. G. (2017). Agency Theory. *Review Of Theory And Evidence On Problems And Perspectives.*, 10, 74–95.

Pandey, A. (2023). Generative AI in teaching and learning: Prompt engineering and towards digital equity. *INTEGRITY, OPEN SCIENCE AND ARTIFICIAL INTELLIGENCE IN ACADEMIA AND BEYOND: MEETING AT THE CROSSROADS.* https://doi.org/DOI: 10.30525/978-9934-26-397-2-34

Pant, S., & Hsu, C. (1995, May). Strategic information systems planning: a review. In *Information Resources Management Association International Conference* (Vol. 3, No. 2, pp. 432-441).

Park, S.-C. (2018). The Fourth Industrial Revolution and implications for innovative cluster policies. *AI & Society*, 33(3), 433–445. DOI: 10.1007/s00146-017-0777-5

Patel, B. (2023). The Future of Mortgages: Evaluating the Potential of Blockchain and Generative AI for Reducing Costs and Streamlining Processes.

Patil, D. (2017). Internet of things and security challenges in wireless sensor network. *Asian Journal of Engineering and Applied Technology*, 6(1), 14–18. DOI: 10.51983/ajeat-2017.6.1.816

Patil, D. C.. (2014). Mechanical property evaluation of an Al-2024 alloy subjected to HPT processing. *IOP Conference Series: Materials Science and Engineering*, IOP Publishing. DOI: 10.1088/1757-899X/63/1/012085

Patil, D. D., Dhotre, D. R., Gawande, G. S., Mate, D. S., Shelke, M. V., & Bhoye, T. S. (2024). Transformative trends in generative ai: Harnessing large language models for natural language understanding and generation. *International Journal of Intelligent Systems and Applications in Engineering*, 12(4s), 309–319.

Patnaik, S., Rangarajan, N., Knechtel, J., Sinanoglu, O., & Rakheja, S. (2019). Spin-orbit torque devices for hardware security: From deterministic to probabilistic regime. *IEEE Transactions on Computer-Aided Design of Integrated Circuits and Systems*, 39(8), 1591–1606. DOI: 10.1109/TCAD.2019.2917856

Patten, T., & Jacobs, P. (1994). Natural-language processing. *IEEE Expert*, 9(1), 35. DOI: 10.1109/64.295134

Patterson, J., & Gibson, A. (2017). *Deep learning: A practitioner's approach.* O'Reilly Media, Inc.

Paulraj, P., & Neelamegam, A. (2014, January). Improving business intelligence based on frequent itemsets using k-means clustering algorithm. In Networks and Communications (NetCom2013) Proceedings of the Fifth International Conference on Networks & Communications (pp. 243-254). Cham: Springer International Publishing.

Perera, P., Silva, R., & Perera, I. (2017, September). Improve software quality through practicing DevOps. In 2017 seventeenth international conference on advances in ICT for emerging regions (ICTer) (pp. 1-6). IEEE.

Pesovski, I., Santos, R., Henriques, R., & Trajkovik, V. (2024). Generative ai for customizable learning experiences. *Sustainability (Basel)*, 16(7), 3034. DOI: 10.3390/su16073034

Petcu, A., Pahontu, B., Frunzete, M., & Stoichescu, D. A. (2023). A secure and decentralized authentication mechanism based on Web 3.0 and Ethereum blockchain technology. *Applied Sciences (Basel, Switzerland)*, 13(4), 2231. DOI: 10.3390/app13042231

Peters, D., Vold, K., Robinson, D., & Calvo, R. A. (2020). Responsible AI—Two frameworks for ethical design practice. *IEEE Transactions on Technology and Society*, 1(1), 34–47. DOI: 10.1109/TTS.2020.2974991

Peterson, J. (2012). *Customisation Of Fashion Products Using Complete Garment Technology*. Tampere University Of Technology.

Ploennigs, J., & Berger, M. (2024). Automating computational design with generative AI. *Civil Engineering Design*, 6(2), 41–52. DOI: 10.1002/cend.202400006

Pollastri, G., Baldi, P., Fariselli, P., & Casadio, R. (2002). Prediction of coordination number and relative solvent accessibility in proteins. *Proteins*, 47(2), 142–153.

Pon-Barry, H., & Shieber, S. M. (2011). Recognizing uncertainty in speech. *EURASIP Journal on Advances in Signal Processing*, 2011(1), 251753. DOI: 10.1155/2011/251753

Posoldova, A. (2020). Machine learning pipelines: From research to production. *IEEE Potentials*, 39(6), 38–42. DOI: 10.1109/MPOT.2020.3016280

Price, P., Tepperman, J., Iseli, M., Duong, T., Black, M., Wang, S., Boscardin, C., Heritage, M., David Pearson, S., Narayanan, S., & Alwan, A. (2009). Assessment of emerging reading skills in young native speakers and language learners. *Speech Communication*, 51(10), 968–984. DOI: 10.1016/j.specom.2009.05.001

Priyanga, G. (2023). The effects of artificial intelligence on digital marketing. ShodhKosh. *Journal of Visual and Performing Arts*, 4, 158–167.

Priya, S., Bhadra, S., Chimalakonda, S., & Venigalla, A. S. M. (2024). ML-Quest: A game for introducing machine learning concepts to K-12 students. *Interactive Learning Environments*, 32(1), 229–244. DOI: 10.1080/10494820.2022.2084115

Qamar, F., Kazmi, S. H. A., Ariffin, K. A. Z., Tayyab, M., & Nguyen, Q. N. (2024). Multi-antenna arrays based massive-mimo for b5g/6g: State-of- the-art, challenges and future research directions.

Qasim, M., Mahmood, D., Bibi, A., Masud, M., Ahmed, G., Khan, S., Jhanjhi, N. Z., & Hussain, S. J. (2022). PCA-based advanced local octa-directional pattern (ALODP-PCA): A texture feature descriptor for image retrieval. *Electronics (Basel)*, 11(2), 202. DOI: 10.3390/electronics11020202

Qin, Z. (2021). Research on cross-border E-commerce third-party logistics model based on machine learning algorithm. *Solid State Technology*, 64, 1454–1461.

Qumer, S. M., & Ikrama, S. (2022). Poppy gustafsson: redefining cybersecurity through ai. *The Case for Women*, 1–38.

Qureshi, J. (2024). *AI-Powered Cloud-Based E-Commerce: Driving Digital Business Transformation Initiatives* (No. 2024012214). *Preprints*. DOI: 10.20944/ preprints202401.2214.v1

Rabbani, M. R., Sarea, A., Khan, S., & Abdullah, Y. (2022). Ethical concerns in artificial intelligence (AI): The role of RegTech and Islamic finance. In *Artificial Intelligence for Sustainable Finance and Sustainable Technology: Proceedings of ICGER 2021 1* (pp. 381-390). Springer International Publishing.

Radanliev, P., De Roure, D., & Santos, O. (2023). Red Teaming Generative AI/ NLP, the BB84 quantum cryptography protocol and the NIST-approved Quantum-Resistant Cryptographic Algorithms. *arXiv Preprint arXiv:2310.04425*. DOI: 10.36227/techrxiv.24153183.v1

Raimi, L., Kah, J. M., & Tariq, M. U. (2022). The Discourse of Blue Economy Definitions, Measurements, and Theories: Implications for Strengthening Academic Research and Industry Practice. In Raimi, L., & Kah, J. (Eds.), *Implications for Entrepreneurship and Enterprise Development in the Blue Economy* (pp. 1–17). IGI Global., DOI: 10.4018/978-1-6684-3393-5.ch001

Raimi, L., Tariq, M. U., & Kah, J. M. (2022). Diversity, Equity, and Inclusion as the Future Workplace Ethics: Theoretical Review. In Raimi, L., & Kah, J. (Eds.), *Mainstreaming Diversity, Equity, and Inclusion as Future Workplace Ethics* (pp. 1–27). IGI Global., DOI: 10.4018/978-1-6684-3657-8.ch001

Rajan, J. G., & Ganesh, R. S. (2022, October). Hardware based data security techniques in IoT: A review. In 2022 3rd International Conference on Smart Electronics and Communication (ICOSEC) (pp. 408-413). IEEE.

Raji, M. A., Olodo, H. B., Oke, T. T., Addy, W. A., Ofodile, O. C., & Oyewole, A. T. (2024). E-commerce and consumer behavior: A review of AI-powered personalization and market trends. GSC Advanced Research and Reviews, 18(3), 066-077.

Rampášek, M. (2023). AI CYBERSECURITY STANDARDISATION AND ITS OVERLAP WITH DSA AND CRA. *Acta Facultatis Iuridicae Universitatis Comenianae*, 42(2), 14–14. DOI: 10.62874/afi.2023.2.08

Rana, M. S., & Shuford, J. (2024). Ai in healthcare: Transforming patient care through predictive analytics and decision support systems. *Journal of Artificial Intelligence General Science (JAIGS) ISSN: 3006-4023, 1* (1).

Rane, N., Choudhary, S., & Rane, J. (2023). Integrating Building Information Modelling (BIM) with ChatGPT, Bard, and similar generative artificial intelligence in the architecture, engineering, and construction industry: applications, a novel framework, challenges, and future scope. *Bard, and similar generative artificial intelligence in the architecture, engineering, and construction industry: applications, a novel framework, challenges, and future scope (November 22, 2023).*

Rane, N. (2023). Role of ChatGPT and similar generative artificial intelligence (AI) in construction industry. *Available atSSRN* 4598258. DOI: 10.2139/ssrn.4598258

Ranganath, V.-P., & Mitra, J. (2020). Are free android app security analysis tools effective in detecting known vulnerabilities? *Empirical Software Engineering*, 25(1), 178–219. DOI: 10.1007/s10664-019-09749-y

Raso, F. A., Hilligoss, H., Krishnamurthy, V., Bavitz, C., & Kim, L. (2018). Artificial intelligence & human rights: Opportunities & risks. *Berkman Klein Center Research Publication*(2018-6).

Rasyad, F., Kongguasa, H. A., & Onggususilo, N. C., Anderies, Kurniawan, A., & Gunawan, A. A. (2023). A systematic literature review of generative adversarial network potential in AI artwork. *2023 International Conference on Computer Science, Information Technology and Engineering (ICCoSITE)*. https://doi.org/DOI: 10.1109/ICCoSITE57641.2023.10127706

Ratani, S., Phatta, D., Phalke, D., Varun, N., & Aher, A. (2024, February). Web Sculptor-Generative AI Based Comprehensive Web Development Framework. In 2024 IEEE International Conference on Computing, Power and Communication Technologies (IC2PCT) (Vol. 5, pp. 1729-1732). IEEE.

Ravi, H. (2021). Innovation in banking: Fusion of artificial intelligence and block-chain. *Asia Pacific Journal of Innovation and Entrepreneurship*, 15(1), 51–61. DOI: 10.1108/APJIE-09-2020-0142

Rawindaran, N., Jayal, A., & Prakash, E. (2021). Machine learning cyberse- curity adoption in small and medium enterprises in developed countries. *Computers*, 10(11), 150. DOI: 10.3390/computers10110150

Razavi, A., van den Oord, A., & Vinyals, O. (2019). Generating Diverse High-Fidelity Images with VQ-VAE-2. *Advances in Neural Information Processing Systems, 32*. https://proceedings.neurips.cc/paper/2019/hash/5f8e2fa1718d1bbcadf1cd9c7a54fb8c-Abstract.html

Reddy, R. T., Pati, P. B., Deepa, K., & Sangeetha, S. T. (2023, April). Flight Delay Prediction Using Machine Learning. In 2023 IEEE 8th International Conference for Convergence in Technology (I2CT) (pp. 1-5). IEEE.

Reddy, R. D., Katkam, S., & Rao, C. R. S. (2022). Cyber Attacks Detection using Machine Learning. *NeuroQuantology: An Interdisciplinary Journal of Neuroscience and Quantum Physics*, 20(19), 4388.

Rehman, T., Tariq, N., Ashraf, M., & Humayun, M. (2024). *Network Intrusion Detection to Mitigate Jamming and Spoofing Attacks Using Federated Leading: A Comprehensive Survey*. Cybersecurity Measures for Logistics Industry Framework.

Reilly, J., McCarthy, K., McGinty, L., & Smyth, B. (2004, December). Incremental critiquing. In *International Conference on Innovative Techniques and Applications of Artificial Intelligence* (pp. 101-114). London: Springer London.

Reimann, L. M., Hanel, L., Sisejkovic, D., Merchant, F., & Leupers, R. (2021, October). Qflow: Quantitative information flow for security-aware hardware design in verilog. In 2021 IEEE 39th International Conference on Computer Design (ICCD) (pp. 603-607). IEEE.

Reis, D. A., ... (2012). Effect of artificial aging on the mechanical properties of an aerospace aluminum alloy 2024. Defect and Diffusion Forum, Trans Tech Publ. DOI: 10.4028/www.scientific.net/DDF.326-328.193

Rekha, K. S. S., Mathur, S., Sadhukhan, S., & Jangiti, J. (2022). Student Stress Prediction Using Machine Learning Algorithms And Comprehensive Analysis. *NeuroQuantology : An Interdisciplinary Journal of Neuroscience and Quantum Physics*, 20(14), 895.

Renggli, C., Rimanic, L., Gürel, N. M., Karlaš, B., Wu, W., & Zhang, C. (2021). A data quality-driven view of mlops. arXiv preprint arXiv:2102.07750.

Ren, S., Choi, T.-M., Lee, K.-M., & Lin, L. (2020). Intelligent service capacity allocation for cross-border-E-commerce related third-party-forwarding logistics operations: A deep learning approach. *Transportation Research Part E, Logistics and Transportation Review*, 134, 101834. DOI: 10.1016/j.tre.2019.101834

Res, J., Homoliak, I., Perešíni, M., Smrčka, A., Malinka, K., & Hanacek, P. (2024). *Enhancing Security of AI-Based Code Synthesis with GitHub Copilot via Cheap and Efficient Prompt-Engineering* (arXiv:2403.12671). arXiv. http://arxiv.org/abs/2403.12671

Reshmi, T. (2021). Information security breaches due to ransomware attacks-a systematic literature review. *International Journal of Information Man- agement Data Insights, 1* (2), 100013.

Richards, G. S., & Duxbury, L. (2015). Work-group knowledge acquisition in knowledge intensive public-sector organizations: An exploratory study. *Journal of Public Administration: Research and Theory*, 25(4), 1247–1277.

Riesen, T., Hall, S., Keeton, B., & Snyder, A. (2023). Internal Consistency Of The Customized Employment Discovery Fidelity Scale: A Preliminary Study. *Rehabilitation Counseling Bulletin*, 66(3), 195–202. DOI: 10.1177/00343552211043259

Rodrigues-da-Silva, L. H., & Crispim, J. A. (2014). The project risk management process, a preliminary study. *Procedia Technology*, 16, 943–949.

Role of wireless sensor networks in emerging communication technologies: A review. (2016). *Emerging Communication Technologies Based on Wireless Sensor Networks*, 30-53. https://doi.org/DOI: 10.1201/b20085-8

Ronanki, K. (2023). Towards an AI-centric Requirements Engineering Framework for Trustworthy AI. *2023 IEEE/ACM 45th International Conference on Software Engineering: Companion Proceedings (ICSE-Companion)*, 278–280. DOI: 10.1109/ICSE-Companion58688.2023.00075

Ruf, P., Madan, M., Reich, C., & Ould-Abdeslam, D. (2021). Demystifying mlops and presenting a recipe for the selection of open-source tools. *Applied Sciences (Basel, Switzerland)*, 11(19), 8861. DOI: 10.3390/app11198861

Russell, S. J., & Norvig, P. (2016). *Artificial intelligence: a modern approach.* Pearson.

Russo, D. (2024). Navigating the complexity of generative ai adoption in software engineering. *ACM Transactions on Software Engineering and Methodology*, 33(5), 1–50. DOI: 10.1145/3652154

Rütz, M., & Wedel, F. (2019). DevOps: A systematic literature review. *Twenty-Seventh European Conference on Information Systems (ECIS2019)*, 1-16.

Sachan, S., Yang, J.-B., Xu, D.-L., Benavides, D. E., & Li, Y. (2020). An Explainable Ai Decision-Support-System To Automate Loan Underwriting. [Samaila, M. G. Internet Of Things Hardware Platform Security Advisor.]. *Expert Systems with Applications*, 144, 113100. DOI: 10.1016/j.eswa.2019.113100

Sahu, K., & Srivastava, R. (2018). 2019. Revisiting software reliability. *Data Management, Analytics and Innovation. Proceedings of ICDMAI*, 1, 221–235.

Salanitri, F. P. FROM CENTRALIZATION TO COLLABORATION: HARNESSING GENERATIVE MODELS IN FEDERATED LEARNING FOR MEDICAL IMAGE ANALYSIS.

Saleh, M., Jhanjhi, N. Z., & Abdullah, A. (2020, February). Proposing a privacy protection model in case of civilian drone. In 2020 22nd International Conference on Advanced Communication Technology (ICACT) (pp. 596-602). IEEE.

Saleh, M., Jhanjhi, N., & Abdullah, A. (2020, February). Fatima-tuz-Zahra, "Proposing a privacy protection model in case of civilian drone,". In *Proc. 22nd Int. Conf. Adv. Commun. Technol.(ICACT)* (pp. 596-602).

Sambasivan, N., & Veeraraghavan, R. (2022). The deskilling of domain expertise in ai development. In *Proceedings of the 2022 chi conference on human factors in computing systems* (pp. 1–14). DOI: 10.1145/3491102.3517578

Sampayo, M., & Peças, P. (2022). CPSD2: A new approach for cyber-physical systems design and development. *Journal of Industrial Information Integration*, 28, 100348. DOI: 10.1016/j.jii.2022.100348

Sanchez, P. (2022). Amazons3R: Get Amazon S3 data via the 'Windsor.ai' API. *CRAN: Contributed Packages*. https://doi.org/DOI: 10.32614/CRAN.package.amazons3R

Sangaiah, A. K., Javadpour, A., Ja'fari, F., Pinto, P., & Chuang, H.-M. (2023). Privacy-aware and ai techniques for healthcare based on k-anonymity model in internet of things. *IEEE Transactions on Engineering Management*.

Santhakumar, G., Takale, D. G., Tyagi, S., Anitha, R., Tiwari, M., & Dhanraj, J. A. (2024). Analysis of Multimodality fusion of medical image segmentation employing deep learning. *Human Cancer Diagnosis and Detection Using Exascale Computing*, 171-183. https://doi.org/DOI: 10.1002/9781394197705.ch11

Sarker, I. H. (2021). Deep learning: A comprehensive overview on techniques, taxonomy, applications and research directions. *SN Computer Science*, 2(6), 420. DOI: 10.1007/s42979-021-00815-1 PMID: 34426802

Sarker, I. H. (2021). Machine learning: Algorithms, real-world applications and research directions. *SN Computer Science*, 2(3), 160. DOI: 10.1007/s42979-021-00592-x PMID: 33778771

Sarker, I. H., Furhad, M. H., & Nowrozy, R. (2021). Ai-driven cybersecurity: An overview, security intelligence modeling and research directions. *SN Computer Science*, 2(3), 173. DOI: 10.1007/s42979-021-00557-0 PMID: 33778771

Sauvola, J., Tarkoma, S., Klemettinen, M., Riekki, J., & Doermann, D. (2024). Future of software development with generative AI. *Automated Software Engineering*, 31(1), 26. DOI: 10.1007/s10515-024-00426-z

Sayeeshwari, S., & Prabhu, E. (2022, July). A simple countermeasure to mitigate buffer overflow attack using minimalistic hardware-integrated software simulation for FPGA. In *2022 IEEE International Conference on Electronics, Computing and Communication Technologies (CONECCT)* (pp. 1-4). IEEE.

Schatz, D., Bashroush, R., & Wall, J. (2017). Towards a more representative definition of cyber security. *Journal of Digital Forensics. Security and Law*, 12, 8.

Schetinger, V., Di Bartolomeo, S., El-Assady, M., McNutt, A., Miller, M., Passos, J. P. A., & Adams, J. L. (2023, June). Doom or deliciousness: Challenges and opportunities for visualization in the age of generative models. *Computer Graphics Forum*, 42(3), 423–435.

Schmitt, M. (2023). Securing the digital world: Protecting smart infrastructures and digital industries with artificial intelligence (ai)-enabled malware and intrusion detection. *Journal of Industrial Information Integration*, 36, 100520. DOI: 10.1016/j.jii.2023.100520

Schulman, J., Moritz, P., Levine, S., Jordan, M., & Abbeel, P. (2015). Preprint repository arXiv achieves milestone million uploads. *Physics Today*.

Sebastiani, F. (2002). Machine learning in automated text categorization. *ACM Computing Surveys*, 34(1), 1–47. DOI: 10.1145/505282.505283

Seeger, P. M., Yahouni, Z., & Alpan, G. (2022). Literature review on using data mining in production planning and scheduling within the context of cyber physical systems. *Journal of Industrial Information Integration*, 28, 100371. DOI: 10.1016/j.jii.2022.100371

Sennan, S., Somula, R., Luhach, A., Deverajan, G., Alnumay, W., Jhanjhi, N., & Sharma, P. (2021). Energy efficient optimal parent selection based routing protocol for Internet of Things using firefly optimization algorithm. [Cybersecurity Issues and Challenges in the Drone Industry. IGI Global.]. *Transactions on Emerging Telecommunications Technologies*, 32(8), e4171. DOI: 10.1002/ett.4171

Seo, Y. W., Lee, K. C., & Lee, S. (2017). Decision Quality Of The Research Project Evaluation Mechanism By Using Particle Swarm Optimization. *Management Decision*, 55(4), 745–765. DOI: 10.1108/MD-03-2016-0141

Sewak, M., Sahay, S. K., & Rathore, H. (2023). Deep reinforcement learning in the advanced cybersecurity threat detection and protection. *Information Systems Frontiers*, 25(2), 589–611.

Shafique, M. A., Malik, B. H., Mahmood, Y., Cheema, S. N., Hameed, K., & Tabassum, S. (2017). Determinants impacting the adoption of e- government information systems and suggesting cloud computing migra- tion framework. *International Journal of Advanced Computer Science and Applications*, 8(9).

Shah, I. A. (2024). Drone Industry Security Issues and Challenges in the Context of IoD. *Cybersecurity Issues and Challenges in the Drone Industry*, 310-323.

Shah, I. A. (2024). Privacy and security challenges in unmanned aerial vehicles (UAVs). Cybersecurity in the Transportation Industry, 93-115.

Shah, I. A. and N. Z. Jhanjhi (2024). "Cybersecurity Issues and Challenges in the Drone Industry."

Shah, I. A., ... (2024). Enabling Explainable AI in Cybersecurity Solutions. Advances in Explainable AI Applications for Smart Cities, IGI Global: 255-275.

Shah, I. A., ... (2024). Industry 4.0: Use of Digitalization in Healthcare. Advances in Computational Intelligence for the Healthcare Industry 4.0, IGI Global: 174-193.

Shah, I. A., ... (2024). IoT Devices in Drones: Security Issues and Future Challenges. Cybersecurity Issues and Challenges in the Drone Industry, IGI Global: 217-235.

Shah, I. A., ... (2024). IoT Smart Healthcare Security Challenges and Solutions. Advances in Computational Intelligence for the Healthcare Industry 4.0, IGI Global: 234-247.

Shah, I. A., ... (2024). Logistics Industry in the Context of the Blockchain Technology. Navigating Cyber Threats and Cybersecurity in the Logistics Industry, IGI Global: 214-235.

Shah, I. A., ... (2024). Logistics With the Internet of Things: Challenges, Perspectives, and Applications. Navigating Cyber Threats and Cybersecurity in the Logistics Industry, IGI Global: 172-195.

Shah, I. A., ... (2024). Use of Deep Learning Applications for Drone Technology. Cybersecurity Issues and Challenges in the Drone Industry, IGI Global: 128-147.

Shah, I. A., et al. (2024). "Supply Chain Management Security Issues and Challenges in the Context of AI Applications." 59-89.

Shah, I. A., et al. (2024). "Use of Emerging Technologies in Healthcare 4.0." 280-296.

Shah, I. A., Jhanjhi, N. Z., & Brohi, S. (2024). Cybersecurity issues and challenges in civil aviation security. Cybersecurity in the Transportation Industry, 1-23.

Shah, I. A., Jhanjhi, N. Z., & Ray, S. K. (2024). IoT Devices in Drones: Security Issues and Future Challenges. In *Cybersecurity Issues and Challenges in the Drone Industry* (pp. 217-235). IGI Global.

Shah, I. A., Laraib, A., Ashraf, H., & Hussain, F. (2024). Drone Technology: Current Challenges and Opportunities. Cybersecurity Issues and Challenges in the Drone Industry, 343-361.

Shah, I. A., Laraib, A., Ashraf, H., & Hussain, F. (2024c). Drone Technology: Current Challenges and Opportunities. Cybersecurity Issues and Challenges in the Drone Industry, 343-361.

Shah, I. A., Laraib, A., Ashraf, H., & Hussain, F. (2024e). Drone Technology: Current Challenges and Opportunities. Cybersecurity Issues and Challenges in the Drone Industry, 343-361.

Shah, I. A., Laraib, A., Ashraf, H., & Hussain, F. (2024f). Drone Technology: Current Challenges and Opportunities. Cybersecurity Issues and Challenges in the Drone Industry, 343-361.

Shah, I. A., Laraib, A., Ashraf, H., & Hussain, F. (2024g). Drone Technology: Current Challenges and Opportunities. Cybersecurity Issues and Challenges in the Drone Industry, 343-361.

Shah, I. A., Murugesan, R. K., & Rajper, S. (2024i). Supply Chain Management Security Issues and Challenges in the Context of AI Applications. Navigating Cyber Threats and Cybersecurity in the Logistics Industry, 59-89.

Shaheed, A., & Kurdy, M. B. (2022). Web application firewall using machine learning and features engineering. *Security and Communication Networks*, 2022, 5280158. DOI: 10.1155/2022/5280158

Shah, I. A., Jhanjhi, N. Z., & Brohi, S. N. (2024). Use of AI-Based Drones in Smart Cities. In *Cybersecurity Issues and Challenges in the Drone Industry* (pp. 362–380). IGI Global. DOI: 10.4018/979-8-3693-0774-8.ch015

Shah, I. A., Jhanjhi, N. Z., & Brohi, S. N. (2024b). *Use of AI-Based Drones in Smart Cities. Cybersecurity Issues and Challenges in the Drone Industry*. IGI Global.

Shah, I. A., Jhanjhi, N. Z., & Rajper, S. (2024b). *Use of Deep Learning Applications for Drone Technology. Cybersecurity Issues and Challenges in the Drone Industry*. IGI Global. DOI: 10.4018/979-8-3693-0774-8

Shah, I. A., Jhanjhi, N. Z., & Ray, S. K. (2024c). *Enabling Explainable AI in Cybersecurity Solutions. Advances in Explainable AI Applications for Smart Cities*. IGI Global.

Shah, I. A., Jhanjhi, N. Z., & Ray, S. K. (2024f). *IoT Devices in Drones: Security Issues and Future Challenges. Cybersecurity Issues and Challenges in the Drone Industry*. IGI Global. DOI: 10.4018/979-8-3693-0774-8.ch009

Shah, I. A., Jhanjhi, N. Z., & Ujjan, R. M. A. (2024e). *Use of AI applications for the drone industry. Cybersecurity Issues and Challenges in the Drone Industry*. IGI Global.

Shah, I. A., Jhanjhi, N. Z., & Ujjan, R. M. A. (2024g). *Drone Technology in the Context of the Internet of Things. Cybersecurity Issues and Challenges in the Drone Industry*. IGI Global.

Shah, I. A., Jhanjhi, N. Z., & Ujjan, R. M. A. (2024h). *Use of AI Applications for the Drone Industry. Cybersecurity Issues and Challenges in the Drone Industry*. IGI Global.

Shah, I. A., Jhanjhi, N., & Ashraf, H. (2024a). *Logistics With the Internet of Things: Challenges, Perspectives, and Applications. Navigating Cyber Threats and Cybersecurity in the Logistics Industry*. IGI Global. DOI: 10.4018/979-8-3693-3816-2.ch006

Shah, I. A., Jhanjhi, N., & Brohi, S. N. (2024b). *IoT Smart Healthcare Security Challenges and Solutions. Advances in Computational Intelligence for the Healthcare Industry 4.0*. IGI Global.

Shah, I. A., Jhanjhi, N., & Brohi, S. N. (2024b). Use of Emerging Technologies in Healthcare 4.0. *Advances in Medical Technologies and Clinical Practice*, 4(0), 280–296. DOI: 10.4018/979-8-3693-2333-5.ch015

Shah, I. A., Jhanjhi, N., & Ray, S. K. (2024a). *Artificial Intelligence Applications in the Context of the Security Framework for the Logistics Industry. Advances in Explainable AI Applications for Smart Cities*. IGI Global.

Shahid, J., Hameed, M. K., Javed, I. T., Qureshi, K. N., Ali, M., & Crespi, N. (2022). A Comparative Study of Web Application Security Parameters: Current Trends and Future Directions. *Applied Sciences (Basel, Switzerland)*, 12(8), 8. Advance online publication. DOI: 10.3390/app12084077

Shah, S. A. A., Ullah, A., Subhan, F., Jhanjhi, N., Masud, M., & Alqhatani, A. (2024). *Truth discovery for mobile workers in edge-assisted mobile crowdsensing*. ICT Express., DOI: 10.1016/j.icte.2024.06.007

Shamrat, F., Asaduzzaman, M., Ghosh, P., Sultan, M. D., & Tasnim, Z. (2020). A web based application for agriculture:"Smart Farming System. *International Journal of Emerging Trends in Engineering Research*, ●●●, 8.

Sharifani, K., & Amini, M. (2023). Machine learning and deep learning: A review of methods and applications. *World Information Technology and Engineering Journal*, 10, 3897–3904.

Sharifonnasabi, F., Jhanjhi, N., Shamshirband, S., & John, J. (2021). Bone age measurement using a hybrid HCNN-KNN model: a case study on dental panoramic images.

Sharma, A., et al. (2022). "Recent trends in AI-based intelligent sensing." **11**(10): 1661.

Sharma, A., Dyrkolbotn, G. O., Øverlier, L., Waltoft-Olsen, A. J., Franke, K., & Katsikas, S. (2022). *A state-of-the-art reverse engineering approach for combating hardware security vulnerabilities at the system and PCB level in IoT devices. 2022 IEEE Physical Assurance and Inspection of Electronics (PAINE)*. IEEE.

Sharma, A., & Kumar, S. (2023). Machine learning and ontology-based novel semantic document indexing for information retrieval. *Computers & Industrial Engineering*, 176, 108940. DOI: 10.1016/j.cie.2022.108940

Sharma, R., Singh, A., Jhanjhi, N., Masud, M., Jaha, E. S., & Verma, S. (2022). Plant Disease Diagnosis and Image Classification Using Deep Learning. *Computers, Materials & Continua*, ●●●, 71. DOI: 10.32604/cmc.2022.020017

Shields, K. (2015). Cybersecurity: Recognizing the risk and protecting against attacks. *NC Banking Inst.*, 19, 345.

Shihadeh, F. (2021). A Conceptual Framework of Financial Inclusion: The Links with Individuals, SMEs, and Banks. In *The Big Data-Driven Digital Economy: Artificial and Computational Intelligence* (pp. 285–300). Springer International Publishing. DOI: 10.1007/978-3-030-73057-4_22

Shi, J., Du, Q., Lin, F., Li, Y., Bai, L., Fung, R. Y., & Lai, K. K. (2020). Coordinating the supply chain finance system with buyback contract: A capital-constrained newsvendor problem. *Computers & Industrial Engineering*, 146, 106587. DOI: 10.1016/j.cie.2020.106587

Shin, H., Park, S., Kim, L., Kim, J., Kim, T., Song, Y., & Lee, S. (2023). The Future Service Scenarios Of 6g Telecommunications Technology. *Telecommunications Policy*, ●●●, 102678.

Shin, H., Sindi, N., Lee, Y., Ka, J., Song, J. Y., & Kim, J. (2022). XDesign: Integrating Interface Design into Explainable AI Education. *Proceedings of the 53rd ACM Technical Symposium on Computer Science Education* V. 2, 1097. DOI: 10.1145/3478432.3499052

Shiohira, K. (2021). *Understanding the impact of artificial intelligence on skills development. education 2030.* UNESCO-UNEVOC International Centre for Technical and Vocational Education and Training.

Shi, Y., Wang, T., & Alwan, L. C. (2020). Analytics for cross-border e-commerce: Inventory risk management of an online fashion retailer. *Decision Sciences*, 51(6), 1347–1376. DOI: 10.1111/deci.12429

Shou, Y., Hu, W., Kang, M., Li, Y., Park, Y. W. J. I. M., & Systems, D. (2018). Risk Management And Firm Performance. *The Moderating Role Of Supplier Integration.*, 118, 1327–1344.

Shuford, J. (2024). Examining Ethical Aspects of AI: Addressing Bias and Equity in the Discipline. *Journal of Artificial Intelligence General Science (JAIGS) ISSN:3006-4023*, 3(1), Article 1. DOI: 10.60087/jaigs.vol03.issue01.p124

Si, C., Zhang, Y., Yang, Z., Liu, R., & Yang, D. (2024, March 5). *Design2Code: How Far Are We From Automating Front-End Engineering?* arXiv.Org. https://arxiv.org/abs/2403.03163v1

Siddique, S., Hridoy, A. A. I., Khushbu, S. A., & Das, A. K. (2022, October). Cvd: An improved approach of software vulnerability detection for object oriented programming languages using deep learning. In *Proceedings of the Future Technologies Conference* (pp. 145-164). Cham: Springer International Publishing.

Sidhu, B. K., Singh, K., & Sharma, N. (2022). A machine learning approach to software model refactoring. *International Journal of Computers and Applications*, 44(2), 166–177. DOI: 10.1080/1206212X.2020.1711616

Sidhu, S., Mohd, B. J., & Hayajneh, T. (2019). Hardware security in IoT devices with emphasis on hardware trojans. *Journal of Sensor and Actuator Networks*, 8(3), 42. DOI: 10.3390/jsan8030042

Silva, L. C., Zagatti, F. R., Sette, B. S., Dos Santos Silva, L. N., Lucrédio, D., Silva, D. F., & De Medeiros Caseli, H. Benchmarking machine learning solutions in production. 2020 19th IEEE International Conference on Machine Learning and Applications (ICMLA), 2020. IEEE, 626-633.

Sindiramutty, S. R., Jhanjhi, N. Z., Tan, C. E., Khan, N. A., Shah, B., & Manchuri, A. R. (2024). *Cybersecurity Measures for Logistics Industry. Navigating Cyber Threats and Cybersecurity in the Logistics Industry.* IGI Global.

Singh, R. (2021). A study of artificial intelligence and e-commerce ecosystem–a customer's perspective. *International Journal of Research in Engineering. Science and Management*, 4(2), 78–87.

Sinha, A. R., Singla, K., & Victor, T. M. M. (2023). Artificial intelligence and machine learning for cybersecurity applications and challenges. *Risk Detection and Cyber Security for the Success of Contemporary Computing*, 109–146.

Sinha, G., & Kant, K. S. (2018). Performance of modified auditory features for speech signal-an empirical study for non-intrusive speech quality assessment using signal based model. *2018 4th International Conference on Recent Advances in Information Technology (RAIT).* https://doi.org/DOI: 10.1109/RAIT.2018.8388997

Siqueira, J. C. D. S. (2023). *Autonomous Incident Response.*

Siraj, M., ... (2024). Addressing Issues and Challenges Using AI in Pharmacy. Advances in Computational Intelligence for the Healthcare Industry 4.0, IGI Global: 22-41.

Siraj, M., & Muhammad, G. (2023). Is Chatbot Marketing Have A Relationship With Electronic Word Of Mouth? A Mediating Role Of The Customer-Brand Relationship. *Journal Of Management Sciences*, 10(2), 80–94.

Sisejkovic, D., Merchant, F., Reimann, L. M., & Leupers, R. (2021). Deceptive logic locking for hardware integrity protection against machine learning attacks. *IEEE Transactions on Computer-Aided Design of Integrated Circuits and Systems*, 41(6), 1716–1729. DOI: 10.1109/TCAD.2021.3100275

Sleimi, M. T., & Emeagwali, O. L. (2017). Do employee attitudes mediate the relationship between strategic human resource management practices and organizational effectiveness? A SEM based investigation using SMART-PLS software. *Business and Economic Horizons*, 13(1), 42–59.

Sodiya, E. O., Amoo, O. O., Umoga, U. J., Atadoga, A., Sodiya, E. O., Amoo, O. O., Umoga, U. J., & Atadoga, A. (2024). AI-driven personalization in web content delivery: A comparative study of user engagement in the USA and the UK. *World Journal of Advanced Research and Reviews*, 21(2), 2. Advance online publication. DOI: 10.30574/wjarr.2024.21.2.0502

Soehnchen, C., Rietz, A., Weirauch, V., Meister, S., & Henningsen, M. (2023). Creating an intercultural user-Centric Design for a Digital Sexual Health Education App for Young women in Resource-Poor regions of Kenya: Qualitative self-extended double Diamond Model for requirements Engineering Analysis. *JMIR Formative Research*, 7, e50304. DOI: 10.2196/50304 PMID: 37921860

Solanki, T., & Panda, B. (2022, June). SpecPref: High performing speculative attacks resilient hardware prefetchers. In *2022 IEEE International Symposium on Hardware Oriented Security and Trust (HOST)* (pp. 57-60). IEEE.

Song, B., Zhou, R., & Ahmed, F. (2024). Multi-modal machine learning in engineering design: A review and future directions. *Journal of Computing and Information Science in Engineering*, 24(1), 010801. DOI: 10.1115/1.4063954

Soni, N., Sharma, E. K., Singh, N., & Kapoor, A. (2019). Impact of artificial intelligence on businesses: from research, innovation, market deployment to future shifts in business models. arXiv preprint arXiv:1905.02092.

Soni, N., Sharma, E. K., Singh, N., & Kapoor, A. (2020). Artificial intelligence in business: From research and innovation to market deployment. *Procedia Computer Science*, 167, 2200–2210. DOI: 10.1016/j.procs.2020.03.272

Sönmez, F. Ö., & Kiliç, B. G. (2021). Holistic web application security visualization for multi-project and multi-phase dynamic application security test results. *IEEE Access : Practical Innovations, Open Solutions*, 9, 25858–25884. DOI: 10.1109/ACCESS.2021.3057044

Souppaya, M., Scarfone, K., & Dodson, D. (2022). Secure software development framework (ssdf) version 1.1. *NIST Special Publication*, 800, 218. DOI: 10.6028/NIST.SP.800-218

Spair, R. (2024, January 21). Revolutionizing Web Design: The Power of Generative AI Websites. *Medium*. https://medium.com/@rickspair/revolutionizing-web-design-the-power-of-generative-ai-websites-08d548b46e21

Spjuth, O., Frid, J., & Hellander, A. (2021). The machine learning life cycle and the cloud: Implications for drug discovery. *Expert Opinion on Drug Discovery*, 16(9), 1071–1079. DOI: 10.1080/17460441.2021.1932812 PMID: 34057379

Sprung, G., Schweighofer, M., Anderle, F., Gürtler, F., & Uhl, M. (2023). Project desart: Using generative AI to create satellite images for an AR sand table. *ICERI Proceedings*. https://doi.org/DOI: 10.21125/iceri.2023.2044

Sreejith, R., & Sinimole, K. (2024). User-centric evaluation of EHR software through NLP-driven investigation: Implications for product development and user experience. *Journal of Open Innovation*, 10(1), 100206. DOI: 10.1016/j.joitmc.2023.100206

Sridhar, V., Rani, S., Pareek, P. K., & Bhambri, P. (2024). Evolution of IoT in various application domains. In Sridhar, V., Rani, S., Pareek, P. K., Bhambri, P., & Elngar, A. A. (Eds.), *Blockchain for IoT systems: Concept, framework and applications* (1st ed., pp. 13–22). Chapman and Hall/CRC., DOI: 10.1201/9781003460367-2

Srinivasan, K., Garg, L., Chen, B.-Y., Alaboudi, A. A., Jhanjhi, N., Chang, C.-T., Prabadevi, B., & Deepa, N. (2021). Expert System for Stable Power Generation Prediction in Microbial Fuel Cell. *Intelligent Automation & Soft Computing*, •••, 30. DOI: 10.32604/iasc.2021.018380

Stamp, M. (2022). *Introduction to machine learning with applications in information security*. Chapman and Hall/CRC. DOI: 10.1201/9781003264873

Stanciu, V., & R^ında͵su, S.-M. (2021). Artificial intelligence in retail: Benefits and risks associated with mobile shopping applications. *Amfiteatru Economic*, 23(56), 46–64. DOI: 10.24818/EA/2021/56/46

Strauss, A. L. (2017). *The discovery of grounded theory: Strategies for qualitative research*. Routledge.

Student stress prediction using machine learning algorithms and comprehensive analysis. (2022). *NeuroQuantology, 20*(14), 895-906. https://doi.org/DOI: 10.48047/nq.2022.20.14.NQ880126

Stütz, T., Kowar, T., Kager, M., Tiefengrabner, M., Stuppner, M., Blechert, J., & Ginzinger, S. (2015). Smartphone based stress prediction. In User Modeling, Adaptation and Personalization: 23rd International Conference, UMAP 2015, Dublin, Ireland, June 29—July 3, 2015. [Springer International Publishing.]. *Proceedings*, 23, 240–251.

Sultana, N. M., & Srinivas, K. Survey on centric data protection method for cloud storage application. *2021 International Conference on Computational Intelligence and Computing Applications (ICCICA)*, 2021. IEEE, 1-8. DOI: 10.1109/ICCI-CA52458.2021.9697235

Sun, J., Liao, Q. V., Muller, M., Agarwal, M., Houde, S., Talamadupula, K., & Weisz, J. D. (2022). Investigating Explainability of Generative AI for Code through Scenario-based Design. *27th International Conference on Intelligent User Interfaces*, 212–228. DOI: 10.1145/3490099.3511119

Swed, S., Alibrahim, H., Elkalagi, N. K. H., Nasif, M. N., Rais, M. A., Nashwan, A. J., & Shoib, S. (2022). Knowledge, attitude, and practice of artificial intelligence among doctors and medical students in Syria: A cross-sectional online survey. *Frontiers in Artificial Intelligence*, 5, 1011524.

Szabó, Z., & Bilicki, V. (2023). A New Approach to Web Application Security: Utilizing GPT Language Models for Source Code Inspection. *Future Internet*, 15(10), 10. Advance online publication. DOI: 10.3390/fi15100326

Szewczyk, P., 2019. Application of blockchain technology in supply chain management. *Zeszyty Naukowe. Organizacja i Zarządzanie/Politechnika Śląska*.

Tabrizchi, H., & Kuchaki Rafsanjani, M. (2020). A survey on security challenges in cloud computing: Issues, threats, and solutions. *The Journal of Supercomputing*, 76(12), 9493–9532. DOI: 10.1007/s11227-020-03213-1

Taddeo, M., McCutcheon, T., & Floridi, L. (2019). Trusting artificial intelligence in cybersecurity is a double-edged sword. *Nature Machine Intelligence*, 1(12), 557–560. DOI: 10.1038/s42256-019-0109-1

Talaei Khoei, T., & Kaabouch, N. (2023). Machine Learning: Models, Challenges, and Research Directions. *Future Internet*, 15(10), 332. DOI: 10.3390/fi15100332

Talwani, S., Singla, J., Mathur, G., Malik, N., Jhanjhi, N., Masud, M., & Aljahdali, S. (2022). Machine-Learning-Based Approach for Virtual Machine Allocation and Migration. [s Note: MDPI stays neutral with regard to jurisdictional claims in published....]. *Electronics (Basel)*, 11(19), 3249. DOI: 10.3390/electronics11193249

Tamburri, D. A. (2020, September). Sustainable mlops: Trends and challenges. In 2020 22nd international symposium on symbolic and numeric algorithms for scientific computing (SYNASC) (pp. 17-23). IEEE.

Tan, D. C. (2005). *The Statistical Properties Of Technical Trading Rules*. Loughborough University.

Tandon, N., & Bhambri, P. (2013). *Novel approach for drug discovery using neural network back propagation algorithm: An optimum drug discovery approach* (Vol. 1). GRIN Publishers.

Tao, Z., & Ye, Q. (2020). The application of artificial intelligence in computer web technology in the era of massive data. *Journal of Physics: Conference Series*, 1574(1), 012020. DOI: 10.1088/1742-6596/1574/1/012020

Tapscott, D., & Tapscott, A. (2016). *Blockchain revolution: how the technology behind Bitcoin is changing money, business, and the world*. Penguin.

Tariq, M. U. (2024). Multidisciplinary Service Learning in Higher Education: Concepts, Implementation, and Impact. In S. Watson (Ed.), Applications of Service Learning in Higher Education (pp. 1-19). IGI Global. DOI: 10.4018/979-8-3693-2133-1.ch001

Tariq, M. U. (2024). Emerging Trends and Innovations in Blockchain-Digital Twin Integration for Green Investments: A Case Study Perspective. In Jafar, S., Rodriguez, R., Kannan, H., Akhtar, S., & Plugmann, P. (Eds.), *Harnessing Blockchain-Digital Twin Fusion for Sustainable Investments* (pp. 148–175). IGI Global., DOI: 10.4018/979-8-3693-1878-2.ch007

Tariq, M. U. (2024). Emotional Intelligence in Understanding and Influencing Consumer Behavior. In Musiolik, T., Rodriguez, R., & Kannan, H. (Eds.), *AI Impacts in Digital Consumer Behavior* (pp. 56–81). IGI Global., DOI: 10.4018/979-8-3693-1918-5.ch003

Tariq, M. U. (2024). Empowering Student Entrepreneurs: From Idea to Execution. In Cantafio, G., & Munna, A. (Eds.), *Empowering Students and Elevating Universities With Innovation Centers* (pp. 83–111). IGI Global., DOI: 10.4018/979-8-3693-1467-8.ch005

Tariq, M. U. (2024). Enhancing Cybersecurity Protocols in Modern Healthcare Systems: Strategies and Best Practices. In Garcia, M., & de Almeida, R. (Eds.), *Transformative Approaches to Patient Literacy and Healthcare Innovation* (pp. 223–241). IGI Global., DOI: 10.4018/979-8-3693-3661-8.ch011

Tariq, M. U. (2024). Equity and Inclusion in Learning Ecosystems. In Al Husseiny, F., & Munna, A. (Eds.), *Preparing Students for the Future Educational Paradigm* (pp. 155–176). IGI Global., DOI: 10.4018/979-8-3693-1536-1.ch007

Tariq, M. U. (2024). Fintech Startups and Cryptocurrency in Business: Revolutionizing Entrepreneurship. In Kankaew, K., Nakpathom, P., Chnitphattana, A., Pitchayadejanant, K., & Kunnapapdeelert, S. (Eds.), *Applying Business Intelligence and Innovation to Entrepreneurship* (pp. 106–124). IGI Global., DOI: 10.4018/979-8-3693-1846-1.ch006

Tariq, M. U. (2024). Leveraging Artificial Intelligence for a Sustainable and Climate-Neutral Economy in Asia. In Ordóñez de Pablos, P., Almunawar, M., & Anshari, M. (Eds.), *Strengthening Sustainable Digitalization of Asian Economy and Society* (pp. 1–21). IGI Global., DOI: 10.4018/979-8-3693-1942-0.ch001

Tariq, M. U. (2024). Metaverse in Business and Commerce. In Kumar, J., Arora, M., & Erkol Bayram, G. (Eds.), *Exploring the Use of Metaverse in Business and Education* (pp. 47–72). IGI Global., DOI: 10.4018/979-8-3693-5868-9.ch004

Tariq, M. U. (2024). Revolutionizing Health Data Management With Blockchain Technology: Enhancing Security and Efficiency in a Digital Era. In Garcia, M., & de Almeida, R. (Eds.), *Emerging Technologies for Health Literacy and Medical Practice* (pp. 153–175). IGI Global., DOI: 10.4018/979-8-3693-1214-8.ch008

Tariq, M. U. (2024). The Role of Emerging Technologies in Shaping the Global Digital Government Landscape. In Guo, Y. (Ed.), *Emerging Developments and Technologies in Digital Government* (pp. 160–180). IGI Global., DOI: 10.4018/979-8-3693-2363-2.ch009

Tariq, M. U. (2024). The Transformation of Healthcare Through AI-Driven Diagnostics. In Sharma, A., Chanderwal, N., Tyagi, S., Upadhyay, P., & Tyagi, A. (Eds.), *Enhancing Medical Imaging with Emerging Technologies* (pp. 250–264). IGI Global., DOI: 10.4018/979-8-3693-5261-8.ch015

Tariq, M. U., & Ismail, M. U. S. B. (2024). AI-powered COVID-19 forecasting: A comprehensive comparison of advanced deep learning methods. *Osong Public Health and Research Perspectives*, 15(2), 2210–9099. DOI: 10.24171/j.phrp.2023.0287 PMID: 38621765

Tarleton, N. (2010). Coherent extrapolated volition: a meta-level approach to machine ethics. *The Singularity Institute, Berkeley, CA, University Stanford, CA, 94305.*

Tata Sutabri, T. S. (2023). Design of A Web-Based Social Network Information System. *International Journal of Artificial Intelligence Research*, 6, 310–316.

Taye, M. M. (2023). Understanding of machine learning with deep learning: Architectures, workflow, applications and future directions. *Computers*, 12(5), 91. DOI: 10.3390/computers12050091

Tayyab, M., Marjani, M., Jhanjhi, N., Hashem, I. A. T., & Usmani, R. S. A. (2022). A watermark-based secure model for data security against security attacks for machine learning algorithms. *J. Eng. Sci. Technol. Special Issue on IAC2021*, 24–37.

Tayyab, M., Mumtaz, M., Jhanjhi, N. Z., & Muzammal, S. M. (2024). Industry 4.0: The digital revolution unleashing sustainable supply chains. In *Digital transformation for improved industry and supply chain performance* (pp. 54–69). IGI Global.

Tayyab, M., Mumtaz, M., Jhanjhi, N. Z., & Muzammal, S. M. (2024). Industry 4.0: The Digital Revolution Unleashing Sustainable Supply Chains. In *Digital Transformation for Improved Industry and Supply Chain Performance* (pp. 54–69). IGI Global. DOI: 10.4018/979-8-3693-5375-2.ch003

Tayyab, M., Mumtaz, M., Muzammal, S. M., & Jhanjhi, N. Z. (2024). Swarm Security: Tackling Threats in the Age of Drone Swarms. In Cybersecurity Issues and Challenges in the Drone Industry (pp. 324-342). IGI Global.

Tayyab, M., Mumtaz, M., Muzammal, S. M., & Jhanjhi, N. Z. (2024). Swarm Security: Tackling Threats in the Age of Drone Swarms. In *Cybersecurity Issues and Challenges in the Drone Industry* (pp. 324–342). IGI Global. https://www.igi-global.com/chapter/swarm-security/340082

Tayyab, M., Mumtaz, M., Muzammal, S. M., & Jhanjhi, N. Z.. (2024). Swarm security: Tackling threats in the age of drone swarms. In *Cybersecurity issues and challenges in the drone industry* (pp. 324–342). IGI Global. DOI: 10.4018/979-8-3693-0774-8.ch013

Tekerek, A. (2021). A novel architecture for web-based attack detection using convolutional neural network. *Computers & Security*, 100, 102096. DOI: 10.1016/j.cose.2020.102096

Tella, A., Ukwoma, S. C., & Kayode, A. I. (2020). A two models modification for determining cloud computing adoption for web-based services in academic libraries in Nigeria. *Journal of Academic Librarianship*, 46(6), 102255. DOI: 10.1016/j.acalib.2020.102255

Tepperman, J., Lee, S., Narayanan, S. S., & Alwan, A. (2011). A generative student model for scoring word reading skills. *IEEE Transactions on Audio, Speech, and Language Processing*, 19(2), 348–360. DOI: 10.1109/TASL.2010.2047812

Terna, P., Maggiora, M., & Battistoni, L. (2016). Emerging cryptocurrency trust in an agent–based model.

Thakur, K., Barker, H. G., & Pathan, A.-S. K. (2024). *Artificial Intelligence and Large Language Models: An Introduction to the Technological Future.* Chapman and Hall/CRC., DOI: 10.1201/9781003474173

Thangam, T., Gayathri, G., & Madhubala, T. (2017, April). A novel logic locking technique for hardware security. In *2017 IEEE International Conference on Electrical, Instrumentation and Communication Engineering (ICEICE)* (pp. 1-7). IEEE.

The rise of AI threats and cybersecurity: Predictions for 2024. (2024, February 15). World Economic Forum. https://www.weforum.org/agenda/2024/02/what-does-2024 -have-in-store-for-the-world-of-cybersecurity/

Thorleiksdóttir, T. (2021). *Understanding Human Potentials for Evaluating Generative Models* [Master Thesis, ETH Zurich]. DOI: 10.3929/ethz-b-000507443

Thota, C., Mavromoustakis, C. X., & Mastorakis, G. (2023). RDSF—Responsive Data-Sharing Framework for User-Centric Internet of Vehicles Assisted Healthcare Systems. *Multimedia Tools and Applications*, ●●●, 1–24. DOI: 10.1007/s11042-023-14387-0

Tian, J., Wang, B., Li, T., Shang, F., & Cao, K. (2020). Coordinated cyber-physical attacks considering DoS attacks in power systems. *International Journal of Robust and Nonlinear Control*, 30(11), 4345–4358. DOI: 10.1002/rnc.4801

Tiefenau, C., Häring, M., Krombholz, K., & Von Zezschwitz, E. (2020). Security, availability, and multiple information sources: Exploring update behavior of system administrators. In *Sixteenth Symposium on Usable Privacy and Security (SOUPS 2020)* (pp. 239-258).

Tivari, G., Khara, D., Dave, D., & Patel, V. (2024). Enhancing Reality: Exploring the Potential of Generative Artificial Intelligence. *International Journal Of Scientific Research In Engineering And Management*, 8(7), 1–13. DOI: 10.55041/IJSREM36378

Tiwari, S. (2022). Concepts and strategies for machine learning. Current studies in basic sciences engineering and technology, 45-54.

Toma, A., Krayani, A., Marcenaro, L., Gao, Y., & Regazzoni, C. S. (2020). Deep Learning for Spectrum Anomaly Detection in Cognitive mmWave Radios. *2020 IEEE 31st Annual International Symposium on Personal, Indoor and Mobile Radio Communications*, 1–7. DOI: 10.1109/PIMRC48278.2020.9217240

Torfi, A., Shirvani, R. A., Keneshloo, Y., Tavaf, N., & Fox, E. A. (2020). Nat- ural language processing advancements by deep learning: A survey. *arXiv preprint arXiv:2003.01200.*

Törnqvist, A., & Martinsson, H. (2023). A User-Centric Monitoring System to Enhance the Development of Web-Based Products: A User-Centric Monitoring System to Enhance the Development of Web-Based Products.

Torricelli, M., Martino, M., Baronchelli, A., & Aiello, L. M. (2024). *The role of interface design on prompt-mediated creativity in Generative AI* (No. arXiv:2312.00233). arXiv. /arXiv.2312.00233DOI: 10.1145/3614419.3644000

Toschi, F., & Sega, M. (2019). *Flowing matter.* Springer Nature. DOI: 10.1007/978-3-030-23370-9

Touretzky, D., Gardner-Mccune, C., & Seehorn, D. (2023). Machine learning and the five big ideas in AI. *International Journal of Artificial Intelligence in Education,* 33(2), 233–266. DOI: 10.1007/s40593-022-00314-1

Tschider, C. A. (2018). Regulating the internet of things: Discrimination, privacy, and cybersecurity in the artificial intelligence age. *Denv. L. Rev.,* 96, 87.

Tu"regu"n, N. (2019). Impact of technology in financial reporting: The case of amazon go. *Journal of Corporate Accounting & Finance,* 30(3), 90–95. DOI: 10.1002/jcaf.22394

Turban, E., Outland, J., King, D., Lee, J. K., Liang, T. P., Turban, D. C., ... & Turban, D. C. (2018). Intelligent (smart) E-commerce. Electronic commerce 2018: A managerial and social networks perspective, 249-283.

Türegün, N. (2019). Impact of technology in financial reporting: The case of Amazon Go. *Journal of Corporate Accounting & Finance,* 30(3), 90–95.

Ujjan, R. M. A., Taj, I., & Brohi, S. N. (2022). *E-Government Cybersecurity Modeling in the Context of Software-Defined Networks. Cybersecurity Measures for E-Government Frameworks.* IGI Global.

Upadhyay, U., & Jain, A. (2019). *Removal of Batch Effects using Generative Adversarial Networks* (No. arXiv:1901.06654). arXiv. http://arxiv.org/abs/1901.06654

Vaigandla, K. K., Vanteru, M. K., & Siluveru, M. (2024). An Extensive Examination of the IoT and Blockchain Technologies in Relation to their Applications in the Healthcare Industry. *Mesopotamian Journal of Computer Science,* 2024, 1–14. DOI: 10.58496/MJCSC/2024/001

Van Liebergen, B. J. J. O. F. T. 2017. Machine Learning: A Revolution In Risk Management And Compliance? 45, 60-67.

Van Riet, J., Malavolta, I., & Ghaleb, T. A. (2023). Optimize along the way: An industrial case study on web performance. *Journal of Systems and Software*, 198, 111593. DOI: 10.1016/j.jss.2022.111593

Van Straaten, L. (2014). An appreciative inquiry of selected elements of staff well-being at a higher education institution (Doctoral dissertation, University of the Free State).

Vanini, P., Rossi, S., Zvizdic, E., & Domenig, T. (2023). Online payment fraud: From anomaly detection to risk management. *Financial Innovation*, 9(1), 66. DOI: 10.1186/s40854-023-00470-w

Vaza, R. N., Prajapati, R., Rathod, D., & Vaghela, D. (2022). Developing a novel methodology for virtual machine introspection to classify unknown malware functions. *Peer-to-Peer Networking and Applications*, 15(1), 793–810. DOI: 10.1007/s12083-021-01281-5

Veeraiah, V., Rajaboina, N. B., Rao, G. N., Ahamad, S., Gupta, A., & Suri, C. S. (2022, April). Securing online web application for IoT management. In 2022 2nd International Conference on Advance Computing and Innovative Technologies in Engineering (ICACITE) (pp. 1499-1504). IEEE.

Vegesna, V. V. (2023). Privacy-preserving techniques in ai-powered cyber se- curity: Challenges and opportunities. *International Journal of Machine Learning for Sustainable Development*, 5(4), 1–8.

Verma, S., Sharma, R., Deb, S., & Maitra, D. (2021). Artificial intelligence in marketing: Systematic review and future research direction. *International Journal of Information Management Data Insights*, 1(1), 100002. DOI: 10.1016/j.jjimei.2020.100002

Vermesan, O., & Bacquet, J. (2017). *Cognitive Hyperconnected Digital Transformation: Internet of Things Intelligence Evolution*. River Publishers.

Vigneswaran, R. K., Vinayakumar, R., Soman, K. P., & Poornachandran, P. (2018, July). Evaluating shallow and deep neural networks for network intrusion detection systems in cyber security. In 2018 9th International conference on computing, communication and networking technologies (ICCCNT) (pp. 1-6). IEEE.

Villarán, C., & Beltrán, M. (2022). User-centric privacy for identity federations based on a recommendation system. *Electronics (Basel)*, 11(8), 1238. DOI: 10.3390/electronics11081238

Villegas-Ch, W., & García-Ortiz, J. (2023). Toward a Comprehensive Framework for Ensuring Security and Privacy in Artificial Intelligence. *Electronics (Basel)*, 12(18), 18. Advance online publication. DOI: 10.3390/electronics12183786

Vinayakumar, R., Poornachandran, P., & Soman, K. P. (2018a). Scalable framework for cyber threat situational awareness based on domain name systems data analysis. Big data in engineering applications, 113-142.

Vinayakumar, R., Soman, K., & Poornachandran, P. (2018b). Evaluating deep learning approaches to characterize and classify malicious URL's. *Journal of Intelligent & Fuzzy Systems*, 34(3), 1333–1343. DOI: 10.3233/JIFS-169429

Vinayakumar, R., Soman, K., Poornachandran, P., Mohan, V. S., & Kumar, A. D. (2019). ScaleNet: Scalable and hybrid framework for cyber threat situational awareness based on DNS, URL, and email data analysis. *Journal of Cyber Security and Mobility*, 8(2), 189–240. DOI: 10.13052/jcsm2245-1439.823

Vinayakumar, R., Soman, K., Poornachandran, P., & Sachin Kumar, S. (2018c). Detecting Android malware using long short-term memory (LSTM). *Journal of Intelligent & Fuzzy Systems*, 34(3), 1277–1288. DOI: 10.3233/JIFS-169424

Vizgirda, V., Zhao, R., & Goel, N. (2024). SocialGenPod: Privacy-Friendly Generative AI Social Web Applications with Decentralised Personal Data Stores. *Companion Proceedings of the ACM Web Conference 2024*, 1067–1070. DOI: 10.1145/3589335.3651251

von Garrel, J., & Jahn, C. (2023). Design framework for the implementation of ai-based (service) business models for small and medium-sized manufac- turing enterprises. *Journal of the Knowledge Economy*, 14(3), 3551–3569. DOI: 10.1007/s13132-022-01003-z

Voronov, S., Tang, S., Amert, T., & Anderson, J. H. (2021). *Ai meets real- time: Addressing real-world complexities in graph response-time analysis. In 2021 ieee real-time systems symposium (rtss)*.

Vuppalapati, C., Ilapakurti, A., Chillara, K., Kedari, S., & Mamidi, V. (2020). *Automating tiny ml intelligent sensors devops using microsoft azure. 2020 ieee international conference on big data (big data)*. IEEE.

Waheed, S., Hamid, B., Jhanjhi, N., Humayun, M., & Malik, N. A. (2019). Improving knowledge sharing in distributed software development. *IJACSA). International Journal of Advanced Computer Science and Applications*, 10.

Wakil, K., Jawawi, D., & Isa, M. (2015). *Analyzing Modern Web Applications to Recognize Features-based Web Engineering Methods*.

Wakil, K., & Jawawi, D. N. A. (2018). A New Adaptive Model for Web Engineering Methods to Develop Modern Web Applications. *Proceedings of the 2018 International Conference on Software Engineering and Information Management*, 32–39. DOI: 10.1145/3178461.3178468

Wang, J., Luo, X., Cao, L., He, H., Huang, H., Xie, J., Jatowt, A., & Cai, Y. (2024). Is Your AI-Generated Code Really Secure? Evaluating Large Language Models on Secure Code Generation with CodeSecEval. *arXiv Preprint arXiv:2407.02395*.

Wang, X., Wan, Z., Hekmati, A., Zong, M., Alam, S., Zhang, M., & Krishnamachari, B. (2024). IoT in the Era of Generative AI: Vision and Challenges. *arXiv preprint arXiv:2401.01923*.

Wang, W., & Siau, K. (2019). Artificial intelligence, machine learning, automation, robotics, future of work and future of humanity: A review and research agenda. [JDM]. *Journal of Database Management*, 30(1), 61–79. DOI: 10.4018/JDM.2019010104

Wang, X., Wu, R., Ma, J., Long, G., & Han, J. (2018). Research on vulnerability detection technology for web mail system. *Procedia Computer Science*, 131, 124–130. DOI: 10.1016/j.procs.2018.04.194

Wang, Y. (2024). Research on Big Data Encryption Algorithm System for Online Education Based on Artificial Intelligence. *Proceedings of the 2024 International Conference on Computer and Multimedia Technology*, 492–498. DOI: 10.1145/3675249.3675334

Wang, Y., Pan, Y., Yan, M., Su, Z., & Luan, T. H. (2023). A Survey on ChatGPT: AI–Generated Contents, Challenges, and Solutions. *IEEE Open Journal of the Computer Society*, 4, 280–302. DOI: 10.1109/OJCS.2023.3300321

Wang, Z.-F., Ren, Y.-W., Cao, Z.-Y., & Zhang, L.-Y. (2023). Lrbft: Improvement Of Practical Byzantine Fault Tolerance Consensus Protocol For Blockchains Based On Lagrange Interpolation. *Peer-to-Peer Networking and Applications*, 16(2), 690–708. DOI: 10.1007/s12083-022-01431-3

Waqas, A. J. P. S. S. R. (2024). The Evaluation of Economic Performance. *Cross-Nation Analysis.*, 8(3), 204–217.

Wei, J., Courbis, A.-L., Lambolais, T., Dray, G., & Maalej, W. (2024, June 19). *On AI-Inspired UI-Design*. arXiv.Org. https://arxiv.org/abs/2406.13631v1

Wei, J., Courbis, A.-L., Lambolais, T., Xu, B., Bernard, P. L., & Dray, G. (2023). Boosting GUI Prototyping with Diffusion Models. *2023 IEEE 31st International Requirements Engineering Conference (RE)*, 275–280. DOI: 10.1109/RE57278.2023.00035

West, D. M. (2018). *The future of work: Robots, ai, and automation.* Brookings Institution Press.

Williams, E. C., Gopalan, N., Rhee, M., & Tellex, S. (2018) Learning to Parse Natural Language to Grounded Reward Functions with Weak Supervision. *IEEE International Conference on Robotics and Automation (ICRA).* DOI: 10.1109/ICRA.2018.8460937

Williams, R., & Yampolskiy, R. (2021). Understanding and avoiding ai failures: A practical guide. *Philosophies,* 6(3), 53. DOI: 10.3390/philosophies6030053

Willman, A. (2024). Adoptions and Effects of Combining Agile Software Development and DevOps Practices–A Literature Review.

Winfield, A. F., & Jirotka, M. (2018). Ethical governance is essential to building trust in robotics and artificial intelligence systems. *Philosophical Transactions. Series A, Mathematical, Physical, and Engineering Sciences,* 376(2133), 20180085. DOI: 10.1098/rsta.2018.0085 PMID: 30323000

Wong, M., Ong, Y., Gupta, A., Bali, K. K., & Chen, C. (2023). Prompt evolution for generative AI: A classifier-guided approach. *2023 IEEE Conference on Artificial Intelligence (CAI).* https://doi.org/DOI: 10.1109/CAI54212.2023.00105

Wood, L., Egger, M., Gluud, L. L., Schulz, K. F., Jüni, P., Altman, D. G., Gluud, C., Martin, R. M., Wood, A. J. G., & Sterne, J. A. C. (2008). Empirical evidence of bias in treatment effect estimates in controlled trials with different interventions and outcomes: Meta-epidemiological study. *BMJ (Clinical Research Ed.),* 336(7644), 601–605. DOI: 10.1136/bmj.39465.451748.AD PMID: 18316340

Wright, S. A., & Schultz, A. E. (2018). The rising tide of artificial intelligence and business automation: Developing an ethical framework. *Business Horizons,* 61(6), 823–832. DOI: 10.1016/j.bushor.2018.07.001

Wu, C., Haihong, E., & Song, M. (2020, January). An automatic artificial intelligence training platform based on kubernetes. In *Proceedings of the 2020 2nd International Conference on Big Data Engineering and Technology* (pp. 58-62).

Wu, J., Huang, Z., Hu, Z., & Lv, C. (2023). Toward Human-in-the-Loop AI: Enhancing Deep Reinforcement Learning via Real-Time Human Guidance for Autonomous Driving. *Engineering (Beijing),* 21, 75–91. DOI: 10.1016/j.eng.2022.05.017

Wyman, O. (2017). Next Generation. *Risk Management.*

Xiang, Y., Wang, L., & Liu, N. (2017). Coordinated attacks on electric power systems in a cyber-physical environment. *Electric Power Systems Research*, 149, 156–168. DOI: 10.1016/j.epsr.2017.04.023

Xiong, M. (2022). *Artificial Intelligence and Causal Inference*. Chapman and Hall/CRC., DOI: 10.1201/9781003028543

Xu, H., Padilla, O., Wang, D., & Li, M. (2021). Changepoints: A collection of change-point detection methods. *CRAN: Contributed Packages*. https://doi.org/DOI: 10.32614/CRAN.package.changepoints

Xu, J., Yang, T., Zhuang, S., Li, H., & Lu, W. (2024). *AI-based financial transaction monitoring and fraud prevention with behaviour prediction.*

Xu, J. (2022). *MLOps in the financial industry: Philosophy practices and tools. Future and Fintech, the, Abcdi and Beyond*. World Scientific.

Xu, M., Du, H., Niyato, D., Kang, J., Xiong, Z., Mao, S., Han, Z., Jamalipour, A., Kim, D. I., Shen, X., Leung, V. C. M., & Poor, H. V. (2024). Unleashing the power of edge-cloud generative ai in mobile networks: A survey of aigc services. *IEEE Communications Surveys and Tutorials*, 26(2), 1127–1170. DOI: 10.1109/COMST.2024.3353265

Yadav, U. S., Gupta, B. B., Peraković, D., Peñalvo, F. J. G., & Cvitić, I. (2022). Security and privacy of cloud-based online online social media: A survey. In *Sustainable management of manufacturing systems in industry 4.0* (pp. 213–236). Springer International Publishing.

Yadav, V. K., & Dadhich, M. (2022). *Machine Learning in Cyber Physical Systems for Agriculture: Crop Yield Prediction Using Cyber Physical Systems and Machine Learning. Real-Time Applications of Machine Learning in Cyber-Physical Systems*. IGI Global.

Yang, L., Tian, M., Xin, D., Cheng, Q., & Zheng, J. (2024). AI-Driven Anonymization: Protecting Personal Data Privacy While Leveraging Machine Learning. *arXiv Preprint arXiv:2402.17191.*

Yang, J., Wang, R., Guan, X., Hassan, M. M., Almogren, A., & Alsanad, A. (2020). AI-enabled emotion-aware robot: The fusion of smart clothing, edge clouds and robotics. *Future Generation Computer Systems*, 102, 701–709. DOI: 10.1016/j.future.2019.09.029

Yang, K. (2024). Quality. In *The Era Of Industry 4.0: Integrating Tradition And Innovation In The Age Of Data And Ai*. John Wiley & Sons.

Yang, Y. (2020). RETRACTED ARTICLE: Research on the optimization of the supplier intelligent management system for cross-border e-commerce platforms based on machine learning. *Information Systems and e-Business Management*, 18(4), 851–870. DOI: 10.1007/s10257-019-00402-1

Yang, Y., Wang, S., Wen, M., & Xu, W. (2021). Reliability modeling and evaluation of cyber-physical system (CPS) considering communication failures. *Journal of the Franklin Institute*, 358(1), 1–16. DOI: 10.1016/j.jfranklin.2018.09.025

Yang, Y., Zheng, K., Wu, B., Yang, Y., & Wang, X. (2020). Network Intrusion Detection Based on Supervised Adversarial Variational Auto-Encoder With Regularization. *IEEE Access : Practical Innovations, Open Solutions*, 8, 42169–42184. DOI: 10.1109/ACCESS.2020.2977007

Yaseen, A. (2023). Ai-driven threat detection and response: A paradigm shift in cybersecurity. *International Journal of Information and Cybersecurity*, 7(12), 25–43.

Yildirim, S., Lee, C., Lee, S., Potamianos, A., & Narayanan, S. (2005) Detecting politeness and frustration state of a child in a conversational computer game. *Proc. Eurospeech Conf.*, 2209–2212. DOI: 10.21437/Interspeech.2005-700

Yildirim, S., Narayanan, S., & Potamianos, A. (2011). Detecting emotional state of a child in a conversational computer game. *Computer Speech & Language*, 25(1), 29–44. DOI: 10.1016/j.csl.2009.12.004

Yongli, G., Qi, D., & Zhipeng, C. (2024). Leveraging the Synergy of IPv6, Generative AI, and Web Engineering to Create a Big Data-driven Education Platform. *Journal of Web Engineering*, 23, 197–226. DOI: 10.13052/jwe1540-9589.2321

York, E. (2023, October). Evaluating chatgpt: Generative ai in ux design and web development pedagogy. In *Proceedings of the 41st ACM International Conference on Design of Communication* (pp. 197-201).

Yu, L., Wei, W., Guo, J., & Qin, X. (2022). Construction of cross border E-commerce comprehensive training curriculum system based on virtual simulation. In The 2021 International Conference on Machine Learning and Big Data Analytics for IoT Security and Privacy: SPIoT-2021 Volume 1 (pp. 707-714). Springer International Publishing.

Yu, P., Xu, H., Hu, X., & Deng, C. (2023, October). Leveraging generative AI and large Language models: A Comprehensive Roadmap for Healthcare Integration. [). MDPI.]. *Health Care*, 11(20), 2776. PMID: 37893850

Yu, S. Y., Yasaei, R., Zhou, Q., Nguyen, T., & Al Faruque, M. A. (2021, December). HW2VEC: A graph learning tool for automating hardware security. In *2021 IEEE International Symposium on Hardware Oriented Security and Trust (HOST)* (pp. 13-23). IEEE.

Yu, Z., Theisen, C., Williams, L., & Menzies, T. (2019). Improving vulnerability inspection efficiency using active learning. *IEEE Transactions on Software Engineering*, 47(11), 2401–2420. DOI: 10.1109/TSE.2019.2949275

Zador, A. M. (2019). A critique of pure learning and what artificial neural networks can learn from animal brains. *Nature Communications*, 10(1), 3770. DOI: 10.1038/s41467-019-11786-6 PMID: 31434893

Zafar, F., Khan, A., Suhail, S., Ahmed, I., Hameed, K., Khan, H. M., . . . Anjum, A. (2017). Trustworthy data: A survey, taxonomy and future trends of secure provenance schemes. *Journal of Network and Computer Applications, 94*, 50-68. Retrieved from https://www.sciencedirect.com/science/article/pii/S1084804517302229 doi: https://doi.org/https://doi.org/10.1016/j.jnca.2017.06.003

Zagane, M., Abdi, M. K., & Alenezi, M. (2020). Deep learning for software vulnerabilities detection using code metrics. *IEEE Access : Practical Innovations, Open Solutions*, 8, 74562–74570. DOI: 10.1109/ACCESS.2020.2988557

Zaheer, A., Tahir, S., Humayun, M., Almufareh, M. F., & Jhanjhi, N. Z. (2022, November). A novel Machine learning technique for fake smart watches advertisement detection. In 2022 14th International Conference on Mathematics, Actuarial Science, Computer Science and Statistics (MACS) (pp. 1-5). IEEE.

Zaman, N., Khan, A. R., & Salih, M. Designing of Energy aware Quality of Service (QoS) based routing protocol for Efficiency Improvement in Wireless Sensor Network (WSN).

Zamanov, R., et al. (2023). "Accretion in the recurrent nova T CrB: Linking the superactive state to the predicted outburst." **680**: L18.

Zarate, J. C. (2015). *The cyber financial wars on the horizon.* Foundation for the Defense of Democracies.

Zavolokina, L., Dolata, M., & Schwabe, G. (2016). The FinTech phenomenon: Antecedents of financial innovation perceived by the popular press. *Financial Innovation*, 2(1), 1–16. DOI: 10.1186/s40854-016-0036-7

Zawacki-Richter, O., Marín, V. I., Bond, M., & Gouverneur, F. (2019). Systematic review of research on artificial intelligence applications in higher education – where are the educators? *International Journal of Educational Technology in Higher Education*, 16(1), 39. Advance online publication. DOI: 10.1186/s41239-019-0171-0

Zeadally, S., Adi, E., Baig, Z., & Khan, I. A. (2020). Harnessing artificial intelligence capabilities to improve cybersecurity. *IEEE Access : Practical Innovations, Open Solutions*, 8, 23817–23837. DOI: 10.1109/ACCESS.2020.2968045

Zeebaree, I. (2024). The Distributed Machine Learning in Cloud Computing and Web Technology: A Review of Scalability and Efficiency. *Journal of Information Technology and Informatics*, 3(1).

Zekos, G. I., & Zekos, G. I. J. E. (2021). *Law Of Artificial Intelligence: Finance, E. I., Risk Management & Governance*. Ai Risk Management.

Zeng, X., He, C., & Jiang, Y. (2023). Investigating the Advancements in Generative Models. *2023 International Conference on Artificial Intelligence and Automation Control (AIAC)*, 347–351. DOI: 10.1109/AIAC61660.2023.00037

Zhai, X., Chu, X., Chai, C.S., Jong, M.S., Istenič, A., Spector, M., Liu, J., Yuan, J., & Li, Y. (2021). A Review of Artificial Intelligence (AI) in Education from 2010 to 2020. *Complex., 2021*, 8812542:1-8812542:18.

Zhang, F., & Yang, Y. (2021). Trust model simulation of cross border e-commerce based on machine learning and Bayesian network. *Journal of Ambient Intelligence and Humanized Computing*, 1–11.

Zhang, J. J., Liu, K., Khalid, F., Hanif, M. A., Rehman, S., Theocharides, T., & Garg, S. (2019, June). Building robust machine learning systems: Current progress, research challenges, and opportunities. In *Proceedings of the 56th Annual Design Automation Conference 2019* (pp. 1-4).

Zhang, K., & Aslan, A. B. (2021). AI technologies for education: Recent research & future directions. *Computers and Education: Artificial Intelligence*, 2, 100025. DOI: 10.1016/j.caeai.2021.100025

Zhang, K., Huang, Y., Du, Y., & Wang, L. (2017). Facial expression recognition based on deep evolutional spatial-temporal networks. *IEEE Transactions on Image Processing*, 26(9), 4193–4203. DOI: 10.1109/TIP.2017.2689999 PMID: 28371777

Zhang, N. (2018). Smart logistics path for cyber-physical systems with internet of things. *IEEE Access : Practical Innovations, Open Solutions*, 6, 70808–70819. DOI: 10.1109/ACCESS.2018.2879966

Zhang, R., Ai, X., & Li, H. (2023). How To Design Subsidy Policies For Clean Energy Projects? A Study On "Coal-To-Gas" Project In China. *Resources Policy*, 85, 103928. DOI: 10.1016/j.resourpol.2023.103928

Zhang, R., Fang, L., He, X., & Wei, C. (2023). *The Whole Process of E-commerce Security Management System*. The Whole Process of E-commerce Security Management System., DOI: 10.1007/978-981-19-9458-6

Zhang, T., Hasegawa-Johnson, M., & Levinson, S. (2006). Cognitive state classification in a spoken tutorial dialogue system. *Speech Communication*, 48(6), 616–632. DOI: 10.1016/j.specom.2005.09.006

Zhang, Y., Guo, Z., Lv, J., & Liu, Y. (2018). A framework for smart production-logistics systems based on CPS and industrial IoT. *IEEE Transactions on Industrial Informatics*, 14(9), 4019–4032. DOI: 10.1109/TII.2018.2845683

Zhang, Y., Wu, X. Y., & Kwon, O. K. (2015). Research on kruskal crossover genetic algorithm for multi-objective logistics distribution path optimization. *International Journal of Multimedia and Ubiquitous Engineering*, 10(8), 367–378. DOI: 10.14257/ijmue.2015.10.8.36

Zhang, Z.. (2024). NTIRE 2024 Challenge on Bracketing Image Restoration and Enhancement: Datasets Methods and Results. *Proceedings of the IEEE/CVF Conference on Computer Vision and Pattern Recognition*. DOI: 10.1109/CVPRW63382.2024.00620

Zhao, C., Du, H., Niyato, D., Kang, J., Xiong, Z., Kim, D. I., & Letaief, K. B. (2024). Generative AI for Secure Physical Layer Communications: A Survey. *arXiv preprint arXiv:2402.13553*.

Zhao, X. (2018, October). A Study on the Applications of Big Data in Cross-border E-commerce. In 2018 IEEE 15th International Conference on e-Business Engineering (ICEBE) (pp. 280-284). IEEE.

Zhao, H., Chen, H., & Yoon, H. (2023). Enhancing text classification models with generative AI-aided data augmentation. *2023 IEEE International Conference On Artificial Intelligence Testing (AITest)*. https://doi.org/DOI: 10.1109/AITest58265.2023.00030

Zhao, J., & Gómez Fariñas, B. (2023). Artificial intelligence and sustainable decisions. *European Business Organization Law Review*, 24(1), 1–39. DOI: 10.1007/s40804-022-00262-2

Zhao, Y., Li, Y., Zhang, X., Geng, G., Zhang, W., & Sun, Y. (2019). A survey of networking applications applying the software defined networking concept based on machine learning. *IEEE Access : Practical Innovations, Open Solutions*, 7, 95397–95417. DOI: 10.1109/ACCESS.2019.2928564

Zheng, X.-L., Zhu, M.-Y., Li, Q.-B., Chen, C.-C., & Tan, Y.-C. (2019). Finbrain: When Finance Meets Ai 2.0. *Frontiers Of Information Technology & Electronic Engineering*, 20(7), 914–924. DOI: 10.1631/FITEE.1700822

Zheng, Z., Xie, S., Dai, H. N., Chen, X., & Wang, H. (2018). Blockchain challenges and opportunities: A survey. *International Journal of Web and Grid Services*, 14(4), 352–375. DOI: 10.1504/IJWGS.2018.095647

Zhou, M., Abhishek, V., Derdenger, T., Kim, J., & Srinivasan, K. (2024, March 5). *Bias in Generative AI*. arXiv.Org. https://arxiv.org/abs/2403.02726v1

Zhou, Y., Yu, Y., & Ding, B. (2020, October). Towards mlops: A case study of ml pipeline platform. In 2020 International conference on artificial intelligence and computer engineering (ICAICE) (pp. 494-500). IEEE.

Zhou, B. (2024). *Social Paradigm Shift Promoted by Generative Models: A Study on the Trend from Result-Oriented to Process-Oriented Paradigm*. OSF. DOI: 10.31219/osf.io/qswzc

Zhou, M., Chen, J., Liu, Y., Ackah-Arthur, H., Chen, S., Zhang, Q., & Zeng, Z. (2019). A method for software vulnerability detection based on improved control flow graph. *Wuhan University Journal of Natural Sciences*, 24(2), 149–160. DOI: 10.1007/s11859-019-1380-z

Zhu, C., Yan, Y., Guo, P., & Li, J. (2018, August). Leveraging 3D packaging technology to enhance integrated circuits security and reliability. In 2018 19th International Conference on Electronic Packaging Technology (Icept) (pp. 766-769). IEEE.

Zhu, W., & Shi, M. (2021). Research on the development path of a cross-European e-commerce logistics mode under the background of "internet plus". *Wireless Communications and Mobile Computing*, 2021(1), 1–7. DOI: 10.1155/2021/6964302

Ziegler, E., Urban, T., Brown, D., Petts, J., Pieper, S. D., Lewis, R., Hafey, C., & Harris, G. J. (2020). Open health imaging foundation viewer: An extensible open-source framework for building web-based imaging applications to support cancer research. *JCO Clinical Cancer Informatics*, 4(4), 336–345. DOI: 10.1200/CCI.19.00131 PMID: 32324447

Žigienė, G., Rybakovas, E., & Alzbutas, R. J. S. (2019).. . *Artificial Intelligence Based Commercial Risk Management Framework For Smes.*, 11, 4501.

Zulaikha, S., Mohamed, H., Kurniawati, M., Rusgianto, S., & Rusmita, S. A. (2020). Customer predictive analytics using artificial intelligence. *The Singapore Economic Review*, ●●●, 1–12. DOI: 10.1142/S0217590820480021

About the Contributors

Noor Zaman Jhanjhi is currently working as Associate Professor, Director Center for Smart society 5.0 [CSS5], & Cluster Head for Cybersecurity, at the School of Computer Science and Engineering, Taylor's University, Malaysia. He is supervising a great number of Postgraduate students, mainly in cybersecurity for Data Science. Dr Jhanjhi serves as Associate Editor and Editorial Assistant Board for several reputable journals, received Outstanding Associate Editor Award for IEEE ACCESS for 2020, PC member for several conferences, guest editor for the reputed journals. He is awarded globally as a top 1% reviewer by Publons (WoS). His collective research Impact factor is 400 plus. He has Patents on his account, edited/authored 35 plus research books published by world-class publishers. He is an external Ph.D./Master thesis examiner/evaluator globally, completed more than 22 internationally funded research grants. Served as a keynote speaker for several conferences, presented Webinars, chaired conference sessions, provided Consultancy internationally. His research areas include Cybersecurity, IoT security, Wireless security, Data Science, Software Engineering, UAVs.

***

Pankaj Bhambri is affiliated with the Department of Information Technology at Guru Nanak Dev Engineering College in Ludhiana. Additionally, he fulfills the role of the Convener for his Departmental Board of Studies. He possesses nearly two decades of teaching experience. His research work has been published in esteemed worldwide and national journals, as well as conference proceedings. Dr. Bhambri has garnered extensive experience in the realm of academic publishing, having served as an editor for a multitude of books in collaboration with esteemed publishing houses such as CRC Press, Elsevier, Scrivener, and Bentham Science. In addition to his editorial roles, he has demonstrated his scholarly prowess by authoring numerous books and contributing chapters to distinguished publishers within the academic community. Dr. Bhambri has been honored with several prestigious accolades, including the ISTE Best Teacher Award in 2023 and 2022, the I2OR National Award in 2020, the Green ThinkerZ Top 100 International Distinguished Educators award in 2020, the I2OR Outstanding Educator Award in 2019, the SAA Distinguished Alumni Award in 2012, the CIPS Rashtriya Rattan Award in 2008, the LCHC Best Teacher Award in 2007, and numerous other commendations from various government and non-profit organizations. He has provided guidance and oversight for numerous research projects and dissertations at the postgraduate and Ph.D. levels. He successfully organized a diverse range of educational programmes, securing financial backing from esteemed institutions such as the AICTE, the TEQIP, among others. Dr. Bhambri's areas of interest encompass machine learning, bioinformatics, wireless sensor networks, and network security.

Mansoor Ebrahim received his MSc from Queen Mary, University of London, UK. He obtained his Ph.D. (Computing) from Sunway University, Malaysia. He is currently associated with Iqra University, Pakistan as HoD (Software Engineering). His current research interests focus on Computer vision, image and video analysis and compression, optimization, image cryptography and IoT. He has more than 15 years of academic and research experience. He served as a Mentor and instructor various institutions in UK and has work as a Research associate for MOSTI in Malaysia. He is the author of over 40+ peer-reviewed international journal and conference publications. He is also external supervisor in various international universities. He is the reviewer of various international indexed journals. He has also conducted various workshops and tutorials. He has also received various national and international research grants. He is a professional engineer and IEEE senior member.

Praveen Gujjar is an academician with 13 years of teaching experience. He has served in engineering and management institute. His research article is published in science direct.

Khizar Hameed was a Research Fellow at Charles Sturt University (CSU) and holds a PhD in Information Technology from the University of Tasmania, specializing in the security and privacy of IoT networks using Blockchain technology. With a strong background in applied cryptography, neural cryptography, and Post-Quantum Blockchain Security, he has published and presented research at international IEEE conferences and serves as an academic reviewer for esteemed journals. His work focuses on securing IoT systems through innovative approaches like smart contracts, AI/ML, and blockchain integration. He also brings extensive teaching experience as a former Lecturer at UMT and contributes to industry and academic projects in IT security and cloud technologies

Vani Hiremani is currently working as an Assistant Professor in the Department of Computer Science and Engineering at Symbiosis Institute of Technology, Deemed University, Pune. She has completed her Master of Technology in Computer Science and Engineering from BEC Bagalkot, Autonomous College under Visveswaraya Technological University Karnataka and PhD in Computer Science and Engineering from Birla Institute of Technology, MESRA. She has more than 12 years of teaching and research experience. She has published more than 30 peer reviewed papers on various national and international journals of repute. She has delivered invited talk at various national and international seminars, conference, symposium, and workshop. She is member of many national and international societies. She is also member in various program committees of many International conference and chaired the session. She is also editor of many International and National Journal of high repute. She has also conducted many workshops in her organization on various topic.

Imtiaz Hussain is Associate Dean of Faculty of Engineering, Sciences and Technology, Iqra University, Karachi.

Muneeba Khan Dedicated physical therapist with a passion for providing exceptional patient care. Skilled in assessing and treating various musculoskeletal conditions through evidence-based techniques. Committed to promoting functional independence and enhancing quality of life for individuals of all ages. Seeking a challenging position to utilize my expertise and contribute to a collaborative healthcare team to utilize my skills and continue helping patients on their journey to recovery.

Nasrullah Khan is a distinguished PhD scholar in Management Sciences and a Senior Lecturer at Dewan University. With a profound dedication to academic excellence, Nasrullah has accumulated extensive experience throughout his career. His journey in academia has been marked by a commitment to advancing knowledge in management sciences, coupled with a passion for teaching and mentoring. As a senior lecturer, Nasrullah has played a pivotal role in shaping the educational experiences of students, contributing to their academic and professional growth. His career reflects a deep-seated dedication to both scholarly pursuits and the enhancement of educational practices.

Adil Liaquat is a seasoned IT Manager with a diploma in Information Technology, currently overseeing technology operations at a leading import-export company. Leveraging his expertise in IT, Adil ensures the company's systems are efficient, secure, and aligned with global business needs. His strategic approach and leadership in implementing and optimizing technology solutions have significantly enhanced operational efficiency and contributed to the company's success. With a passion for continuous learning and a keen understanding of the intersection between technology and international trade, Adil stands out as a vital asset in his field.

Poornima Mahadevappa is a distinguished researcher and educator specializing in edge computing, cybersecurity, and IoT. With 5 years of research experience, 5 years of IT industry exposure, and 2 years in academia, she brings a rich blend of expertise to her work. Presently, her research endeavours centre around cutting-edge technologies like edge computing, with a focus on integrating edge nodes to support sustainability in cloud infrastructure. Her scholarly pursuits also encompass cybersecurity and IoT, where she explores innovative strategies to address threats and optimize performance in Edge computing based IoT applications. As a Lecturer at Taylor's University, Malaysia, she is dedicated to advancing knowledge and fostering innovation in these pivotal areas, making significant contributions to both academic discourse and technological progress.

Syeda Mariam Muzammal holds a PhD in Computer Science from Taylor's University in Malaysia. With a passion for academia and a wealth of industry experience, Dr. Syeda has made significant contributions to the field through teaching and research. As a seasoned educator, she imparts knowledge to both undergraduate and postgraduate students. In research, her focus spans various cutting-edge domains. A trailblazer in the Internet of Things (IoT), Dr. Syeda explores the intricacies of IoT systems and their applications. Cybersecurity and Network Security are integral aspects of her research, where a profound understanding of threats and defenses is cultivated. Routing protocols, an essential component of network communication, are a subject of expertise for her. In the ever-evolving landscape of technology, Dr. Syeda is at the forefront of research in Machine Learning, trust-based security, and Blockchain. She has overall 10 years of professional, academic, and research experience, with a number of research publications in well-reputed journals and conferences.

Rachna Rana is working as Associate Professor in the Department of Computer Science & Engineering at Ludhiana Group of Colleges in Ludhiana. She possesses nearly two decades of teaching experience. Her areas of interest includes machine learning, wireless sensor networks, and network security.

Abdul Rehman is a dedicated academic with a solid foundation in commerce, having completed his Master of Commerce degree. He is currently furthering his expertise by pursuing an MBA, demonstrating his commitment to expanding his knowledge in business and management. Alongside his studies, Abdul serves as a lecturer in the BBA HRM program at SBB Dewan University. His dual role as an educator and a student reflects his passion for learning and teaching, as well as his drive to excel in the field. Through this blend of theoretical knowledge and practical experience, he is well-prepared to make significant contributions to the business world.

Muzzammil Siraj, an accomplished professional with an MBA in Marketing and a Pharm.D. from Hamdard University, currently serves as a Lecturer at Dewan University. With a deep commitment to shaping the future of marketing professionals, he specializes in exploring the intersection of Chatbot Marketing, Electronic Word of Mouth (eWOM), and Customer-Brand Relationships. His scholarly contributions include a notable publication, "Is Chatbot Marketing related to Electronic Word of Mouth? A Mediating Role of the Customer-Brand Relationship," demonstrating his expertise in advancing marketing knowledge. Siraj's research extends to the innovative use of AI in various industries, including pharmacy and banking. He has contributed to significant works such as "Addressing Issues and Challenges Using AI in Pharmacy" and "The Impact of Investment in AI on Bank Performance: Empirical Evidence from Pakistan's Banking Sector." Passionate about fostering innovative approaches in marketing and healthcare, he actively seeks collaborations, speaking engagements, and research opportunities to explore the dynamic intersections of academia and industry.

Preethi Srivathsa, received a bachelor's degree in computer science and engineering from VTU, Karnataka in 2008, a master's degree in computer science and engineering from VTU, Karnataka 2013, and a philosophy of doctorate degree in Computer Science and Engineering from Presidency University, Bangalore in 2022, respectively. She has a total of 15 years of Teaching experience. She is currently working as an Assistant Professor-Senior Scale in the Department of Information Technology, Manipal Institute of Technology, Bengaluru, Manipal Academy of Higher Education, Manipal, India. Her research areas include the Internet of Things, Computer Architecture, and cryptography. She has many papers to her credit in reputed international journals, national journals, and conferences. She has been serving as a reviewer for highly respected journals.

Muhammad Usman Tariq has more than 16+ year's experience in industry and academia. He has authored more than 200+ research articles, 100+ case studies, 50+ book chapters and several books other than 4 patents. He has been working as a consultant and trainer for industries representing six sigma, quality, health and safety, environmental systems, project management, and information security standards. His work has encompassed sectors in aviation, manufacturing, food, hospitality, education, finance, research, software and transportation. He has diverse and significant experience working with accreditation agencies of ABET,

ACBSP, AACSB, WASC, CAA, EFQM and NCEAC. Additionally, Dr. Tariq has operational experience in incubators, research labs, government research projects, private sector startups, program creation and management at various industrial and academic levels. He is Certified Higher Education Teacher from Harvard University, USA, Certified Online Educator from HMBSU, Certified Six Sigma Master Black Belt, Lead Auditor ISO 9001 Certified, ISO 14001, IOSH MS, OSHA 30, and OSHA 48. He has been awarded Principal Fellowship from Advance HE UK & Chartered Fellowship of CIPD.

Index

A

AI 3, 37, 59, 63, 64, 65, 66, 67, 68, 70,
71, 72, 73, 74, 75, 76, 80, 81, 83, 84,
85, 86, 87, 88, 89, 90, 94, 95, 96, 97,
98, 99, 100, 101, 102, 103, 104, 105,
106, 107, 108, 109, 110, 111, 112,
113, 114, 115, 116, 117, 118, 119,
120, 121, 122, 123, 124, 125, 126,
127, 128, 130, 145, 147, 148, 149,
150, 151, 153, 154, 155, 157, 158,
161, 162, 167, 168, 169, 171, 172,
176, 179, 180, 183, 186, 187, 188,
189, 190, 191, 193, 194, 195, 196,
197, 198, 200, 202, 203, 204, 205,
206, 207, 208, 209, 210, 211, 212,
213, 214, 215, 216, 217, 220, 221,
223, 224, 225, 226, 227, 228, 229,
230, 231, 232, 233, 234, 235, 236,
237, 238, 239, 252, 255, 256, 257,
258, 261, 262, 263, 264, 265, 267,
269, 271, 284, 285, 286, 287, 288,
289, 290, 291, 292, 293, 294, 297,
298, 299, 300, 301, 308, 309, 310,
311, 312, 313, 314, 315, 316, 317,
318, 319, 320, 321, 322, 323, 324,
325, 326, 327, 328, 329, 330, 331,
332, 333, 334, 335, 336, 338, 339,
340, 341, 342, 343, 344, 345, 346,
347, 348, 349, 350, 351, 352, 353,
354, 355, 356, 357, 358, 359, 361,
362, 363, 364, 365, 366, 367, 368,
369, 370, 371, 372, 373, 374, 375,
376, 377, 378, 379, 380, 381, 382,
383, 384, 385, 386, 387, 388, 389,
390, 391, 392, 393, 394, 395, 396,
397, 398, 399, 400, 401, 402, 403,
404, 405, 406, 407, 408, 409, 410,
411, 412, 413, 414, 415, 416, 417,
418, 419, 420, 421, 422, 423, 424,
425, 426, 427, 428, 430, 431, 432,
434, 437, 438, 441, 442, 445, 446,
447, 451, 454, 457, 458, 459, 471,
472, 473, 474, 475, 476, 477, 478, 479,
480, 481, 482, 483, 484, 485
AI improves human lives. Artificial
intelligence has the potential to
improve economic growth and raise
everyone's standard of living. People
and businesses everywhere are eager
to invest in human resources 64, 204
AI Integration 84, 96, 122, 196, 224, 229,
230, 231, 232, 233, 234, 235, 236,
310, 390, 401
AI Models 130, 197, 211, 224, 225, 227,
228, 229, 256, 288, 292, 308, 310,
312, 315, 316, 319, 321, 332, 339,
340, 341, 343, 345, 347, 348, 350,
363, 364, 366, 368, 369, 372, 373,
374, 375, 383, 385, 386, 387, 388,
389, 390, 391, 393, 394, 395, 396, 402,
405, 414, 425, 473, 474, 476, 477, 478
also known as vulnerability mapping 129
and buyers. Without a doubt 64, 204
and data security 129, 363
and e-business is crucial to continuously
providing customers with the easiest
way to purchase goods and services.
Moreover 204
and effective web components inside
a React ecosystem to meet these
difficulties. By doing this 242, 260
and interactive web interface components
that can adapt to the constantly shifting
needs of users in terms of security 241
and interface speed. One of the most
important components of any modern
web application is secure user login and
permission. Stronger authentication is
required to protect user data and the
integrity of apps 241
and payment gateway vulnerabilities 203,
269
and privacy-preserving technologies as
possible ways to improve the security
of e-commerce platforms. The data
that is being presented highlights how
important it is for technology 203
and reducing vulnerabilities in an
environment. It involves assigning

software high priority and promptly addressing risks to stop data breaches and cyberattacks. Considering the nature of the hardware 129

and Redux. Therefore 242, 260

and user awareness to come together to provide a safe and reliable online purchasing environment. To strengthen the digital marketplace against the challenges presented by a constantly changing cyber landscape 203

and user-friendly web applications remains a major problem in the constantly evolving field of web development. Web application developers must provide modular 241

Artificial Intelligence 31, 33, 38, 45, 57, 59, 63, 64, 65, 66, 67, 70, 71, 72, 78, 83, 84, 85, 89, 93, 94, 95, 97, 98, 99, 100, 101, 102, 103, 105, 106, 107, 108, 109, 111, 112, 125, 127, 128, 130, 147, 151, 157, 161, 165, 167, 168, 169, 170, 174, 175, 176, 177, 178, 179, 180, 181, 182, 185, 187, 188, 190, 191, 193, 194, 195, 196, 199, 201, 202, 204, 205, 206, 208, 209, 210, 211, 214, 215, 216, 219, 221, 224, 227, 238, 250, 252, 255, 257, 258, 263, 264, 265, 267, 281, 282, 284, 285, 288, 289, 290, 291, 298, 318, 321, 322, 323, 325, 326, 328, 329, 330, 331, 332, 340, 341, 354, 355, 357, 358, 361, 362, 365, 372, 377, 379, 407, 411, 413, 416, 422, 424, 426, 427, 428, 429, 430, 431, 432, 433, 434, 435, 437, 438, 445, 446, 447, 453, 454, 457, 458, 459, 462, 463, 466, 472, 473, 474, 476, 482, 483, 485

as worries over data privacy and cybersecurity grow. Though there are a number of these solutions on the market 241, 259

Automated Web Design 297, 301, 310, 320

Automation 9, 33, 39, 58, 70, 76, 108, 109, 124, 137, 138, 142, 221, 231, 233, 249, 257, 263, 294, 299, 300, 310, 311,

318, 320, 325, 330, 331, 336, 343, 349, 350, 356, 392, 403, 411, 413, 418, 421, 434, 438, 446, 451, 455, 459, 467, 468, 476, 477, 482

B

Blockchain 34, 87, 147, 148, 149, 150, 151, 153, 154, 155, 157, 158, 159, 181, 189, 190, 204, 213, 239, 296, 316, 317, 323, 327, 346, 347, 353, 356, 378, 401, 425, 428, 429, 430, 431, 451, 453, 484

blockchain payment gateway 204, 213

businesses try to increase their profit margins without sacrificing the quality of their products. Conversely 204

Business Innovation 223, 226, 231, 235

Business Security Models 129, 131

C

categorizing 129

Cloud-based and cyber attacks in E-commerce 204

Code Generation 235, 309, 312, 316, 331, 339, 342, 344, 351, 358

Content Generation 297, 298, 300, 311, 333, 347, 349, 352, 472, 475

Cost Reduction 149, 153, 334

customers successfully fulfil their needs and desires at home. AI provides answers for a wide range of issues that both consumers and business owners face. Computer-based information can benefit economic growth 204

Cyber Security 9, 38, 39, 46, 57, 66, 172, 204, 210, 213, 216, 218, 220, 256, 285, 286, 289, 290, 291, 292, 293, 326, 353, 356, 390, 423, 426, 427, 428, 429, 430, 431, 433, 473, 478, 481

cybersecurity Issues and Challenges 37, 59, 81, 105, 145, 157, 158, 220, 238, 239, 283, 329, 357, 378, 434, 453, 454

143, 144, 145, 156, 158, 186, 201,
210, 215, 218, 221, 238, 255, 257,
266, 295, 323, 353, 356, 357, 378,
401, 426, 428, 429, 434, 446, 447,
448, 451, 454, 483

issues can be solved 21, 241, 253

is the continuous process of identifying 129

L

large-scale data transfer capabilities 241

legislation 203, 212, 256, 291, 380, 394

M

Machine Learning 1, 3, 4, 5, 6, 9, 10, 18,
19, 21, 22, 23, 26, 28, 29, 30, 32, 33,
34, 35, 39, 43, 45, 48, 58, 59, 60, 63,
64, 65, 66, 67, 68, 76, 77, 78, 87, 88,
98, 99, 100, 101, 103, 105, 132, 146,
171, 178, 186, 195, 202, 209, 210,
213, 216, 218, 219, 220, 221, 241,
242, 245, 246, 247, 249, 250, 251,
253, 255, 256, 258, 259, 261, 262,
263, 264, 265, 266, 269, 271, 272,
273, 276, 278, 280, 281, 282, 283,
284, 287, 289, 291, 294, 295, 296,
298, 300, 301, 310, 311, 317, 321,
322, 323, 332, 340, 343, 348, 349,
353, 355, 359, 379, 381, 384, 408,
409, 410, 411, 417, 419, 420, 421,
422, 424, 426, 428, 431, 432, 433,
434, 438, 441, 447, 448, 451, 453,
459, 465, 472, 479, 482, 484

Machine Learning Approaches 19, 21, 30,
33, 241, 245, 246, 249, 273

Machine Learning Models 1, 29, 88, 249,
261, 264, 269, 271, 289, 310, 311,
317, 332, 348

machine learning teaches itself how to
accomplish a task over time and
then assists people in performing
that activity. The capacity to design
effective 241

managers 64, 84, 91, 198, 204

Mitigation Measures 213, 293

ML 4, 9, 22, 23, 48, 63, 64, 68, 127, 130,
132, 144, 171, 241, 242, 250, 262, 266,
267, 270, 282, 286, 316, 348, 379,
381, 382, 383, 384, 385, 390, 391,
397, 398, 399, 409, 410, 417, 420,
424, 430, 438, 448, 459, 465

N

network 6, 8, 30, 33, 34, 38, 42, 49, 57,
58, 60, 78, 98, 99, 101, 129, 132, 137,
157, 168, 169, 170, 171, 172, 184,
185, 207, 213, 247, 249, 250, 259,
261, 262, 264, 273, 274, 281, 284,
287, 294, 295, 296, 307, 308, 317,
330, 380, 381, 382, 384, 385, 386,
389, 391, 392, 393, 397, 398, 399,
400, 401, 408, 409, 410, 411, 412,
414, 416, 417, 419, 420, 421, 423,
424, 429, 430, 435, 442, 443, 450,
451, 452, 455, 476, 483, 484

NLG 459, 461

NLP 30, 227, 262, 286, 299, 311, 350,
354, 356, 379, 381, 383, 384, 386,
409, 410, 417, 424, 455, 457, 458,
459, 460, 462, 463, 464, 465, 466, 467

NLU 459, 460

O

OpenAI 162, 224, 227, 229, 312, 315,
339, 344, 458

organizations 3, 9, 28, 42, 64, 68, 88, 89,
98, 104, 109, 111, 120, 123, 126, 130,
164, 166, 168, 169, 172, 174, 175,
177, 179, 180, 181, 183, 184, 196,
204, 207, 211, 237, 248, 273, 285,
286, 290, 291, 292, 317, 319, 332,
337, 342, 349, 380, 381, 390, 391,
392, 394, 395, 397, 403, 404, 405,
406, 407, 409, 411, 413, 414, 415,
448, 471, 473, 474, 479, 481

P

Pakistan 41, 83, 84, 85, 90, 96, 97, 104,
147, 157, 193, 203, 223, 238, 269,
361, 377, 379, 437

Phishing attacks 203, 204, 213, 417, 419, 420
Physical Therapy 361, 366, 367, 369, 374
PLS SEM 200
prioritizing 129, 292, 404, 416
Privacy 8, 30, 32, 33, 34, 35, 38, 57, 60, 69, 88, 89, 134, 138, 144, 194, 196, 197, 203, 211, 214, 219, 241, 256, 259, 266, 274, 278, 282, 288, 291, 314, 315, 316, 317, 319, 321, 327, 331, 332, 336, 337, 338, 341, 344, 345, 346, 347, 348, 350, 351, 353, 354, 357, 358, 359, 374, 377, 380, 391, 394, 395, 405, 406, 412, 413, 414, 415, 416, 425, 429, 431, 434, 449, 451, 452, 455, 456, 474, 476, 481

R

Ransomware attacks 204, 380, 381, 393, 432
React 195, 241, 242, 259, 260, 392, 395, 396, 397, 398, 411, 423
reusable 241, 242, 260
Risk Management 60, 83, 84, 88, 89, 93, 94, 95, 98, 99, 101, 102, 103, 104, 105, 106, 156, 157, 196, 201, 216, 221

S

safe 8, 36, 135, 151, 203, 241, 242, 248, 259, 260, 287, 291, 365, 443
Security 1, 2, 3, 4, 5, 6, 8, 9, 12, 14, 15, 16, 18, 20, 21, 26, 27, 28, 30, 31, 32, 33, 34, 35, 36, 37, 38, 39, 45, 46, 57, 58, 59, 60, 66, 67, 68, 69, 89, 95, 103, 104, 114, 116, 117, 118, 129, 130, 131, 132, 133, 134, 135, 137, 138, 139, 140, 141, 142, 143, 144, 145, 146, 149, 150, 151, 157, 158, 161, 162, 163, 164, 165, 166, 167, 168, 169, 170, 171, 172, 173, 174, 175, 176, 177, 178, 179, 180, 181, 182, 183, 184, 185, 186, 187, 189, 194, 201, 203, 204, 210, 211, 213, 214, 216, 218, 220, 222, 225, 226, 227, 228, 238, 239, 241, 242, 243, 244, 245, 246, 247, 248, 249, 253, 254, 256, 259, 263, 266, 269, 270, 271, 272, 273, 274, 275, 276, 277, 278, 281, 283, 284, 285, 286, 287, 289, 290, 291, 292, 293, 295, 315, 316, 321, 322, 323, 325, 326, 328, 329, 331, 332, 337, 338, 339, 340, 341, 342, 343, 344, 346, 347, 348, 349, 350, 351, 352, 353, 354, 355, 356, 357, 358, 363, 374, 377, 378, 379, 380, 381, 382, 383, 384, 385, 386, 387, 388, 389, 390, 391, 392, 393, 394, 395, 396, 397, 398, 399, 400, 401, 402, 403, 404, 405, 406, 407, 408, 409, 411, 413, 414, 415, 416, 418, 419, 420, 421, 422, 423, 424, 425, 426, 427, 428, 429, 430, 431, 432, 433, 434, 437, 439, 440, 441, 442, 443, 444, 448, 449, 450, 451, 452, 453, 454, 455, 456, 473, 474, 475, 476, 477, 478, 479, 480, 481, 483
Security Testing 35, 36, 118, 182, 338, 339, 451, 478
Semi-supervised Learning 4, 5, 24, 253, 277
Smart PLS 91, 95, 102, 149, 198
Software Vulnerabilities 1, 3, 4, 5, 9, 10, 13, 16, 21, 23, 25, 26, 27, 28, 29, 30, 31, 32, 33, 35, 36, 39, 243, 244, 245, 246, 253, 271, 272, 275, 276, 277, 409, 440, 441
SPSS 147, 151, 230
studies 6, 8, 10, 12, 13, 14, 23, 28, 44, 45, 56, 70, 74, 97, 100, 107, 119, 120, 123, 150, 176, 205, 215, 220, 224, 226, 228, 229, 230, 236, 246, 252, 253, 257, 274, 275, 276, 284, 318, 331, 335, 338, 344, 350, 351, 383, 395, 398, 416, 431, 441, 445, 446, 463, 464
such as phishing attacks 203

T

the emergence of an AI-ready business does not translate into a rise in the need for mechanical expertise. The use of electronic commerce has made

Printed in the United States
by Baker & Taylor Publisher Services

Printed in the United States
by Baker & Taylor Publisher Services